Vauxhall Astra Owners Workshop Manual

Steve Rendle

Models covered
Vauxhall Astra models with petrol engines, including
special/limited editions;
Saloon, Hatchback, Estate and Van
1389 cc, 1598 cc & 1998 cc (inc. 16V)

Also covers Opel Astra range, including 1796 cc engine
Does not cover Diesel engines
For information on 1992 Convertible and Astramax Van models,
see OWM 1136

ABCDE
FGHIJ
KLMNO
PQRST

Haynes
THE BOOK ®

Haynes Publishing Group
Sparkford Nr Yeovil
Somerset BA22 7JJ England

Haynes Publications, Inc
861 Lawrence Drive
Newbury Park
California 91320 USA

Acknowledgements

Thanks are due to Champion Spark Plug, who supplied the illustrations showing spark plug conditions, to Holt Lloyd Limited who supplied the illustrations showing bodywork repair, and to Duckhams Oils, who provided lubrication data. Certain other illustrations are the copyright of Vauxhall Motors Ltd, and are used with their permission. Thanks are also due to Sykes-Pickavant Limited, who provided some of the workshop tools, and to all those people at Sparkford who helped in the production of this manual.

© **Haynes Publishing Group 1993**

A book in the **Haynes Owners Workshop Manual Series**

Printed by J. H. Haynes & Co. Ltd., Sparkford, Nr Yeovil, Somerset BA22 7JJ, England

ISBN 1 85010 832 3

British Library Cataloguing in Publication Data
A catalogue record for this book is available from the British Library.

We take great pride in the accuracy of information given in this manual, but vehicle manufacturers make alterations and design changes during the production run of a particular vehicle of which they do not inform us. No liability can be accepted by the authors or publishers for loss, damage or injury caused by any errors in, or omissions from, the information given.

Restoring and Preserving our Motoring Heritage

Few people can have had the luck to realise their dreams to quite the same extent and in such a remarkable fashion as John Haynes, Founder and Chairman of the Haynes Publishing Group.

Since 1965 his unique approach to workshop manual publishing has proved so successful that millions of Haynes Manuals are now sold every year throughout the world, covering literally thousands of different makes and models of cars, vans and motorcycles.

A continuing passion for cars and motoring led to the founding in 1985 of a Charitable Trust dedicated to the restoration and preservation of our motoring heritage. To inaugurate the new Museum, John Haynes donated virtually his entire private collection of 52 cars.

Now with an unrivalled international collection of over 210 veteran, vintage and classic cars and motorcycles, the Haynes Motor Museum in Somerset is well on the way to becoming one of the most interesting Motor Museums in the world.

A 70 seat video cinema, a cafe and an extensive motoring bookshop, together with a specially constructed one kilometre motor circuit, make a visit to the Haynes Motor Museum a truly unforgettable experience.

Every vehicle in the museum is preserved in as near as possible mint condition and each car is run every six months on the motor circuit.

Enjoy the picnic area set amongst the rolling Somerset hills. Peer through the William Morris workshop windows at cars being restored, and browse through the extensive displays of fascinating motoring memorabilia.

From the 1903 Oldsmobile through such classics as an MG Midget to the mighty 'E' Type Jaguar, Lamborghini, Ferrari Berlinetta Boxer, and Graham Hill's Lola Cosworth, there is something for everyone, young and old alike, at this Somerset Museum.

Haynes Motor Museum

Situated mid-way between London and Penzance, the Haynes Motor Museum is located just off the A303 at Sparkford, Somerset (home of the Haynes Manual) and is open to the public 7 days a week all year round, except Christmas Day and Boxing Day.

Contents

Spark plug condition and bodywork repair colour pages between pages 32 and 33

Vauxhall Astra CD Saloon

Vauxhall Astra GLS Hatchback

Vauxhall Astra GLS Estate

Vauxhall Astra GSi 16V

About this manual

Its aim

The aim of this manual is to help you get the best value from your vehicle. It can do so in several ways. It can help you decide what work must be done (even should you choose to get it done by a garage), provide information on routine maintenance and servicing, and give a logical course of action and diagnosis when random faults occur. However, it is hoped that you will use the manual by tackling the work yourself. On simpler jobs it may even be quicker than booking the car into a garage and going there twice, to leave and collect it. Perhaps most important, a lot of money can be saved by avoiding the costs a garage must charge to cover its labour and overheads.

The manual has drawings and descriptions to show the function of the various components so that their layout can be understood. Then the tasks are described and photographed in a clear step-by-step sequence.

Its arrangement

The manual is divided into Chapters, each covering a logical sub-division of the vehicle. The Chapters are each divided into Sections, numbered with single figures, eg 5; the Sections are divided into paragraphs, or into sub-sections and paragraphs.

It is freely illustrated, especially in those parts where there is a detailed sequence of operations to be carried out. There are two forms of illustration: figures and photographs. The figures are numbered in sequence with decimal numbers, according to their position in the Chapter -- eg Fig. 6.4 is the fourth drawing/illustration in Chapter 6.

Photographs carry the same number (either individually or in related groups) as the Section and paragraph to which they relate.

There is an alphabetical index at the back of the manual as well as a contents list at the front. Each Chapter is also preceded by its own individual contents list.

References to the 'left' or 'right' of the vehicle are in the sense of a person in the driver's seat facing forward.

Unless otherwise stated, nuts and bolts are removed by turning anti-clockwise, and tightened by turning clockwise.

Vehicle manufacturers continually make changes to specifications and recommendations, and these, when notified, are incorporated into our manuals at the earliest opportunity.

We take great pride in the accuracy of information given in this manual, but vehicle manufacturers make alterations and design changes during the production run of a particular vehicle of which they do not inform us. No liability can be accepted by the authors or publishers for loss, damage or injury caused by any errors in, or omissions from, the information given.

Project vehicles

The main project vehicle used in the preparation of this manual, and appearing in many of the photographic sequences was a 1992 Vauxhall Astra 1.6 GLS 5-door Hatchback. Additional work was carried out and photographed on a 1992 Vauxhall Astra 1.4 LS Saloon, a 1992 Vauxhall Astra 1.4 Expression 3-door Hatchback, and a 1992 Vauxhall Astra 2.0 GSi 16V Hatchback.

Introduction to the Vauxhall/Opel Astra

The Astra covered by this manual was first introduced to the European market in Autumn 1991. Although mechanically there is a fundamental similarity to the previous Astra/Belmont/Kadett models, the later version is much improved and refined in all respects. This manual covers models fitted with petrol engines, but other models in the range are available with diesel engines.

Five petrol engines are available in the Astra range, although not all of the engines are available in all markets. The engines available are 1.4, 1.6, 1.8 and 2.0 litre single overhead camshaft (SOHC) versions, and a 2.0 litre double overhead camshaft (DOHC) version, which is fitted to the performance-orientated GSi model. All of the engines use fuel injection, and are fitted with a range of emission control systems, with the exception of a 1.4 litre carburettor engine available in certain markets. All the engines are of a well-proven design and, provided regular maintenance is carried out, are unlikely to give trouble.

The Astra is available in 4-door Saloon, 3- and 5-door Hatchback,

Estate and Van bodystyles (although the GSi model is only available in Hatchback form), with a wide range of fittings and interior trim depending on the model specification.

Fully-independent front suspension is fitted, with the components attached to a subframe assembly; the rear suspension is semi-independent, with a torsion beam and trailing arms.

A five-speed manual gearbox is fitted as standard to all models, and four-speed electronically-controlled automatic transmission is available as an option on certain models.

A wide range of standard and optional equipment is available within the Astra range to suit most tastes, including an anti-lock braking system.

For the home mechanic, the Astra is a straightforward vehicle to maintain, and most of the items requiring frequent attention are easily accessible.

General dimensions and weights

Dimensions
Overall length:
    Saloon models .... 4239 mm
    Hatchback models (except GSi) .... 4051 mm
    GSi models .... 4086 mm
    Estate and Van models .... 4278 mm
Overall width (all models – excluding door mirrors) .... 1688 mm
Overall width (all models – including door mirrors) .... 1795 mm
Overall height:
    Saloon and Hatchback models .... 1410 mm
    Estate models (without roof rails) .... 1475 mm
    Estate models (with roof rails) .... 1525 mm
    Van models (without roof rails) .... 1490 mm
    Van models (with roof rails) .... 1540 mm
Wheelbase (all models) .... 2517 mm
Turning circle .... 9.8 metres
Weights
Kerb weight:*
    Saloon models .... 960 to 1090 kg
    Hatchback models .... 930 to 1125 kg
    Estate models .... 995 to 1127 kg
    Van models .... 1030 to 1050 kg
Exact kerb weights depend upon model and specification.

Maximum gross vehicle weight .... Refer to VIN plate
Maximum roof rack load .... 100 kg
Maximum towing hitch downward load (noseweight) .... 75 kg
Maximum towing weights .... Refer to a Vauxhall/Opel dealer for latest recommendations

Jacking, towing and wheel changing

Jacking

The jack supplied with the vehicle tool kit should only be used for changing the roadwheels – *'Wheel changing'* later in this Section. When carrying out any other kind of work, raise the vehicle using a hydraulic jack, and always supplement the jack with axle stands positioned under the vehicle jacking points.

When using a hydraulic jack or axle stands, always position the jack head or axle stand head under one of the relevant jacking points (note that the jacking points for use with a hydraulic jack and axle stands are different to those for use with the vehicle jack). **Do not** jack the vehicle under the sump or any of the steering or suspension components. The jacking points and axle stand positions are shown in the accompanying illustrations. **Never** *work under, around, or near a raised vehicle, unless it is adequately supported in at least two places.*

Towing

Towing eyes are fitted to the front and rear of the vehicle for attachment of a tow rope. Note that on GSi models, the towing eyes are covered by plastic covers, which must be unclipped for access to the towing eyes (photos). Always turn the ignition key to position 'II' when the vehicle is being towed, so that the steering lock is released and the direction indicator and brake lights are operational.

Before being towed, release the handbrake and place the gear lever in neutral on manual gearbox models, or 'N' on automatic transmission models. Note that greater-than-usual pedal pressure will be required to operate the brakes, since the vacuum servo unit is only operational with the engine running. Similarly, on models with power steering, greater-than-usual steering effort will be required.

Note that a vehicle with automatic transmission should always be towed forwards. To avoid damage to the automatic transmission, do not tow the car any faster than 50 mph (80 km/h), or any further than 60 miles (100 km). Where it can be arranged, models with automatic transmission should ideally be towed with the front wheels off the ground, particularly if a transmission fault is suspected.

Wheel changing

To change a wheel, remove the spare wheel and jack (located under the carpet or cover panel in the floor of the luggage compartment), apply the handbrake and place chocks at the front and rear of the wheel diagonally opposite the one to be changed. On automatic transmission models, place the selector lever in position 'P'. Make sure that the vehicle is located on firm level ground, and then slightly loosen the wheel nuts with the brace provided (where applicable, remove the trim first). Locate the jack head in the jacking point nearest to the wheel to be changed, and raise the jack by turning the handle. Note that the lug on the jack head must engage with the cut-out in the jacking point. On GSi models, plastic covers must be unclipped for access to the jacking points (photo). When the wheel is clear of the ground, remove the nuts (and trim where applicable) and lift off the wheel. Fit the spare wheel (and trim where applicable) and moderately tighten the nuts. Lower the vehicle, and then tighten the nuts fully. Refit the trim where applicable. With the spare wheel in position, remove the chock and stow the jack and tools.

Front jacking point for hydraulic jack or axle stands

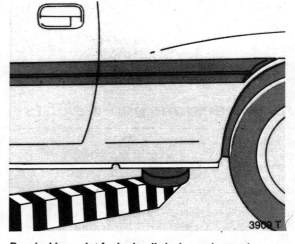

Rear jacking point for hydraulic jack or axle stands

Front towing eye – all models except GSi

Plastic cover unclipped to expose front towing eye – GSi model

Plastic cover removed and jack engaged with jacking point – GSi model

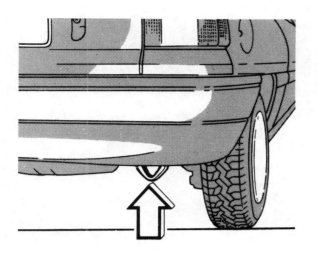

Rear towing eye – Hatchback model (not GSi)

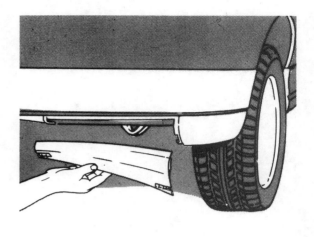

Plastic cover unclipped to expose rear towing eye – GSi model

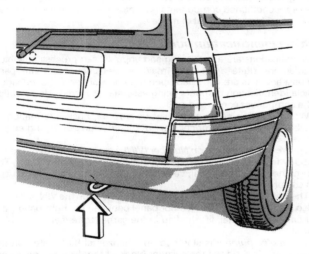

Rear towing eye – Estate and Van models

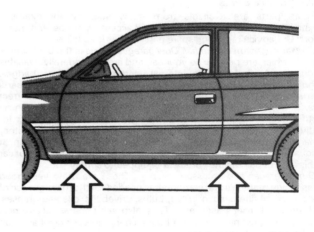

Jacking points for use with vehicle jack when wheel changing

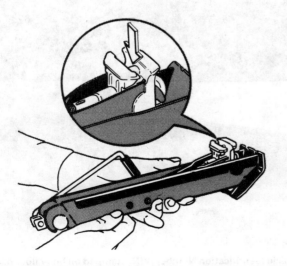

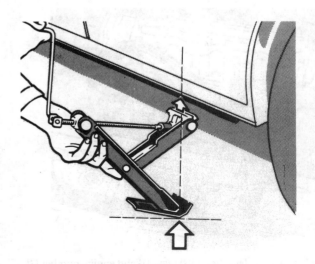

Locate the vehicle jack on level ground and engage the lug on the jack head with the cut-out in the jacking point

Buying spare parts and vehicle identification numbers

Buying spare parts

Spare parts are available from many sources; for example, Vauxhall/Opel garages, other garages and accessory shops, and motor factors. Our advice regarding spare part sources is as follows.

Officially appointed Vauxhall/Opel garages – This is the best source for parts which are peculiar to your car, and are not generally available (eg complete cylinder heads, internal gearbox components, badges, interior trim, etc.). It is also the only place at which you should buy parts if the vehicle is still under warranty. To be sure of obtaining the correct parts, it will be necessary to give the storeman your car's vehicle identification number, and if possible, take the old parts along for positive identification. Many parts are available under a factory exchange scheme – any parts returned should always be clean. It obviously makes good sense to go straight to the specialists on your car for this type of part, as they are best equipped to supply you.

Other garages and accessory shops – These are often very good places to buy materials and components needed for the maintenance of your car (eg oil filters, spark plugs, bulbs, drivebelts, oils and greases, touch-up paint, filler paste, etc). They also sell general accessories, usually have convenient opening hours, charge lower prices and can often be found not far from home.

Motor factors – Good factors will stock all the more important components which wear out comparatively quickly (eg exhaust systems, brake pads, seals and hydraulic parts, clutch components,

bearing shells, pistons, valves, etc.). Motor factors will often provide new or reconditioned components on a part exchange basis – this can save a considerable amount of money.

Vehicle identification numbers

Modifications are a continuing and unpublicised process in vehicle manufacture, quite apart from major model changes. Spare parts manuals and lists are compiled upon a numerical basis, the individual vehicle identification numbers being essential to correct identification of the component concerned.

When ordering spare parts, always give as much information as possible. Quote the car model, year of manufacture, body and engine numbers as appropriate.

The *Vehicle Identification Number (VIN) plate* is riveted to the top of the body front panel, and can be viewed once the bonnet is open. The plate carries the VIN number, vehicle weight information and paint and trim colour codes

The *Vehicle Identification Number (VIN)* is given on the VIN plate, and is also stamped into the body floor panel between the right-hand front seat and the sill panel; lift the flap in the carpet to reveal the number (photo).

The *engine number* is stamped on a horizontal flat located on the exhaust manifold side of the cylinder block, at the distributor/coil end. The first part of the engine number gives the engine code – eg 'C 16 SE'.

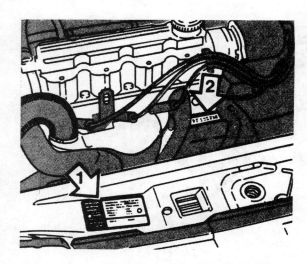

Vehicle Identification Number (VIN) plate (1) and engine number (2) locations

Vehicle Identification Number (VIN) stamped on body floor panel

Safety first!

However enthusiastic you may be about getting on with the job in hand, do take the time to ensure that your safety is not put at risk. A moment's lack of attention can result in an accident, as can failure to observe certain elementary precautions. There will always be new ways of having accidents, and the following points do not pretend to be a comprehensive list of all dangers; they are intended rather to make you aware of the risks and to encourage a safety-conscious approach to all work you carry out on your vehicle.

Essential DOs and DON'Ts

DON'T rely on a single jack when working underneath the vehicle. Always use reliable additional means of support, such as axle stands, securely placed under a structural part of the vehicle that you know will not give way.

DON'T attempt to loosen or tighten high-torque nuts (eg wheel hub nuts) while the vehicle is on a jack; it may be pulled off.

DON'T start the engine without first ascertaining that the transmission is in neutral (or 'Park' where applicable) and the handbrake applied.

DON'T suddenly remove the filler cap from a hot cooling system - cover it with a cloth and release the pressure gradually first, or you may get scalded by escaping coolant.

DON'T attempt to drain oil, automatic transmission fluid, or coolant until you are sure it has cooled sufficiently to avoid scalding you.

DON'T grasp any part of the engine, exhaust or catalytic converter without first ascertaining that it is sufficiently cool to avoid burning you.

DON'T allow brake fluid or antifreeze to contact vehicle paintwork.

DON'T syphon toxic liquids such as fuel, brake fluid or antifreeze by mouth, or allow them to remain on your skin.

DON'T inhale dust - it may be injurious to health (see *Asbestos* below).

DON'T allow any spilt oil or grease to remain on the floor - wipe it up straight away, before someone slips on it.

DON'T use ill-fitting spanners or other tools which may slip and cause injury.

DON'T attempt to lift a heavy component which may be beyond your capability - get assistance.

DON'T rush to finish a job, or take unverified short cuts.

DON'T allow children or animals in or around an unattended vehicle.

DON'T park vehicles with catalytic converters over combustible materials such as dry grass, oily rags, etc if the engine has recently been run. As catalytic converters reach extremely high temperatures, any such materials in close proximity may ignite.

DON'T run vehicles equipped with catalytic converters without the exhaust system heat shields fitted.

DO wear eye protection when using power tools such as an electric drill, sander, bench grinder etc, and when working under the vehicle.

DO use a barrier cream on your hands prior to undertaking dirty jobs - it will protect your skin from infection as well as making the dirt easier to remove afterwards; but make sure your hands aren't left slippery. Note that long term contact with used engine oil can be a health hazard.

DO keep loose clothing (cuffs, tie etc) and long hair well out of the way of moving mechanical parts.

DO remove rings, wristwatch etc, before working on the vehicle - especially the electrical system.

DO ensure that any lifting tackle or jacking equipment used has a safe working load rating adequate for the job, and is used precisely as recommended by the manufacturer.

DO keep your work area tidy - it is only too easy to fall over articles left lying around.

DO get someone to check periodically that all is well when working alone on the vehicle.

DO carry out work in a logical sequence and check that everything is correctly assembled and tightened afterwards.

DO remember that your vehicle's safety affects that of yourself and others. If in doubt on any point, get specialist advice.

IF, in spite of following these precautions, you are unfortunate enough to injure yourself, seek medical attention as soon as possible.

Asbestos

Certain friction, insulating, sealing, and other products - such as brake linings, brake bands, clutch linings, gaskets, etc - contain asbestos. *Extreme care must be taken to avoid inhalation of dust from such products since it is hazardous to health.* If in doubt, assume that they *do* contain asbestos.

Fire

Remember at all times that petrol is highly flammable. Never smoke, or have any kind of naked flame around, when working on the vehicle. But the risk does not end there - a spark caused by an electrical short-circuit, by two metal surfaces contacting each other, by careless use of tools, or even by static electricity built up in your body under certain conditions, can ignite petrol vapour, which in a confined space is highly explosive. The vapour produced by spilling oil or hydraulic fluid onto hot metal, such as an exhaust manifold, can also be flammable or explosive.

Whenever possible disconnect the battery earth terminal before working on any part of the fuel or electrical system, and never risk spilling fuel on to a hot engine or exhaust. Catalytic converters run at extremely high temperatures, and consequently can be an additional fire hazard. Observe the precautions outlined elsewhere in this section.

It is recommended that a fire extinguisher of a type suitable for fuel and electrical fires is kept handy in the garage or workplace at all times. Ideally a suitable extinguisher should also be carried in the vehicle. Never try to extinguish a fuel or electrical fire with water. If a vehicle fire does occur, take note of the remarks below about hydrofluoric acid.

Note: *Any reference to a 'torch' appearing in this manual should always be taken to mean a hand-held battery-operated electric lamp or flashlight. It does NOT mean a welding/gas torch or blowlamp.*

Hydrofluoric acid

Hydrofluoric acid is extremely corrosive. It is formed when certain types of synthetic rubber, which may be found in O-rings, oil seals, brake hydraulic system seals, fuel hoses etc, are exposed to temperatures above 400°C. The obvious circumstance in which this could happen on a vehicle is in the case of a fire. The rubber does not burn but changes into a charred or sticky substance which contains the acid. *Once formed, the acid remains dangerous for years. If it gets onto the skin it may be necessary to amputate the limb concerned.*

When dealing with a vehicle which has suffered a fire, or with components salvaged from such a vehicle, always wear protective gloves and discard them carefully after use. Bear this in mind if obtaining components from a car breaker.

Fumes

Certain fumes are highly toxic and can quickly cause unconsciousness and even death if inhaled to any extent, especially if inhalation takes place through a lighted cigarette or pipe. Petrol vapour comes into this category, as do the vapours from certain solvents such as trichloroethylene. Any draining or pouring of such volatile fluids should be done in a well ventilated area.

When using cleaning fluids and solvents, read the instructions carefully. Never use materials from unmarked containers - they may give off poisonous vapours.

Never run the engine of a motor vehicle in an enclosed space such as a garage. Exhaust fumes contain carbon monoxide which is extremely poisonous; if you need to run the engine, always do so in the open air or at least have the rear of the vehicle outside the workplace. Although vehicles fitted with catalytic converters have greatly reduced toxic exhaust emissions, the above precautions should still be observed.

If you are fortunate enough to have the use of an inspection pit, never drain or pour petrol, and never run the engine, while the vehicle is standing over it; the fumes, being heavier than air, will concentrate in the pit with possibly lethal results.

The battery

Batteries which are sealed for life require special precautions which are normally outlined on a label attached to the battery. Such precautions are primarily related to situations involving battery charging and jump starting from another vehicle.

With a conventional battery, never cause a spark, or allow a naked light, in close proximity to it. It will normally be giving off a certain amount of hydrogen gas, which is highly explosive.

Whenever possible disconnect the battery earth terminal before working on the fuel or electrical systems.

If possible, loosen the filler plugs or cover when charging the battery from an external source. Do not charge at an excessive rate or the battery may burst. Special care should be taken with the use of high charge-rate boost chargers to prevent the battery from overheating.

Take care when topping up and when carrying the battery. The acid electrolyte, even when diluted, is very corrosive and should not be allowed to contact clothing, eyes or skin.

Always wear eye protection when cleaning the battery to prevent the caustic deposits from entering your eyes.

The vehicle electrical system

Take care when making alterations or repairs to the vehicle wiring. Electrical faults are the commonest cause of vehicle fires. Make sure that any accessories are wired correctly using an appropriately rated fuse and wire of adequate current-carrying capacity. When possible avoid the use of 'piggy-back' or self-splicing connectors to power additional electrical equipment from existing feeds; make up a new feed with its own fuse instead.

When considering the current which a new circuit will have to handle, do not overlook the switch, especially when planning to use an existing switch to control additional components – for instance, if spotlights are to be fed via the main lighting switch. For preference a relay should be used to switch heavy currents. If in doubt consult an auto electrical specialist.

Any wire which passes through a body panel or bulkhead must be protected from chafing with a grommet or similar device. A wire which is allowed to chafe bare against the bodywork will cause a short-circuit and possibly a fire.

Mains electricity and electrical equipment

When using an electric power tool, inspection light, diagnostic equipment etc, which works from the mains, always ensure that the appliance is correctly connected to its plug and that, where necessary, it is properly earthed. Do not use such appliances in damp conditions and, again, beware of creating a spark or applying excessive heat in the vicinity of fuel or fuel vapour. Also ensure that the appliances meet the relevant national safety standards.

Ignition HT voltage

A severe electric shock can result from touching certain parts of the ignition system, such as the HT leads, when the engine is running or being cranked, particularly if components are damp or the insulation is defective. Where an electronic ignition system is fitted, the HT voltage is much higher and could prove fatal, especially to wearers of cardiac pacemakers.

Jacking and vehicle support

The jack provided with the vehicle is designed primarily for emergency wheel changing, and its use for servicing and overhaul work on the vehicle is best avoided. Instead, a more substantial workshop jack (trolley jack or similar) should be used. Whichever type is employed, it is essential that additional safety support is provided by means of axle stands designed for this purpose. Never use makeshift means such as wooden blocks or piles of house bricks, as these can easily topple or, in the case of bricks, disintegrate under the weight of the vehicle. Further information on the correct positioning of the jack and axle stands is provided in the *'Jacking, towing and wheel changing'* section.

If removal of the wheels is not required, the use of drive-on ramps is recommended. Caution should be exercised to ensure that they are correctly aligned with the wheels, and that the vehicle is not driven too far along them so that it promptly falls off the other ends or tips the ramps.

General repair procedures

Whenever servicing, repair or overhaul work is carried out on the car or its components, it is necessary to observe the following procedures and instructions. This will assist in carrying out the operation efficiently and to a professional standard of workmanship.

Joint mating faces and gaskets

When separating components at their mating faces, never insert screwdrivers or similar implements into the joint between the faces in order to prise them apart. This can cause severe damage which results in oil leaks, coolant leaks, etc upon reassembly. Separation is usually achieved by tapping along the joint with a soft-faced hammer in order to break the seal. However, note that this method may not be suitable where dowels are used for component location.

Where a gasket is used between the mating faces of two components, ensure that it is renewed on reassembly and fit it dry unless otherwise stated in the repair procedure. Make sure that the mating faces are clean and dry with all traces of old gasket removed. When cleaning a joint face, use a tool which is not likely to score or damage the face, and remove any burrs or nicks with an oilstone or fine file.

Make sure that tapped holes are cleaned with a pipe cleaner and keep them free of jointing compound, if this is being used, unless specifically instructed otherwise.

Ensure that all orifices, channels or pipes are clear and blow through them, preferably using compressed air.

Oil seals

Oil seals can be removed by levering them out with a wide flat-bladed screwdriver or similar implement. Alternatively, a number of self-tapping screws may be screwed into the seal and these used as a purchase for pliers or some similar device in order to pull the seal free.

Whenever an oil seal is removed from its working location, either individually or as part of an assembly, it should be renewed.

The very fine sealing lip of the seal is easily damaged and will not seal if the surface it contacts is not completely clean and free from scratches, nicks or grooves. If the original sealing surface of the component cannot be restored, and the manufacturer has not made provision for slight relocation of the seal relative to the sealing surface, the component should be renewed.

Protect the lips of the seal from any surface which may damage them in the course of fitting. Use tape or a conical sleeve where possible. Lubricate the seal lips with oil before fitting and, on dual-lipped seals, fill the space between the lips with grease.

Unless otherwise stated, oil seals must be fitted with their sealing lips toward the lubricant to be sealed.

Use a tubular drift or block of wood of the appropriate size to install the seal and, if the seal housing is shouldered, drive the seal down to the shoulder. If the seal housing is unshouldered, the seal should be fitted with its face flush with the housing top face (unless otherwise instructed).

Screw threads and fastenings

Seized nuts, bolts and screws are quite a common occurrence where corrosion has set in, and the use of penetrating oil or releasing fluid will often overcome this problem if the offending item is soaked for a while before attempting to release it. The use of an impact driver may also provide a means of releasing such stubborn fastening devices when used in conjunction with the appropriate screwdriver bit or socket. If none of these methods works, it may be necessary to resort to the careful application of heat, or the use of a hacksaw or nut splitter device.

Studs are usually removed by locking two nuts together on the threaded part and then using a spanner on the lower nut to unscrew the stud. Studs or bolts which have broken off below the surface of the component in which they are mounted can sometimes be removed using a proprietary stud extractor. Always ensure that a blind tapped hole is completely free from oil, grease, water or other fluid before installing the bolt or stud. Failure to do this could cause the housing to crack due to the hydraulic action of the bolt or stud as it is screwed in.

When tightening a castellated nut to accept a split pin, tighten the nut to the specified torque, where applicable, and then tighten further to the next split pin hole. Never slacken the nut to align the split pin hole unless stated in the repair procedure.

When checking or retightening a nut or bolt to a specified torque setting, slacken the nut or bolt by a quarter of a turn, and then retighten to the specified setting. However, this should not be attempted where angular tightening has been used.

For some screw fastenings, notably cylinder head bolts or nuts, torque wrench settings are no longer specified for the latter stages of tightening, 'angle-tightening' being called up instead. Typically, a fairly low torque wrench setting will be applied to the bolts/nuts in the correct sequence, followed by one or more stages of tightening through specified angles.

Locknuts, locktabs and washers

Any fastening which will rotate against a component or housing in the course of tightening should always have a washer between it and the relevant component or housing.

Spring or split washers should always be renewed when they are used to lock a critical component such as a big-end bearing retaining bolt or nut. Locktabs which are folded over to retain a nut or bolt should always be renewed.

Self-locking nuts can be reused in non-critical areas, providing resistance can be felt when the locking portion passes over the bolt or stud thread. However, it should be noted that self-locking stiffnuts tend to lose their effectiveness after long periods of use, and in such cases should be renewed as a matter of course.

Split pins must always be replaced with new ones of the correct size for the hole.

When thread-locking compound is found on the threads of a fastener which is to be re-used, it should be cleaned off with a wire brush and solvent, and fresh compound applied on reassembly.

Special tools

Some repair procedures in this manual entail the use of special tools such as a press, two or three-legged pullers, spring compressors etc. Wherever possible, suitable readily available alternatives to the manufacturer's special tools are described, and are shown in use. In some instances, where no alternative is possible, it has been necessary to resort to the use of a manufacturer's tool and this has been done for reasons of safety as well as the efficient completion of the repair operation. Unless you are highly skilled and have a thorough understanding of the procedures described, never attempt to bypass the use of any special tool when the procedure described specifies its use. Not only is there a very great risk of personal injury, but expensive damage could be caused to the components involved.

Environmental considerations

When disposing of used engine oil, brake fluid, antifreeze etc, give due consideration to any detrimental environmental effects. Do not, for instance, pour any of the above liquids down drains into the general sewage system or onto the ground to soak away. Many local council refuse tips provide a facility for waste oil disposal as do some garages. If none of these facilities are available, consult your local Environmental Health Department for further advice.

With the universal tightening-up of legislation regarding the emission of environmentally harmful substances from motor vehicles, most current vehicles have tamperproof devices fitted to the main adjustment points of the fuel system. These devices are primarily designed to prevent unqualified persons from adjusting the fuel/air mixture with the chance of a consequent increase in toxic emissions. If such devices are encountered during servicing or overhaul, they should, wherever possible, be renewed or refitted in accordance with the vehicle manufacturer's requirements or current legislation.

Tools and working facilities

Introduction

A selection of good tools is a fundamental requirement for anyone contemplating the maintenance and repair of a motor vehicle. For the owner who does not possess any, their purchase will prove a considerable expense, offsetting some of the savings made by doing-it-yourself. However, provided that the tools purchased meet the relevant national safety standards and are of good quality, they will last for many years and prove an extremely worthwhile investment.

To help the average owner to decide which tools are needed to carry out the various tasks detailed in this manual, we have compiled three lists of tools under the following headings: *Maintenance and minor repair*, *Repair and overhaul*, and *Special*. Newcomers to practical mechanics should start off with the *Maintenance and minor repair* tool kit and confine themselves to the simpler jobs around the vehicle. Then, as confidence and experience grow, more difficult tasks can be undertaken, with extra tools being purchased as, and when, they are needed. In this way, a *Maintenance and minor repair* tool kit can be built up into a *Repair and overhaul* tool kit over a considerable period of time without any major cash outlays. The experienced do-it-yourselfer will have a tool kit good enough for most repair and overhaul procedures and will add tools from the *Special* category when it is felt that the expense is justified by the amount of use to which these tools will be put.

Maintenance and minor repair tool kit

The tools given in this list should be considered as a minimum requirement if routine maintenance, servicing and minor repair operations are to be undertaken. We recommend the purchase of combination spanners (ring one end, open-ended the other); although more expensive than open-ended ones, they do give the advantages of both types of spanner.

Combination spanners:
Metric – 8, 9, 10, 11, 12, 13, 14, 15, 17 & 19 mm
Adjustable spanner – 35 mm jaw (approx)
Engine sump/gearbox/rear axle drain plug key (where applicable)
Spark plug spanner (with rubber insert)
Spark plug gap adjustment tool

Set of feeler gauges
Brake adjuster spanner (where applicable)
Brake bleed nipple spanner
Screwdrivers:
Flat blade – approx 100 mm long x 6 mm dia
Cross blade – approx 100 mm long x 6 mm dia
Combination pliers
Hacksaw (junior)
Tyre pump
Tyre pressure gauge
Grease gun (where applicable)
Oil can
Oil filter removal tool
Fine emery cloth
Wire brush (small)
Funnel (medium size)

Repair and overhaul tool kit

These tools are virtually essential for anyone undertaking any major repairs to a motor vehicle, and are additional to those given in the *Maintenance and minor repair* list. Included in this list is a comprehensive set of sockets. Although these are expensive, they will be found invaluable as they are so versatile – particularly if various drives are included in the set. We recommend the half-inch square-drive type, as this can be used with most proprietary torque wrenches. If you cannot afford a socket set, even bought piecemeal, then inexpensive tubular box spanners are a useful alternative.

The tools in this list will occasionally need to be supplemented by tools from the *Special* list.

Sockets (or box spanners) to cover range in previous list
Reversible ratchet drive (for use with sockets) (photo).
Extension piece, 250 mm (for use with sockets)
Universal joint (for use with sockets)
Torque wrench (for use with sockets)
Self-locking grips
Ball pein hammer
Soft-faced mallet (plastic/aluminium or rubber)

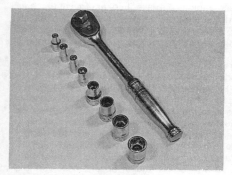

Sockets and reversible ratchet drive

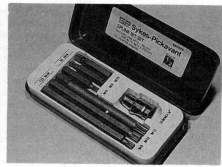

Spline bit set

Spline key set

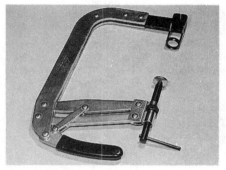

Valve spring compressor

Piston ring compressor

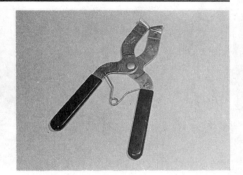

Piston ring removal/installation tool

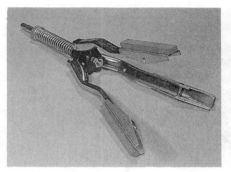

Cylinder bore hone

Three-legged hub and bearing puller

Micrometer set

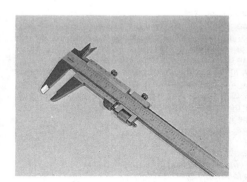

Vernier calipers

Dial test indicator and magnetic stand

Stroboscopic timing light

Compression testing gauge

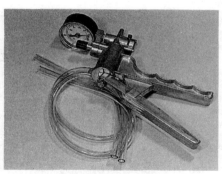

Vacuum pump and gauge

Bush and bearing removal/installation set

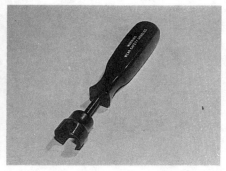

Brake shoe steady spring cup removal tool

Clutch plate alignment set

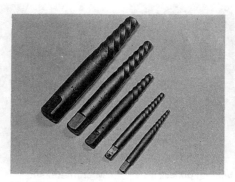

Stud extractor set

Tap and die set

Screwdrivers:
     Flat blade – long & sturdy, short (chubby), and narrow (electrician's) types
     Cross blade – Long & sturdy, and short (chubby) types
Pliers:
     Long-nosed
     Side cutters (electrician's)
     Circlip (internal and external)
Cold chisel – 25 mm
Scriber
Scraper
Centre-punch
Pin punch
Hacksaw
Brake hose clamp
Brake/clutch bleeding kit
Selection of twist drills
Steel rule/straight-edge
Allen keys (inc. splined/Torx type) (photos).
Selection of files
Wire brush
Axle stands
Jack (strong trolley or hydraulic type)
Light with extension lead

Special tools

The tools in this list are those which are not used regularly, are expensive to buy, or which need to be used in accordance with their manufacturers' instructions. Unless relatively difficult mechanical jobs are undertaken frequently, it will not be economic to buy many of these tools. Where this is the case, you could consider clubbing together with friends (or joining a motorists' club) to make a joint purchase, or borrowing the tools against a deposit from a local garage or tool hire specialist. It is worth noting that many of the larger DIY superstores now carry a large range of special tools for hire at modest rates.

The following list contains only those tools and instruments freely available to the public, and not those special tools produced by the vehicle manufacturer specifically for its dealer network. You will find occasional references to these manufacturers' special tools in the text of this manual. Generally, an alternative method of doing the job without the vehicle manufacturers' special tool is given. However, sometimes there is no alternative to using them. Where this is the case and the relevant tool cannot be bought or borrowed, you will have to entrust the work to a franchised garage.

     Valve spring compressor (photo).
     Valve grinding tool
     Piston ring compressor (photo).
     Piston ring removal/installation tool (photo).
     Cylinder bore hone (photo).
     Balljoint separator
     Coil spring compressors (where applicable)
     Two/three-legged hub and bearing puller (photo).
     Impact screwdriver
     Micrometer and/or vernier calipers (photos).
     Dial test indicator (photo).
     Stroboscopic timing light (photo).
     Dwell angle meter/tachometer
     Universal electrical multi-meter
     Cylinder compression gauge (photo).
     Hand-operated vacuum pump and gauge (photo).
     Bush and bearing removal/installation set (photo).
     Brake shoe steady spring cup removal tool (photo).
     Clutch plate alignment set (photo).
     Stud extractors (photo).
     Tap and die set (photo).
     Lifting tackle
     Trolley jack

Buying tools

For practically all tools, a tool factor is the best source since he will have a very comprehensive range compared with the average garage or accessory shop. Having said that, accessory shops often offer excellent quality tools at discount prices, so it pays to shop around.

Remember, you don't have to buy the most expensive items on the shelf but it is always advisable to steer clear of the very cheap tools. There are plenty of good tools around at reasonable prices, but always aim to purchase items which meet the relevant national safety standards. If in doubt, ask the proprietor or manager of the shop for advice before making a purchase.

Care and maintenance of tools

Having purchased a reasonable tool kit, it is necessary to keep the tools in a clean and serviceable condition. After use, always wipe off any dirt, grease and metal particles using a clean, dry cloth, before putting the tools away. Never leave them lying around after they have been used. A simple tool rack on the garage or workshop wall for items such as screwdrivers and pliers is a good idea. Store all normal spanners and sockets in a metal box. Any measuring instruments, gauges, meters, etc, must be carefully stored where they cannot be damaged or become rusty.

Take a little care when tools are used. Hammer heads inevitably become marked and screwdrivers lose the keen edge on their blades from time to time. A little timely attention with emery cloth or a file will soon restore items like this to a good serviceable finish.

Working facilities

Not to be forgotten when discussing tools is the workshop itself. If anything more than routine maintenance is to be carried out, some form of suitable working area becomes essential.

It is appreciated that many an owner mechanic is forced by circumstances to remove an engine or similar item without the benefit of a garage or workshop. Having done this, any repairs should always be done under the cover of a roof.

Wherever possible, any dismantling should be done on a clean, flat workbench or table at a suitable working height.

Any workbench needs a vice; one with a jaw opening of 100 mm is suitable for most jobs. As mentioned previously, some clean dry storage space is also required for tools, as well as for any lubricants, cleaning fluids, touch-up paints and so on, which become necessary.

Another item which may be required, and which has a much more general usage, is an electric drill with a chuck capacity of at least 8 mm. This, together with a good range of twist drills, is virtually essential for fitting accessories.

Last, but not least, always keep a supply of old newspapers and clean, lint-free rags available, and try to keep any working area as clean as possible.

Spanner jaw gap and bolt size comparison table

Jaw gap – in (mm)	Spanner size	Bolt size
0.197 (5.00)	5 mm	M 2.5
0.216 (5.50)	5.5 mm	M 3
0.218 (5.53)	$\frac{7}{32}$ in AF	
0.236 (6.00)	6 mm	M 3.5
0.250 (6.35)	$\frac{1}{4}$ in AF	
0.275 (7.00)	7 mm	M 4
0.281 (7.14)	$\frac{9}{32}$ in AF	
0.312 (7.92)	$\frac{5}{16}$ in AF	
0.315 (8.00)	8 mm	M 5
0.343 (8.71)	$\frac{11}{32}$ in AF	
0.375 (9.52)	$\frac{3}{8}$ in AF	
0.394 (10.00)	10 mm	M 6
0.406 (10.32)	$\frac{13}{32}$ in AF	
0.433 (11.00)	11 mm	M 7
0.437 (11.09)	$\frac{7}{16}$ in AF	$\frac{1}{4}$ in SAE
0.468 (11.88)	$\frac{15}{32}$ in AF	
0.500 (12.70)	$\frac{1}{2}$ in AF	$\frac{5}{16}$ in SAE
0.512 (13.00)	13 mm	M8
0.562 (14.27)	$\frac{9}{16}$ in AF	$\frac{3}{8}$ in SAE
0.593 (15.06)	$\frac{19}{32}$ in AF	
0.625 (15.87)	$\frac{5}{8}$ in AF	$\frac{7}{16}$ in SAE
0.669 (17.00)	17 mm	M 10
0.687 (17.44)	$\frac{11}{16}$ in AF	
0.709 (19.00)	19 mm	M 12
0.750 (19.05)	$\frac{3}{4}$ in AF	$\frac{1}{2}$ in SAE
0.781 (19.83)	$\frac{25}{32}$ in AF	
0.812 (20.62)	$\frac{13}{16}$ in AF	
0.866 (22.00)	22 mm	M 14
0.875 (22.25)	$\frac{7}{8}$ in AF	$\frac{9}{16}$ in SAE
0.937 (23.79)	$\frac{15}{16}$ in AF	$\frac{5}{8}$ in SAE
0.945 (24.00)	24 mm	M 16
0.968 (24.58)	$\frac{31}{32}$ in AF	
1.000 (25.40)	1 in AF	$\frac{11}{16}$ in SAE
1.062 (26.97)	$1\frac{1}{16}$ in AF	$\frac{3}{4}$ in SAE
1.063 (27.00)	27 mm	M 18
1.125 (28.57)	$1\frac{1}{8}$ in AF	
1.182 (30.00)	30 mm	M 20
1.187 (30.14)	$1\frac{3}{16}$ in AF	
1.250 (31.75)	$1\frac{1}{4}$ in AF	$\frac{7}{8}$ in SAE
1.260 (32.00)	32 mm	M 22
1.312 (33.32)	$1\frac{5}{16}$ in AF	
1.375 (34.92)	$1\frac{3}{8}$ in AF	
1.418 (36.00)	36 mm	M 24
1.437 (36.49)	$1\frac{7}{16}$ in AF	1 in SAE
1.500 (38.10)	$1\frac{1}{2}$ in AF	
1.615 (41.00)	41 mm	M 27

Booster battery (jump) starting

When jump starting a car using a booster battery, observe the following precautions.

(a) Before connecting the booster battery, make sure that the ignition is switched off.
(b) Ensure that all electrical equipment (lights, heater, wipers, etc.) is switched off.
(c) Make sure that the booster battery is the same voltage as the discharged one in the vehicle.
(d) If the battery is being jump started from the battery in another vehicle, the two vehicles MUST NOT TOUCH each other.
(e) Make sure that the transmission is in Neutral (manual gearbox) or Park (automatic transmission).

Connect one jump lead between the positive (+) terminals of the two batteries. Connect the other jump lead first to the negative (–) terminal of the booster battery, and then to a good earthing point on the vehicle to be started, such as a bolt or bracket on the engine block, at least 45 cm from the battery if possible. Make sure that the jump leads will not come into contact with the fan, drivebelts or other moving parts of the engine.

Start the engine using the booster battery, then with the engine running at idle speed, disconnect the jump leads in the reverse order of connection.

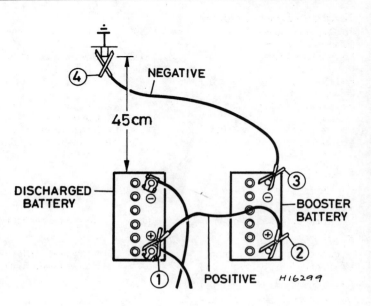

Jump start lead connections for negative-earth vehicles – connect leads in order shown

Conversion factors

Length (distance)

Inches (in)	X	25.4	= Millimetres (mm)	X	0.0394	= Inches (in)
Feet (ft)	X	0.305	= Metres (m)	X	3.281	= Feet (ft)
Miles	X	1.609	= Kilometres (km)	X	0.621	= Miles

Volume (capacity)

Cubic inches (cu in; in^3)	X	16.387	= Cubic centimetres (cc; cm^3)	X	0.061	= Cubic inches (cu in; in^3)
Imperial pints (Imp pt)	X	0.568	= Litres (l)	X	1.76	= Imperial pints (Imp pt)
Imperial quarts (Imp qt)	X	1.137	= Litres (l)	X	0.88	= Imperial quarts (Imp qt)
Imperial quarts (Imp qt)	X	1.201	= US quarts (US qt)	X	0.833	= Imperial quarts (Imp qt)
US quarts (US qt)	X	0.946	= Litres (l)	X	1.057	= US quarts (US qt)
Imperial gallons (Imp gal)	X	4.546	= Litres (l)	X	0.22	= Imperial gallons (Imp gal)
Imperial gallons (Imp gal)	X	1.201	= US gallons (US gal)	X	0.833	= Imperial gallons (Imp gal)
US gallons (US gal)	X	3.785	= Litres (l)	X	0.264	= US gallons (US gal)

Mass (weight)

Ounces (oz)	X	28.35	= Grams (g)	X	0.035	= Ounces (oz)
Pounds (lb)	X	0.454	= Kilograms (kg)	X	2.205	= Pounds (lb)

Force

Ounces-force (ozf; oz)	X	0.278	= Newtons (N)	X	3.6	= Ounces-force (ozf; oz)
Pounds-force (lbf; lb)	X	4.448	= Newtons (N)	X	0.225	= Pounds-force (lbf; lb)
Newtons (N)	X	0.1	= Kilograms-force (kgf; kg)	X	9.81	= Newtons (N)

Pressure

Pounds-force per square inch (psi; lbf/in^2; lb/in^2)	X	0.070	= Kilograms-force per square centimetre (kgf/cm^2; kg/cm^2)	X	14.223	= Pounds-force per square inch (psi; lbf/in^2; lb/in^2)
Pounds-force per square inch (psi; lbf/in^2; lb/in^2)	X	0.068	= Atmospheres (atm)	X	14.696	= Pounds-force per square inch (psi; lbf/in^2; lb/in^2)
Pounds-force per square inch (psi; lbf/in^2; lb/in^2)	X	0.069	= Bars	X	14.5	= Pounds-force per square inch (psi; lbf/in^2; lb/in^2)
Pounds-force per square inch (psi; lbf/in^2; lb/in^2)	X	6.895	= Kilopascals (kPa)	X	0.145	= Pounds-force per square inch (psi; lbf/in^2; lb/in^2)
Kilopascals (kPa)	X	0.01	= Kilograms-force per square centimetre (kgf/cm^2; kg/cm^2)	X	98.1	= Kilopascals (kPa)
Millibar (mbar)	X	100	= Pascals (Pa)	X	0.01	= Millibar (mbar)
Millibar (mbar)	X	0.0145	= Pounds-force per square inch (psi; lbf/in^2; lb/in^2)	X	68.947	= Millibar (mbar)
Millibar (mbar)	X	0.75	= Millimetres of mercury (mmHg)	X	1.333	= Millibar (mbar)
Millibar (mbar)	X	0.401	= Inches of water (inH$_2$O)	X	2.491	= Millibar (mbar)
Millimetres of mercury (mmHg)	X	0.535	= Inches of water (inH$_2$O)	X	1.868	= Millimetres of mercury (mmHg)
Inches of water (inH$_2$O)	X	0.036	= Pounds-force per square inch (psi; lbf/in^2; lb/in^2)	X	27.68	= Inches of water (inH$_2$O)

Torque (moment of force)

Pounds-force inches (lbf in; lb in)	X	1.152	= Kilograms-force centimetre (kgf cm; kg cm)	X	0.868	= Pounds-force inches (lbf in; lb in)
Pounds-force inches (lbf in; lb in)	X	0.113	= Newton metres (Nm)	X	8.85	= Pounds-force inches (lbf in; lb in)
Pounds-force inches (lbf in; lb in)	X	0.083	= Pounds-force feet (lbf ft; lb ft)	X	12	= Pounds-force inches (lbf in; lb in)
Pounds-force feet (lbf ft; lb ft)	X	0.138	= Kilograms-force metres (kgf m; kg m)	X	7.233	= Pounds-force feet (lbf ft; lb ft)
Pounds-force feet (lbf ft; lb ft)	X	1.356	= Newton metres (Nm)	X	0.738	= Pounds-force feet (lbf ft; lb ft)
Newton metres (Nm)	X	0.102	= Kilograms-force metres (kgf m; kg m)	X	9.804	= Newton metres (Nm)

Power

Horsepower (hp)	X	745.7	= Watts (W)	X	0.0013	= Horsepower (hp)

Velocity (speed)

Miles per hour (miles/hr; mph)	X	1.609	= Kilometres per hour (km/hr; kph)	X	0.621	= Miles per hour (miles/hr; mph)

Fuel consumption

Miles per gallon, Imperial (mpg)	X	0.354	= Kilometres per litre (km/l)	X	2.825	= Miles per gallon, Imperial (mpg)
Miles per gallon, US (mpg)	X	0.425	= Kilometres per litre (km/l)	X	2.352	= Miles per gallon, US (mpg)

Temperature

Degrees Fahrenheit = (°C x 1.8) + 32   Degrees Celsius (Degrees Centigrade; °C) = (°F − 32) x 0.56

It is common practice to convert from miles per gallon (mpg) to litres/100 kilometres (l/100km), where mpg (Imperial) x l/100 km = 282 and mpg (US) x l/100 km = 235

Fault diagnosis

Contents

Introduction

The vehicle owner who does his or her own maintenance according to the recommended service schedules should not have to use this section of the manual very often. Modern component reliability is such that, provided those items subject to wear or deterioration are inspected or renewed at the specified intervals, sudden failure is comparatively rare. Faults do not usually just happen as a result of sudden failure, but develop over a period of time. Major mechanical failures in particular are usually preceded by characteristic symptoms over hundreds or even thousands of miles. Those components which do occasionally fail without warning are often small and easily carried in the vehicle.

With any fault finding, the first step is to decide where to begin investigations. Sometimes this is obvious, but on other occasions a little detective work will be necessary. The owner who makes half a dozen haphazard adjustments or replacements may be successful in curing a fault (or its symptoms), but will be none the wiser if the fault recurs and ultimately may have spent more time and money than was necessary. A calm and logical approach will be found to be more satisfactory in the long run. Always take into account any warning signs or abnormalities that may have been noticed in the period preceding the fault – power loss, high or low gauge readings, unusual smells, etc – and remember that failure of components such as fuses or spark plugs may only be pointers to some underlying fault.

The pages which follow provide an easy reference guide to the more common problems which may occur during the operation of the vehicle. These problems and their possible causes are grouped under headings denoting various components or systems, such as Engine, Cooling system, etc. The Chapter and/or Section which deals with the problem is also shown in brackets. Whatever the fault, certain basic principles apply. These are as follows:

Verify the fault. This is simply a matter of being sure that you know what the symptoms are before starting work. This is particularly important if you are investigating a fault for someone else who may not have described it very accurately.

Don't overlook the obvious. For example, if the vehicle won't start, is there petrol in the tank? (Don't take anyone else's word on this particular point, and don't trust the fuel gauge either!) If an electrical fault is indicated, look for loose or broken wires before digging out the test gear.

Cure the disease, not the symptom. Substituting a flat battery with a fully charged one will get you off the hard shoulder, but if the underlying cause is not attended to, the new battery will go the same way. Similarly, changing oil-fouled spark plugs for a new set will get you moving again, but remember that the reason for the fouling (if it wasn't simply an incorrect grade of plug) will have to be established and corrected.

Don't take anything for granted. Particularly, don't forget that a 'new' component may itself be defective (especially if it's been rattling around in the boot for months), and don't leave components out of a fault diagnosis sequence just because they are new or recently fitted. When you do finally diagnose a difficult fault, you'll probably realise that all the evidence was there from the start.

1   Engine

Engine fails to rotate when attempting to start
- Battery terminal connections loose or corroded (Chapter 1).
- Battery discharged or faulty (Chapter 12).
- Broken, loose or disconnected wiring in the starting circuit (Chapter 12).
- Defective starter solenoid or switch (Chapter 12).
- Defective starter motor (Chapter 12).
- Flywheel ring gear or starter pinion teeth loose or broken (Chapter 2 or 12).
- Engine earth strap broken or disconnected (Chapter 2 or 12).
- Automatic transmission not in Park/Neutral position or starter inhibitor switch faulty (Chapter 7, Part B).

Engine rotates but will not start
- Fuel tank empty.
- Battery discharged (engine rotates slowly) (Chapter 12).
- Battery terminal connections loose or corroded (Chapter 1).
- Ignition components damp or damaged (Chapter 1 or 5).
- Broken, loose or disconnected wiring in the ignition circuit (Chapter 1 or 5).
- Worn, faulty or incorrectly-gapped spark plugs (Chapter 1).
- Choke mechanism sticking, incorrectly adjusted, or faulty – carburettor engine only (Chapter 4, Part A).
- Fuel injection system fault (Chapter 4, Part B).
- Major mechanical failure (eg camshaft drive) (Chapter 2).

Engine difficult to start when cold
- Battery discharged (Chapter 12).
- Battery terminal connections loose or corroded (Chapter 1).
- Worn, faulty or incorrectly-gapped spark plugs (Chapter 1).
- Choke mechanism sticking, incorrectly adjusted, or faulty – carburettor engine only (Chapter 4, Part A).
- Fuel injection system fault (Chapter 4, Part B).
- Other ignition system fault (Chapter 1 or 5).
- Low cylinder compressions (Chapter 2, Part A).

Engine difficult to start when hot
- Air filter element dirty or clogged (Chapter 1).
- Choke mechanism sticking, incorrectly-adjusted, or faulty – carburettor engine only (Chapter 4, Part A).
- Carburettor float chamber flooding – where applicable (Chapter 4, Part A).
- Fuel injection system fault (Chapter 4, Part B).
- Low cylinder compressions (Chapter 2, Part A).

Starter motor noisy or excessively-rough in engagement
- Flywheel ring gear or starter pinion teeth loose or broken (Chapter 2 or 12).
- Starter motor mounting bolts loose or missing (Chapter 12).
- Starter motor internal components worn or damaged (Chapter 12).

Engine starts but stops immediately
- Insufficient fuel reaching carburettor – where applicable (Chapter 4).
- Blocked carburettor jet(s) or internal passages – where applicable (Chapter 4, Part A).

- Fuel injection system fault (Chapter 4, Part B).
- Loose or faulty electrical connections in the ignition circuit (Chapter 1 or 5).
- Vacuum leak at the carburettor or inlet manifold/throttle body, as applicable (Chapter 4).

Engine idles erratically
- Incorrectly-adjusted idle speed and/or mixture settings (Chapter 1).
- Fuel injection system fault (Chapter 4, Part B).
- Air filter element clogged (Chapter 1).
- Vacuum leak at the carburettor/fuel injection unit, inlet manifold/throttle body or associated hoses (Chapter 4).
- Worn, faulty or incorrectly-gapped spark plugs (Chapter 1).
- Faulty or worn hydraulic valve lifters (Chapter 2, Part B).
- Uneven or low cylinder compressions (Chapter 2, Part A).
- Camshaft lobes worn (Chapter 2).
- Timing belt incorrectly tensioned (Chapter 2, Part A).

Engine misfires at idle speed
- Worn, faulty or incorrectly-gapped spark plugs (Chapter 1).
- Faulty spark plug HT leads (Chapter 1).
- Incorrectly-adjusted idle mixture settings (Chapter 1).
- Incorrect ignition timing (Chapter 1).
- Vacuum leak at the carburettor/fuel injection unit, inlet manifold/throttle body or associated hoses (Chapter 4).
- Fuel injection system fault (Chapter 4, Part B).
- Distributor cap cracked or tracking internally – where applicable (Chapter 1).
- Faulty or worn hydraulic valve lifters (Chapter 2, Part B).
- Uneven or low cylinder compressions (Chapter 2, Part A).
- Disconnected, leaking or perished crankcase ventilation hoses (Chapter 4).

Engine misfires throughout the driving speed range
- Blocked carburettor jet(s) or internal passages – where applicable (Chapter 4, Part A).
- Carburettor incorrectly-adjusted or worn – where applicable (Chapter 1 or Chapter 4, Part A).
- Fuel injection system fault (Chapter 4, Part B).
- Fuel filter choked (Chapter 1).
- Fuel pump faulty (Chapter 4).
- Fuel tank vent blocked or fuel pipes restricted (Chapter 4).
- Vacuum leak at the carburettor/fuel injection unit, inlet manifold/throttle body or associated hoses (Chapter 4).
- Worn, faulty or incorrectly-gapped spark plugs (Chapter 1).
- Faulty spark plug HT leads (Chapter 1).
- Distributor cap cracked or tracking internally – where applicable (Chapter 1).
- Faulty ignition coil (Chapter 5).
- Uneven or low cylinder compressions (Chapter 2, Part A).

Engine hesitates on acceleration
- Worn, faulty or incorrectly-gapped spark plugs (Chapter 1).
- Carburettor accelerator pump faulty – where applicable (Chapter 4, Part A).
- Blocked carburettor jets or internal passages – where applicable (Chapter 4, Part A).
- Fuel injection system fault (Chapter 4, Part B).
- Vacuum leak at the carburettor/fuel injection unit, inlet manifold/throttle body or associated hoses (Chapter 4).
- Carburettor incorrectly-adjusted or worn – where applicable (Chapter 1 or Chapter 4, Part A).

Engine stalls
- Incorrectly-adjusted idle speed and/or mixture settings (Chapter 1).
- Blocked carburettor jet(s) or internal passages – where applicable (Chapter 4, Part A).
- Vacuum leak at the carburettor/fuel injection unit, inlet manifold/throttle body or associated hoses (Chapter 4).
- Fuel injection system fault (Chapter 4, Part B).
- Fuel filter choked (Chapter 1).
- Fuel pump faulty (Chapter 4).
- Fuel tank vent blocked or fuel pipes restricted (Chapter 4).

Engine lacks power
- Incorrect ignition timing (Chapter 1).

- Carburettor incorrectly-adjusted or worn – where applicable (Chapter 1 or Chapter 4, Part A).
- Fuel injection system fault (Chapter 4, Part B).
- Timing belt incorrectly fitted or tensioned (Chapter 2, Part A).
- Fuel filter choked (Chapter 1).
- Fuel pump faulty (Chapter 4).
- Uneven or low cylinder compressions (Chapter 2, Part A).
- Worn, faulty or incorrectly-gapped spark plugs (Chapter 1).
- Vacuum leak at the carburettor/fuel injection unit, inlet manifold/throttle body or associated hoses (Chapter 4).
- Brakes binding (Chapter 1 or 9).
- Clutch slipping – where applicable (Chapter 6).
- Automatic transmission fluid level incorrect (Chapter 1).

Engine backfires

- Ignition timing incorrect (Chapter 1).
- Timing belt incorrectly fitted or tensioned (Chapter 2, Part A).
- Carburettor incorrectly-adjusted or worn – where applicable (Chapter 1 or Chapter 4, Part A).
- Vacuum leak at the carburettor/fuel injection unit, inlet manifold/throttle body or associated hoses (Chapter 4).

Oil pressure warning light illuminated with engine running

- Low oil level or incorrect grade (Chapter 1).
- Faulty low oil pressure warning light switch (Chapter 12).
- Worn engine bearings and/or oil pump (Chapter 2).
- High engine operating temperature (Chapter 3).
- Oil pressure relief valve defective (Chapter 2).
- Oil pick-up strainer clogged (Chapter 2).

Engine runs-on after switching off

- Idle speed excessively high (Chapter 1).
- Excessive carbon build-up in engine (Chapter 2).
- High engine operating temperature (Chapter 3).
- Carburettor fault – where applicable (Chapter 4, Part A).
- Fuel injection system fault (Chapter 4, Part B).

Engine noises

Pre-ignition (pinking) or knocking during acceleration or under load
- Ignition timing incorrect (Chapter 1).
- Incorrect grade of fuel (Chapter 4).
- Vacuum leak at the carburettor/fuel injection unit, inlet manifold/throttle body or associated hoses (Chapter 4).
- Excessive carbon build-up in engine (Chapter 2).
- Worn or damaged distributor or other ignition system component (Chapter 5).
- Carburettor incorrectly-adjusted or worn – where applicable (Chapter 1 or Chapter 4, Part A).
- Fuel injection system fault (Chapter 4, Part B).

Whistling or wheezing noises
- Leaking inlet manifold, throttle body, carburettor, or fuel injection unit gasket (Chapter 4).
- Leaking exhaust manifold gasket or pipe-to-manifold joint (Chapter 1).
- Leaking vacuum hose (Chapter 4, 5 or 9).
- Blowing cylinder head gasket (Chapter 2).

Tapping or rattling noises
- Faulty or worn hydraulic valve lifters (Chapter 2, Part B).
- Worn valve gear or camshaft (Chapter 2).
- Incorrectly-adjusted or worn timing belt (Chapter 2, Part A).
- Ancillary component fault (water pump, alternator etc) (Chapter 3 or 12).

Knocking or thumping noises
- Worn big-end bearings (regular heavy knocking, perhaps less under load) (Chapter 2, Part B).
- Worn main bearings (rumbling and knocking, perhaps worsening under load) (Chapter 2, Part B).
- Piston slap (most noticeable when cold) (Chapter 2).
- Ancillary component fault (alternator, water pump etc) (Chapter 3 or 12).

2   Cooling system

Overheating
- Insufficient coolant in system (Chapter 3).
- Thermostat faulty (Chapter 3).
- Radiator core blocked or grille restricted (Chapter 3).
- Electric cooling fan or fan switch faulty (Chapter 3).
- Timing belt worn, or incorrectly-adjusted (Chapter 2, Part A).
- Ignition timing incorrect (Chapter 1).
- Inaccurate temperature gauge sender (Chapter 3).
- Airlock in cooling system (Chapter 1).

Overcooling
- Thermostat faulty (Chapter 3).
- Inaccurate temperature gauge sender (Chapter 3).

External coolant leakage
- Deteriorated or damaged hoses or hose clips (Chapter 1).
- Radiator core or heater matrix leaking (Chapter 3).
- Water pump seal leaking (Chapter 3).
- Boiling due to overheating (Chapter 3).
- Core plug leaking (Chapter 2).

Internal coolant leakage
- Leaking cylinder head gasket (Chapter 2).
- Cracked cylinder head or cylinder bore (Chapter 2).

Corrosion
- Infrequent draining and flushing (Chapter 1).
- Incorrect antifreeze mixture or inappropriate type (Chapter 1).

3   Fuel and exhaust system

Excessive fuel consumption
- Air filter element dirty or clogged (Chapter 1).
- Carburettor incorrectly-adjusted or worn – where applicable (Chapter 1 or Chapter 4, Part A).
- Fuel injection system fault (Chapter 4).
- Ignition timing incorrect (Chapter 1).
- Tyres under-inflated (Chapter 1).

Fuel leakage and/or fuel odour
- Damaged or corroded fuel tank, pipes or connections (Chapter 1).
- Carburettor float chamber flooding – where applicable (Chapter 4, Part A).
- Damaged or faulty fuel injection system component (Chapter 4, Part B).

Excessive noise or fumes from exhaust system
- Leaking exhaust system or manifold joints (Chapter 1).
- Leaking, corroded or damaged silencers or pipe (Chapter 1).
- Broken mountings causing body or suspension contact (Chapter 1).

4   Clutch

Pedal travels to floor – no pressure or very little resistance
- Broken clutch cable (Chapter 6).
- Incorrect clutch cable adjustment (Chapter 1).
- Broken clutch release bearing or fork (Chapter 6).
- Broken diaphragm spring in clutch pressure plate (Chapter 6).

Clutch fails to disengage (unable to select gears)
- Incorrect clutch cable adjustment (Chapter 1).
- Clutch friction disc sticking on gearbox input shaft splines (Chapter 6).
- Clutch friction disc sticking to flywheel or pressure plate (Chapter 6).
- Faulty pressure plate assembly (Chapter 6).
- Gearbox input shaft seized in crankshaft spigot bearing (Chapter 2).

- Clutch release mechanism worn or incorrectly assembled (Chapter 6).

Clutch slips (engine speed increases with no increase in vehicle speed)

- Incorrect clutch cable adjustment (Chapter 6).
- Clutch friction disc linings excessively worn (Chapter 6).
- Clutch friction disc linings contaminated with oil or grease (Chapter 6).
- Faulty pressure plate or weak diaphragm spring (Chapter 6).

Judder as clutch is engaged

- Clutch friction disc linings contaminated with oil or grease (Chapter 6).
- Clutch friction disc linings excessively worn (Chapter 6).
- Clutch cable sticking or frayed (Chapter 6).
- Faulty or distorted pressure plate or diaphragm spring (Chapter 6).
- Worn or loose engine or gearbox mountings (Chapter 2).
- Clutch friction disc hub or gearbox input shaft splines worn (Chapter 6 or 7).*

Noise when depressing or releasing clutch pedal

- Worn clutch release bearing (Chapter 6).
- Worn or dry clutch pedal bushes (Chapter 6).
- Faulty pressure plate assembly (Chapter 6).
- Pressure plate diaphragm spring broken (Chapter 6).
- Broken clutch friction disc cushioning springs (Chapter 6).

5 Manual gearbox

Noisy in neutral with engine running

- Input shaft bearings worn (noise apparent with clutch pedal released but not when depressed) (Chapter 7).*
- Clutch release bearing worn (noise apparent with clutch pedal depressed, possibly less when released) (Chapter 6).

Noisy in one particular gear

- Worn, damaged or chipped gear teeth (Chapter 7).*

Difficulty engaging gears

- Clutch fault (Chapter 6).
- Worn or damaged gear linkage (Chapter 7).
- Incorrectly-adjusted gear linkage (Chapter 7).
- Worn synchroniser units (Chapter 7).*

Jumps out of gear

- Worn or damaged gear linkage (Chapter 7).
- Incorrectly-adjusted gear linkage (Chapter 7).
- Worn synchroniser units (Chapter 7).*
- Worn selector forks (Chapter 7).*

Vibration

- Lack of oil (Chapter 1).
- Worn bearings (Chapter 7).*

Lubricant leaks

- Leaking differential side oil seal (Chapter 7).
- Leaking housing joint (Chapter 7).*
- Leaking input shaft oil seal (Chapter 7).

Although the corrective action necessary to remedy the symptoms described is beyond the scope of the home mechanic, the above information should be helpful in isolating the cause of the condition so that the owner can communicate clearly with a professional mechanic.

6 Automatic transmission

Note: *Due to the complexity of the automatic transmission, it is difficult for the home mechanic to properly diagnose and service this unit. For problems other than the following, the vehicle should be taken to a dealer service department or automatic transmission specialist.*

Fluid leakage

- Automatic transmission fluid is usually deep red in colour. Fluid leaks should not be confused with engine oil, which can easily be blown onto the transmission by air flow.
- To determine the source of a leak, first remove all built-up dirt and grime from the transmission housing and surrounding areas, using a degreasing agent or by steam-cleaning. Drive the vehicle at low speed so air flow will not blow the leak far from its source. Raise and support the vehicle, and determine where the leak is coming from. The following are common areas of leakage.
  (a) Oil pan (Chapter 7).
  (b) Dipstick tube (Chapter 1 or 7).
  (c) Transmission-to-fluid cooler fluid pipes/unions (Chapter 7).

Transmission fluid brown or has burned smell

- Transmission fluid level low, or fluid in need of renewal (Chapter 1 or 7).

General gear selection problems

- Chapter 7, Part B, deals with checking and adjusting the selector linkage on automatic transmissions. The following are common problems which may be caused by a poorly-adjusted linkage.
  (a) Engine starting in gears other than Park or Neutral.
  (b) Indicator on gear selector lever pointing to a gear other than the one actually being used.
  (c) Vehicle moves when in Park or Neutral.
  (d) Poor gearshift quality or erratic gear changes.
- Refer to Chapter 7, Part B for the selector linkage adjustment procedure.
- Faulty electronic control system (Chapter 7, Part B).

Transmission will not downshift (kickdown) with accelerator pedal fully depressed

- Low transmission fluid level (Chapter 1).
- Incorrect selector mechanism adjustment (Chapter 7, Part B).
- Faulty electronic control system (Chapter 7, Part B).

Engine will not start in any gear, or starts in gears other than Park or Neutral

- Incorrect starter/inhibitor switch adjustment (Chapter 7, Part B).
- Incorrect selector mechanism adjustment (Chapter 7, Part B).
- Faulty electronic control system (Chapter 7, Part B).

Transmission slips, shifts roughly, is noisy or has no drive in forward or reverse gears

- There are many probable causes for the above problems, but the home mechanic should be concerned with only one possibility – fluid level. Before taking the vehicle to a dealer or transmission specialist, check the fluid level as described in Chapter 1. Correct the fluid level as necessary, or have the fluid changed if needed. If the problem persists, professional help will be necessary.

7 Driveshafts

Clicking or knocking noise on turns (at slow speed on full-lock)

- Lack of constant velocity joint lubricant (Chapter 8).
- Worn outer constant velocity joint (Chapter 8).

Vibration when accelerating or decelerating

- Worn inner constant velocity joint (Chapter 8).
- Bent or distorted driveshaft (Chapter 8).

8 Braking system

Note: *Before assuming that a brake problem exists, make sure that the tyres are in good condition and correctly inflated, the front wheel alignment is correct, and the vehicle is not loaded with weight in an unequal manner. Apart from checking the condition of all pipe and hose connections, any faults occurring on the anti-lock braking system should be referred to a Vauxhall/Opel dealer for diagnosis.*

Vehicle pulls to one side under braking

- Worn, defective, damaged or contaminated front or rear brake pads/shoes on one side (Chapter 1).
- Seized or partially-seized front or rear brake caliper/wheel cylinder piston (Chapter 9).
- A mixture of brake pad/shoe lining materials fitted between sides (Chapter 1 or 9).
- Brake caliper mounting bolts loose (Chapter 9).
- Worn or damaged steering or suspension components (Chapter 10).

Noise (grinding or high-pitched squeal) when brakes applied

- Brake pad or shoe friction lining material worn down to metal backing (Chapter 1).
- Excessive corrosion of brake disc or drum – may be apparent after the vehicle has been standing for some time (Chapter 1).
- Foreign object (stone chipping, etc.) trapped between brake disc and disc shield (Chapter 9).

Excessive brake pedal travel

- Inoperative rear brake self-adjuster mechanism (Chapter 9).
- Faulty master cylinder (Chapter 9).
- Air in hydraulic system (Chapter 9).
- Faulty vacuum servo unit (Chapter 9).

Brake pedal feels spongy when depressed

- Air in hydraulic system (Chapter 9).
- Deteriorated flexible rubber brake hoses (Chapter 9).
- Master cylinder mounting nuts loose (Chapter 9).
- Faulty master cylinder (Chapter 9).

Excessive brake pedal effort required to stop vehicle

- Faulty vacuum servo unit (Chapter 9).
- Disconnected, damaged or insecure brake servo vacuum hose (Chapter 9).
- Primary or secondary hydraulic circuit failure (Chapter 9).
- Seized brake caliper or wheel cylinder piston(s) (Chapter 9).
- Brake pads or brake shoes incorrectly fitted (Chapter 1 or 9).
- Incorrect grade of brake pads or brake shoes fitted (Chapter 1 or 9).
- Brake pads or brake shoe linings contaminated (Chapter 9).

Judder felt through brake pedal or steering wheel when braking

- Excessive run-out or distortion of front discs or rear drums (Chapter 9).
- Brake pad or brake shoe linings worn (Chapter 1).
- Brake caliper or rear brake backplate mounting bolts loose (Chapter 9).
- Wear in suspension or steering components or mountings (Chapter 10).

Brakes binding

- Seized brake caliper or wheel cylinder piston(s) (Chapter 9).
- Incorrectly-adjusted handbrake mechanism or linkage (Chapter 9).
- Faulty master cylinder (Chapter 9).

Rear wheels locking under normal braking

- Rear brake shoe linings contaminated (Chapter 1 or 9).
- Faulty brake pressure regulator (Chapter 9).

9 Suspension and steering systems

Note: *Before diagnosing suspension or steering faults, be sure that the trouble is not due to incorrect tyre pressures, mixtures of tyre types or binding brakes.*

Vehicle pulls to one side

- Defective tyre (Chapter 1).
- Excessive wear in suspension or steering components (Chapter 10).
- Incorrect front wheel alignment (Chapter 10).
- Accident damage to steering or suspension components (Chapter 10).

Wheel wobble and vibration

- Front roadwheels out of balance (vibration felt mainly through the steering wheel) (Chapter 10).
- Rear roadwheels out of balance (vibration felt throughout the vehicle) (Chapter 10).
- Roadwheels damaged or distorted (Chapter 10).
- Faulty or damaged tyre (Chapter 1).
- Worn steering or suspension joints, bushes or components (Chapter 10).
- Wheel bolts loose (Chapter 1).

Excessive pitching and/or rolling around corners or during braking

- Defective shock absorbers (Chapter 10).
- Broken or weak coil spring and/or suspension component (Chapter 10).
- Worn or damaged anti-roll bar or mountings (Chapter 10).

Wandering or general instability

- Incorrect front wheel alignment (Chapter 10).
- Worn steering or suspension joints, bushes or components (Chapter 10).
- Roadwheels out of balance (Chapter 10).
- Faulty or damaged tyre (Chapter 1).
- Wheel bolts loose (Chapter 1).
- Defective shock absorbers (Chapter 10).

Excessively-stiff steering

- Lack of steering gear lubricant (Chapter 10).
- Seized tie-rod end balljoint or suspension balljoint (Chapter 10).
- Broken or incorrectly-adjusted power steering pump drivebelt (Chapter 1).
- Incorrect front wheel alignment (Chapter 10).
- Steering rack or column bent or damaged (Chapter 10).

Excessive play in steering

- Worn steering column bearing or flexible coupling (Chapter 10).
- Worn steering tie-rod end balljoints (Chapter 10).
- Worn steering gear (Chapter 10).
- Worn steering or suspension joints, bushes or components (Chapter 10).

Lack of power assistance

- Broken or incorrectly-adjusted power steering pump drivebelt (Chapter 1).
- Incorrect power steering fluid level (Chapter 1).
- Restriction in power steering fluid hoses (Chapter 10).
- Faulty power steering pump (Chapter 10).
- Faulty steering gear (Chapter 10).

Tyre wear excessive

Tyres worn on inside or outside edges
- Tyres under-inflated (wear on both edges) (Chapter 1).
- Incorrect camber or castor angles (wear on one edge only) (Chapter 10).
- Worn steering or suspension joints, bushes or components (Chapter 10).
- Excessively-hard cornering.
- Accident damage.

Tyre treads exhibit feathered edges
- Incorrect toe setting (Chapter 10).

Tyres worn in centre of tread
- Tyres over-inflated (Chapter 1).

Tyres worn on inside and outside edges
- Tyres under-inflated (Chapter 1).

Tyres worn unevenly
- Tyres out of balance (Chapter 1).
- Excessive wheel or tyre run-out (Chapter 1).
- Worn shock absorbers (Chapter 10).
- Faulty tyre (Chapter 1).

10 Electrical system

Note: *For problems associated with the starting system, refer to the faults listed under 'Engine' earlier in this Section.*

Battery will not hold a charge for more than a few days
- Battery defective internally (Chapter 12).
- Battery terminal connections loose or corroded (Chapter 1).
- Alternator drivebelt worn or incorrectly-adjusted (Chapter 1).
- Alternator not charging at correct output (Chapter 12).
- Alternator or voltage regulator faulty (Chapter 12).
- Short-circuit causing continual battery drain (Chapter 12).

Ignition warning light remains illuminated with engine running
- Alternator drivebelt broken, worn, or incorrectly-adjusted (Chapter 1).
- Alternator brushes worn, sticking, or dirty (Chapter 12).
- Alternator brush springs weak or broken (Chapter 12).
- Internal fault in alternator or voltage regulator (Chapter 12).
- Broken, disconnected, or loose wiring in charging circuit (Chapter 12).

Ignition warning light fails to come on
- Warning light bulb blown (Chapter 12).
- Broken, disconnected, or loose wiring in warning light circuit (Chapter 12).
- Alternator faulty (Chapter 12).

Lights inoperative
- Bulb blown (Chapter 12).
- Corrosion of bulb or bulbholder contacts (Chapter 12).
- Blown fuse (Chapter 12).
- Faulty relay (Chapter 12).
- Broken, loose, or disconnected wiring (Chapter 12).
- Faulty switch (Chapter 12).

Instrument readings inaccurate or erratic
Instrument readings increase with engine speed
- Faulty voltage regulator (Chapter 12).

Fuel or temperature gauges give no reading
- Faulty gauge sender unit (Chapter 3 or 4).
- Wiring open-circuit (Chapter 12).
- Faulty gauge (Chapter 12).

Fuel or temperature gauges give continuous maximum reading
- Faulty gauge sender unit (Chapter 3 or 4).
- Wiring short-circuit (Chapter 12).
- Faulty gauge (Chapter 12).

Horn inoperative or unsatisfactory in operation
Horn operates all the time
- Horn push either earthed or stuck down (Chapter 12).
- Horn cable to horn push earthed (Chapter 12).

Horn fails to operate
- Blown fuse (Chapter 12).
- Cable or cable connections loose, broken or disconnected (Chapter 12).
- Faulty horn (Chapter 12).

Horn emits intermittent or unsatisfactory sound
- Cable connections loose (Chapter 12).
- Horn mountings loose (Chapter 12).
- Faulty horn (Chapter 12).

Windscreen/tailgate wipers inoperative or unsatisfactory in operation
Wipers fail to operate or operate very slowly
- Wiper blades stuck to screen, or linkage seized or binding (Chapter 12).
- Blown fuse (Chapter 12).
- Cable or cable connections loose, broken or disconnected (Chapter 12).
- Faulty relay (Chapter 12).
- Faulty wiper motor (Chapter 12).

Wiper blades sweep over too large or too small an area of the glass
- Wiper arms incorrectly positioned on spindles (Chapter 12).
- Excessive wear of wiper linkage (Chapter 12).
- Wiper motor or linkage mountings loose or insecure (Chapter 12).

Wiper blades fail to clean the glass effectively
- Wiper blade rubbers worn or perished (Chapter 1).
- Wiper arm tension springs broken, or arm pivots seized (Chapter 12).
- Insufficient windscreen washer additive to adequately remove road film (Chapter 1).

Windscreen/tailgate washers inoperative or unsatisfactory in operation
One or more washer jets inoperative
- Blocked washer jet (Chapter 12).
- Disconnected, kinked or restricted fluid hose (Chapter 12).
- Insufficient fluid in washer reservoir (Chapter 1).

Washer pump fails to operate
- Broken or disconnected wiring or connections (Chapter 12).
- Blown fuse (Chapter 12).
- Faulty washer switch (Chapter 12).
- Faulty washer pump (Chapter 12).

Washer pump runs for some time before fluid is emitted from jets
- Faulty one-way valve in fluid supply hose (Chapter 12).

Electric windows inoperative or unsatisfactory in operation
Window glass will only move in one direction
- Faulty switch (Chapter 11).

Window glass slow to move
- Incorrectly-adjusted door glass guide channels (Chapter 11).
- Regulator seized or damaged, or in need of lubrication (Chapter 11).
- Door internal components or trim fouling regulator (Chapter 11).
- Faulty motor (Chapter 11).

Window glass fails to move
- Incorrectly-adjusted door glass guide channels (Chapter 11).
- Blown fuse (Chapter 12).
- Faulty relay (Chapter 12).
- Broken or disconnected wiring or connections (Chapter 11 or 12).
- Faulty motor (Chapter 11).

Central locking system inoperative or unsatisfactory in operation
Complete system failure
- Blown fuse (Chapter 12).
- Faulty relay (Chapter 12).
- Broken or disconnected wiring or connections (Chapter 11 or 12).

Latch locks but will not unlock, or unlocks but will not lock
- Faulty master switch (Chapter 11).
- Broken or disconnected latch operating rods or levers (Chapter 11).
- Faulty relay (Chapter 12).

One motor fails to operate
- Broken or disconnected wiring or connections (Chapter 11 or 12).
- Faulty motor (Chapter 11).
- Broken, binding or disconnected lock operating rods or levers (Chapter 11).
- Fault in door lock (Chapter 11).

MOT test checks

Introduction

Motor vehicle testing has been compulsory in Great Britain since 1960, when the Motor Vehicle (Tests) Regulations were first introduced. At that time, testing was only applicable to vehicles ten years old or older, and the test itself only covered lighting equipment, braking systems and steering gear. Current vehicle testing is far more extensive and, in the case of private vehicles, is now an annual inspection commencing three years after the date of first registration. Test standards are becoming increasingly stringent; for details of changes, consult the latest edition of the MOT Inspection Manual (available from HMSO or bookshops).

This section is intended as a guide to getting your vehicle through the MOT test. It lists all the relevant testable items, how to check them yourself, and what is likely to cause the vehicle to fail. Obviously it will not be possible to examine the vehicle to the same standard as the professional MOT tester, who will be highly experienced in this work and will have all the necessary equipment available. However, working through the following checks will provide a good indication as to the condition of the vehicle, and will enable you to identify any problem areas before submitting the vehicle for the test. Where a component is found to need repair or renewal, reference should be made to the appropriate Chapter in the manual, where further information will be found.

The following checks have been sub-divided into four categories as follows.

(a) Checks carried out from the driver's seat.
(b) Checks carried out with the vehicle on the ground.
(c) Checks carried out with the vehicle raised and with the wheels free to rotate.
(d) Exhaust emission checks.

In most cases, the help of an assistant will be necessary to carry out these checks thoroughly.

Checks carried out from the driver's seat

Handbrake (Chapter 1 or 9)

Test the operation of the handbrake by pulling on the lever until the handbrake is in the normal fully-applied position. Ensure that the travel of the lever (the number of clicks of the ratchet) is not excessive before full resistance of the braking mechanism is felt. If so, this would indicate incorrect adjustment of the rear brakes, or incorrectly-adjusted handbrake cables.

With the handbrake fully applied, tap the lever sideways, and make sure that it does not release, which would indicate wear in the ratchet and pawl. Release the handbrake, and move the lever from side to side to check for excessive wear in the pivot bearing. Check the security of the lever mountings, and make sure that there is no corrosion of any part of the body structure within 30 cm of the lever mounting. If the lever mountings cannot be readily seen from inside the vehicle, carry out this check later when working underneath.

Footbrake (Chapter 1 or 9)

Check that the brake pedal is sound, without visible defects such as excessive wear of the pivot bushes or broken or damaged pedal pad. Check also for signs of fluid leaks on the pedal, floor or carpets, which would indicate failed seals in the brake master cylinder.

Depress the brake pedal slowly at first, then rapidly until sustained pressure can be held. Maintain this pressure and check that the pedal does not creep down to the floor which would again indicate problems with the master cylinder. Release the pedal, wait a few seconds then depress it once until firm resistance is felt. Check that this resistance occurs near the top of the pedal travel. If the pedal travels nearly to the floor before firm resistance is felt, this would indicate incorrect brake adjustment resulting in 'insufficient reserve travel' of the footbrake. If firm resistance cannot be felt, ie the pedal feels spongy, this would indicate that air is present in the hydraulic system, which will necessitate complete bleeding of the system.

Check that the servo unit is operating correctly by depressing the brake pedal several times to exhaust the vacuum. Keep the pedal depressed and start the engine. As soon as the engine starts, the brake pedal resistance will be felt to alter. If this is not the case, there may be a leak from the brake servo vacuum hose, or the servo unit itself may be faulty.

Steering wheel and column (Chapter 10)

Examine the steering wheel for fractures or looseness of the hub, spokes or rim. Move the steering wheel from side to side and then up and down, in relation to the steering column. Check that the steering wheel is not loose on the column, indicating wear in the column splines or a loose steering wheel retaining nut. Continue moving the steering wheel as before, but also turn it slightly from left to right. Check that there is no abnormal movement of the steering wheel, indicating excessive wear in the column upper support bearing, universal joint(s) or flexible coupling.

Windscreen and mirrors (Chapter 11)

The windscreen must be free of cracks or other damage which will seriously interfere with the driver's field of view, or which will prevent the windscreen wipers from operating properly. Small stone chips are acceptable. Any stickers, dangling toys or similar items must also be clear of the field of view.

Rear view mirrors must be secure, intact and capable of being adjusted. The nearside (passenger side) door mirror is not included in the test unless the interior mirror cannot be used – for instance, in the case of a van with blacked-out rear windows.

Seat belts and seats (Chapter 11)

Note: *The following checks are applicable to all seat belts, front and rear. Front seat belts must be of a type that will restrain the upper part of the body; lap belts are not acceptable. Various combinations of seat belt types are acceptable at the rear.*

Carefully examine the seat belt webbing for cuts, or any signs of

Check the security of all seat belt mountings – upper mounting shown with trim cover removed

Shake the roadwheel vigorously to check for excess play in the wheel bearings and suspension components

Inspect the constant velocity joint gaiters (1) and retaining clips (2)

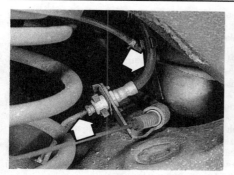

Check the braking system pipes and hoses (arrowed) for signs of damage or deterioration

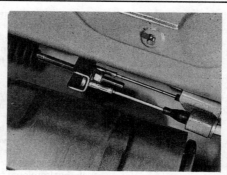

Check the handbrake cables for signs of fraying, and for secure mounting

Check the condition of the exhaust system (typical system shown), paying particular attention to the mountings

serious fraying or deterioration. If the seat belt is of the retractable type, pull the belt all the way out and examine the full extent of the webbing.

Fasten and unfasten the belt, ensuring that the locking mechanism holds securely and releases properly when intended. If the belt is of the retractable type, check also that the retracting mechanism operates correctly when the belt is released.

Check the security of all seat belt mountings and attachments which are accessible, without removing any trim or other components, from inside the vehicle (photo). Any serious corrosion, fracture or distortion of the body structure within 30 cm of any mounting point will cause the vehicle to fail. Certain anchorages will not be accessible or even visible from inside the vehicle; in this instance, further checks should be carried out later, when working underneath. If any part of the seat belt mechanism is attached to the front seat, then the seat mountings are treated as anchorages and must also comply as above.

The front seats themselves must be securely attached so that they cannot move unexpectedly, and the backrests must lock in the upright position.

Doors (Chapter 11)

Both front doors must be able to be opened and closed from outside and inside, and must latch securely when closed. In the case of a pick-up, the tailgate must be securely attached and capable of being securely fastened.

Electrical equipment (Chapter 12)

Switch on the ignition and operate the horn. The horn must operate, and produce a clear sound audible to other road users. Note that a gong, siren or two-tone horn fitted as an alternative to the manufacturer's original equipment is not acceptable.

Check the operation of the windscreen washers and wipers. The washers must operate with adequate flow and pressure, and with the jets adjusted so that the liquid strikes the windscreen near the top of the glass.

Operate the windscreen wipers in conjunction with the washers, and check that the blades cover their designed sweep of the windscreen without smearing. The blades must effectively clean the glass so that the driver has an adequate view of the road ahead, and to the front nearside and offside of the vehicle. If the screen smears or does not clean adequately, it is advisable to renew the wiper blades before the MOT test.

Depress the footbrake with the ignition switched on, and have your assistant check that both rear stop-lights operate, and are extinguished when the footbrake is released. If one stop-light fails to operate, it is likely that a bulb has blown or there is a poor electrical contact at, or near, the bulbholder. If both stop-lights fail to operate, check for a blown fuse, faulty stop-light switch or possibly two blown bulbs. If the lights stay on when the brake pedal is released, it is possible that the switch is at fault.

Checks carried out with the vehicle on the ground

Vehicle identification

Front and rear number plates must be in good condition, securely fitted and easily read. Letters and numbers must be correctly spaced, with the gap between the group of numbers and the group of letters at least double the gap between adjacent numbers and letters.

The vehicle identification number on the plate under the bonnet

must be legible. It will be checked during the test as part of the measures taken to prevent the fraudulent acquisition of certificates.

Electrical equipment (Chapter 12)

Switch on the sidelights, and check that both front and rear sidelights and the number plate lights are illuminated, and that the lenses and reflectors are secure and undamaged. This is particularly important at the rear, where a cracked or damaged lens would allow a white light to show to the rear, which is unacceptable. Note in addition that any lens which is excessively dirty, either inside or out, such that the light intensity is reduced, could also constitute a fail.

Switch on the headlights, and check that both dipped beam and main beam units are operating correctly and at the same light intensity. If either headlight shows signs of dimness, this is usually attributable to a poor earth connection or severely-corroded internal reflector. Inspect the headlight lenses for cracks or stone damage. Any damage to the headlight lens will normally constitute a fail, but this is very much down to the tester's discretion. Bear in mind that with all light units, they must operate correctly when first switched on. It is not acceptable to tap a light unit to make it operate.

The headlights must not only be aligned so as not to dazzle other road users when switched to dipped beam, but also so as to provide adequate illumination of the road. This can only be accurately checked using optical beam-setting equipment, so if you have any doubts about the headlight alignment, it is advisable to have this professionally checked and if necessary reset, before the MOT test.

With the ignition switched on, operate the direction indicators and check that they show amber lights to the front and to the rear, that they flash at the rate of between one and two flashes per second, and that the 'tell-tale' on the instrument panel also functions. Operation of the sidelights and stop-lights must not affect the indicators - if it does, the cause is usually a bad earth at the rear light cluster. Similarly check the operation of the hazard warning lights, which must work with the ignition on and off. Examine the lenses for cracks or damage as described previously.

Check the operation of the rear foglight(s). The test only concerns itself with the statutorily-required foglight, which is the one on the offside. The light must be secure, and emit a steady red light. The warning light on the instrument panel or in the switch must also work.

Footbrake (Chapter 1 or 9)

From within the engine compartment, examine the brake pipes for signs of leaks, corrosion, insecurity, chafing or other damage, and check the master cylinder and servo unit for leaks, security of their mountings or excessive corrosion in the vicinity of the mountings. The master cylinder reservoir must be secure; if it is of the translucent type, the fluid level must be between the upper and lower level markings.

Turn the steering as necessary so that the right-hand front brake flexible hose can be examined. Inspect the hose carefully for any sign of cracks or deterioration of the rubber. This will be most noticeable if the hose is bent in half, and is particularly common where the rubber portion enters the metal end fitting. Turn the steering onto full-left then full-right lock, and ensure that the hose does not contact the wheel, tyre, or any part of the steering or suspension mechanism. While your assistant depresses the brake pedal firmly, check the hose for any bulges or fluid leaks under pressure. Now repeat these checks on the left-hand front hose. Should any damage or deterioration be noticed, renew the hose.

Steering mechanism and suspension (Chapter 10)

Have your assistant turn the steering wheel from side to side slightly, up to the point where the steering gear just begins to transmit this movement to the roadwheels. Check for excessive free play between the steering wheel and the steering gear, which would indicate wear in the steering column joints, wear or insecurity of the steering column-to-steering gear coupling, or insecurity, incorrect adjustment, or wear in the steering gear itself. Generally speaking, free play greater than 1.3 cm for vehicles with rack-and-pinion type steering or 7.6 cm for vehicles with steering box mechanisms, should be considered excessive.

Have your assistant turn the steering wheel more vigorously in each direction, up to the point where the roadwheels just begin to turn. As this is done, carry out a complete examination of all the steering joints, linkages, fittings and attachments. Any component that shows signs of wear, damage, distortion, or insecurity should be renewed or attended to accordingly. On vehicles equipped with power steering, also check that the power steering pump is secure, that the pump drivebelt is in satisfactory condition and correctly adjusted, that there are no fluid leaks or damaged hoses, and that the system operates correctly. Additional checks can be carried out later with the vehicle raised, when there will be greater working clearance underneath.

Check that the vehicle is standing level, and at approximately the correct ride height. Ensure that there is sufficient clearance between the suspension components and the bump stops to allow full suspension travel over bumps.

Shock absorbers (Chapter 10)

Depress each corner of the vehicle in turn, and then release it. If the shock absorbers are in good condition, the corner of the vehicle will rise and then settle in its normal position. If there is no noticeable damping effect from the shock absorber, and the vehicle continues to rise and fall, then the shock absorber is defective and the vehicle will fail. A shock absorber which has seized will also cause the vehicle to fail.

Exhaust system (Chapter 1 or 4)

Start the engine, and with your assistant holding a rag over the tailpipe, check the entire system for leaks, which will appear as a rhythmic fluffing or hissing sound at the source of the leak. Check the effectiveness of the silencer by ensuring that the noise produced is of a level to be expected from a vehicle of similar type. Providing that the system is structurally sound, it is acceptable to cure a leak using a proprietary exhaust system repair kit or similar method.

Checks carried out with the vehicle raised and with the wheels free to rotate

Jack up the front and rear of the vehicle, and securely support it on axle stands positioned at suitable load-bearing points under the vehicle structure. Position the stands clear of the suspension assemblies, ensuring that the wheels are clear of the ground and that the steering can be turned onto full-right and full-left lock.

Steering mechanism (Chapter 10)

Examine the steering rack rubber gaiters for signs of splits, lubricant leakage or insecurity of the retaining clips. If power steering is fitted, check for signs of deterioration, damage, chafing or leakage of the fluid hoses, pipes or connections. Also check for excessive stiffness or binding of the steering, a missing split pin or locking device, or any severe corrosion of the body structure within 30 cm of any steering component attachment point.

Have your assistant turn the steering onto full-left then full-right lock. Check that the steering turns smoothly without undue tightness or roughness, and that no part of the steering mechanism, including a wheel or tyre, fouls any brake flexible or rigid hose or pipe, or any part of the body structure.

On vehicles with four-wheel steering, similar considerations apply to the rear wheel steering linkages. However, it is permissible for a rear wheel steering system to be inoperative, provided that the rear wheels are secured in the straight-ahead position and that the front wheel steering system is operating effectively.

Front and rear suspension and wheel bearings (Chapter 1 or 10)

Starting at the front right-hand side of the vehicle, grasp the roadwheel at the 3 o'clock and 9 o'clock positions, and shake it vigorously. Check for any free play at the wheel bearings, suspension balljoints, or suspension mountings, pivots and attachments. Check also

for any serious deterioration of the rubber or metal casing of any mounting bushes, or any distortion, deformation or severe corrosion of any components. Look for missing split pins, tab washers or other locking devices on any mounting or attachment, or any severe corrosion of the vehicle structure within 30 cm of any suspension component attachment point.

If any excess free play is suspected at a component pivot point, this can be confirmed by using a large screwdriver or similar tool to lever between the mounting and the component attachment. This will confirm whether the wear is in the pivot bush, its retaining bolt or in the mounting itself (the bolt holes can often become elongated).

Now grasp the wheel at the 12 o'clock and 6 o'clock positions, shake it vigorously and repeat the previous inspection (photo). Rotate the wheel, and check for roughness or tightness of the front wheel bearing such that imminent failure of the bearing is indicated.

Carry out all the above checks at the other front wheel, and then at both rear wheels.

Roadsprings and shock absorbers (Chapter 10)

On vehicles with strut type suspension units, examine the strut assembly for signs of serious fluid leakage, corrosion or severe pitting of the piston rod, or damage to the casing. Check also for security of the mounting points.

If coil springs are fitted, check that the spring ends locate correctly in their spring seats, that there is no severe corrosion of the spring, and that it is not cracked, broken or in any way damaged.

If the vehicle is fitted with leaf springs, check that all leaves are intact, that the axle is securely attached to each spring, and that there is no wear or deterioration of the spring eye mountings, bushes, or shackles.

The same general checks apply to vehicles fitted with other suspension types, such as torsion bars, hydraulic displacer units etc. In all cases, ensure that all mountings and attachments are secure, that there are no signs of excessive wear, corrosion, cracking, deformation or damage to any component or bush, and that there are no fluid leaks or damaged hoses or pipes (hydraulic types).

Inspect the shock absorbers for signs of serious fluid leakage. (Slight seepage of fluid is normal for some types of shock absorber, and is not a reason for failing.) Check for excessive wear of the mounting bushes or attachments, or damage to the body of the unit.

Driveshafts (Chapter 8)

With the steering turned onto full lock, rotate each front wheel in turn and inspect the constant velocity joint gaiters for splits or damage (photo). Also check the gaiter is securely attached to its respective housings by clips or other methods of retention.

Continue turning the wheel, and check that each driveshaft is straight with no sign of damage.

Braking system (Chapter 1 or 9)

If possible, without dismantling, check for wear of the brake pads and the condition of the discs. Ensure that the friction lining material has not worn excessively, and that the discs are not fractured, pitted, scored or worn excessively.

Carefully examine all the rigid brake pipes underneath the vehicle, and the flexible hoses at the rear. Check the pipes for signs of excessive corrosion, chafing or insecurity, and the flexible hoses for signs of bulging under pressure, chafing, splits or deterioration (photo).

Look for signs of hydraulic fluid leaks at the brake calipers or on the brake backplates, indicating failed hydraulic seals in the components concerned.

Slowly spin each wheel, while your assistant depresses the footbrake then releases it. Ensure that each brake is operating, and that the wheel is free to rotate when the pedal is released. It is not possible to test brake efficiency without special equipment, but (traffic and local conditions permitting) a road test can be carried out to check that the vehicle pulls up in a straight line.

Examine the handbrake mechanism, and check for signs of frayed or broken cables, excessive corrosion, or wear or insecurity of the linkage (photo). Have your assistant operate the handbrake, while you check that the mechanism works on each relevant wheel and releases fully without binding.

Fuel and exhaust systems (Chapter 1 or 4)

Inspect the fuel tank, fuel pipes, hoses and unions (including the unions at the pump, filter and carburettor). All components must be secure and free from leaks. The fuel filler cap must also be secure and of an appropriate type.

Examine the exhaust system over its entire length checking for any damaged, broken or missing mountings, security of the pipe retaining clamps and condition of the system with regard to rust and corrosion (photo).

Wheels and tyres (Chapter 1 or 10)

Carefully examine each tyre in turn, on both the inner and outer walls and over the whole of the tread area, and check for signs of cuts, tears, lumps, bulges, and for separation of the tread and exposure of the ply or cord due to wear or other damage. Check also that the tyre bead is correctly seated on the wheel rim, and that the tyre valve is sound and properly seated. Spin the wheel, and check that it is not excessively distorted or damaged, particularly at the bead rim.

Check that the tyres are of the correct size for the vehicle, and that they are of the same size and type on each axle. (Having a 'space saver' spare tyre in use is not acceptable.) The tyres should also be inflated to the specified pressures.

Using a suitable gauge, check the tyre tread depth. The current legal requirement states that the tread pattern must be visible over the whole tread area, and must be of a minimum depth of 1.6 mm over at least three-quarters of the tread width. It is acceptable for some wear of the inside or outside edges of the tyre to be apparent, but this wear must be in one even circumferential band, and the tread must be visible. Any excessive wear of this nature may indicate incorrect front wheel alignment, which should be checked before the tyre becomes excessively worn. See the appropriate Chapters for further information on tyre wear patterns and front wheel alignment.

Body corrosion

Check the condition of the entire vehicle structure for signs of corrosion in any load-bearing areas. For the purpose of the MOT test, all chassis box sections, side sills, crossmembers, pillars, suspension, steering, braking system and seat belt mountings and anchorages should all be considered as load-bearing areas. As a general guide, any corrosion which has seriously reduced the metal thickness of a load-bearing area to weaken it, is likely to cause the vehicle to fail. Should corrosion of this nature be encountered, professional repairs are likely to be needed.

Body damage or corrosion which causes sharp or otherwise dangerous edges to be exposed will also cause the vehicle to fail.

Exhaust emission checks

Have the engine at normal operating temperature, and make sure that the preliminary conditions for checking idle speed and mixture (ignition system in good order, air filter element clean, etc) have been met.

Before any measurements are carried out, raise the engine speed to around 2500 rpm, and hold it at this speed for 20 seconds. Allow the engine speed to return to idle, and watch for smoke emissions from the exhaust tailpipe. If the idle speed is obviously much too high, or if dense blue or clearly-visible black smoke comes from the tailpipe for more than 5 seconds, the vehicle will fail. As a rule of thumb, blue smoke signifies oil being burnt (worn valve stem oil seals, valve guides, piston rings or bores), while black smoke signifies unburnt fuel (dirty air cleaner element, mixture extremely rich, or other carburettor or fuel injection system fault).

If the idle speed and smoke emission are satisfactory, an exhaust gas analyser capable of measuring carbon monoxide (CO) and hydrocarbons (HC) is now needed. The following paragraphs assume that such an instrument can be hired or borrowed – it is unlikely to be economic for the home mechanic to buy one. Alternatively, a local garage may agree to perform the check for a small fee.

CO emissions (mixture)

Current MOT regulations specify a maximum CO level at idle of 4.5% for vehicles first used after August 1983. The CO level specified by the vehicle maker is well inside this limit.

If the CO level cannot be reduced far enough to pass the test (and assuming that the fuel and ignition systems are otherwise in good condition) it is probable that the carburettor is badly worn, or that there is some problem in the fuel injection system. On carburettors with an automatic choke, it may be that the choke is not releasing as it should.

It is possible for the CO level to be within the specified maximum for MOT purposes but well above the maximum specified by the manufacturer. The tester is entitled to draw attention to this, but it is not in itself a reason for failing the vehicle.

HC emissions

With the CO emissions within limits, HC emissions must be no more than 1200 ppm (parts per million). If the vehicle fails this test at idle, it can be re-tested at around 2000 rpm; if the HC level is then 1200 ppm or less, this counts as a pass.

Excessive HC emissions can be caused by oil being burnt, but they are more likely to be due to unburnt fuel. Possible reasons include:

(a)   Spark plugs in poor condition or incorrectly-gapped.
(b)   Ignition timing incorrect.
(c)   Valve clearances incorrect.
(d)   Engine compression low.

Note that excessive HC levels in the exhaust gas can cause premature failure of the catalytic converter (when fitted).

Chapter 1 Routine maintenance and servicing

Contents

Specifications

Note: *For details of engine code location, refer to 'Buying spare parts and vehicle identification numbers'.*

Engine
Oil filter type .... Champion G102

Cooling system

Antifreeze mixtures (antifreeze to Vauxhall/Opel specification GME L 6):	**Antifreeze**	**Water**
Protection to –10°C	20%	80%
Protection to –20°C	34%	66%
Protection to –30°C	44%	56%
Protection to –40°C	52%	48%

Fuel system
Note: *All speeds given are for manual gearbox models – no information available for automatic transmission models at time of writing.*

Idle speed:
  Carburettor engine (14 NV) .... 900 to 950 rpm
  Fuel injection engines:*
    C 14 NZ .... 830 to 990 rpm
    C 14 SE .... 820 to 980 rpm
    C 16 NZ .... 780 to 940 rpm
    C 16 SE .... 820 to 980 rpm
    C 18 NZ .... 750 to 910 rpm
    C 20 NE .... 770 to 930 rpm
    C 20 XE .... 860 to 1020 rpm
Controlled by electronic control unit – no adjustment possible

Idle mixture CO content:
  Carburettor engine .... 0.5 to 1.5%
  Fuel injection engines (all models) .... 0.4% or less
Fuel octane requirement (refer to Chapter 4 Specifications for further details):
  Carburettor engine .... 97 RON leaded (ie 4-star) or 95 RON unleaded (ie unleaded Premium)
  Fuel injection engines (all models) .... 95 RON unleaded (ie unleaded Premium)

Ignition system
Firing order 1–3–4–2
Location of No 1 cylinder .... Crankshaft pulley (timing belt) end
Direction of crankshaft rotation .... Clockwise
Direction of distributor rotor arm rotation .... Clockwise

Ignition system

Ignition timing (stroboscopic, at idle speed, with vacuum hose disconnected):
    Carburettor engine .... 5° BTDC
    Fuel-injection engines:*
        All except 2.0 litre engines .... 10° BTDC
        C 20 NE (SOHC) engine .... 13 to 17° BTDC
        C 20 XE (DOHC) engine .... 14 to 18° BTDC
Controlled by electronic control unit – no adjustment possible
Spark plugs:
    Type:
        All SOHC engines .... Champion RN7YCC
        DOHC engine .... Champion RC9MCC
    Electrode gap (all models).. 0.8 mm

Now RN9YYCC (handwritten)

Clutch

Clutch pedal travel:
    Right-hand-drive models .... 134 to 141 mm
    Left-hand-drive models .... 125 to 132 mm

Braking system

Minimum front brake pad lining thickness (including backing plate) .... 7.0 mm
Minimum rear brake pad lining thickness (including backing plate).......... 7.0 mm
Minimum rear brake shoe lining thickness .... 0.5 mm above rivet heads

Suspension and steering

Power steering pump drivebelt deflection .... 10.0 mm

Tyre pressures (cold) – normal load:*	Front	Rear
1.4 and 1.6 litre engine models:		
Saloon and Hatchback models	1.9 bars (27 lbf/in²)	1.6 bars (23 lbf/in²)
Estate and Van models	1.9 bars (24 lbf/in²)	1.7 bars (24 lbf/in²)
1.8 litre engine models:		
Saloon and Hatchback models	2.1 bars (30 lbf/in²)	1.8 bars (26 lbf/in²)
Estate and Van models	2.1 bars (30 lbf/in²)	1.9 bars (27 lbf/in²)
2.0 litre engine models:		
All models except GSi, Estate and Van)	2.3 bars (33 lbf/in²)	2.0 bars (29 lbf/in²)
GSi models	2.3 bars (33 lbf/in²)	2.2 bars (32 lbf/in²)
Estate and Van models	2.1 bars (30 lbf/in²)	1.9 bars (27 lbf/in²)
Tyre pressures (cold) – full-load:		
1.4 and 1.6 litre engine models:		
Saloon and Hatchback models	2.1 bars (30 lbf/in²)	2.3 bars (33 lbf/in²)
Estate and Van models	2.1 bars (30 lbf/in²)	3.0 bars (43 lbf/in²)
1.8 litre models:		
Saloon and Hatchback models	2.3 bars (33 lbf/in²)	2.5 bars (36 lbf/in²)
Estate and Van models	2.3 bars (33 lbf/in²)	3.2 bars (46 lbf/in²)
2.0 litre models:		
Saloon and Hatchback models	2.5 bars (36 lbf/in²)	2.7 bars (39 lbf/in²)
Estate and Van models	2.3 bars (33 lbf/in²)	3.2 bars (46 lbf/in²)

A 'normal' load is considered to be up to 3 passengers and light luggage

Electrical system

Alternator drivebelt deflection.. 10.0 mm

Torque wrench settings

	Nm	lbf ft
Engine oil drain plug	45	33
Outer timing belt covers	4	3
Thermostat housing bolts:		
1.4 and 1.6 litre engines................................	10	7
1.8 and 2.0 litre models.................................	15	11
Coolant temperature sender – 1.4 and 1.6 litre engines ...	10	7
Spark plugs	25	18
Roadwheel bolts	90	66
Power steering pump mounting bolts – 1.8 and 2.0 litre engine models:		
Bolts 'A' and 'C' in Fig. 1.7	25	18
Bolts 'B' in Fig. 1.7	40	30
Alternator mounting nuts and bolts:		
M8 size..	25	18
M10 size..	35	26

Lubricants, fluids and capacities

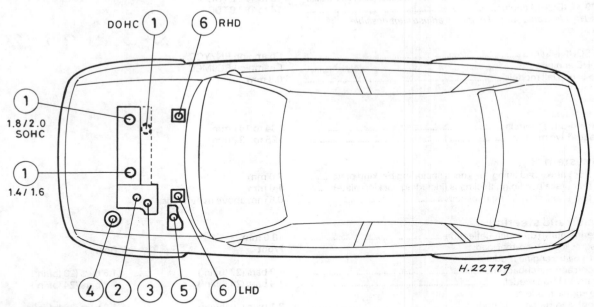

Lubricants and fluids

Component or system	Lubricant type/specification	Duckhams recommendation
1 Engine	Multigrade engine oil, viscosity range SAE 10W/40 to 20W/50, to API SF/CC, SF/CD or SG/CD	Duckhams QXR, Hypergrade, or 10W/40 Motor Oil
2 Manual gearbox	Vauxhall/Opel gear oil No 19 40 750 or 19 40 759	Duckhams Hypoid 80 or Hypoid 75W/90S
3 Automatic transmission	Dexron II type automatic transmission fluid	Duckhams Uni-Matic or D-Matic
4 Power steering fluid reservoir	Vauxhall/Opel fluid No 19 40 691 or 19 40 699	Duckhams Uni-Matic or D-Matic
5 Cooling system	Clean water and antifreeze to Vauxhall/Opel specification GME L 6	Duckhams Universal Antifreeze and Summer Coolant
6 Brake fluid reservoir	Hydraulic fluid to DOT 4	Duckhams Universal Brake and Clutch Fluid

Capacities

Engine oil
Capacity (including filter):
  1.4 and 1.6 litre engines.. 3.5 litres
  1.8 and 2.0 litre SOHC engines.. 4.0 litres
  DOHC engine .... 4.5 litres
Difference between MAX and MIN dipstick marks................... 1.0 litre
Cooling system
1.4 litre engines... 5.8 litres
1.6 litre engines... 5.6 litres
1.8 litre engine.. 7.0 litres
2.0 litre SOHC engine .... 6.5 litres
DOHC engine .... 6.9 litres
Fuel tank:
Saloon and Hatchback models .... 52.0 litres
Estate and Van models .... 50.0 litres
Manual gearbox
F 10/5 and F 13/5 gearboxes.. 1.6 litres
F 16/5 and F 20/5 gearboxes.. 1.3 litres
Automatic transmission
Drain and refill .... 3.0 to 3.5 litres
Power steering fluid reservoir .... 1.0 litre

Are your plugs trying to tell you something?

Normal.
Grey-brown deposits, lightly coated core nose. Plugs ideally suited to engine, and engine in good condition.

Heavy Deposits.
A build up of crusty deposits, light-grey sandy colour in appearance.
Fault: Often caused by worn valve guides, excessive use of upper cylinder lubricant, or idling for long periods.

Lead Glazing.
Plug insulator firing tip appears yellow or green/yellow and shiny in appearance.
Fault: Often caused by incorrect carburation, excessive idling followed by sharp acceleration. Also check ignition timing.

Carbon fouling.
Dry, black, sooty deposits.
Fault: over-rich fuel mixture.
Check: carburettor mixture settings, float level, choke operation, air filter.

Oil fouling.
Wet, oily deposits. Fault: worn bores/piston rings or valve guides; sometimes occurs (temporarily) during running-in period.

Overheating.
Electrodes have glazed appearance, core nose very white – few deposits. Fault: plug overheating. Check: plug value, ignition timing, fuel octane rating (too low) and fuel mixture (too weak).

Electrode damage.
Electrodes burned away; core nose has burned, glazed appearance. Fault: pre-ignition. Check: for correct heat range and as for 'overheating'.

Split core nose.
(May appear initially as a crack). Fault: detonation or wrong gap-setting technique. Check: ignition timing, cooling system, fuel mixture (too weak).

WHY DOUBLE COPPER IS BETTER FOR YOUR ENGINE.

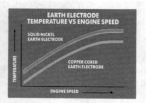

Unique Trapezoidal Copper Cored Earth Electrode — 50% Larger Spark Area — Copper Cored Centre Electrode

Champion Double Copper plugs are the first in the world to have copper core in both centre <u>and</u> earth electrode. This innovative design means that they run cooler by up to 100°C – giving greater efficiency and longer life. These double copper cores transfer heat away from the tip of the plug faster and more efficiently. Therefore, Double Copper runs at cooler temperatures than conventional plugs giving improved acceleration response and high speed performance with no fear of pre-ignition.

TRAPEZOIDAL COPPER CORED EARTH ELECTRODE
NEW TRAPEZOIDAL COPPER CORED EARTH ELECTRODE   CONVENTIONAL SOLID NICKEL ALLOY EARTH ELECTRODE
50% INCREASE IN SPARK AREA

EARTH ELECTRODE TEMPERATURE VS ENGINE SPEED
SOLID NICKEL EARTH ELECTRODE
COPPER CORED EARTH ELECTRODE
TEMPERATURE
ENGINE SPEED

Champion Double Copper plugs also feature a unique trapezoidal earth electrode giving a 50% increase in spark area. This, together with the double copper cores, offers greatly reduced electrode wear, so the spark stays stronger for longer.

 FASTER COLD STARTING

 FOR UNLEADED OR LEADED FUEL

 ELECTRODES UP TO 100°C COOLER

 BETTER ACCELERATION RESPONSE

 LOWER EMISSIONS

 50% BIGGER SPARK AREA

 THE LONGER LIFE PLUG

Plug Tips/Hot and Cold.
Spark plugs must operate within well-defined temperature limits to avoid cold fouling at one extreme and overheating at the other.
Champion and the car manufacturers work out the best plugs for an engine to give optimum performance under all conditions, from freezing cold starts to sustained high speed motorway cruising.
Plugs are often referred to as hot or cold. With Champion, the higher the number on its body, the hotter the plug, and the lower the number the cooler the plug.

Plug Cleaning
Modern plug design and materials mean that Champion no longer recommends periodic plug cleaning. Certainly don't clean your plugs with a wire brush as this can cause metal conductive paths across the nose of the insulator so impairing its performance and resulting in loss of acceleration and reduced m.p.g.
However, if plugs are removed, always carefully clean the area where the plug seats in the cylinder head as grit and dirt can sometimes cause gas leakage.
Also wipe any traces of oil or grease from plug leads as this may lead to arcing.

CHAMPION

DOUBLE ◀◀ COPPER

1 This photographic sequence shows the steps taken to repair the dent and paintwork damage shown above. In general, the procedure for repairing a hole will be similar; where there are substantial differences, the procedure is clearly described and shown in a separate photograph.

2 First remove any trim around the dent, then hammer out the dent where access is possible. This will minimise filling. Here, after the large dent has been hammered out, the damaged area is being made slightly concave.

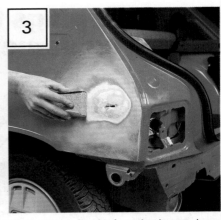

3 Next, remove all paint from the damaged area by rubbing with coarse abrasive paper or using a power drill fitted with a wire brush or abrasive pad. 'Feather' the edge of the boundary with good paintwork using a finer grade of abrasive paper.

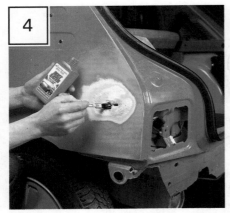

4 Where there are holes or other damage, the sheet metal should be cut away before proceeding further. The damaged area and any signs of rust should be treated with Turtle Wax Hi-Tech Rust Eater, which will also inhibit further rust formation.

5 *For a large dent or hole* mix Holts Body Plus Resin and Hardener according to the manufacturer's instructions and apply around the edge of the repair. Press Glass Fibre Matting over the repair area and leave for 20-30 minutes to harden. Then ...

5A ... brush more Holts Body Plus Resin and Hardener onto the matting and leave to harden. Repeat the sequence with two or three layers of matting, checking that the final layer is lower than the surrounding area. Apply Holts Body Plus Filler Paste as shown in Step 5B.

5B *For a medium dent*, mix Holts Body Plus Filler Paste and Hardener according to the manufacturer's instructions and apply it with a flexible applicator. Apply thin layers of filler at 20-minute intervals, until the filler surface is slightly proud of the surrounding bodywork.

5C *For small dents and scratches* use Holts No Mix Filler Paste straight from the tube. Apply it according to the instructions in thin layers, using the spatula provided. It will harden in minutes if applied outdoors and may then be used as its own knifing putty.

6 Use a plane or file for initial shaping. Then, using progressively finer grades of wet-and-dry paper, wrapped round a sanding block, and copious amounts of clean water, rub down the filler until glass smooth. 'Feather' the edges of adjoining paintwork.

7

Protect adjoining areas before spraying the whole repair area and at least one inch of the surrounding sound paintwork with Holts Dupli-Color primer.

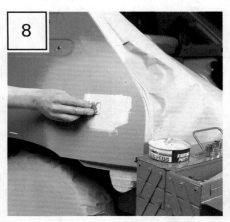

8

Fill any imperfections in the filler surface with a small amount of Holts Body Plus Knifing Putty. Using plenty of clean water, rub down the surface with a fine grade wet-and-dry paper – 400 grade is recommended – until it is really smooth.

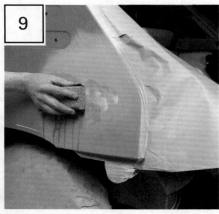

9

Carefully fill any remaining imperfections with knifing putty before applying the last coat of primer. Then rub down the surface with Holts Body Plus Rubbing Compound to ensure a really smooth surface.

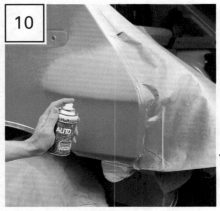

10

Protect surrounding areas from overspray before applying the topcoat in several thin layers. Agitate Holts Dupli-Color aerosol thoroughly. Start at the repair centre, spraying outwards with a side-to-side motion.

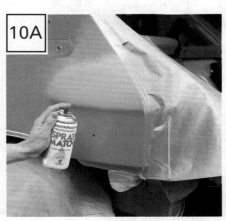

10A

If the exact colour is not available off the shelf, local Holts Professional Spraymatch Centres will custom fill an aerosol to match perfectly.

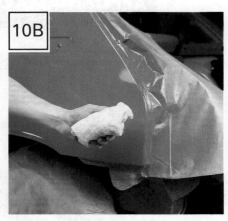

10B

To identify whether a lacquer finish is required, rub a painted unrepaired part of the body with wax and a clean cloth.

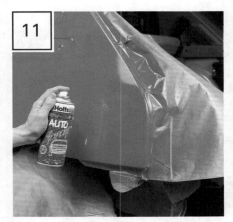

11

If *no* traces of paint appear on the cloth, spray Holts Dupli-Color clear lacquer over the repaired area to achieve the correct gloss level.

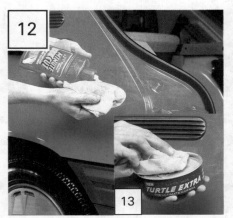

12

13

The paint will take about two weeks to harden fully. After this time it can be 'cut' with a mild cutting compound such as Turtle Wax Minute Cut prior to polishing with a final coating of Turtle Wax Extra.

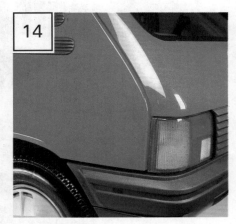

14

When carrying out bodywork repairs, remember that the quality of the finished job is proportional to the time and effort expended.

HAYNES
No1 for DIY

Haynes publish a wide variety of books besides the world famous range of *Haynes Owners Workshop Manuals*. They cover all sorts of DIY jobs. Specialist books such as the *Improve and Modify* series and the *Purchase and DIY Restoration Guides* give you all the information you require to carry out everything from minor modifications to complete restoration on a number of popular cars. In addition there are the publications dealing with specific tasks, such as the *Car Bodywork Repair Manual* and the *In-Car Entertainment Manual*. The *Household DIY* series gives clear step-by-step instructions on how to repair everyday household objects ranging from toasters to washing machines.

Whether it is under the bonnet or around the home there is a Haynes Manual that can help you save money. Available from motor accessory stores and bookshops or direct from the publisher.

Maintenance schedule

Introduction

This Chapter is designed to help the DIY owner maintain the Astra with the goals of maximum economy, safety, reliability and performance in mind.

On the following pages is a master maintenance schedule, listing the servicing requirements, and the intervals at which they should be carried out as recommended by the manufacturers. The operations are listed in the order in which the work can be most conveniently undertaken. For example, all the operations which are performed from within the engine compartment are grouped together, as are all those which require the vehicle to be raised and supported for access to the suspension and underbody. Alongside each operation in the schedule is a reference which directs the user to the relevant Sections in this Chapter covering maintenance procedures, or to other Chapters in the Manual where the operations are described and illustrated in greater detail. Specifications for all the maintenance operations, together with a list of lubricants, fluids and capacities, are provided at the beginning of this Chapter. Refer to the accompanying photographs of the engine compartment and the underbody of the vehicle for the locations of the various components.

Servicing your vehicle in accordance with the mileage/time maintenance schedule, using the step-by-step procedures provided, will result in a planned maintenance programme that should produce a long and reliable service life. Bear in mind that it is a comprehensive plan, so maintaining some items but not others at the specified intervals will not produce the same results.

The first step in this maintenance programme is to prepare yourself before the actual work begins. Read through all the procedures to be undertaken, then obtain all the parts, lubricants and any additional tools required.

Check the bodywork for damage and corrosion (Section 10)
Check the headlight beam alignment (Chapter 12)
Check the rear brake pressure-regulating valve adjustment – where applicable (Section 8)
Check rear suspension level control system pressure – where applicable (Section 9)
Perform a road test to check all the vehicle systems (Section 12)

Operations with the vehicle raised and supported

Check the front and rear (where applicable) brake pads, calipers and discs (Section 8)
Check the braking system flexible hoses and metal pipes (Section 8)
Renew the braking system hydraulic fluid (Section 8)
Check the condition of the underbody corrosion protection (Section 10)

Operations in the engine compartment

Renew the engine oil and filter (Section 1)
Renew the pollen filter (Section 2)
Check the idle speed and mixture, where possible (Section 3)
Check the condition of the HT leads, distributor cap and rotor arm, as applicable (Section 4)
Check the ignition timing, where possible (Section 4)
Check the condition of all emission control system components (Chapter 4, Part C)
Check the alternator drivebelt tension (Section 11)
Check the power steering drivebelt tension – where applicable (Section 11)

Every 250 miles (400 km) or weekly

Operations internal and external

Visually examine the tyres for tread depth, and wear or damage (Section 9)
Check and if necessary adjust the tyre pressures (Section 9)
Check the operation of the horn, all lights, and the wipers and washers (Section 11)

Operations in the engine compartment

Check the engine oil level (Section 1)
Check the engine coolant level (Section 2)
Check the brake fluid level (Section 8)
Check the power steering fluid level – where applicable (Section 9)
Check the windscreen/tailgate washer fluid level (Section 11)
Check the condition of the battery (Section 11)

Every 9000 miles (15 000 km) or 12 months – whichever comes first

Carry out the weekly checks, then carry out the following:

Operations internal and external

Check under the vehicle for signs of fluid leakage
Check the tightness of the roadwheel bolts (Section 9)

Every 18 000 miles (30 000 km) or 24 months – whichever comes first

In addition to the weekly checks and the items listed under the 9000 mile service heading, carry out the following:

Operations internal and external

Check the clutch cable adjustment/clutch pedal travel (Section 5)
Lubricate all door/bonnet/boot lid/tailgate hinges and locks (Section 10)
Check the condition and operation of the seat belts (Section 11)

Operations with the vehicle raised and supported

Check the rear brake shoes, drums and wheel cylinders – where applicable (Section 8)
Check the condition of the front suspension and steering components, particularly the rubber gaiters and seals (Section 9)
Check the condition of the rear suspension components (Section 9)
Check the condition of the driveshaft joint gaiters, and the driveshaft joints (Section 7)

Operations in the engine compartment

Renew the air cleaner filter element (Section 3)
Renew the spark plugs (Section 4)
Renew the fuel filter (Section 3)
Check the manual gearbox oil level – where applicable (Section 6)
Check the automatic transmission fluid level – where applicable (Section 6)
Renew the coolant – optional, no renewal intervals specified by Vauxhall/Opel (Section 2)

Every 36 000 miles (60 000 km) or 4 years – whichever comes first

In addition to the weekly checks, and the items listed under the 9000 and 18 000 mile service headings, carry out the following:

Operation in the engine compartment

Check the condition and tension of the timing belt and renew if necessary – compulsory for 1.8 and 2.0 litre SOHC engines, optional for all other engines (Section 1)

Every 72 000 miles (120 000 km) or 8 years – whichever comes first

In addition to the weekly checks, and the items listed under the 9000 and 18 000 mile service headings, carry out the following:

Operation in the engine compartment

Renew the timing belt – DOHC engines only (Chapter 2)

Engine compartment component locations (airbox removed) – 1.4 litre single-point fuel injection (C 14 NZ) engine

1   VIN plate
2   Air cleaner casing
3   Suspension strut top cover
4   Washer fluid reservoir
5   Brake fluid reservoir
6   Alternator

7   Throttle cable
8   Tie-rods
9   Fuel injection unit
10 Coolant expansion tank
11 Clutch cable
12 Ignition coil

13 Battery positive lead
14 Battery negative lead
15 Battery condition indicator
16 Distributor
17 Radiator
18 Cooling fan motor

19 Engine oil level dipstick
20 Engine oil filler cap
21 Oxygen sensor
22 Air cleaner hot air tube

Engine compartment component locations – 1.6 litre multi-point fuel injection (C 16 SE) engine

1 VIN plate
2 Air cleaner casing
3 Suspension strut top cover
4 Washer fluid reservoir
5 Brake fluid reservoir
6 Throttle body

7 Inlet manifold
8 Tie-rods
9 Throttle cable
10 Coolant expansion tank
11 Clutch cable
12 Battery positive lead

13 Battery negative lead
14 Battery condition indicator
15 Power steering fluid
    reservoir
16 Ignition coil
17 Radiator

18 Cooling fan motor
19 Engine oil level dipstick
20 Engine oil filler cap
21 Fuel injectors
22 Fuel rail

Engine compartment component locations – 2.0 litre DOHC (C 20 XE) engine

1 VIN plate
2 Air cleaner casing
3 Suspension strut top cover
4 Windscreen/tailgate washer
   fluid reservoir
5 Brake fluid reservoir
6 Air mass meter

7 Airbox
8 Fuse/relay box
9 Coolant expansion tank
10 Headlight washer fluid
    reservoir
11 ABS hydraulic modulator

12 Ignition coil
13 Battery positive lead
14 Battery negative lead
15 Battery condition indicator
16 Power steering fluid
    reservoir

17 Distributor
18 Radiator
19 Engine oil level dipstick
20 Spark plug cover
21 Throttle cable
22 Engine oil filler cap

Front underbody view – 1.6 litre multi-point fuel injection (C 16 SE) engine

1   Brake caliper
2   Anti-roll bar securing nut
3   Suspension lower arm
4   Catalytic converter

5   Subframe
6   Power steering fluid cooler
    pipes
7   Oil filter

8   Clutch cover plate
9   Differential cover plate
10 Engine oil drain plug
11 Driveshaft

12 Rear engine/gearbox
    mounting-to-subframe
    nuts
13 Exhaust sprung joint

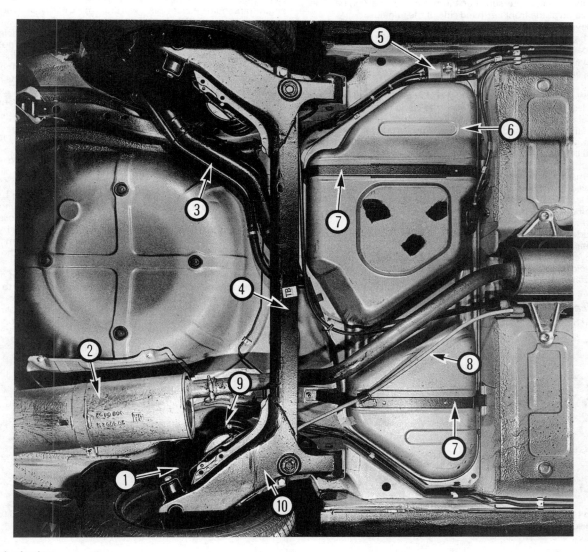

Rear underbody view

1 Shock absorber
2 Exhaust expansion box
3 Fuel tank filler pipe
4 Torsion beam
5 Fuel filter
6 Fuel tank
7 Fuel tank securing straps
8 Handbrake cable
9 Coil spring
10 Trailing arm

Maintenance procedures

1 Engine

Engine oil level check

1   The engine oil level is checked using a dipstick which extends through a tube and into the sump at the bottom of the engine. The dipstick is located at the front left-hand side of the engine.

2   The oil level should be checked with the vehicle standing on level ground and before the vehicle is driven, or at least 5 minutes after the engine has been stopped. If the oil level is checked immediately after driving the vehicle, some of the oil will remain in the upper engine components and oil galleries, resulting in an inaccurate reading on the dipstick.

3   Withdraw the dipstick from the tube, and wipe all the oil from the end with a clean rag or paper towel. Insert the clean dipstick back into the tube as far as it will go, then withdraw it once more. Note the oil level on the end of the dipstick. Add oil as necessary until the level is between the upper (maximum) mark and lower (minimum) mark on the dipstick. Note that 1.0 litre of oil will be required to raise the level from the lower mark to the upper mark (photo).

4   Always maintain the level between the two dipstick marks. If the level is allowed to fall below the lower mark, oil starvation may result which could lead to severe engine damage. If the engine is overfilled by adding too much oil, this may result in oil-fouled spark plugs, oil leaks, or oil seal failures.

5   Oil is added to the engine after removing the filler cap (twist it through a quarter turn anti-clockwise and withdraw it) from the engine camshaft cover (photo). It is advisable to use an oil can with a spout or a funnel, to avoid spillage. Always use the correct grade and type of oil as shown in 'Lubricants, fluids and capacities'.

Engine oil and filter renewal

6   Frequent oil and filter changes are the most important preventative

maintenance procedures which can be undertaken by the DIY owner. As engine oil ages, it becomes diluted and contaminated, which leads to premature engine wear.

7   Before starting this procedure, gather together all the necessary tools and materials (photo). Also make sure that you have plenty of clean rags and newspapers handy to mop up any spills. Ideally, the engine oil should be warm, as it will drain more easily, and more built-up sludge will be removed with it. Take care not to touch the exhaust or any other hot parts of the engine when working under the vehicle. To avoid any possibility of scalding, and to protect yourself from possible skin irritants and other harmful contaminants in used engine oils, it is advisable to wear gloves when carrying out this work. Access to the underside of the vehicle will be greatly improved if it can be raised on a lift, driven onto ramps, or jacked up and supported on axle stands. Whichever method is chosen, make sure that the vehicle remains level, or if it is at an angle, that the drain plug is at the lowest point. The drain plug is located in the rear face of the sump.

8   Remove the oil filler cap from the camshaft cover (twist it through a quarter turn anti-clockwise and withdraw it).

9   On DOHC engine models, release the securing clips, and remove the access hatch from the engine undershield for access to the oil drain plug (photo).

10   Using a spanner, or preferably a suitable socket and bar, slacken the drain plug about half a turn (photos). Position the draining container under the drain plug, then remove the plug completely. If possible, try to keep the plug pressed into the sump while unscrewing it by hand the last couple of turns. As the plug releases from the threads, move it away sharply so that the stream of oil from the sump runs into the container, not up your sleeve!

11   Allow some time for the oil to drain, noting that it may be necessary to reposition the container as the oil flow slows to a trickle.

12   After all the oil has drained, wipe the drain plug and the sealing washer with a clean rag. Examine the condition of the sealing washer, and renew it if it shows signs of scoring or other damage which may

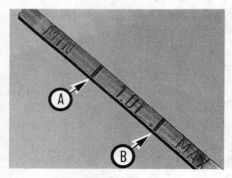

1.3 Engine oil level dipstick MIN (A) and MAX (B) marks

1.5 Topping-up the engine oil level

1.7 Tools and materials required for engine oil and filter renewal

1.9 Removing the engine undershield – DOHC engine model

1.10A Loosening the oil drain plug – SOHC engine

1.10B Engine oil drain plug – DOHC engine

1.14 Removing the access hatch for access to the oil filter – DOHC engine model

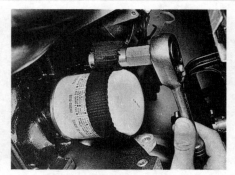

1.16A Using an oil filter removal tool to slacken the filter – SOHC engine

1.16B Using an oil filter removal tool to slacken the filter – DOHC engine

prevent an oil-tight seal. Clean the area around the drain plug opening and refit the plug complete with the washer. Tighten the plug securely, preferably to the specified torque using a torque wrench.

13   The oil filter is located at the front left-hand side of the engine on 1.4 and 1.6 litre engines, or on the right-hand side of the engine on 1.8 and 2.0 litre engines. On 1.8 and 2.0 litre models, improved access to the oil filter can be obtained by jacking up the front of the vehicle (if not already done) and removing the right-hand roadwheel.

14   On DOHC engine models, release the securing clips, and remove the access hatch from the right-hand side of the engine undershield for access to the oil filter (photo).

15   Move the container into position under the oil filter.

16   Use an oil filter removal tool to slacken the filter initially, then unscrew it by hand the rest of the way (photos). Empty the oil from the old filter into the container.

17   Use a clean rag to remove all oil, dirt and sludge from the filter sealing area on the engine. Check the old filter to make sure that the rubber sealing ring has not stuck to the engine. If it has, carefully remove it.

18   Apply a light coating of clean engine oil to the sealing ring on the new filter, then screw the filter into position on the engine. Tighten the filter firmly by hand only – **do not** use any tools.

19   Remove the old oil and all tools from under the vehicle then, if applicable, lower the vehicle to the ground.

20   Fill the engine through the filler hole in the camshaft cover, using the correct grade and type of oil, as described earlier in this Section. Pour in half the specified quantity of oil first, then wait a few minutes for the oil to drain into the sump. Continue to add oil a small quantity at a time until the level is up to the lower mark on the dipstick. Adding a further 1.0 litre will bring the level up to the upper mark on the dipstick.

21   Start the engine and run it for a few minutes, while checking for leaks around the oil filter seal and the sump drain plug. Note that there may be a delay of a few seconds before the low oil pressure warning light goes out when the engine is first started, as the oil circulates through the new oil filter and the engine oil galleries before the pressure builds up.

22   On DOHC engine models, refit the access hatches to the engine undershield after checking for oil leaks.

23   Stop the engine and wait a few minutes for the oil to settle in the sump once more. With the new oil circulated and the filter now completely full, recheck the level on the dipstick and add more oil as necessary.

24   Dispose of the used engine oil safely with reference to 'General repair procedures' in the preliminary Sections of this Manual.

Timing belt condition and tension check

Note: *Although Vauxhall/Opel only specify an interval for checking the tension of the timing belt on 1.8 and 2.0 litre SOHC engines, it is strongly recommended that the following checks are carried out for all models at the intervals specified in the 'Maintenance schedule'. These precautionary checks are recommended to prevent the possibility of serious engine damage which may occur if the belt is worn, or if the belt breaks in service. It is up to the individual owner to decide whether or not to follow this advice. Consult a Vauxhall/Opel dealer for further advice if in doubt.*

25   Remove the upper outer timing belt cover (or the one-piece outer cover on DOHC engines) as described in Part A of Chapter 2.

26   Ensure that the gearbox/transmission is in neutral, then using a suitable spanner or socket on the crankshaft pulley/sprocket bolt (as applicable), rotate the crankshaft so that the full length of the timing belt can be progressively checked. Examine the belt carefully for any signs of uneven wear, splitting or oil contamination and renew it if there is the slightest doubt about its condition.

27   At the same time as checking the timing belt condition, the timing belt tension should be checked, as described in Part A of Chapter 2. Vauxhall/Opel only specify this check for 1.8 and 2.0 litre engines, but it is strongly recommended that it is carried out on all engines as a precautionary measure. It is up to the individual owner to decide whether or not to follow this advice. Consult a Vauxhall/Opel dealer for advice if in doubt.

28   On completion of the checks, refit the timing belt cover(s).

Timing belt renewal

29   On DOHC engine models, the timing belt **must** be renewed at the specified intervals. The renewal of the timing belt on other models is up to the discretion of the owner, but it is strongly recommended that the belt is inspected at regular intervals as described previously in this Section, and that the belt is renewed if there is the slightest doubt about its condition. If the belt breaks while the engine is running, serious and expensive engine damage may result. For details of timing belt renewal, refer to Chapter 2.

General engine checks

Valve clearances – general

30   It is necessary for a clearance to exist between the tip of each valve stem and the valve operating mechanism, to allow for the expansion of the various engine components as the engine reaches normal operating temperature.

31   On many older engines, this meant that the valve clearances (also known as 'tappet' clearances) had to be checked and adjusted regularly.

32   The engines covered in this manual, however, employ hydraulic valve lifters ('tappets') which use the engine lubrication system oil pressure to automatically take up the clearance between each camshaft lobe and its respective valve stem. Therefore there is no need for regular checking and inspection of the valve clearances, but it is important that only good-quality oil of the recommended viscosity and specification is used in the engine, and that this oil is changed at the recommended intervals. If the oil is allowed to deteriorate, particles of dirt or 'sludge' may block or reduce the oil feed to the valve lifters, which may cause one or more of the valve lifters to fail, possibly resulting in expensive engine damage.

33   On starting the engine from cold, or if the vehicle has been standing for several days, there may be a slight delay while oil pressure builds up in the engine, especially in the valve lifters. This may cause a rattling noise from the top of the engine for a few seconds after start-up. Care should be taken not to damage the engine by running it at high speed until all the valve lifters have refilled with oil, and are operating normally.

34   If the valve clearances are though to be noisy, or if a light rattle persists from the top end of the engine after it has reached normal operating temperature, take the vehicle to a Vauxhall/Opel dealer for advice. A qualified technician will be able to tell whether the noise is typical for the engine's mileage and age, or whether a genuine fault exists. If any valve lifter is faulty, it must be renewed.

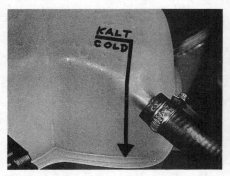

2.2 Coolant expansion tank level markings   **2.4 Topping-up the coolant level**   **2.7 Lifting the pollen filter from its housing**

General checks

35   Visually inspect the engine joint faces, gaskets and seals for any signs of coolant or oil leaks. Pay particular attention to the areas around the camshaft cover, cylinder head, oil filter and sump joint faces. Bear in mind that over a period of time, some very slight seepage from these areas is to be expected – what you are really looking for is any indication of a serious leak. If a leak is apparent, renew the offending gasket or oil seal by referring to the appropriate Chapters in this manual.
36   Also check the security and condition of all the engine-related pipes and hoses. Check the routing of all hoses and pipes, and if any cable ties or clips are broken, or appear to be missing, renew them. Clips which are broken or missing can lead to chafing of the hoses pipes or wiring, which could cause more serious problems in the future.

2   Cooling, heating and ventilation systems

Coolant level check

Warning: *DO NOT attempt to remove the expansion tank pressure cap when the engine is hot, as there is a very great risk of scalding.*

1   All vehicles covered by this manual are equipped with a pressurised cooling system. A coolant expansion tank, located at the rear left-hand side of the engine compartment, is connected by hoses to the cooling system. The tank allows for expansion of the coolant as the engine temperature increases, and enables monitoring of the coolant level.
2   The coolant level in the expansion tank should be checked regularly. The level in the tank varies with the temperature of the engine. When the engine is cold, the coolant level should be up to the 'KALT' (or 'COLD') mark on the side of the tank (photo). When the engine is hot, the level will rise slightly above the mark.
3   If topping-up is necessary, wait until the engine is cold, then cover the expansion tank cap with a wad of rag, and slowly turn the cap anti-clockwise to relieve the pressure in the cooling system (a hissing sound will normally be heard). Wait until any pressure remaining in the system is released, then continue to turn the cap until it can be removed.
4   Add a mixture of water and antifreeze (see 'Antifreeze mixture' later in this Section) through the expansion tank filler neck, until the coolant reaches the level mark (photo). Refit the cap, turning it clockwise as far as it will go to secure.
5   With a sealed type cooling system, the addition of coolant should only be necessary at very infrequent intervals. If frequent topping-up is required, it is likely that there is a leak in the system. Check the radiator, all hoses and joint faces for any sign of staining or dampness, and rectify as necessary. If no leaks can be found, it is advisable to have the cooling system pressure-tested by a dealer or suitably-equipped garage, as this can often detect a small leak not previously visible.

Pollen filter renewal

6   Open the bonnet, and remove the scuttle water deflector panels, noting how they are located over the flanges on the scuttle.
7   Release the securing clips at the front of the now-exposed pollen filter, and carefully lift the filter from its housing (photo).

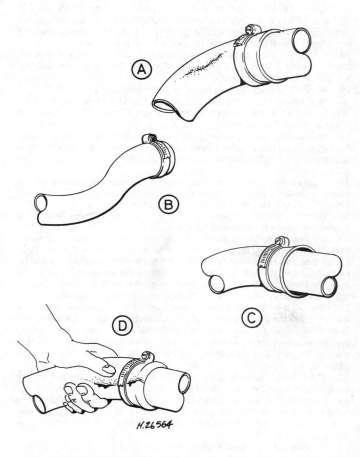

Fig. 1.1 Coolant hose inspection (Sec 2)

A   *Check hose for chafed or burned areas; these may lead to a sudden and costly failure*
B   *A soft hose indicates inside deterioration, leading to contamination of the cooling system and clogging of the radiator*

C   *A hardened hose can fail at any time; tightening the clamps will not seal the joint or prevent leaks*
D   *A swollen hose or one with oil-soaked ends indicates contamination from oil or grease. Cracks and breaks can be easily seen by squeezing the hose*

8   Fit the new filter using a reversal of the removal procedure, ensuring that the water deflector panels are correctly located on the scuttle.

General cooling system checks

9   The engine should be cold for the cooling system checks, so perform the following procedure before driving the vehicle or after the engine has been stopped for at least three hours.
10   Remove the expansion tank filler cap as described previously in this Section, and clean it thoroughly inside and out with a rag. Also clean the filler neck on the expansion tank. The presence of rust or corrosion in the filler neck indicates that the coolant should be renewed. The coolant inside the expansion tank should be clean and transparent. If it is rust-coloured, drain and flush the system, and refill with a fresh coolant mixture.
11   Carefully check the cooling system hoses along their entire length. Renew any hose which is cracked, swollen or deteriorated. Cracks will show up better if the hose is squeezed. Pay close attention to the hose clips which secure the hoses to the cooling system components. Hose clips can pinch and puncture hoses, resulting in cooling system leaks. If wire type hose clips are used, it may be a good idea to replace them with screw-type clips.
12   Inspect all the cooling system components (hoses, joint faces, etc.) for leaks. A leak in the cooling system will usually show up as white or rust-coloured deposits on the area adjoining the leak. Where any problems of this nature are found on system components, renew the component or gasket with reference to Chapter 3.
13   Clean the front of the radiator with a soft brush to remove all insects, leaves, etc., imbedded in the radiator fins (remove the radiator grille panel for access as described in Chapter 11). Be extremely careful not to damage the radiator fins, and don't cut your fingers on them.

Cooling system draining

Warning: *Wait until the engine is cold before starting this procedure. Do not allow antifreeze to come in contact with your skin, or with the painted surfaces of the vehicle. Rinse off spills immediately with plenty of water. Never leave antifreeze lying around in an open container, or in a puddle in the driveway or garage floor. Children and pets are attracted by its sweet smell, but antifreeze is fatal if ingested. Refer to the note at the beginning of the 'Antifreeze mixtures' sub-Section before proceeding.*

14   To drain the cooling system, remove the expansion tank filler cap as described previously in this Section.
15   On DOHC engine models, remove the engine undershield with reference to Chapter 11.
16   Position a suitable container beneath the radiator bottom hose connection, then slacken the hose clip and ease the hose from the radiator stub. If the hose joint has not been disturbed for some time, it will be necessary to manipulate the hose to break the joint. Allow the coolant to drain into the container.
17   As no cylinder block drain plug is fitted, and the radiator bottom hose may be situated above the bottom of the radiator, the system cannot be drained completely. Care should therefore be taken when refilling the system to maintain antifreeze strength.
18   If the coolant has been drained for a reason other than renewal, then provided it is clean and less than two years old, it can be re-used. Note that Vauxhall/Opel do not specify renewal intervals for the coolant installed in the system when the vehicle is new, so renewal is up to the discretion of the owner.

Cooling system flushing

19   If coolant renewal has been neglected, or if the antifreeze mixture has become diluted, then in time, the cooling system may gradually lose efficiency, as the coolant passages become restricted due to rust, scale deposits, and other sediment. The cooling system efficiency can be restored by flushing the system clean.
20   The radiator should be flushed independently of the engine, to avoid unnecessary contamination.
21   To flush the radiator, disconnect the top hose at the radiator, then insert a garden hose into the radiator top inlet. Direct a flow of clean water through the radiator, and continue flushing until clean water emerges from the radiator bottom outlet (the bottom radiator hose should have been disconnected to drain the system). If after a reasonable period, the water still does not run clear, the radiator can be flushed with a good proprietary cleaning agent such as Holts Radflush or Holts Speedflush. It is important that the cleaning agent

manufacturer's instructions are followed carefully. If the contamination is particularly bad, insert the hose in the radiator bottom outlet, and flush the radiator in reverse ('reverse-flushing').
22   To flush the engine, proceed as follows, according to engine type.

1.4 and 1.6 litre engine models

23   Remove the thermostat as described in Chapter 3, then temporarily refit the thermostat cover.
24   With the radiator top and bottom hoses disconnected from the radiator, insert a hose into the radiator bottom hose. Direct a clean flow of water through the engine, and continue flushing until clean water emerges from the radiator top hose.
25   On completion of flushing, refit the thermostat with reference to Chapter 3, and reconnect the hoses.

1.8 and 2.0 litre engine models

26   Remove the thermostat and cover assembly, as described in Chapter 3.
27   With the radiator bottom hose disconnected from the radiator, insert a hose into the radiator bottom hose. Direct a flow of clean water through the engine, and continue flushing until clean water emerges from the thermostat housing. It is advisable to place a sheet of plastic under the thermostat housing to deflect water away from the engine and surrounding components during the flushing process.
28   On completion of flushing, refit the thermostat and cover assembly, reconnect the hoses and remove the plastic sheet.

Cooling system filling

29   Before attempting to fill the cooling system, make sure that all hoses and clips are in good condition, and that the clips are tight. Note that an antifreeze mixture must be used all year round, to prevent corrosion of the alloy engine components.
30   On 1.4 and 1.6 litre engine models, disconnect the wire and unscrew the coolant temperature sender from the inlet manifold (photo).
31   Remove the expansion tank cap, and fill the system by slowly pouring the coolant into the expansion tank to prevent airlocks from forming.
32   If the coolant is being renewed, begin by pouring in a couple of litres of water, followed by the correct quantity of antifreeze, then top-up with more water.
33   On 1.4 and 1.6 litre engine models, refit the coolant temperature sender when coolant free of air bubbles emerges from the orifice in the inlet manifold (photo).
34   Top-up the coolant level to the 'KALT' (or 'COLD') mark on the expansion tank, then refit the expansion tank cap.
35   Start the engine and run it until it reaches normal operating temperature, then stop the engine and allow it to cool.

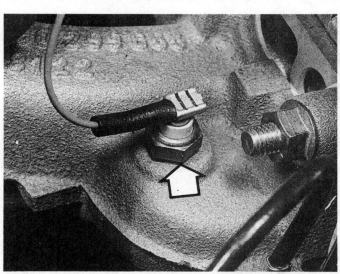

2.30 On 1.4 and 1.6 litre engines, remove the coolant temperature sender (arrowed) from the inlet manifold before filling the cooling system – single-point fuel injection engine shown

2.33 On 1.4 and 1.6 litre engines, refit the coolant temperature sender when coolant free of air bubbles emerges from the orifice (arrowed) – multi- point fuel injection engine shown

36   Check for leaks, particularly around disturbed components. Check the coolant level in the expansion tank, and top-up if necessary. Note that the system must be cold before an accurate level is indicated in the expansion tank. If the expansion tank cap is removed while the engine is still warm, cover the cap with a thick cloth and unscrew the cap slowly to gradually relieve the system pressure (a hissing sound will normally be heard). Wait until any pressure remaining in the system is released, then continue to turn the cap until it can be removed.
37   On DOHC engine models, refit the engine undershield on completion.

Antifreeze mixture

Note: *Vauxhall/Opel do not recommend renewal intervals for the antifreeze mixture, as the mixture used to fill the system when the vehicle is new is designed to last the lifetime of the vehicle. However, it is strongly recommended that the coolant is renewed the intervals specified in the 'Maintenance schedule', as a precaution against possible engine corrosion problems. This is particularly advisable if the coolant has been renewed previously, using an antifreeze other than that specified by Vauxhall/Opel. With many antifreeze types, the corrosion inhibitors become progressively less effective with age. It is up to the individual owner whether or not to follow this advice.*

38   Always use an ethylene-glycol based antifreeze which is suitable for use in mixed-metal cooling systems. The quantity of antifreeze and levels of protection are indicated in the Specifications.
39   Before adding antifreeze, the cooling system should be completely drained, preferably flushed, and all hoses and clips checked for condition and security.
40   After filling with antifreeze, a label should be attached to the radiator or expansion tank stating the type and concentration of antifreeze used, and the date installed. Any subsequent topping-up should be made with the same type and concentration of antifreeze.
41   Do not use engine antifreeze in the windscreen/tailgate washer system, as it will cause damage to the vehicle paintwork. A screenwash such as Turtle Wax High Tech Screen Wash should be added to the washer system in the quantities recommended on the bottle.

3   Fuel and exhaust systems

Warning: *Certain procedures in this Section require the removal of fuel lines and connections, which may result in some fuel spillage. Before carrying out any operation on the fuel system, refer to the precautions given in 'Safety first!' at the beginning of this manual, and follow them implicitly. Petrol is a highly-dangerous and volatile liquid, and the precautions necessary when handling it cannot be overstressed.*

Idle speed and mixture adjustment
Carburettor engine

Note: *Certain adjustment points in the fuel system are protected by tamperproof caps, plugs or seals. In some territories, it is an offence to drive a vehicle with broken or missing tamperproof seals. Before disturbing a tamperproof seal, check that no local or national laws will be broken by doing so, and fit a new tamperproof seal after adjustment is complete, where required by law. Do not break tamperproof seals on an engine which is still under warranty. To carry out the adjustments, an accurate tachometer and an exhaust gas analyser (CO meter) will be required.*

1   In order to check the idle speed and mixture adjustment, the following conditions must be met.

   (a)   *The engine must be at normal operating temperature.*
   (b)   *All electrical consumers (cooling fan, heater blower, headlights, etc) must be switched off.*
   (c)   *The ignition timing and spark plug gaps must be correctly adjusted – see Section 4.*
   (d)   *The throttle cable free play must be correctly adjusted – see Chapter 4.*
   (e)   *The air intake components must be free from leaks, and the air cleaner filter element must be clean.*
   (f)   *The fast idle speed adjustment screw must not touch the fast idle cam during the procedure.*

2   Connect a tachometer and an exhaust gas analyser to the vehicle in accordance with the manufacturer's instructions.
3   Start the engine and run it an 2000 rpm for approximately 30 seconds, then allow it to idle. If the idle speed is outside the specified limits, adjust by means of the throttle stop screw (photo).
4   When the idle speed is correct, check the CO level in the exhaust gas. If it is outside the specified limits, adjust by means of the idle mixture adjustment screw (photo). Turn the screw in very small increments until the CO level is correct.
5   With the idle mixture correct, readjust the idle speed if necessary.
6   If the cooling fan cuts in during the adjustment procedure, stop the adjustments and proceed when the cooling fan stops.
7   When both idle speed and mixture are correctly set, stop the engine and disconnect the test equipment.
8   Fit new tamperproof seals to the adjustment screws, where this is required by law.

Fuel injection engines

9   On all fuel injection engines, the idle speed and mixture are controlled by the electronic control unit (ECU), and no adjustment is possible. If any problems are suspected, the vehicle should be taken to a Vauxhall/Opel dealer who will have the necessary specialist test equipment to carry out system checks and fault diagnosis. Refer to Chapter 4 for further details of the fuel injection systems.

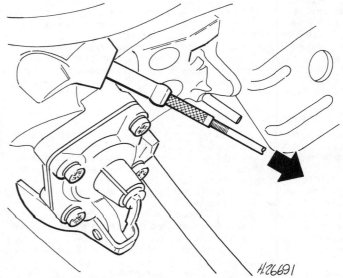

Fig. 1.2 Removing the fuel filter from the carburettor fuel inlet pipe (Sec 3)

3.3 Carburettor idle speed adjustment (throttle stop) screw (arrowed)

3.4 Tamperproof plug (arrowed) covering carburettor idle mixture adjustment screw

Air cleaner filter element renewal

10   The air cleaner assembly is located at the front right-hand side of the engine compartment.

11   Release the clips securing the cover to the air cleaner casing, then lift the cover sufficiently to remove the element (photos).

12   Wipe clean the inside surfaces of the cover and the main casing, and check that there is no foreign matter visible in the inlet duct.

13   Fit the new element, noting that the rubber locating flange should be uppermost, then refit the air cleaner cover and secure with the clips.

Fuel filter renewal

Carburettor engine

14   The fuel filter is located in the carburettor fuel inlet pipe.

15   Disconnect the trunking from the air cleaner, then disconnect the vacuum pipe and breather hose from the airbox. Extract the three securing screws and lift off the airbox, complete with air trunking.

16   Place a wad of rag under the fuel inlet pipe at the carburettor to catch any fuel which may be spilled during the procedure.

17   Disconnect the fuel inlet hose from the carburettor. Be prepared for fuel spillage, and clamp or plug the end of the hose to reduce unnecessary fuel loss. Take adequate fire precautions.

18   To remove the filter, carefully screw an M3 bolt approximately 5.0 mm into the end of the filter, and pull on the bolt to withdraw the filter from the end of the inlet pipe – see Fig. 1.2.

19   Push the new filter into the inlet pipe, ensuring that it engages securely, then reconnect the fuel inlet hose, and refit the airbox.

Fuel injection engines

20   The fuel filter is located on a bracket attached to the right-hand side of the fuel tank (photo).

21   Clamp the fuel hoses at either end of the filter to minimise fuel loss

when the hoses are disconnected, then place a suitable container beneath the filter to catch the fuel which will be released.

22   Disconnect the fuel hoses from the filter. Be prepared for fuel spillage, and take adequate fire precautions.

23   Note the orientation of the filter (note the orientation of any flow direction markings which may appear on the filter body), then unscrew the clamp bolt, and withdraw the filter from its bracket. Note that the filter will still contain some petrol, which should be drained safely into a suitable container. Dispose of the old filter safely.

24   Position the new filter in the retaining strap, ensuring that it is orientated correctly (make sure that the flow direction arrow(s) are correctly orientated, where applicable), then tighten the retaining strap screw to secure the filter.

25   Reconnect the hoses to the filter.

26   Run the engine and check for leaks on completion. If leakage is evident, stop the engine immediately, and rectify the problem without delay.

General fuel system checks

27   The fuel system is most easily checked with the vehicle raised on a hoist or suitably supported on axle stands, so the components underneath are readily visible and accessible.

28   If the smell of petrol is noticed while driving or after the vehicle has been parked in the sun, the system should be thoroughly inspected immediately.

29   Remove the petrol tank filler cap and check for damage, corrosion and an unbroken sealing imprint on the gasket. Renew the cap if necessary.

30   With the vehicle raised, inspect the petrol tank and filler neck for punctures, cracks and other damage. The connection between the filler neck and tank is especially critical. Sometimes a rubber filler neck or

3.11A Release the clips securing the cover to the air cleaner casing ...

3.11B ... then lift the cover sufficiently to remove the element

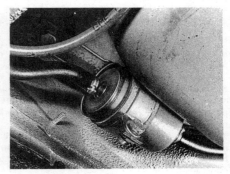

3.20 Fuel filter location

connecting hose will leak due to loose retaining clamps or deteriorated rubber.

31   Carefully check all rubber hoses and metal fuel lines leading away from the petrol tank. Check for loose connections, deteriorated hoses, crimped lines and other damage. Pay particular attention to the vent pipes and hoses which often loop up around the filler neck and can become blocked or crimped. Follow the lines to the front of the vehicle, carefully inspecting them all the way. Renew damaged sections as necessary.

32   From within the engine compartment, check the security of all fuel hose attachments, and inspect the fuel hoses and vacuum hoses for kinks, chafing and deterioration.

33   Check the operation of the throttle linkage, and lubricate the linkage components with a few drops of light oil.

Exhaust system check

34   With the engine cold (at least an hour after the vehicle has been driven), check the complete exhaust system from the engine to the end of the tailpipe. The exhaust system is most easily checked with the vehicle raised on a hoist or suitably supported on axle stands, so that the exhaust components are readily visible and accessible.

35   Check the exhaust pipes and connections for evidence of leaks, severe corrosion and damage. Make sure that all brackets and mountings are in good condition and tight. Leakage at any of the joints or in other parts of the system will usually show up as a black sooty stain in the vicinity of the leak. Holts Flexiwrap and Holts Gun Gum exhaust repair systems can be used for effective repairs to exhaust pipes and silencer boxes, including ends and bends. Holts Flexiwrap is an MOT-approved permanent exhaust repair. Holts Firegum is suitable for the assembly of all exhaust system joints.

36   Rattles and other noises can often be traced to the exhaust system, especially the brackets and mountings. Try to move the pipes and silencers. If the components are able to come into contact with the body or suspension parts, secure the system with new mountings or if possible, separate the joints and twist the pipes as necessary to provide additional clearance.

4   Ignition system

Warning: *Voltages produced by an electronic ignition system are considerably higher than those produced by conventional systems. Extreme care must be taken when working on the system with the ignition switched on. Persons with surgically-implanted cardiac pacemaker devices should keep well clear of the ignition circuits, components and test equipment.*

HT leads, distributor cap and rotor arm checks

1   To check the HT leads, proceed as follows.

2   On DOHC engine models, unscrew the two securing bolts, and withdraw the spark plug cover from the camshaft cover for access to the spark plug HT leads.

3   Ensure that the leads are numbered before removing them to avoid confusion when refitting. Working on each HT lead in turn, pull the end of the lead from the spark plug by gripping the end connector, not the lead, otherwise the lead connection may be fractured.

4   Check inside the connector for signs of corrosion, which will look like a white crusty powder. Push the connector back onto the spark plug, ensuring that it is a tight fit on the plug. If it is not, remove the lead again, and use pliers to carefully crimp the metal terminal inside the connector until it fits securely on the end of the spark plug.

5   Using a clean rag, wipe the entire length of the lead to remove any built-up dirt and grease. Once the lead is clean, check for burns, cracks and other damage. Do not bend the lead excessively, or pull the lead lengthwise – the conductor inside might break.

6   Disconnect the other end of the lead from the distributor cap, or coil, as applicable. Again, pull only on the connector. Check for corrosion and a tight fit, as described previously for the spark plug end of the lead. Refit the lead securely on completion.

7   Check the remaining HT leads one at a time, in the same way, including the lead from the distributor cap to the coil, where applicable.

8   If new HT leads are required, purchase a set for your specific vehicle and engine type.

9   On models fitted with a distributor, loosen the securing screws, or release the securing clips, as applicable, and remove the distributor cap

4.9 Releasing a distributor cap securing clip

(photo). Wipe the cap clean inside and out, and carefully inspect it for signs of cracks, 'tracking' (indicated by thin black lines running between the contacts) and worn, corroded, burnt or loose contacts. Check that the carbon brush in the centre of the cap is not worn, that it moves freely, and stands proud of the surface of the cap. Renew the cap if any faults are found. When fitting a new cap, remove the HT leads from the old cap one at a time, and fit them to the new cap in the exact same location – do not simultaneously remove all the leads from the old cap, as it is easy to fit the leads to the new cap in the wrong order, resulting in the wrong cylinder firing order.

10   Where applicable, remove the rotor arm, noting that on certain models the rotor arm is secured by screws. Examine the rotor arm for corrosion, cracks or other damage. If the metal portion of the rotor arm is badly burnt or loose, renew the rotor arm. If slightly burnt or corroded, it may be cleaned with a fine file.

11   Note that it is common practice to renew the distributor cap and rotor arm whenever new HT leads are fitted.

12   Even with the ignition system in first-class condition, some engines may still occasionally experience poor starting attributable to damp ignition components. To disperse moisture, Holts Wet Start can be very effective. Holts Damp Start can be used for providing a sealing coat to exclude moisture from the ignition system, and in extreme difficulty, Holts Cold Start will help to start a car when only a very poor spark occurs.

Ignition timing check and adjustment
Carburettor engine

Note: *A tachometer and a timing light will be required during this procedure.*

13   Start the engine and run it until it reaches normal operating temperature, then switch off.

14   Disconnect the vacuum pipe from the distributor vacuum unit.

15   Connect a tachometer and a stroboscopic timing light to the engine, in accordance with the equipment manufacturer's instructions. Note that the timing light should be connected to No 1 cylinder HT circuit (No 1 cylinder is nearest the timing belt end of the engine).

16   Start the engine, and check that the idle speed is between 700 and 1000 rpm.

17   Point the timing light at the timing pointer on the rear timing belt cover, and check that the pointer is aligned with the upper notch in the crankshaft pulley, representing 5° BTDC. Note that there are two notches on the pulley representing 5° and 10° BTDC – see Fig. 5.1 in Chapter 5.

18   If the notches and the pointer are not aligned as previously described, loosen the distributor clamp nut and turn the distributor body slightly in the required direction to align the notches and pointer.

19   Tighten the distributor clamp nut, and check that the notches and pointer are still aligned.

20   Stop the engine and disconnect the timing light and the tachometer, then reconnect the vacuum pipe to the distributor vacuum diaphragm unit.

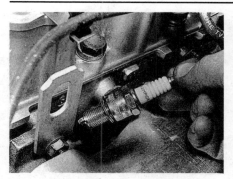

4.27A Removing a spark plug – SOHC engine

4.27B Removing a spark plug – DOHC engine

4.32A Measuring a spark plug electrode gap using a feeler gauge

4.32B Measuring a spark plug electrode gap using a wire gauge

4.33 Adjusting a spark plug electrode gap using a special tool

Fuel injection engines

21   No adjustment of the ignition timing is possible on fuel injection engines, as the adjustment is carried out automatically by the electronic control unit.

22   If a fault is suspected, the ignition timing can be checked by a Vauxhall/Opel dealer, using specialist dedicated test equipment.

Spark plug renewal

23   The correct functioning of the spark plugs is vital for the correct running and efficiency of the engine. It is essential that the plugs fitted are appropriate for the engine, and a suitable type is specified at the beginning of this Chapter. If this type is used and the engine is in good condition, the spark plugs should not need attention between scheduled replacement intervals. Spark plug cleaning is rarely necessary, and should not be attempted unless specialised equipment is available, as damage can easily be caused to the firing ends.

24   To remove the plugs, first open the bonnet, then on DOHC engine models, unscrew the two securing bolts, and withdraw the spark plug cover from the camshaft cover.

25   If necessary, mark the HT leads 1 to 4, to correspond to the cylinder the lead serves (No 1 cylinder is nearest the timing belt end of the engine). Pull the HT leads from the plugs by gripping the end connectors, not the leads, otherwise the lead connections may be fractured.

26   It is advisable to remove any dirt from the spark plug recesses using a clean brush, vacuum cleaner or compressed air, before removing the plugs, to prevent the dirt dropping into the cylinders.

27   Unscrew the plugs using a spark plug spanner, a suitable box spanner or a deep socket and extension bar (photos). Keep the socket in alignment with the spark plugs, otherwise if it is forcibly moved to either side, the porcelain top of the spark plug may be broken off. As each plug is removed, examine it as follows.

28   Examination of the spark plugs will give a good indication of the condition of the engine. If the insulator nose of the spark plug is clean and white, with no deposits, this is indicative of a weak mixture or too hot a plug (a hot plug transfers heat away from the electrode slowly, while a cold plug transfers heat away quickly).

29   If the tip and insulator nose are covered with hard black-looking deposits, then this is indicative that the idle mixture is too rich. Should the plug be black and oily, then it is likely that the engine is fairly worn, as well as the mixture being too rich.

30   If the insulator nose is covered with light-tan to greyish-brown deposits, then the mixture is correct and it is likely that the engine is in good condition.

31   The spark plug gap is of considerable importance as, if it is too large or too small, the size of the spark and its efficiency will be seriously impaired. For the best results, the spark plug gap should be set in accordance with the Specifications at the beginning of this Chapter.

32   To set the spark plug gap, measure the gap between the electrodes with a feeler gauge, and then bend open, or closed, the outer plug electrode until the correct gap is achieved (photos). The centre electrode should never be bent, as this may crack the insulation and cause plug failure, if nothing worse.

33   Special spark plug electrode gap adjusting tools are available from most motor accessory shops (photo).

34   Before fitting the spark plugs, check that the threaded connector sleeves on the top of the plug are tight, and that the plug exterior surfaces and threads are clean.

35   Screw in the spark plugs by hand where possible, then tighten them to the specified torque. Take extra care to enter the plug threads correctly, as the cylinder head is of light alloy construction.

36   Reconnect the HT leads in their correct order, and on DOHC engine models, refit the spark plug cover to the camshaft cover.

5   Clutch

Clutch cable adjustment/clutch pedal travel check

1   Working inside the vehicle, ensure that the clutch pedal is in its normal rest position, then measure the distance from the centre of the top edge of the pedal to the lowest point of the steering wheel. Fully depress the pedal, and repeat the measurement (photos). The measurements can be taken using a suitable strip of wood or metal, as the important figure is the *difference* between the two measurements, ie the movement (stroke) of the pedal.

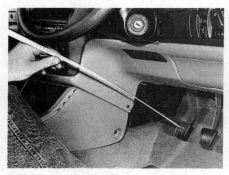

5.1A Measure the distance from the centre of the top edge of the pedal to the lowest point of the steering wheel ...

5.1B ... then fully depress the pedal and repeat the measurement

5.3 Removing the clip from the clutch cable threaded rod. Threaded rod adjuster flats arrowed

2   The difference between the two measurements must be as given in the Specifications – if not, adjust the clutch cable as follows to achieve the specified pedal movement.
3   Working in the engine compartment, remove the clip from the threaded rod at the clutch release arm on the gearbox, then turn the threaded rod as required, using a spanner on the flats provided (photo). Turn the rod clockwise to increase pedal movement, or anti-clockwise to decrease pedal movement. Recheck the pedal movement, and then refit the clip to the threaded rod on completion.
4   On a vehicle in which the clutch has covered a high mileage, it may no longer be possible to adjust the cable to achieve the specified pedal movement, and this indicates that the clutch friction disc requires renewal. Note that when correctly adjusted, the clutch pedal will rest slightly higher than the brake pedal – it is incorrect for the two pedals to be in alignment. If the pedals are aligned, the cable requires adjustment. Note also that there should be no play in the clutch pedal.

6   Manual gearbox and automatic transmission

Manual gearbox oil level check

1   On DOHC engine models, remove the engine undershield as described in Chapter 11.
2   Ensure that the vehicle is standing on a level surface.
3   Working underneath the vehicle, unscrew the gearbox oil level plug, which is located in the rear left of the differential housing on F 10/5 and F 13/5 type gearboxes, and in the rear right of the differential housing on F 16/5 and F 20/5 type gearboxes (photos).

4   If necessary, top-up with oil through the breather/filler orifice in the gear selector cover. Unscrew the breather/filler plug, and top-up with the specified grade of oil, until oil just begins to run from the level plug orifice (photos). Refit the level plug and the breather/filler plug on completion.
5   On DOHC engine models, refit the engine undershield.

Automatic transmission fluid level check

6   To check the fluid level, the vehicle must be parked on level ground with the handbrake applied.
7   If the transmission fluid is cold (ie, if the engine is cold), start the engine and allow it to idle for one minute, then complete the following checking procedure within a further two minutes.
8   With the engine idling, fully depress the brake pedal and move the gear selector lever smoothly through all positions, finishing in position 'P'.
9   With the engine still idling, withdraw the transmission fluid level dipstick (located at the left-hand side of the engine compartment, next to the battery), wipe it clean with a lint-free rag, re-insert it and withdraw it again.
10   If the transmission fluid was cold at the beginning of the procedure, the fluid level should be between the 'MIN' and 'MAX' marks on the side of the dipstick marked '+20°C'. Note that 0.25 litres of fluid is required to raise the level from the 'MIN' to the 'MAX' mark.
11   If the transmission fluid was at operating temperature at the beginning of the procedure (ie, if the vehicle has been driven for at least 12 miles/20 km), the fluid level should be between the 'MIN' and 'MAX' marks on the side of the dipstick marked '+80°C'. Note that 0.5 litres of fluid is required to raise the level from the 'MIN' to the 'MAX' mark.

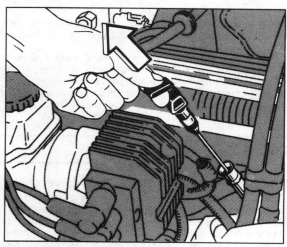

Fig. 1.3 Withdrawing the automatic transmission fluid level dipstick (Sec 6)

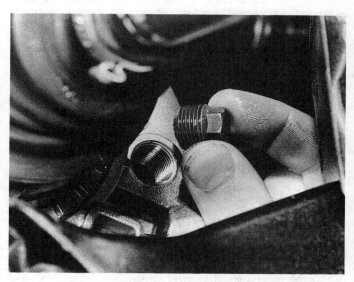

6.3A Removing the gearbox oil level plug – F 13/5 type gearbox

6.3B Gearbox oil level plug (arrowed) – F 16/5 type gearbox (viewed from below, with driveshaft removed)

6.4A Unscrew the breather/filler plug ...

6.4B ... and top-up with the specified grade of oil

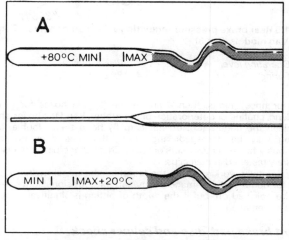

Fig. 1.4 Automatic transmission fluid level dipstick markings (Sec 6)

A   Markings for fluid at operating temperature

B   Markings for cold fluid

7.1 Check the condition of the driveshaft joint gaiters (A) and their retaining clips (B)

12   If topping-up is necessary, stop the engine, and top-up with the specified type of fluid through the dipstick tube.

13   Re-check the level, and refit the dipstick on completion.

7   Driveshafts

Driveshaft joint gaiters and driveshaft joint check

1   With the vehicle raised and securely supported on stands, turn the steering onto full-lock, then slowly rotate each front roadwheel. Inspect the condition of the outer constant velocity (CV) joint rubber gaiters while squeezing the gaiters to open out the folds. Check for signs of cracking, splits or deterioration of the rubber, which may allow the grease to escape and lead to water and grit entering the joint. Also check the security and condition of the retaining clips (photo). Repeat these checks on the inner CV joints. If any damage or deterioration is found, the gaiters should be renewed as described in Chapter 8.

2   At the same time, check the general condition of the CV joints themselves by first holding the driveshaft and attempting to rotate the wheel. Repeat this check by holding the inner joint and attempting to rotate the driveshaft. Any appreciable movement indicates wear in the joints, wear in the driveshaft splines or a loose front hub nut.

8   Braking system

Hydraulic fluid level check

Note: *Hydraulic fluid is poisonous; wash off immediately and thoroughly in the case of skin contact, and seek immediate medical advice if any fluid is swallowed or gets into the eyes. Certain types of hydraulic fluid are inflammable, and may ignite when allowed into contact with hot components; when servicing any hydraulic system, it is safest to assume that the fluid is inflammable, and to take precautions against the risk of fire as when handling petrol. Hydraulic fluid is also an effective paint stripper, and will attack certain plastics; if any is spilt, it should be washed off immediately using copious quantities of fresh water. Finally, it is hygroscopic (it absorbs moisture from the air) – old fluid may be contaminated and unfit for further use. When topping-up or renewing the fluid, always use the recommended type, and ensure that it comes from a freshly-opened, sealed container.*

1   The brake master cylinder and fluid reservoir are mounted on the front of the vacuum servo unit in the engine compartment. The maximum and minimum fluid level marks are indicated on the side of the reservoir, and the fluid level should be maintained between these marks at all times.

2   If topping-up is necessary, first wipe the area around the filler cap with a clean rag before removing the cap. When adding fluid, pour it carefully into the reservoir to avoid spilling it on surrounding painted surfaces. Be sure to use only the specified brake hydraulic fluid, since mixing different types of fluid can cause damage to the system (photo). See *'Lubricants, fluids and capacities'* at the beginning of this Chapter.

8.2 Topping-up the brake fluid level

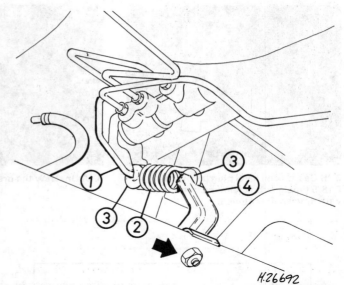

Fig. 1.5 Rear brake pressure-regulating valve components – Estate and Van models (Sec 8)

1   *Operating lever*   3   *Plastic bushes*
2   *Spring*   4   *Bracket*

3   When adding fluid, it is a good idea to inspect the reservoir for contamination. The system should be drained and refilled if deposits, dirt particles or contamination can be seen in the fluid.
4   After filling the reservoir to the correct level, make sure that the cap is refitted securely, to avoid leaks and the entry of foreign matter.
5   The fluid level in the master cylinder reservoir will drop slightly as the brake pads and shoes (where applicable) wear down during normal operation. If the reservoir requires repeated replenishing to maintain the correct level, this is an indication of a hydraulic leak somewhere in the system, which should be investigated immediately.

Hydraulic fluid renewal

6   The procedure is similar to that for the bleeding of the hydraulic system as described in Chapter 9, except that the brake fluid reservoir should be emptied by syphoning, using a (clean) old battery hydrometer or similar before starting, and allowance should be made for the old fluid to be expelled from the circuit when bleeding each section of the circuit.

Rear brake pressure-regulating valve check – Estate and Van models

7   To check the adjustment of the valve, the vehicle must be unladen – ie there should be no luggage or passengers in the vehicle, and the fuel tank should be a maximum of half-full. On models fitted with manual rear suspension level control, check that the system is pressurised to a minimum of 0.8 bars (see Section 9).
8   The vehicle must be standing on its wheels.
9   To check the operation of the valve, fully depress the brake pedal, then quickly release it.
10   The valve operating lever (see Fig. 1.5) should move. If the lever does not move, the valve is faulty, and should be renewed.
11   To adjust the valve, ensure that the valve operating lever is resting against its stop – if necessary, press the operating lever up to its stop, towards the front of the vehicle. The ends of the spring should lie in the plastic bushes in the valve operating lever and the bracket on the rear suspension torsion beam, and the spring should be free of play, and free from tension.
12   If necessary, loosen the nut securing the spring bracket to the rear suspension torsion beam, and move the bracket backwards or forwards as necessary until the spring is free of play and free from tension. Tighten the bracket securing nut on completion of adjustment.

Braking system hose and pipe check

13   The brake hydraulic system consists of a number of metal hydraulic pipes which run from the master cylinder to the front and rear brake assemblies, and the hydraulic modulator on models with an anti-lock braking system (ABS). Flexible hoses are fitted between the pipes and the front and rear brake assemblies, to allow for steering and suspension movement.
14   When checking the system, first look for signs of leakage at the

pipe or hose unions, then examine the flexible hoses for signs of cracking, chafing or deterioration of the rubber. Bend the hoses sharply between the fingers (but do not actually bend them double, or the casing may be damaged) and check that this does not reveal previously-hidden cracks, cuts or splits. Check that pipes and hoses are securely fastened in their clips.
15   Carefully working along the length of the metal hydraulic pipes, look for dents, kinks, damage of any sort, or corrosion. Light corrosion can be polished off, but if the depth of pitting is significant, the pipe must be renewed.

Front brake pad, disc and caliper check

16   Jack up the front of the vehicle, support securely on axle stands, then remove the roadwheels (see ‘*Jacking, towing and wheel changing*’).
17   For a quick check, the thickness of friction material remaining on each pad can be measured through the slot in the front of the caliper body. If the friction material on any pad is worn to the specified minimum thickness or less, all four pads must be renewed (see Chapter 9).
18   For a comprehensive check, the brake pads should be removed and cleaned. This will allow the operation of the caliper to be checked, and the condition of the brake disc itself to be fully examined on both sides (see Chapter 9).

Rear brake pad, disc and caliper check

19   Proceed as described for the front brakes in paragraphs 16 to 18 inclusive, but jack up the rear of the vehicle, and check the friction material thickness through the slot in the rear of the caliper body.

Rear brake shoe, drum and wheel cylinder check

20   Jack up the rear of the vehicle and support it securely on axle stands (see ‘*Jacking, towing and wheel changing*’).
21   For a quick check, the thickness of friction material remaining on one of the brake shoes can be observed through the hole in the brake backplate which is exposed by prising out the sealing grommet (photo). If a rod of the same diameter as the specified minimum friction material thickness is placed against the shoe friction material, the amount of wear can be assessed. A torch or inspection light will probably be required to help observation. If the friction material on any shoe is worn down to the specified minimum thickness or less, all four shoes must be renewed.
22   For a comprehensive check, the brake drum should be removed and cleaned. This will allow the wheel cylinders to be checked, and the condition of the brake drum itself to be fully examined (see Chapter 9).

8.21 Removing the sealing grommet from the inspection hole in the rear brake backplate

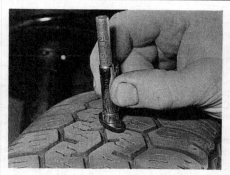

9.1 Checking a tyre tread depth with a depth gauge

9.3 Checking a tyre pressure with a tyre pressure gauge

9   Suspension and steering

Wheel and tyre maintenance and tyre pressure checks

1   The original tyres on all Astra vehicles are equipped with tread wear safety bands which will appear when the tread depth reaches approximately 1.6 mm. Tread wear can be monitored with a simple, inexpensive device known as a tread depth indicator gauge (photo).

2   Wheels and tyres should give no real problems in use, provided that a close eye is kept on them with regard to excessive wear or damage. To this end, the following points should be noted.

3   Ensure that tyre pressures are checked regularly and maintained correctly. Checking should be carried out with the tyres cold, and **not** immediately after the vehicle has been in use (photo). If the pressures are checked with the tyres hot, an apparently-high reading will be obtained owing to heat expansion. **Under no circumstances** should an attempt be made to reduce the pressures to the quoted cold reading in this instance, or effective under-inflation will result.

4   Note any abnormal tread wear with reference to Fig. 1.6. Tread pattern irregularities such as feathering, flat spots and more wear on one side than the other are indications of front wheel alignment and/or balance problems. If any of these conditions are noted, they should be rectified as soon as possible.

5   Under-inflation will cause overheating of the tyre owing to excessive flexing of the casing, and the tread will not sit correctly on the road surface. This will cause a consequent loss of adhesion and excessive wear, not to mention the danger of sudden tyre failure due to heat build-up.

6   Over-inflation will cause rapid wear of the centre part of the tyre tread, coupled with reduced adhesion, harsher ride, and the danger of shock damage occurring in the tyre casing.

7   Regularly check the tyres for damage in the form of cuts or bulges, especially in the sidewalls. Remove any nails or stones embedded in the tread before they penetrate the tyre to cause deflation. If removal of a nail does reveal that the tyre has been punctured, refit the nail so that its point of penetration is marked. Then immediately change the wheel and have the tyre repaired by a tyre dealer. Do not drive on a tyre in such a condition. If in any doubt as to the possible consequences of any damage found, consult your local tyre dealer for advice.

8   Periodically remove the wheels and clean any dirt or mud from the inside and outside surfaces. Examine the wheel rims for signs of rusting,

Condition	Probable cause	Corrective action	Condition	Probable cause	Corrective action
Shoulder wear	• Underinflation (wear on both sides) • Incorrect wheel camber (wear on one side) • Hard cornering	• Check and adjust pressure • Repair or renew suspension parts • Reduce speed	**Feathered edge** **Toe wear**	• Incorrect toe setting	• Adjust front wheel alignment
Centre wear	• Overinflation	• Measure and adjust pressure	**Uneven wear**	• Incorrect camber or castor • Malfunctioning suspension • Unbalanced wheel • Out-of-round brake disc/drum	• Repair or renew suspension parts • Repair or renew suspension parts • Balance tyres • Machine or renew disc/drum

Fig. 1.6 Tyre tread wear patterns and causes (Sec 9)

corrosion or other damage. Light alloy wheels are easily damaged by 'kerbing' whilst parking, and similarly steel wheels may become dented or buckled. Renewal of the wheel is very often the only course of remedial action possible.

9   The balance of each wheel and tyre assembly should be maintained to avoid excessive wear, not only to the tyres but also to the steering and suspension components. Wheel imbalance is normally signified by vibration through the vehicle's bodyshell, although in many cases it is particularly noticeable through the steering wheel. Conversely, it should be noted that wear or damage in suspension or steering components may cause excessive tyre wear. Out-of-round or out-of-true tyres, damaged wheels and wheel bearing wear/maladjustment also fall into this category. Balancing will not usually cure vibration caused by such wear.

10   Wheel balancing may be carried out with the wheel either on or off the vehicle. If balanced on the vehicle, ensure that the wheel-to-hub relationship is marked in some way prior to subsequent wheel removal so that the relationship can be maintained when the wheel is refitted.

11   General tyre wear is influenced to a large degree by driving style – harsh braking and acceleration or fast cornering will all produce more rapid tyre wear. Interchanging of tyres may result in more even wear, however it is worth bearing in mind that if this is completely effective, the added expense is incurred of replacing simultaneously a complete set of tyres – this may prove financially restrictive for many owners.

12   Front tyres may wear unevenly as a result of wheel misalignment. The front wheels should always be correctly aligned according to the settings specified by the vehicle manufacturer.

13   Legal restrictions apply to many aspects of tyre fitting and usage and in the UK this information is contained in the Motor Vehicle Construction and Use Regulations. It is suggested that a copy of these regulations is obtained from your local police if in doubt as to current legal requirements with regard to tyre type and condition, minimum tread depth, etc.

Power steering fluid level check

14   The power steering fluid level is checked with a dipstick attached to the reservoir filler cap. The reservoir is located at the front left-hand side of the engine compartment, next to the battery.

15   The fluid level should be checked with the engine stopped.

16   Unscrew the filler cap from the top of the reservoir, and wipe all the fluid from the end with a clean rag or paper towel. Refit the reservoir filler cap, then remove it once more. Note the fluid level on the dipstick. When the engine is cold, the fluid level should be up to the lower mark on the dipstick. When the engine is at normal operating temperature, the fluid level should be up to the upper mark on the dipstick (photo).

17   Top-up with the specified type of fluid if necessary (photo), and securely refit the reservoir filler cap on completion.

18   If frequent topping-up proves to be necessary, this indicates that there is a leak in the hydraulic system, which should be located and rectified without delay.

Roadwheel bolt tightness check

19   Using a torque wrench on each wheel bolt in turn, ensure that the bolts are tightened to the specified torque.

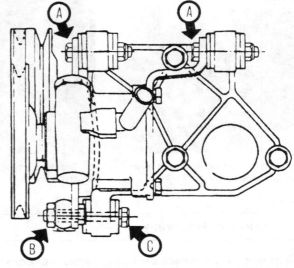

Fig. 1.7 Mounting and adjuster bolts (arrowed) must be loosened to adjust power steering pump drivebelt tension – 1.8 and 2.0 litre engine models (Sec 9)

For A, B and C see 'Torque wrench settings'

Rear suspension level control system pressure check

20   The rear suspension level control system pressure is checked using a tyre pressure gauge on the inflation valve located in the rear right-hand side of the luggage compartment floor. The check should be carried out with the vehicle unladen.

21   Remove the cap from the valve, and check that the system pressure is 0.8 bars (11.6 lbf/in^2). The pressure must never be allowed to drop below this value, even with the vehicle unladen. Adjust if necessary using a tyre pump.

Power steering pump drivebelt check, adjustment and renewal

1.4 and 1.6 litre engine models

22   On 1.4 and 1.6 litre engine models, the power steering pump is driven by the alternator drivebelt. Drivebelt checking, adjustment and renewal procedures are given in Section 11.

1.8 and 2.0 litre engine models

23   Correct tensioning of the drivebelt will ensure that it has a long life. Beware, however, of overtightening, as this can cause excessive wear in the pump.

24   The belt should be inspected along its entire length regularly, and if it is found to be worn, frayed or cracked, it should be renewed as a precaution against breakage in service.

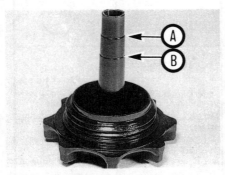

9.16 Power steering fluid level dipstick markings

A   *Level with engine cold*
B   *Level with engine at operating temperature*

9.17 Topping-up the power steering fluid level

9.27 Adjusting the length of the power steering pump threaded rod – 1.8 and 2.0 litre engine models

25   Although special tools are available for measuring the belt tension, a good approximation can be achieved if the belt is tensioned so that there is approximately 10.0 mm of free movement under firm thumb pressure at the mid-point of the belt run between pulleys. If in doubt, err on the slack side, as an excessively-tight belt may cause damage to the pump.
26   If adjustment is required, or if the belt is to be renewed, slacken the adjuster and mounting bolts shown in Fig. 1.7.
27   Slacken the adjuster nuts, and adjust the length of the threaded rod in order to tension or remove the belt as desired (photo).
28   Where applicable, fit the new belt around the pulleys, then tension the belt as described previously.
29   Tighten the adjuster nuts, and tighten the adjuster and mounting bolts to the specified torque on completion.
30   If a new drivebelt has been fitted, recheck the tension after a few hundred miles.

Front suspension and steering component check

31   Raise the front of the vehicle and securely support it on axle stands (see 'Jacking, towing and wheel changing').
32   Visually inspect the balljoint dust covers and the steering gear gaiters for splits, chafing or deterioration. Any wear of these components will cause loss of lubricant, and may allow water to enter the components, resulting in rapid deterioration of the balljoints or steering gear.
33   On vehicles equipped with power steering, check the fluid hoses for chafing or deterioration, and the pipe and hose unions for fluid leaks. Also check for signs of fluid leakage under pressure from the steering gear rubber gaiters, which would indicate failed fluid seals within the steering gear.
34   Grasp each roadwheel at the 12 o'clock and 6 o'clock positions and try to rock it (photo). Very slight free play may be felt, but if the movement is appreciable, further investigation is necessary to determine the source. Continue rocking the wheel while an assistant depresses the footbrake. If the movement is now eliminated or significantly reduced, it is likely that the hub bearings are at fault. If the free play is still evident with the footbrake depressed, then there is wear in the suspension joints or mountings.
35   Now grasp each wheel at the 9 o'clock and 3 o'clock positions, and try to rock it as before. Any movement felt now may again be caused by wear in the hub bearings or the steering track-rod end balljoints. If the track-rod end balljoint is worn, the visual movement will be obvious.
36   Using a large screwdriver or flat bar, check for wear in the suspension mounting bushes by levering between the relevant suspension component and its attachment point. Some movement is to be expected, as the mountings are made of rubber, but excessive wear should be obvious. Also check the condition of any visible rubber bushes, looking for splits, cracks or contamination of the rubber.
37   Check for any signs of fluid leakage around the suspension

9.34 Rocking a roadwheel to check steering/suspension component wear

strut/shock absorber bodies, or from the rubber gaiters around the piston rods. Should any fluid be noticed, the suspension strut/shock absorber is defective internally, and should be renewed.
Note: *Suspension struts/shock absorbers should always be renewed in pairs on the same axle.*
38   With the vehicle standing on its wheels, have an assistant turn the steering wheel back and forth about an eighth of a turn each way. There should be very little, if any, lost movement between the steering wheel and roadwheels. If this is not the case, closely observe the joints and mountings previously described, but in addition check the steering column rubber coupling for wear, and also check the steering gear itself.
39   The efficiency of each suspension strut/shock absorber may be checked by bouncing the vehicle at each corner. Generally speaking, the body will return to its normal position and stop after being depressed. If it rises and returns on a rebound, the suspension strut/shock absorber is probably suspect. Also examine the suspension strut/shock absorber upper and lower mountings for any signs of wear.

Rear suspension component check

40   Chock the front wheels, then jack up the rear of the vehicle and support securely on axle stands (see 'Jacking, towing and wheel changing').
41   Visually inspect the rear suspension components for any signs of obvious wear or damage. Pay particular attention to the rubber mounting bushes and renew if necessary (see Chapter 10).
42   Grasp each roadwheel at the 12 o'clock and 6 o'clock positions, and try to rock it. Any excess movement indicates incorrect adjustment or wear in the wheel bearings. Wear may also be accompanied by a rumbling sound when the wheel is spun, or a noticeable roughness if the wheel is turned slowly. The wheel bearing is integral with the rear hub unit, and if worn, the complete assembly must be renewed as described in Chapter 10.
43   Check the rear shock absorbers in a similar manner to that described previously for the front shock absorbers.

10   Bodywork and fittings

Bodywork damage/corrosion check

1   Once the car has been washed and all tar spots and other surface blemishes have been cleaned off, carefully check all paintwork, looking closely for chips or scratches. Pay particular attention to vulnerable areas such as the front panels (bonnet and spoiler), and around the wheel arches. Any damage to the paintwork must be rectified as soon as possible, to comply with the terms of the manufacturer's anti-corrosion warranties; check with a Vauxhall/Opel dealer for details.
2   If a chip or light scratch is found which is recent and still free from rust, it can be touched-up using the appropriate touch-up stick which can be obtained from Vauxhall/Opel dealers. Any more serious damage, or rusted stone chips, can be repaired as described in Chapter 11, but if damage or corrosion is so severe that a panel must be renewed, seek professional advice as soon as possible.
3   Always check that the door and ventilation opening drain holes and pipes are completely clear, so that water can drain out.

Underbody corrosion protection check

4   The wax-based underbody protective coating should be inspected annually, preferably just prior to Winter, when the underbody should be washed down as thoroughly as possible without disturbing the protective coating (see Chapter 11, Section 2, regarding the use of steam cleaners). Any damage to the coating should be repaired using a suitable wax-based sealer. If any of the body panels are disturbed for repair or renewal, do not forget to replace the coating and to inject wax into door panels, sills and box sections, to maintain the level of protection provided by the vehicle manufacturer.

Seat belt check

5   Carefully examine the seat belt webbing for cuts or any signs of serious fraying or deterioration. If the seat belt is of the retractable type, pull the belt all the way out, and examine the full extent of the webbing.

6   The seat belts are designed to lock up during a sudden stop or impact, yet allow free movement during normal driving. Fasten and unfasten the belt, ensuring that the locking mechanism holds securely and releases properly when intended. Check also that the retracting mechanism operates correctly when the belt is released.

Hinge and lock lubrication

7   Lubricate the hinges of the bonnet, doors and tailgate or boot lid (as applicable) with a light general-purpose oil. Similarly, lubricate all latches, locks and lock strikers. At the same time, check the security and operation of all the locks, adjusting them if necessary (see Chapter 11).
8   Lightly lubricate the bonnet release mechanism and cable with a suitable grease.

11   Electrical system

Battery check and maintenance

Caution: *Before carrying out any work on the vehicle battery, read through the precautions given in 'Safety first!' at the beginning of this manual.*
1   A 'maintenance-free' battery is standard equipment on all vehicles covered by this manual. Although this type of battery has many advantages over the older refillable type, and never requires the addition of distilled water, it should still be routinely maintained according to the following procedure.
2   The battery is located at the front right-hand corner of the engine compartment. The exterior of the battery should be inspected periodically for damage such as a cracked case or cover.
3   Check the tightness of the battery cable clamps to ensure good electrical connections, and check the entire length of each cable for cracked insulation and frayed wiring.
4   If corrosion (visible as white, fluffy deposits) is evident, remove the cables from the battery terminals, clean them with a small wire brush, then refit them. Corrosion can be kept to a minimum by applying a layer of petroleum jelly to the clamps and terminals after they are reconnected.
5   Make sure that the battery tray is in good condition, and that the retaining clamp is tight.
6   Corrosion on the tray, retaining clamp and the battery itself can be removed with a solution of water and baking soda. Thoroughly rinse all cleaned areas with plain water.
7   Any metal parts of the vehicle damaged by corrosion should be covered with a zinc-based primer, then painted.
8   Further information on the battery, charging, and jump starting, can be found in Chapter 12 and in the preliminary sections of this manual.

Alternator drivebelt check, adjustment and renewal

Checking and adjustment

9   Correct tensioning of the alternator drivebelt will ensure that it has a long life. Beware, however, of overtightening, as this can cause excessive wear in the alternator.
10   On 1.4 and 1.6 litre models with power steering, the alternator drivebelt also drives the power steering pump.
11   Disconnect the air intake trunking from the air cleaner, and the airbox or the throttle body, as applicable, and remove it for improved access.
12   The belt should be inspected along its entire length regularly, and if it is found to be worn, frayed or cracked, it should be renewed as a precaution against breakage in service. It is advisable to carry a spare drivebelt of the correct type in the vehicle at all times.
13   Although special tools are available for measuring the belt tension, a good approximation can be achieved if the belt is tensioned so that there is approximately 13.0 mm of free movement at the mid-point of the longest run between pulleys. If in doubt, err on the slack side, as an excessively-tight belt may cause damage to the alternator.
14   If adjustment is required, loosen the alternator upper and lower mounting nuts and bolts, and with the mounting bolts just holding the unit firm, lever the alternator away from the engine using a wooden lever at the mounting bracket until the correct tension is achieved, then tighten the mounting nuts and bolts. On no account lever at the free end of the alternator, as serious internal damage could be caused to the alternator.

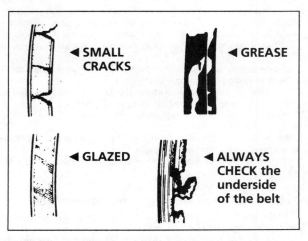

Fig. 1.8 Examine the alternator drivebelt for signs of wear, deterioration or contamination (Sec 11)

Renewal

15   To remove the belt on 1.8 and 2.0 litre engine models, first remove the power steering pump drivebelt as described in Section 9.
16   Disconnect the air intake trunking from the air cleaner, and the airbox or the throttle body, as applicable, and remove it for improved access. Loosen the alternator upper and lower mounting nuts and bolts sufficiently to allow the alternator to pivot towards the engine.
17   Slide the belt from the pulleys (photo).
18   Fit the new belt around the pulleys, and take up the slack in the belt by swinging the alternator away from the engine and lightly tightening the mounting nuts and bolts.
19   Tension the drivebelt as described previously in this sub-Section, and recheck the tension after a few hundred miles.
20   On 1.8 and 2.0 litre engine models, refit and tension the power steering pump drivebelt, as described in Section 9.

Horn, lights and direction indicators operational check

21   Check the operation of all electrical equipment, ie horn, lights, direction indicators, etc. Refer to the appropriate Sections of Chapter 12 for details if any of the circuits are found to be inoperative.
22   Visually check all accessible wiring connectors, harnesses and retaining clips for security, and for signs of chafing or damage. Rectify any faults found.

Windscreen/tailgate wiper blade check and renewal

23   Check the condition of the wiper blades. If they are cracked or show any signs of deterioration, or if the glass swept area smears, renew the blades. For maximum effectiveness, the wiper blades should be renewed annually as a matter of course.
24   To remove a wiper blade, pull the arm away from the glass until it locks. Swivel the blade through 90°, then squeeze the locking tabs, and detach the blade from the arm (photo). When fitting the new blade, make sure that the blade locks securely into the arm, and that the blade is orientated correctly.

Windscreen/tailgate/headlight washer system check

25   The fluid reservoir for the windscreen and tailgate washer system (where fitted) is located at the rear right-hand corner of the engine compartment. On models with a headlight washer system, the fluid reservoir is located under the left-hand front wheel arch, with the filler tube protruding into the rear left-hand corner of the engine compartment (photo).
26   Check, and if necessary top-up, the washer fluid level in the reservoir. When topping-up the reservoir, a screenwash such as Turtle Wax High Tech Screen Wash should be added in the quantities recommended on the bottle.
27   **Never** use engine antifreeze in the washer fluid, as it can damage the vehicle paintwork.
28   Check the security of the pump wires and the washer tubing.
29   Check the operation of the washers. If a jet is blocked, it can be

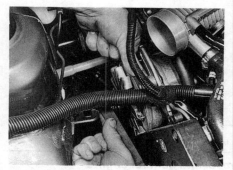

11.17 Sliding the drivebelt from the alternator pulley – 1.6 litre engine model with power steering

11.24 Wiper blade locking tabs (arrowed)

11.25 Headlight washer fluid reservoir filler neck (arrowed)

cleared using a thin wire probe or a pin. Adjust the nozzles using a pin if necessary, aiming the spray at a point slightly above the centre of the swept area, to allow for the spray being deflected down by the air flow when the car is moving.

12   Road test

Instruments and electrical equipment

1   Check the operation of all instruments and electrical equipment.
2   Make sure that all instruments read correctly, and switch on all electrical equipment in turn to check that it functions properly.

Steering and suspension

3   Check for any abnormalities in the steering, suspension, handling or road feel.
4   Drive the vehicle and check that there are no unusual vibrations or noises.
5   Check that the steering feels positive, with no excessive 'sloppiness', or roughness, and check for any suspension noises when cornering and driving over bumps.

Drivetrain

6   Check the performance of the engine, clutch (where applicable), gearbox/transmission and driveshafts.
7   Listen for any unusual noises from the engine, clutch and gearbox/transmission.
8   Make sure that the engine runs smoothly when idling, and that there is no hesitation when accelerating.
9   Check that, where applicable, the clutch action is smooth and

progressive, that the drive is taken up smoothly, and that the pedal travel is not excessive. Also listen for any noises when the clutch pedal is depressed.
10   On manual gearbox models, check that all gears can be engaged smoothly without noise, and that the gear lever action is not abnormally vague or 'notchy'.
11   On automatic transmission models, make sure that all gearchanges occur smoothly without snatching, and without an increase in engine speed between changes. Check that all the gear positions can be selected with the vehicle at rest. If any problems are found, they should be referred to a Vauxhall/Opel dealer.
12   Listen for a metallic clicking sound from the front of the vehicle as the vehicle is driven slowly in a circle with the steering on full-lock. Carry out this check in both directions. If a clicking noise is heard, this indicates wear in a driveshaft joint, in which case renew the joint if necessary.

Check the operation and performance of the braking system

13   Make sure that the vehicle does not pull to one side when braking, and that the wheels do not lock prematurely when braking hard.
14   Check that there is no vibration through the steering when braking.
15   Check that the handbrake operates correctly without excessive movement of the lever, and that it holds the vehicle stationary on a slope.
16   Test the operation of the brake servo unit as follows. Depress the footbrake four or five times to exhaust the vacuum, then start the engine. As the engine starts, there should be a noticeable 'give' in the brake pedal as vacuum builds up. Allow the engine to run for at least two minutes and then switch it off. If the brake pedal is now depressed again, it should be possible to detect a hiss from the servo as the pedal is depressed. After about four or five applications, no further hissing should be heard and the pedal should feel considerably harder.

Chapter 2 Engine

Contents

Specifications

Single overhead camshaft (SOHC) engines
Engine (general)

Type	Four-cylinder, in-line, water-cooled. Single belt-driven overhead camshaft, acting on hydraulic valve lifters

Manufacturer's engine codes:*
1.4 litre carburettor engine	14 NV
1.4 litre single-point fuel injection engine	C 14 NZ
1.4 litre multi-point fuel injection engine	C 14 SE
1.6 litre single-point fuel injection engine	C 16 NZ
1.6 litre multi-point fuel injection engine	C 16 SE
1.8 litre engine	C 18 NZ
2.0 litre engine	C 20 NE

Bore:
1.4 litre engines	77.600 mm
1.6 litre engines	79.000 mm
1.8 litre engine	84.800 mm
2.0 litre engine	86.000 mm

Stroke:
1.4 litre engines	73.400 mm
1.6 litre engines	81.500 mm
1.8 litre engine	79.500 mm
2.0 litre engine	86.000 mm

Capacity:
1.4 litre engines	1389 cc
1.6 litre engines	1598 cc
1.8 litre engine	1796 cc
2.0 litre engine	1998 cc
Firing order	1–3–4–2 (No 1 cylinder at timing belt end)
Direction of crankshaft rotation	Clockwise

Engine (general) – continued

Compression ratio:
14 NV and C 14 NZ engines	9.4 : 1
C 14 SE engine	10.0 : 1
C 16 NZ engine, C 18 NZ and C 20 NE engines	9.2 : 1
C 16 SE engine	9.8 : 1

Maximum power:
14 NV engine	55 kW at 5800 rpm
C 14 NZ engine	44 kW at 5200 rpm
C 14 SE engine	60 kW at 5800 rpm
C 16 NZ engine	55 kW at 5200 rpm
C 16 SE engine	74 kW at 5800 rpm
C 18 NZ engine	66 kW at 5400 rpm
C 20 NE engine	85 kW at 5400 rpm

Maximum torque:
14 NV engine	110 Nm at 3000 rpm
C 14 NZ engine	103 Nm at 2800 rpm
C 14 SE engine	113 Nm at 3400 rpm
C 16 NZ engine	125 Nm at 2800 rpm
C 16 SE engine	135 Nm at 3400 rpm
C 18 NZ engine	145 Nm at 3000 rpm
C 20 NE engine	170 Nm at 2600 rpm

Maximum compression pressure difference between cylinders............. 1.0 bar

For details of engine code location, see 'Buying spare parts and vehicle identification numbers'

Cylinder block

Material	Cast iron
Maximum cylinder bore ovality	0.013 mm
Maximum cylinder bore taper	0.013 mm
Maximum permissible rebore oversize	0.500 mm

Cylinder bore diameters:

	Bore diameter	Identification mark
1.4 litre engines:		
Production size 1	77.555 to 77.565 mm	6
	77.565 to 77.575 mm	7
	77.575 to 77.585 mm	8
Production size 2	77.585 to 77.595 mm	99
	77.595 to 77.605 mm	00
	77.605 to 77.615 mm	01
	77.615 to 77.625 mm	02
Production size 4	77.665 to 77.675 mm	07
0.5 mm oversize	78.065 to 78.075 mm	7 + 0.5
1.6 litre engines:		
Production size 1	78.945 to 78.955 mm	5
	78.955 to 78.965 mm	6
	78.965 to 78.975 mm	7
	78.975 to 78.985 mm	8
Production size 2	78.985 to 78.995 mm	99
	78.995 to 79.005 mm	00
	79.005 to 79.015 mm	01
	79.015 to 79.025 mm	02
Production size 3	79.025 to 79.035 mm	03
	79.035 to 79.045 mm	04
	79.045 to 79.055 mm	05
	79.055 to 79.065 mm	06
Production size 4	79.065 to 79.075 mm	07
	79.075 to 79.085 mm	08
	79.085 to 79.095 mm	09
	79.095 to 79.105 mm	1
0.5 mm oversize	79.645 to 79.475 mm	7 + 0.5
	79.475 to 79.485 mm	8 + 0.5
	79.485 to 79.495 mm	9 + 0.5
	79.495 to 79.505 mm	0 + 0.5
1.8 litre engine:		
Production size 2	84.780 mm	8
	84.790 mm	99
	84.800 mm	00
	84.810 mm	01
	84.820 mm	02
0.5 mm oversize	85.270 mm	7 + 0.5
2.0 litre engine:		
Production size 2	85.980 mm	8
	85.990 mm	99
	86.000 mm	00
	86.010 mm	01
	86.020 mm	02
0.5 mm oversize	86.470 mm	7 + 0.5

Crankshaft and bearings

	1.4 and 1.6 litre	1.8 and 2.0 litre
Number of main bearings... 5		
Main bearing journal diameter:		
Standard...	54.972 to 54.985 mm	57.982 to 57.995 mm
0.25 mm undersize	54.722 to 54.735 mm	57.732 to 57.745 mm
0.50 mm undersize	54.472 to 54.485 mm	57.482 to 57.495 mm
Main bearing shell colour codes (all models):	**Bearing cap shells**	**Cylinder block shells**
Standard...	Brown	Green
0.25 mm undersize	Brown/blue	Green/blue
0.50 mm undersize	Brown/white	Green/white
Centre (thrust) main bearing journal width:	**1.4 and 1.6 litre**	**1.8 and 2.0 litre**
Standard...	26.000 to 26.052 mm	25.850 to 25.900 mm
0.25 mm undersize	26.200 to 26.252 mm	26.050 to 26.100 mm
0.50 mm undersize	26.400 to 26.452 mm	26.250 to 26.300 mm
Big-end bearing journal diameter:	**1.4 and 1.6 litre**	**1.8 and 2.0 litre**
Standard...	42.971 to 42.987 mm	48.970 to 48.988 mm
0.25 mm undersize	42.271 to 42.737 mm	48.720 to 48.738 mm
0.50 mm undersize	42.471 to 42.487 mm	48.470 to 48.488 mm
Big-end bearing shell colour codes (all models):		
Standard...	None	
0.25 mm undersize	Blue	
0.50 mm undersize	White	
Maximum main and big-end bearing journal out-of-round (all engines) ..	0.040 mm	
Main bearing running clearance:		
1.4 and 1.6 litre	0.025 to 0.050 mm	
1.8 and 2.0 litre	0.015 to 0.040 mm	
Big-end bearing running clearance:		
1.4 and 1.6 litre	0.019 to 0.071 mm	
1.8 and 2.0 litre	0.006 to 0.031 mm	
Crankshaft endfloat:		
1.4 and 1.6 litre	0.100 to 0.200 mm	
1.8 and 2.0 litre	0.050 to 0.152 mm	
Connecting rod endfloat:		
1.4 and 1.6 litre	0.110 to 0.240 mm	
1.8 and 2.0 litre	0.070 to 0.240 mm	

Pistons

Piston-to-bore clearance:	
New	0.020 mm
After rebore (oversize)	0.010 to 0.030 mm

Note: *Piston diameters – pistons carry identification marks corresponding to those listed previously for cylinder bore diameters. The appropriate piston diameter is 0.020 mm less than the corresponding bore diameter.*

Piston rings

Number of rings (per piston)..	2 compression, 1 oil control
Ring end gap:	
Compression..	0.300 to 0.500 mm
Oil control (top and bottom sections)	0.400 to 1.400 mm
Ring gap offset (to gap of adjacent ring)*	180°

**For oil control ring sections, see text Section 40*

Cylinder head

	1.4 and 1.6 litre	1.8 and 2.0 litre
Material..	Light alloy	
Maximum permissible distortion of sealing face	0.025 mm	
Overall height of cylinder head (sealing surface to sealing surface)..........	96.000 ± 0.100 mm	
Valve seat width:	**1.4 and 1.6 litre**	**1.8 and 2.0 litre**
Inlet...	1.300 to 1.400 mm	1.000 to 1.500 mm
Exhaust..	1.700 to 1.800 mm	1.700 to 2.200 mm

Camshaft

Camshaft bearing journal diameter:	Standard	0.1 mm undersize
1.4 and 1.6 litre engines:		
No 1	39.435 to 39.455 mm	
No 2	39.685 to 39.705 mm	
No 3	39.935 to 39.955 mm	
No 4	40.185 to 40.205 mm	
No 5	40.435 to 40.455 mm	
1.8 and 2.0 litre engines:	**Standard**	**0.1 mm undersize**
No 1	42.455 to 42.470 mm	42.355 to 42.370 mm
No 2	42.705 to 42.720 mm	42.605 to 42.620 mm
No 3	42.955 to 42.970 mm	42.855 to 42.870 mm
No 4	43.205 to 43.220 mm	43.105 to 43.120 mm
No 5	43.455 to 43.470 mm	43.355 to 43.370 mm

Camshaft (continued)

Camshaft bearing diameter in housing:

1.4 and 1.6 litre engines:

No 1	39.500 to 39.525 mm
No 2	39.750 to 39.775 mm
No 3	40.000 to 40.025 mm
No 4	40.250 to 40.275 mm
No 5	40.500 to 40.525 mm

1.8 and 2.0 litre engines:

	Standard	**0.1 mm undersize**
No 1	42.500 to 42.525 mm	42.400 to 42.425 mm
No 2	42.750 to 42.775 mm	42.650 to 42.675 mm
No 3	43.000 to 43.025 mm	42.900 to 42.925 mm
No 4	43.250 to 43.275 mm	43.150 to 43.175 mm
No 5	43.500 to 43.525 mm	43.400 to 43.425 mm
Maximum permissible radial run-out	0.030 mm	
Endfloat	0.090 to 0.210 mm	

Timing belt

Tension using gauge KM-510-A (1.8 and 2.0 litre engines – see text Section 7):

New belt, cold	4.5
New belt, warm	7.5
Used belt, cold	2.5
Used belt, warm	7.0

Valves and guides

	Inlet	**Exhaust**
Stem diameter (all engines):		
Standard	6.998 to 7.012 mm	6.978 to 6.992 mm
0.075 mm oversize	7.037 to 7.087 mm	7.053 to 7.067 mm
0.150 mm oversize	7.148 to 7.162 mm	7.128 to 7.142 mm
0.250 mm oversize	7.248 to 7.262 mm	7.228 to 7.242 mm
Valve guide bore (all engines):		
Standard	7.030 to 7.050 mm	
0.075 mm oversize	7.105 to 7.125 mm	
0.150 mm oversize	7.180 to 7.200 mm	
0.250 mm oversize	7.280 to 7.300 mm	
Maximum permissible valve stem play in guide (all engines):		
Inlet	0.018 to 0.052 mm	
Exhaust	0.038 to 0.072 mm	
Valve seat angle (all engines)	44°	
Valve clearances	Automatic adjustment by hydraulic valve lifters	

Flywheel

Maximum permissible lateral run-out of starter ring gear	0.500 mm
Refinishing limit – maximum depth of material which may be removed from clutch friction surface	0.300 mm

Lubrication system

Minimum permissible oil pressure at idle speed, with engine at operating temperature (oil temperature of at least 80°C)	1.5 bars
Oil pump type	Gear type, driven from crankshaft
Oil pump clearances:	
Inner-to-outer gear teeth clearance (backlash) – all engines	0.100 to 0.200 mm
Gear-to-housing clearance (endfloat):	
1.4 and 1.6 litre engines	0.080 to 0.150 mm
1.8 and 2.0 litre engines	0.030 to 0.100 mm

Torque wrench settings

	Nm	**lbf ft**
Camshaft cover bolts	8	6
Crankshaft pulley bolt (1.4 and 1.6 litre engines):		
M10 bolt with 23.0 mm thread length	55	41
M10 bolt with 30.0 mm thread length:*		
Stage 1	55	41
Stage 2	Angle-tighten a further 45° to 60°	Angle-tighten a further 45° to 60°
M12 bolt:*		
Stage 1	90	66
Stage 2	Angle-tighten a further 30° to 45°	Angle-tighten a further 30° to 45°
Crankshaft pulley-to-sprocket bolts (1.8 and 2.0 litre engines)	20	15
Outer timing belt cover bolts	4	3
Rear timing belt cover bolts:		
1.4 and 1.6 litre engines	12	9
1.8 and 2.0 litre engines	6	4
Coolant pump bolts:		
1.4 and 1.6 litre engines	8	6
1.8 and 2.0 litre engines	25	18
Camshaft sprocket bolt	45	33
Crankshaft sprocket bolt (1.8 and 2.0 litre engines):*		
Stage 1	130	96
Stage 2	Angle-tighten a further 40° to 50°	Angle-tighten a further 40° to 50°
Timing belt tension indicator bolt (1.4 and 1.6 litre engines)	20	15

Torque wrench settings (continued)

	Nm	lbf ft
Cylinder head bolts:*		
1.4 and 1.6 litre engines:		
Stage 1	25	18
Stage 2	Angle-tighten a further 60°	Angle-tighten a further 60°
Stage 3	Angle-tighten a further 60°	Angle-tighten a further 60°
Stage 4	Angle-tighten a further 30°	Angle-tighten a further 30°
Stage 5 (engine warm)	Angle-tighten a further 30°	Angle-tighten a further 30°
1.8 and 2.0 litre engines:		
Stage 1	25	18
Stage 2	Angle-tighten a further 60°	Angle-tighten a further 60°
Stage 3	Angle-tighten a further 60°	Angle-tighten a further 60°
Stage 4	Angle-tighten a further 60°	Angle-tighten a further 60°
Stage 5 (engine warm)	Angle-tighten a further 30°	Angle-tighten a further 30°
Fuel pump-to-camshaft housing bolts (carburettor engine)	18	13
Camshaft thrustplate bolts	8	6
Sump drain plug	45	33
Oil pick-up pipe-to-oil pump bolts	8	6
Oil pick-up pipe bracket-to-cylinder block bolt	8	6
Sump bolts:		
1.4 and 1.6 litre engines	8	6
1.8 and 2.0 litre engines	5	4
Oil pump bolts	6	4
Oil pressure relief valve plug	30	22
Flywheel/driveplate bolts:*		
1.4 and 1.6 litre engines:		
Stage 1	35	26
Stage 2	Angle-tighten a further 30° to 45°	Angle-tighten a further 30° to 45°
1.8 and 2.0 litre engines:		
Stage 1	65	48
Stage 2	Angle-tighten a further 30° to 45°	Angle-tighten a further 30° to 45°
Engine-to-gearbox/transmission bolts	75	55
Right-hand engine mounting-to-body bolts	65	48
Right-hand engine mounting-to-engine bracket bolts	35	26
Left-hand engine/transmission mounting-to-transmission bracket bolts	60	44
Left-hand engine/transmission mounting-to-body bolts*	65	48
Rear engine/transmission mounting-to-crossmember bolts	40	30
Rear engine/transmission mounting-to-transmission bracket bolts	45	33
Engine/transmission mounting bracket-to-engine/transmission bolts	60	44
Alternator mounting bracket-to-engine bolts:		
M8 bolts	25	18
M10 bolts	40	30
Alternator-to-mounting bracket bolts:		
M8 bolts	25	18
M10 bolts	40	30
Alternator-to-adjuster bracket bolt	25	18
Exhaust manifold hot air shroud bolts	8	6
Inlet and exhaust manifold nuts	22	16
Power steering pump pulley bolts	25	18
Power steering pump bolts	30	18
Thermostat housing bolts:		
1.4 and 1.6 litre engines	10	7
1.8 and 2.0 litre engines	15	11
Starter motor bolts:		
1.4 and 1.6 litre engines	25	18
1.8 and 2.0 litre engines:		
Engine side	45	33
Transmission side	75	55
Spark plugs	25	18
Main bearing cap bolts:*		
1.4 and 1.6 litre engines:		
Stage 1	50	37
Stage 2	Angle-tighten a further 45° to 60°	Angle-tighten a further 45° to 60°
1.8 and 2.0 litre engines:		
Stage 1	50	37
Stage 2	Angle-tighten a further 40° to 50°	Angle-tighten a further 40° to 50°
Big-end bearing cap bolts:		
1.4 and 1.6 litre engines:		
Bolts with 15.0 mm thread length	28	21
Bolts with 40.0 mm thread length:*		
Stage 1	25	18
Stage 2	Angle-tighten a further 30°	Angle-tighten a further 30°
1.8 and 2.0 litre engines:*		
Stage 1	35	26
Stage 2	Angle-tighten a further 45° to 60°	Angle-tighten a further 45° to 60°

*Use new bolts

Double overhead camshaft (DOHC) engine
Engine (general)
Type.. Four-cylinder in-line, water-cooled. Double belt-driven overhead camshafts, acting on hydraulic valve lifters
Manufacturer's engine code... C 20 XE
Bore... 86.000 mm
Stroke... 86.000 mm
Capacity .... 1998 cc
Firing order.. 1–3–4–2 (No 1 cylinder at timing belt end)
Direction of crankshaft rotation .... Clockwise
Compression ratio .... 10.5 : 1
Maximum power .... 110 kW at 6000 rpm
Maximum torque.. 196 Nm at 4800 rpm
Maximum compression pressure difference between cylinders............ 1.0 bar

Cylinder block
All specifications as given for SOHC engines, except for the following:
Cylinder bore diameters:

Bore diameter	Identification mark
85.975 to 85.985 mm	8
85.985 to 85.995 mm	99
85.995 to 86.005 mm	00
86.005 to 86.015 mm	01
86.015 to 86.025 mm	02
86.465 to 86.475 mm	7 + 0.5
86.475 to 86.485 mm	8 + 0.5
86.485 to 86.495 mm	9 + 0.5
86.495 to 86.505 mm	0 + 0.5

Production size 1 — (Production size 1, Production size 2, 0.5 mm oversize rows correspond above)

Production size 1 ....
Production size 2 ....
0.5 mm oversize ....

Crankshaft and bearings
All specifications as given for 1.8 and 2.0 litre SOHC engines, except for the following:
Centre (thrust) main bearing journal width:
   Standard.. 25.950 to 26.002 mm
   0.25 mm undersize .... 26.150 to 26.202 mm
   0.5 mm undersize .... 26.350 to 26.402 mm

Pistons
Piston-to-bore clearance .... 0.020 to 0.040 mm
Note: *Piston diameters – pistons carry identification marks corresponding to those listed previously for cylinder bore diameters. The appropriate piston diameter is 0.030 mm less than the corresponding bore diameter.*

Piston rings
All specifications as given for SOHC engines

Cylinder head
All specifications as given for SOHC engines, except for the following:
Overall height of cylinder head (sealing surface to sealing surface).......... 135.630 mm
Valve seat width:
   Inlet.. 1.000 to 1.400 mm
   Exhaust... 1.400 to 1.800 mm

Camshafts
Camshaft bearing journal diameter .... 27.939 to 27.960 mm
Camshaft bearing diameter in cylinder head and bearing caps.................. 28.000 to 28.021 mm
Maximum permissible radial run-out .... 0.040 mm
Endfloat.. 0.040 to 0.144 mm

Valves and guides
Stem diameter:

	Inlet	Exhaust
Standard	6.955 to 6.970 mm	6.945 to 6.960 mm
0.075 mm oversize	7.030 to 7.045 mm	7.020 to 7.035 mm
0.150 mm oversize	7.105 to 7.120 mm	7.095 to 7.110 mm

Valve guide bore:
   Standard.. 7.000 to 7.015 mm
   0.075 mm oversize .... 7.075 to 7.090 mm
   0.150 mm oversize .... 7.150 to 7.165 mm
Maximum permissible valve stem play in guide:
   Inlet.. 0.030 to 0.060 mm
   Exhaust... 0.040 to 0.070 mm
Valve seat angle .... 44° 44'
Valve clearances .... Automatic adjustment by hydraulic valve lifters

Flywheel
All specifications as given for 1.8 and 2.0 litre SOHC engines

Lubrication system
All specifications as given for 1.8 and 2.0 litre SOHC engines

Torque wrench settings

All specifications as given for 2.0 litre SOHC engine, except for the following:

	Nm	lbf ft
Outer timing belt cover bolts	8	6
Camshaft sprocket bolt:*		
Stage 1	50	37
Stage 2	Angle-tighten a further 40° to 50°	Angle-tighten a further 40° to 50°
Crankshaft sprocket bolt:*		
Stage 1	250	185
Stage 2	Angle-tighten a further 40° to 50°	Angle-tighten a further 40° to 50°
Timing belt tensioner pulley and idler pulley bolts:*		
Stage 1	25	18
Stage 2	Angle-tighten a further 45° to 60°	Angle-tighten a further 45° to 60°
Cylinder head bolts:*		
Stage 1	25	18
Stage 2	Angle-tighten a further 65°	Angle-tighten a further 65°
Stage 3	Angle-tighten a further 65°	Angle-tighten a further 65°
Stage 4	Angle-tighten a further 65°	Angle-tighten a further 65°
Stage 5 (engine warm)	Angle-tighten a further 30° to 45°	Angle-tighten a further 30° to 45°
Camshaft bearing cap nuts:		
Main (M8)	20	15
Rear (M6)	10	7
Sump bolts	15	11
Flywheel bolts:*		
Stage 1	65	48
Stage 2	Angle-tighten a further 40° to 50°	Angle-tighten a further 40° to 50°
Engine mounting bracket-to-engine bolts	75	55
Power steering pump bracket-to-engine bolts	40	30
Crankcase breather tube-to-engine bolts	25	18

Use new bolts

Part A: In-car engine repair procedures

1 General information

How to use this Chapter

This Part of Chapter 2 describes the repair procedures which can reasonably be carried out on the engine while it remains in the vehicle. If the engine has been removed from the vehicle and is being dismantled as described in Part B, any preliminary dismantling procedures can be ignored.

Note that while it may be possible physically to overhaul items such as the piston/connecting rod assemblies while the engine is in the vehicle, such tasks are not usually carried out as separate operations, and usually require the execution of several additional procedures (not to mention the cleaning of components and of oilways); for this reason, all such tasks are classed as major overhaul procedures, and are described in Part B of this Chapter.

Part B describes the removal of the engine/transmission unit from the vehicle, and the full overhaul procedures which can then be carried out.

For ease of reference, all specifications are given in one Specifications Section at the beginning of the Chapter.

Engine description

The engine is of four-cylinder in-line, single or double overhead camshaft type (depending on model), and is mounted transversely at the front of the vehicle.

The crankshaft runs in five shell-type bearings, and the centre bearing incorporates thrust bearing shells to control crankshaft endfloat.

The connecting rods are attached to the crankshaft by horizontally-split shell-type big-end bearings. On single overhead camshaft (SOHC) engines, the pistons are attached to the connecting rods by gudgeon pins, which are an interference fit in the connecting rod small-end bores. On double overhead camshaft (DOHC) engines, the gudgeon pins are fully-floating, and are secured by circlips. The aluminium-alloy pistons are fitted with three piston rings – two compression rings and an oil control ring.

The camshaft on SOHC engines is driven from the crankshaft by a toothed composite-rubber belt. Each cylinder has two valves (one inlet and one exhaust), operated via rocker arms which are supported at their pivot ends by hydraulic self-adjusting valve lifters (tappets).

On DOHC engines, both camshafts are driven from the crankshaft by a single toothed composite-rubber belt. Each cylinder has four valves (two inlet and two exhaust), operated directly from the camshafts via hydraulic self-adjusting valve lifters. One camshaft operates the inlet valves, and the other operates the exhaust valves.

The inlet and exhaust valves are each closed by a single valve spring, and operate in guides pressed into the cylinder head.

A gear-type oil pump is located in a housing attached to the front of the cylinder block, and is driven directly from the crankshaft. A full-flow type oil filter is fitted, and DOHC models are equipped with a remotely-mounted oil cooler.

The distributor (where fitted) is driven directly from the end of the camshaft (the exhaust camshaft in the case of DOHC engines), and on carburettor models, the mechanical fuel pump is operated from the front end of the camshaft. The coolant pump is located at the front of the cylinder block, and is driven by the timing belt.

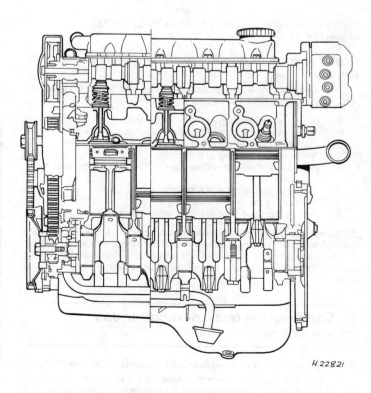

H.22822

H.22821

Fig. 2.1 Front sectional view of a 1.6 litre (C 16 SE) engine (Sec 1)   **Fig. 2.2 Side sectional view of a 1.6 litre (C 16 SE) engine (Sec 1)**

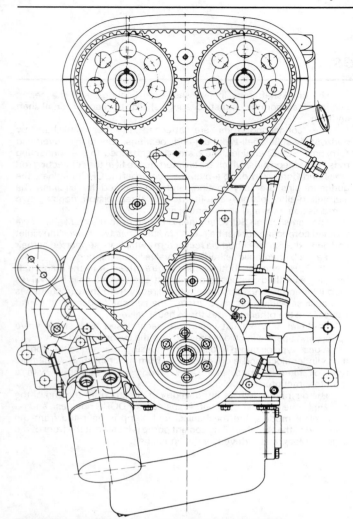

Fig. 2.3 Front sectional view of 2.0 litre DOHC (C 20 XE) engine (Sec 1)

Repair operations possible with the engine in the vehicle

The following operations can be carried out without having to remove the engine from the vehicle.

(a)   *Removal and refitting of the cylinder head.*
(b)   *Removal and refitting of the timing belt and sprockets.*
(c)   *Removal and refitting of the camshaft.*
(d)   *Removal and refitting of the sump.*
(e)   *Removal and refitting of the big-end bearings, connecting rods, and pistons*.*
(f)   *Removal and refitting of the oil pump.*
(g)   *Renewal of the engine mountings.*
(h)   *Removal and refitting of the flywheel/driveplate.*

*Although the operation marked with an asterisk can be carried out with the engine in the vehicle (after removal of the sump), it is preferable for the engine to be removed, in the interests of cleanliness and improved access. For this reason, the procedure is described in Part B of this Chapter.

2   Compression test – description and interpretation

Note: *A suitable compression gauge will be required to carry out this test.*

1   When engine performance is down, or if misfiring occurs which cannot be attributed to the ignition or fuel systems, a compression test

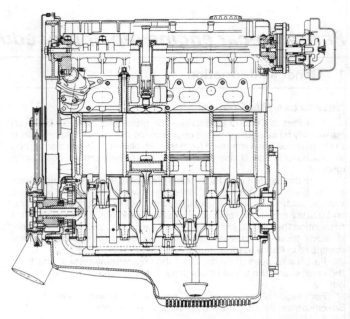

Fig. 2.4 Side sectional view of 2.0 litre DOHC (C 20 XE) engine (Sec 1)

can provide diagnostic clues as to the engine's condition. If the test is performed regularly, it can give warning of trouble before any other symptoms become apparent. **Note:** *The engine must be at normal operating temperature, and the battery must be fully charged for this test. Refer to the precautions to be observed when working on models equipped with a catalytic converter (see Chapter 4) before proceeding.*
2   Remove all of the spark plugs from the engine (see Chapter 1).
3   Disconnect the wiring plug from the ignition coil (on models with separate LT wire connections to the coil, disconnect the wire from terminal '15' on the coil), and on fuel injection models, remove the fuel pump relay (see Chapter 12).
4   Fit a compression tester to the No 1 spark plug hole (No 1 cylinder is nearest the timing belt end of the engine) – the type of tester which screws into the plug thread is to be preferred (photo).
5   Have an assistant hold the accelerator pedal fully depressed, at the same time cranking the engine over for approximately four seconds on the starter motor; after one or two revolutions, the compression pressure reading on the gauge should build up to a maximum figure and then stabilise. Record the highest reading obtained.
6   Repeat the test on the remaining cylinders, recording the pressure in each.

2.4 Compression tester fitted to No 1 spark plug hole

7   All cylinders should produce very similar pressures; any difference greater than that specified indicates the existence of a fault. Note that the compression should build up quickly in a healthy engine; low compression on the first stroke, followed by gradually increasing pressure on successive strokes, indicates worn piston rings. A low compression reading on the first stroke, which does not build up during successive strokes, indicates leaking valves or a blown head gasket (a cracked head could also be the cause). Deposits on the undersides of the valve heads can also cause low compression.

8   If the pressure in any cylinder is significantly lower than that in the remaining cylinders, carry out the following test to isolate the cause. Introduce a teaspoonful of clean engine oil into the relevant cylinder through its spark plug hole and repeat the test.

9   If the addition of oil temporarily improves the compression pressure, this indicates that bore or piston wear is responsible for the pressure loss. No improvement suggests that leaking or burnt valves, or a blown head gasket may be to blame.

10   A low reading from two adjacent cylinders is almost certainly due to the head gasket having blown between them; the presence of coolant in the engine oil will confirm this.

11   If one cylinder is about 20 percent lower than the others, and the engine has a slightly rough idle, a worn camshaft lobe could be the cause.

12   If the compression reading is unusually high, the combustion chambers are probably coated with carbon deposits. If this is the case, the cylinder head should be removed and decarbonised (see Part B of this Chapter).

13   On completion of the test, refit the spark plugs and reconnect the ignition coil wiring, as applicable.

3 Top dead centre (TDC) for No 1 piston – locating

1   Top dead centre (TDC) is the highest point in the cylinder that a piston reaches as the crankshaft turns. Each piston reaches TDC at the

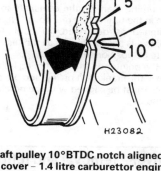

Fig. 2.5 Crankshaft pulley 10°BTDC notch aligned with pointer on rear timing belt cover – 1.4 litre carburettor engine (Sec 3)

end of the compression stroke, and again at the end of the exhaust stroke, however for the purpose of timing the engine, TDC refers to the position of No 1 piston at the end of its compression stroke. On all engines in this Manual, No 1 piston and cylinder are at the timing belt end of the engine.

2   All engine overhaul procedures use the factory timing marks, which vary according to engine type.

3   Disconnect both battery leads.

4   Remove the outer timing belt cover (it is only necessary to remove the upper cover on SOHC engines), as described in Section 6.

5   Using a suitable spanner or socket on the crankshaft pulley or sprocket bolt (as applicable – note that on manual gearbox models, the crankshaft can be turned by engaging top gear and pushing the vehicle backwards or forwards as necessary), rotate the crankshaft to bring No 1 piston to TDC as follows, according to engine type.

6   **All engines except 1.4 litre carburettor engines and DOHC engines** – the pointer on the timing belt cover must be aligned with the notch in the crankshaft pulley, or the timing mark on the TDC sensor wheel, as applicable, and the timing mark on the camshaft sprocket must be aligned with the notch in the timing belt rear cover (photos).

3.6A TDC pointer on timing belt cover aligned with timing notch in TDC sensor wheel (arrows) – 1.6 litre multi-point fuel injection engine

3.6B TDC pointer on timing belt cover aligned with timing notch in crankshaft pulley (arrows) – 2.0 litre SOHC engine

3.6C Timing mark on camshaft sprocket aligned with notch in timing belt rear cover (arrows) – 1.6 litre fuel injection engine

3.8A Timing pointer on rear timing belt cover aligned with notch in crankshaft pulley (circled) – DOHC engine

3.8B Timing marks on camshaft sprocket aligned with notches in camshaft cover (arrows) – DOHC engine

7 **1.4 litre carburettor engines** – the pointer on the rear timing belt cover must be aligned with the 10° BTDC notch in the crankshaft pulley (see Fig. 2.5), and the timing mark on the camshaft sprocket must be aligned with the notch in the timing belt rear cover. Note that when the timing marks are aligned as described, although No 1 piston is positioned 10° BTDC, this is acceptable for all the tasks in this manual requiring No 1 piston to be positioned at TDC.

8 **DOHC engines** – the pointer on the rear timing belt cover must be aligned with the notch in the crankshaft pulley, and the timing marks on the camshaft sprockets must be aligned with the notches in the top of the camshaft cover (photos).

4 Camshaft cover – removal and refitting

1.4 and 1.6 litre engines

Removal

1 Disconnect the breather hose(s) from the stub(s) on the camshaft cover (photos).

2 Take note of the positions of any brackets and/or clips secured by the camshaft cover bolts, then unscrew and remove the bolts, along with the clips and/or brackets, as applicable (photo).

3 Lift the camshaft cover from the cylinder head (photo). If the cover is stuck, do not lever between the cover and camshaft housing mating surfaces – if necessary, gently tap the cover sideways to free it. Where applicable, recover the gasket/rubber seal.

Refitting

4 Before commencing refitting, examine the inside of the cover for a build-up of oil sludge or any other contamination, and if necessary clean the cover with paraffin, or a water-soluble solvent. Dry the cover thoroughly before refitting.

5 Where applicable, examine the condition of the rubber seal, and if necessary renew it. Note that on certain models, the seal rests in a groove in the cover, and a tag on the seal engages with the notch in the

cover when the seal is correctly positioned (photo). If a cork gasket was fitted, it should always be renewed on refitting.

6 Thoroughly clean the mating faces of the camshaft housing and the cover.

7 Position the cover on the camshaft housing, noting that the breather pipe stubs should be nearest the timing belt end of the engine.

8 Refit the securing bolts, ensuring that any clips and/or brackets are in place under their heads as noted before removal, and tighten the bolts to the specified torque in a diagonal sequence.

9 Reconnect the breather hose(s) to the stub(s) on the cover.

1.8 and 2.0 litre SOHC engines

Note: *A new gasket must be used when refitting the camshaft cover.*

Removal

10 Proceed as described previously in this Section for 1.4 and 1.6 litre engines, but recover the gasket.

Refitting

11 Where applicable, examine the condition of the crankcase ventilation filter inside the camshaft cover, and clean using paraffin or a water-soluble solvent if clogging is evident.

12 Thoroughly clean the mating faces of the camshaft housing and the cover.

13 Fit the cover using a new gasket, noting that the breather hose stub should point towards the timing belt end of the engine.

14 Proceed as described in paragraphs 8 and 9.

2.0 litre DOHC engines

Removal

15 Remove the outer timing belt cover, as described in Section 6.

16 Disconnect the breather hoses from the camshaft cover (photo).

17 Using an Allen key, or a hexagon bit, unscrew the two securing bolts and withdraw the spark plug cover (photo). If necessary, mark the spark plug HT leads for position (to avoid confusion when refitting) then disconnect them from the plugs, and unclip them from the end of the camshaft cover.

4.1A Disconnect the breather hoses ...

4.1B ... from the camshaft cover – 1.6 litre engine

4.2 Note the positions of any brackets and clips (arrowed) secured by the camshaft cover bolts – 1.6 litre engine

4.3 Lifting the camshaft cover from the cylinder head

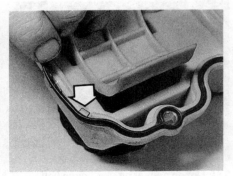

4.5 Tag on seal (arrowed) engages with notch in camshaft cover – 1.6 litre engine

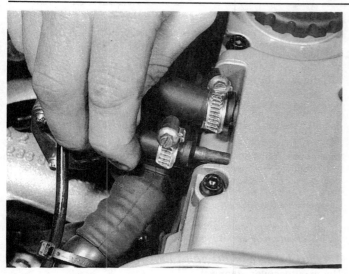

4.16 Disconnecting a breather hose from the rear of the camshaft cover – DOHC engine

18   Using an Allen key or a hexagon bit, unscrew the twenty securing bolts, and withdraw the camshaft cover (photo).
19   Recover the one-piece rubber gasket (photo).

Refitting

20   Before commencing refitting, examine the inside of the cover for a build-up of oil sludge or any other contamination, and if necessary clean the cover with paraffin, or a water-soluble solvent. Dry the cover thoroughly before refitting.
21   Thoroughly clean the mating faces of the camshaft cover and cylinder head.
22   Examine the condition of the camshaft cover rubber seal, and if necessary renew it.

23   Refit the camshaft cover, then refit the securing bolts, and tighten them to the specified torque.
24   Refit the HT leads to the spark plugs (ensuring that they are refitted to their correct cylinders), then clip the leads to the end of the camshaft cover, refit the camshaft cover and tighten the securing bolts.
25   Reconnect the breather hoses to the camshaft cover.
26   Refit the outer timing belt cover, as described in Section 6.

---

5   Crankshaft pulley – removal and refitting

Note: *On 1.4 and 1.6 litre engines, a new securing bolt may be required when refitting the crankshaft pulley – see text.*

Removal

1   Disconnect the battery negative lead.
2   For improved access, raise the front right-hand side of the vehicle and support securely on axle stands (see *'Jacking, towing and wheel changing'*). Remove the roadwheel.
3   Unscrew the securing screws and/or remove the plastic clips, as applicable, and withdraw the underwing shield (photo).
4   If necessary, rotate the crankshaft (using a suitable socket or spanner on the crankshaft pulley or sprocket bolt, as applicable) until the relevant timing marks align (see Section 3).
5   On 1.8 and 2.0 litre engine models, remove the power steering pump drivebelt as described in Chapter 10.
6   Remove the alternator drivebelt as described in Chapter 12.
7   To prevent the crankshaft from turning as the pulley bolt is unscrewed, either select top gear and have an assistant apply the brakes hard (manual gearbox models only), or remove the starter motor and lock the ring gear teeth using a suitable tool.
8   **On 1.4 and 1.6 litre engines,** unscrew the pulley bolt and recover the washer fitted behind it, then remove the pulley (photo).
9   **On 1.8 and 2.0 litre SOHC engines,** unscrew the four bolts securing the pulley to the crankshaft sprocket, using a suitable Allen key or hexagon bit, then remove the pulley.
10   **On 2.0 litre DOHC engines,** unscrew the six bolts securing the

4.17 Withdrawing the spark plug cover – DOHC engine

4.18 Unscrewing a camshaft cover securing bolt – DOHC engine

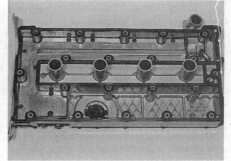

4.19 Camshaft cover removed to show one-piece rubber gasket – DOHC engine

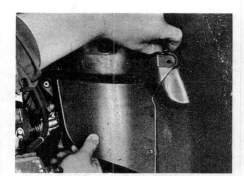

5.3 Withdrawing the underwing shield – 1.6 litre engine model

5.8 Removing the crankshaft pulley bolt and washer – 1.6 litre engine model

5.10 Crankshaft pulley and securing bolts (viewed through wheel arch with wheel removed) – DOHC engine

pulley to the crankshaft sprocket, using a suitable splined bit, then remove the pulley (photo).

Refitting

11   On refitting, ensure that the notch in the pulley fits over the locating lug on the crankshaft sprocket.
12   On 1.4 and 1.6 litre engines, it may be necessary to use a new bolt to secure the pulley, depending on the type of bolt originally fitted – see Specifications.
13   Prevent the crankshaft from turning as during removal, then fit the pulley securing bolt(s), ensuring that the washer is in place under the bolt head where applicable.
14   Tighten the bolt(s) to the specified torque, in stages where applicable – see Specifications.
15   Refit and tension the alternator drivebelt, as described in Chapter 12.
16   On 1.8 and 2.0 litre engine models, refit and tension the power steering pump drivebelt as described in Chapter 10.
17   Refit the underwing shield.
18   Refit the roadwheel, and lower the vehicle to the ground.
19   Reconnect the battery negative lead.

6   Timing belt covers – removal and refitting

1.4 and 1.6 litre carburettor and single-point fuel injection engines

Upper outer cover – removal
1   If desired, for improved access, remove the air cleaner assembly, as described in Chapter 4.
2   If necessary, to allow access for further work (eg, if the timing belt is to be removed), remove the alternator drivebelt as described in Chapter 12. Similarly, on models with power steering, remove the power steering pump pulley, and loosen the pump securing bolts to enable the pump to be moved away from the timing belt cover. There is no need to disconnect the fluid pipes. Note that if the timing belt is to be removed, the power steering pump must be removed completely.
3   Unscrew the securing bolt, and unclip the upper timing belt cover from the rear cover and lower cover.

Upper outer cover – refitting
4   Refitting is a reversal of removal, but where applicable, refit and tension the alternator drivebelt as described in Chapter 12.

Lower outer cover – removal
5   For improved access, raise the front right-hand side of the vehicle, and support securely on axle stands (see *'Jacking, towing and wheel changing'*). Remove the roadwheel.
6   Remove the underwing shield (see Chapter 11).
7   Remove the crankshaft pulley as described in Section 5.
8   Unscrew the two securing bolts, and unclip the lower timing belt cover from the upper cover and rear cover.

Lower outer cover – refitting
9   Refitting is a reversal of removal, but where applicable, refit the crankshaft pulley using a new securing bolt as described in Section 5.

Rear cover – removal
10   Remove the outer covers as described previously in this Section, but note that where applicable, the power steering pump must be removed completely, as described in Chapter 10.
11   Remove the timing belt as described in Section 7.
12   Remove the timing belt sprockets as described in Section 8.
13   Unscrew the securing bolt, and remove the timing belt tension indicator assembly from the cylinder block.
14   Unscrew and remove the screws securing the rear timing belt cover to the camshaft housing and cylinder block, then withdraw the cover.

Rear cover – refitting
15   Refitting is a reversal of removal, bearing in mind the following points.
   (a)   *Refit and tension the timing belt as described in Section 7.*
   (b)   *Refit the outer timing belt covers as described previously in this Section.*
   (c)   *Where applicable, refit the power steering pump, and bleed the fluid circuit as described in Chapter 10.*

1.4 and 1.6 litre multi-point fuel injection engines

Upper outer cover – removal
16   Disconnect the battery negative lead.
17   For improved access, remove the air cleaner assembly, as described in Chapter 4.
18   Remove the alternator drivebelt, as described in Chapter 12.
19   On models with power steering, remove the power steering pump pulley, and loosen the pump securing bolts to enable the pump to be moved away from the timing belt cover. There is no need to disconnect the fluid pipes.
20   Unscrew the three securing bolts, and unclip the lower edge of the upper cover from the lower cover. Withdraw the upper cover (photos).

Upper outer cover – refitting
21   Refitting is a reversal of removal, but refit and tension the alternator drivebelt as described in Chapter 12.

Lower outer cover – removal
22   Disconnect the battery negative lead.
23   For improved access, raise the front right-hand side of the vehicle, and support securely on axle stands (see *'Jacking, towing and wheel changing'*). Remove the roadwheel.
24   Remove the underwing shield (see Chapter 11).
25   Remove the crankshaft pulley as described in Section 5.
26   Where applicable, unclip the TDC sensor wiring from the lower timing belt cover.
27   Unscrew the four securing bolts, and remove the lower timing belt cover.

Lower outer cover – refitting
28   Refitting is a reversal of removal, but where applicable, refit the crankshaft pulley using a new securing bolt as described in Section 5.

Rear cover – removal
29   Proceed as described in paragraphs 10 to 13 inclusive.
30   Unscrew the two upper and two lower screws securing the rear timing belt cover (photo).

6.20A Unscrew the three securing bolts (arrowed) ...

6.20B ... and withdraw the upper timing belt cover – 1.6 litre multi-point fuel injection engine

6.30 Unscrewing a rear timing belt cover upper securing screw – 1.6 litre multi-point fuel injection engine

6.31 TDC sensor wiring clipped to rear of rear timing belt cover – 1.6 litre multi-point fuel injection engine

31   Withdraw the rear cover, and where applicable, unclip the TDC sensor wiring from the rear of the cover (photo).

Rear cover – refitting

32   Proceed as described in paragraph 15.

1.8 and 2.0 litre SOHC engines

Upper outer cover – removal

33   Disconnect the battery negative lead.
34   If desired, for improved access, remove the air cleaner assembly as described in Chapter 4.
35   Remove the power steering pump drivebelt as described in Chapter 10.
36   Remove the alternator drivebelt as described in Chapter 12.
37   Disconnect the wiring from the temperature gauge sender.
38   Release the securing clips, and remove the upper timing belt cover.

Upper outer cover – refitting

39   Refitting is a reversal of removal, but refit and tension the alternator drivebelt as described in Chapter 12.

Lower outer (coolant pump) cover – removal

40   Remove the upper timing belt cover as described previously in this Section, then unclip the lower cover from the coolant pump.

Lower outer (coolant pump) cover – refitting

41   Refitting is a reversal of removal, but refit and tension the alternator drivebelt as described in Chapter 12.

Rear cover – removal

42   Remove the outer timing belt covers as described previously in this Section.
43   Remove the timing belt as described in Section 7.
44   Remove the timing belt sprockets as described in Section 8.
45   Where applicable, disconnect the wiring plug from the TDC sensor, and unclip the wiring from the rear belt cover.
46   Unscrew the two upper and two lower securing bolts, and withdraw the cover, manipulating it from the smaller rear cover on the coolant pump.
47   If desired, the smaller rear belt cover can be removed from the coolant pump, after unscrewing the securing bolt, by rotating it to disengage it from the retaining flange on the pump.

Rear cover – refitting

48   Refitting is a reversal of removal, but refit and tension the timing belt as described in Section 7.

2.0 litre DOHC engines

Outer cover – removal

49   Disconnect the battery negative lead.
50   For improved access to the timing belt cover bolts, remove the air cleaner assembly as described in Chapter 4.
51   Remove the alternator drivebelt, as described in Chapter 12.
52   Remove the three securing screws, and withdraw the outer timing belt cover. Recover the rubber grommets if they are loose (photos).

Outer cover – refitting

53   Refitting is a reversal of removal, but examine the condition of the rubber seal on the cover, and renew if necessary (photo). Ensure that the rubber grommets are in place in the cover securing screw holes, and refit and tension the alternator drivebelt as described in Chapter 12.

Rear cover – removal

54   Remove the outer timing belt cover as described previously in this Section.
55   Remove the timing belt, as described in Section 7.
56   Remove the timing belt sprockets, as described in Section 8 of this Chapter.
57   Remove the timing belt tensioner and the idler pulley, as described in Section 10.
58   Unscrew the upper and middle studs for the timing belt outer cover screws. Note that the upper stud simply unscrews from the cylinder head, but the middle stud is secured by a bolt.
59   Unscrew the two upper and single lower right-hand rear belt cover securing bolts (photos), and withdraw the rear belt cover.

Rear cover – refitting

60   Refitting is a reversal of removal, bearing in mind the following points.

(a) Refit the belt tensioner and the idler pulley as described in Section 10.
(b) Refit the timing belt sprockets as described in Section 8.
(c) Refit and tension the alternator drivebelt as described in Section 12.

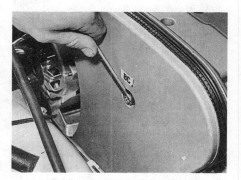

6.52A Unscrewing an outer timing belt cover securing screw – DOHC engine

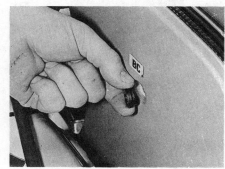

6.52B Recover the rubber grommets if they are loose – DOHC engine

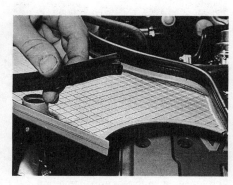

6.53 Removing the rubber seal from the outer timing belt cover – DOHC engine

6.59A Timing belt outer cover screw upper stud (1) and rear belt cover upper securing bolts (2) – DOHC engine

6.59B Rear timing belt cover lower right-hand securing bolt (arrowed) – DOHC engine

7 Timing belt – removal, refitting and adjustment

1.4 and 1.6 litre engines

Removal

1 Disconnect the battery negative lead.
2 Remove the outer timing belt covers as described in Section 6, but note that, where applicable, the power steering pump must be removed completely.
3 Turn the crankshaft to bring No 1 piston to top dead centre, as described in Section 3 (if necessary, temporarily refit the crankshaft pulley and its securing bolt to enable the timing mark to be viewed and the crankshaft to be turned).
4 Insert a suitable tool (such as a pin punch) into the hole in the timing belt tension indicator arm, then lever the arm clockwise to its stop, and lock in position by inserting the tool into the corresponding hole in the tension indicator backplate (photo). Leave the tool in position to lock the tension indicator until the belt is refitted.
5 Loosen the three coolant pump securing bolts, using a suitable Allen key or hexagon bit, then turn the pump to relieve the tension in the timing belt.
6 Slide the timing belt from the sprockets, and withdraw it from the engine (photo). Take note of any arrows marked on the belt to indicate the direction of rotation.

Refitting

7 Ensure that No 1 piston is still positioned at top dead centre, as

described in Section 3. Note that the arrow cast into the front face of the crankshaft sprocket must be aligned with the corresponding notch in the bottom of the rear timing belt cover (photo).
8 Refit the timing belt around the sprockets, starting at the crankshaft sprocket.
9 Adjust the timing belt tension, as described in paragraphs 13 to 22 inclusive.
10 Refit the outer timing belt covers, as described in Section 6.
11 Where applicable, refit the power steering pump, as described in Chapter 10.
12 On completion, reconnect the battery negative lead, and where applicable, bleed the power steering fluid circuit, as described in Chapter 10.

Adjustment

Note: *The engine must be cold when carrying out checking and adjustment of the timing belt tension.*

13 With the outer timing belt covers removed as described in Section 6, proceed as follows.
14 Turn the crankshaft to bring No 1 piston to top dead centre, as described in Section 3 (if necessary, temporarily refit the crankshaft pulley and its bolt to enable the timing mark to be viewed and the crankshaft to be turned).
15 If desired, to make the crankshaft easier to turn during the following procedure, remove the spark plugs as described in Chapter 1.
16 Loosen the three coolant pump securing bolts, using a suitable Allen key or hexagon bit, but do not remove them.
17 Turn the coolant pump clockwise to increase the belt tension until the tensioner indicator arm moves fully clockwise to its stop (ie the

7.4 Using a pin punch to lock the timing belt tensioner indicator arm in position – 1.6 litre engine

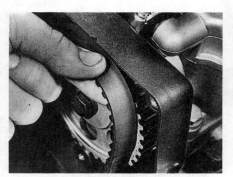

7.6 Sliding the timing belt from the camshaft sprocket – 1.6 litre engine

7.7 Arrow on crankshaft sprocket aligned with notch in rear timing belt cover (arrows) with No 1 piston at TDC – 1.6 litre engine

7.17 Using special tool KM-421-A to turn the coolant pump –
1.6 litre engine

7.27 Loosening a coolant pump securing bolt – 2.0 litre SOHC
engine

holes in the indicator arm and the tensioner backplate are aligned). Note
that a special tool is available to turn the coolant pump (Vauxhall/Opel
tool KM-421-A or equivalent) (photo).
18   Tighten the coolant pump securing bolts sufficiently to prevent
the pump from moving during the following operation.
19   Using a suitable socket or spanner on the crankshaft pulley bolt,
turn the crankshaft clockwise through two complete revolutions, until
No 1 piston is again positioned at top dead centre. Turn the crankshaft
smoothly without jerking, to avoid the belt jumping on the pulleys.
20   Carefully turn the coolant pump anti-clockwise to slacken the belt,
until the tension indicator pointer is positioned in the centre of the 'V' on
the tensioner backplate – see Fig. 2.6, then tighten the coolant pump
securing bolts to the specified torque.
21   Turn the crankshaft clockwise through two complete revolutions,
as described previously, and check that the tension indicator pointer is
still positioned as described in paragraph 20 – if not, the procedure
described in paragraphs 16 to 20 inclusive must be repeated until the
pointer aligns correctly.
22   On completion, refit the spark plugs (where applicable), and refit
the outer timing belt covers as described in Section 6.

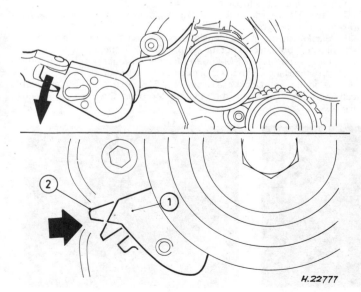

Fig. 2.6 Turn the coolant pump (special tool shown) anti-clockwise
until the tension indicator pointer (1) is positioned in the centre of
the 'V' (2) – 1.4 and 1.6 litre engines (Sec 7)

1.8 and 2.0 litre SOHC engines
Removal
Note: *A suitable puller may be required to remove the crankshaft
sprocket.*

23   Disconnect the battery negative lead.
24   Remove the outer timing belt covers, as described in Section 6.
25   Turn the crankshaft to bring No 1 cylinder to top dead centre, using
a suitable socket or spanner on the crankshaft sprocket bolt, as
described in Section 3.
26   Remove the crankshaft pulley, as described in Section 5.
27   Loosen the three coolant pump securing bolts, using a suitable
Allen key or hexagon bit (photo), then turn the pump to relieve the
tension in the timing belt.
28   Slide the timing belt from the sprockets, and withdraw it from the
engine. Take note of any arrows marked on the belt to indicate the
direction of rotation.

Refitting
29   Ensure that No 1 cylinder is still positioned at top dead centre, as
described in Section 3.
30   Refit the timing belt around the sprockets, starting at the
crankshaft sprocket.
31   Adjust the timing belt tension, as described in paragraphs 35 to 47,
or 48 to 52, as applicable.
32   Refit the crankshaft pulley, as described in Section 5.
33   Refit the outer timing belt covers, as described in Section 6.
34   On completion, reconnect the battery negative lead.

Adjustment using Vauxhall/Opel tool KM-510-A
Note: *The tension of a new belt must be adjusted with the engine cold.
The tension of a used belt must be checked with the engine at normal
operating temperature. The manufacturers specify the use of a special
gauge, Vauxhall/Opel tool KM-510-A, for checking the timing belt
tension. If access to a suitable gauge cannot be obtained, it is strongly
recommended that the vehicle is taken to a Vauxhall/Opel dealer to have
the belt tension checked at the earliest opportunity.*

35   With the outer timing belt covers removed as described in
Section 6, proceed as follows.
36   If desired, to make the crankshaft easier to turn during the
following procedure, remove the spark plugs as described in Chapter 1.
37   Read the instructions supplied with the gauge before proceeding.
38   Turn the crankshaft through at least quarter of a turn clockwise,
using a suitable socket or spanner on the crankshaft sprocket bolt.
39   Place the locked gauge at the centre of the belt run between the
coolant pump and the camshaft sprocket. The gauge should locate on
the timing belt as shown in Fig. 2.7.
40   Slowly release the operating lever on the gauge, then lightly tap
the gauge two or three times, and note the reading on the scale (photo).
41   If the reading is not as specified, loosen the three coolant pump

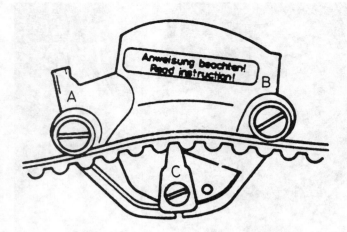

Fig. 2.7 Tension gauge KM-510-A correctly positioned on timing belt. Belt must pass through points A, B and C – 2.0 litre SOHC engine (Sec 7)

securing bolts, using a suitable Allen key or hexagon bit (if not already done), and rotate the coolant pump in the required direction to achieve the desired reading on the gauge. Rotate the pump clockwise to increase the belt tension, or anti-clockwise to decrease the tension. Note that a special tool is available to turn the coolant pump (Vauxhall/Opel tool KM-421-A or equivalent).

42   Lightly tighten the coolant pump securing bolts sufficiently to prevent the pump from moving.
43   Remove the tensioning gauge, and turn the crankshaft through on complete revolution clockwise.
44   Re-check the belt tension as described in paragraphs 39 and 40.
45   If the tension is not as specified, repeat paragraphs 41 to 44 inclusive until the desired, consistent reading is obtained.
46   On completion of adjustment, remove the checking gauge, and tighten the coolant pump bolts to the specified torque.
47   Refit the spark plugs (where applicable), and refit the outer timing belt covers as described in Section 6.

Approximate adjustment

Note: *Refer to the note at the beginning of the previous sub-Section before proceeding.*

48   With the outer timing belt covers removed as described in Section 6, proceed as follows.
49   If the special gauge is not available, the timing belt tension can be checked approximately by twisting the belt between the thumb and forefinger, at the centre of the run between the coolant pump and the camshaft sprocket. It ought to be just possible to twist the belt through 90° using moderate pressure (photo).
50   If adjustment is necessary, proceed as described previously for adjustment using the special gauge (ie, adjust the tension by moving the coolant pump), but have the belt tension checked by a Vauxhall/Opel dealer at the earliest opportunity.

51   If in doubt, err on the tight side when adjusting the tension, as if the belt is too slack, it may jump on the sprockets, which could result in serious engine damage.
52   Ensure that the coolant pump bolts are tightened to the specified torque before refitting the outer timing belt covers as described in Section 6.

2.0 litre DOHC engines

Note: *Whenever the timing belt is slackened, it must be renewed; never refit a used belt.*

Removal

Note: *A suitable puller may be required to remove the crankshaft sprocket.*
53   Disconnect the battery negative lead.
54   Remove the outer timing belt cover, as described in Section 6.
55   Turn the crankshaft to bring No 1 cylinder to top dead centre, using a suitable socket or spanner on the crankshaft sprocket bolt, as described in Section 3.
56   Remove the crankshaft pulley, as described in Section 5.
57   Loosen the securing bolt (photo), release the timing belt tensioner pulley, then slide the belt from the sprockets and pulleys.

Refitting

58   Temporarily refit the crankshaft pulley, and check that No 1 piston is still positioned at top dead centre, as described in Section 3.
59   Remove the crankshaft pulley, then fit a **new** timing belt around the sprockets and pulleys, starting at the crankshaft sprocket.
60   Refit the crankshaft pulley.
61   Adjust the timing belt tension as described in paragraphs 64 to 73, or 74 to 79 inclusive.
62   Refit the outer timing belt cover, as described in Section 6.
63   Reconnect the battery negative lead.

Adjustment using Vauxhall/Opel tool KM-666

Note: *The manufacturers specify the use of a special adjustment wrench, Vauxhall/Opel tool KM-666 for adjusting the timing belt tension. If access to this tool cannot be obtained, an approximate adjustment can be achieved using the method described in paragraph 74 onwards; however, it is emphasised that the vehicle should be taken to a Vauxhall/Opel dealer at the earliest opportunity to have the tension adjusted using the special tool. Do not drive the vehicle over any long distance until the belt tension has been adjusted using the special tool. No checking of 'fitted' (in-use) timing belt adjustment is specified, and the following adjustment procedure applies only to a newly-fitted belt – the adjustment must be carried out with the engine cold.*

64   With the outer timing belt cover removed as described in Section 6, proceed as follows.
65   Turn the crankshaft to bring No 1 piston to top dead centre, as described in Section 3.
66   Slacken the timing belt tensioner pulley bolt, then remove the bolt, and fit a new bolt, but do not fully tighten it at this stage.
67   Fit the special tool KM-666 to the belt tensioner pulley mounting plate, in accordance with the tool manufacturer's instructions.
68   Working anti-clockwise from the TDC mark on the exhaust camshaft sprocket, mark the seventh tooth on the sprocket – see Fig. 2.8.

7.40 Note the reading on the scale of the tension gauge – 2.0 litre SOHC engine

7.49 Checking the timing belt tension by twisting the belt through 90° between thumb and forefinger – 2.0 litre SOHC engine

7.57 Loosening the timing belt tensioner pulley securing bolt – DOHC engine

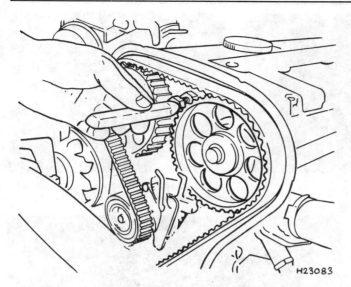

Fig. 2.8 Working anti-clockwise from the TDC mark on the exhaust camshaft sprocket, mark the seventh tooth on the sprocket – DOHC engine (Sec 7)

69 Turn the crankshaft clockwise until the mark made in paragraph 68 is aligned with the TDC notch in the camshaft cover. The crankshaft must be turned evenly and without jerking, to prevent the timing belt from jumping on the sprockets and pulleys.

70 Tighten the new tensioner pulley bolt to the specified torque in the two stages given in the Specifications.

71 Remove special tool KM-666.

72 Turn the crankshaft clockwise until the TDC marks on the camshaft sprockets are aligned with the notches in the camshaft cover, and check that the crankshaft pulley TDC mark is aligned with the pointer on the rear timing belt cover.

73 Refit the outer timing belt cover as described in Section 6.

Approximate adjustment

Note: *Refer to the note at the beginning of the previous sub-Section before proceeding.*

74 Proceed as described in paragraphs 64 to 66 inclusive.

75 Have an assistant press the tensioner pulley against the belt until the belt can just be twisted through 45°, using moderate thumb pressure with the thumb and forefinger, on the longest belt run between the exhaust camshaft sprocket and the belt idler pulley.

76 Have the assistant hold the tensioner pulley in position, and tighten the new tensioner pulley bolt to the specified torque in the two stages given in the Specifications.

77 Turn the crankshaft clockwise through two complete revolutions, and check that, with the crankshaft pulley TDC mark aligned with the pointer on the rear timing belt cover, the TDC marks on the camshaft sprockets are still aligned with the notches in the camshaft cover.

78 Refit the outer timing belt cover as described in Section 6.

79 Have the belt tension adjusted by a Vauxhall/Opel dealer using the manufacturer's special tool at the earliest opportunity.

8 Timing belt sprockets – removal and refitting

Note: *This Section describes the removal and refitting of individual components. If more than one sprocket is to be removed, begin by removing the timing belt (see Section 7), then remove the relevant sprockets, ignoring the preliminary steps given in this Section.*

SOHC engines

Camshaft sprocket – removal

1 With the outer timing belt covers removed as described in Section 6, proceed as follows.

2 Turn the crankshaft to bring No 1 piston to top dead centre, as described in Section 3.

3 On 1.4 and 1.6 litre engines, insert a suitable tool (such as a pin punch) into the hole in the timing belt tension indicator arm, then lever the arm clockwise to its stop, and lock in position by inserting the tool into the corresponding hole in the tension indicator backplate. Leave the tool in position to lock the tension indicator until the camshaft sprocket is refitted.

4 Loosen the three coolant pump securing bolts, using a suitable Allen key or hexagon bit, then turn the pump to relieve the tension in the timing belt.

5 The camshaft must be prevented from turning as the sprocket bolt is unscrewed, and this can be achieved in one of two ways as follows.

(a) *Make up a tool similar to that shown, and use it to hold the sprocket stationary by means of the holes in the sprocket face (photo).*

(b) *Remove the camshaft cover as described in Section 4, and prevent the camshaft from turning by holding it with a suitable spanner on the flats provided between Nos 3 and 4 camshaft lobes (see photo 8.9).*

6 Unscrew the camshaft sprocket bolt and withdraw it, noting the washer under the bolt head.

7 Withdraw the sprocket from the end of the camshaft, manipulating the timing belt from the sprocket as it is withdrawn.

Camshaft sprocket – refitting

8 Commence refitting by offering the camshaft sprocket to the camshaft, making sure that the lug on the end of the camshaft engages with the corresponding hole in the camshaft sprocket (photo).

9 Refit the sprocket securing bolt, ensuring that the washer is in place, and tighten the bolt to the specified torque, preventing the camshaft from turning as during removal (photo).

10 Where applicable, refit the camshaft cover as described in Section 4.

11 Ensure that the TDC marks on the camshaft sprocket and crankshaft sprocket are still aligned (No 1 piston at TDC) as described in Section 3, then slip the timing belt over the camshaft sprocket.

8.5 Improvised tool being used to hold the camshaft sprocket stationary – SOHC engine

8.8 Lug (1) on camshaft engages with hole (2) in sprocket – SOHC engine

8.9 Tightening the camshaft sprocket securing bolt while holding the camshaft using a spanner on the camshaft flats – SOHC engine

8.19A Remove the crankshaft sprocket, ...

8.19B ... Woodruff key ...

8.19C ... and thrustwasher from the end of the crankshaft – 2.0 litre SOHC engine

12   Adjust the timing belt tension as described in Section 7.
13   Refit the outer timing belt covers as described in Section 6.

Crankshaft sprocket – removal

Note: *A suitable puller may be required to remove the sprocket on 1.8 and 2.0 litre models.*

14   With the outer timing belt covers removed as described in Section 6, proceed as follows.
15   Turn the crankshaft to bring No 1 piston to top dead centre, as described in Section 3.
16   Remove the crankshaft pulley, as described in Section 5.
17   On 1.8 and 2.0 litre engines, the crankshaft sprocket bolt must now be unscrewed. To prevent the crankshaft from turning as the sprocket bolt is unscrewed, either select top gear and have an assistant apply the brakes hard (manual gearbox models only), or remove the starter motor and jam the ring gear teeth using a suitable tool. Unscrew the sprocket bolt (taking care as it is very tight) and recover the washer from under the bolt head.
18   Proceed as described in paragraphs 3 and 4, then slip the timing belt from the sprocket.
19   Remove the sprocket from the end of the crankshaft, using a suitable puller if necessary. Where applicable, recover the Woodruff key and the thrustwasher from the end of the crankshaft (photos).

Crankshaft sprocket – refitting

Note: *On 1.4 and 1.6 litre engines, a new securing bolt may be required when refitting the crankshaft pulley – see Section 5. On 1.8 and 2.0 litre models, a new securing bolt will be required when refitting the crankshaft sprocket – see Section 3.*

20   On 1.4 and 1.6 litre engines, where applicable refit the Woodruff key to the end of the crankshaft, then refit the crankshaft sprocket with the locating flange and locating lug for the crankshaft pulley outermost (photo).
21   On 1.8 and 2.0 litre engines, where applicable refit the thrustwasher and the Woodruff key to the end of the crankshaft, then refit the crankshaft sprocket, and tighten a new securing bolt to the specified torque in the two stages given in the Specifications. Ensure that the washer is in place under the bolt head, and prevent the engine from turning as during removal.
22   Ensure that the TDC marks on the camshaft sprocket and

8.20 Refitting the crankshaft pulley with locating flange and locating lug for pulley (arrowed) outermost

crankshaft sprocket are still aligned (No 1 piston at TDC) as described in Section 3 (temporarily refit the crankshaft pulley if necessary), then slip the timing belt over the crankshaft sprocket.
23   Refit the crankshaft pulley as described in Section 3.
24   Adjust the timing belt tension as described in Section 7.
25   Refit the outer timing belt covers as described in Section 6.

DOHC engines

Camshaft sprocket – removal

26   Remove the timing belt as described in Section 7.
27   The camshaft must be prevented from turning as the sprocket bolt is unscrewed, and this can be achieved as described in paragraph 5 of this Section, noting that the flats provided to hold the camshaft stationary are located in front of No 1 cam lobe (photo).

8.27 Spanner positioned to counterhold exhaust camshaft – DOHC engine

8.28 Withdrawing the camshaft sprocket bolt and washer ...

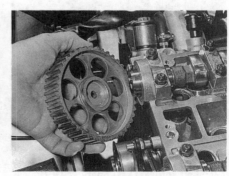

8.29 ... and the sprocket – DOHC engine

9.2 Withdrawing the timing belt tension indicator – 1.6 litre engine

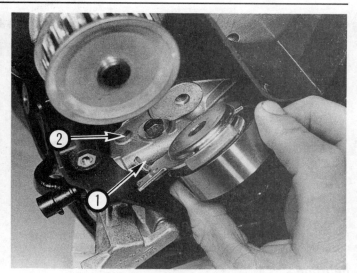

9.3 Lug (1) on tension indicator backplate must engage with hole (2) in oil pump – 1.6 litre engine (shown with engine removed from vehicle)

28   Unscrew the camshaft sprocket bolt and withdraw it, noting the washer under the bolt head (photo).
29   Withdraw the sprocket from the end of the camshaft (photo).

Camshaft sprocket – refitting

Note: *A new camshaft sprocket securing bolt and a new timing belt must be used on refitting.*

30   Commence refitting by offering the camshaft sprocket to the camshaft, making sure that the lug on the end of the camshaft engages with the corresponding hole in the camshaft sprocket.
31   Fit a new sprocket securing bolt, ensuring that the washer is in place, and tighten the bolt to the specified torque in the two stages given in the Specifications, preventing the camshaft from turning as during removal.
32   Fit a new timing belt and adjust the tension, as described in Section 7.

Crankshaft sprocket – removal

33   Remove the timing belt as described in Section 7.
34   The crankshaft sprocket bolt must now be unscrewed. To prevent the crankshaft from turning as the sprocket bolt is unscrewed, either select top gear and have an assistant apply the brakes hard (manual gearbox models only), or remove the starter motor and jam the ring gear teeth using a suitable tool.
35   Using a suitable Torx socket, unscrew the sprocket bolt (taking care as it is very tight) and recover the washer from under the bolt head.
36   Withdraw the sprocket from the end of the crankshaft, using a suitable puller if necessary.

Crankshaft sprocket – refitting

Note: *A new camshaft sprocket securing bolt and a new timing belt must be used on refitting.*

37   Refit the crankshaft sprocket to the end of the crankshaft.
38   Apply a little grease to the threads of a new sprocket securing bolt, and tighten it to the specified torque in the two stages given in the Specifications. Ensure that the washer is in place under the bolt head, and prevent the crankshaft from turning as during removal.
39   Fit a new timing belt, and adjust the tension as described in Section 7.

9   Timing belt tension indicator (1.4 and 1.6 litre engines) – removal and refitting

Removal

1   Remove the timing belt as described in Section 7.
2   Unscrew the central securing bolt, and withdraw the tension indicator (photo).

Refitting

3   Refit the tension indicator, ensuring that the lug on the indicator backplate engages with the corresponding hole in the oil pump (photo).
4   Refit the tension indicator securing bolt, and tighten it to the specified torque.
5   Refit and tension the timing belt, and adjust the tension as described in Section 7.

10   Timing belt tensioner and idler pulley (DOHC engines) – removal and refitting

Removal

1   Remove the timing belt as described in Section 7.
2   To remove the belt tensioner or the idler pulley, simply unscrew the securing bolt from the centre of the pulley, then withdraw the tensioner assembly or pulley, as applicable (photo). Recover the spacer sleeve from the bolt.

10.2 Timing belt pulley components – DOHC engine

1   *Tensioner pulley securing bolt*
2   *Tensioner pulley mounting plate*
3   *Idler pulley securing bolt*

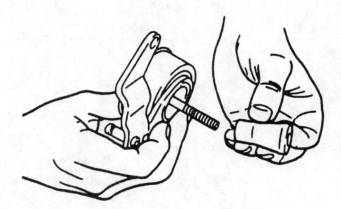

Fig. 2.9 Belt tensioner pulley and spacer sleeve. Note that smaller diameter of spacer fits against pulley – DOHC engine (Sec 10)

Refitting

Note: *The pulley securing bolt(s) must be renewed on refitting, and a new timing belt must be fitted.*

3   Refit the belt tensioner or idler pulley, as applicable, using a new bolt, noting that the spacer sleeve should be fitted with the smaller diameter against the pulley.

4   Tighten the securing bolt to the specified torque in the two stages given in the Specifications, except when refitting the belt tensioner, in which case do not fully tighten the bolt until the timing belt has been fitted and tensioned.

5   Fit a new timing belt, and adjust the tension as described in Section 7.

11 Camshaft oil seals – renewal

SOHC engines

Front oil seal

1   Remove the camshaft sprocket as described in Section 8.

2   Punch or drill a small hole in the centre of the now-exposed oil seal.

3   Screw in a self-tapping screw, and pull on the screw with pliers to extract the seal (photo).

4   Clean the oil seal seat with a wooden or plastic scraper.

5   Wind a thin band of tape around the end of the camshaft, to protect the lips of the new oil seal as it is fitted.

6   Grease the lips of the new seal, and drive it into position until it is flush with the housing, using a suitable socket or tube (photo). Take care not to damage the seal lips during fitting.

7   Carefully remove the tape from the end of the camshaft.

8   Refit the camshaft sprocket as described in Section 8.

Rear oil seal – 1.4 and 1.6 litre engines

9   Remove the distributor, or coil, as applicable, from the end of the camshaft housing, as described in Chapter 5.

10   On 1.4 litre engines, and 1.6 litre single-point fuel injection engines (see Chapter 4), the camshaft rear oil seal takes the form of an O-ring on the rear of the distributor body. Prise off the old O-ring using a screwdriver (photo), then fit the new O-ring, and refit the distributor as described in Chapter 5.

11   On 1.6 litre multi-point fuel injection engines, the camshaft rear oil seal takes the form of an O-ring on the rear of the coil mounting plate. Unscrew the three coil mounting plate securing bolts, and withdraw the plate from the end of the camshaft housing (photo). Prise off the old O-ring using a screwdriver, then fit the new O-ring, and refit the coil mounting plate. Refit the coil to the mounting plate, with reference to Chapter 5 if necessary.

11.3 Extracting the camshaft front oil seal using a self-tapping screw – 1.6 litre engine

11.6 Fitting a new camshaft front oil seal using a large socket – 1.6 litre engine

11.10 Removing the O-ring/camshaft rear oil seal from the rear of the distributor – 1.4 litre engine

11.11 Coil mounting plate removed for access to O-ring/camshaft rear oil seal (arrowed) – 1.6 litre multi-point fuel injection engine (shown with camshaft housing removed from engine)

11.13 Removing the camshaft rear oil seal – 2.0 litre engine (shown with camshaft housing removed from engine)

11.19 Removing a camshaft front oil seal – DOHC engine

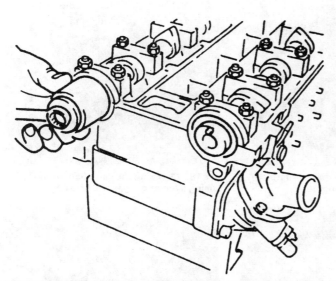

Fig. 2.10 Using the camshaft sprocket bolt, washer, and a suitable tube to fit a new camshaft front oil seal – DOHC engine (Sec 11)

Rear oil seal – 1.8 and 2.0 litre engines

12   Remove the distributor components, as described in Chapter 5.
13   Prise the seal from the camshaft housing (photo).
14   Clean the oil seal seat with a wooden or plastic scraper.
15   Grease the lips of the new seal, and drive it into position until it is flush with the end of the camshaft housing, using a suitable socket or tube. Take care not to damage the seal lips during fitting.
16   Refit the distributor components as described in Chapter 5.

DOHC engines

Front oil seal

17   Remove the relevant camshaft sprocket as described in Section 8.
18   Punch or drill a small hole in the centre of the now-exposed oil seal.
19   Screw in a self-tapping screw, and pull on the screw with pliers to extract the seal (photo).
20   Clean the oil seal seat with a wooden or plastic scraper.
21   Ensure that the locating peg for the sprocket in the end of the camshaft is uppermost.
22   Grease the lips of the new seal, then fit the seal using a tube or socket of suitable diameter with a washer and the camshaft sprocket bolt. Screw the camshaft sprocket bolt into the end of the camshaft to draw the oil seal into position on its shoulder – see Fig. 2.10.
23   Refit the camshaft sprocket as described in Section 8.

Rear oil seal

24   No rear camshaft oil seals are fitted to DOHC engines, although an O-ring is fitted to the rear of the distributor body (the distributor is driven from the end of the exhaust camshaft).
25   To renew the O-ring, remove the distributor as described in Chapter 5, then prise off the old O-ring using a screwdriver. Fit the new O-ring, and refit the distributor as described in Chapter 5.

12   Camshaft(s) – removal, inspection and refitting

SOHC engines
Removal

1   The camshaft can only be removed without disturbing the housing if a special tool (Vauxhall/Opel No 603 850, or equivalent) is available to depress the cam followers whilst the camshaft is withdrawn.
2   Assuming that such a tool is not available, the camshaft housing must be removed. Since the cylinder head bolts must be removed, it is strongly recommended that a new cylinder head gasket is fitted. If the gasket is not renewed, and it 'blows' on reassembly, the cylinder head will have to be removed in order to renew the gasket, and another new set of bolts will have to be obtained for refitting. *You have been warned!*
3   Removal and refitting of the camshaft housing is described in Section 13 along with cylinder head removal and refitting. If it is decided not to disturb the cylinder head, the relevant paragraphs referring specifically to cylinder head removal and refitting can be ignored, and it is strongly recommended that the cylinder head is clamped to the cylinder block using four head bolts and some spacers to reduce the possibility of the seal between the head and the block being broken.
4   With the camshaft housing removed, proceed as follows.
5   On carburettor engines, remove the fuel pump as described in Chapter 4.
6   Remove the distributor, distributor components, or coil (as applicable) from the end of the housing.
7   On 1.6 litre multi-point fuel injection engines, unscrew the three securing bolts, and remove the coil mounting plate from the end of the camshaft housing.
8   On 1.8 and 2.0 litre engines, prise out the camshaft rear oil seal.
9   Working at the distributor/coil end of the camshaft, unscrew the two camshaft thrustplate securing bolts, using a suitable Allen key or hexagon bit (photo).
10   Withdraw the thrustplate, noting which way round it is fitted (photo).
11   Carefully withdraw the camshaft from the distributor/coil end of the housing, taking care not to damage the bearing journals (photo).

Inspection

12   With the camshaft removed, examine the bearings in the camshaft housing for signs of obvious wear or pitting. If evident, a new camshaft housing will probably be required. Also check that the oil supply holes in the camshaft housing are free from obstructions (photo).
13   The camshaft itself should show no marks or scoring on the journal or cam lobe surfaces. If evident, renew the camshaft. Note that if the camshaft is renewed, all the rocker arms should also be renewed.
14   Check the camshaft thrustplate for signs of wear or grooves, and renew if evident.

Refitting

Note: *The front (and rear, where applicable) camshaft oil seal(s) should be renewed on refitting.*

15   It is advisable to renew the camshaft front oil seal as a matter of course if the camshaft has been removed. Prise out the old seal using a screwdriver, and tap in the new seal until it is flush with the housing, using a suitable socket or tube.

12.9 Camshaft thrustplate and securing bolts – 1.6 litre engine

12.10 Removing the camshaft thrustplate – 2.0 litre SOHC engine

12.11 Withdrawing the camshaft from the housing – 2.0 litre SOHC engine

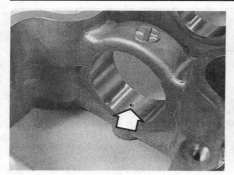

12.12 Oil supply hole (arrowed) in camshaft housing

12.18A Tightening a camshaft thrustplate securing bolt – 1.6 litre engine

12.18B Checking the camshaft endfloat using a feeler gauge – 1.6 litre engine

12.29 Corresponding identification marks (arrowed) on camshaft bearing cap and cylinder head – DOHC engine

12.31 Exhaust camshaft rear bearing cap securing nuts (arrowed) – DOHC engine

12.32 Removing a camshaft bearing cap – DOHC engine

16   Commence refitting by liberally oiling the bearings in the housing, and also the oil seal lip.

17   Carefully insert the camshaft into the housing from the distributor/coil end, taking care to avoid damage to the bearings.

18   Refit the thrustplate, and tighten the securing bolts. Check the camshaft endfloat by inserting a feeler gauge between the thrustplate and the camshaft end flange. If the endfloat exceeds that specified, renew the thrustplate (photos).

19   On 1.8 and 2.0 litre engines, fit a new camshaft rear oil seal to the housing, using a suitable socket or tube. The oil seal should be flush with the end of the camshaft housing.

20   On 1.6 litre multi-point fuel injection engines, examine the condition of the O-ring on the rear of the coil mounting plate, and renew it if necessary, then refit the coil mounting plate.

21   Refit the distributor, distributor components or coil, as applicable, as described in Chapter 5.

22   On carburettor engines, refit the fuel pump as described in Chapter 4.

23   Where applicable, remove the bolts and spacers clamping the cylinder head to the block.

24   Refit the camshaft housing, as described in Section 13.

25   If a new camshaft has been fitted, it is important to observe the following running-in schedule (unless otherwise specified by the manufacturer) immediately after initially starting the engine:

    (a)   One minute at 2000 rpm.
    (b)   One minute at 1500 rpm.
    (c)   One minute at 3000 rpm.
    (d)   One minute at 2000 rpm.

26   Change the engine oil (but not the filter, unless due in any case) approximately 600 miles (1000 km) after fitting a new camshaft.

DOHC engines

Removal

27   Remove the relevant camshaft sprocket as described in Section 8.

28   If the exhaust camshaft is to be removed, remove the distributor as described in Chapter 5.

29   Check the camshaft bearing caps for identification marks, and if none are present, make corresponding marks on the bearing caps and the top surface of the cylinder head using a centre-punch. Note the

orientation of the bearing caps before removal, as they must be refitted in exactly the same positions from which they are removed. The inlet camshaft caps are usually numbered 1 to 5, and the exhaust camshaft caps 6 to 11, with corresponding numbers cast into the cylinder head (photo).

30   Before removing the camshaft, check the endfloat using a dial gauge or a feeler gauge. If the endfloat is outside the specified limits, the camshaft must be renewed.

31   Loosen the relevant camshaft bearing caps in half-turn stages – ie, loosen all the nuts by half a turn, then loosen all the nuts by a further half turn and so on (this is necessary to slowly relieve the tension in the valve springs). Note that the exhaust camshaft rear bearing cap, which also supports the distributor, is secured by four nuts (photo).

32   Remove the bearing cap nuts (noting the washers under them) and the bearing caps, then carefully lift the relevant camshaft from the cylinder head, complete with the oil seal (photo).

Inspection

33   With the camshaft removed, examine the bearing surfaces in the cylinder head for signs of obvious wear or pitting. If evident, the cylinder head and all the bearing caps must be renewed as a matched set, as it is not possible to renew the bearings individually.

34   The camshaft should show no marks or scoring on the journal or cam lobe surfaces. If evident, renew the camshaft.

35   It is advisable to renew the camshaft front oil seal as a matter of course. Prise the old seal from the front of the camshaft and discard it.

Refitting

36   Commence refitting by liberally coating the contact faces of the hydraulic valve lifters with molybdenum disulphide paste.

37   Coat the mating faces of the bearing cap which house the oil seal (No 1 or 6, depending on which camshaft has been removed), and in the case of the exhaust camshaft, the bearing cap which houses the distributor drive (No 11) with suitable sealing compound (Vauxhall/Opel No 15 04 201, or equivalent).

38   Oil the bearing surfaces and the lobes of the camshaft, then place the camshaft in position on the cylinder head with the sprocket locating pin uppermost.

39   Refit the bearing caps in their original positions as noted during removal.

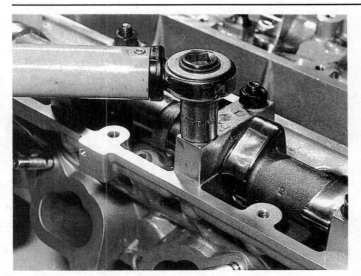

12.40 Tightening a camshaft bearing cap securing nut – DOHC engine

40   Fit the bearing cap washers and nuts, and tighten the nuts progressively to the specified torque in half-turn stages (as when loosening) (photo). Note that when refitting the exhaust camshaft, the two smaller rear bearing cap securing nuts should be tightened after all the main camshaft bearing cap nuts have been tightened. Note also that the two smaller nuts should be tightened to a lower torque wrench setting than the main nuts.
41   Lubricate the lips of a new camshaft front oil seal with a little grease, and fit the oil seal as described in Section 11.
42   Where applicable, refit the distributor as described in Chapter 5.
43   Refit the camshaft sprocket as described in Section 8.

13   Cylinder head – removal and refitting

SOHC engines
Removal
Note: *The engine must be cold when removing the cylinder head.*

1   Disconnect the battery negative lead.
2   Drain the cooling system as described in Chapter 1.
3   Disconnect the exhaust downpipe from the manifold, with reference to Chapter 4.
4   The cylinder head can be removed complete with the manifolds, or the manifolds can be detached from the cylinder head prior to removal, with reference to Chapter 4. If no work is to be carried out on the inlet manifold, it can be unbolted from the cylinder head and supported to one side out of the way, thus avoiding the need to disconnect the relevant hoses, pipes and wiring.
5   If the cylinder head is to be removed complete with the manifolds, disconnect all relevant hoses, pipes and wiring from the inlet manifold and associated components, with reference to Chapter 4. On carburettor engines, disconnect the hot air hose from the shroud on the exhaust manifold.
6   If the inlet manifold is to be left in the engine compartment, proceed as follows – otherwise, proceed to paragraph 15.
7   Disconnect the air cleaner trunking from the airbox on the carburettor or fuel injection unit, or directly from the throttle body (as applicable).
8   Disconnect the camshaft cover breather hose(s) from the camshaft cover (photo).
9   Where applicable, on fuel injection models, unbolt the wiring harness earth lead(s) from the camshaft housing (photo).
10   On 1.4 and 1.6 litre models, disconnect the crankcase breather hose from the stub at the rear of the camshaft housing (photo).
11   Loosen the alternator mountings, then unbolt the upper alternator mounting bracket from the inlet manifold (photo).
12   Where applicable, unclip the fuel injector wiring harness from the brackets on the camshaft cover, then separate the two halves of the

13.8 Loosening a camshaft cover breather hose clamp – 2.0 litre SOHC engine

13.9 Unbolting a wiring harness earth lead from the camshaft housing – 1.6 litre multi-point fuel injection engine

13.10 Loosening the crankcase breather hose clamp from the camshaft housing stub – 1.6 litre engine

13.11 Unbolt the upper alternator mounting bracket (bolt arrowed) from the inlet manifold

13.12A Unclip the fuel injector wiring harness from the brackets on the camshaft cover ...

13.12B ... then separate the two halves of the wiring connector – 1.6 litre multi-point fuel injection engine

13.13 Inlet manifold moved to one side to enable removal of the cylinder head – 1.6 litre multi-point fuel injection engine

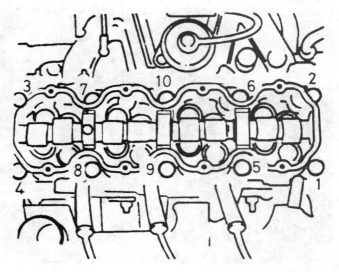

Fig. 2.11 Cylinder head bolt loosening sequence – SOHC engines (Sec 13)

harness connector, and release the connector from the clip on the camshaft cover (photos).
13   Make a final check to ensure that all necessary hoses, pipes and wires have been disconnected, then unscrew the securing nuts, noting the location of any brackets (eg, engine lifting bracket) attached to the studs in the cylinder head, and lift the inlet manifold from the cylinder head. Ensure that the manifold is properly supported, taking care not to strain any of the hoses, pipes and wires, etc, which are still connected (photo).
14   Recover the manifold gasket from the cylinder head.
15   If desired, remove the exhaust manifold with reference to Chapter 4.
16   Remove the camshaft sprocket as described in Section 8.
17   Unscrew the two upper rear timing belt cover securing bolts from the camshaft housing.
18   Disconnect the HT leads from the spark plugs and the coil, labelling them if necessary to aid refitting, and where applicable remove the distributor cap with reference to Chapter 1. Where applicable, disconnect the distributor or coil (1.6 litre multi-point fuel injection models) wiring plug.
19   If not already done, disconnect the crankcase breather hose from the camshaft housing, and on 1.8 and 2.0 litre engines, unscrew the bolt securing the crankcase breather tube bracket to the end of the cylinder head (photos).
20   Disconnect the coolant hose(s) from the thermostat housing (photo).
21   On carburettor models, disconnect the fuel hoses from the fuel pump. Be prepared for fuel spillage, and plug or clamp the open ends of the hoses to prevent further fuel loss and dirt ingress.
22   Where applicable, disconnect the wiring plug from the coolant temperature sensor in the end of the cylinder head (photo).

23   Make a final check to ensure that all relevant hoses, pipes and wires, etc, have been disconnected.
24   Working from the outside inwards in a spiral pattern as shown in Fig. 2.11, loosen all the cylinder head bolts by a quarter of a turn, then loosen all the bolts by half a turn, and finally loosen and remove the bolts. Recover the washers.
25   Lift the camshaft housing from the cylinder head (photo). If necessary, tap the housing gently with a soft-faced mallet to free it from the cylinder head, but **do not** lever at the mating faces. Note that the camshaft housing is located on dowels.
26   Lift the cylinder head from the cylinder block (photo). If necessary, tap the cylinder head gently with a soft-faced mallet to free it from the block, but **do not** lever at the mating faces. Note that the cylinder head is located on dowels.
27   Lift the rocker arms and their thrust pads from the cylinder head, keeping them in order so that they can be refitted in their original positions (photos).
28   Lift the hydraulic valve lifters from the cylinder head, and keep the lifters in order, so that they can be refitted in their original positions (photo).
29   Recover the cylinder head gasket and discard it.

Refitting

Note: *A new cylinder head gasket and new cylinder head bolts must be used on refitting, and a suitable sealant (Vauxhall/Opel No 15 03 166, or equivalent) will be required to coat the camshaft housing-to-cylinder head mating faces.*

30   Clean the cylinder head and block mating faces, and the camshaft housing and cylinder head mating faces, by careful scraping. Take care not to damage the cylinder head and camshaft housing, which are made

13.19A Disconnecting the crankcase breather hose from the camshaft housing – 2.0 litre SOHC engine

13.19B Unbolting the crankcase breather tube bracket from the cylinder head – 2.0 litre SOHC engine

13.20 Disconnecting the coolant hose from the thermostat housing – 1.6 litre engine

13.22 Disconnecting the wiring plug from the coolant temperature sensor – 1.6 litre multi-point fuel injection engine

13.25 Lifting the camshaft housing from the cylinder head – 1.6 litre multi-point fuel injection engine

13.26 Lifting the cylinder head from the cylinder block – 1.6 litre multi-point fuel injection engine

13.27A Lift the rocker arms ...

13.27B ... and their thrust pads from the cylinder head – 1.6 litre engine

13.28 Lift the hydraulic valve lifters from the cylinder head – 1.6 litre engine

13.31A Cylinder head gasket 'OBEN/TOP' markings

13.31B Cylinder head gasket correctly located over dowels (arrowed) in cylinder block – 1.6 litre engine (shown with engine removed from vehicle)

13.34 Lubricate the valve lifter contact faces with molybdenum disulphide grease – 1.6 litre engine

of light alloy and are easily scored. Cover the coolant passages and other openings with masking tape or rag to prevent dirt and carbon falling in. Mop out all the oil from the bolt holes; if oil is left in the holes, hydraulic pressure could crack the block when the bolts are refitted.

31   Commence refitting by locating a new cylinder head gasket on the block so that the word 'OBEN' or 'TOP' can be read from above (photos).

32   With the mating faces scrupulously clean, locate the cylinder head on the block so that the positioning dowels engage in their holes.

33   Before refitting the hydraulic valve lifters, it is advisable to dismantle and clean them as described in Section 30 in Part B of this Chapter.

34   Refit the hydraulic valve lifters, thrust pads and rocker arms to the cylinder head in their original positions. Liberally oil the valve lifter bores. Lubricate the contact faces of the valve lifters, thrust pads and rocker arms with a little molybdenum disulphide grease (photo).

35   Temporarily refit the crankshaft sprocket, and ensure that the

timing marks are still positioned with No 1 piston at top dead centre (see Section 3).

36   Apply sealing compound (Vauxhall/Opel No 15 03 166, or equivalent) to the cylinder head top mating face (photo), then refit the camshaft housing to the cylinder head.

37   Fit the **new** cylinder head bolts, ensuring that the washers are in place under their heads, and screw the bolts in by hand as far as possible (photo).

38   Tighten the bolts working from the inside outwards in a spiral pattern as shown in Fig. 2.12. Tighten the bolts in the four stages given in the Specifications – ie, tighten all bolts to the Stage 1 torque, then tighten all bolts to Stage 2 and so on (photos).

39   Further refitting is a reversal of the removal procedure, bearing in mind the following points.

40   Ensure that the ignition HT leads are reconnected to their correct cylinders.

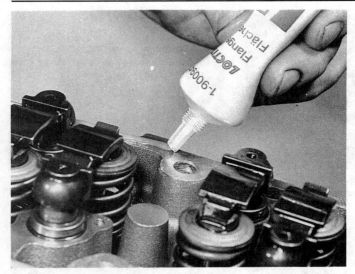

13.36 Apply sealing compound to the cylinder head top mating face – 1.6 litre engine

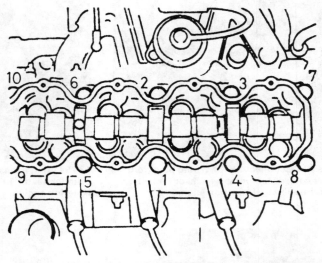

Fig. 2.12 Cylinder head bolt tightening sequence – SOHC engines (Sec 13)

41   Refit the camshaft sprocket as described in Section 8.
42   Where applicable, refit the manifolds to the cylinder head with reference to Chapter 4, using new gaskets.
43   Reconnect the exhaust downpipe to the manifold, using a new gasket, with reference to Chapter 4.
44   Refit the upper alternator mounting bracket to the inlet manifold, and then adjust the alternator drivebelt tension as described in Chapter 12.
45   Refill the cooling system as described in Chapter 1.
46   On completion, check that all relevant hoses, pipes and wires, etc, have been reconnected.
47   When the engine is started, check for signs of leaks.
48   Once the engine has reached normal operating temperature, check and if necessary adjust the idle speed and mixture (where possible), as described in Chapter 4, and finally tighten the cylinder head bolts to the Stage 5 setting.

DOHC engines

Removal

Note: *The engine must be cold when removing the cylinder head.*

49   Disconnect the battery negative lead.
50   Drain the cooling system as described in Chapter 1.
51   Remove the front section of the exhaust system as described in Chapter 4.
52   The cylinder head can be removed complete with the inlet manifold, or the inlet manifold can be detached from the cylinder head prior to removal, with reference to Chapter 4. If no work is to be carried out on the inlet manifold, it can be unbolted from the cylinder head and supported to one side out of the way, thus avoiding the need to disconnect the relevant hoses, pipes and wiring.

53   If the cylinder head is to be removed complete with the inlet manifold, disconnect all relevant hoses, pipes and wiring from the inlet manifold and associated components, with reference to Chapter 4, and unbolt the manifold support bracket from the manifold (photo). Loosen the alternator mountings, then unbolt the upper alternator mounting from the inlet manifold.
54   If the inlet manifold is to be left in the engine compartment, proceed as follows – otherwise, proceed to paragraph 65.
55   Disconnect the wiring plug from the airflow meter, and the breather hose from the airbox on the throttle body, then disconnect the air cleaner trunking and remove the airflow meter/airbox assembly from the throttle body, with reference to Chapter 4 if necessary.
56   Disconnect the end of the throttle cable from the throttle valve lever, then unbolt the throttle cable support bracket and remove it from the inlet manifold.
57   Unscrew the two earth lead securing nuts from the fuel rail (one at each end of the rail) and disconnect the three earth leads.
58   Disconnect the wiring plug from the throttle position switch.
59   Pull up on the wiring harness housing, and disconnect the wiring plugs from the fuel injectors by compressing the retaining clips. Move the wiring harness to one side.
60   Disconnect the two breather hoses from the rear of the camshaft cover (photo).
61   Loosen the alternator mountings, then unbolt the upper alternator mounting from the inlet manifold.
62   Unbolt the manifold support bracket from the manifold.
63   Make a final check to ensure that all necessary hoses, pipes and wires have been disconnected, then unscrew the securing nuts and lift the inlet manifold from the cylinder head. Ensure that the manifold is properly supported, taking care not to strain any of the hoses, pipes and wires, etc, which are still connected.

13.37 Fit new cylinder head bolts, ensuring that the washers are in place – 2.0 litre engine

13.38A Tighten the cylinder head bolts to the specified torque ...

13.38B ... then through the specified angle – 2.0 litre engine

13.53 Unbolting the inlet manifold support bracket from the manifold (viewed from underneath) – DOHC engine

13.67 Removing the timing belt outer cover upper stud – DOHC engine

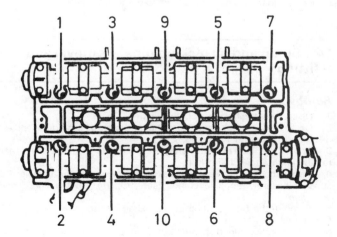

Fig. 2.13 Cylinder head bolt loosening sequence – DOHC engine (Sec 13)

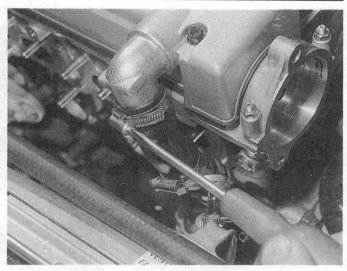

13.60 Disconnecting the larger breather hose from the rear of the camshaft cover – DOHC engine

64   Recover the manifold gasket from the cylinder head.
65   Remove the camshaft sprockets as described in Section 8.
66   Remove the timing belt tensioner, and the idler pulley, as described in Section 10.
67   Unscrew the upper and middle studs for the timing belt outer cover screws. Note that the upper stud simply unscrews from the cylinder head, but the middle stud is secured by a bolt (photo).
68   Unscrew the two upper rear timing belt cover securing bolts from the cylinder head.
69   Remove the distributor cap and HT leads with reference to Chapter 5.
70   Disconnect the distributor wiring plug.
71   Disconnect the coolant hose from the left-hand side of the cylinder head.
72   Unscrew the bolt securing the crankcase breather tube bracket to the end of the cylinder head.
73   Disconnect the radiator top hose from the thermostat housing, and disconnect the wiring plugs from the temperature gauge sender and the coolant temperature sensor (both located in the thermostat housing) (photo).
74   Make a final check to ensure that all relevant hoses, pipes and wires have been disconnected.
75   Using a suitable Torx socket, and working in the order shown in Fig. 2.13, loosen all the cylinder head bolts by a quarter of a turn, then loosen all the bolts by half a turn, and finally loosen and remove the bolts. Recover the washers (photo).
76   Lift the cylinder head from the cylinder block (photo). If necessary, tap the cylinder head gently with a soft-faced mallet to free it from the block, but **do not** lever at the mating faces. Note that the cylinder head is located on dowels.
77   Recover the cylinder head gasket and discard it.

Refitting
Note: *A new cylinder head gasket, new cylinder head bolts, and a new timing belt must be used on refitting.*

78   Clean the cylinder head and block mating faces by careful scraping. Take care not to damage the cylinder head, which is made of light alloy and is easily scored. Cover the coolant passages and other openings with masking tape or rag, to prevent dirt and carbon falling in. Mop out all the oil from the bolt holes; if oil is left in the holes, hydraulic pressure could crack the block when the bolts are refitted.
79   Commence refitting by locating a new cylinder head gasket on the block so that the word 'OBEN' or 'TOP' is uppermost at the timing belt end of the engine (photo).
80   With the mating faces scrupulously clean, locate the cylinder head on the block so that the positioning dowels engage in their holes.
81   Temporarily refit the crankshaft pulley and the camshaft sprockets, and ensure that No 1 piston is still positioned at top dead centre (see Section 3).

13.73 Disconnecting the radiator top hose from the thermostat housing – DOHC engine

13.75 Removing a cylinder head bolt and washer – DOHC engine

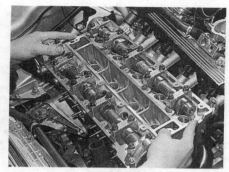

13.76 Lifting the cylinder head from the cylinder block – DOHC engine

13.79 New cylinder head gasket in position – DOHC engine

13.83A Tighten the cylinder head bolts to the specified torque ...

13.83B ... and then through the specified angle – DOHC engine

82   Fit the **new** cylinder head bolts, ensuring that the washers are in place under their heads, and screw the bolts in *by hand* as far as possible.

83   Tighten the bolts in the order shown in Fig. 2.14. Tighten the bolts in the four stages given in the Specifications – ie, tighten all bolts to the Stage 1 torque, then tighten all bolts to Stage 2, and so on (photos).

84   Further refitting is a reversal of removal, bearing in mind the following points.

85   Refit the timing belt tensioner and idler pulley as described in Section 10.

86   Refit the camshaft sprockets as described in Section 8.

87   Fit a new timing belt and tension it as described in Section 7.

88   Where applicable, refit the inlet manifold to the cylinder head with reference to Chapter 4, using a new gasket.

89   Refit the front section of the exhaust system as described in Chapter 4, using a new gasket.

90   Refit the upper alternator mounting to the inlet manifold (where applicable), then adjust the alternator drivebelt tension as described in Chapter 12.

91   Refill the cooling system as described in Chapter 1.

92   On completion, check that all relevant hoses, pipes and wires, etc, have been reconnected.

93   When the engine is started, check for signs of leaks.

94   Once the engine has reached normal operating temperature, finally tighten the cylinder head bolts to the Stage 5 setting.

14   Sump and oil pick-up pipe – removal and refitting

Removal

1   Disconnect the battery negative lead.

2   On DOHC engine models, remove the engine undershield as described in Chapter 11, Section 25.

3   Drain the engine oil, with reference to Chapter 1 if necessary, then refit and tighten the drain plug.

4   Apply the handbrake, then jack up the front of the vehicle and support securely on axle stands (see 'Jacking, towing and wheel changing').

5   Remove the front section of the exhaust system as described in Chapter 4.

6   Where applicable, disconnect the wiring from the oil level sensor mounted in the sump.

7   Unscrew the securing bolts, and remove the engine-to-gearbox/transmission blanking plate from the bellhousing (photo).

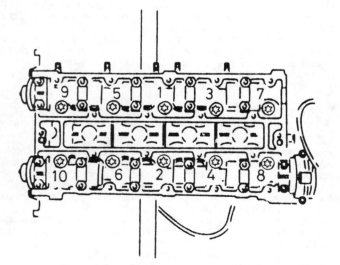

Fig. 2.14 Cylinder head bolt tightening sequence – DOHC engine (Sec 13)

14.7 Removing the engine-to-gearbox/transmission blanking plate from the bellhousing – 2.0 litre engine

14.8 Withdrawing the sump – 1.6 litre engine

14.10 Removing the bracket securing the oil pick-up pipe to the cylinder block – 2.0 litre SOHC engine

14.13 Applying sealing compound to the joint between the oil pump and cylinder block – 2.0 litre SOHC engine

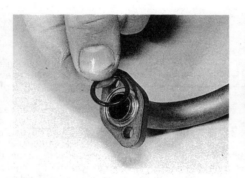

14.15A Fit a new O-ring to the oil pick-up pipe ...

14.15B ... and refit the pick-up pipe to the oil pump – 1.6 litre engine

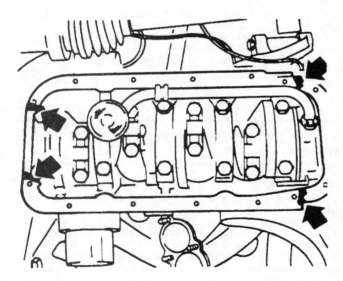

Fig. 2.15 Apply sealing compound to oil pump and rear main bearing cap joints before refitting sump – SOHC engine shown (Sec 14)

8 Unscrew the securing bolts, and withdraw the sump (photo). If necessary, tap the sump with a soft-faced mallet to free it from the cylinder block – **do not** lever between the sump and cylinder block mating faces. Note that on 1.8 and 2.0 litre engines, the sump baffle will probably be pulled away from the cylinder block with the sump, but cannot be removed until the bracket securing the oil pick-up pipe has been removed.

9 Recover the gasket.

10 On 1.8 and 2.0 litre engines, to remove the sump baffle, unbolt the bracket securing the oil pick-up pipe to the cylinder block (photo). The baffle can then be manipulated over the oil pick-up pipe. Recover the sump baffle gasket.

11 If desired, the oil pick-up pipe can be removed by unscrewing the single bolt securing the support bracket to the cylinder block (if not already done), and the two bolts securing the end of the pipe to the oil pump. Recover the O-ring.

Refitting

Note: *A new sump gasket and sump baffle gasket (1.8 and 2.0 litre engines) must be used on refitting. Suitable sealant (Vauxhall/Opel No 15 03 294, or equivalent) will be required to coat the cylinder block face (see text) and suitable thread-locking compound will be required to coat the sump securing bolt threads.*

12 Clean all traces of old gasket from the mating faces of the cylinder block, sump baffle (where applicable), and sump.

13 Commence refitting by applying sealing compound (Vauxhall/Opel No 15 03 294, or equivalent) to the joints between the oil pump and cylinder block, and the rear main bearing cap and cylinder block – see Fig. 2.15 (photo).

14 On 1.8 and 2.0 litre engines, fit a new sump baffle gasket, if necessary applying a little sealing compound to hold it in place, then offer the sump baffle up to the cylinder block, manipulating it over the oil pick-up pipe where applicable. Locate the remaining gasket on the sump baffle, but do not use sealing compound.

15 If the oil pick-up pipe has been removed, refit it to the oil pump using a new O-ring (photos).

16 Where applicable, refit the bracket securing the oil pick-up pipe to the cylinder block, ensuring that it passes through the relevant hole in the sump baffle on 1.8 and 2.0 litre engines.

17 Coat the sump securing bolts with thread-locking compound, then refit the sump, and tighten the securing bolts to the specified torque.

18 Further refitting is a reversal of removal, but refit the front section of the exhaust system with reference to Chapter 4, and on completion, refill the engine with oil as described in Chapter 1.

15.4 Oil cooler pipe unions at oil pump –
DOHC engine

15.8 Locate a new oil pump gasket on the
cylinder block – 2.0 litre SOHC engine

15.10 Refitting the oil pump – 1.6 litre
engine (shown with engine removed from
vehicle)

1   Tape wound around crankshaft
2   Flats on crankshaft engage with inner
    oil pump gear

15   Oil pump – removal and refitting

Removal

1   Remove the rear timing belt cover as described in Section 6.
2   Remove the sump, oil pick-up pipe and sump baffle (where applicable) as described in Section 14.
3   On 1.8 and 2.0 litre engines, unscrew the oil filter from its mounting on the oil pump, with reference to Chapter 1 if necessary.
4   On DOHC engines, disconnect the oil cooler pipe unions from the oil pump, and move the pipes to one side out of the way (photo).
5   Disconnect the wiring from the oil pressure switch mounted in the oil pump.
6   On DOHC engines, remove the spacer washer from the end of the crankshaft.
7   Remove the securing bolts, and withdraw the oil pump from the cylinder block. Recover the gasket.

Refitting

Note: *A new oil pump gasket, a new front crankshaft oil seal, and on 1.8 and 2.0 litre engines, a new oil filter must be used on refitting. On DOHC engines, suitable sealing compound (Vauxhall/Opel No 15 04 200, or equivalent) will be required to coat the face of the crankshaft spacer washer.*

Fig. 2.16 Oil pump securing bolts (arrowed) and crankshaft spacer ring (A) – DOHC engine (Sec 15)

8   Thoroughly clean the mating faces of the oil pump and cylinder block, then locate a new gasket on the block (photo).
9   Wind a thin layer of tape around the front edge of the crankshaft, to prevent damage to the oil seal lips as the pump is refitted.
10 With a new oil seal fitted to the pump, as described in Section 16, grease the oil seal lips, then refit the pump, ensuring that the inner gear engages with the flats on the crankshaft (photo).
11 Tighten the securing bolts to the specified torque, then carefully remove the tape from the front of the crankshaft.
12 On DOHC engines, coat the oil pump mating face of the spacer washer with sealing compound (Vauxhall/Opel No 15 04 200, or equivalent), then push the washer onto the end of the crankshaft until it is seated against the end of the oil pump.
13 Reconnect the wiring to the oil pressure switch.
14 On DOHC engines, reconnect the oil cooler pipes to the oil pump, and tighten the unions.
15 On 1.8 and 2.0 litre engines, fit a new oil filter, with reference to Chapter 1.
16 Refit the sump baffle (where applicable), oil pick-up pipe and sump, as described in Section 14.
17 Refit the rear timing belt cover as described in Section 6.

16   Oil pump – dismantling, inspection and reassembly

Dismantling

1   With the oil pump removed as described in Section 15, proceed as follows.
2   Remove the securing screws (photo) and withdraw the rear cover. The screws may be very tight, in which case it may be necessary to use an impact driver to remove them.
3   The oil pressure relief valve components can be removed from the pump by unscrewing the cap. Withdraw the cap, sealing ring, spring and plunger (photo).
4   Prise the crankshaft front oil seal from the pump using a screwdriver.

Inspection

5   Check the clearance between the inner and outer gear teeth (backlash) using a feeler gauge (photo).
6   Check the clearance between the edges of the gears and the housing (endfloat) using a straight edge and a feeler gauge (photo).
7   If any of the clearances are outside the specified limits, renew the components as necessary.
8   Examine the pressure relief valve spring and plunger, and renew if any sign of damage or wear is evident.

16.2 Removing an oil pump rear cover
securing screw

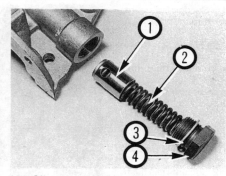

16.3 Oil pressure relief valve components

1 Plunger   3 Sealing ring
2 Spring   4 Plug

16.5 Check the clearance between the inner
and outer gear teeth ...

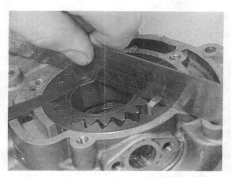

16.6 ... and between the edges of the gears
and the housing

16.11 Gear outer face identification mark
(arrowed)

16.13 Fitting a new crankshaft front oil seal
to the oil pump

Reassembly

Note: *A new pressure relief valve sealing ring should be used on reassembly, and suitable sealing compound (Vauxhall/Opel No 15 03 166, or equivalent) will be required to coat the pump housing mating face.*

9   Ensure that the interior of the pump body is scrupulously clean before commencing reassembly.
10   Discard the old pressure relief valve sealing ring, then thoroughly clean the pressure relief valve components, and lubricate them with clean engine oil before refitting. Use a new sealing ring.
11   Ensure that the gears are clean, then lubricate them with clean engine oil, and refit them to the pump body, noting that the outer gear is marked with a punch dot to indicate its outer face (ie, the face nearest the pump cover) (photo).
12   Ensure that the mating faces of the rear cover and the pump

housing are clean, then coat the pump housing mating face with sealing compound (Vauxhall/Opel No 15 03 166, or equivalent), and refit the rear cover. Refit and tighten the securing screws.
13   Fit a new crankshaft front oil seal to the recess in the pump body, using a suitable socket or tube, so that the seal is flush with the outer face of the housing (photo).

17   Crankshaft oil seals – renewal

Front oil seal

Note: *On DOHC engines, suitable sealing compound (Vauxhall/Opel No 15 04 200, or equivalent) will be required to coat the face of the crankshaft spacer washer.*

17.5 Using a self-tapping screw and a pair
of pliers to extract the crankshaft front oil
seal – 1.6 litre engine

17.8 Tapping a new crankshaft front oil seal
into position – 1.6 litre engine

17.15 Fitting a new crankshaft rear oil seal.
Note tape on end of crankshaft (viewed
with engine removed from vehicle and
sump removed)

1   Remove the crankshaft sprocket as described in Section 8. Ensure that, where applicable, the Woodruff key is removed from the end of the crankshaft.
2   On 1.8 and 2.0 litre SOHC engines, remove the rear timing belt cover with reference to Section 6.
3   On DOHC engines, remove the spacer washer from the end of the crankshaft.
4   Punch or drill a small hole in the centre of the now-exposed oil seal.
5   Screw in a self-tapping screw, and pull on the screw with pliers to extract the seal (photo). Several attempts may be necessary. Be careful not to damage the sealing face of the crankshaft.
6   Clean the oil seal seat with a wooden or plastic scraper.
7   Wind a thin band of tape around the end of the crankshaft to protect the lips of the new oil seal as it is fitted.
8   Grease the lips of the new seal, and tap it into position until it is flush with the outer face of the oil pump body, using a suitable socket or tube (photo). Take care not to damage the seal lips during fitting.
9   Carefully remove the tape from the end of the crankshaft.
10   On DOHC engines, coat the oil pump mating face of the spacer washer with sealing compound (Vauxhall/Opel No 15 04 200, or equivalent), then push the washer onto the end of the crankshaft until it is seated against the end of the oil pump.
11   On 1.8 and 2.0 litre engines, refit the rear timing belt cover, with reference to Section 6.
12   Where applicable, refit the Woodruff key, and refit the crankshaft sprocket, as described in Section 8.

Rear oil seal

13   Remove the flywheel/driveplate as described in Section 18.
14   Proceed as described in paragraphs 4 to 6 inclusive of this Section.
15   Grease the lips of the new seal, then tap the seal into position using a suitable tube, until flush with the outer faces of the cylinder block and rear main bearing cap (photo).
16   Refit the flywheel/driveplate as described in Section 18.

18 Flywheel/driveplate – removal, inspection and refitting

Removal

1   Remove the starter motor as described in Chapter 12.
2   Remove the clutch as described in Chapter 6, or the automatic transmission as described in Chapter 7, as applicable.
3   If the gearbox is still attached to the engine, remove the clutch release bearing and its guide sleeve, as described in Chapter 6.
4   Although the flywheel bolt holes are offset so that the flywheel can only be fitted in one position, it will make refitting easier if alignment marks are made between the flywheel and the end of the crankshaft.
5   Prevent the flywheel from turning by jamming the ring gear teeth using a suitable tool. Access is most easily obtained through the starter motor aperture.
6   Unscrew the securing bolts, and remove the flywheel (photo). *Take care, as the flywheel is heavy.*

18.6 Removing the flywheel – 1.6 litre engine

Inspection

7   If the teeth on the flywheel starter ring are badly worn, or if some are missing, then it will be necessary to remove the ring and fit a new one.
8   The old ring can be split with a cold chisel, after making a cut with a hacksaw blade between two gear teeth. Take great care not to damage the flywheel during this operation, and use eye protection at all times. Once the ring has been split, it will spread apart, and can be lifted from the flywheel.
9   The new ring gear must be heated to 180 to 230°C (356 to 446°F) and unless facilities for heating by oven or flame are available, leave the fitting to a Vauxhall/Opel dealer or engineering works. The new ring gear must not be overheated during this work, or the temper of the metal will be affected.
10   The ring should be tapped gently down onto its register, and left to cool naturally – the contraction of the metal on cooling will ensure that it is a secure and permanent fit.
11   If the clutch friction disc contact surface of the flywheel is scored, or on close inspection, shows signs of small hair cracks (caused by overheating), it may be possible to have the flywheel surface-ground, provided the overall thickness of the flywheel is not reduced too much. Consult a Vauxhall/Opel dealer or a specialist engine repairer, and if grinding is not possible, renew the flywheel complete.

Refitting

Note: *New flywheel securing bolts must be used on refitting.*

12   Offer the flywheel to the end of the crankshaft, and align the previously-made marks on the flywheel and crankshaft.
13   Fit new flywheel securing bolts, and tighten them to the two stages given in the Specifications, whilst preventing the flywheel from turning as during removal (photos).

18.13A Tool for preventing flywheel from turning, using engine-to-gearbox bolt – 1.6 litre engine

18.13B Tighten the flywheel securing bolts to the specified torque ...

18.13C ... and then through the specified angle – 1.6 litre engine

14   Where applicable, refit the clutch release bearing and its guide sleeve, as described in Chapter 6.
15   Refit the clutch as described in Chapter 6, or the automatic transmission as described in Chapter 7, as applicable.
16   Refit the starter motor as described in Chapter 12.

19   Engine/transmission mountings – inspection and renewal

Inspection

1   To improve access, raise the front of the vehicle and support it securely on axle stands (see *'Jacking, towing and wheel changing'*).
2   Check the mounting rubbers to see if they are cracked, hardened or separated from the metal at any point. Renew the mounting if any such damage or deterioration is evident.
3   Check that all the mounting securing nuts and bolts are securely tightened, using a torque wrench to check if possible.
4   Using a large screwdriver, or a similar tool, check for wear in the mountings by carefully levering against them to check for free play. Where this is not possible, enlist the aid of an assistant to move the engine/gearbox/transmission unit back and forth, and from side to side, while you observe the mountings. While some free play is to be expected, even from new components, excessive wear should be obvious. If excessive free play is found, check first to see that the securing nuts and bolts are correctly tightened, then renew any worn components as described below.

Renewal

Right-hand mounting

Note: *Suitable thread-locking compound will be required to coat the threads of the mounting block-to-body bolts on refitting.*

5   On DOHC engine models, remove the engine undershield, with reference to Chapter 11, Section 25.
6   If not already done, apply the handbrake, then raise the front of the vehicle and support securely on axle stands (see *'Jacking, towing and wheel changing'*).
7   Attach suitable lifting tackle to the engine lifting brackets on the cylinder head, and support the weight of the engine.
8   Working under the vehicle, unbolt the engine mounting bracket from the cylinder block, and unbolt the mounting block from the body, then withdraw the bracket/mounting assembly (photo).
9   Unbolt the mounting block from the bracket.
10   Fit the new mounting block to the bracket, and tighten the securing bolts to the specified torque.
11   Refit the mounting bracket to the cylinder block, and tighten the securing bolts to the specified torque.
12   Coat the threads of the mounting block-to-body bolts with suitable thread-locking compound, then refit them and tighten to the specified torque.
13   Disconnect the lifting tackle and hoist from the engine.
14   On DOHC engine models, refit the engine undershield.

19.8 Right-hand engine mounting bracket (1) and mounting block (2) – 1.6 litre engine (viewed from underneath)

15   Lower the vehicle to the ground.

Left-hand mounting

Note: *New mounting block-to-body bolts must be used on refitting.*

16   Proceed as described in paragraphs 5 to 7 inclusive.
17   Working under the vehicle, unbolt the engine/transmission mounting bracket from the transmission, and unbolt the mounting block from the body, then withdraw the bracket/mounting assembly (photo).
18   Unbolt the mounting from the bracket.
19   Fit the new mounting block to the bracket, and tighten the securing bolts to the specified torque.
20   Before refitting the bracket/mounting assembly, check that the original bolts which secured the mounting block to the body rotate freely in their threaded bores in the body. If necessary, re-cut the threaded bores using an M10 x 1.25 mm tap.
21   Refit the mounting bracket to the transmission, and tighten the securing bolts to the specified torque.
22   Fit **new** mounting block-to-body bolts, and tighten them to the specified torque.
23   Proceed as described in paragraphs 13 to 15 inclusive.

Rear mounting

24   Proceed as described in paragraphs 5 to 7 inclusive.
25   Working under the vehicle, unbolt the mounting block from the front subframe and the mounting bracket, and withdraw the mounting block (photos).
26   Fit the new mounting block to the subframe and mounting bracket, and tighten the securing bolts to the specified torque.
27   Proceed as described in paragraphs 13 to 15 inclusive.

19.17 Left-hand engine/transmission mounting bracket (1) and mounting block (2) – 1.6 litre engine (viewed from underneath)

19.25A Rear engine mounting block-to-front subframe nuts (arrowed) – viewed from underneath

19.25B Rear engine mounting bracket (arrowed) – 1.6 litre engine (viewed from underneath)

**20.3 Oil cooler pipe bracket viewed through front bumper –
DOHC engine**

**20.4 Oil cooler pipe union (1) and oil cooler securing nut (2) viewed
through front bumper – DOHC engine**

20   Oil cooler (DOHC engine) – removal and refitting

Removal

1   To gain sufficient access to enable the oil cooler to be removed, the
radiator must be removed, as described in Chapter 3, or alternatively,
the front bumper must be removed, as described in Chapter 11.
2   With the appropriate components removed for access, unscrew the
oil cooler pipe unions from the oil cooler. Be prepared for oil spillage, and
plug the open ends of the pipes, to prevent further oil leakage and dirt
ingress.
3   If necessary, unclip the oil cooler pipes from their brackets, to allow
sufficient space for the oil cooler to be removed (photo).
4   Unscrew the two securing nuts, and withdraw the oil cooler from its
mounting brackets (photo).

Refitting

5   Refitting is a reversal of removal, but on completion, check and if
necessary top-up the engine oil level, as described in Chapter 1.

Part B: Engine removal and general engine overhaul procedures

21 General information

1 This Part of Chapter 2 includes details of engine removal and refitting, and general overhaul procedures for the cylinder head, cylinder block/crankcase and internal engine components.

2 The information ranges from advice concerning preparation for an overhaul and the purchase of replacement parts, to detailed step-by-step procedures covering removal, inspection, renovation and refitting of internal engine components.

3 The following Sections have been compiled based on the assumption that the engine has been removed from the vehicle. For information concerning in-vehicle engine repair, as well as information on the removal and refitting of the external components necessary to facilitate overhaul, refer to Part A of this Chapter, and to Section 28 of this Part.

22 Engine overhaul – general information

1 It is not always easy to determine when, or if, an engine should be completely overhauled, as a number of factors must be considered. Also bear in mind that it may prove more economical to purchase a reconditioned engine than to carry out a full overhaul, however this cannot be accurately determined until the engine has been fully dismantled.

2 High mileage is not necessarily an indication that an engine overhaul is required, while low mileage does not preclude the need for an overhaul. Frequency of servicing is the most important consideration. An engine which has had regular and frequent oil and filter changes, in addition to the other specified maintenance (see Chapter 1), is likely to give many thousands of miles of reliable service. Conversely, a neglected engine may require an overhaul very early in its life.

3 Excessive oil consumption is an indication that piston rings, valve seals and/or valve guides are in need of attention. Make sure that oil leaks are not responsible before deciding that the piston rings and/or valve guides are worn. Perform a cylinder compression check to determine the extent of the work required (see Part A of this Chapter).

4 Check the oil pressure using a suitable oil pressure gauge fitted in place of the engine oil pressure switch (follow the equipment manufacturer's instructions), and compare it with the figure given in the Specifications. If the oil pressure is extremely low, the main and big-end bearings and/or the oil pump are probably worn.

5 Loss of power, rough running, knocking or metallic engine noises, excessive valve gear noise, or high fuel consumption may also point to the need for an overhaul, especially if all the conditions are present at the same time. If a complete service does not remedy the situation, overhaul is the only course of action available.

6 A full engine overhaul involves restoring the specifications (clearances, endfloats, etc) of the internal components to the standards used in a new engine. During a complete overhaul, the pistons and piston rings are renewed, and the cylinder bores are reconditioned. New main bearings and big-end bearings are generally fitted, and if necessary, the crankshaft may be reground to compensate for wear in the bearing journals. The valves should also be inspected and serviced as well, since they are usually in less-than-perfect condition if the engine has reached the stage where overhaul is required. Always pay careful attention to the condition of the oil pump when overhauling the engine, and renew it if in any doubt as to its serviceability. If a complete overhaul is carried out, the end result should be to the standard of a new engine, and should provide many trouble-free miles of service. **Note:** *Critical cooling system components such as the hoses, thermostat and water pump should be carefully inspected and if necessary renewed when an engine is overhauled. The radiator should be checked carefully to ensure that it is not clogged or leaking.*

7 Before beginning engine overhaul, carefully read through all the procedures involved to familiarize yourself with the scope and requirements of the job. Overhauling an engine is not difficult if you follow all of the instructions carefully, have the necessary tools and equipment ready to hand, and pay close attention to all the recommended specifications. However, engine overhaul can be time-consuming; plan on the vehicle being off the road for a minimum of two weeks, especially if parts must be taken to an engineering works for repair or reconditioning. Check on the availability of new parts, and make sure that any necessary special tools and equipment are obtained in advance. Most work can be done with typical hand tools, although a number of precision measuring instruments will be required to inspect parts in order to determine whether renewal is required. Often, an engineering works will handle the inspection of parts and offer advice concerning reconditioning and renewal. **Note:** *Always wait until the engine has been completely dismantled and all components, especially the cylinder block, have been inspected before deciding which service and repair operations must be entrusted to an engineering works. Since the condition of the cylinder block will be the major factor to consider when determining whether to overhaul the original engine or buy a reconditioned unit, do not purchase parts or have overhaul work done on other components until the block has been thoroughly inspected. As a general rule, time is the primary cost of an overhaul, so it does not pay to fit worn or sub- standard parts.*

8 As a final note, to ensure maximum life and minimum trouble from an overhauled engine, everything must be assembled with care in a spotlessly-clean environment.

23 Engine removal – methods and precautions

If you have decided to remove an engine for overhaul or major repair work, several preliminary steps should be taken. Locating a suitable place to work is extremely important. Adequate working space, along with storage space for the vehicle, will be required. If a garage is not available, at the very least a flat, level, clean work surface is required. Cleaning the engine compartment and engine before beginning the removal procedure will help to keep tools clean and organized. An engine hoist or an A-frame will also be required. Make sure that the equipment is rated in excess of the combined weight of the engine and transmission. Safety is of primary importance, considering the potential hazards involved in lifting the engine out of the vehicle. If the engine is being removed by a novice, an assistant should be available. Advice and aid from someone more experienced would also be helpful. There are many instances when one person cannot simultaneously perform all of the operations required when lifting the engine out of the vehicle. Plan the operation carefully before beginning. Obtain all of the tools and equipment required prior to beginning the job. Equipment necessary to perform engine removal and installation safely and with relative ease includes (in addition to an engine hoist) a heavy-duty trolley jack, complete sets of spanners and sockets as described in the preliminary Sections of this manual, wooden blocks, and plenty of rags and cleaning solvent to cope with spilled oil, coolant and fuel. If the hoist is to be hired, make sure that you arrange for it in advance, and perform all of the operations possible without it beforehand. This will save you money and time. Plan for the vehicle to be out of use for some time. An engineering works may be required to perform some of the work which the DIY enthusiast cannot accomplish without special equipment. These establishments often have a busy schedule, so it would be a good idea to consult them before removing the engine, in order to gain a rough estimate of the amount of time required to overhaul or repair components which may require attention. Always be extremely careful when removing and refitting the engine. Serious injury can result from careless actions. By planning ahead and taking plenty of time, the job (although major) can be accomplished successfully.

24.8 Disconnecting the brake servo vacuum hose from the inlet manifold – multi-point fuel injection engine

24.10 Disconnecting the MAP sensor vacuum hose from the throttle body – multi-point fuel injection engine

24.11 Disconnecting a coolant hose from the throttle body – multi-point fuel injection engine

24 Engine – removal and refitting (leaving manual gearbox in vehicle)

Removal

1 Disconnect both battery leads.
2 Remove the bonnet as described in Chapter 11, and on DOHC engine models, remove the engine undershield.
3 Drain the cooling system as described in Chapter 1, and remove the radiator as described in Chapter 3.
4 Drain the engine oil as described in Chapter 1 and, on 1.8 and 2.0 litre models, remove the oil filter.
5 Remove the air cleaner assembly from the body panel, and remove the air inlet trunking and the airbox from the carburettor or throttle body (as applicable), with reference to Chapter 4. Where applicable, on carburettor and single-point fuel injection models, disconnect the hot air hose from the exhaust manifold hot air shroud and the air cleaner, and remove the hose.
6 Remove the alternator as described in Chapter 12.
7 Where applicable, remove the power steering pump as described in Chapter 10.
8 Disconnect the brake servo vacuum hose from the inlet manifold (photo).
9 Disconnect the throttle cable from the throttle lever and the bracket on the carburettor or inlet manifold, as applicable.
10 Disconnect the vacuum pipe(s) from the carburettor or throttle body (as applicable), noting their locations (photo).

11 Disconnect the coolant hose(s) from the inlet manifold and/or throttle body, as applicable (photo).
12 On carburettor models, disconnect the coolant hoses from the automatic choke housing, and disconnect the wiring from the automatic choke heater and the choke pull-down solenoid. Where applicable, also disconnect the airbox vacuum pipe from the carburettor.
13 Depressurise the fuel system as described in Chapter 4, then disconnect the fuel hoses from the fuel pump and vapour separator on carburettor models, or from the fuel injection unit or the pipes on the inlet manifold, as applicable, on fuel injection models. Be prepared for fuel spillage, and take adequate fire precautions. Plug or clamp the open ends of the pipes and hoses to prevent dirt ingress and further fuel leakage.
14 On fuel injection models, disconnect all relevant wiring connections and plugs, noting their locations, and move the fuel injection wiring harness to one side. Where applicable, release the securing clips and withdraw the wiring harness from the brackets on the camshaft cover.
15 Disconnect the heater coolant hoses from the coolant gallery at the rear of the cylinder block, and from the cylinder head or inlet manifold, as applicable (photo).
16 On DOHC engine models, disconnect the oil cooler pipe unions from the oil pump.
17 Disconnect the wiring from the following components (if not already done). Note that on certain models, a large single plug can be disconnected in order to separate the engine wiring loom from the main wiring harness (the connector can usually be found clipped to a bracket on the battery tray). This will leave the wiring loom attached to the

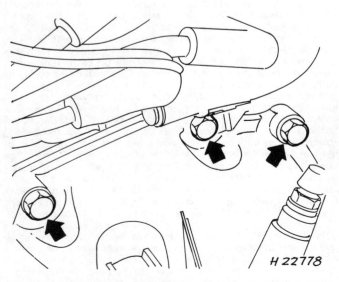
Fig. 2.17 Three upper engine-to-gearbox bolts (arrowed) (Sec 24)

24.15 Disconnecting the coolant hose (arrowed) from the inlet manifold – multi-point fuel injection engine

**24.28 Right-hand engine mounting bracket (arrowed) –
SOHC engine**

**24.30 Lifting the engine from the vehicle – 1.6 litre multi-point fuel
injection engine**

engine, avoiding the need to remove the plugs and connections from
individual components.

   (a) *Starter motor.*
   (b) *Distributor/coil (as applicable, note HT lead positions).*
   (c) *Oil pressure switch.*
   (d) *TDC sensor (where applicable).*
   (e) *Oil level sensor (where applicable).*
   (f) *Knock sensor (DOHC engine models).*
   (g) *Coolant temperature sensor (where applicable).*
   (h) *Temperature gauge sender.*

18   Make a final check to ensure that all relevant hoses, pipes and
wires have been disconnected, and that they are positioned clear of the
engine.
19   Unscrew and remove the three upper engine-to-gearbox bolts
accessible from the engine compartment, noting the locations of any
brackets which may be secured by the bolts.
20   If not already done, apply the handbrake, then jack up the front of
the vehicle and support securely on axle stands (see *'Jacking, towing
and wheel changing'*).
21   Remove the crankshaft pulley, with reference to Section 5 in
Part A.
22   Remove the front section of the exhaust system, as described in
Chapter 4.
23   On models where it is possible to remove the clutch with the
engine and gearbox in the vehicle (see Chapter 6), remove the clutch as
described in Chapter 6.
24   On models where it is not possible to remove the clutch with the
engine and gearbox in the vehicle (see Chapter 6), pull the gearbox input
shaft from engagement with the splined hub of the clutch friction disc.
This procedure is described in Chapter 6, Section 4 as part of the clutch
removal procedure for models where it is possible to remove the clutch
with the engine and gearbox in the vehicle.
25   Unbolt and remove the gearbox bellhousing cover plate.
26   Attach a suitable hoist and lifting tackle to the engine lifting
brackets on the cylinder head, and support the weight of the engine.
27   Support the gearbox using a trolley jack with an interposed block
of wood to spread the load.
28   Unbolt the right-hand engine mounting from the cylinder block
and the body, and withdraw the mounting bracket (photo).
29   Unscrew and remove the four lower engine-to-gearbox bolts
(again noting the location of any brackets which may be secured by the
bolts), then manipulate the engine as necessary to separate it from the
gearbox. Note that the gearbox locates on dowels in the cylinder block.
30   Carefully raise the hoist, and lift the engine from the vehicle, taking
care not to damage any of the surrounding components in the engine
compartment (photo).
31   With the engine removed, the gearbox can be supported by
placing a suitable length of wood between the bellhousing and the front
suspension subframe. Once the wooden support is in place, remove the
trolley jack from under the gearbox.

Refitting

Note: *Suitable thread-locking compound will be required to coat the
threads of the right-hand engine mounting-to-body bolts.*

32   With the front of the vehicle raised and supported on axle stands,
support the gearbox with a trolley jack and interposed block of wood,
and remove the previously-positioned support from between the
gearbox bellhousing and the subframe.
33   Support the engine with the hoist and lifting tackle, and gently
lower the engine into position in the engine compartment.
34   Mate the engine and the gearbox together, ensuring that the
gearbox locates on the dowels in the cylinder block, then refit the three
upper engine-to-gearbox bolts (ensuring that any brackets noted during
removal are in place) – do not fully tighten the bolts at this stage.
35   Refit the four lower engine-to-gearbox bolts (again ensuring that
any brackets noted during removal are in place), but again do not fully
tighten them at this stage.
36   Fit the right-hand engine mounting bracket to the cylinder block,
and tighten its securing bolts to the specified torque.
37   Coat the engine mounting-to-body bolts with thread-locking
compound, then manipulate the engine and gearbox as necessary to
enable the bolts to be fitted. Fit the bolts and tighten them to the
specified torque.
38   Tighten all the engine-to-gearbox bolts to the specified torque,
then disconnect the lifting tackle and hoist from the engine, and remove
the trolley jack from beneath the gearbox.
39   Refit the gearbox bellhousing cover plate.
40   Refit the clutch, where applicable, as described in Chapter 6,
and/or engage the gearbox input shaft with the splined hub of the clutch
friction disc (as described in Chapter 6, Section 4).
41   Refit the front section of the exhaust system, as described in
Chapter 4.
42   Refit the crankshaft pulley, with reference to Section 5 in Part A.
43   Lower the vehicle to the ground.
44   Refit and reconnect all relevant pipes, wires and hoses, etc, using a
reversal of the removal procedure described in paragraphs 8 to 17
inclusive.
45   Where applicable, refit the power steering pump, and on 1.8 and
2.0 litre models, tension the pump drivebelt, as described in Chapter 10.
46   Refit the alternator and tension the drivebelt, as described in
Chapter 12.
47   Refit the air cleaner components, with reference to Chapter 4 if
necessary, and where applicable on carburettor models, reconnect the
hot air hose to the exhaust manifold hot air shroud.
48   Fill the engine with oil, and where applicable fit a new oil filter, as
described in Chapter 1.
49   Refit the radiator as described in Chapter 3, and refill the cooling
system as described in Chapter 1.
50   Refit the bonnet as described in Chapter 11, and on DOHC engine
models, refit the engine undershield.

25.2 Gear selector rod clamp sleeve (arrowed)

51   Reconnect the battery leads.
52   On completion, where applicable bleed the power steering fluid circuit as described in Chapter 10.

25   Engine/manual gearbox assembly – removal and refitting

Removal

1   Proceed as described in Section 24, paragraphs 1 to 17 inclusive.
2   Working in the engine compartment, make alignment marks between the gear selector rod and the clamp sleeve, then loosen the clamp bolt, and disconnect the gear selector rod from the clamp sleeve (photo).
3   Remove the retaining clip, then slide the clutch cable from the release lever, pushing the release lever back towards the bulkhead if necessary to allow the cable to be disconnected. Pull the cable support from the bracket on the gearbox casing, then move the cable to one side out of the way, taking note of its routing.
4   Disconnect the wiring from the reversing light switch, which is located at the front of the gearbox casing.
5   Unscrew the securing sleeve, and disconnect the speedometer cable from the gearbox.
6   Unscrew the retaining nut, and disconnect the earth strap from the gearbox endplate.
7   Make a final check to ensure that all relevant pipes, hoses, wires, etc, have been disconnected, and that they are positioned clear of the engine and gearbox.
8   Proceed as described in Section 24, paragraphs 20 to 22 inclusive.
9   Disconnect the inboard ends of the driveshafts from the differential, with reference to the relevant paragraphs of Chapter 8, Section 2. Be prepared for oil spillage as the driveshafts are withdrawn, and plug the apertures in the differential, to prevent further loss of oil and dirt ingress. Support the driveshafts by suspending them with wire or string – **do not** allow them to hand down under their own weight.
10   Attach a hoist and suitable lifting tackle to the engine lifting brackets on the cylinder head, and support the weight of the engine.
11   Remove the left-hand engine/gearbox mounting completely by unscrewing the two bolts securing the rubber mounting to the vehicle body, and the three bolts securing the mounting bracket to the gearbox.
12   Unbolt the right-hand engine mounting from the body and from the cylinder block, and withdraw the mounting bracket.
13   Working under the vehicle, unscrew and remove the two nuts securing the engine/gearbox rear mounting to the front subframe, and the three bolts securing the mounting bracket to the gearbox, then withdraw the mounting bracket.
14   Carefully swing the engine/gearbox assembly across the engine compartment as necessary, to allow the assembly to be lifted vertically

from the vehicle by raising the hoist. Take care not to damage any of the surrounding components in the engine compartment.
15   With the engine/gearbox assembly removed, support the assembly on suitable blocks of wood positioned on a workbench, or failing that, on a clean area of the workshop floor.
16   Clean away any external dirt using paraffin or a water-soluble solvent and a stiff brush.
17   Unbolt and remove the gearbox bellhousing cover plate.
18   Ensure that both engine and gearbox are adequately supported, then unscrew and remove the engine-to-gearbox bolts, noting the locations of any brackets which may be secured by the bolts.
19   Carefully withdraw the gearbox from the engine, ensuring that the weight of the gearbox is not allowed to hang on the input shaft while it is engaged with the clutch friction disc. Note that the gearbox locates on dowels positioned in the cylinder block.

Refitting

Note: *New bolts must be used to secure the left-hand engine/gearbox mounting to the body on refitting, and new locking plates must be used on the bolts securing the rear engine/gearbox mounting to the gearbox. Suitable thread-locking compound will be required to coat the threads of the right-hand engine mounting-to-body bolts. An M10 x 1.25 mm tap may be required during this procedure – see text.*

20   Before commencing the refitting operations, check that the two original bolts which secure the left-hand engine/gearbox rubber mounting to the vehicle body rotate freely in their threaded bores in the body. If necessary, re-cut the threaded bores using an M10 x 1.25 mm tap.
21   On models where the clutch can be removed and refitted with the engine and gearbox in the vehicle, if the clutch has been removed, it will prove easier to refit after the engine/gearbox assembly has been refitted to the vehicle.
22   Carefully offer the gearbox to the engine until the bellhousing is located on the dowels in the cylinder block, then refit the engine-to-gearbox bolts, and tighten them to the specified torque. Make sure that any brackets secured by the bolts are correctly positioned as noted before removal. If the clutch is still bolted to the flywheel, ensure that the weight of the gearbox is not allowed to hang on the input shaft as it is engaged with the clutch friction disc.
23   If the clutch is in place, refit the gearbox bellhousing cover plate.
24   With the front of the vehicle raised and supported on axle stands, support the engine/gearbox assembly with the hoist and lifting tackle, then gently lower it into position in the engine compartment.
25   Working under the vehicle, refit the rear engine/gearbox mounting to the gearbox, using new locking plates under the bolt heads, and tighten the bolts to the specified torque.
26   Fit the two bolts securing the engine/gearbox rear mounting to the front subframe, but do not fully tighten them at this stage.
27   Fit the right-hand engine mounting bracket to the cylinder block, and tighten the securing bolts to the specified torque.
28   Coat the right-hand engine mounting-to-body bolts with thread-locking compound, then fit the bolts, but do not fully tighten them at this stage.
29   Fit the left-hand gearbox mounting bracket to the gearbox, and tighten the securing bolts to the specified torque.
30   Fit new left-hand gearbox mounting-to-body bolts, and tighten them to the specified torque.
31   Tighten the right-hand engine mounting and the rear engine/gearbox mounting-to-front subframe bolts to their specified torques, then remove the lifting tackle and the hoist from the engine.
32   Where applicable, the clutch can now be fitted, and/or the gearbox input shaft can be pressed into engagement with the splined hub of the clutch friction disc, as described in Chapter 6. Refit the gearbox bellhousing cover plate, where applicable.
33   Reconnect the inboard ends of the driveshafts to the differential, with reference to the relevant paragraphs in Chapter 8, Section 2, using new snap-rings.
34   Refit the front section of the exhaust system, as described in Chapter 4.
35   Refit the crankshaft pulley, with reference to Section 5 in Part A.
36   Reconnect the gearbox earth strap, and tighten the securing nut.
37   Lower the vehicle to the ground.
38   Reconnect the speedometer cable to the gearbox, and tighten the securing sleeve.
39   Reconnect the reversing light switch wiring.

40 Refit the clutch cable to the bracket on the gearbox casing, then reconnect the cable to the release lever, and adjust the cable as described in Chapter 6. Ensure that the cable is routed as noted during removal.
41 Reconnect the gear selector rod to the clamp sleeve, ensuring that the marks made before disconnection are aligned, and tighten the clamp bolt.
42 Proceed as described in Section 24, paragraphs 44 to 49 inclusive.
43 Top-up the gearbox oil level, as described in Chapter 1.
44 Refit the bonnet as described in Chapter 11, and on DOHC engine models, refit the engine undershield.
45 Reconnect the battery leads.

26 Engine – removal and refitting (leaving automatic transmission in vehicle)

Removal

1 Proceed as described in Section 24, paragraphs 1 to 17 inclusive.
2 Make a final check to ensure that all relevant hoses, pipes and wires have been disconnected, and that they are positioned clear of the engine.
3 Unscrew and remove the three upper engine-to-transmission bolts, accessible from the engine compartment, noting the location of any brackets which may be secured by the bolts.
4 Proceed as described in Section 24, paragraphs 20 to 22 inclusive.
5 Unbolt and remove the transmission bellhousing cover plate.
6 If the original torque converter and driveplate are to be refitted, make alignment marks between the torque converter and the driveplate, to ensure that the components are reassembled in their original positions.
7 Working through the bottom of the bellhousing, unscrew the three torque converter-to-driveplate bolts. It will be necessary to turn the crankshaft using a suitable spanner or socket on the crankshaft pulley or sprocket bolt (as applicable), to gain access to each bolt in turn through the aperture. Use a screwdriver or a similar tool to jam the driveplate ring gear, preventing the driveplate from rotating as the bolts are loosened. Discard the bolts.
8 Attach a suitable hoist and lifting tackle to the engine lifting brackets on the cylinder head, and support the weight of the engine.
9 Support the transmission using a trolley jack with an interposed block of wood to spread the load.
10 Unbolt the right-hand engine mounting from the cylinder block and the body, and withdraw the mounting bracket.
11 Unscrew and remove the lower engine-to-transmission bolts, then manipulate the engine as necessary to separate it from the transmission, noting that the transmission locates on dowels in the cylinder block. Ensure that the torque converter is held firmly in place in the transmission casing as the engine and transmission are separated, otherwise it could fall out, resulting in fluid spillage and possible damage. Retain the torque converter while the engine is removed by bolting a strip of metal across the transmission bellhousing end face.
12 Carefully raise the hoist, and lift the engine from the vehicle, taking care not to damage any of the surrounding components in the engine compartment.
13 With the engine removed, the transmission can be supported by placing a suitable length of wood between the bellhousing and the front suspension subframe. Once the wooden support is in place, remove the trolley jack from under the transmission.

Refitting

Note: *New torque converter-to-driveplate bolts must be used on refitting, and if the original torque converter is being used, an M10 x 1.25 mm tap will be required. Suitable thread-locking compound will be required to coat the threads of the right-hand engine mounting-to-body bolts.*

14 With the front of the vehicle raised and supported on axle stands, support the transmission with a trolley jack and interposed block of wood, and remove the previously-positioned support from between the transmission bellhousing and the subframe.
15 If the original torque converter is still in place, commence refitting by recutting the torque converter-to-driveplate bolt threads in the torque converter using an M10 x 1.25 mm tap.

16 Support the engine with the hoist and lifting tackle, and gently lower the engine into position in the engine compartment.
17 Where applicable, remove the strip of metal retaining the torque converter in the transmission casing, and hold the torque converter in position as the engine is mated to the transmission.
18 Ensure that the transmission locates on the dowels in the cylinder block, then refit the three upper engine-to-transmission bolts (ensuring that any brackets are in place as noted before removal) – do not fully tighten the bolts at this stage.
19 Refit the lower engine-to-transmission bolts (again ensuring that any brackets are in place), but again do not fully tighten them at this stage.
20 Fit the right-hand engine mounting bracket to the cylinder block, and tighten its securing bolts to the specified torque.
21 Coat the engine mounting-to-body bolts with thread-locking compound, then manipulate the engine and transmission as necessary to enable the bolts to be fitted. Fit the bolts and tighten them to the specified torque.
22 Tighten all the engine-to-transmission bolts to the specified torque, then disconnect the lifting tackle and hoist from the engine, and remove the trolley jack from beneath the transmission.
23 If the original torque converter and driveplate have been refitted, carefully turn the crankshaft to align the marks made before removal, before fitting the torque converter-to-driveplate bolts.
24 Fit **new** torque converter-to-driveplate bolts, and tighten them to the specified torque. Turn the crankshaft for access to each bolt in turn, and prevent the driveplate from turning as during removal.
25 Refit the transmission bellhousing cover plate.
26 Proceed as described in Section 24, paragraphs 41 to 52 inclusive.
27 Check the transmission fluid level and top-up if necessary, as described in Chapter 1.

27 Engine/automatic transmission assembly – removal and refitting

Removal

1 Proceed as described in Section 24, paragraphs 1 to 17 inclusive.
2 To reduce fluid spillage as the driveshafts are withdrawn from the transmission, drain the transmission fluid as described in Chapter 7, Section 14.
3 Unscrew the securing sleeve, and disconnect the speedometer cable from the transmission.
4 If not already done, apply the handbrake, then jack up the front of the vehicle and support securely on axle stands (see 'Jacking, towing and wheel changing').
5 Remove the crankshaft pulley, with reference to Section 5 in Part A.
6 Remove the front section of the exhaust system, as described in Chapter 4.
7 Disconnect the transmission fluid cooler hoses either at the transmission or at the radiator, noting their routing. Clamp or plug the hoses to minimise fluid loss and dirt ingress.
8 Disconnect the transmission wiring harness connector, and unbolt the two wiring harness brackets from the transmission casing.
9 Disconnect the vent hose from the transmission (the vent hose is located below the battery tray), noting its routing.
10 Remove the retaining clamp and the washer, and disconnect the selector cable from the actuating lever on the transmission. Move the cable to one side away from the transmission.
11 Make a final check to ensure that all relevant pipes, hoses, wires, etc, have been disconnected, and that they are positioned clear of the engine and transmission.
12 Proceed as described in Section 25, paragraphs 9 to 14 inclusive, substituting 'transmission' for 'gearbox'.
13 With the engine/transmission assembly removed, support the assembly on suitable blocks of wood positioned on a workbench, or failing that, on a clean area of the workshop floor.
14 Clean away any external dirt using paraffin or a water-soluble solvent and a stiff brush.
15 Unbolt and remove the transmission bellhousing cover plate.
16 If the original torque converter and driveplate are to be refitted, make alignment marks between the torque converter and the driveplate, to ensure that the components are reassembled in their original positions.

17   Ensure that both the engine and transmission are adequately supported, then working through the bottom of the bellhousing, unscrew the three torque converter-to-driveplate bolts. It will be necessary to turn the crankshaft using a suitable spanner or socket on the crankshaft pulley or sprocket bolt (as applicable), to gain access to each bolt in turn through the aperture. Use a screwdriver or a similar tool to jam the driveplate ring gear, preventing the driveplate from rotating as the bolts are loosened. Discard the bolts.

18   Unscrew and remove the engine-to-transmission bolts, noting the locations of any brackets which may be secured by the bolts.

19   Carefully pull the engine and transmission apart, ensuring that the torque converter is held firmly in place in the transmission casing, otherwise it could fall out, resulting in fluid spillage and possible damage. It may be necessary to rock the units slightly to separate them. If the transmission is to be left removed for some time, retain the torque converter by bolting a strip of metal across the bellhousing end face.

Refitting

Note: *New torque converter-to-driveplate bolts must be used on refitting. New bolts must be used to secure the left-hand engine/gearbox mounting to the body on refitting, and new locking plates must be used on the bolts securing the rear engine/gearbox mounting to the gearbox. Suitable thread-locking compound will be required to coat the threads of the right-hand engine mounting-to-body bolts. An M10 x 1.25 mm tap may be required during this procedure – see text.*

20   If the original torque converter is being refitted, commence refitting by recutting the torque converter-to-driveplate bolt threads in the torque converter using an M10 x 1.25 mm tap.

21   If a new transmission is being fitted, the manufacturers recommend that the radiator fluid cooler passages are flushed clean before the new transmission is installed. Ideally, compressed air should be used (in which case, ensure that adequate safety precautions are taken); alternatively, the cooler can be flushed with clean automatic transmission fluid until all the old fluid has been expelled, and fresh fluid runs clear from the cooler outlet.

22   Check that the two original bolts which secure the left-hand engine/transmission rubber mounting to the vehicle body rotate freely in their threaded bores in the body. If necessary, re-cut the threaded bores using an M10 x 1.25 mm tap.

23   Carefully offer the transmission to the engine until the bellhousing is located on the dowels in the cylinder block (ensure that the torque converter is held firmly in place in the transmission casing as the engine and transmission are connected), then refit the engine-to-transmission bolts, and tighten them to the specified torque. Make sure that any brackets secured by the bolts are correctly positioned as noted before removal.

24   If the original torque converter and driveplate are being refitted, carefully turn the crankshaft to align the marks made before removal, before fitting the torque converter-to-driveplate bolts.

25   Fit **new** torque converter-to-driveplate bolts, and tighten them to the specified torque. Turn the crankshaft for access to each bolt in turn, and prevent the driveplate from turning as during removal.

26   Refit the transmission bellhousing cover plate.

27   Attach the lifting tackle to the engine/transmission assembly, then lower the assembly into the engine compartment, and reconnect the mountings as described in Section 25, paragraphs 24 to 31 inclusive, substituting 'transmission' for 'gearbox'.

28   Reconnect the inboard ends of the driveshafts to the differential, with reference to the relevant paragraphs in Chapter 8, Section 2, using new snap-rings.

29   Reconnect the transmission vent hose, ensuring that it is routed as noted before removal.

30   Reconnect the selector cable to the actuating lever on the transmission, and adjust the cable as described in Chapter 7.

31   Refit the transmission wiring harness brackets, and reconnect the transmission wiring harness connector.

32   Reconnect the transmission fluid cooler hoses, using new sealing washers where applicable, and making sure that they are correctly routed.

33   Refit the front section of the exhaust system, as described in Chapter 4.

34   Refit the crankshaft pulley, with reference to Section 5 in Part A.

35   Lower the vehicle to the ground.

36   Reconnect the speedometer cable, and tighten the securing sleeve.

37   Proceed as described in Section 24, paragraphs 44 to 49 inclusive.

38   Refill the transmission with the correct quantity and type of fluid, through the dipstick tube.

39   Refit the bonnet as described in Chapter 11, and on DOHC engine models, refit the engine undershield.

40   Make a final check to ensure that all hoses, pipes and wires have been correctly reconnected.

41   Reconnect the battery leads.

42   On completion, where applicable bleed the power steering fluid circuit as described in Chapter 10, and top-up the automatic transmission fluid level as described in Chapter 1.

28   Engine overhaul – dismantling sequence

1   It is far easier to dismantle and work on the engine if it is mounted on a portable engine stand. These stands can often be hired from a tool hire shop. Depending on the type of stand used, the flywheel/driveplate may have to be removed from the engine to allow the engine stand bolts to be tightened into the end of the cylinder block.

2   If a stand is not available, it is possible to dismantle the engine while supported on blocks on a sturdy workbench or on the floor. Be extra-careful not to tip or drop the engine when working without a stand.

3   Before starting the overhaul procedure, the external engine ancillary components must be removed (this is the case even if a reconditioned engine is to be fitted, in which case, the components from the old engine must be transferred to the reconditioned unit). These components include the following.

    (a)   Alternator and mounting bracket (see Chapter 12).
    (b)   Starter motor (see Chapter 12).
    (c)   Rear coolant gallery and hoses.
    (d)   Inlet and exhaust manifolds (see Chapter 4).
    (e)   Oil filter (see Chapter 1).
    (f)   Distributor/coil components (as applicable), HT leads and spark plugs (see Chapter 1 or 5).
    (g)   Engine mounting (see Section 19 in Part A).
    (h)   Oil pressure switch (see Chapter 12).
    (i)   Crankcase breather tube.
    (j)   Engine lifting brackets.
    (k)   TDC sensor and bracket (where applicable) (see Chapter 5).
    (l)   Coolant temperature sensor (where applicable) (see Chapter 5).
    (m)   Knock sensor (DOHC engines) (see Chapter 5).
    (n)   Thermostat and cover (1.8 and 2.0 litre engines) (see Chapter 3).
    (o)   Fuel pump (1.4 litre carburettor models) (see Chapter 4).
    (p)   Power steering pump mounting bracket (1.8 and 2.0 litre engines) (see Chapter 10).
    (q)   Power steering pump (where applicable – 1.4 and 1.6 litre engines) (see Chapter 10).
    (r)   Wiring harnesses.
    (s)   Dipstick.

Note: *When removing the ancillary components from the engine, pay close attention to details which may be helpful or important during refitting. Note the fitted position of gaskets, seals, spacers, washers, bolts and other small items.*

4   If a 'short' engine is being obtained (which consists of the cylinder block, crankshaft, pistons and connecting rods all assembled as a unit), then the cylinder head, sump, timing belt (SOHC engines only), and possibly other components (such as the oil pump) will have to be removed from the old unit and fitted to the new unit.

5   If a complete overhaul is being planned, the engine can be dismantled using the following sequence.

    (a)   Inlet and exhaust manifolds (see Chapter 4).
    (b)   Timing belt and sprockets (see Sections 7 and 8 in Part A).
    (c)   Cylinder head (see Section 13 in Part A).
    (d)   Flywheel/driveplate (see Section 18 in Part A).
    (e)   Sump (see Section 14 in Part A).
    (f)   Oil pump (see Section 15 in Part A).
    (g)   Piston/connecting rod assemblies (see Section 32).
    (h)   Crankshaft (see Section 33).

29.1 Removing the thermostat housing from the cylinder head – 2.0 litre SOHC engine

29.2 Using a rubber suction plunger tool to remove a valve lifter – DOHC engine

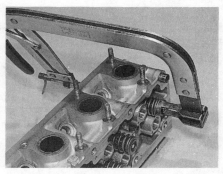

29.3 Valve spring compressor tool fitted to No 1 exhaust valve – 2.0 litre SOHC engine

6   Before beginning the dismantling and overhaul procedures, make sure that all of the correct tools have been obtained. Refer to the preliminary Sections at the beginning of this manual for further information.

29 Cylinder head – dismantling

Note: *New and reconditioned cylinder heads are available from the manufacturers and from engine overhaul specialists. Due to the fact that some specialist tools are required for the dismantling and inspection procedures, and new components may not be readily available, it may be more practical and economical for the home mechanic to purchase a reconditioned head rather than to dismantle, inspect and recondition the*

29.5 Extracting a split collet – SOHC engine

original head. A valve spring compressor tool will be required for this operation.

1   With the cylinder head removed as described in Section 13 in Part A, clean away all external dirt, and remove the following components, if not already done.

(a)   Remove the manifolds (see Chapter 4).
(b)   Remove the spark plugs (see Chapter 5).
(c)   Remove the thermostat housing (photo), and on 1.4 and 1.6 litre engines, the thermostat (see Chapter 3).
(d)   On DOHC engines, remove the camshafts (see Section 12 in Part A).

2   On DOHC engines, remove the hydraulic valve lifters from their bores using a rubber suction plunger tool (photo) – do not invert the cylinder head in order to remove the valve lifters. Keep the valve lifters upright at all times (oil groove at the bottom – see Fig. 2.18), and immerse them in order of removal in a container of clean engine oil until they are to be refitted.
3   To remove a valve, fit a valve spring compressor tool. Ensure that the arms of the compressor tool are securely positioned on the head of the valve and the spring cap (photo).
4   Compress the valve spring to relieve the pressure of the spring cap acting on the collets. If the spring cap sticks to the valve stem, support the compressor tool and give the end a light tap with a soft-faced mallet to help free the spring cap.
5   Extract the two split collets, then slowly release the compressor tool (photo).

Fig. 2.18 The valve lifters should be kept upright, with the oil groove (arrowed) at the bottom – DOHC engine (Sec 29)

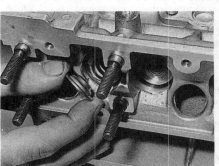

29.6A Remove the spring cap, ...

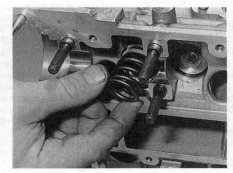

29.6B ... spring, ...

29.6C ... valve stem oil seal (arrowed), ...

29.6D ... and spring seat, ...

29.6E ... then extract the valve – DOHC engine

29.7 Place each valve assembly in a labelled polythene bag

6   Remove the spring cap, spring, valve stem oil seal, and the spring seat, then withdraw the valve through the combustion chamber (photos).

7   Repeat the procedure for the remaining valves, keeping all components in strict order so that they can be refitted in their original positions, unless all the components are to be renewed. If the components are to be kept and used again, place each valve assembly in a labelled polythene bag or a similar small container. Note that as with cylinder numbering, the valves are normally numbered from the timing belt end of the engine (photo). Make sure that on DOHC engines, the valve components are identified as inlet and exhaust, as well as numbered.

30 Cylinder head and valve components – cleaning and inspection

1   Thorough cleaning of the cylinder head and valve components, followed by a detailed inspection, will enable a decision to be made on whether further work is necessary before reassembling the components.

Cleaning

2   Scrape away all traces of old gasket material and sealing compound from the cylinder head surfaces. Take care not to damage the cylinder head surfaces, as the head is made of light alloy.

3   Scrape away the carbon from the combustion chambers and ports, then wash the cylinder head thoroughly with paraffin or a suitable solvent.

4   Scrape off any heavy carbon deposits that may have formed on the valves, then use a power-operated wire brush to remove deposits from the valve heads and stems.

Inspection

Note: Be sure to perform all the following inspection procedures before concluding that the services of a machine shop or engine overhaul specialist are required. Make a list of all items that require attention.

Cylinder head

5   Inspect the head very carefully for cracks, evidence of coolant leakage, and other damage. If cracks are found, a new cylinder head should be obtained.

6   Use a straight-edge and feeler blade to check that the cylinder head surface is not distorted (photo). If the specified distortion limit is exceeded, it may be possible to have the cylinder head resurfaced, provided that the overall height of the head is not reduced to less than the specified minimum.

7   Examine the valve seats in each of the combustion chambers. If the seats are severely pitted, cracked or burned, then they will need to be recut by an engine overhaul specialist. If only slight pitting is evident, this can be removed by grinding the valve heads and seats together with coarse then fine grinding paste, as described later in this Section.

8   If the valve guides are worn, indicated by a side-to-side motion of the valve, the guides can be reamed, and valves with oversize stems can be fitted. This work is best carried out by an engine overhaul specialist. A dial gauge may be used to determine whether the amount of side play of a valve exceeds the specified maximum.

9   Check the valve lifter bores in the cylinder head for wear. If excessive wear is evident, the cylinder head must be renewed. Also check the valve lifter oil holes in the cylinder head for obstructions.

10   On 1.8 and 2.0 litre engines, an oil pressure regulating valve is fitted to the oil gallery in the cylinder head (photo). This valve can be renewed if it appears to be damaged, or if its operation is suspect, and access is gained via the circular plug covering the end of the valve. The old valve must be crushed, then its remains extracted, and a thread (M10) cut in the valve seat to allow removal using a suitable bolt. A new valve and plug can then be driven into position. In view of the intricacies of this operation, it is probably best to have the valve renewed by a Vauxhall/Opel dealer if necessary.

11   On 1.8 and 2.0 litre SOHC engines, always renew the sealing ring between the cylinder head and the thermostat housing when the head is removed for overhaul (photo). Reference to Chapter 3 will show that a considerable amount of work is involved if it is wished to renew the sealing ring with the cylinder head installed.

Valves

Warning: The exhaust valves fitted to DOHC engines are filled with sodium to improve heat transfer. Sodium is a highly-reactive metal, which will ignite or explode spontaneously on contact with water (including water vapour in the air). Valves containing sodium must NOT be disposed of with ordinary scrap – seek advice from a Vauxhall/Opel dealer if the valves are to be disposed of.

12   Examine the head of each valve for pitting, burning, cracks and general wear, and check the valve stem for scoring and wear ridges. Rotate the valve, and check for any obvious indication that it is bent. Look for pitting and excessive wear on the end of each valve stem. If the valve appears satisfactory at this stage, measure the valve stem diameter at several points using a micrometer (photo). Any significant difference in the readings obtained indicates wear of the valve stem. Should any of these conditions be apparent, the valve(s) must be renewed. If the valves are in satisfactory condition, they should be ground (lapped) onto their respective seats to ensure a smooth gas-tight seal.

13   Valve grinding is carried out as follows. Place the cylinder head upside-down on a bench, with a block of wood at each end to give clearance for the valve stems.

14   Smear a trace of coarse carborundum paste on the seat face in the cylinder head, and press a suction grinding tool onto the relevant valve head. With a semi-rotary action, grind the valve head to its seat, lifting the valve occasionally to redistribute the grinding paste (photo). When a dull, matt, even surface is produced on the faces of both the valve seat and the valve, wipe off the paste and repeat the process with fine carborundum paste. A light spring placed under the valve head will greatly ease this operation. When a smooth unbroken ring of light grey matt finish is produced on both the valve and seat faces, the grinding operation is complete. Carefully clean away every trace of grinding paste, taking great care to leave none in the ports or in the valve guides. Clean the valves and valve seats with a paraffin-soaked rag, then with a clean rag, and finally, if an air line is available, blow the valves, valve guides and cylinder head ports clean.

Valve components

15   Check that all the valve springs are intact. If any one is broken, all should be renewed.

16   If possible, check the free height of the springs against new ones,

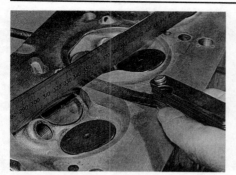
30.6 Checking the cylinder head surface for distortion

30.10 Cylinder head oil pressure regulating valve (1) and plug (2) – 2.0 litre SOHC engine

30.11 Renewing the thermostat housing sealing ring – 2.0 litre SOHC engine

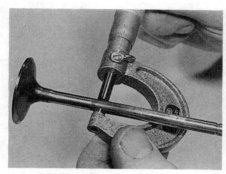
30.12 Measuring a valve stem diameter

30.14 Grinding-in a valve seat

then stand each spring on a flat surface and check it for squareness. If a spring is found to be too short, or damaged in any way, renew all the springs as a set. Springs suffer from fatigue, and it is a good idea to renew them even if they look serviceable.

Rocker arm components – SOHC engines

17   Check the rocker arm and thrust pad faces (the areas that contact the valve lifters and valve stems) for pits, wear, score-marks or any indication that the surface-hardening has worn through. Check the rocker arm camshaft contact faces in the same manner. Clean the oil hole in the top of each rocker arm using a length of wire. Renew any rocker arms or thrust pads which appear suspect.

Valve lifters – SOHC engines

18   Proceed as described in paragraph 9.
19   On engines which have covered a high mileage, or for which the service history (particularly oil changes) is suspect, it is possible for the valve lifters to suffer internal contamination, which in extreme cases may result in increased engine top-end noise and wear. To minimise the possibility of problems occurring later in the life of the engine, it is advisable to dismantle and clean the hydraulic valve lifters as follows whenever the cylinder head is overhauled. Note that no spare parts are available for the valve lifters, and if any of the components are unserviceable, the complete assembly must be renewed (photo).
20   Carefully pull the collar from the top of the valve lifter cylinder. It should be possible to remove the collar by hand – if a tool is used, take care not to distort the collar.
21   Withdraw the plunger from the cylinder, and recover the spring.
22   Using a small screwdriver, carefully prise the cap from the base of the plunger. Recover the spring and ball from under the cap, taking care not to lose them as the cap is removed.
23   Carefully clean all the components using paraffin or a suitable solvent, paying particular attention to the machined surfaces of the cylinder (internal surfaces), and piston (external surfaces). Thoroughly dry all the components using a lint-free cloth. Carefully examine the springs for damage or distortion – the complete valve lifter must be renewed if the springs are not in perfect condition.
24   Lubricate the components sparingly with clean engine oil of the correct grade (see Chapter 1), then reassemble as follows.

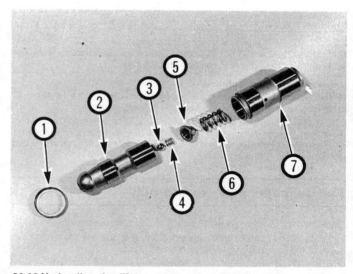
30.19 Hydraulic valve lifter components – SOHC engine

1   Collar
2   Plunger
3   Ball
4   Small spring
5   Plunger cap
6   Large spring
7   Cylinder

25   Invert the plunger, and locate the ball on its seat in the base of the plunger (photo).
26   Locate the smaller spring on its seat in the plunger cap, then carefully refit the cap and spring, ensuring that the spring locates on the ball. Carefully press around the flange of the cap, using a small screwdriver if necessary, until the flange is securely located in the groove in the base of the plunger (photos).
27   Locate the larger spring over the plunger cap, ensuring that the spring is correctly seated, and slide the plunger and spring assembly into the cylinder (photos).

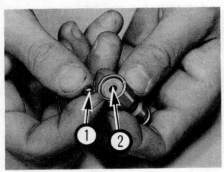

30.25 Locate the ball (1) on its seat (2) in the base of the plunger

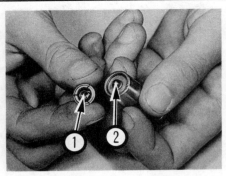

30.26A Spring (1) located in plunger cap, and ball (2) located on seat in plunger

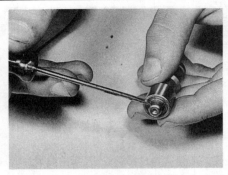

30.26B Locate the cap flange in the plunger groove

30.27A Locate the spring over the plunger cap ...

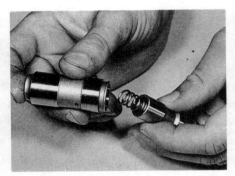

30.27B ... then slide the plunger and spring assembly into the cylinder

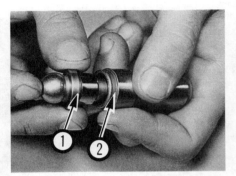

30.28 Slide the collar (1) over the top of the plunger and engage with the groove (2) in the cylinder

28   Slide the collar over the top of the plunger, and carefully compress the plunger by hand, until the collar can be pushed down to engage securely with the groove in the cylinder (photo).

Valve lifters – DOHC engines

Note: *The valve lifters should always be stored upright in a container of clean engine oil while removed from the cylinder head.*

29   Inspect the valve lifters for obvious signs of wear on the contact faces, and check the valve lifter oil holes for obstructions, particularly for oil sludge. If excessive wear is evident (this is unlikely), all the valve lifters must be renewed as a set.

31   Cylinder head – reassembly

Note: *New valve stem oil seals should be used on reassembly.*

1   With all the components cleaned, starting at one end of the cylinder head, fit the valve components as follows (photo).

2   Insert the appropriate valve into its guide (if new valves are being fitted, insert each valve into the location to which it has been ground), ensuring that the valve stem is well-lubricated with clean engine oil (photo). If the original components are being refitted, all components must be refitted in their original positions.

3   Fit the spring seat (photo).

4   New valve stem oil seals should be supplied with a fitting sleeve, which fits over the collet groove in the valve stem, to prevent damage to the oil seal as it is slid down the valve stem (photo). If no sleeve is supplied, wind a short length of tape round the top of the valve stem to cover the collet groove.

5   Lubricate the valve stem oil seal with clean engine oil, then push the oil seal down the valve stem using a suitable tube or socket until the seal is fully engaged with the spring seat (photos). Remove the fitting sleeve or the tape, as applicable, from the valve stem.

6   Fit the valve spring and the spring cap (photos).

7   Fit the spring compressor tool, and compress the valve spring until the spring cap passes beyond the collet groove in the valve stem.

8   Apply a little grease to the collet groove, then fit the split collets into

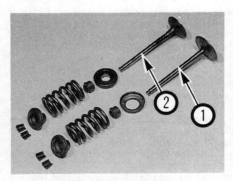

31.1 Inlet (1) and exhaust (2) valve components – SOHC engine

31.2 Inserting an exhaust valve into its guide – SOHC engine

31.3 Fitting a valve seat (exhaust valve shown) – SOHC engine

31.4 Slide the oil seal fitting sleeve down the valve stem ...

31.5A ... then fit the valve stem oil seal ...

31.5B ... and push onto the spring seat using a suitable socket – SOHC engine

31.6A Fit the valve spring ...

31.6B ... and spring cap

31.8 Use a little grease to hold the split collets in place

the groove, with the narrow ends nearest the spring. The grease should hold them in the groove (photo).

9   Slowly release the compressor tool, ensuring that the collets are not dislodged from the groove. When the compressor is fully released, give the top of the valve assembly a tap with a soft-faced mallet to settle the components.

10   Repeat the procedure for the remaining valves, ensuring that if the original components are being used, they are all refitted in their original positions.

11   On DOHC engines, refit the hydraulic valve lifters to the cylinder head in their original positions. Liberally oil the valve lifter bores, and if new valve lifters are being fitted, initially immerse each one in a container of clean engine oil and compress it (by hand) several times to charge it.

12   Refit the following components as applicable (if desired these components can be refitted after refitting the cylinder head).

(a) On DOHC engines, refit the camshafts (see Section 12 in Part A).

(b) Refit the thermostat housing (complete with thermostat on 1.4 and 1.6 litre engines), using a new sealing ring, where applicable (photo) – see Chapter 3.

(c) Refit the spark plugs (see Chapter 5).

(d) Refit the manifolds (see Chapter 4).

31.12 Fitting a new thermostat housing sealing ring – DOHC engine

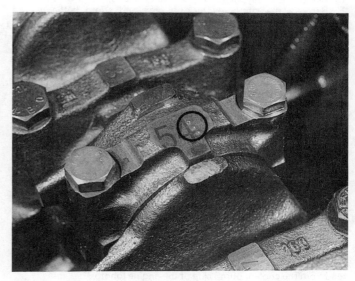

32.3 Big-end cap centre punch identification marks (circled). Note that lug on bearing cap faces flywheel end of engine – 2.0 litre SOHC engine

33.6 Check the crankshaft endfloat using a dial gauge ...

33.7 ... or a feeler gauge – 2.0 litre SOHC engine

33.8 Main bearing cap identification marks (arrowed) – 1.6 litre engine

32 Piston/connecting rod assembly – removal

1 Remove the cylinder head as described in Section 13 in Part A.
2 Remove the sump, oil pick-up pipe and sump baffle (where applicable), as described in Section 14 in Part A.
3 If the connecting rods and big-end caps are not marked to indicate their positions in the cylinder block (ie cylinder numbers), centre-punch them at adjacent points either side of the cap/rod joint. Note to which side of the engine the marks face (photo).
4 Unscrew the big-end cap bolts from the first connecting rod, and remove the cap. If the bearing shells are to be re-used, tape the cap and the shell together.
5 Check the top of the cylinder bore for a wear ridge. If evident, carefully scrape it away with a ridge reamer tool, otherwise as the piston is pushed out of the block, the piston rings may jam against the ridge.
6 Place the wooden handle of a hammer against the bottom of the connecting rod, and push the piston/rod assembly up and out of the cylinder bore. Recover the bearing shell, and tape it to the connecting rod if it is to be re-used.
7 Remove the remaining three assemblies in a similar way. Rotate the crankshaft as necessary to bring the big-end bolts to the most accessible position.

33 Crankshaft – removal

1 Remove the cylinder head as described in Section 13 in Part A.
2 Remove the sump, oil pick-up pipe and sump baffle (where applicable), as described in Section 14 in Part A.
3 Remove the oil pump as described in Section 15.
4 Remove the pistons and connecting rods, as described in Section 32. If no work is to be done on the pistons and connecting rods, there is no need to push the pistons out of the cylinder bores.
5 Invert the engine so that the crankshaft is uppermost.
6 Before removing the crankshaft, check the endfloat using a dial gauge in contact with the end of the crankshaft. Push the crankshaft fully one way and then zero the gauge. Push the crankshaft fully the other way, and check the endfloat (photo). The result should be compared with the specified limit, and will give an indication as to whether new thrust bearing shells are required.
7 If a dial gauge is not available, a feeler gauge can be used to measure crankshaft endfloat. Push the crankshaft fully towards one end of the crankcase, and insert a feeler gauge between the thrust flange of the centre main bearing shell and the machined surface of the crankshaft web (photo). Before measuring, ensure that the crankshaft is fully forced towards one end of the crankcase, to give the widest possible gap at the measuring location.
8 The main bearing caps are numbered 1 to 4 from the timing belt end of the engine. The rear (flywheel end) cap is not marked. To ensure that the caps are refitted the correct way round, note that the numbers are read from the coolant pump side of the engine (photo).
9 Unscrew and remove the main bearing cap bolts, and tap off the bearing caps. If the bearing shells are to be re-used, tape them to their respective caps.

33.10 Lifting the crankshaft from the crankcase

10 Lift the crankshaft from the crankcase (photo).
11 Extract the upper bearing shells, and identify them for position if they are to be re-used.

34 Cylinder block/crankcase – cleaning and inspection

Cleaning

1 For complete cleaning, ideally the core plugs should be removed, where fitted. Drill a small hole in the plugs, then insert a self-tapping screw and pull out the plugs using a pair of grips or a slide hammer. Also remove all external components (senders, sensors, brackets, etc).
2 Note that, where applicable, the rubber plug located next to the bellhousing flange on the cylinder block covers the aperture for the installation of a diagnostic TDC sensor (used by Vauxhall/Opel dealers). The sensor, when connected to a suitable monitoring unit, indicates TDC from the position of the pins set into the crankshaft balance weight.
3 Scrape all traces of gasket from the cylinder block, taking particular care not to damage the cylinder head and sump mating faces.
4 Remove all oil gallery plugs, where fitted. The plugs are usually very tight – they may have to be drilled out and the holes re-tapped. Use new plugs when the engine is reassembled.
5 If the block is extremely dirty, it should be steam-cleaned.
6 If the block has been steam-cleaned, clean all oil holes and oil galleries one more time on completion. Flush all internal passages with warm water until the water runs clear, dry the block thoroughly and wipe all machined surfaces with a light oil. If you have access to compressed air, use it to speed the drying process, and to blow out all the oil holes and galleries. **Warning:** *Wear eye protection when using compressed air!*

7 If the block is relatively clean, an adequate cleaning job can be achieved with hot soapy water and a stiff brush. Take plenty of time, and do a thorough job. Regardless of the cleaning method used, be sure to clean all oil holes and galleries very thoroughly, dry the block completely, and coat all machined surfaces with light oil.

8 The threaded holes in the cylinder block must be clean, to ensure accurate torque readings when tightening fixings during reassembly. Run the correct-size tap (which can be determined from the size of the relevant bolt which fits in the hole) into each of the holes to remove rust, corrosion, thread sealant or other contamination, and to restore damaged threads. If possible, use compressed air to clear the holes of debris produced by this operation. Do not forget to clean the threads of all bolts and nuts as well.

9 After coating the mating surfaces of the new core plugs with suitable sealant, fit them to the cylinder block. Make sure that they are driven in straight and seated correctly, or leakage could result. Special tools are available for this purpose, but a large socket, with an outside diameter which will just fit into the core plug, will work just as well.

10 Where applicable, apply suitable sealant to the new oil gallery plugs, and insert them into the relevant holes in the cylinder block. Tighten the plugs securely.

11 If the engine is to be left dismantled for some time, refit the main bearing caps, tighten the bolts finger-tight, and cover the cylinder block with a large plastic bag to keep it clean and prevent corrosion.

Inspection

12 Visually check the block for cracks, rust and corrosion. Look for stripped threads in the threaded holes (it may be possible to re-cut stripped threads using a suitable tap). If there has been any history of internal coolant leakage, it may be worthwhile asking an engine overhaul specialist to check the block using special equipment. If defects are found, have the block repaired if possible, otherwise renewal may be the only solution.

13 Examine the cylinder bores for taper, ovality, scoring and scratches. Start by carefully examining the top of the cylinder bores. If they are at all worn, a very slight ridge will be found on the thrust side. This marks the top of the piston ring travel.

14 Measure the bore diameter of each cylinder at the top (just under the wear ridge), centre and bottom of the cylinder bore, parallel to the crankshaft axis.

15 Next, measure the bore diameter at the same three locations, at right-angles to the crankshaft axis. Compare the results with the figures given in the Specifications.

16 Repeat the procedure for the remaining cylinders.

17 If the cylinder wear exceeds the permitted tolerances, or if the cylinder walls are badly scored or scuffed, then the cylinders will have to be rebored by a suitably-qualified specialist, and new oversize pistons will have to be fitted. In this case, note the following points.

(a) *Pistons and cylinder bores are closely matched in production. The actual diameter of the piston is indicated by numbers on its crown (photo); the same numbers on the crankcase indicate the cylinder bore diameter.*

(b) *After reboring has taken place, the cylinder bores should be measured accurately, and oversize pistons selected from the grades available to give the specified piston-to-bore clearance.*

(c) *For grading purposes, the piston diameter is measured across the bottom of the skirt.*

18 If the bore wear is marginal, and within the specified tolerances, new special piston rings can be fitted to offset the wear.

19 If this is the case, the bores should be honed in order to allow the new rings to bed in correctly and provide the best possible seal. The conventional type of hone has spring-loaded stones, and is used with a power drill. You will also need some paraffin or honing oil and rags. The hone should be moved up and down the cylinder bore to produce a crosshatch pattern, and plenty of honing oil should be used. Ideally, the cross-hatch lines should intersect at approximately a 60° angle. Do not remove more material than is necessary to produce the required finish. If new pistons are being fitted, the piston manufacturers may specify a finish with a different angle, so their instructions should be followed. Do not withdraw the hone from the cylinder while it is still being turned – stop it first. After honing a cylinder, wipe out all traces of the honing oil. An engine overhaul specialist will be able to carry out this work at moderate cost, if required.

35 Piston/connecting rod assembly – inspection

1 Before the inspection process can begin, the piston/connecting rod assemblies must be cleaned, and the original piston rings removed from the pistons.

2 Carefully expand the old rings over the top of the pistons. The use of two or three old feeler gauges will be helpful in preventing the rings dropping into empty grooves (photo).

3 Scrape away all traces of carbon from the top of the piston. A hand-held wire brush or a piece of fine emery cloth can be used once the majority of the deposits have been scraped away.

4 Remove the carbon from the ring grooves in the piston, using an old ring. Break the ring in half to do this (be careful not to cut your fingers – piston rings are sharp). Be very careful to remove only the carbon deposits – do not remove any metal, and do not nick or scratch the sides of the ring grooves.

5 Once the deposits have been removed, clean the piston/connecting rod assembly with paraffin or a suitable solvent, and dry thoroughly. Make sure that the oil return holes in the ring grooves are clear.

6 If the pistons and cylinder bores are not damaged or worn excessively, and if the cylinder block does not need to be rebored, the original pistons can be refitted. Normal piston wear shows up as even

34.17 Piston diameter marking (arrowed) on piston crown

35.2 Using a feeler gauge to aid removal of a piston ring

vertical wear on the piston thrust surfaces, and slight looseness of the top ring in its groove. New piston rings should always be used when the engine is reassembled.

7   Carefully inspect each piston for cracks around the skirt, at the gudgeon pin bosses, and at the piston ring lands.

8   Look for scoring and scuffing on the thrust faces of the piston skirt, holes in the piston crown, and burned areas at the edge of the crown. If the skirt is scored or scuffed, the engine may have been suffering from overheating, and/or abnormal combustion ('pinking') which caused excessively-high operating temperatures. The cooling and lubrication systems should be checked thoroughly. A hole in the piston crown, or burned areas at the edge of the piston crown indicates that abnormal combustion (pre-ignition, 'pinking', knocking, or detonation) has been occurring. If any of the above problems exist, the causes must be investigated and corrected, or the damage will occur again. The causes may include leaks in the intake air tracts, incorrect fuel/air mixture, or incorrect ignition timing.

9   Corrosion of the piston, in the form of pitting, indicates that coolant has been leaking into the combustion chamber and/or the crankcase. Again, the cause must be corrected, or the problem may persist in the rebuilt engine.

10   Check the piston-to-bore clearance by measuring the cylinder bore (see Section 34) and the piston diameter. Measure the piston across the bottom of the skirt, at a 90° angle to the gudgeon pin. Subtract the piston diameter from the bore diameter to obtain the clearance. If this is greater than the figures given in the Specifications, the block will have to be rebored, and new pistons and rings fitted.

11   On SOHC engines, check the fit of the gudgeon pin by twisting the piston and connecting rod in opposite directions. Any noticeable play indicates excessive wear, which must be corrected. If the pistons or connecting rods are to be renewed, it is necessary to have this work carried out by a Vauxhall/Opel dealer or a suitable engine overhaul specialist, who will have the necessary tooling to remove the gudgeon pins.

12   On DOHC engines, inspect the gudgeon pin circlips for security and signs of damage, and renew if necessary.

13   Examine the mating faces of the big-end caps and connecting rods to see if they have ever been filed, in a mistaken attempt to take up bearing wear. This is extremely unlikely, but if evident, the offending connecting rods and caps must be renewed.

14   Check the alignment of the connecting rods visually, and if the rods are not straight, take them to an engine overhaul specialist for a more detailed check.

36.7 Measuring the diameter of a crankshaft journal

measurement at each end of the journal, near the webs, to determine if the journal is tapered. If the crankshaft journals are damaged, tapered, out-of-round or excessively-worn, the crankshaft will have to be reground and undersize bearings fitted.

8   Check the oil seal contact surfaces at each end of the crankshaft for wear and damage. If the seal has worn an excessive groove in the surface of the crankshaft, consult an engine overhaul specialist, who will be able to advise whether a repair is possible or whether a new crankshaft is necessary.

9   Where applicable, check the teeth of the TDC sensor wheel for damage. If evident, the sensor wheel can be renewed after unscrewing the three securing bolts – in this case, consult a Vauxhall/Opel dealer, as it may be necessary to have the crankshaft assembly balanced before reassembling the engine.

10   Similarly, where applicable, check the condition of the pins in the front crankshaft balance weight, which serve as detent points for the plug-in diagnostic sensor used by Vauxhall/Opel dealers.

37 Main and big-end bearings – inspection

1   Even though the main and big-end bearings should be renewed during engine overhaul, the old bearings should be retained for close examination, as they may reveal valuable information about the condition of the engine. The bearing shells carry identification marks to denote their size in the form of a colour code, or a letter/number code marked on the back of the shell (photos). If the shells are to be renewed, without carrying out any crankshaft regrinding, the old shells should be taken along when obtaining new shells to ensure that the correct shells are obtained.

2   Bearing failure occurs because of lack of lubrication, the presence of dirt or other foreign particles, overloading the engine, or corrosion. If a bearing fails, the cause must be found and eliminated before the engine is reassembled, to prevent the failure from happening again.

3   To examine the bearing shells, remove them from the cylinder block, the main bearing caps, the connecting rods and the big-end bearing caps, and lay them out on a clean surface in the same order as they were fitted to the engine. This will enable any bearing problems to be matched with the corresponding crankshaft journal.

4   Dirt and other foreign particles can enter the engine in a variety of ways. Contamination may be left in the engine during assembly, or it may pass through filters or the crankcase ventilation system. Normal engine wear produces small particles of metal, which can eventually cause problems. If particles find their way into the lubrication system, it is likely that they will eventually be carried to the bearings. Whatever the source, these foreign particles often end up embedded in the soft bearing material, and are easily recognized. Large particles will not embed in the bearing, and will score or gouge the bearing and journal.

36 Crankshaft – inspection

1   Clean the crankshaft using paraffin or a suitable solvent, and dry it, preferably with compressed air if available. **Warning:** *Wear eye protection when using compressed air!* Be sure to clean the oil holes with a pipe cleaner or similar probe, to ensure that they are not obstructed.

2   Check the main and big-end bearing journals for uneven wear, scoring, pitting and cracking.

3   Big-end bearing wear is accompanied by distinct metallic knocking when the engine is running (particularly noticeable when the engine is pulling from low revs), and some loss of oil pressure.

4   Main bearing wear is accompanied by severe engine vibration and rumble – getting progressively worse as engine revs increase – and again by loss of oil pressure.

5   Check the bearing journal for roughness by running a finger lightly over the bearing surface. Any roughness (which will be accompanied by obvious bearing wear) indicates that the crankshaft requires regrinding.

6   If the crankshaft has been reground, check for burrs around the crankshaft oil holes (the holes are usually chamfered, so burrs should not be a problem unless regrinding has been carried out carelessly). Remove any burrs with a fine file or scraper, and thoroughly clean the oil holes as described previously.

7   Using a micrometer, measure the diameter of the main and big-end bearing journals, and compare the results with the Specifications at the beginning of this Chapter (photo). By measuring the diameter at a number of points around each journal's circumference, you will be able to determine whether or not the journal is out-of-round. Take the

37.1A Typical main bearing shell ...

37.1B ... and main thrust bearing shell identification marks –
1.6 litre engine

To prevent possible contamination, clean all parts thoroughly, and keep everything spotlessly-clean during engine assembly. Once the engine has been installed in the vehicle, ensure that regular engine oil and filter changes are carried out at the recommended intervals.

5   Lack of lubrication (or lubrication breakdown) has a number of interrelated causes. Excessive heat (which thins the oil), overloading (which squeezes the oil from the bearing face), and oil leakage (from excessive bearing clearances, worn oil pump or high engine speeds) all contribute to lubrication breakdown. Blocked oil passages, which may be the result of misaligned oil holes in a bearing shell, will also starve a bearing of oil and destroy it. When lack of lubrication is the cause of bearing failure, the bearing material is wiped or extruded from the steel backing of the bearing. Temperatures may increase to the point where the steel backing turns blue from overheating.

6   Driving habits can have a definite effect on bearing life. Full-throttle, low-speed operation (labouring the engine) puts very high loads on bearings, which tends to squeeze out the oil film. These loads cause the bearings to flex, which produces fine cracks in the bearing face (fatigue failure). Eventually the bearing material will loosen in places, and tear away from the steel backing. Regular short journeys can lead to corrosion of bearings because insufficient engine heat is produced to drive off the condensed water and corrosive gases which form inside the engine. These products collect in the engine oil, forming acid and sludge. As the oil is carried to the bearings, the acid attacks and corrodes the bearing material.

7   Incorrect bearing installation during engine assembly will also lead to bearing failure. Tight-fitting bearings leave insufficient bearing lubrication clearance, and will result in oil starvation. Dirt or foreign particles trapped behind a bearing shell results in high spots on the bearing which can lead to failure.

8   If new bearings are to be fitted, the bearing running clearances should be measured before the engine is finally reassembled, to ensure that the correct bearing shells have been obtained (see Sections 40 and 41). If the crankshaft has been reground, the engineering works which carried out the work will advise on the correct-size bearing shells to suit the work carried out. If there is any doubt as to which bearing shells should be used, seek advice from a Vauxhall/Opel dealer.

38   Engine overhaul – reassembly sequence

1   Before reassembly begins, ensure that all necessary new parts have been obtained (particularly gaskets, and various bolts which must be renewed), and that all the tools required are available. Read through the entire procedure to familiarise yourself with the work involved, and to ensure that all items necessary for reassembly of the engine are to hand. In addition to all normal tools and materials, a thread-locking compound

will be required. A tube of RTV sealing compound will also be required, to seal certain joint faces which are not fitted with gaskets.

2   In order to save time and avoid problems, engine reassembly can be carried out in the following order.

(a)   Piston rings (see Section 39).
(b)   Crankshaft and main bearings (see Section 40).
(c)   Piston/connecting rod assemblies (see Section 41).
(d)   Oil pump (see Section 15 in Part A).
(e)   Sump (see Section 14 in Part A).
(f)   Cylinder head, valve lifters, camshafts and rocker components (where applicable) (see Sections 12 and 13 in Part A).
(g)   Timing belt and sprockets (see Sections 7 and 8 in Part A).
(h)   Flywheel/driveplate (see Section 18 in Part A).
(i)   Engine external components.

39   Piston rings – refitting

1   Before refitting the new piston rings, the ring end gaps must be checked as follows.

2   Lay out the piston/connecting rod assemblies and the new piston ring sets, so that the ring sets will be matched with the same piston and cylinder during the end gap measurement and subsequent engine reassembly.

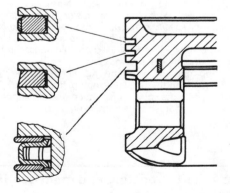

Fig. 2.19 Sectional view showing correct orientation of piston rings – all engines (Sec 39)

39.5 Measuring a piston ring end gap using a feeler gauge

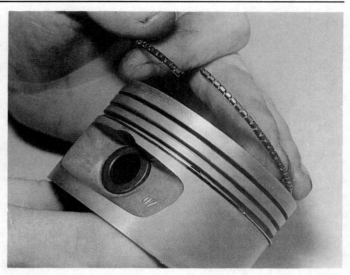

39.10 Fitting an oil control spreader ring

3   Insert the top ring into the first cylinder, and push it down the bore using the top of the piston. This will ensure that the ring remains square with the cylinder walls. Position the ring near the bottom of the cylinder bore, at the lower limit of ring travel.

4   Measure the end gap using feeler gauges.

5   Repeat the procedure with the ring at the top of the cylinder bore, at the upper limit of its travel, and compare the measurements with the figures given in the Specifications (photo).

6   If the gap is too small (unlikely if genuine Vauxhall/Opel parts are used), it must be enlarged or the ring ends may contact each other during engine operation, causing serious damage. Ideally, new piston rings providing the correct end gap should be fitted, but as a last resort, the end gap can be increased by filing the ring ends very carefully with a fine file. Mount the file in a vice equipped with soft jaws, slip the ring over the file with the ends contacting the file face, and slowly move the ring to remove material from the ends – take care, as piston rings are sharp, and are easily broken.

7   With new piston rings, it is unlikely that the end gap will be too large, and if the gaps are too large, check that you have the correct rings for your engine and for the particular cylinder bore size.

8   Repeat the checking procedure for each ring in the first cylinder, and then for the rings in the remaining cylinders. Remember to keep rings, pistons and cylinders matched up.

9   Once the ring end gaps have been checked and if necessary corrected, the rings can be fitted to the pistons.

10   The oil control ring (lowest one on the piston) is composed of three sections, and should be installed first. Fit the lower steel ring, then the spreader ring, followed by the upper steel ring (photo).

11   With the oil control ring components installed, the second (middle) ring can be fitted. It is usually stamped with a mark ('TOP') which must face up, towards the top of the piston. **Note:** *Always follow the instructions supplied with the new piston ring sets – different manufacturers may specify different procedures. Do not mix up the top and middle rings, as they have different cross-sections.* Using two or three old feeler blades, as for removal of the old rings, carefully slip the ring into place in the middle groove.

12   Fit the top ring in the same manner, ensuring that, where applicable, the mark on the ring is facing up. If a stepped ring is being fitted, fit the ring with the smaller diameter of the step uppermost.

13   Repeat the procedure for the remaining pistons and rings.

40   Crankshaft – refitting and main bearing running clearance check

1   Refitting the crankshaft is the first step in the engine reassembly procedure. It is assumed at this point that the cylinder block and

crankshaft have been cleaned, inspected and repaired or reconditioned as necessary.

2   Position the cylinder block with the sump mating face uppermost.

Main bearing running clearance check

Note: *When finally refitting the crankshaft, new main bearing cap bolts must be used. However, when checking the bearing running clearance, the original bolts should be used, and then discarded. A vernier dial indicator, an internal micrometer, or 'Plastigage' will be required for this check – see text.*

3   Clean the bearing shells and the bearing recesses in both the cylinder block and main bearing caps. If new shells are being fitted, ensure that all traces of the protective grease are cleaned off using paraffin. Wipe the shells dry with a clean lint-free cloth.

4   Note that the central bearing shells have thrust flanges which control crankshaft endfloat. If the original bearing shells are being re-used, they must be refitted to their original locations in the block and caps (photos).

5   Before the crankshaft can be permanently installed, the main bearing running clearance should be checked, and this can be done in either of two ways. One method is to fit the main bearing caps to the cylinder block, with bearing shells in place. With the original cap retaining bolts tightened to the specified torque, measure the internal diameter of each assembled pair of bearing shells using a vernier dial indicator or an internal micrometer. If the diameter of each corresponding crankshaft journal is measured and then subtracted from the bearing internal diameter, the result will give the main bearing running clearance. The second (and more accurate) method is to use an American product known as 'Plastigage'. This consists of a fine thread of perfectly-round plastic, which is compressed between the bearing cap shell and the crankshaft journal. When the bearing cap is removed, the deformed plastic can be measured with a special card gauge supplied with the Plastigage kit. The running clearance is determined from this gauge. Plastigage is sometimes difficult to obtain in this country, but enquiries at one of the larger specialist chains of quality motor factors should produce the name of a stockist in your area. The procedure for using Plastigage is as follows.

6   With the upper main bearing shells in place in the cylinder block, carefully lay the crankshaft in position. Do not use any lubricant; the crankshaft journals and bearing shells must be perfectly clean and dry.

7   Cut several pieces of the appropriate-size Plastigage (they should be slightly shorter than the width of the main bearings) and place one piece on each crankshaft journal axis (photo).

8   With the bearing shells in position in the caps, fit the caps to their original locations. Take care not to disturb the Plastigage.

9   Starting with the centre main bearing and working outwards, tighten the main bearing cap bolts (use the original bolts) progressively to their specified torque. Do not rotate the crankshaft at any time during this operation.

10   Remove the bearing cap bolts and carefully lift off the caps,

40.4A Main bearing shell (A) and central main bearing shell (B) with thrust flange

40.4B Fitting a main bearing shell to the cylinder block

40.7 Lay the length of Plastigage on the journal to be measured, parallel to the crankshaft centre line

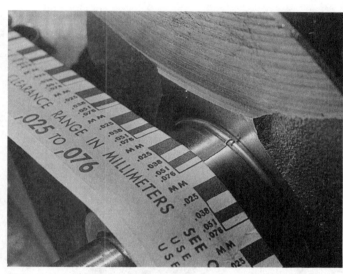

40.11 Using the scale on the envelope provided to check (at its widest point) the width of the crushed Plastigage and measure the bearing running clearance

dirt or oil was trapped between the bearing shells and the caps or block when the clearance was measured. If the Plastigage was wider at one end than at the other, the crankshaft journal may be tapered.

13 Carefully remove all traces of the Plastigage material from the crankshaft and bearing shells, using a fingernail or other improvised tool which is unlikely to score the shells.

Final crankshaft refitting

Note: *New main bearing cap bolts must be used when refitting the crankshaft. Suitable sealants (Vauxhall/Opel Nos 15 03 294 and 15 04 201, or equivalents) will be required to coat the front and rear main bearing caps.*

14 Carefully lift the crankshaft out of the cylinder block once more.

15 Lubricate the lips of a new crankshaft rear oil seal, and carefully slip it over the rear of the crankshaft. Do this carefully, as the seal lips are very delicate. Ensure that the open side of the seal faces the inside of the engine.

16 Liberally lubricate each bearing shell in the cylinder block (photo), and lower the crankshaft into position. Check that the rear oil seal is positioned correctly.

17 If necessary, seat the crankshaft using light taps from a soft-faced mallet on the crankshaft balance webs.

18 Lubricate the bearing shells in the bearing caps, and the crankshaft journals, then fit Nos 2, 3 and 4 bearing caps, and tighten the new bolts as far as possible by hand.

19 Fill the side grooves of the front (where applicable – not all engines have grooves in the front main bearing cap) and rear main bearing caps with RTV jointing compound (Vauxhall/Opel part No 15 03 294, or equivalent), and coat the lower surfaces of the bearing caps with sealing compound (Vauxhall/Opel part No 15 04 201, or equivalent). Fit the bearing caps, and tighten the new bolts as far as possible by hand. Ensure that the front main bearing cap is exactly flush with the end face of the cylinder block (photos).

20 Working from the centre main bearing cap outwards, tighten the bearing cap bolts to the specified torque in the two stages given in the Specifications; ie tighten all bolts to Stage 1, then tighten all bolts to Stage 2 (photos).

keeping them in order. Do not disturb the Plastigage or rotate the crankshaft. If any of the bearing caps are difficult to remove, free them by carefully tapping with a soft-faced mallet.

11 Compare the width of the deformed Plastigage on each journal with the scale printed on the card gauge to obtain the main bearing running clearance (photo).

12 If the clearance is not as specified, the bearing shells may be the wrong size (or excessively-worn if the original shells are being re-used). Before deciding that different size shells are required, make sure that no

40.16 Lubricate the main bearing shells before fitting the crankshaft

40.19A Fill the side grooves of the rear main bearing cap with RTV jointing compound ...

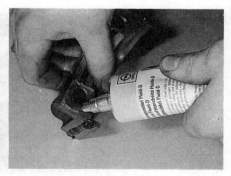

40.19B ... and the lower surfaces with sealing compound

40.19C Fitting the centre main bearing cap

40.20A Tighten the main bearing cap bolts to the specified torque ...

40.20B ... then through the specified angle – 2.0 litre SOHC engine

21   When all bolts have been fully tightened, inject further RTV jointing compound into the side grooves of the front (where applicable) and rear main bearing caps until it is certain that they are full.
22   Now rotate the crankshaft, and check that it turns freely, with no signs of binding or tight spots.
23   Check the crankshaft endfloat with reference to Section 33.
24   Refit the pistons and connecting rods as described in Section 41.
25   Refit the oil pump as described in Section 15 in Part A.
26   Refit the sump baffle (where applicable), oil pick-up pipe and sump, as described in Section 14 in Part A.
27   Refit the cylinder head as described in Section 13 in Part A.

41   Piston/connecting rod assembly – refitting and big-end bearing running clearance check

1   Clean the backs of the big-end bearing shells and the recesses in the connecting rods and big-end caps. If new shells are being fitted, ensure

that all traces of the protective grease are cleaned off using paraffin. Wipe the shells, caps and connecting rods dry with a lint-free cloth.
2   Press the bearing shells into the connecting rods and caps in their correct positions.

Big-end bearing running clearance check

Note: *When finally refitting the piston/connecting rod assemblies, new big-end bearing cap bolts must be used. However, when checking the bearing running clearance, the original bolts should be used, and then discarded. A piston ring compressor tool will be required for this operation.*

3   Lubricate No 1 piston and piston rings, and check that the ring gaps are correctly positioned. The gap in the lower steel ring of the oil control ring should be offset 25.0 to 50.0 mm to the right of the spreader ring gap, and the upper steel ring gap should be offset by the same distance to the left of the spreader ring gap. The upper compression ring should be positioned with the ring gap offset by 180° to the lower compression ring gap.
4   Liberally lubricate cylinder bore with clean engine oil.

41.5A Piston crown arrow must point towards timing belt end of engine – 1.6 litre engine

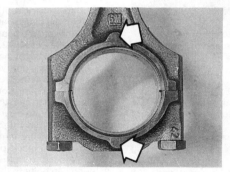

41.5B Lugs (arrowed) on connecting rod and big-end cap must point towards flywheel end of engine – 1.6 litre engine

41.5C Tapping a piston into its bore – 1.6 litre engine

41.9A Tighten the big-end bearing cap bolts to the specified torque ...

41.9B ... then through the specified angle – 1.6 litre engine

5   Fit a ring compressor to No 1 piston, then insert the piston and connecting rod into the cylinder bore so that the base of the compressor stands on the block. With the crankshaft big-end bearing journal positioned at its lowest point, tap the piston carefully into the cylinder bore with the wooden handle of a hammer, and at the same time guide the connecting rod onto the bearing journal. Note that the arrow or notch, as applicable, on the piston crown should point towards the timing belt end of the engine, and the lugs on the connecting rod and big-end bearing cap should point towards the flywheel end of the engine (photos). The oil spray hole in the connecting rod should be on the coolant pump side of the engine.

6   To measure the big-end bearing running clearance, refer to the information contained in Section 40, as the same general procedures apply. If the Plastigage method is being used, ensure that the big-end bearing journal and the bearing shells are clean and dry, then engage the connecting rod with the bearing journal. Lay the Plastigage strip on the bearing journal, fit the bearing cap in its original location (noting that the lug on the bearing cap should point towards the flywheel end of the engine), then tighten the original bearing cap bolts to the specified torque. Do not rotate the crankshaft during this operation. Remove the bearing cap, and check the running clearance by measuring the Plastigage as previously described.

7   Repeat the checking procedures on the remaining piston/connecting rod assemblies.

Final piston/connecting rod assembly refitting

Note: *New big-end bearing cap bolts must be used when refitting the piston/connecting rod assemblies.*

8   After checking the running clearance of all the big-end bearings and taking any corrective action necessary, clean off all traces of Plastigage from the bearing shells and journals.

9   Liberally lubricate the bearing journals and bearing shells, and refit the bearing caps once more, ensuring correct positioning as previously described. Tighten the new bearing cap bolts to the specified torque in the two stages given in the Specifications; ie tighten all bolts to Stage 1, then tighten all bolts to Stage 2 (photos).

10   After refitting each piston/connecting rod assembly, rotate the crankshaft, and check that it turns freely, with no signs of binding or tight spots.

11   Refit the sump baffle (where applicable), oil pick-up pipe and sump, as described in Section 14 in Part A.

12   Refit the cylinder head as described in Section 13 in Part A.

42 Engine – initial start-up after overhaul

1   With the engine refitted to the vehicle, check the engine oil and coolant levels.

2   With the spark plugs removed and the ignition system disabled by disconnecting the coil LT lead, or wiring plug (as applicable), crank the engine over on the starter until the oil pressure light goes out. This may take a few seconds as the new oil filter fills with oil.

3   Refit the spark plugs, and connect all the HT leads.

4   Start the engine, noting that this may take a little longer than usual as fuel is pumped to the engine. If a new camshaft has been fitted to SOHC engine models, pay careful attention to the running-in procedure given in Section 12 in Part A.

5   While the engine is idling, check for fuel, coolant and oil leaks. Where applicable, check the power steering and/or automatic transmission fluid pipe/hose unions for leakage. Do not be alarmed if there are some odd smells and smoke from parts getting hot and burning off oil deposits.

6   Keep the engine idling until hot coolant is felt circulating through the radiator top hose, indicating that the engine is at normal operating temperature, then check the ignition timing (where possible – see Chapter 1), and if necessary adjust the idle speed and mixture (where possible – see Chapter 1).

7   Stop the engine, and if the cylinder head has been removed, tighten the bolts to the Stage 5 torque setting.

8   Allow the engine to cool, then recheck the oil and coolant levels, and top-up as necessary.

9   If new pistons, rings or bearings have been fitted, the engine must be run-in at reduced speeds and loads for the first 500 miles (800 km). Do not operate the engine at full-throttle, or allow it to labour in any gear during this period. It is beneficial to change the engine oil and filter at the end of this period.

Chapter 3
Cooling, heating and ventilation systems

Contents

Specifications

System type	Pressurised, with front-mounted radiator, remote expansion tank, and electric cooling fan. Coolant pump driven by timing belt

Thermostat
Type..	Wax
Start-to-open temperature (all models).......................................	92°C
Fully-open temperature (all models)	107°C

Electric cooling fan
Switches on at (all models)..	100°C
Switches off at	95°C

Torque wrench settings

	Nm	lbf ft
Coolant pump bolts:		
1.4 and 1.6 litre engines..	8	6
1.8 and 2.0 litre engines..	25	18
Thermostat housing bolts (1.4 and 1.6 litre engines)	10	7
Thermostat cover bolts (1.8 and 2.0 litre engines).......................	8	6

1 Cooling system – general information and precautions

General information

Engine cooling is achieved using a pump-assisted system, in which the coolant is pressurised. The system consists of a radiator, a coolant pump driven by the engine timing belt, an electric cooling fan, a thermostat, an expansion tank, and connecting hoses.

The system works in the following way. Cold coolant from one side of the radiator, which is mounted at the front of the engine compartment, passes to the coolant pump, which forces the coolant through the coolant passages in the cylinder block and cylinder head. The coolant absorbs heat from the engine, and then returns to the radiator via the heater system. As the coolant flows across the radiator, it is cooled, and the cycle is repeated.

Air flows through the radiator, to cool the radiator as a result of the vehicle's forward motion. However, if the coolant temperature exceeds a given figure, a temperature-sensitive switch in the radiator switches on the electric cooling fan, to increase the airflow through the radiator. The fan only operates when necessary, with a consequent reduction in noise and energy consumption.

To reduce the time taken for the engine to warm up when starting from cold, the thermostat, located in the cylinder head outlet, prevents coolant flowing to the radiator until the temperature has risen sufficiently. Instead, the outflow from the cylinder head bypasses the radiator and is redirected around the engine. When the temperature reaches a given figure, the thermostat opens, to allow coolant to flow to the radiator. The thermostat is operated by the expansion of a temperature-sensitive wax capsule.

An expansion tank is incorporated in the system, to allow for coolant expansion. The system is topped-up through a filler cap on the expansion tank.

On models fitted with automatic transmission, the radiator incorporates a heat exchanger to cool the automatic transmission fluid.

Precautions

Warning: *Do not attempt to remove the expansion tank filler cap or disturb any part of the cooling system while the engine is hot, as there is a high risk of scalding. If the expansion tank filler cap must be removed before the engine and radiator have fully cooled (even though this is NOT recommended) the pressure in the cooling system must first be relieved. Cover the cap with a thick layer of cloth, to avoid scalding, and slowly unscrew the filler cap until a hissing sound can be heard. When the hissing has stopped, indicating that the pressure has reduced, slowly unscrew the filler cap until it can be removed; if more hissing sounds are heard, wait until they have stopped before unscrewing the cap completely. At all times, keep well away from the filler cap opening.*

Warning: *Do not allow antifreeze to come into contact with skin or painted surfaces of the vehicle. Rinse off spills immediately with plenty of water. Never leave antifreeze lying around in an open container or in a puddle on the driveway or garage floor. Children and pets are attracted by its sweet smell, but antifreeze can be fatal if ingested.*

Warning: *If the engine is hot, the electric cooling fan may start rotating even if the engine is not running, so be careful to keep hands, hair and loose clothing well clear when working in the engine compartment.*

2.3 Disconnecting the radiator top hose

2 Cooling system hoses – disconnection and renewal

Note: *Refer to the warnings given in Section 1 of this Chapter before proceeding.*

1 If the checks described in Chapter 1 reveal a faulty hose, it must be renewed as follows.

2 First drain the cooling system (see Chapter 1). If the coolant is not due for renewal, it may be re-used if it is collected in a clean container.

3 To disconnect a hose, use a screwdriver to slacken the clips, then move them along the hose, clear of the relevant inlet/outlet. Carefully work the hose free (photo). While the hoses can be removed with relative ease when new, or when hot, **do not** attempt to disconnect any part of the system while it is still hot.

4 Note that the radiator inlet and outlet stubs are fragile; do not use excessive force when attempting to remove the hoses. If a hose proves to be difficult to remove, try to release it by rotating the ends on the relevant inlet/outlet before attempting to free it. If all else fails, cut the hose with a sharp knife, then slit it so that it can be peeled off in two pieces. Although this may prove expensive if the hose is otherwise undamaged, it is preferable to buying a new radiator.

5 When fitting a hose, first slide the clips onto the hose, then work the hose into position. If clamp type clips were originally fitted, it is a good idea to replace them with screw type clips when refitting the hose. If the hose is stiff, use a little soapy water as a lubricant, or soften the hose by soaking it in hot water.

6 Work the hose into position, checking that it is correctly routed, then slide each clip along the hose until it passes over the flared end of the relevant inlet/outlet, before tightening the clip securely.

7 Refill the cooling system with reference to Chapter 1.

8 Check thoroughly for leaks as soon as possible after disturbing any part of the cooling system.

3 Radiator – removal, inspection and refitting

Removal

Note: *Refer to the warnings given in Section 1 of this Chapter before proceeding. Minor leaks from the radiator can be cured without removing the radiator, using a product such as Holts Radweld.*

1 The radiator can be removed complete with the cooling fan and shroud if there is no need to disturb the fan. If desired, the fan and its shroud can be removed from the radiator with reference to Section 6.

2 Disconnect the battery negative lead.

3 Drain the cooling system as described in Chapter 1.

4 Where applicable, disconnect the wiring plugs from the cooling fan and the cooling fan switch mounted in the bottom right-hand side of the radiator.

5 Disconnect the top hose from the radiator.

6 On models with automatic transmission, clamp the transmission fluid cooler hoses, then disconnect them from the cooler in the side of the radiator. Be prepared for fluid spillage, and plug the open ends of the cooler and hoses immediately, to minimise fluid loss and prevent dirt ingress.

7 Unscrew the two top radiator mounting bracket securing bolts, and lift the brackets from the radiator rubber mountings (photo).

8 Lift the radiator to disengage the lower securing lugs, and withdraw it from the vehicle (photo).

Inspection

9 If the radiator has been removed due to suspected blockage, reverse-flush it as described in Chapter 1. Clean dirt and debris from the radiator fins, using an air line (in which case, wear eye protection) or a soft brush. Be careful, as the fins are easily damaged, and are sharp.

3.7 Removing a top radiator mounting bracket

3.8 Withdrawing the radiator

3.14 Radiator mounting rubber (arrowed) in lower body panel

5.3 Lifting off the thermostat housing to expose the thermostat (arrowed) – 1.6 litre engine

5.10A Withdraw the thermostat cover complete with the thermostat ...

5.10B ... and recover the O-ring – 2.0 litre SOHC engine

10   If necessary, a radiator specialist can perform a 'flow test' on the radiator, to establish whether an internal blockage exists.
11   A leaking radiator must be referred to a specialist for permanent repair. Do not attempt to weld or solder a leaking radiator, as damage to the plastic components may result.
12   In an emergency, minor leaks from the radiator can be cured by using a suitable radiator sealant in accordance with its manufacturer's instructions with the radiator *in situ*.
13   If the radiator is to be sent for repair or renewed, remove all hoses, and the cooling fan switch.
14   Inspect the condition of the radiator mounting rubbers, and renew them if necessary (photo).

Refitting

Note: *Where applicable, new sealing rings must be used when reconnecting the automatic transmission fluid cooler hoses.*

15   Refitting is a reversal of removal, bearing in mind the following points.
16   Ensure that the radiator rubber mountings are in good condition and renew if necessary, and ensure that the lower securing lugs engage correctly as the radiator is refitted.
17   Where applicable, use new sealing rings when reconnecting the automatic transmission fluid cooler hoses, and on completion check and if necessary top-up the fluid level as described in Chapter 1.
18   Refill the cooling system as described in Chapter 1.

4   Expansion tank – removal and refitting

Removal

Note: *Refer to the warnings given in Section 1 of this Chapter before proceeding.*

1   Where applicable, disconnect the battery negative lead, and disconnect the coolant level sensor wiring plug from the expansion tank filler cap.
2   Unscrew the two securing nuts, and lift the expansion tank clear of the body for access to the two coolant hose connections.
3   Where applicable, unclip the octane coding plug assembly from the side of the expansion tank.
4   Disconnect the hose from the side of the tank, then clamp or plug the hose, and suspend it as high as possible above the height of the engine to prevent coolant loss.
5   Position a suitable container beneath the tank, then disconnect the bottom hose and allow the contents of the tank to drain into the container. Clamp or plug the bottom hose, then suspend the hose as high as possible above the engine to prevent coolant loss.
6   Withdraw the expansion tank from the engine compartment.

Refitting

7   Refitting is a reversal of removal, but on completion, check and if necessary top-up the coolant level, as described in Chapter 1. The coolant drained from the expansion tank during removal can be re-used, provided that it has not been contaminated.

5   Thermostat – removal, testing and refitting

Removal

1.4 and 1.6 litre engines

1   Partially drain the cooling system with reference to Chapter 1.
2   Remove the rear timing belt cover as described in Chapter 2.
3   Unscrew and remove the two thermostat housing securing bolts, and lift off the thermostat housing (photo).
4   If desired, disconnect the coolant hose from the thermostat housing, and remove the housing.
5   Withdraw the thermostat from the cylinder head, noting that coolant may be released from the radiator bottom outlet as the thermostat is withdrawn, even though the cooling system has been partially drained.
6   Remove the sealing ring from the edge of the thermostat.
7   The thermostat can be tested, as described later in this Section.

1.8 and 2.0 litre engines

8   Partially drain the cooling system with reference to Chapter 1.
9   Disconnect the radiator top hose from the thermostat cover.
10   Unscrew and remove the three thermostat cover securing bolts, and withdraw the cover complete with the thermostat. Recover the O-ring (photos).
11   If desired, the thermostat can be tested as described later in this Section.
12   Note that if it is necessary to renew the thermostat, the complete cover and thermostat must be renewed as an assembly, as the two components are not available separately.

Testing

13   A rough test of the thermostat may be made by suspending it with a piece of string in a container full of water. Heat the water to bring it to

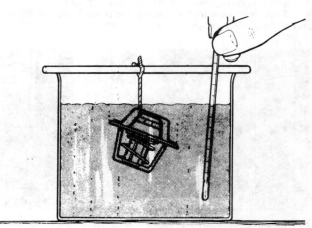

Fig. 3.1 Testing the thermostat opening temperature (Sec 5)

5.14 View of thermostat showing opening temperature markings

6.1 Cooling fan thermostatic switch (arrowed)

6.6 Disconnecting the cooling fan wiring plug

6.7A Cooling fan shroud securing bolt (arrowed) – DOHC engine

6.7B Withdrawing the cooling fan shroud assembly – 1.6 litre engine

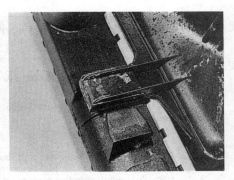

6.10 Ensure that the left-hand lower end of the fan shroud locates correctly in the clip on the radiator

the boil – the thermostat must open by the time the water boils. If not, renew it.

14   If a thermometer is available, the precise opening temperature of the thermostat may be determined, and compared with the figures given in the Specifications. The opening temperature is also marked on the thermostat (photo).

15   A thermostat which fails to close as the water cools must also be renewed.

Refitting

1.4 and 1.6 litre engines

16   Refitting is a reversal of removal, using a new sealing ring, and bearing in mind the following points.

17   Ensure that the lugs on the thermostat engage with the corresponding cut-outs in the cylinder head.

18   Refit the rear timing belt cover as described in Chapter 2.

19   Refill the cooling system with reference to Chapter 1.

1.8 and 2.0 litre engines

20   Refitting is a reversal of removal, but use a new O-ring, and on completion refill the cooling system, with reference to Chapter 1.

6   Electric cooling fan – testing, removal and refitting

Testing

1   The cooling fan is supplied with current via the ignition switch and fuse 11 (which may be mounted in the fusebox, or under the fusebox, depending on model – see Chapter 12). The circuit is completed by the cooling fan thermostatic switch, which is mounted in the lower right-hand side of the radiator (photo).

2   If the fan does not appear to work, run the engine until normal

operating temperature is reached, then allow it to idle. If the fan does not cut in within a few minutes, switch off the ignition and disconnect the wiring plug from the cooling fan switch. Bridge the two contacts in the wiring plug using a length of spare wire, and switch on the ignition. If the fan now operates, the switch is probably faulty and should be renewed.

3   If the fan still fails to operate, check that full battery voltage is available at the brown and white wire terminal of the switch; if not, then there is a fault in the feed wire to the switch (possibly due to a fault in the fan motor, or a blown fuse). If there is no problem with the feed, check that there is continuity between the switch brown wire terminal and a good earth point on the body; if not, then the earth connection is faulty and must be re-made.

4   If the switch and the wiring are in good condition, the fault must lie in the motor itself. The motor can be checked by disconnecting it from the wiring loom, and connecting a 12-volt supply directly to it. If the motor is faulty, it must be renewed, as no spares are available.

Removal

5   Disconnect the battery negative lead.

6   Disconnect the wiring from the cooling fan (photo).

7   Unscrew the two fan shroud securing bolts, then tilt the assembly back slightly towards the engine, and withdraw it upwards away from the radiator (photos).

8   To separate the fan motor from the shroud, unscrew the three securing nuts.

9   No spare parts are available for the motor, and if the unit is faulty, it must be renewed.

Refitting

10   Refitting is a reversal of removal, but ensure that the left-hand lower end of the fan shroud locates correctly in the clip on the radiator (photo).

11   On completion, start the engine and run it until it reaches normal operating temperature, then continue to run the engine and check that the cooling fan cuts in and functions correctly.

7.10A Coolant temperature gauge sender (arrowed) – 1.6 litre engine with multi-point fuel injection

7.10B Coolant temperature gauge sender location (arrowed) – 2.0 litre SOHC engine

7.10C Coolant temperature gauge sender location (arrowed) – 2.0 litre DOHC engine

7 Cooling system electrical switches – testing, removal and refitting

Electric cooling fan thermostatic switch

Testing
1   Testing of the switch is described in Section 6, as part of the electric cooling fan test procedure.

Removal
2   The switch is located in the lower right-hand side of the radiator. The engine and radiator should be cold before removing the switch.
3   Either partially drain the cooling system (as described in Chapter 1) to just below the level of the switch, or have ready a suitable plug which can be used to plug the switch aperture in the radiator while the switch is removed. If a plug is used, take great care not to damage the radiator, and do not use anything which will allow foreign matter to enter the radiator.
4   Disconnect the battery negative lead.
5   Disconnect the wiring plug from the switch.
6   Carefully unscrew the switch from the radiator, and recover the sealing ring.

Refitting
7   Refitting is a reversal of removal, but use a new sealing ring, and refill the cooling system as described in Chapter 1.
8   On completion, start the engine and run it until it reaches normal operating temperature, then continue to run the engine and check that the cooling fan cuts in and functions correctly.

Coolant temperature gauge sender

Testing
9   The coolant temperature gauge, mounted in the instrument panel, is fed with a stabilised voltage supply from the instrument panel feed (via the ignition switch and a fuse), and its earth is controlled by the sender.
10   The sender is screwed into the inlet manifold on 1.4 and 1.6 litre engines, and into the thermostat housing on 1.8 and 2.0 litre engines (photos). The sender contains a thermistor, which consists of an electronic component whose electrical resistance decreases at a predetermined rate as its temperature rises. When the coolant is cold, the sender resistance is high, current flow through the gauge is reduced, and the gauge needle points towards the blue (cold) end of the scale. If the sender is faulty, it must be renewed.
11   If the sender develops a fault, first check the other instruments; if they do not work at all, check the instrument panel electrical feed. If the readings are erratic, there may be a fault in the voltage stabiliser, which will necessitate renewal of the stabiliser (see Chapter 12). If the fault lies in the temperature gauge alone, check it as follows.
12   If the gauge needle remains at the 'cold' end of the scale, disconnect the sender wire, and earth it to the cylinder head. If the needle then deflects when the ignition is switched on, the sender unit is proved faulty, and should be renewed. If the needle still does not move, remove the instrument panel (Chapter 12) and check the continuity of

the brown/white wire between the sender unit and the gauge, and the feed to the gauge unit. If continuity is shown, and the fault still exists, then the gauge is faulty, and the gauge unit should be renewed.
13   If the gauge needle remains at the 'hot' end of the scale, disconnect the sender wire. If the needle then returns to the 'cold' end of the scale when the ignition is switched on, the sender unit is proved faulty and should be renewed. If the needle still does not move, check the remainder of the circuit as described previously.

Removal
Note: *Suitable sealant will be required to coat the sender threads when refitting.*

14   Partially drain the cooling system, as described in Chapter 1, to minimise coolant spillage.
15   Disconnect the battery negative lead.
16   Disconnect the wiring from the switch, then unscrew the switch from its location.

Refitting
17   Refitting is a reversal of removal, bearing in mind the following points.
18   Coat the threads of the sender with suitable sealant before fitting.
19   Top-up the cooling system as described in Chapter 1.
20   On completion, start the engine and check the operation of the temperature gauge. Also check for coolant leaks.

Coolant level sensor

Testing
21   On models fitted with a coolant level sensor, the sensor is located in the coolant expansion tank, and is an integral part of the expansion tank cap.
22   To test the sensor, with the engine cold, slowly unscrew the expansion tank cap to relieve any pressure in the cooling system.
23   Fully unscrew the cap, and carefully withdraw it, complete with the sensor.
24   Hold the cap/sensor assembly vertically, clear of the coolant in the expansion tank, taking care not to strain the wiring, then have an assistant switch on the ignition (do not start the engine).
25   Have your assistant observe the check control panel on the dashboard, which should indicate 'Coolant level'.
26   Switch off the ignition, and refit the cap/sensor assembly, then switch on the ignition again, and check that the check control panel does not indicate a problem.
27   If the sensor does not operate as described, check the wiring for obvious signs of damage.
28   If the wiring appears to be intact, further fault diagnosis must be entrusted to a Vauxhall/Opel dealer. Note that if the sensor is renewed, the cap and sensor must be renewed as an assembly.

Removal
29   The engine must be cold before attempting to remove the expansion tank cap.
30   Disconnect the battery negative lead.
31   Disconnect the wiring from the terminals on top of the expansion tank cap.

8.4 Withdrawing the coolant pump – 1.6 litre engine (O-ring arrowed)

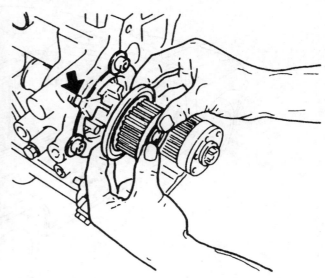

Fig. 3.2 Lugs (arrowed) on coolant pump and cylinder block must be aligned – DOHC engines (Sec 8)

32   Slowly unscrew the expansion tank cap to relieve any pressure in the cooling system, then withdraw the cap/sensor assembly.
33   Note that the sensor is an integral part of the cap, and the two cannot be separated.

Refitting

34   Refitting is a reversal of removal.

Coolant temperature sensor

35   Where fitted, this switch is part of the fuel injection system, and details can be found in Chapter 4.

8   Coolant pump – removal and refitting

1.4 and 1.6 litre engines

Note: *A new pump O-ring will be required when refitting, and suitable waterproof grease (Vauxhall/Opel No 19 70 206, or equivalent) will be required to coat the pump mounting face in the cylinder block.*

Removal

1   Drain the cooling system with reference to Chapter 1.
2   Remove the rear timing belt cover as described in Chapter 2.
3   Unscrew and remove the three coolant pump securing bolts.
4   Withdraw the coolant pump from the cylinder block, and recover the O-ring (photo). It may be necessary to tap the pump lightly with a soft-faced hammer to free it from the cylinder block.
5   No overhaul of the pump is possible, and if faulty, the unit must be renewed.

Refitting

6   Before refitting the pump, smear the pump mounting face in the cylinder block with a waterproof grease (Vauxhall/Opel No 19 70 206, or equivalent).
7   Fit the pump using a new O-ring, but do not fully tighten the pump securing bolts until the timing belt has been fitted and tensioned (Chapter 2).
8   Refit the rear timing belt cover as described in Chapter 2.
9   Refill the cooling system as described in Chapter 1.

1.8 and 2.0 litre engines

Note: *A new pump O-ring will be required when refitting, and suitable waterproof grease (Vauxhall/Opel No 19 70 206, or equivalent) will be required to coat the pump mounting face in the cylinder block. On DOHC engines, a new timing belt must be used on refitting (see Chapter 2).*

Removal

10   Drain the cooling system with reference to Chapter 1.
11   Remove the timing belt, as described in Chapter 2, and on DOHC engines, remove the timing belt rear cover.
12   On SOHC engines, unscrew and remove the bolt securing the smaller timing belt rear cover on the coolant pump to the cylinder block.
13   Proceed as described in paragraphs 3 to 5 inclusive.
14   If desired, the timing belt rear cover can be removed from the pump by rotating the cover to release it from the flange on the pump.

Refitting

15   Before refitting the pump, smear the pump mounting face in the cylinder block with a waterproof grease (Vauxhall/Opel No 19 70 206, or equivalent).
16   Fit the pump using a new O-ring, and on DOHC engines, ensure that the lugs on the pump and the cylinder block are aligned before tightening the pump securing bolts – see Fig. 3.2. On SOHC engine models, refit and tighten the bolt securing the smaller timing belt rear cover on the coolant pump to the cylinder block, but do not fully tighten the pump securing bolts until the timing belt has been fitted and tensioned (Chapter 2).
17   On DOHC engines, refit the timing belt rear cover, as described in Chapter 2.
18   Fit the timing belt, as described in Chapter 2 (on DOHC engines, a new timing belt must be fitted).
19   Refill the cooling system as described in Chapter 1.

9   Heating and ventilation system – general information

The heating/ventilation system consists of a pollen filter, a three-speed blower motor (housed in the engine compartment), face-level vents in the centre and at each end of the facia, and air ducts to the front and rear footwells.

The control unit is located in the facia, and the controls operate flap valves to deflect and mix the air flowing through the various parts of the heating/ventilation system. The flap valves are contained in the air distribution housing, which acts as a central distribution unit, passing air to the various ducts and vents.

Cold air enters the system through the grille at the rear of the engine compartment, and passes through the pollen filter. If required, the airflow is boosted by the blower, and then flows through the various ducts, according to the settings of the controls. Stale air is expelled through ducts behind the rear bumper. If warm air is required, the cold air is passed over the heater matrix, which is heated by the engine coolant.

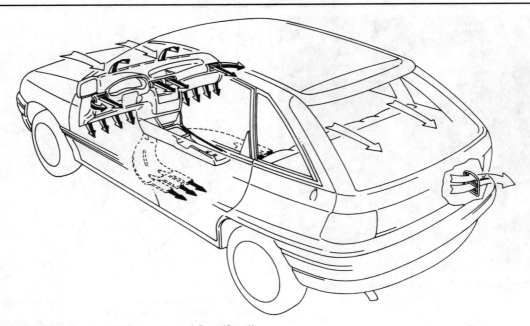

Fig. 3.3 Schematic view of heating/ventilation system airflow (Sec 9)

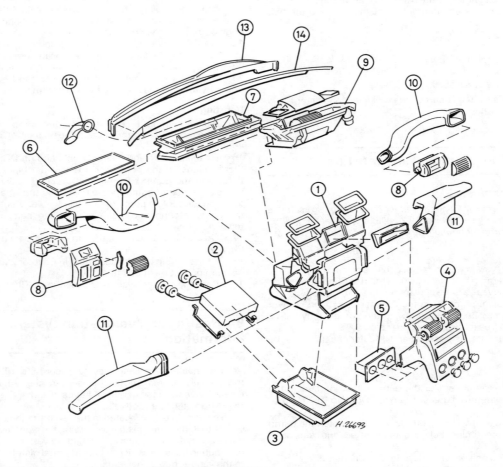

Fig. 3.4 Heating/ventilation system components – left-hand-drive model shown (Sec 9)

1	Air distribution housing	5	Heater/ventilation control
2	Heater matrix		unit
3	Heater matrix lower cover	6	Pollen filter
4	Facia centre panel assembly	7	Pollen filter housing

1 Air distribution housing
2 Heater matrix
3 Heater matrix lower cover
4 Facia centre panel assembly

5 Heater/ventilation control
   unit
6 Pollen filter
7 Pollen filter housing

8 Passenger's side
   ventilation nozzle housing
9 Heater blower motor
   assembly
10 Driver's side air duct

11 Centre air duct
12 Water drain tube
13 Water deflector
14 Windscreen cowl panel

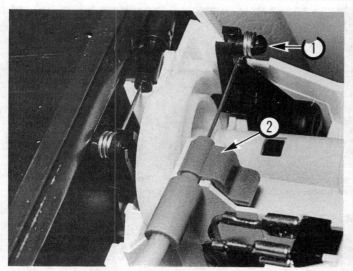

10.3 Heater/ventilation control unit withdrawn to expose control cable end connection (1) and securing clip (2)

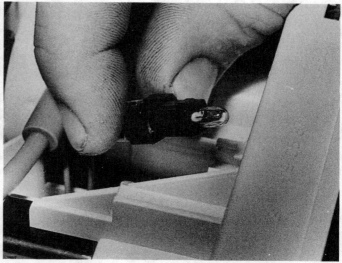

10.7 Pulling the heater control switch illumination bulbholder from the rear of the control unit

A recirculation switch enables the outside air supply to be closed off, while the air inside the vehicle is recirculated. This can be useful to prevent unpleasant odours entering from outside the vehicle, but should only be used briefly, as the recirculated air inside the vehicle will soon deteriorate.

Certain models may be fitted with heated front seats. The heat is produced by electrically-heated mats in the seat and backrest cushions. The temperature is regulated automatically by a thermostat, and cannot be adjusted.

10 Heater/ventilation components – removal and refitting

Heater/ventilation control unit

Removal
1 Remove the facia centre panel assembly, as described in Chapter 11.
2 Carefully pull the heater/ventilation control unit forwards from the facia, taking care not to strain the control cables and wiring.
3 Release the securing clips, and disconnect the control cables from the air distribution and temperature control switches (two cables on the air distribution switch, one cable on the temperature switch), noting their locations (photo).
4 Disconnect the wiring plug from the rear of the unit.
5 Disconnect the vacuum pipes from the rear of the air recirculation switch, noting their locations.
6 The heater/ventilation control unit can now be withdrawn from the vehicle.
7 If desired, the control switch illumination bulb can be renewed by disconnecting the wires, and pulling the bulbholder from the rear of the control unit (photo). The bulb is a push-fit in the bulbholder.
8 The blower motor switch and the air recirculation switch can be removed from the control unit by releasing the securing clips. The blower motor securing clips are accessible from the rear of the switch, and the air recirculation switch securing clips are accessible from the front of the switch after removing the switch knob.

Refitting
9 Refitting is a reversal of removal, bearing in mind the following points.
10 Ensure that the control cables are securely reconnected in their correct locations, and that the cable runs are free from kinks and obstructions. Check the operation of the controls before finally refitting the facia centre panel assembly.
11 Refit the facia centre panel assembly as described in Chapter 11.

Heater/ventilation control cables – renewal

Lower air distribution control cable
12 Pull the heater/ventilation control unit forwards from the facia, as described previously in this Section.
13 Release the securing clips, and disconnect the cable from the rear of the control unit.
14 Follow the run of the cable behind the facia, taking note of its routing, and disconnect the cable from the lever on the air distribution housing. Note that the method of fastening is the same as that used at the control unit.
15 Fit the new cable using a reversal of the removal procedure, noting the following points.
16 Ensure that the cable is correctly routed, and free from kinks and obstructions, and make sure that the cable securing clips are fastened correctly.
17 Refit the control unit as described previously in this Section.

Upper air distribution control cable
18 Remove the instrument panel, as described in Chapter 12.
19 Proceed as described in paragraphs 12 and 13 of this Section.
20 Follow the run of the cable behind the facia, taking note of its routing, and working through the instrument panel aperture, disconnect the end of the cable from the lever on the air distribution housing. Note that the method of fastening is the same as that used at the control unit.
21 Proceed as described in paragraphs 15 to 17 of this Section.
22 Refit the instrument panel as described in Chapter 12.

Air temperature control cable
23 Release the securing clips, and remove the lower cover panel from under the passenger's side facia.
24 Where applicable, remove the securing screws, and withdraw the oddments tray from under the glovebox.
25 Proceed as described in paragraphs 12 and 13 of this Section.
26 Follow the run of the cable behind the facia, taking note of its routing, and working up behind the passenger's footwell, disconnect the end of the cable from the lever on the air distribution housing. Note that the method of fastening is the same as that used at the control unit.
27 Proceed as described in paragraphs 15 to 17 of this Section.
28 Refit the glovebox and the facia lower cover panel using a reversal of the removal procedure.

Heater blower motor

Removal
29 Disconnect the battery negative lead.
30 Remove the pollen filter, as described in Chapter 1.
31 Remove the windscreen wiper arms, with reference to Chapter 12 if necessary.
32 Remove the windscreen cowl panel, as described in Chapter 11.

10.33 Disconnecting the heater blower motor wiring plug

10.34 Disconnecting a vacuum pipe from the connector in the blower motor housing

10.35A Pollen filter housing assembly securing bolts (arrowed)

10.35B Withdrawing the pollen filter housing assembly from the scuttle

10.36 Removing the blower motor upper cover

10.37 Heater blower motor wires (1) and motor securing screw (2)

33   Disconnect the blower motor wiring plug, then prise the wiring grommet from the pollen filter housing, and pull the wiring through the aperture in the housing (photo).
34   Similarly, disconnect the vacuum pipes from the connector at the front of the housing, noting their routing (photo).
35   Unscrew the four securing bolts (two at the front, and two at the rear), and manipulate the pollen filter housing assembly from the scuttle (photos).
36   Release the two securing clips, and remove the blower motor upper cover (photo).
37   Disconnect the two blower motor wires from the blower motor resistor, then remove the two blower motor securing screws, and carefully withdraw the motor assembly from its location (photo).

Refitting
38   Refitting is a reversal of removal, bearing in mind the following points.
39   Ensure that the wiring and the vacuum pipes are securely reconnected and correctly routed.
40   Ensure that all panels are securely refitted, and that the weatherstrips are correctly engaged with the panels.
41   Refit the windscreen wiper arms with reference to Chapter 12.

Heater blower motor resistor
Removal
42   Remove the pollen filter, as described in Chapter 1, to expose the resistor.
43   Remove the single securing screw, then disconnect the wiring, and remove the resistor (photos).

Refitting
44   Refitting is a reversal of removal.

Heater matrix
Removal
45   Either drain the cooling system as described in Chapter 1, or, working in the engine compartment, clamp the heater hoses at the bulkhead to reduce coolant loss when the hoses are disconnected.
46   Place a suitable container beneath the heater hoses, then disconnect the hoses from the heater matrix stubs. Allow the coolant to drain into the container.
47   Remove the centre console, as described in Chapter 11.
48   Carefully detach the two tubes from the bottom of the air ducts in front of the heater matrix housing (photo).

10.43A Heater blower motor resistor securing screw (1) and wiring plugs (2)

10.43B Removing the heater blower motor resistor

10.48 Detach the two tubes (arrowed) from the bottom of the air ducts

10.49A Remove the front ...

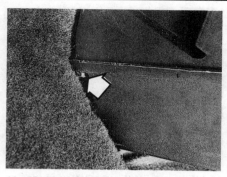

10.49B ... and rear heater matrix lower cover securing screws ...

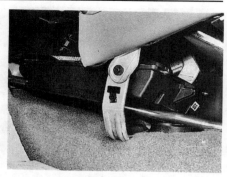

10.49C ... and lower the cover

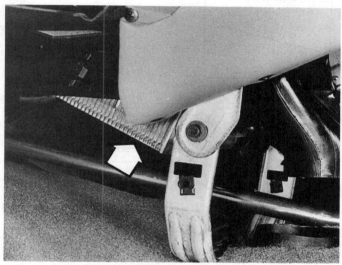

10.51 Withdraw the heater matrix (arrowed) from its housing

49 Remove the five screws securing the heater matrix lower cover (the front screw also secures the air ducts), then lift up the air ducts to enable the lower cover to be withdrawn (photos).
50 At this stage, it is advisable to lay a piece of plastic sheeting or similar under the heater matrix to prevent any coolant which may be released as the matrix is withdrawn from damaging the carpet.
51 Carefully withdraw the heater matrix from its housing (noting that the metal fins are sharp, and can easily be damaged), and withdraw it from the vehicle (photo).

Refitting

52 Refitting is a reversal of removal, noting the following points.
53 Make sure that the tubes are securely refitted to the air ducts.

54 Ensure that the coolant hoses are securely reconnected to the heater matrix stubs.
55 On completion, where applicable, refill the cooling system as described in Chapter 1.

Air recirculation vacuum unit

Removal

56 Remove the glove compartment, as described in Chapter 11.
57 Reach up behind the facia, and locate the vacuum unit (photo); access is limited.
58 Unclip the actuating rod from the end of the unit, and disconnect the vacuum hose.
59 Unclip the vacuum unit from its mounting.

Refitting

60 Refitting is a reversal of removal.

11 Heater/ventilation vents – removal and refitting

Ventilation nozzles

Removal

1 Carefully release the relevant nozzle from the facia, using a screwdriver with a piece of card under the blade, to avoid damage to the facia trim, then withdraw the nozzle (photo).

Refitting

2 Simply push the nozzle into its housing in the facia until the securing lugs click into place.

Driver's side ventilation nozzle housing

Removal

3 Remove the steering column shrouds, as described in Chapter 11.
4 Remove the instrument panel surround, as described in Chapter 11.

10.57 Air recirculation vacuum unit

11.1 Removing a facia ventilation nozzle

11.7 Removing the driver's side ventilation nozzle housing upper securing screw

11.8 Removing the ventilation nozzle housing securing clip

11.9 Withdrawing the ventilation nozzle housing from the facia

11.10 Levering the headlight aim adjustment switch from the ventilation nozzle housing

5   Remove the ventilation nozzle, as described previously in this Section.
6   Remove the lighting rotary switch, as described in Chapter 12.
7   Remove the upper nozzle housing securing screw (located at the top of the nozzle aperture), and the lower securing screw (located at the bottom of the lighting switch aperture) (photo).
8   Carefully pull out the housing securing clip, accessible from behind the left-hand side (right-hand-drive models), or the right-hand side (left-hand-drive models) of the housing, as applicable (photo).
9   Carefully withdraw the housing from the facia, and unclip the wiring plugs from the rear of the housing (photo).
10   If desired, the remaining switches can be removed from the housing by carefully pushing them out through the front of the housing from behind (photo).

Refitting

11   Refitting is a reversal of removal, but ensure that the housing engages correctly with the air duct in the facia.

Passenger's side ventilation nozzle housing
Removal

12   Remove the glovebox, as described in Chapter 11.
13   Remove the ventilation nozzle, as described previously in this Section.
14   Remove the upper housing securing screw (located at the top of the nozzle aperture), and the lower securing screw (located at the bottom of the housing, in the glovebox aperture), then carefully withdraw the housing from the facia.

Refitting

15   Refitting is a reversal of removal, but ensure that the housing engages correctly with the air duct in the facia.

12   Heated front seat components – removal and refitting

Heater switch
Removal

1   Disconnect the battery negative lead.

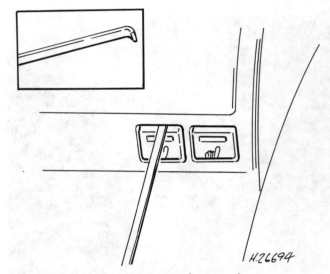

Fig. 3.5 Hooked tool used to remove front seat heater switches (Sec 12)

2   Using a suitable length of wire, make up a hooked tool similar to that shown in Fig. 3.5.
3   Carefully slide the tool round the top edge of the switch to release the securing lugs, then pull the switch forwards from the centre console.
4   Disconnect the wiring plug from the rear of the switch, and remove the switch.

Refitting

5   Refitting is a reversal of removal.

Heater mat

6   For access to the heater mats, the seat must be dismantled, and the upholstery must be removed (by unstitching). The procedure for this involves removing the seat back, which is secured by rivets.
7   Due to the difficulty involved in removing the upholstery, and the possible risk of injury to the vehicle occupants, should the seat be reassembled incorrectly, this task is considered to be beyond the scope of this manual.

Chapter 4
Fuel, exhaust and emission control systems

Contents

Specifications

Part A: Carburettor engines
Fuel grade
Note: *Fuel grade names (eg; 'Regular', 'Premium', 'Super', etc.) may vary depending on territory – if in doubt, check the RON number before use.*
Fuel octane requirement:

Unleaded..	95 RON (Premium) or 98 RON (Super or 'Super Plus')
Leaded	97 RON or 98 RON (4-star)

Fuel pump

Type..	Mechanical

Carburettor (general)

Type..	Pierburg 2E3
Application*..	14 NV engine
Choke type	Automatic

*For details of engine code location, see 'Buying spare parts and vehicle identification numbers'.

Carburettor data

Idle speed	925 ± 25 rpm
Idle mixture CO content	1.0 ± 0.5%
Fast idle speed	2200 to 2600 rpm
Choke valve gap	1.5 to 3.5 mm
Choke pull-down gap:	
'Small'	1.7 to 2.1 mm
'Large'	2.5 to 2.9 mm
Idle fuel jet	45
Idle air bleed	130

	Primary	Secondary
Venturi diameter	20.0 mm	24.0 mm
Main jet	X95	X110

Torque wrench settings

	Nm	lbf ft
Fuel pump bolts	18	13
Fuel tank mounting strap nuts	20	15
Inlet manifold nuts	22	16
Exhaust manifold nuts	22	16
Exhaust downpipe-to-manifold bolts	25	18

Part B: Fuel injection engines

General

System type:*	
C 14 NZ, C 16 NZ and C 18 NZ engines	Multec single-point fuel injection
C 14 SE and C 16 SE engines	Multec multi-point fuel injection
C 20 NE engine	Motronic M 1.5.2 fuel injection
C 20 XE engine	Motronic M 2.5 fuel injection

*For details of engine code location, see 'Buying spare parts and vehicle identification numbers'.

Fuel grade

Note: Fuel grade names (eg; 'Regular', 'Premium', 'Super', etc.) may vary depending on territory – if in doubt, check the RON number before use.

Fuel octane requirement:	
C 14 NZ, C 16 NZ, C 18 NZ and C 20 NE engines	95 RON ('Premium') or 91 RON ('Regular') unleaded
C 14 SE and C 16 SE engines	95 RON ('Premium'), 98 RON ('Super' or 'Super Plus') or 91 RON ('Regular')* unleaded
C 20 XE engine**	95 RON ('Premium'), 98 RON ('Super' or 'Super Plus') or 91 RON ('Regular') unleaded

*91 RON unleaded fuel may be used after fitting special octane coding plug (95/91 RON) available from Vauxhall/Opel dealers.
**The knock control system on the C 20 XE engine automatically adjusts the engine ignition system according to the type of fuel used.

Fuel pump

Type	Electric, mounted in fuel tank
Delivery quantity	85.0 litres/hour at 12 volts

Multec single-point fuel injection system data

Fuel pressure (pressure regulator vacuum hose connected)	0.76 bars
Idle speed:	
C 14 NZ engine	830 to 990 rpm
C 16 NZ engine	780 to 940 rpm
C 18 NZ engine	750 to 910 rpm
Idle mixture CO content (all engines)	0.4% maximum

Multec multi-point fuel injection system data

Fuel pressure (pressure regulator vacuum hose connected)	3.0 bars
Idle speed:	
C 14 SE engine	820 to 980 rpm
C 16 SE engine	No information available at time of writing
Idle mixture CO content (all engines)	0.4% maximum
Crankshaft speed/position sensor-to-sensor wheel air gap	1.0 ± 0.7 mm

Motronic M 1.5.2 fuel injection system data

Fuel pressure (pressure regulator vacuum hose connected)	3.0 bars
Idle speed	770 to 930 rpm
Idle mixture CO content	0.4% maximum

Motronic M 2.5 fuel injection system data

Fuel pressure (pressure regulator vacuum hose connected)	3.0 bars
Idle speed	860 to 1020 rpm
Idle mixture CO content	0.4% maximum

Torque wrench settings

	Nm	lbf ft
Single-point fuel injection unit-to-inlet manifold nuts	22	16
Single-point fuel injection unit upper section securing screws	6	4
Coolant temperature sensor:		
All except C 20 NE and C 20 XE engines	20	15
C 20 NE engine	10	7
C 20 XE engine	11	8
Oxygen sensor (all engines)	30	22

Part A: Carburettor engine

1 General information and precautions

General information

The fuel system on carburettor models comprises a fuel tank, a fuel pump, a vapour separator (not fitted to all models), a downdraught carburettor, and a thermostatically-controlled air cleaner.

The fuel tank is mounted under the rear of the vehicle, forward of the rear suspension. The tank is ventilated to the atmosphere, and is filled from the right-hand side of the vehicle through a simple filler pipe. The fuel gauge sender unit is mounted inside the tank.

The fuel pump is a mechanical diaphragm type, operated by a pushrod which is in turn actuated by a lobe on the camshaft.

The fuel vapour separator (where fitted) is used to stabilise the fuel supply to the carburettor. Vapour is purged from the carburettor fuel supply, thus improving hot starting qualities.

The carburettor is a Pierburg 2E3 type, a full description of which is given in Section 12.

The air cleaner has a vacuum-controlled air intake, supplying a blend of hot and cold air to suit the prevailing engine operating conditions. Further details are given in Section 2.

Precautions

Certain adjustment points in the fuel system are protected by tamperproof caps, plugs or seals. In some territories, it is an offence to drive a vehicle with broken of missing tamperproof seals. Before disturbing a tamperproof seal, check that no local or national laws will be broken by doing so, and fit a new tamperproof seal after adjustment is complete where this is required by law. Do not break tamperproof seals on a vehicle which is still under warranty.

When working on fuel system components, scrupulous cleanliness must be observed, and care must be taken not to introduce any foreign matter into fuel lines or components. Carburettors in particular are delicate instruments, and care should be taken not to disturb any components unnecessarily. Before attempting work on a carburettor, ensure that the relevant spares are available. If persistent problems are encountered, it is recommended that the advice of a Vauxhall/Opel dealer or carburettor specialist is sought. Most dealers will be able to provide carburettor re-jetting and servicing facilities, and if necessary it should be possible to purchase a reconditioned carburettor.

Refer to Chapter 5, Section 1 for precautions to be observed when working on vehicles fitted with electronic control units.

Warning: *Many of the procedures in this Chapter require the removal of fuel lines and connections which may result in some fuel spillage. Before carrying out any operation on the fuel system refer to the precautions given in 'Safety first!' at the beginning of this manual, and follow them implicitly. Petrol is a highly-dangerous and volatile liquid, and the precautions necessary when handling it cannot be overstressed.*

2 Air cleaner intake air temperature control system – testing

1 The air cleaner is thermostatically-controlled, to provide air at the most suitable temperature for combustion with minimum exhaust emission levels.

2 The optimum air temperature is achieved by drawing in cold air from an air intake at the front of the vehicle, and blending it with hot air from a shroud on the exhaust manifold. The proportion of hot air and cold air is varied by the position of a flap valve in the air cleaner intake spout, which is controlled by a vacuum diaphragm unit. The vacuum applied to the diaphragm type is regulated by a heat sensor located within the air cleaner body.

3 To check the operation of the air temperature control, the engine must be cold. First check the position of the flap valve. Disconnect the hot air tube from the air cleaner spout, and check (by probing with a finger) that the flap is closed to admit only cold air from outside the vehicle (photos). Start the engine, and check that the flap now opens to admit only hot air from the exhaust manifold.

4 Temporarily reconnect the hot air tube to the air cleaner spout.

5 Run the engine until it reaches normal operating temperature.

6 Disconnect the hot air tube once more, and check that the flap is now closed to admit only cold air from outside the vehicle, or in hot weather, a mixture of hot and cold air. Reconnect the hot air tube after making the check.

7 If the flap does not function correctly, the air cleaner must be renewed, as parts are not available individually.

3 Air cleaner housing assembly – removal and refitting

Removal

1 Disconnect the air hose from the airbox on the carburettor.

2 Remove the air cleaner filter element, as described in Chapter 1.

3 Slacken the air cleaner housing assembly securing nuts (one front and one rear), and pull the assembly from the body panel.

Refitting

4 Refitting is a reversal of removal.

2.3A Exhaust manifold-to-air cleaner hot air tube

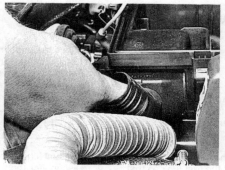
2.3B Checking the operation of the air cleaner flap valve

4.7 Disconnecting a fuel hose from the fuel pump

4.8 Withdrawing the fuel pump and plastic insulating block

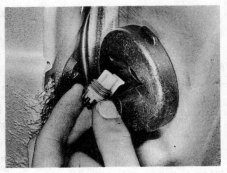

5.6 Disconnecting the wiring plug from the fuel gauge sender unit

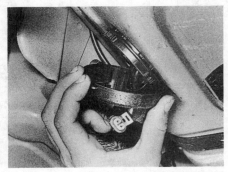

5.7 Pulling the plastic cover from the fuel gauge sender unit

4   Fuel pump – testing, removal and refitting

Note: *Refer to the warning note in Section 1 before proceeding.*

Testing

1   Disconnect the ignition coil HT lead.
2   Place a wad of clean rag under the pump outlet, then disconnect the pump outlet hose. Be prepared for fuel spillage, and take adequate fire precautions.
3   Have an assistant crank the engine on the starter. Well-defined spurts of fuel should be ejected from the pump outlet – if not, the pump is probably faulty (or the tank is empty). Dispose of the fuel-soaked rag safely.
4   No spare parts are available for the pump, and if faulty, the unit must be renewed.

Removal

5   The fuel pump is located at the right-hand end of the camshaft housing.
6   Disconnect the battery negative lead.
7   Disconnect the fuel hoses from the pump (photo). If necessary, label the hoses so that they can be reconnected to their original locations. Be prepared for fuel spillage, and take adequate fire precautions. Plug the open ends of the hoses to prevent dirt ingress and further fuel spillage.
8   Unscrew the two securing bolts, and withdraw the pump from the camshaft housing (photo).
9   Recover the plastic insulating block.

Refitting

10   Refitting is a reversal of removal, but ensure that the fuel hoses are reconnected to their correct locations as noted during removal, and tighten the securing bolts to the specified torque.
11   Run the engine and check for leaks on completion. If leakage is evident, stop the engine immediately and rectify the problem without delay. Note that the engine may take a longer time than usual to start when the pump has been removed as the pump refills with fuel.

5   Fuel gauge sender unit – removal and refitting

Note: *Refer to the warning in Section 1 before proceeding.*

Removal

1   Disconnect the battery negative lead.
2   Siphon out any remaining fuel in the tank through the filler pipe. Siphon the fuel into a clean metal container which can be sealed.
3   Chock the front wheels, then jack up the rear of the vehicle and support securely on axle stands (see *'Jacking, towing and wheel changing'*).
4   The sender unit is located in the front face of the fuel tank.
5   Make alignment marks on the sender unit and the fuel tank so that the unit can be refitted in its original position.
6   Disconnect the wiring plug from the sender unit (photo).

7   Pull back the plastic cover (photo), then disconnect the fuel hose(s) from the sender unit. Be prepared for fuel spillage, and take adequate fire precautions. Plug the open end(s) of the hose(s) to prevent dirt ingress and further fuel loss.
8   To remove the sender unit, engage a flat piece of metal as a lever between two of the slots on the sender unit rim, and turn the sender unit anti-clockwise.
9   Withdraw the unit carefully, to avoid bending the float arm.
10   Recover the sealing ring.

Refitting

11   Refitting is a reversal of removal, bearing in mind the following points.
12   Examine the condition of the sealing ring and renew if necessary.
13   Ensure that the marks made on the sender unit and fuel tank before removal are aligned.
14   Ensure that the hoses are reconnected to their correct locations as noted during removal.
15   On completion, fill the fuel tank, then run the engine and check for leaks. Also check that the fuel gauge reads correctly. If leakage is evident, stop the engine immediately and rectify the problem without delay. Note that the engine may take a longer time than usual to start when the sender unit has been removed, as the fuel pump refills with fuel.

6   Fuel vapour separator – removal and refitting

Note: *Refer to the warning in Section 1 before proceeding.*

Removal

1   Where fitted, the vapour separator is located on a bracket attached to the side of the carburettor.
2   Note the locations of the three fuel hoses, labelling them if necessary to aid refitting, then disconnect the hoses from the vapour separator. Be prepared for fuel spillage, and take adequate fire precautions. Clamp or plug the open ends of the hoses, to prevent dirt ingress and further fuel spillage.
3   Remove the two securing screws, and lift the vapour separator from its bracket.

Refitting

4   Check the body of the separator for cracks or leaks before refitting, and renew if necessary.
5   Refitting is a reversal of removal, but ensure that the three fuel hoses are connected to their correct locations as noted during removal.

7   Fuel filter – renewal

1   The fuel filter is located in the carburettor fuel inlet pipe.
2   Disconnect the trunking from the air cleaner, then disconnect the vacuum pipe and breather hose from the airbox. Extract the three securing screws and lift off the airbox, complete with air trunking.

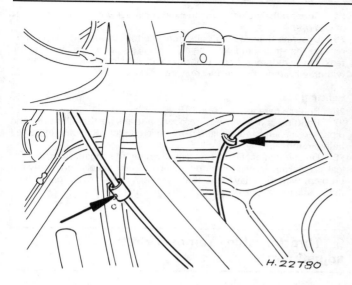

Fig. 4.1 Handbrake cables (arrowed) clipped to fuel tank and tank securing strap – Saloon and Hatchback models (Sec 8)

3   Place a wad of rag under the fuel inlet pipe at the carburettor to catch any fuel which may be spilled during the procedure.
4   Disconnect the fuel inlet hose from the carburettor. Be prepared for fuel spillage, and clamp or plug the end of the hose to reduce unnecessary fuel loss. Take adequate fire precautions.
5   To remove the filter, carefully screw an M3 bolt approximately 5.0 mm into the end of the filter, and pull on the bolt to withdraw the filter from the end of the inlet pipe – see Fig. 4.4.
6   Push the new filter into the inlet pipe, ensuring that it engages securely, then reconnect the fuel inlet hose, and refit the airbox.

8   Fuel tank – removal and refitting

Note: *Refer to the warning in Section 1 before proceeding.*

Saloon and Hatchback models
Removal
1   Disconnect the battery negative lead.
2   Proceed as described in Section 5, paragraphs 1 to 3 inclusive.
3   Disconnect the exhaust system front flexible joint (see Section 23). Suspend the front section of the exhaust system with wire or string from the underbody.
4   Disconnect the rear section of the exhaust system from its rubber mountings, and allow it to rest on the rear suspension torsion beam. It is advisable to support the centre section of the exhaust system with wire or string from the underbody to avoid straining the system.
5   Release the handbrake cables from the clips on the tank (right-hand cable) and tank securing strap (left-hand cable), and move them clear of the tank. On certain models, it may be necessary to slacken the cable adjuster to enable the cables to be moved clear of the tank (see Chapter 9).
6   Where applicable, remove the fuel filter from the side of the fuel tank, with reference to Section 7.
7   Clamp the fuel hose(s) running to the fuel gauge sender unit (located in the right-hand side of the tank), then position a suitable container under the sender unit to catch the fuel which will be released as the hose(s) is/are disconnected.
8   Pull back the plastic cover, then disconnect the hose(s) from the sender unit. Be prepared for fuel spillage, and take adequate fire precautions.
9   Disconnect the wiring plug from the fuel gauge sender unit.
10   Disconnect the filler and vent hoses from the rear of the fuel tank (photo).
11   Support the weight of the fuel tank on a jack with interposed block of wood.

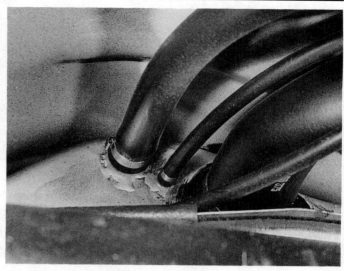

8.10 Filler and vent hose connections at rear of fuel tank – Hatchback model

12   Unscrew the securing nuts from the tank mounting straps (photo), then remove the straps and lower the tank sufficiently to enable the disconnection of the remaining vent hose(s).
13   With the aid of an assistant, carefully lower the tank, and withdraw it from under the vehicle. Note that as the tank is withdrawn, some residual fuel may be released.

Refitting
14   If the tank contains sediment or water, it may be cleaned out using two or three rinses with clean fuel. Shake vigorously using several changes of fuel, but before doing so, remove the fuel gauge sender unit, as described in Section 5. *This procedure should be carried out in a well-ventilated area, and it is vital to take adequate fire precautions.*
15   Any repairs to the fuel tank should be carried out by a professional. **Do not** under any circumstances attempt to weld or solder a fuel tank. Removal of all residual fuel vapours requires several hours of specialist cleaning.
16   Refitting is a reversal of removal, bearing in mind the following points.
17   Ensure that all hoses and pipes are securely reconnected to their correct locations, as noted before removal.
18   Where applicable, refit the fuel filter with reference to Section 7.
19   If the handbrake cable adjuster has been slackened, adjust the handbrake cables as described in Chapter 9.

8.12 Fuel tank mounting strap nut

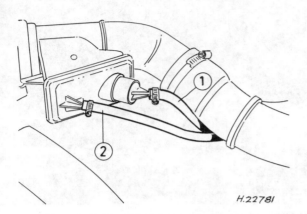

Fig. 4.2 Disconnect the hoses (1 and 2) from the fuel filler assembly – Estate and Van models (Sec 8)

20   On completion, fill the fuel tank, then run the engine and check for leaks. If leakage is evident, stop the engine immediately and rectify the problem without delay. Note that the engine may take a longer time than usual to start, as the pump refills with fuel.

Estate and Van models

Removal

21   Proceed as described in Section 5, paragraphs 1 to 3 inclusive.
22   Disconnect the filler and vent hoses from the side of the tank.
23   Disconnect the hoses shown in Fig. 4.2 from the fuel filler assembly.

24   Support the weight of the fuel tank on a jack with interposed block of wood.
25   Unscrew the securing bolts from the tank mounting straps, then remove the straps, and with the aid of an assistant, carefully lower the tank and withdraw it from under the vehicle. Note that as the tank is withdrawn, some residual fuel may be released.

Refitting

26   Refer to paragraphs 14 and 15.
27   Refitting is a reversal of removal, but ensure that all hoses and pipes are securely reconnected to their correct locations, as noted before removal.
28   On completion, fill the fuel tank, then run the engine and check for leaks. If leakage is evident, stop the engine immediately and rectify the problem without delay. Note that the engine may take a longer time than usual to start, as the pump refills with fuel.

9   Throttle cable – removal, refitting and adjustment

Removal

1   Disconnect the air trunking from the air cleaner, then disconnect the vacuum pipe and breather hose from the airbox.
2   Extract the three securing screws (photo) and lift off the airbox, complete with the air trunking.
3   Extract the clip from the cable end fitting at the bracket on the carburettor, then slide the cable end grommet from the bracket (photos).
4   Slide the cable end from the throttle valve lever on the carburettor.
5   Working inside the vehicle, release the securing clips, and remove the lower trim panel from the driver's footwell (photo).
6   Pull the cable retainer from the top of the pedal, and disconnect the cable end from the pedal.
7   Make a careful note of the cable routing, then withdraw the cable through the bulkhead into the engine compartment.

9.2 Removing an airbox securing screw

9.3A Extract the throttle cable end clip ...

9.3B ... and slide the grommet from the bracket

9.5 Removing the lower trim panel from the driver's footwell

9.12 Throttle pedal stop screw

10.3 Throttle pedal pivot assembly – circlip arrowed

Refitting

8 Refitting is a reversal of removal, bearing in mind the following points.
9 Ensure that the cable is correctly routed, as noted before removal.
10 Ensure that the bulkhead grommet is correctly seated in its aperture.
11 On completion, check the throttle mechanism for satisfactory operation, and if necessary adjust the cable, as described in the following paragraphs.

Adjustment

12 Two points of cable adjustment are provided. A stop screw is located on the pedal arm to control the fully-released position of the pedal stop, and a clip is located on a threaded section of the cable sheath at the bracket on the carburettor, to adjust the cable free play (photo).
13 The cable should be adjusted so that when the throttle pedal is released, there is very slight free play in the cable at the carburettor end.
14 Check that when the throttle pedal is fully depressed, the throttle valve is fully open. Adjust the position of the clip on the cable sheath, and the pedal stop screw, to achieve the desired results.

10 Throttle pedal – removal and refitting

Removal

1 Working inside the vehicle, release the securing clips, and remove the lower trim panel from the driver's footwell.
2 Pull the cable retainer from the top of the pedal, and disconnect the cable end from the pedal.
3 Extract the circlip from the right-hand end of the pedal pivot shaft, then slide out the pivot shaft from the left-hand side of the pedal pivot bracket (photo). Recover the pivot bushes and the pedal return spring.

Refitting

4 Before refitting the pedal components, examine the pivot bushes for wear, and renew if necessary.
5 Refitting is a reversal of removal, but on completion check the throttle mechanism for satisfactory operation, and check the throttle cable adjustment, as described in Section 9.

11 Unleaded petrol – general information and usage

Note: *The information given in this Section is correct at the time of writing, and applies only to petrols currently available in the EC. If in any*

doubt as to the suitability of petrol, or if using the vehicle outside the EC, consult a Vauxhall/Opel dealer or one of the motoring organisations for advice on the petrols available, and their suitability for your vehicle.

Vauxhall/Opel recommend the use of 95 RON (Premium) unleaded petrol in carburettor Astra models; 98 RON (Super or 'Super Plus') unleaded petrol can be used without modification.
97 or 98 RON leaded (4-star) petrol can be used without modification in carburettor models not equipped with a catalytic converter. **Do not** use leaded petrol in models equipped with a catalytic converter, or the (expensive) catalyst unit will be ruined.

12 Carburettor – general information

The Pierburg 2E3 carburettor is of twin-venturi, fixed-jet sequential throttle type (photos). The primary throttle valve operates alone except at high speeds and loads, when the secondary throttle valve is operated, until at full-throttle, both are fully open. This arrangement allows good fuel economy during light acceleration and cruising, but also gives maximum power at full-throttle. The secondary throttle valve is vacuum-operated, according to the vacuum produced in the primary venturi. The primary throttle barrel and venturi diameters are smaller than their secondary counterparts. The carburettor is a complicated instrument, with various refinements and sub-systems added to achieve improved driveability, economy and exhaust emission levels.

A separate idle system operates independently from the main jet system, supplying fuel via the mixture control screw.

The main jets are calibrated to suit engine requirements at mid-range throttle openings. To provide the necessary fuel enrichment at full-throttle, a vacuum-operated power valve is used. The valve provides extra fuel under the low vacuum conditions associated with wide throttle openings.

To provide an enriched mixture during acceleration, an accelerator pump delivers extra fuel to the primary main venturi. The accelerator pump is operated mechanically by a cam on the throttle linkage.

A fully-automatic choke is fitted, operated by a coolant and electrically-heated bi-metal coil. When the engine is cold, the bi-metal coil is fully wound up, holding the choke plate (fitted to the primary barrel) closed. As the engine warms up, the bi-metal coil is heated and therefore unwinds, progressively opening the choke plate. A vacuum-operated pull-down system is employed, whereby, if the engine is under choke but is only cruising (ie not under heavy load), the choke plate is opened against the action of the bi-metal coil. The pull-down system prevents an over-rich mixture, which would otherwise reduce fuel economy and may cause unnecessary engine wear when the engine is cold. A secondary pull-down solenoid is fitted, which operates in conjunction with the main diaphragm unit to modify the pull-down characteristics, improving fuel economy.

An unusual feature of the Pierburg carburettor is that the float level is set in production, and cannot be adjusted.

12.1A Side view of carburettor, showing accelerator pump (1) and main choke pull-down diaphragm unit (2)

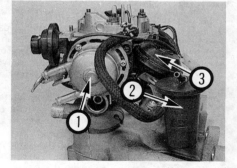

12.1B Side view of carburettor, showing automatic choke housing (1), vapour separator (2) and secondary throttle valve (3)

12.1C Side view of carburettor, showing secondary choke pull-down solenoid (1) and power valve (2)

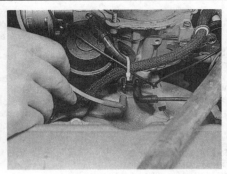

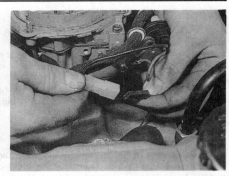

13.5 Disconnecting the coolant hoses from the automatic choke housing

13.6 Disconnecting a vacuum pipe from the front of the carburettor

13.7 Disconnecting the choke heater wiring plug

13 Carburettor – removal and refitting

Note: *Refer to the warning in Section 1 before proceeding. New gasket(s) must be used when refitting the carburettor.*

Removal

1   Disconnect the battery negative lead.
2   Disconnect the trunking from the air cleaner, then disconnect the vacuum pipe and breather hose from the airbox. Extract the three securing screws and lift off the airbox, complete with air trunking.
3   Disconnect the fuel supply hose from the carburettor, or disconnect the fuel supply and return hoses from the vapour separator, as applicable. Be prepared for fuel spillage, and take adequate fire precautions. Clamp or plug the end of the hose(s), to prevent dirt ingress and further fuel spillage.
4   Extract the clip from the throttle cable end fitting at the bracket on the carburettor, then slide the cable end grommet from the bracket, and slide the cable end from the throttle valve lever.
5   Disconnect the coolant hoses from the automatic choke housing, noting their locations as an aid to refitting (photo). Be prepared for coolant spillage, and clamp or plug the hoses, or secure them with their ends facing upwards, to prevent further coolant loss.
6   Disconnect the two vacuum pipes from the front of the carburettor, noting their locations and routing for use when refitting (photo).
7   Disconnect the choke heater wiring plug (photo).
8   Unscrew the three securing nuts, and withdraw the carburettor from the inlet manifold studs (photo).
9   Recover the gasket(s) and insulator block which fit between the carburettor and the inlet manifold.

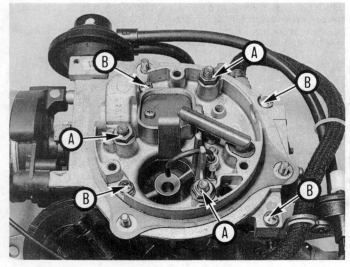

13.8 Carburettor securing nuts (A) and top cover securing screws (B)

Refitting

10   Refitting is a reversal of removal, but renew the gasket(s).
11   On completion, carry out the following checks and adjustments.
12   Check the throttle cable free play and adjust if necessary, as described in Section 9.
13   Check and if necessary top-up the coolant level, as described in Chapter 1.
14   Check and if necessary adjust the idle speed and mixture, as described in Chapter 1.

14 Carburettor – fault diagnosis, overhaul and adjustments

Note: *Refer to the warning in Section 1 before proceeding. All gaskets and seals should be renewed on reassembly.*

Fault diagnosis

1   Faults with the carburettor are usually associated with dirt entering the float chamber and blocking the jets, causing a weak mixture or power failure within a certain engine speed range. If this is the case, then a thorough clean will normally cure the problem. If the carburettor is well worn, uneven running may be caused by air entering through the throttle valve spindle bearings.
2   If a carburettor fault is suspected, always check first (where possible) that the ignition timing is correct, and that the spark plugs are in good condition and correctly gapped. Also check that the throttle cable is correctly adjusted, and that the air cleaner filter element is clean. Bear in mind that it is possible that one of the hydraulic valve lifters may be faulty, resulting in an incorrect valve clearance.
3   If careful checking of all the preceding points produces no improvement, the carburettor should be removed for cleaning and overhaul.

Overhaul and adjustments

Note: *All gaskets and seals should be renewed on reassembly.*

4   The following paragraphs describe cleaning and adjustment procedures which can be carried out by the home mechanic after the carburettor has been removed from the inlet manifold (see Section 13). If the carburettor is worn or damaged, it should either be renewed or overhauled by a specialist, who will be able to restore the carburettor to its original calibration.
5   With the carburettor removed as described in Section 13, clean all external dirt from the carburettor, then remove the four carburettor top cover securing screws, noting their locations, as two different lengths of screw are used.
6   Lift off the top cover, and recover the gasket.
7   Access to the carburettor jets in the top cover can now be obtained – see Fig. 4.3.
8   Blow through the jets and drillings with compressed air (wear eye protection), or air from a foot pump – do not probe them with wire. If the jets are to be removed, unscrew them carefully using suitable tools of the correct size.

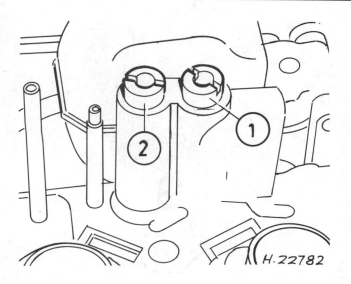

Fig. 4.3 Carburettor main jets in top cover (Sec 14)

1   Primary main jet   *2   Secondary main jet*

9   Remove the fuel filter from the inlet pipe by carefully screwing an M3 bolt approximately 5.0 mm into the end of the filter, and pulling on the bolt to withdraw the filter from the end of the inlet pipe. Push a new filter into the inlet pipe, ensuring that it engages securely.
10   Carefully clean any foreign matter from the float chamber.
11   Removal and refitting of the float and automatic choke unit, and renewal of the various diaphragm units, is described in the following Sections.
12   Further dismantling is not recommended.
13   Reassemble in the reverse order to dismantling. Use new gaskets and seals throughout.
14   Refit the carburettor as described in Section 13.

15   Carburettor needle valve and float – removal, inspection and refitting

Note: *Refer to the warning in Section 1 before proceeding. A new carburettor top cover gasket should be used on refitting. A tachometer and an exhaust gas analyser will be required to check the idle speed and mixture on completion.*

Removal

1   Disconnect the battery negative lead.
2   Disconnect the air trunking from the air cleaner, then disconnect the vacuum pipe and breather hose from the airbox.
3   Extract the three securing screws and lift off the airbox, complete with the air trunking.
4   Thoroughly clean all external dirt from the carburettor.
5   Disconnect the fuel supply hose at the carburettor. Be prepared for fuel spillage, and take adequate fire precautions. Plug the end of hose, to prevent dirt ingress and further fuel spillage.
6   Identify the automatic choke coolant hose locations as an aid to refitting, then disconnect the hoses. Be prepared for coolant spillage, and clamp or plug the hoses, or secure them with their ends facing upwards to prevent further coolant loss.
7   Disconnect the choke heater wiring plug.
8   Disconnect the two vacuum hoses from the choke pull-down unit.
9   Remove the four carburettor top cover securing screws, noting their locations, as two different lengths of screw are used.
10   Lift off the top cover, and recover the gasket.

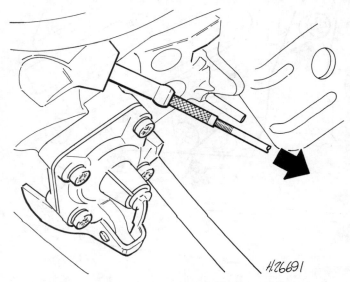

Fig. 4.4 Removing the fuel filter from the carburettor fuel inlet pipe (Sec 14)

11   Using a suitable pin punch, tap the float retaining pin from the base of the top cover, and lift out the float and needle valve.

Inspection

12   Inspect the components for damage, and renew as necessary. Check the needle valve for wear, and check the float for leaks by shaking it to see if it contains petrol.

Refitting

13   Clean the mating faces of the carburettor body and top cover.
14   Refitting is a reversal of removal, bearing in mind the following points.
15   After refitting, check the float and needle valve for full and free movement. Note that no adjustment of the float is possible.
16   Use a new gasket between the top cover and the carburettor body.
17   Ensure that all hoses, pipes and wires are correctly reconnected.
18   On completion, check and if necessary top-up the coolant level, as described in Chapter 3, and check and if necessary adjust the idle speed and mixture, as described in Chapter 1.

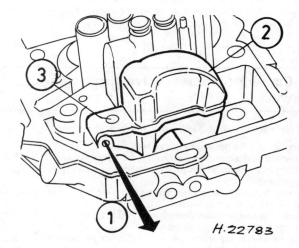

Fig. 4.5 Carburettor float assembly in top cover (Sec 15)

1   Float retaining pin   3   Needle valve
2   Float

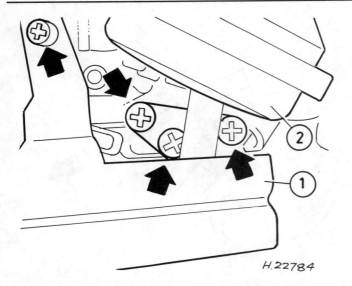

H.22784

Fig. 4.6 Carburettor secondary throttle valve vacuum diaphragm unit (Sec 16)

1 Bracket   *2 Diaphragm unit*

16 Carburettor secondary throttle valve vacuum diaphragm – renewal

Note: *The diaphragm unit must be renewed in its entirety, as no spares are available.*

1   Proceed as described in Section 15, paragraphs 2 and 3.
2   Disconnect the diaphragm unit vacuum pipe from the carburettor.
3   Prise the diaphragm operating rod balljoint from the secondary throttle valve linkage.
4   Where applicable, remove the two securing screws and lift the vapour separator from the bracket. Move the vapour separator to one side, taking care not to strain the fuel hoses.
5   If necessary, for improved access remove the choke housing as described in Section 19, paragraph 2 and 3.
6   Remove the four securing screws, and withdraw the diaphragm unit, complete with its bracket from the carburettor body – see Fig. 4.6.
7   Fit the new diaphragm using a reversal of the removal procedure.
8   Where applicable, when refitting the choke bi-metal housing, ensure that the bi-metal spring is correctly engaged with the choke lever, and align the marks on the bi-metal housing and choke housing as noted before removal.

17 Carburettor power valve diaphragm – renewal

Note: *Refer to the warning in Section 1 before proceeding.*

1   Disconnect the battery negative lead.
2   Proceed as described in Section 15, paragraphs 2 and 3.
3   Thoroughly clean all external dirt from the area around the power valve housing.
4   Remove the two securing screws, and lift off the power valve cover, spring, and diaphragm assembly.
5   Clean the mating faces of the cover and housing.
6   Fit the new diaphragm as follows.
7   Locate the spring on the cover and diaphragm assembly, ensuring that it is correctly seated, then press the diaphragm assembly and cover together. Note that the vacuum hole in the diaphragm must align with the corresponding holes in the housing flange and cover.
8   Further fitting is a reversal of removal, but ensure that the diaphragm is correctly seated.

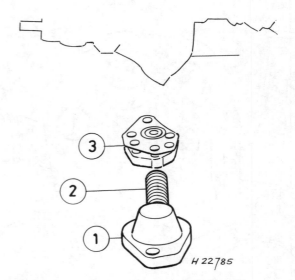

H 22785

Fig. 4.7 Carburettor power valve components (Sec 17)

1 Cover   *3 Diaphragm assembly*
2 Spring

18 Carburettor accelerator pump diaphragm – renewal

Note: *Refer to the warning in Section 1 before proceeding.*

1   Proceed as described in Section 15, paragraphs 1 to 3.
2   Thoroughly clean all external dirt from the area around the accelerator pump housing.
3   Remove the four securing screws, and lift off the accelerator pump cover. Recover the diaphragm, spring, valve retainer and valve. Note the orientation of the valve retainer.
4   Clean the mating faces of the cover and housing.
5   Check the condition of the valve, and renew if necessary.
6   Commence fitting of the new diaphragm by locating the valve, valve retainer and spring in the housing. Note that the valve retainer can

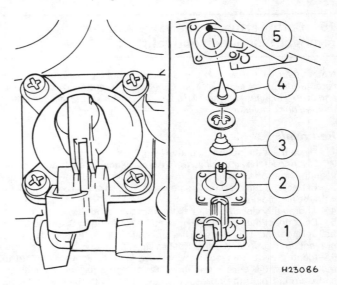

H23086

Fig. 4.8 Carburettor accelerator pump components (Sec 18)

1 Cover with operating lever   *4 Valve*
2 Diaphragm   *5 Air passage*
3 Spring

only be fitted in one position. The larger diameter of the spring should rest against the valve retainer.

7   Locate the diaphragm on the housing, ensuring that the spring is correctly seated, and refit the cover. Tighten the cover securing screws progressively to avoid distorting the diaphragm.

8   Further fitting is a reversal of removal.

---

19   Carburettor automatic choke unit – removal, refitting and adjustment

Note: *Refer to the warning in Section 1 before proceeding. A tachometer and an exhaust gas analyser will be required to check the idle speed and mixture on completion. If the coolant housing is removed, new O-rings must be used on refitting.*

Removal

1   Proceed as described in Section 15, paragraphs 1 to 3.

2   Note the position of the bi-metal housing alignment marks as an aid to refitting, if necessary making additional marks for clarity, then remove the three securing screws and lift off the bi-metal housing. Place the housing to one side, taking care not to strain the coolant hoses or electric choke heater wiring.

3   Remove the three screws securing the choke housing to the carburettor body, and withdraw the choke assembly, taking care not to bend the choke operating rod.

4   If it is necessary to remove the bi-metal housing for renewal, proceed as follows; otherwise proceed to paragraph 8.

5   Identify the automatic choke coolant hose locations as an aid to refitting, then disconnect the hoses. Be prepared for coolant spillage, and clamp or plug the hoses, or secure them with their ends facing upwards, to prevent further loss of coolant.

6   Disconnect the wiring from the electric choke heater, and withdraw the bi-metal housing.

7   The coolant housing can be separated from the bi-metal housing by unscrewing the central securing bolt. Recover the O-rings from under the bolt head, and from the rim of the coolant housing.

Refitting

8   Commence refitting by locating the choke assembly on the carburettor body, ensuring that the lever on the choke assembly engages with the choke operating rod. Tighten the three securing screws.

9   Check and if necessary adjust the choke valve gap and the fast idle cam position, as described later in this Section.

10   Connect the bi-metal spring to the choke lever, position the bi-metal housing and the choke housing as noted during removal, then tighten the securing screws.

11   Where applicable, refit the coolant housing to the bi-metal housing, using new O-rings if necessary, and reconnect the coolant hoses and the electric choke heater wiring.

12   Further refitting is a reversal of removal, bearing in mind the following points.

13   If the coolant hoses have been disconnected, check the coolant level, as described in Chapter 1.

14   Check and if necessary adjust the fast idle speed, as described later in this Section.

Adjustment

Choke valve gap

15   With the bi-metal housing removed as described previously in this Section, proceed as follows.

16   Press the choke operating lever fully clockwise, and retain it in position with a rubber band – see Fig. 4.10.

17   Move the throttle lever to the fully-open position, and measure the choke valve gap between the lower side of the choke plate and the wall of the primary barrel. Check that the gap is as given in the Specifications.

18   If necessary, adjust the choke valve gap by bending the segment (2) in Fig. 4.10. If the gap is too small, enlarge the gap (B) in Fig. 4.10 by levering with a screwdriver. If the gap is too large, decrease gap (B) using a pair of pliers.

19   If no further adjustments are to be carried out, refit the bi-metal housing as described previously in this Section.

Fast idle cam position

20   With the bi-metal housing removed, and the choke valve gap ('A' in Fig. 4.11) correctly set as described previously in this Section, proceed as follows.

21   Open the throttle valve, then close the choke valve using light finger pressure on the choke drive lever – see Fig. 4.11. Close the throttle valve.

22   Check that the fast idle speed adjustment screw is resting against the stop on the second-highest step of the fast idle cam.

23   If adjustment is required, first check that the choke return spring is correctly positioned, then adjust by bending the lever (2) in Fig. 4.11.

24   Refit the bi-metal housing as described previously in this Section.

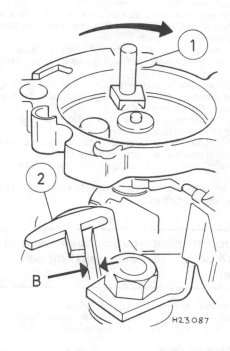

Fig. 4.10 Choke valve gap adjustment (Sec 19)

1   *Choke operating lever*   B   *See text*
2   *Adjuster segment*

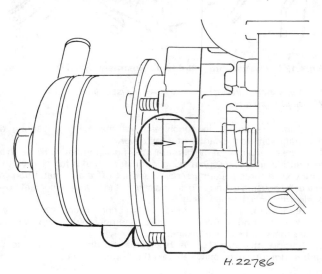

Fig. 4.9 Carburettor automatic choke bi-metal housing alignment marks (circled) (Sec 19)

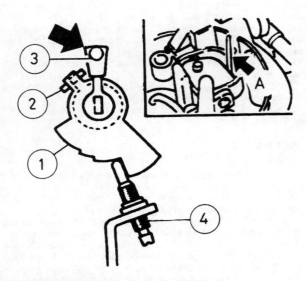

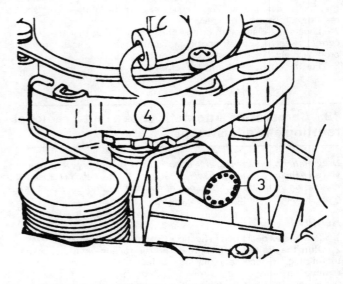

Fig. 4.11 Fast idle cam adjustment (Sec 19)

1   Fast idle cam
2   Adjustment lever
3   Choke drive lever

*4   Fast idle speed adjustment
     screw*
A   See text

Fig. 4.12 Fast idle speed adjustment (Sec 19)

*3   Fast idle speed adjustment
     screw*

*4   Fast idle cam – screw
     positioned on second-
     highest step*

Fast idle speed adjustment

Note: *To carry out the adjustment, an accurate tachometer and an exhaust gas analyser will be required.*

25   Check the idle speed and mixture, as described in Chapter 1. The idle speed **must** be correct before attempting to check or adjust the fast idle speed.
26   With the engine at normal operating temperature, and a tachometer connected in accordance with the equipment manufacturer's instructions, proceed as follows.
27   Position the fast idle speed adjustment screw on the second-highest step of the cam – see Fig. 4.12.
28   Start the engine without touching the throttle pedal, and check that the fast idle speed is as specified. If adjustment is required, stop the engine, and proceed as follows.
29   Remove the tamperproof cap from the fast idle speed adjustment screw – ensure that no local or national laws are being broken by doing so (photo).
30   Ensure that the adjustment screw is still resting on the second-highest step of the fast idle cam, then start the engine, again without touching the throttle pedal.
31   Turn the adjustment screw using a suitable screwdriver, until the specified fast idle speed is obtained.
32   If the cooling fan cuts in during the adjustment procedure, stop the adjustments, and proceed when the cooling fan stops.
33   On completion of adjustment, stop the engine and disconnect the tachometer.
34   Fit a new tamperproof cap to the fast idle speed adjustment screw, where this is required by law.

Fig. 4.13 Choke vacuum pull-down adjustment (Sec 19)

1   Adjustment screw
2   Diaphragm unit

A   Twist drill

3   Using a suitable pin punch, tap out the roll pin securing the diaphragm unit to the carburettor top cover.
4   Note the position of the bi-metal housing alignment marks as an aid to refitting (if necessary making additional marks for clarity) then remove the three securing screws, and lift off the bi-metal housing. Place the housing to one side, taking care not to strain the coolant hoses or electric choke heater wiring.
5   Remove the three securing screws securing the choke assembly to the carburettor body. Allow the choke assembly to drop down, but do not disconnect the choke linkage.
6   Remove the star clip which secures the diaphragm unit to the carburettor top cover, and withdraw the diaphragm unit.

20   Carburettor automatic choke vacuum pull-down units – removal, refitting and adjustment

Note: *Refer to the warning in Section 1 before proceeding. If the main diaphragm unit is removed, a new star clip (securing the main diaphragm unit to the carburettor top cover) will be required on refitting.*

Main diaphragm unit

Removal

1   Proceed as described in Section 15, paragraphs 1 to 3.
2   Disconnect the diaphragm unit vacuum pipes.

Refitting

7   Refitting is a reversal of removal, but use a new star clip to secure the diaphragm unit to the carburettor top cover. Before refitting the

19.29 Tamperproof cap (arrowed) covering fast idle speed adjustment screw

20.11 Secondary choke pull-down solenoid securing screw and earth lead

20.17 Checking the vacuum pull-down gap using a twist drill

airbox to the top of the carburettor, check and if necessary adjust the choke pull-down as described later in this Section.

Secondary pull-down solenoid

Removal

8   This unit operates in conjunction with the main diaphragm unit.
9   To remove the solenoid unit, first proceed as described in Section 15, paragraphs 1 to 3.
10   Disconnect the diaphragm unit vacuum pipe.
11   Disconnect the wiring plug, then unscrew the securing screw, and withdraw the solenoid unit and its mounting bracket from the carburettor. Note that the securing screw also secures the wiring plug earth lead (photo).

Refitting

12   Refitting is a reversal of removal, but ensure that the wiring plug earth lead is in place under the solenoid bracket securing screw.

Vacuum pull-down adjustment

13   With the airbox removed from the top of the carburettor as described in Section 15, paragraphs 2 and 3, proceed as follows.
14   Note the position of the bi-metal housing alignment marks as an aid to refitting (if necessary making additional marks for clarity) then remove the three securing screws, and lift off the bi-metal housing. Place the housing to one side, taking care not to strain the coolant hoses or electric choke heater wiring.
15   Position the fast idle speed adjustment screw on the highest step of the fast idle cam, and check that the choke valve is closed.
16   Move the pull-down arm towards the diaphragm unit by pushing on the adjustment screw until resistance is felt. Hold the arm in this position.
17   Using a drill shank of appropriate diameter, or a similar item, measure the clearance between the lower side of the choke plate and the wall of the primary barrel (photo). Check that the clearance is as given for the 'small' choke pull-down gap in the Specifications.
18   If adjustment is necessary, turn the adjustment screw in the appropriate direction, using a suitable Allen key, until the clearance is correct.
19   Now push the pull-down arm towards the diaphragm unit as far as its stop, and hold the arm in this position.

20   As before, measure the clearance between the lower side of the choke plate and the wall of the primary barrel. Check that the clearance is as given for the 'large' choke pull-down gap in the Specifications.
21   If adjustment is necessary, turn the adjustment screw in the appropriate direction until the clearance is correct.
22   Connect the bi-metal spring to the choke lever, position the bi-metal housing on the choke housing, and loosely fit the securing screws. Align the marks on the bi-metal housing and the choke housing as noted during removal, then tighten the securing screws.
23   Refit the airbox to the top of the carburettor on completion.

21 Inlet manifold – removal and refitting

Note: *Refer to the warning in Section 1 before proceeding. A new manifold gasket must be used on refitting.*

Removal

1   Disconnect the battery negative lead.
2   Drain the cooling system as described in Chapter 1.
3   Proceed as described in Section 13, paragraphs 2 to 7 inclusive, ignoring the reference to coolant spillage in paragraph 5.
4   Disconnect the coolant hose from the rear of the manifold (photo).
5   Where applicable, disconnect the camshaft cover breather hose from the rear of the manifold (photo).
6   Unscrew the union and disconnect the brake servo vacuum hose from the manifold.
7   Disconnect the wiring from the temperature gauge sender.
8   Unscrew and remove the top alternator mounting nut and bolt.
9   Disconnect and remove the stub hose which connects the crankcase breather tube to the rear of the camshaft housing.
10   Make a final check to ensure that all relevant hoses, pipes and wires have been disconnected.
11   Unscrew the securing nuts, and withdraw the manifold from the cylinder head (photo). Note the position of the rear engine lifting bracket, which is secured by one of the manifold nuts, and recover the manifold gasket.
12   It is possible that some of the manifold studs may be unscrewed from the cylinder head when the manifold securing nuts are unscrewed.

21.4 Disconnecting the coolant hose ...

21.5 ... and the camshaft cover breather hose (arrowed) from the inlet manifold

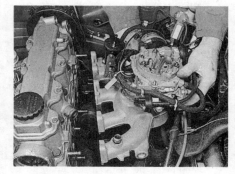

21.11 Withdrawing the inlet manifold

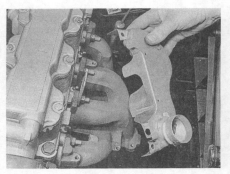

22.4 Withdrawing the exhaust manifold hot air shroud

22.7A Unscrew the exhaust manifold securing nuts, noting the location of the engine lifting bracket

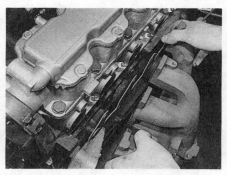

22.7B Withdrawing the exhaust manifold and gasket

In this event, the studs should be screwed back into the cylinder head once the manifold has been removed, using two manifold nuts locked together.

13   If desired, the carburettor can be removed from the manifold, with reference to Section 13.

Refitting

14   Refitting is a reversal of removal, bearing in mind the following points.

15   If the carburettor has been removed from the manifold, refit it using a new gasket.

16   If the alternator mounting bracket has been unbolted from the manifold, refit it before refitting the manifold, as access to the securing bolt is limited once the manifold is in place.

17   Refit the manifold using a new gasket, and ensure that the engine lifting bracket is in place under the relevant manifold nut.

18   Ensure that all relevant hoses, pipes and wires are correctly reconnected.

19   Refill the cooling system as described in Chapter 1.

20   Check the throttle cable free play and adjust if necessary, as described in Section 9.

21   If the carburettor has been disturbed, check and if necessary adjust the idle speed and mixture, as described in Chapter 1.

22   Exhaust manifold – removal and refitting

Note: *New manifold-to-cylinder head and manifold-to-downpipe gaskets must be used on refitting.*

Removal

1   Disconnect the battery negative lead.

2   Disconnect the HT leads from the spark plugs, if necessary labelling them to ensure refitting to their correct cylinders.

3   Loosen the clamp screw and disconnect the air cleaner hot air tube from the shroud on the manifold.

4   Remove the securing screws and withdraw the hot air shroud from the manifold (photo).

5   Working under the manifold, unscrew and remove the four bolts securing the exhaust downpipe to the manifold.

6   Separate the downpipe from the manifold, and support with wire or string. Do not allow the front section of the exhaust system to hang under its own weight. Recover the gasket.

7   Unscrew the securing nuts, and withdraw the manifold from the cylinder head. Note the position of the front engine lifting bracket, which is secured by one of the manifold studs, and recover the manifold gasket (photos).

8   Refer to Section 21, paragraph 12.

Refitting

9   Refit the manifold using a new gasket, and ensure that the engine lifting bracket is in place under the relevant manifold nut.

10   Reconnect the exhaust downpipe to the manifold, using a new gasket.

11   Further refitting is a reversal of removal.

23   Exhaust system – general information and component renewal

General information

1   Periodically, the exhaust system should be checked for signs of leaks or damage. Also inspect the system rubber mountings, and renew if necessary.

2   Small holes or cracks can be repaired using proprietary exhaust repair products, such as Holts Flexiwrap and Holts Gun Gum.

3   The original factory-fitted exhaust system consists of four separate sections, all of which can be renewed individually.

4   Before renewing an individual section of the exhaust system, it is wise to inspect the remaining sections. If corrosion or damage is evident on more than one section of the system, it may prove more economical to renew the entire system.

5   Individual sections of the system can be renewed as follows.

Component renewal

Note: *All relevant gaskets and/or sealing rings should be renewed on refitting.*

Front section

6   Raise the vehicle, and support securely on axle stands (see *'Jacking, towing and wheel changing'*).

7   Unscrew the two securing bolts, and disconnect the exhaust front section from the front expansion box at the flexible joint. Recover the sealing ring and the springs (photo).

8   Unbolt the exhaust front section from the bracket on the cylinder block (photo).

23.7 Exhaust front section-to-front expansion box flexible joint

23.8 Exhaust front section-to-cylinder block bracket

23.10 Use a new sealing ring when connecting the exhaust flexible joint

23.16 Exhaust centre section-to-rear section clamp

9   Unscrew and remove the bolts securing the downpipe to the exhaust manifold, and withdraw the exhaust front section. Recover the downpipe-to-manifold gasket, and where applicable, recover the springs from the bolts.
10   Refitting is a reversal of removal, but use a new gasket when reconnecting the downpipe to the manifold, and a new sealing ring when connecting the flexible joint (photo).

Front expansion box

11   Proceed as described in paragraphs 6 and 7.
12   Unscrew the securing bolts (and nuts, where applicable), and disconnect the front expansion box from the exhaust centre section. Recover the sealing ring/gasket and, where applicable, the springs.
13   Withdraw the expansion box from under the vehicle.
14   Refitting is a reversal of removal, but use new sealing rings/gaskets as applicable.

Centre section

15   Raise the vehicle, and support securely on axle stands (see 'Jacking, towing and wheel changing').

16   Unscrew the clamp bolt, and disconnect the exhaust centre section from the rear section (photo). If necessary, tap round the joint with a hammer to break the seal, and gently prise the two sections apart. Note that the end of the centre section fits inside the rear section, to form a sleeve joint.
17   Unscrew the securing bolts (and nuts, where applicable), and disconnect the exhaust centre section from the front expansion box. Recover the sealing ring/gasket and, where applicable, the springs.
18   Release the exhaust centre section from its rubber mountings on the underbody, and withdraw it from the vehicle.
19   Refitting is a reversal of removal, but use a new sealing ring when connecting the flexible joint, and lubricate the pipes with exhaust assembly paste when connecting the centre section to the rear section.

Rear section

20   Proceed as described in paragraphs 15 and 16.
21   Release the exhaust rear section from its rubber mountings on the underbody, and withdraw it from the vehicle.
22   Refitting is a reversal of removal, but lubricate the pipes with exhaust assembly paste when connecting the rear section to the centre section.

Part B: Fuel injection engines

24 General information and precautions

General information

Three different basic types of fuel injection system are used in the Astra range, these being Multec single-point fuel injection, Multec multi-point fuel injection, and Bosch Motronic fuel injection. The systems are described in further detail in Section 35.

Fuel is supplied from a tank mounted under the rear of the vehicle, by an electric fuel pump mounted in the tank. The fuel passes through a filter, to the fuel injection system, which incorporates various sensors, actuators, and an electronic control unit.

The inducted air passes through an air cleaner, which incorporates a paper filter element to filter out potentially-harmful particles (serious internal engine damage can be caused if foreign particles enter through the air intake system). On single-point fuel injection engines, the air cleaner has a vacuum-controlled air intake, supplying a blend of hot and cold air to suit the prevailing engine operating conditions.

The electronic control unit controls both the fuel injection system and the ignition system, integrating the two into a complete engine management system. Refer to Chapter 5 for details of the ignition side of the system.

The exhaust system is similar to that described for carburettor models in Part A of this Chapter, but a catalytic converter is incorporated to reduce exhaust gas emissions.

Precautions

Refer to the precautions and warning given in Section 1 in Part A of this Chapter, but note that the fuel injection system is pressurised – extra care must be taken when disconnecting the fuel lines. When disconnecting a fuel line union or hose, loosen the union or clamp screw slowly, to avoid a sudden release of pressure which may cause the fuel to spray out.

On models with single-point fuel injection, before disconnecting any fuel lines, the system must be depressurised by removing the fuel pump relay (see Chapter 12), and cranking the engine on the starter motor for at least 5 seconds.

After carrying out any work involving disconnection of fuel lines, it is advisable to check the connections for leaks, pressurising the system by switching the ignition on and off several times.

Electronic control units are very sensitive components, and certain precautions must be taken, to avoid damage to the unit when working on a vehicle equipped with an engine management system, as follows.

When carrying out welding operations on the vehicle using electric welding equipment, the battery and alternator should be disconnected.

Although the underbonnet-mounted modules will tolerate normal underbonnet conditions, they can be adversely affected by excess heat or moisture. If using welding equipment or pressure-washing equipment in the vicinity of an electronic module, take care not to direct heat, or jets of water or steam, at the module. If this cannot be avoided, remove the module from the vehicle, and protect its wiring plug with a plastic bag.

Before disconnecting any wiring, or removing components, always ensure that the ignition is switched off.

Do not attempt to improvise fault diagnosis procedures using a test light or multimeter, as irreparable damage could be caused to the module.

After working on fuel injection/engine management system components, ensure that all wiring is correctly reconnected before reconnecting the battery or switching on the ignition.

25 Air cleaner intake air temperature control system (single-point fuel injection engines) – testing

Refer to Section 2 in Part A of this Chapter.

26 Air cleaner housing assembly – removal and refitting

1   Refer to Section 3 in Part A of this Chapter, noting the following.
2   On models with Motronic M 1.5.2 fuel injection, note that the air mass meter is attached to the air cleaner cover, and the air intake temperature sensor is located in the air trunking. Disconnect the battery negative lead, and disconnect the relevant sensor wiring plug when removing the air cleaner cover or the air trunking.
3   On certain models, the base of the air cleaner housing (photo) clips into a resonator box mounted under the front wing. The resonator box can be removed as follows.
4   Remove the front wheel arch liner, as described in Chapter 11.
5   Remove the single securing screw, and lower the resonator box from the wheel arch (photo).
6   Refitting is a reversal of removal.

27 Fuel pump – testing, removal and refitting

Note: *Refer to the precautions given in Section 24 before proceeding. A new gasket must be used on refitting the pump, and suitable sealing compound will be required to coat the securing bolt threads.*

Saloon and Hatchback models

Testing

1   If the pump is functioning, it should be possible to hear it 'buzzing' by listening under the rear of the vehicle when the ignition is switched on. Unless the engine is started, the fuel pump should switch off after approximately one second. If the noise produced is excessive, this may be due to a faulty pump.
2   If the pump appears to have failed completely, check the wiring to the pump, and check the appropriate fuse and relay.
3   To test the performance of the pump, special equipment is required, and it is recommended that any suspected faults are referred to a Vauxhall/Opel dealer.

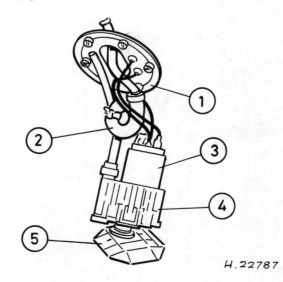

H.22787

Fig. 4.14 Fuel pump assembly (Sec 27)

1	Mounting plate	4	Rubber sleeve
2	Fuel hose	5	Fuel filter
3	Pump		

26.3 Removing the air cleaner housing – 1.6 litre multi-point fuel injection engine

26.5 Withdrawing the air cleaner resonator box from under the wheel arch

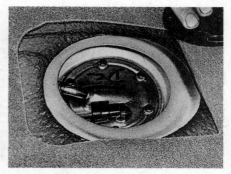

27.9 Plastic cover removed to expose fuel pump – Hatchback model

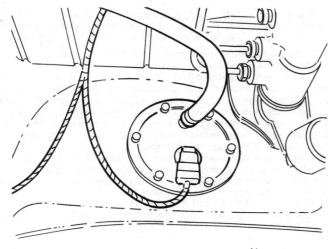

H.22788

Fig. 4.15 Fuel pump location in fuel tank – Estate and Hatchback models (Sec 27)

Removal

4   On models with single-point fuel injection, depressurize the fuel system by removing the fuel pump relay (see Chapter 12), and cranking the engine on the starter motor for at least 5 seconds.

5   Disconnect the battery negative lead.

6   Siphon out any remaining fuel in the tank through the filler pipe. Siphon the fuel into a clean metal container which can be sealed.

7   Fold the rear sear cushions forwards.

8   Lift the carpet panel on the right-hand side of the floor to expose the plastic fuel pump cover.

9   Carefully prise the plastic cover from the floor to expose the fuel pump (photo).

10   Disconnect the pump wiring plug.

11   Release the hose clip, and carefully disconnect the fuel hose from the top of the pump. Be prepared for fuel spillage, and take adequate fire precautions. Clamp or plug the open end of the hose to prevent dirt ingress and further fuel spillage.

12   Unscrew the six securing bolts and washers, and carefully withdraw the pump assembly from the fuel tank. Again, be prepared for the release of fuel, and take suitable precautions.

13   If required, the fuel pump can be detached from the assembly for renewal as follows.

14   Pull the fuel filter from the bottom of the pump.

15   Release the hose clip, and disconnect the fuel hose from the top of the pump.

16   Take note of the positions of the two pump wires to aid correct refitting, then using a soldering iron, de-solder the two wires from the top of the pump.

17   Carefully slide the pump from its rubber mounting sleeve.

Refitting

18   Refitting is a reversal of removal, bearing in mind the following points.

19   If the pump has been detached from the assembly, make sure that the wires are securely soldered to the pump in their correct locations when reassembling.

20   Inspect the filter at the bottom of the pump for excessive contamination or blockage, and renew if necessary.

21   Use a new pump gasket.

22   Clean the threads of the pump securing bolts thoroughly, and coat them with a suitable sealing compound before refitting.

Estate and Van models

Testing

23   Proceed as described in paragraphs 1 to 3 inclusive.

Removal

24   Chock the front wheels, then jack up the rear of the vehicle and support securely on axle stands (see *'Jacking, towing and wheel changing'*).

25   The fuel pump is located in the front end of the fuel tank, under the vehicle.

26   Proceed as described in paragraphs 10 to 17 inclusive.

Refitting

27   Proceed as described in paragraphs 18 to 22 inclusive.

28   Fuel gauge sender unit – removal and refitting

Refer to Section 5 in Part A of this Chapter.

29   Fuel filter – removal and refitting

Note: *Refer to the precautions given in Section 24 before proceeding.*

Removal

1   The fuel filter is located on a bracket attached to the right-hand side of the fuel tank.

2   Clamp the fuel hoses at either end of the filter to minimise fuel loss when the hoses are disconnected, then place a suitable container beneath the filter to catch the fuel which will be released.

3   Disconnect the fuel hoses from the filter. Be prepared for fuel spillage, and take adequate fire precautions.

31.4A Releasing the throttle cable balljoint clip ...

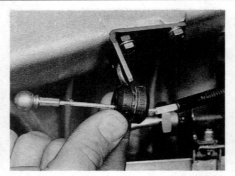

31.4B ... and releasing the cable grommet from its bracket – 1.6 litre multi-point fuel injection engine

33.2 Octane coding plug – shown set for 95 RON petrol

4   Note the orientation of the filter (and the orientation of any flow direction markings which may appear on the filter body), then unscrew the clamp bolt, and withdraw the filter from its bracket. Note that the filter will still contain some petrol, which should be drained safely into a suitable container.

Refitting

5   Refitting is a reversal of removal, ensuring that the filter is orientated as noted before removal.

30   Fuel tank – removal and refitting

Proceed as described in Section 8 in Part A of this Chapter, but disconnect the fuel hose and the wiring plug from the fuel pump, with reference to Section 27.

31   Throttle cable – removal, refitting and adjustment

Removal and refitting

1   Refer to Section 9 in Part A of this Chapter, but note the following.
2   Where applicable, ignore the reference to removing the airbox.
3   For 'carburettor' substitute 'throttle body' or 'fuel injection unit' as applicable, and note that the cable bracket is bolted to the inlet manifold.
4   On all except DOHC engine models, the throttle cable end connects to a balljoint on the throttle valve lever, and is retained by a clip. The cable is also retained by a grommet which locates in a bracket attached to the inlet manifold (photos).

Adjustment

5   Refer to Section 9 in Part A of this Chapter, but for 'carburettor' substitute 'throttle body' or 'fuel injection unit', as applicable.

32   Throttle pedal – removal and refitting

Refer to Section 10 in Part A of this Chapter.

33   Unleaded petrol – general information and usage

Note: *The information given in this Section is correct at the time of writing, and applies only to petrols currently available in the EC. If in any*

doubt as to the suitability of petrol, or if using the vehicle outside the EC, consult a Vauxhall/Opel dealer or one of the motoring organisations for advice on the petrols available, and their suitability for your vehicle.

1   Vauxhall/Opel recommend the use of 95 RON ('Premium') unleaded petrol for all fuel injection Astra models.
2   Certain models (see Specifications) can also be operated on 98 RON ('Super' or 'Super Plus') unleaded petrol, by reversing the position of the octane coding plug in its connector on the battery tray (photo). Where applicable, the plug is marked '95' on one side, which corresponds to the position for use with 95 RON (Premium) unleaded petrol, and '98' on the other side, which corresponds to the position for use with 98 RON ('Super' or 'Super Plus') unleaded petrol.
3   If necessary (for example, when travelling in territories where 95 RON unleaded petrol is not available), certain models (see Specifications) can be operated on 91 RON unleaded petrol by using a special octane coding plug available from Vauxhall/Opel dealers.
4   Leaded petrol **must not** be used in fuel injection models, as irreparable (and expensive) damage will be caused to the catalytic converter.

34   Catalytic converter – general information and precautions

General information

All fuel-injected models are equipped with a catalytic converter, to reduce exhaust gas emissions. The catalytic converter is located in the exhaust system between the exhaust front and centre sections.

The purpose of the catalytic converter is to convert potentially-harmful carbon monoxide gas, oxides of nitrogen, and unburnt hydrocarbons into harmless gases and water vapour before they are released into the atmosphere. The converter consists of a stainless steel canister containing a catalyst-coated honeycomb ceramic. The catalyst comprises a mixture of three precious metals; platinum, palladium and rhodium.

The exhaust gases pass freely through the honeycomb, where the catalyst speeds up the chemical change of the exhaust gases, without being permanently altered itself.

To enable the engine management system to achieve complete combustion of the fuel mixture, and thus to minimise exhaust emissions, an oxygen sensor is fitted in the exhaust gas stream. The sensor monitors the oxygen level in the exhaust gas, and sends a signal to the electronic control module. The module constantly alters the fuel/air mixture within a narrow band to reduce emissions, and to allow the catalytic converter to operate at maximum efficiency. No adjustment of idle mixture is therefore possible on models fitted with a catalytic converter.

Precautions

During operation, the catalytic converter reaches very high temperatures, and this should be borne in mind when parking the car. Try to avoid parking the vehicle on dry grass, etc, which may present a fire hazard if the catalyst is at working temperature.

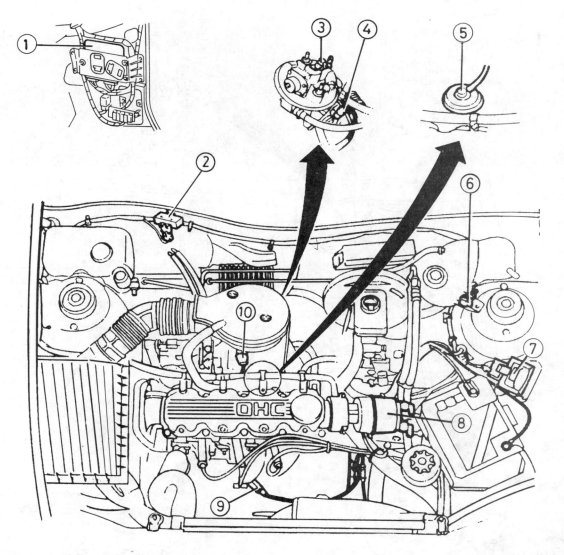

Fig. 4.16 Multec single-point fuel injection system – 1.4 and 1.6 litre engines (Sec 35)

1   *Electronic control unit (in right-hand footwell)*
2   *Manifold absolute pressure (MAP) sensor*
3   *Fuel injector*
4   *Throttle position sensor*
5   *Exhaust gas recirculation valve (1.6 litre engine only)*
6   *Octane rating plug (see Chapter 5)*
7   *Ignition coil*
8   *Distributor*
9   *Exhaust gas oxygen sensor*
10 *Idle speed control motor*

When carrying out any work under the vehicle, bear in mind that the catalyst will take a considerable time to cool down from its working temperature when the engine has been running. Take suitable precautions to avoid the possibility of burns and the risk of fire.

If a fault in the ignition system is suspected, rectify the problem or seek advice as soon as possible, particularly in the case of misfiring, as damage to the catalyst may result.

If unburnt fuel enters the catalytic converter, the fuel may burn in the catalyst, resulting in overheating and serious damage to the converter. To avoid this possibility, the following should be avoided.

(a)   *Frequent cold starts in succession.*
(b)   *Operation of the starter motor for an excessively-long time (fuel is injected during the starting process).*
(c)   *Allowing the fuel level in the fuel tank to become excessively low (an irregular fuel supply may cause overheating).*
(d)   *Starting the engine by push or tow-starting (unburnt fuel may enter the converter). Always use jump leads as an alternative.*

To avoid damage to the catalyst, the engine must be regularly serviced, and unleaded petrol must **always** be used (see Section 33). Leaded petrol will 'poison' the catalyst, and **must not** be used.

35   Fuel injection systems – general information

Multec single-point fuel injection

The system is under the overall control of the Multec engine management system, which also controls the ignition system (see Chapter 5).

Fuel is supplied from the rear-mounted fuel tank by an electric pump mounted in the tank, via a fuel filter to the Multec injection unit. A fuel pressure regulator mounted on the injection unit maintains a constant fuel pressure to the fuel injector. Excess fuel is returned from the regulator to the tank.

The fuel injection unit (resembling a carburettor) houses the throttle valve, idle speed control motor, throttle position sensor, fuel injector, and pressure regulator.

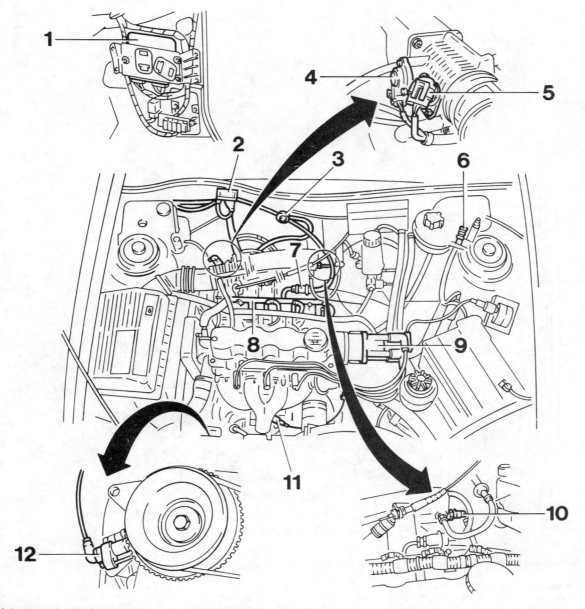

Fig. 4.17 Multec multi-point fuel injection system – 1.4 litre engine (Sec 35)

1	Electronic control unit (in right-hand footwell)	4	Throttle position sensor
2	Manifold absolute pressure (MAP) sensor	5	Idle speed control motor
3	Fuel tank vent valve	6	Octane rating plug (see Chapter 5)
7	Fuel pressure regulator	10	Intake air temperature sensor
8	Fuel injectors	11	Exhaust gas oxygen sensor
9	Distributor	12	Crankshaft speed/position sensor

The duration of the electrical pulse supplied to the fuel injector determines the quantity of fuel injected, and pulse duration is computed by the Multec electronic control unit (ECU) on the basis of information received from the various sensors. These sensors include a throttle position sensor (mounted on the fuel injection unit), a manifold absolute pressure (MAP) sensor, a distributor (1.4 and 1.6 litre engines – supplies information on crankshaft speed/position), a crankshaft speed/position sensor (1.8 litre engine only), a coolant temperature sensor, and an exhaust gas oxygen sensor.

Idle speed is controlled by the idle speed control motor, which regulates the quantity of air bypassing the throttle valve. The motor is controlled by the electronic control unit; there is no provision for the direct adjustment of idle speed.

A catalytic converter is fitted, to reduce harmful exhaust gas emissions.

Multec multi-point fuel injection

The system is under the overall control of the Multec engine management system, which also controls the ignition system (see Chapter 5).

Fuel is supplied from the rear-mounted fuel tank, via a fuel filter and a pressure regulator, to the fuel rail. Excess fuel is returned from the regulator to the tank. The fuel rail acts as a reservoir for the four fuel injectors, which inject fuel into the cylinder inlet tracts, upstream of the inlet valves. The fuel injectors operate in pairs. The injectors for cylinder Nos 1 and 2 operate simultaneously, and similarly the injectors for cylinder Nos 3 and 4 operate simultaneously.

The duration of the electrical pulses to the fuel injectors determines the quantity of fuel injected, and the pulse duration is computed by the Multec electronic control unit (ECU) on the basis of information received

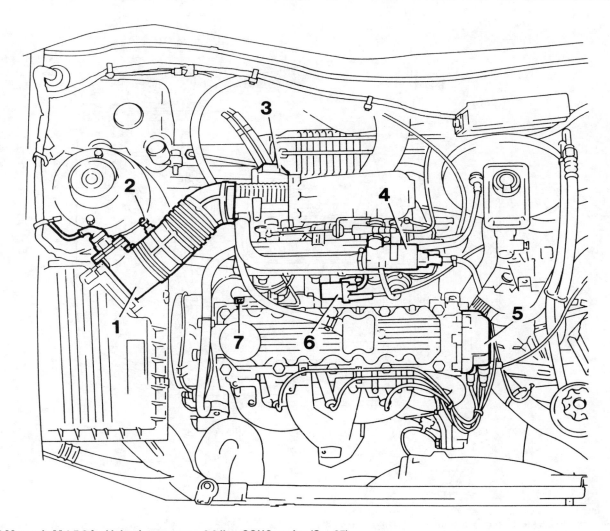

Fig. 4.18 Motronic M 1.5.2 fuel injection system – 2.0 litre SOHC engine (Sec 35)

1	Air mass meter	3	Throttle position sensor	5	Distributor	7	Coolant temperature
2	Intake air temperature sensor	4	Idle speed control valve	6	Fuel tank vent valve		sensor

from the various sensors. These sensors include a throttle position sensor, a manifold absolute pressure (MAP) sensor, a crankshaft speed/position sensor, an intake air temperature sensor, a coolant temperature sensor, and an exhaust gas oxygen sensor.

Inlet air passes from the air cleaner to the inlet manifold via the throttle valve. A sensor in the inlet manifold measures the temperature of the inlet air, and sends a signal to the electronic control unit.

A throttle position sensor enables the electronic control unit to compute the fuel requirements. Information from the throttle position sensor is also used to cut off the fuel supply on the overrun, thus improving fuel economy and reducing exhaust gas emissions.

Idle speed is controlled by the idle speed control motor, which regulates the amount of air bypassing the throttle valve. The motor is controlled by the electronic control unit; there is no provision for the direct adjustment of idle speed.

A catalytic converter is fitted, to reduce harmful exhaust gas emissions.

Bosch Motronic fuel injection

The Bosch Motronic system is available in two versions, depending on model. The Motronic M 1.5.2 system is used on SOHC engines, and the Motronic M 2.5 system is used on DOHC engines. The system is under the overall control of the Motronic engine management system, which also controls the ignition system (see Chapter 5).

Fuel is supplied from the rear-mounted fuel tank by an electric pump mounted in the tank, via a fuel filter and a pressure regulator, to the fuel rail. Excess fuel is returned from the regulator to the tank. The fuel rail acts as a reservoir for the four fuel injectors, which inject fuel into the cylinder inlet tracts, upstream of the inlet valves. On SOHC engines, the fuel injectors receive an electrical pulse once per crankshaft revolution, which operates all four injectors simultaneously. On DOHC engines, sequential fuel injection is used, whereby each injector receives an individual electrical pulse, allowing the four injectors to operate independently, which enables finer control of the fuel supply to each cylinder. The duration of the electrical pulse determines the quantity of fuel injected, and pulse duration is computed by the Motronic module, on the basis of information received from the various sensors.

On SOHC engines, inlet air passes from the air cleaner through a hot-film type air mass meter, before passing to the cylinder inlet tracts via the throttle valve. The electrical current required to maintain the temperature of the hot film panel in the air mass meter is directly proportional to the mass flow rate of the air trying to cool it. The current is converted into a signal which is passed to the Motronic module.

On DOHC engines, inlet air passes from the air cleaner through a hot-wire type air mass meter, before passing to the cylinder inlet tracts via a two- stage throttle body assembly and the electronic traction control throttle housing. The air mass meter operates in a similar manner to that described for SOHC engines. The throttle body contains

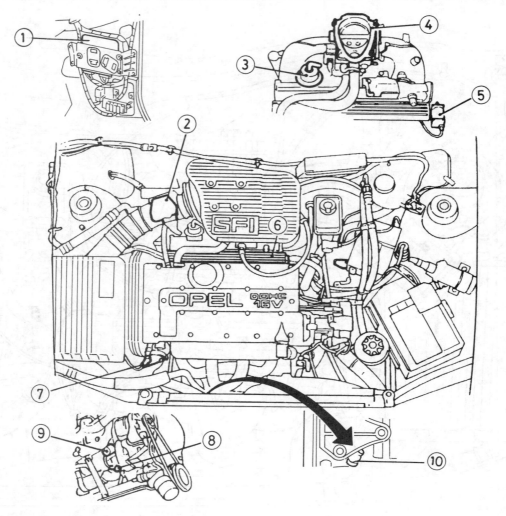

Fig. 4.19 Motronic M 2.5 fuel injection system – DOHC engine (Sec 35)

1	*Electronic control unit (in right-hand footwell)*	*7*	*Coolant temperature sensor*
2	*Air mass meter*	*8*	*Knock sensor*
3	*Fuel pressure regulator*		
4	*Throttle body*	*9*	*Idle speed control valve*
5	*Fuel tank vent valve*	*10*	*Crankshaft speed/position sensor*
6	*Fuel injection wiring harness housing*		

two throttle valves which open progressively, allowing high torque at part-throttle, and high-speed 'breathing' capacity at full-throttle. The electronic traction control (ETC) throttle valve operates independently from the Motronic system, and further details can be found in Section 41.

A throttle position sensor enables the Motronic module to compute the throttle position, and its rate of change. Extra fuel can thus be provided for acceleration when the throttle is opened suddenly. Information from the throttle position sensor is also used to cut off the fuel supply on the overrun, thus improving fuel economy and reducing exhaust gas emissions.

Idle speed is controlled by a variable-orifice solenoid valve, which regulates the amount of air bypassing the throttle valve. The valve is controlled by the Motronic module; there is no provision for the direct adjustment of idle speed.

Additional sensors inform the Motronic module of engine coolant temperature, intake air temperature (SOHC engines), crankshaft speed/position, and exhaust gas oxygen content. On DOHC engines, the Motronic module also receives signals from a cylinder block-mounted knock sensor, which senses 'knocking' (or pre-ignition) just as it begins to occur, enabling the electronic control module to retard the ignition timing, thus preventing engine damage.

A fuel filter is incorporated in the fuel supply line, to ensure that the fuel supplied to the injectors is clean.

A fuel pump cut-off relay is controlled by the Motronic module, which cuts the power to the fuel pump, should the engine stop with the ignition switched on (such as in the event of an accident).

A catalytic converter is fitted, to reduce harmful exhaust gas emissions.

All engines must be operated on unleaded petrol, and leaded petrol **must not** be used, as it will damage the catalyst.

36 Fuel injection system components – testing

1   Apart from the basic electrical tests outlined in Chapter 12, and the ignition system checks given in Chapter 5, the individual fuel system components cannot easily be tested by the home mechanic.

2   If a fault occurs, in most cases, the engine electronic control unit will still allow the engine to run (using a back-up programme of stored values), albeit at reduced efficiency and possibly with reduced driveability. While the fault might be evident to the driver, it could easily be masked by the back-up programme in such a way that fault diagnosis becomes very difficult.

3   The electronic control units have a self-analysis function, which stores fault codes in the module memory, and these fault codes can be

decoded using the specialist test equipment available to a Vauxhall/Opel dealer.

4   If a fault occurs (which may be indicated by the illumination of the engine warning light on the instrument panel), and the cause is not immediately obvious, it is worth carrying out the checks described in the following paragraphs. If these checks do not resolve the problem, the best course of action is to have the complete system checked by a Vauxhall/Opel dealer using the specialist diagnostic equipment.

5   If a fault arises, first check that it is not due to poor maintenance. Check that the air cleaner element is clean, that the spark plugs are in good condition and correctly gapped, that the crankcase ventilation system hoses are clear of obstructions and undamaged (see Part C of this Chapter), and that the throttle cable is correctly adjusted (see Section 31).

6   If the engine is running very roughly, carry out a compression test (see Chapter 2), and bear in mind that one of the hydraulic valve lifters may be faulty, producing an incorrect valve clearance.

7   If the problem is thought to be due to a dirty or blocked fuel injector, try using a proprietary fuel injector cleaning product (which is normally added to the contents of the fuel tank) in accordance with the product manufacturer's instructions.

8   If the fault persists, check the ignition system components (as far as possible), as described in Chapter 5.

9   If the fault is still not eliminated, work methodically through the system, checking all fuses, wiring connectors, wiring, vacuum hoses, looking for any signs of poor connections, damage, dirt, leaks or other faults.

10   Once the system components have been checked for signs of obvious faults, take the vehicle to a suitably-equipped Vauxhall/Opel dealer for the full system to be checked using the specialist diagnostic equipment.

11   **Do not** attempt to check any of the components, particularly the electronic control unit, using anything other than the correct test equipment, as serious (and possibly expensive!) damage to the components could result.

37   Fuel injection system components (Multec single-point fuel injection) – removal and refitting

Airbox

Removal

1   Disconnect the breather hose from the airbox.

2   Disconnect the two vacuum pipes from the airbox, noting their locations.

3   Loosen the clamp screw, and disconnect the air trunking from the end of the airbox.

4   Remove the two securing screws, and lift the airbox from the fuel injection unit. Recover the sealing ring.

Refitting

5   Refitting is a reversal of removal, bearing in mind the following points.

6   Inspect the sealing ring for damage or deterioration, and renew if

necessary. Ensure that the sealing ring locates correctly in the groove in the base of the airbox.

7   Reconnect the vacuum pipes as noted before removal.

Fuel injection unit

Note: *Refer to the precautions given in Section 24 before proceeding. All gaskets and seals must be renewed on refitting, and suitable thread-locking compound will be required to coat the fuel injection unit securing nut threads.*

Removal

8   Depressurise the fuel system by removing the fuel pump relay see Chapter 12), and cranking the engine on the starter motor for a minimum of 5 seconds.

9   Disconnect the battery negative lead.

10   Remove the airbox from the top of the fuel injection unit, as described earlier in this Section.

11   Release the securing lugs, and disconnect the wiring plug from the fuel injector (photo).

12   Remove the rubber seal from the top of the fuel injection unit (if not already done), then slide the fuel injector wiring rubber grommet from the slot in the side of the fuel injection unit (photo). Move the wiring to one side.

13   Disconnect the wiring plugs from the idle speed control motor and the throttle position sensor.

14   Disconnect the fuel feed and return hoses from the fuel injection unit, noting their locations to aid refitting. Be prepared for fuel spillage, and take adequate fire precautions. Clamp or plug the open ends of the hoses to minimise further fuel loss.

15   Disconnect the vacuum hoses from the fuel injection unit, noting their locations and routing to ensure correct refitting.

16   Disconnect the MAP sensor hose from the rear of the fuel injection unit (photo).

17   Disconnect the operating rod from the throttle valve lever (photo).

18   Make a final check to ensure that all relevant hoses and wires have been disconnected to facilitate removal of the fuel injection unit.

19   Unscrew the two securing nuts and recover the washers, and recover the sleeves which fit over the manifold studs, then carefully lift the fuel injection unit from the inlet manifold (photos). Recover the gasket.

20   If desired, the fuel injection unit may now be split into its upper and lower sections by removing the two securing screws (photo). The vacuum hose flange and the fuel hose unions can also be removed if desired.

Refitting

21   Refitting is a reversal of removal, bearing in mind the following points.

22   Where applicable, when reassembling the two sections of the fuel injection unit, use a new gasket. Similarly, where applicable use a new gasket when refitting the vacuum hose flange. If the fuel hose unions have been removed, make sure that the washers are in place when refitting.

23   Refit the fuel injection unit to the manifold using a new gasket, ensuring that the sleeves are in place over the manifold studs. Coat the threads of the securing nuts with a suitable thread-locking compound before fitting. Ensure that the washers are in place under the nuts.

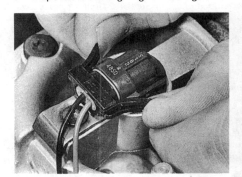

37.11 Releasing the fuel injector wiring plug retaining lugs – single-point fuel injection engine

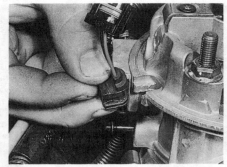

37.12 Sliding the fuel injector wiring rubber grommet from the fuel injection unit

37.16 Disconnecting the MAP sensor hose from the fuel injection unit – single-point fuel injection engine

37.17 Disconnecting the operating rod (arrowed) from the throttle valve lever – single-point fuel injection engine

37.19A Recover the sleeves which fit over the manifold studs – single-point fuel injection engine

37.19B Lifting the fuel injection unit from the inlet manifold

37.20 Removing a fuel injection unit upper-to-lower section securing screw – single-point fuel injection system

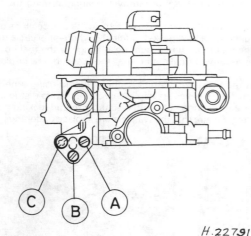

H.22791

Fig. 4.20 Vacuum hose connections at fuel injection unit single-point fuel injection system (Sec 37)

A   *Intake air temperature control*
B   *Exhaust gas recirculation (where applicable)*
C   *Fuel tank vent valve (where applicable)*

24   Ensure that all hoses are reconnected and routed correctly, as noted before removal. Note that the vacuum hoses should be connected as shown in Fig. 4.20.
25   On completion, check and if necessary adjust the throttle cable free play as described in Section 31.

Fuel injector

Note: *Refer to the precautions given in Section 24. If the original injector is being refitted, new O-rings must be used. Suitable thread-locking compound will be required to coat the clamp bracket screw threads.*

Removal

26   Depressurise the fuel system by removing the fuel pump relay (see Chapter 12), and cranking the engine on the starter motor for a minimum of 5 seconds.
27   Disconnect the battery negative lead.
28   Remove the airbox from the top of the fuel injection unit, as described earlier in this Section.
29   Squeeze the securing lugs, and disconnect the wiring plug from the fuel injector.
30   Remove the Torx type securing screw, and withdraw the injector clamp bracket (photos).
31   Carefully withdraw the injector from the fuel injection unit (photo).

Refitting

32   If the original injector is to be refitted, renew the two O-rings at the base of the injector.
33   Carefully install the injector in the fuel injection unit, with the wiring socket pointing towards the clamp bracket screw hole.
34   Refit the injector clamp bracket, ensuring that it engages correctly with the injector (the bracket should engage with the slot below the wiring socket in the injector).
35   Coat the threads of the clamp bracket screw with a suitable thread-locking compound, then refit and tighten the screw (photo).
36   Reconnect the injector wiring plug, and reconnect the battery negative lead.

Fuel pressure regulator

Note: *Refer to the precautions given in Section 24 before proceeding. The pressure regulator diaphragm must be renewed whenever the regulator cover is removed. Suitable thread-locking compound will be required to coat the regulator cover securing bolts.*

Removal

37   Depressurise the fuel system by removing the fuel pump relay (see Chapter 12), and cranking the engine on the starter motor for a minimum of 5 seconds.
38   Remove the airbox from the top of the fuel injection unit, as described earlier in this Section.
39   Unscrew the four Torx type pressure regulator cover securing bolts, and carefully withdraw the cover (photo).
40   Recover the spring seat and spring assembly, and lift out the diaphragm (photo).

Refitting

41   Refitting is a reversal of removal, but ensure that the diaphragm is correctly located in the groove in the fuel injection unit, and coat the

37.30A Remove the securing screw ...

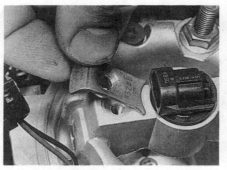

37.30B ... and withdraw the injector clamp bracket – single-point fuel injection system

37.31 Removing the fuel injector. Note O-rings (arrowed) – single-point fuel injection system

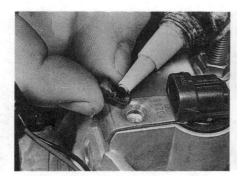

37.35 Coat the fuel injector clamp bracket screw with thread-locking compound – single-point fuel injection system

37.39 Removing the fuel pressure regulator cover – single-point fuel injection system

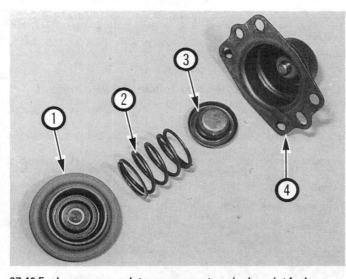

37.40 Fuel pressure regulator components – single-point fuel injection system

| 1 | Diaphragm | 3 | Spring seat |
| 2 | Spring | 4 | Cover |

threads of the cover securing bolts with a suitable thread-locking compound before fitting.

Throttle position sensor

Note: *Suitable thread-locking compound will be required to coat the sensor securing bolt threads on refitting.*

Removal

42   Disconnect the battery negative lead.

43   Remove the airbox from the top of the fuel injection unit, as described earlier in this Section.
44   Disconnect the wiring plug from the throttle position sensor (photo).
45   Remove the two securing screws, and withdraw the sensor from its housing in the fuel injection unit (photo).

Refitting

46   Ensure that the throttle valve is closed, then refit the sensor to the housing, making sure that the sensor arm is correctly engaged with the throttle valve shaft.
47   Coat the sensor securing bolts with suitable thread-locking compound, then insert and tighten them.
48   Further refitting is a reversal of removal.

Idle speed control motor

Note: *A new O-ring must be used on refitting, and suitable thread-locking compound will be required to coat the motor securing bolt threads.*

Removal

49   Disconnect the battery negative lead.
50   Remove the airbox from the top of the fuel injection unit, as described earlier in this Section.
51   Release the securing lugs, and disconnect the wiring plug from the idle speed control motor (photo).
52   Remove the two securing screws, and withdraw the motor from the side of the fuel injection unit. Where applicable, recover the O-ring seal (photos).

Refitting

53   Refitting is a reversal of removal, bearing in mind the following points.
54   To avoid damaging the housing during refitting, the distance between the end of the motor piston and the end face of the motor body flange should not be larger than 28.0 mm (photo). Measure the distance shown, and if greater than specified, carefully push the piston into the motor body as far as its stop.

37.44 Disconnecting the throttle position sensor wiring plug – single-point fuel injection system

37.45 Removing the throttle position sensor – single-point fuel injection engine

37.51 Disconnecting the wiring plug from the idle speed control motor – single-point fuel injection system

37.52A Remove the securing screws ...

37.52B ... and withdraw the idle speed control motor. Note O-ring (arrowed) – single-point fuel injection system

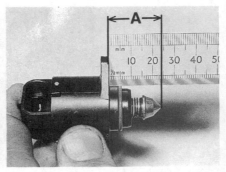

37.54 Measure the distance (A) between the end of the idle speed control motor piston and the end face of the motor body flange – single-point fuel injection system

55   Refit the motor using a new O-ring seal, with the wiring socket facing downwards.

56   Coat the threads of the motor securing bolts with a suitable thread-locking compound before fitting.

Manifold absolute pressure (MAP) sensor

Removal

57   The sensor is located on the engine compartment bulkhead, under the edge of the water deflector (photo).

58   Disconnect the battery negative lead.

59   Lift up the edge of the water deflector for access to the sensor.

60   Disconnect the sensor wiring plug and the vacuum pipe.

61   Pull the sensor upwards to release it from its bracket, and withdraw it from the vehicle.

Refitting

62   Refitting is a reversal of removal.

Crankshaft speed/position sensor (1.8 litre engine)

Note: *A new sealing ring may be required on refitting.*

Removal

63   The sensor is located in the exhaust manifold side of the engine, in

37.57 MAP sensor location (water deflector lifted for access)

37.67 Unscrewing the crankshaft speed/position sensor securing screw (engine mounting bracket and power steering pump removed) – 1.8 litre single-point fuel injection engine

37.68 Examine the crankshaft speed/position sensor O-ring

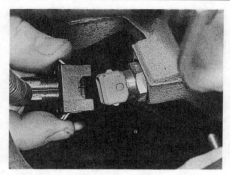

37.73 Disconnecting the coolant temperature sensor wiring plug – 1.4 litre single- point fuel injection engine

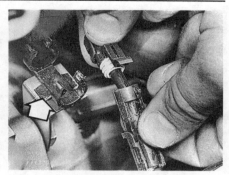

37.77 Disconnecting the oxygen sensor wiring connector. Note connector bracket location on gearbox (arrowed) – 1.4 litre single-point fuel injection engine

37.87A Unscrew the securing nuts ...

37.87B ... and pull the wiring plug bracket from the footwell

the lower cylinder block, behind the oil pump.
64   Disconnect the battery negative lead.
65   Where applicable, release the relevant outer timing belt cover securing clips, and unclip the sensor wiring from the timing belt cover.
66   Disconnect the sensor wiring connector, noting its location.
67   Unscrew the securing screw, and withdraw the sensor from the cylinder block (photo).

Refitting

68   Examine the sensor sealing ring, and renew if necessary (photo).
69   Refitting is a reversal of removal, ensuring that the sensor wiring is correctly located on the timing belt cover (where applicable), and that the wiring connector is correctly located.

Coolant temperature sensor

Note: *A new sealing ring must be used on refitting.*

Removal

70   The sensor is located in the rear right-hand side of the inlet manifold.
71   Disconnect the battery negative lead.
72   Partially drain the cooling system, as described in Chapter 1.
73   Disconnect the sensor wiring plug (photo).
74   Unscrew the sensor, and withdraw it from the inlet manifold. Recover the sealing ring where applicable.

Refitting

75   Refitting is a reversal of removal, but use a new sealing ring, and on completion, top-up the cooling system as described in Chapter 1.

Exhaust gas oxygen sensor

Note: *If the original sensor is to be re-used, the threads must be lubricated with special grease on refitting – see below.*

Removal

76   Start the engine, and run it until it reaches normal operating temperature. Stop the engine.
77   Disconnect the battery negative lead, then disconnect the oxygen sensor wiring plug, noting its location (photo).

78   Using a suitable spanner, unscrew the sensor from the inlet manifold. It is advisable to wear suitable gloves, as the exhaust system will be extremely hot.
79   Withdraw the sensor and its wiring, taking care not to burn the wiring on the exhaust system.

Refitting

80   The sensor must be refitted with the engine and exhaust system still at normal operating temperature.
81   If a new sensor is being fitted, it will be supplied with the threads coated in a special grease, to prevent the sensor seizing in the exhaust manifold.
82   If the original sensor is being refitted, clean the threads carefully. The threads must be coated with Vauxhall/Opel special grease No 19 48 602. Use only the specified grease, which consists of liquid graphite and glass beads. As the exhaust system heats up, the graphite will burn off, leaving the glass beads between the threads to prevent the sensor from seizing.
83   Refitting is a reversal of removal.

Electronic control unit

Note: *On 1.6 and 1.8 litre models, the control unit consists of two components – the basic control unit, and the programme memory, which clips into a circuit board in the control unit. The two components can be renewed independently, if a fault is suspected, but the source of the fault can only be established using specialist test equipment available to a Vauxhall/Opel dealer. On 1.4 litre engines, the two components cannot be separated, and the complete unit must be renewed if a fault is suspected.*

Removal

84   The control unit is located behind the right-hand footwell side/sill trim panel.
85   Disconnect the battery negative lead.
86   Remove the footwell side/sill trim panel, as described in Chapter 11.
87   Where applicable, unscrew the two securing nuts, and pull the wiring plug bracket from the footwell to allow sufficient access to enable the control unit to be withdrawn (photos).

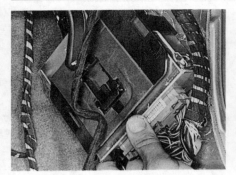

37.90 Lowering the fuel injection control unit and bracket assembly from the footwell

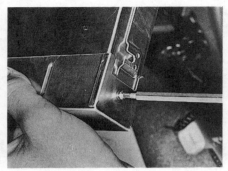

37.92A Remove the control unit rear cover ...

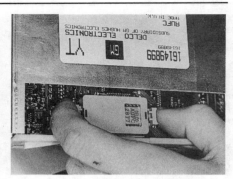

37.92B ... for access to the programme memory

38.2 Loosening an air trunking clamp screw

38.3 Disconnecting a camshaft cover breather hose from the throttle body – Multec multi-point fuel injection system

38.4 Disconnecting the fuel tank vent valve vacuum hose from the throttle body – Multec multi-point fuel injection system

88   On certain left-hand-drive models, it may be necessary to remove the glovebox (see Chapter 11) to allow access to the control unit.
89   Reach up into the footwell and locate the control unit.
90   Unscrew or unclip (as applicable) the control unit bracket, then lower the bracket, and disconnect the wiring plug(s) from the control unit (photo).
91   Unclip the control unit from the bracket, noting its orientation.
92   On 1.6 and 1.8 litre engines, the programme memory can be unclipped from its circuit board in the control unit, after removing the cover from the rear of the control unit. The cover is secured by two screws (photos).

Refitting

93   Refitting is a reversal of removal.

Exhaust gas recirculation valve (1.6 and 1.8 litre engines)

94   Refer to Section 47 in Part C of this Chapter.

Fuel evaporation control system components

95   Refer to Section 47 in Part C of this Chapter.

38   Fuel injection system components (Multec multi-point fuel injection) – removal and refitting

Throttle body

Note: *A new gasket must be used on refitting.*

Removal

1   Disconnect the battery negative lead.

2   Loosen the clamp screws securing the air trunking to the throttle body and the air cleaner cover, then withdraw the air trunking (photo).
3   Disconnect the camshaft cover breather hoses from the throttle body (photo).

38.9 Throttle linkage – Multec multi-point fuel injection system

1   Cable end balljoint
2   Cable grommet
3   Throttle return spring (note orientation)

4   Disconnect the fuel tank vent valve vacuum hose from the throttle body (photo).
5   Disconnect the manifold absolute pressure (MAP) sensor vacuum hose from the throttle body.
6   Disconnect the coolant hoses from the throttle body. Be prepared for coolant spillage, and clamp or plug the open ends of the hoses, to prevent further coolant loss.
7   Disconnect the wiring plugs from the throttle position sensor and the idle speed control motor.
8   Release the securing clip, then disconnect the throttle cable end balljoint from the throttle valve lever.
9   Slide the throttle cable grommet from the bracket on the inlet manifold, then unhook the throttle return spring from the bracket. If desired, unhook the spring from the grommet in the throttle valve linkage, and lay the spring to one side out of the way (in this case, note the orientation of the spring to enable correct refitting) (photo).
10   Make a final check to ensure that all relevant hoses and wires have been disconnected to facilitate removal of the throttle body.
11   Unscrew the four securing nuts, and withdraw the throttle body from the inlet manifold.
12   Recover the gasket.
13   If desired, the throttle position sensor and the idle speed control motor can be removed from the throttle body, as described later in this Section.

Refitting

14   Refitting is a reversal of removal, bearing in mind the following points.
15   Where applicable, refit the throttle position sensor and/or the idle speed control motor, as described later in this Section.
16   Thoroughly clean the mating faces of the throttle body and inlet manifold, and refit the throttle body using a new gasket.
17   Ensure that all wires and hoses are correctly reconnected and routed.
18   Check and if necessary top-up the coolant level, as described in Chapter 1.
19   On completion, check and if necessary adjust the throttle cable free play as described in Section 31.

Fuel injectors

Note: *Refer to the precautions given in Section 24 before proceeding. The seals at both ends of the fuel injector(s) must be renewed on refitting.*

Removal

20   Disconnect the battery negative lead.
21   Place a wad of rag beneath the fuel pipe union at the fuel pressure regulator, and then depressurise the fuel system by slowly loosening the fuel pipe union. Two open-ended spanners will be required in order that one can be used to counterhold the regulator as the union is loosened. Be prepared for fuel spillage, and take adequate fire precautions. Tighten the union when the pressure has been released.
22   Disconnect the wiring plugs from the fuel injectors, then move the wiring clear of the fuel rail (photo).
23   Disconnect the vacuum pipe from the end of the fuel pressure regulator.
24   Remove the two fuel rail securing bolts, then lift the fuel rail complete with fuel injectors sufficiently to enable the injector(s) to be removed (photos). Take care not to strain the fuel hoses which run under the fuel rail. Be prepared for fuel spillage, and take adequate fire precautions.
25   To remove an injector from the fuel rail, prise out the metal securing clip using a screwdriver or a pair of pliers, then pull the injector from the fuel rail (photos).
26   Overhaul of the fuel injectors is not possible, as no spares are available. If faulty, an injector must be renewed.
27   If desired, the fuel rail assembly can be removed from the vehicle, after disconnecting the two fuel hoses, which are connected to fuel supply and return pipes under the fuel rail. Access to the two hoses is most easily obtained from under the vehicle. Mark the hoses for position before disconnecting them, to ensure that they are reconnected correctly.

Refitting

28   Commence refitting by fitting new seals to both ends of the fuel injector(s).
29   Refitting is a reversal of removal, ensuring that all pipes and wires are correctly reconnected.

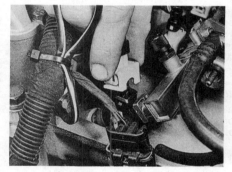

38.22 Disconnecting a fuel injector wiring plug – Multec multi-point fuel injection system

38.24A Fuel rail securing bolts (arrowed) – Multec multi-point fuel injection system

38.24B Lifting the fuel rail from the inlet manifold – Multec multi-point fuel injection system

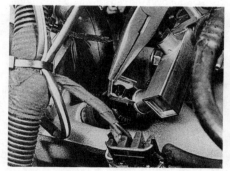

38.25A Removing a fuel injector securing clip – Multec multi-point fuel injection system

38.25B Removing a fuel injector from the fuel rail. O-rings arrowed – Multec multi-point fuel injection system

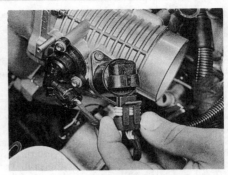

38.32 Loosening the fuel pressure regulator fuel pipe union – Multec multi-point fuel injection system

38.33 Removing the fuel pressure regulator – Multec multi-point fuel injection system

38.40 Disconnecting the idle speed control motor wiring plug – Multec multi-point fuel injection system

Fuel pressure regulator

Note: *Refer to the precautions given in Section 24 before proceeding. New sealing rings must be used on refitting.*

Removal

30   Disconnect the battery negative lead.
31   Disconnect the vacuum hose from the end of the pressure regulator.
32   Place a wad of rag beneath the fuel pipe union on the pressure regulator, then depressurise the fuel system by slowly loosening the union. Be prepared for fuel spillage, and take adequate fire precautions. Two open-ended spanners will be required, in order that one can be used to counterhold the regulator as the union is loosened (photo). Once the pressure has been released, disconnect the fuel pipe from the pressure regulator. Plug the open end of the pipe to prevent fuel loss.
33   Unscrew the securing bolt, and pull the pressure regulator from the fuel pipe and the fuel rail (photo).

Refitting

34   Refitting is a reversal of removal, but use new sealing rings on the regulator connections to the fuel pipe and the fuel rail.

Throttle position sensor

Removal

35   Disconnect the battery negative lead.
36   Release the securing clips, and disconnect the wiring plug from the throttle position sensor.
37   Remove the three securing screws, and withdraw the sensor from the throttle body.

Refitting

38   Refitting is a reversal of removal, but ensure that the sensor wiper engages correctly with the throttle valve shaft, and ensure that the sensor is correctly seated in its location on the throttle body.

Idle speed control motor

Note: *A new sealing ring may be required on refitting.*

Removal

39   Disconnect the battery negative lead.
40   Release the securing clip, and disconnect the wiring plug from the idle speed control motor (photo).
41   Remove the two securing screws, and withdraw the motor. Where applicable, recover the O-ring seal.

Refitting

42   Before refitting the motor, examine the condition of the sealing ring, and renew if necessary.
43   Refitting is a reversal of removal, ensuring that the sealing ring is correctly located, and that the motor wiring socket faces downwards.

Manifold absolute pressure (MAP) sensor

44   Proceed as described in Section 37 for single-point fuel injection engines.

Crankshaft speed/position sensor

Note: *A new sealing ring may be required on refitting.*

Removal

45   The sensor is located in a bracket bolted to the lower cylinder block, on the inlet manifold side of the engine, next to the crankshaft pulley (photo).
46   Disconnect the battery negative lead.
47   Disconnect the sensor wiring connector, which is attached to a bracket on the camshaft cover. Release the connector from the bracket.
48   Access to the sensor is most easily obtained from under the vehicle. If desired, raise the front of the vehicle and support securely on axle stands, as described in *'Jacking, towing and wheel changing'*.
49   Remove the securing screw, and withdraw the sensor from its bracket. Note the routing of the wiring to aid refitting.

Refitting

50   Examine the sensor sealing ring, and renew if necessary.
51   Refitting is a reversal of removal, ensuring that the wiring and the wiring connector are correctly located.
52   On completion, check the gap between the end face of the sensor and the toothed sensor wheel attached to the crankshaft pulley, using a suitable feeler gauge. The gap should be as given in the Specifications. If the gap is not as specified, the sensor mounting bracket must be renewed, as no adjustment is possible.

Coolant temperature sensor

53   Proceed as described in Section 37 for single-point fuel injection engines, but note that the sensor is located in the left-hand end face of the cylinder head, beneath the distributor, or coil (as applicable).

Intake air temperature sensor

Removal

54   The sensor is located in the left-hand end of the inlet manifold plenum chamber.
55   Disconnect the battery negative lead.
56   Disconnect the sensor wiring plug (photo).
57   Unscrew the sensor from the inlet manifold.

Refitting

58   Refitting is a reversal of removal.

Exhaust gas oxygen sensor

59   Proceed as described in Section 37 for single-point fuel injection engines.

Electronic control unit

60   Proceed as described in Section 37 for single-point fuel injection engines, noting that the basic control unit and the programme memory can be renewed independently.

Fuel evaporation control system components

61   Refer to Section 47 in Part C of this Chapter.

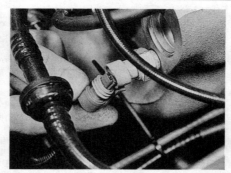

38.45 Crankshaft speed/position sensor location viewed from underneath vehicle (securing bolt arrowed) – Multec multi-point fuel injection system

38.56 Disconnecting the intake air temperature sensor wiring plug – Multec multi-point fuel injection system

39.10 Unhooking the throttle return spring from the bracket on the inlet manifold – Motronic M 1.5.2 fuel injection system

39 Fuel injection system components (Motronic M 1.5.2 fuel injection) – removal and refitting

Throttle body

Note: *A new gasket must be used on refitting.*

Removal

1   Disconnect the battery negative lead.
2   Release the securing clip, and disconnect the wiring plug from the intake air temperature sensor (mounted in the air trunking). Pull on the plug, not on the wiring.
3   Loosen the clamp screws securing the air trunking to the throttle body and the air mass meter, then withdraw the air trunking.
4   Disconnect the idle speed control valve hose from the throttle body.
5   Disconnect the camshaft cover breather hose from the throttle body.
6   Disconnect the fuel tank vent valve vacuum hose from the throttle body.
7   Disconnect the coolant hoses from the throttle body. Be prepared for coolant spillage, and clamp or plug the open ends of the hoses, to prevent further coolant loss.
8   Release the securing clip, and disconnect the wiring plug from the throttle position sensor.
9   Release the securing clip, then disconnect the throttle cable end balljoint from the throttle valve lever.
10   Slide the throttle cable grommet from the bracket on the inlet manifold, then unhook the throttle return spring from the bracket. If desired, unhook the spring from the grommet in the throttle valve linkage, and lay the spring to one side out of the way (in this case, note the orientation of the spring to enable correct refitting) (photo).
11   Make a final check to ensure that all relevant hoses and wires have been disconnected to facilitate removal of the throttle body.
12   Unscrew the four securing nuts (photo), and withdraw the throttle body from the inlet manifold. Access to the lower nuts may be restricted by the two fuel hoses, and it may be necessary to move the hoses to one side to improve access. Take care not to strain the hoses.
13   Recover the gasket.
14   If desired, the throttle position sensor can be removed from the throttle body, as described later in this Section.

Refitting

15   Refitting is a reversal of removal, bearing in mind the following points.
16   Where applicable, refit the throttle position sensor as described later in this Section.
17   Thoroughly clean the mating faces of the throttle body and inlet manifold, and refit the throttle body using a new gasket.
18   Ensure that all wires and hoses are correctly reconnected and routed.
19   Check and if necessary top-up the coolant level, as described in Chapter 1.
20   On completion, check and if necessary adjust the throttle cable free play, as described in Section 31.

Fuel injectors

Note: *Refer to the precautions given in Section 24 before proceeding. The seals at both ends of the fuel injector(s) must be renewed on refitting.*

Removal

21   Disconnect the battery negative lead.
22   Unscrew the union nut, and disconnect the brake servo vacuum hose from the inlet manifold.
23   Remove the idle speed control valve, complete with hoses, as described later in this Section.
24   Disconnect the vacuum hose from the top of the fuel pressure regulator.
25   Disconnect the wiring harness housing from the fuel injectors, and move it to one side, taking care not to strain the wiring. Pull up on the wiring harness housing, and compress the wiring plug securing clips to release the harness housing from the injectors.
26   Place a wad of rag beneath the fuel pressure regulator, then depressurise the fuel system by slowly loosening the clamp screws securing the fuel supply hose to the pressure regulator. Be prepared for fuel spillage, and take adequate fire precautions.
27   Remove the four bolts from the brackets securing the fuel rail to the inlet manifold, then lift the inlet rail complete with fuel injectors sufficiently to enable the injector(s) to be removed. Take care not to strain the fuel hoses. Be prepared for fuel spillage, and take adequate fire precautions.
28   To remove an injector from the fuel rail, prise out the metal securing clip using a screwdriver, then pull the injector from the fuel rail.
29   Overhaul of the fuel injectors is not possible, as no spares are available. If faulty, an injector must be renewed.

39.12 Unscrewing a throttle body securing nut (arrowed) – Motronic M 1.5.2 fuel injection system

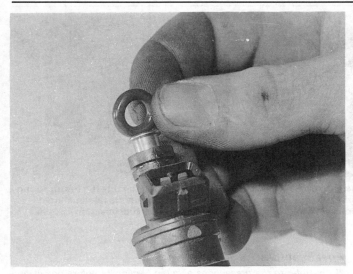

39.30 Fitting a new O-ring to a fuel injector – Motronic M 1.5.2 fuel injection system

Refitting

30   Commence refitting by fitting new seals to both ends of the fuel injector(s) (photo).
31   Refitting is a reversal of removal, ensuring that all hoses, pipes and wires are correctly reconnected.

Fuel pressure regulator

Note: *Refer to the precautions given in Section 24 before proceeding.*

Removal

32   Disconnect the battery negative lead.
33   For improved access, remove the idle speed control valve as described later in this Section, then disconnect the wiring harness from the fuel injectors and move it to one side, taking care not to strain the wiring. Pull on the wiring harness housing, and compress the wiring plug retaining clips to release the harness housing from the injectors.
34   Position a wad of rag beneath the pressure regulator, to absorb any fuel which may be released as the regulator is removed.
35   Slowly loosen the clamp screws and disconnect the fuel hoses from the regulator. Be prepared for fuel spillage, and take adequate fire precautions.
36   Disconnect the vacuum hose from the top of the regulator, and withdraw the regulator.

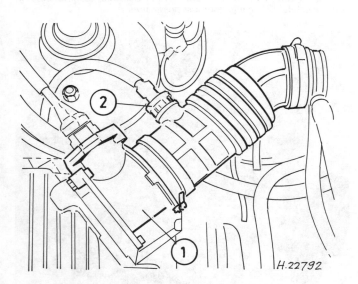

Fig. 4.21 Air mass meter (1) and intake air temperature sensor (2) – Motronic M 1.5.2 fuel injection system (Sec 39)

Refitting

37   Refitting is a reversal of removal.

Air mass meter

Note: *A new sealing ring must be used on refitting, and suitable thread-locking compound will be required to coat the securing bolts.*

Removal

38   Disconnect the battery negative lead.
39   Release the securing clip, and disconnect the wiring plug from the intake air temperature sensor (mounted in the air trunking). Pull on the plug, not on the wiring.
40   Similarly, disconnect the wiring plug from the air mass meter.
41   Loosen the clamp screws securing the air trunking to the throttle body and the air mass meter, then withdraw the air trunking.
42   Remove the air cleaner cover, complete with the air mass meter, with reference to Section 3 in Part A of this Chapter.
43   Unscrew the two securing bolts, and remove the air mass meter from the air cleaner cover. Recover the sealing ring.

Refitting

44   Refitting is a reversal of removal, but use a new sealing ring when fitting the air mass meter to the air cleaner cover, and coat the securing bolts with a suitable thread-locking compound.

Throttle position sensor

45   Proceed as described in Section 38 for Multec multi-point fuel injection engines, noting that the sensor is secured by two screws.

Idle speed control valve

Removal

46   Disconnect the battery negative lead.
47   Release the retaining clip, and disconnect the wiring plug from the idle speed control valve (photo).
48   The valve can be removed complete with its connecting hoses, or separately, leaving the hoses in place.
49   Loosen the relevant clamp screws, then disconnect the hoses and withdraw the valve (photo).

Refitting

50   Refitting is a reversal of removal.

Crankshaft speed/position sensor

51   Proceed as described in Section 37 for the 1.8 litre engine.

Coolant temperature sensor

52   Proceed as described in Section 37 for single-point fuel injection engines, but note that the sensor is located in the end of the thermostat housing on the inlet manifold side of the engine, below the alternator upper mounting bracket (photo).

Intake air temperature sensor

53   Proceed as described in Section 38 for Multec multi-point fuel injection engines, but note that the sensor is located in the air trunking between the inlet manifold and the air mass meter. Take care not to damage the air trunking.

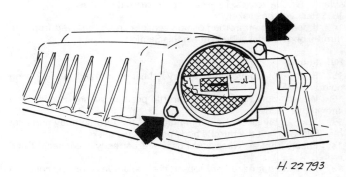

Fig. 4.22 Air mass meter securing screws (arrowed) – Motronic M 1.5.2 fuel injection system (Sec 39)

39.47 Disconnecting the wiring plug from the idle speed control valve – Motronic M 1.5.2 fuel injection system

39.49 Withdrawing the idle speed control valve complete with hoses – Motronic M 1.5.2 fuel injection system

39.52 Disconnecting the coolant temperature sensor wiring plug – Motronic M 1.5.2 fuel injection system

Exhaust gas oxygen sensor

54   Proceed as described in Section 37 for single-point fuel injection engines, but note that the sensor is mounted in the exhaust front section, and access is obtained from underneath the vehicle. If desired, raise the front of the vehicle and support securely on axle stands, as described in '*Jacking, towing and wheel changing*'.

Electronic control unit

55   Proceed as described in Section 37 for single-point fuel injection engines, ignoring the references to the basic control unit and the programme memory.

Fuel evaporation control system components

56   Refer to Section 47 in Part C of this Chapter.

40   Fuel injection system components (Motronic M 2.5 fuel injection) – removal and refitting

Airbox

Note: *Suitable sealant will be required to coat the sealing ring seating area in the airbox on refitting.*

Removal

1   Loosen the clamp screw securing the air trunking to the left-hand side of the air mass meter.
2   Using a suitable Allen key or hexagon bit, unscrew the four bolts securing the airbox to the throttle body (photo).
3   Lift the airbox from the top of the throttle body, and disconnect the hose from the base of the airbox (photo).
4   Withdraw the airbox, and recover the sealing ring from the base of the airbox if it is loose.

Refitting

5   Before commencing refitting, remove the sealing ring from the base of the airbox, if not already done (photo).
6   Examine the sealing ring, and if it is worn or damaged, renew it.
7   Thoroughly clean the sealing ring seating area in the airbox, then liberally coat the seating face with a suitable sealant (Vauxhall/Opel part No 15 04 851, or equivalent).
8   Fit the sealing ring to the airbox, ensuring that it is correctly seated, then refit the assembly using a reversal of the removal procedure.

Main throttle body

Note: *A new gasket must be used on refitting.*

Removal

9   Disconnect the battery negative lead.
10   Remove the airbox/air mass meter assembly from the top of the throttle body, as described previously in this Section.
11   Release the securing clip, and disconnect the wiring plug from the throttle position sensor. Pull on the plug, not on the wiring.
12   Unscrew the retaining nut, and detach the fuel hose bracket from the left-hand side of the throttle body.
13   Slide the throttle cable end from the throttle valve lever (photo).
14   Disconnect the breather hose from the front of the throttle body (photo).
15   Make a final check to ensure that all relevant hoses, pipes and wires have been disconnected and moved clear of the throttle body.
16   Unscrew the four securing nuts, and remove the throttle body from the inlet manifold (photo). Recover the gasket.
17   If desired, the throttle position sensor can be removed from the throttle body, as described later in this Section.
18   **Do not** under any circumstances attempt to adjust the throttle valve linkage. If the throttle valve linkage is faulty, refer the problem to a Vauxhall/Opel dealer.

Refitting

19   Refitting is a reversal of removal, bearing in mind the following points.

40.2 Unscrewing an airbox securing bolt – Motronic M 2.5 fuel injection system

40.3 Disconnecting the hose from the airbox – Motronic M 2.5 fuel injection system

40.5 Removing the sealing ring from the base of the airbox – Motronic M 2.5 fuel injection system

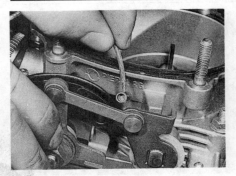

40.13 Disconnecting the throttle cable from the throttle valve lever – Motronic M 2.5 fuel injection system

40.14 Disconnect the breather hose (arrowed) from the throttle body – Motronic M 2.5 fuel injection system

40.16 Two of the main throttle body securing nuts (arrowed) – Motronic M 2.5 fuel injection system

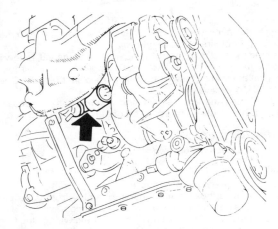

Fig. 4.23 Idle speed control valve location (arrowed) viewed from underneath vehicle – Motronic M 2.5 fuel injection system (Sec 40)

20   Before refitting the throttle body, check the adjustment of the throttle position sensor, as described in paragraphs 65 to 67 inclusive.
21   Thoroughly clean the mating faces of the throttle body and electronic traction control (ETC) throttle housing, and refit the throttle body using a new gasket.
22   Ensure that all hoses, pipes and wires are correctly reconnected and routed.
23   Refit the airbox as described earlier in this Section.
24   On completion, check and if necessary adjust the throttle cable free play, as described in Section 31.

Electronic traction control (ETC) throttle housing

25   Refer to Section 42.

Fuel injectors

Note: *Refer to the precautions given in Section 24 before proceeding. The seals at both ends of the fuel injector(s) must be renewed on refitting.*

Removal

26   Disconnect the battery negative lead.
27   Remove the airbox, as described previously in this Section.
28   Position a wad of rag beneath one of the fuel hose unions on the fuel rail, to absorb the fuel which will be released as the union is disconnected.
29   Slowly loosen the fuel hose union to relieve the pressure in the fuel line, then disconnect the hose from the fuel rail (photo). Be prepared for fuel spillage, and take adequate fire precautions. Clamp or plug the end of the fuel hose, to prevent dirt ingress and further fuel spillage.
30   Repeat paragraphs 28 and 29 for the remaining fuel hose-to-fuel rail union.
31   Disconnect the two breather hoses from the rear of the camshaft cover. Disconnect the larger hose from the throttle body, and remove the hose completely.
32   Disconnect the vacuum pipe from the top of the fuel pressure regulator.
33   Disconnect the wiring plug from the air mass meter. Recover the sealing ring.
34   Disconnect the wiring plug from the throttle position sensor.
35   Slide the end of the throttle cable from the throttle valve lever on the throttle body, then unbolt the cable bracket from the inlet manifold, and move it to one side.
36   Disconnect the wiring harness from the fuel injectors, and move it to one side, taking care not to strain the wiring. Pull up on the wiring harness housing, and compress the wiring plug retaining clips to release the housing from the injectors (photo).
37   Unscrew and remove the two fuel rail securing nuts, and withdraw the fuel rail complete with fuel injectors from the inlet manifold. Note the position of the earth leads on the fuel rail securing studs (photo).
38   To remove an injector from the fuel rail, prise out the metal securing clip, then pull the injector from the fuel rail (photos).

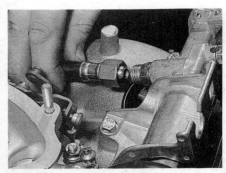

40.29 Disconnecting the fuel supply hose from the fuel rail – Motronic M 2.5 fuel injection system

40.36 Lifting the wiring harness housing from the fuel injectors – Motronic M 2.5 fuel injection system

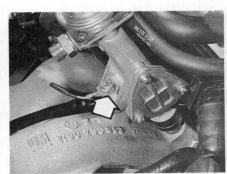

40.37 Fuel rail securing nut (arrowed). Note position of earth lead – Motronic M 2.5 fuel injection system

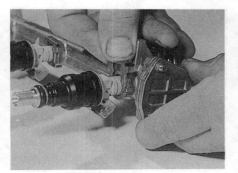

40.38A Prise out the metal securing clip ...

40.38B ... and pull the injector from the fuel rail – Motronic M 2.5 fuel injection system

40.49 Disconnecting the vacuum pipe from the fuel pressure regulator – Motronic M 2.5 fuel injection system

40.57 Disconnecting the wiring plug from the air mass meter – Motronic M 2.5 fuel injection system

40.62 Throttle position sensor (arrowed) – Motronic M 2.5 fuel injection system

39   Overhaul of the fuel injectors is not possible, as no spares are available. If faulty, an injector must be renewed.

Refitting

40   Commence refitting by fitting new seals to both ends of the fuel injector(s).
41   Further refitting is a reversal of removal, bearing in mind the following points.
42   Ensure that all hoses, pipes and wires are correctly reconnected.
43   Refit the airbox as described earlier in this Section.
44   On completion, check and if necessary adjust the throttle cable free play, as described in Section 31.

Fuel pressure regulator

Note: *Refer to the precautions given in Section 24 before proceeding.*

Removal

45   Disconnect the battery negative lead.
46   Remove the airbox from the top of the throttle housing, as described earlier in this Section.
47   Release the retaining clip, and disconnect the wiring plug from the air mass meter. Pull on the plug, not on the wiring. Where applicable, recover the sealing ring.
48   Release the retaining clip, and disconnect the wiring plug from the throttle position sensor.
49   Disconnect the vacuum pipe from the top of the fuel pressure regulator (photo).
50   Position a wad of rag beneath the fuel supply union on the fuel rail, then depressurise the fuel system by slowly loosening the union. Be prepared for fuel spillage, and take adequate fire precautions. Tighten the union when the pressure has been released.
51   Position a wad of rag beneath the regulator, to absorb the fuel which will be released as the regulator is removed.
52   Using a suitable spanner or socket, and working underneath the regulator, unscrew the Torx type securing bolts, then withdraw the regulator. Be prepared for fuel spillage, and take adequate fire precautions.

Refitting

53   Refitting is a reversal of removal, bearing in mind the following points.
54   Ensure that all wires, pipes and hoses are correctly reconnected.
55   Refit the airbox as described earlier in this Section.

Air mass meter

Removal

56   Disconnect the battery negative lead.
57   Release the retaining clip, and disconnect the wiring plug from the air mass meter (photo). Pull on the plug, not on the wiring. Recover the sealing ring, where applicable.
58   Loosen the clamp screws, disconnect the air trunking from either end of the meter, then withdraw the meter.

Refitting

59   Refitting is a reversal of removal, but where applicable, inspect the condition of the wiring plug sealing ring and renew if necessary.

Throttle position sensor

Removal

60   Disconnect the battery negative lead.
61   Remove the airbox and the air mass meter, as described previously in this Section (note that if the connecting air trunking is left in place, the two components can be removed as an assembly).
62   Release the retaining clip, and disconnect the wiring plug from the throttle position sensor (photo).
63   Remove the two securing screws and withdraw the sensor from the throttle body.

Refitting

64   Refit the sensor, but before tightening the securing screws, adjust the position of the sensor as follows.
65   Turn the sensor body anti-clockwise until resistance is felt, then tighten the securing screws.

**40.73 Idle speed control valve (arrowed) –
Motronic M 2.5 fuel injection system**

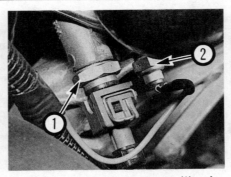

**40.78 Coolant temperature sensor (1) and
temperature gauge sender (2) – Motronic
M 2.5 fuel injection system**

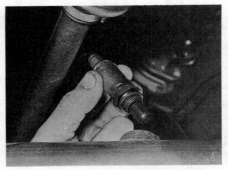

**40.79 Removing the exhaust gas oxygen
sensor – Motronic M 2.5 fuel injection
system**

66   When the throttle valve is opened, an audible click should be noticeable from the sensor, and similarly, this should be repeated as the throttle valve is closed.
67   If necessary, adjust the position of the sensor until a click is heard just as the throttle valve begins to open.
68   Refit the airbox as described earlier in this Section.

Idle speed control valve

Removal
69   Disconnect the battery negative lead.
70   Loosen the clamp screw, and disconnect the hose from underneath the airbox on the throttle body. Remove the clamp from the hose.
71   Apply the handbrake, then jack up the front of the vehicle, and support securely on axle stands (see *'Jacking, towing and wheel changing'*).
72   Remove the engine undershield, as described in Chapter 11.
73   Working underneath the vehicle, disconnect the wiring plug from the idle speed control valve, which is located underneath the inlet manifold, above the starter motor (photo).
74   Loosen the clamp screw and disconnect the remaining idle speed control valve hose from the inlet manifold, then withdraw the valve downwards, complete with the hoses.
75   If the hoses are to be removed from the valve, mark their locations before removal so that they can be correctly reconnected. Once the valve has been refitted, it is extremely difficult to swap the hose positions.

Refitting
76   Refitting is a reversal of removal, but ensure that the valve rests horizontally, with the wiring routed over the top of the coolant hose. If the wiring is routed under the coolant hose, this may cause the valve to be bent downwards, resulting in a restriction or fracture in the air hose to the inlet manifold.

Crankshaft speed/position sensor

77   Proceed as described in Section 37 for the 1.8 litre engine.

Coolant temperature sensor

78   Proceed as described in Section 37 for single-point fuel injection engines, but note that the sensor is located in the thermostat housing, on the exhaust manifold side of the engine (photo).

Exhaust gas oxygen sensor

79   Proceed as described in Section 37 for single-point fuel injection engines, but note that the sensor is mounted in the exhaust front section, and access is obtained from underneath the vehicle, after removing the engine undershield access hatch (photo). If desired, raise the front of the vehicle and support securely on axle stands, as described in *'Jacking, towing and wheel changing'*.

Knock sensor

Removal
80   The sensor is located on the lower inlet manifold side of the

cylinder block, below the idle speed control valve, and (unless the inlet manifold has been removed) is only accessible from below the vehicle.
81   Disconnect the battery negative lead.
82   Apply the handbrake, then jack up the front of the vehicle and support securely on axle stands, as described in *'Jacking, towing and wheel changing'*.
83   Remove the engine undershield, as described in Chapter 11.
84   Disconnect the sensor wiring plug.
85   Unscrew the securing bolt, and withdraw the sensor from the cylinder block.

Refitting
86   Refitting is a reversal of the removal procedure, but make sure that the sensor and its seat are perfectly clean, and that the sensor is secured firmly. Failure to observe these points could result in damage to the engine, as a poorly-mounted sensor will not detect 'knocking', and the appropriate ignition correction will not be applied.

Electronic control unit

87   Proceed as described in Section 37 for single-point fuel injection engines, ignoring the references to the basic control unit and the programme memory.

Fuel evaporation control system components

88   Refer to Section 47 in Part C of this Chapter.

---

41   Electronic traction control system – general information

The electronic traction control (ETC) system is fitted to DOHC engine models, and monitors the traction provided by the driven (front) wheels, preventing the wheels from spinning, regardless of the road conditions and the grip of the tyres. This is particularly beneficial in helping to increase traction when driving on slippery roads due to rain, snow, or ice.
The ETC system is controlled by an electronic control unit, which receives information from the Motronic and ABS system electronic control units. The four ABS wheel sensors (see Chapter 9) continuously monitor the traction of the front wheels by comparing the speeds of the front wheels with those of the rear wheels. Immediately a difference in speed is registered between the front and rear wheels, a signal is fed to the ETC electronic control unit. The ETC control unit activates an auxiliary throttle valve, which reduces the engine speed (and thus torque) to optimum levels in relation to the rotation of the wheels, even though the driver may be applying full-throttle (main throttle valve fully open). In exceptional circumstances, such as when driving away from rest using full-throttle on an icy surface, the ETC control unit supplies a signal to the Motronic control unit to interrupt the fuel injection and ignition systems intermittently, reducing engine torque more rapidly.
The ETC system throttle valve is mounted in a housing fitted between the main throttle body and the inlet manifold. The throttle valve is actuated by a control motor, via a coupling rod. A potentiometer

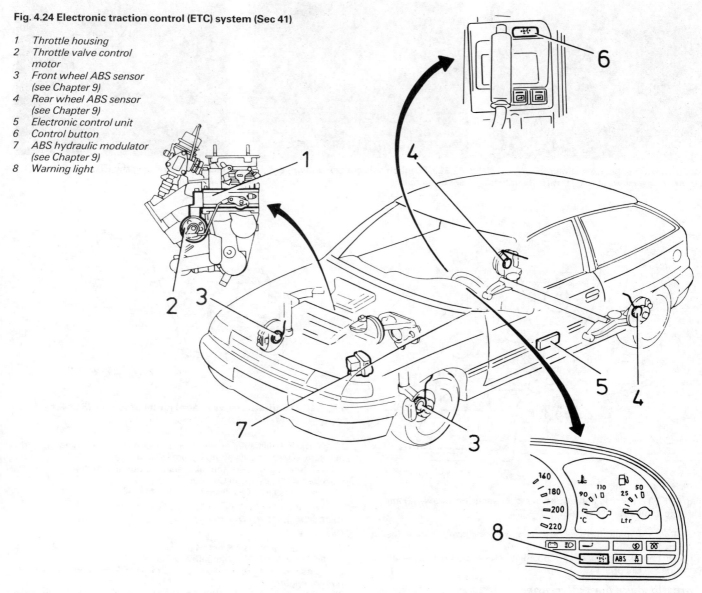

Fig. 4.24 Electronic traction control (ETC) system (Sec 41)

1 Throttle housing
2 Throttle valve control motor
3 Front wheel ABS sensor (see Chapter 9)
4 Rear wheel ABS sensor (see Chapter 9)
5 Electronic control unit
6 Control button
7 ABS hydraulic modulator (see Chapter 9)
8 Warning light

is incorporated in the control motor to provide the ETC control unit with information on the ETC throttle valve position.

If desired, the system can be switched off by using a button mounted in the centre console. This may be beneficial in certain circumstances such as when driving in deep snow, or when 'digging' the vehicle out of soft ground.

42 Electronic traction control system components – removal and refitting

Throttle housing

Note: New gaskets must be used on refitting.

Removal

1 Disconnect the battery negative lead.
2 Remove the main throttle body, as described in Section 40.
3 Disconnect the camshaft cover breather hose from the right-hand side of the ETC throttle valve housing.
4 Disconnect the coolant hoses from the ETC throttle valve housing, noting their locations and routing to aid correct refitting. Be prepared for

coolant spillage, and clamp or plug the open ends of the hoses to minimise coolant loss.
5 Unscrew and remove the two bolts securing the throttle valve control motor to the throttle valve housing.
6 Disconnect the two vacuum hoses from the front of the throttle valve housing, noting their locations to aid refitting.
7 Disconnect the throttle valve actuating rod from the lever on the side of the throttle valve housing.
8 Lift the ETC throttle valve housing from the inlet manifold. Recover the gasket.

Refitting

9 Before commencing refitting, thoroughly clean the mating surfaces of the ETC throttle valve housing and the inlet manifold.
10 Fit the ETC throttle valve housing to the inlet manifold, using a new gasket.
11 Further refitting is a reversal of removal, bearing in mind the following points.
12 Ensure that the coolant hoses are correctly reconnected and routed, as noted before removal.
13 When reconnecting the throttle valve actuating rod to the lever on the throttle valve housing, ensure that the retaining clip engages.
14 When reconnecting the vacuum hoses to the throttle valve housing, ensure that they are correctly positioned as noted previously.

42.23 Throttle valve operating rod connection (arrowed) to ETC throttle valve

42.32 ETC electronic control unit cover securing nuts

42.34 Withdrawing the ETC electronic control unit

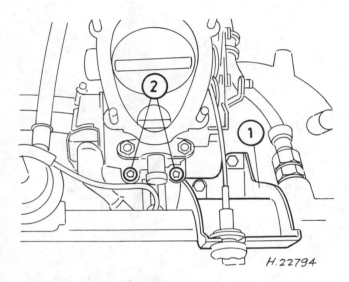

Fig. 4.25 ETC throttle valve control motor securing screws (2) and throttle cable bracket (1) (Sec 42)

15   Refit the main throttle body, using a new gasket, as described in Section 40.
16   On completion, check the coolant level and top-up if necessary, as described in Chapter 1.

Throttle valve control motor

Removal

17   Disconnect the battery negative lead.
18   Remove the airbox from the top of the throttle body, as described in Section 40.
19   Disconnect the crankcase ventilation hose from the main throttle body.
20   Loosen the alternator mounting bolts, then remove the top mounting bolt, slip the drivebelt from the alternator pulley, and swing the alternator to one side, away from the engine.
21   Unscrew the two securing screws, and detach the throttle cable bracket from the inlet manifold.
22   Disconnect the throttle valve control motor wiring plug, which is accessible from the alternator side of the throttle housing.
23   Disconnect the ETC throttle valve operating rod from the throttle valve (photo).
24   Unscrew and remove the two bolts securing the throttle valve control motor to the ETC throttle valve housing, then carefully withdraw the motor assembly – see Fig. 4.25.
25   If the throttle valve operating rod is disconnected from the motor, take careful note of the orientation of the rod, to enable correct refitting.

Refitting

26   Refitting is a reversal of removal, bearing in mind the following points.

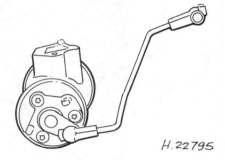

Fig. 4.26 ETC throttle valve control motor assembly (Sec 42)

27   Where applicable, ensure that the throttle valve operating rod is correctly orientated, as noted before removal.
28   Before tightening the alternator mounting bolts, tension the drivebelt as described in Chapter 12.
29   Refit the airbox as described in Section 40.

Electronic control unit

Removal

30   The ETC electronic control unit is located inside the vehicle, next to the left-hand front seat, beneath a cover in the sill.
31   Ensure that the ignition is switched off, then disconnect the battery negative lead.
32   Prise up the two flaps which conceal the control unit cover securing nuts, then remove the securing nuts (photo).
33   Carefully withdraw the control unit cover, noting that it clips into the seat runner cover panel.
34   Pull the control unit from its location, then remove the wiring plug securing screw, release the clips to disconnect the wiring plug, and withdraw the unit (photo).

Refitting

35   Refitting is a reversal of removal, ensuring that the cover engages correctly with the seat runner cover panel.

Manual override switch

Removal

36   The switch is located in the centre console.
37   Disconnect the battery negative lead.
38   Carefully prise the central storage tray from the centre console.
39   Disconnect the wiring from the switch.
40   Carefully push the switch out through the top of the centre console.

Refitting

41   Refitting is a reversal of removal.

43.3 Brake servo hose union nut (1) and wiring connector (2) attached to left-hand end of inlet manifold – single-point fuel injection engine

43.9 Earth wire (arrowed) attached to upper alternator mounting – single-point fuel injection engine

43 Inlet manifold – removal and refitting

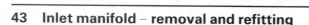

Note: *Refer to the precautions given in Section 24 before proceeding. A new gasket must be used on refitting.*

Models with Multec single-point fuel injection
Removal

1 Proceed as described in Section 37, paragraphs 8 to 16 inclusive.
2 Release the securing clip, then disconnect the throttle cable end balljoint from the throttle valve lever. Slide the throttle cable grommet from the bracket on the inlet manifold, and move the throttle cable to one side out of the way.
3 Unscrew the union nut, and disconnect the brake servo vacuum hose from the inlet manifold (photo).
4 On 1.6 litre engines, disconnect the hose from the exhaust gas recirculation valve.
5 Disconnect the wiring from the temperature gauge sender.
6 Where applicable, disconnect the wiring from the coolant temperature sensor.
7 Separate the two halves of the wiring connector located in the bracket attached to the left-hand end of the inlet manifold. Unclip the connector from the bracket.
8 Partially drain the cooling system as described in Chapter 1, then disconnect the coolant hose from the rear of the inlet manifold. Be prepared for coolant spillage, and plug the open end of the hose to reduce coolant loss.
9 Unscrew and remove the top alternator mounting nut and bolt, noting the location of the earth wire on the bolt (photo).
10 Make a final check to ensure that all relevant hoses, pipes and wires have been disconnected.
11 Unscrew the securing nuts, and withdraw the manifold from the cylinder head. Recover the gasket.
12 It is possible that some of the manifold studs may be unscrewed from the cylinder head when the manifold securing nuts are unscrewed. In this event, the studs should be screwed back into the cylinder head once the manifold has been removed, using two manifold nuts locked together.
13 If desired, the ancillary components can be removed from the manifold with reference to the relevant Sections of this Chapter.

Refitting

14 Refitting is a reversal of removal, bearing in mind the following points.
15 Where applicable, refit any ancillary components to the manifold, with reference to the relevant Sections of this Chapter.
16 If the alternator mounting bracket has been unbolted from the

manifold, refit it before refitting the manifold, as access is limited once the manifold is in place.
17 Refit the manifold using a new gasket, and tighten the securing nuts to the specified torque.
18 Ensure that all relevant hoses, pipes and wires are correctly reconnected and routed.
19 On completion, check and if necessary top-up the coolant level, as described in Chapter 1.
20 Check and if necessary adjust the throttle cable free play, as described in Section 31.

Models with Multec multi-point fuel injection
Removal

21 Disconnect the battery negative lead.
22 Release the securing clip, then disconnect the throttle cable end balljoint from the throttle valve lever. Slide the throttle cable grommet from the bracket on the inlet manifold, and move the throttle cable to one side out of the way.
23 Loosen the clamp screw, and disconnect the air trunking from the throttle body.
24 Unscrew the union nut, and disconnect the brake servo vacuum hose from the inlet manifold (photo).

43.24 Brake servo hose union nut (arrowed) – Multec multi-point fuel injection engine

43.29 Earth lead securing bolts (arrowed) at right-hand end of cylinder head – Multec multi-point fuel injection engine

43.34A Fuel pipe connections (arrowed) under inlet manifold (viewed from underneath vehicle) – Multec multi-point fuel injection engine

43.34B Clamp the fuel hoses (arrowed) to prevent fuel spillage

25   Disconnect the camshaft cover breather hoses from the throttle body.
26   Disconnect the vacuum hoses from the throttle body, noting their locations to aid refitting.
27   Disconnect the coolant hoses from the throttle body (two hoses) and the inlet manifold (one hose), noting their locations to aid refitting. Be prepared for coolant spillage, and clamp or plug the open ends of the hoses, to prevent further coolant loss. Where applicable, unclip the coolant hose from the rear of the manifold.
28   Disconnect the wiring plugs from the throttle position sensor and the idle speed control motor in the throttle housing, and from the intake air temperature sensor in the inlet manifold plenum chamber.
29   Unscrew the two securing bolts, and disconnect the two earth leads from the right-hand end of the cylinder head (photo).
30   Disconnect the earth lead from the engine lifting eye bolt at the left- hand end of the inlet manifold.
31   Disconnect the wiring from the coolant temperature gauge sender in the inlet manifold.
32   Disconnect the wiring plugs from the fuel injectors.
33   Separate the two halves of the wiring connector located in the bracket attached to the upper left-hand inlet manifold stud.
34   Disconnect the fuel hoses from the fuel pipes under the fuel rail, noting their locations to ensure correct refitting. Access is most easily obtained from under the vehicle – if desired, raise the front of the vehicle and support securely on axle stands, as described in *'Jacking, towing and wheel changing'*. Loosen the clamp screws slowly, to release the pressure in the system. Be prepared for fuel spillage, and take adequate fire precautions. Clamp or plug the open ends of the hoses to prevent dirt ingress and further fuel leakage (photos).
35   Unscrew and remove the top alternator mounting nut and bolt.

43.37 Lifting the inlet manifold from the engine – Multec multi-point fuel injection engine

36   Make a final check to ensure that all relevant hoses, pipes and wires have been disconnected.
37   Proceed as described in paragraphs 11 to 13 inclusive (photo).

Refitting
38   Proceed as described in paragraphs 14 to 20 inclusive.

Models with Motronic M 1.5.2 fuel injection
Removal
39   Disconnect the battery negative lead.
40   Remove the idle speed control valve and its hoses, with reference to Section 39 if necessary.
41   Release the securing clip, then disconnect the throttle cable and balljoint from the throttle valve lever. Slide the throttle cable grommet from the bracket on the inlet manifold, and move the cable to one side out of the way.
42   Loosen the clamp screw, and disconnect the air trunking from the throttle body.
43   Unscrew the union nut, and disconnect the brake servo vacuum hose from the inlet manifold.
44   Disconnect the camshaft cover breather hose from the throttle body.
45   Disconnect the coolant hoses from the throttle body. Be prepared for coolant spillage, and clamp or plug the open ends of the hoses to prevent further coolant loss.
46   Disconnect the wiring plug from the throttle position sensor.
47   Disconnect the vacuum pipe from the top of the fuel pressure regulator.
48   Disconnect the wiring harness housing from the fuel injectors, and move it to one side, taking care not to strain the wiring. Pull up on the wiring harness housing, and compress the wiring plug retaining clips to release the harness housing from the injectors.
49   Disconnect the fuel hoses from the fuel rail. Loosen the clamps slowly, to depressurise the fuel system. Be prepared for fuel spillage, and take adequate fire precautions. Clamp or plug the open ends of the hoses, to prevent dirt ingress and further fuel leakage.
50   Unscrew and remove the top alternator mounting nut and bolt.
51   Make a final check to ensure that all relevant hoses, pipes and wires have been disconnected.
52   Proceed as described in paragraphs 11 to 13 inclusive (photos).

Refitting
53   Proceed as described in paragraphs 14 to 20 inclusive.

Models with Motronic M 2.5 fuel injection
Removal
54   Disconnect the battery negative lead.
55   Disconnect the wiring from the air mass meter. Recover the sealing ring, where applicable.
56   Loosen the clamp screw securing the air trunking to the right-hand end of the air mass meter.
57   Using a suitable Allen key or hexagon bit, unscrew the four bolts securing the airbox to the throttle body. Lift the airbox from the throttle body, and disconnect the hose from the base of the airbox, then withdraw the airbox/air mass meter assembly.
58   Disconnect the wiring plug from the throttle position sensor.

43.52A Unscrewing an inlet manifold securing nut – Motronic M 1.5.2 fuel injection engine

43.52B Removing the inlet manifold – Motronic M 1.5.2 fuel injection engine

43.67 Disconnecting the brake servo hose from the inlet manifold – Motronic M 2.5 fuel injection engine

59   Slide the throttle cable end from the throttle valve lever, then pull the cable end grommet from the bracket on the inlet manifold, and move the throttle cable to one side out of the way.

60   Disconnect the two breather hoses from the rear of the camshaft cover. Disconnect the larger hose from the main throttle body, and remove the hose completely.

61   Position a wad of rag beneath one of the fuel hose unions on the fuel rail, to absorb the fuel which will be released as the union is disconnected.

62   Slowly loosen the fuel hose unions, to gradually relieve the pressure in the fuel feed line, then disconnect the hose from the fuel rail. Be prepared for fuel spillage, and take adequate fire precautions. Plug the end of the fuel hose, to prevent dirt ingress and further fuel leakage.

63   Repeat paragraphs 61 and 62 for the remaining fuel hose-to-fuel rail union.

64   Disconnect the vacuum pipes from the front of the ETC throttle housing.

65   Disconnect the coolant hoses from the ETC throttle valve housing, noting their locations and routing to aid correct refitting. Be prepared for coolant spillage, and clamp or plug the open ends of the hoses to minimise coolant loss.

66   Disconnect the wiring harness housing from the fuel injectors, and move it to one side, taking care not to strain the wiring. Pull up on the wiring harness housing, and compress the wiring plug retaining clips to release the housing from the injectors.

67   Unscrew the union nut, and disconnect the brake servo vacuum hose from the left-hand side of the inlet manifold (photo).

68   Unscrew the retaining nut, and remove the fuel hose bracket from the left-hand side of the throttle body.

69   Unscrew the securing nuts, and disconnect the earth leads from the fuel rail securing studs at either end of the fuel rail.

70   Unscrew the securing bolt, and remove the cable/hose bracket from the left-hand end of the inlet manifold.

71   Remove the idle speed control valve, as described in Section 40.

72   Unscrew and remove the top alternator mounting nut and bolt.

73   Make a final check to ensure that all relevant hoses, pipes and wires have been disconnected.

74   Proceed as described in paragraphs 11 to 13 inclusive.

Refitting

75   Proceed as described in paragraphs 14 to 20 inclusive, but additionally, make sure that the ETC throttle housing coolant hoses are correctly routed and reconnected, as noted before removal.

44   Exhaust manifold – removal and refitting

SOHC engines

1   Refer to Section 22 in Part A of this Chapter, bearing in mind the following points (photos).

2   Disconnect the oxygen sensor wiring plug before separating the exhaust downpipe from the manifold.

3   Where applicable, ignore the reference to the air cleaner hot air tube.

DOHC engines

4   On DOHC engine models, a tubular exhaust manifold is fitted, which incorporates the front section of the exhaust system.

5   Refer to Section 45 for details of removal and refitting.

45   Exhaust system – general information and component renewal

General information

SOHC engine models

1   Refer to Section 23 in Part A of this Chapter, noting the following points.

44.1A Exhaust manifold hot air shroud securing bolts (arrowed) – 1.6 litre multi-point fuel injection engine

44.1B Refitting the exhaust manifold – 1.6 litre multi-point fuel injection engine

44.1C Tightening an exhaust manifold securing nut. Note position of engine lifting bracket (arrowed) – 1.6 litre multi-point fuel injection engine

45.6A Exhaust front section-to-manifold joint – 1.4 litre single-point fuel injection engine

45.6B Exhaust front section-to-manifold joint – 1.6 litre multi-point fuel injection engine

45.6C Fitting a new exhaust downpipe-to-manifold gasket – 1.6 litre multi-point fuel injection engine

45.6D Exhaust front section mounting bracket (1) and sprung joint (2) – 1.6 litre multi-point fuel injection engine

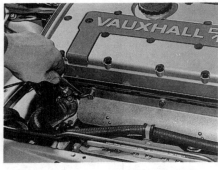

45.13 Unscrewing an exhaust manifold heat shield-to-cylinder head bolt – DOHC engine

2   The original factory-fitted exhaust system consists of four separate sections (including the catalytic converter – see Section 34), all of which can be renewed individually. The manufacturers do not specify any renewal intervals for the catalytic converter. An exhaust gas oxygen sensor is fitted in the exhaust front pipe on 2.0 litre engine models.
3   When inspecting the exhaust system, also inspect the catalytic converter for signs of damage or corrosion. At the same time, inspect oxygen sensor and its wiring for signs of damage.

DOHC engine models
4   Refer to the preceding paragraphs for SOHC engine models, but note that a tubular exhaust manifold is fitted, which incorporates the front section of the exhaust system.

Component renewal
Note: *All relevant gaskets and/or sealing rings should be renewed on refitting.*

Front section – SOHC engine models
5   Disconnect the battery negative lead, and disconnect the oxygen sensor wiring plug, which is usually attached to a bracket secured to one of the top engine-to-gearbox bolts.
6   Refer to Section 23 in Part A of this Chapter, noting that the rear end of the front section must be disconnected from the catalytic converter instead of the front expansion box (photos).
7   Note that certain models have a rigid joint instead of a sprung joint between the exhaust front section and the catalytic converter.

Front section – DOHC engine models
8   Proceed as described in paragraph 5.
9   Raise the vehicle, and support securely on axle stands (see *'Jacking, towing and wheel changing'*).
10   Remove the engine undershield, as described in Chapter 11.
11   Unscrew the two securing bolts, and disconnect the exhaust front section from the catalytic converter at the flexible joint. Recover the sealing ring and springs.

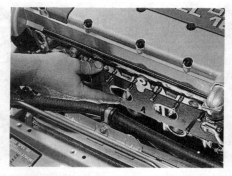

45.17 Fitting a new exhaust manifold gasket – DOHC engine

45.19 Exhaust centre section-to-catalytic converter joint – 1.6 litre multi-point fuel injection engine

12   Unbolt the exhaust front section from the bracket on the cylinder block.

13   Working in the engine compartment, remove the bolts securing the exhaust manifold heat shield to the cylinder head (photo).

14   Unscrew the two lower exhaust manifold securing nuts which also secure the heat shield brackets, and withdraw the heat shield.

15   Unscrew the remaining manifold securing nuts, then withdraw the manifold/exhaust front section from the vehicle. Recover the manifold gasket.

16   It is possible that some of the manifold studs may be unscrewed from the cylinder head when the manifold securing nuts are unscrewed. In this event, the studs should be screwed back into the cylinder head once the manifold has been removed, using two manifold nuts locked together.

17   Refitting is a reversal of removal, but use a new manifold gasket, and use a new sealing ring when reconnecting the flexible joint (photo).

Catalytic converter

18   Proceed as described for the front expansion box in Section 23 in Part A of this Chapter. The internal components of the converter are fragile – take care not to strike it during removal, and do not drop it once removed.

Centre section

19   Refer to Section 23 in Part A of this Chapter, noting that the front end of the centre section must be disconnected from the catalytic converter instead of the front expansion box (photo).

Rear section

20   Refer to Section 23 in Part A of this Chapter.

Part C: Emission control systems

46   General information

All models in the Astra range can be operated on unleaded petrol (models with a catalytic converter can **only** be operated on unleaded petrol), but additionally, various systems may be fitted (depending on model) to reduce the emission of pollution into the atmosphere. The systems are described in more detail in the following paragraphs. Note that all models are fitted with a crankcase emission control system.

Crankcase emission control system

A crankcase ventilation system is fitted to all models, but the systems differ in detail according to model.

Oil fumes and blow-by gases (combustion gases which have passed by the piston rings) are drawn from the crankcase into the area of the cylinder head above the camshaft(s) via a hose. From here, the gases are drawn into the inlet manifold/throttle body (as applicable) and/or the air box on the carburettor/throttle body, where they are mixed with fresh air/fuel mixture and burnt, hence reducing harmful exhaust emissions.

Certain models may have a mesh filter inside the camshaft cover, which should be cleaned in paraffin if clogging is evident.

Exhaust emission control system

To minimise the level of exhaust gas pollutants released into the atmosphere, all fuel-injected models are fitted with a catalytic converter (see Section 34 in Part B of this Chapter), located in the exhaust system. A 'closed loop' system is used, in which an exhaust gas oxygen sensor, mounted in the exhaust manifold or downpipe (depending on model), provides a signal to the fuel system electronic control unit, to enable it adjust the air/fuel mixture ratio within very fine limits. This enables the catalytic converter to operate at its optimum efficiency at all times.

The oxygen sensor senses the level of oxygen in the exhaust gas, which is proportional to the air/fuel mixture ratio. A rich mixture produces exhaust gases with a low oxygen content, and the oxygen content rises as the mixture weakens. The catalyst operates at maximum efficiency when the air/fuel mixture ratio is at the chemically-correct ratio for the complete combustion of petrol, and the output produced by the oxygen sensor allows the electronic control unit to maintain air/fuel ratio very close to the optimum value under all engine operating conditions.

Fuel evaporation control system

To minimise the escape into the atmosphere of unburnt hydrocarbons, a fuel evaporation control system is fitted to certain models. The fuel tank filler cap is sealed, to prevent the release of fuel vapour into the atmosphere, and a charcoal canister is mounted under the right-hand wheel arch, to collect the fuel vapours which would otherwise be released from the tank when the vehicle is parked. The vapours are stored in the canister until a vent valve is operated by manifold vacuum, or by the fuel system electronic control unit (depending on engine type). The vent valve releases the vapours into the engine inlet tract where they are burnt during the normal combustion process.

Exhaust gas recirculation system

The exhaust gas recirculation system is designed to recirculate small quantities of exhaust gas into the inlet tract, and therefore into the combustion process. This process reduces the level of oxides of nitrogen present in the final exhaust gas which is released into the atmosphere. The volume of exhaust gas recirculated is controlled by manifold vacuum via a valve mounted in the inlet manifold.

A tract in the cylinder head allows exhaust gas to pass from the exhaust side of the cylinder head to the exhaust gas recirculation valve in the inlet manifold.

47.10A Unscrewing the charcoal canister clamp nut

47.10B Withdrawing the charcoal canister

47.12 Fuel tank vent valve – single-point fuel injection system

47 Emission control system components – testing and renewal

Crankcase emission control system components

Testing

1   If the system is thought to be faulty, firstly, check that the hoses are unobstructed. On high-mileage vehicles, particularly when regularly used for short journeys, a jelly-like deposit may be evident inside the crankcase emission control system hoses. If excessive deposits are present, the relevant hose(s) should be removed and cleaned.
2   Periodically inspect the system hoses for security and damage, and renew them as necessary. Note that damaged or loose hoses can cause various engine running problems (erratic idle speed, stalling, etc) which can be difficult to trace.

Component renewal

3   The crankcase breather tube can be unbolted from the cylinder block after disconnecting the hose. Use a new gasket when refitting. Note that on certain engines, the dipstick tube is integral with the crankcase breather tube.
4   Certain models have a mesh filter inside the camshaft cover, which should be cleaned in paraffin if clogging is evident. For access to the filter, remove the camshaft cover as described in Chapter 2. The filter can be removed from the camshaft cover for cleaning after unscrewing the securing screws.

Exhaust emission control system

Testing

5   The system can only be tested accurately using Vauxhall/Opel specialist diagnostic equipment. Any suspected faults should be referred to a Vauxhall/Opel dealer.

Component renewal

6   Refer to the relevant Section in Part B of this Chapter.

Fuel evaporation control system

Testing

7   If the system is thought to be faulty, disconnect the hoses from the charcoal canister and vent valve, and check that the hoses are clear by blowing through them. If necessary, clean or renew the hoses.
8   If the vent valve or the charcoal canister itself are thought to be faulty, the only course of action available is renewal.

Charcoal canister – renewal

9   Remove the wheel arch liner from the front right-hand wheel arch, as described in Chapter 11.
10   Unscrew the securing nut, and detach the clamp strap securing the canister to the bracket under the wheel arch. Withdraw the canister and disconnect the hoses (photos).
11   Fit the new canister using a reversal of the removal procedure.

Fuel tank vent valve (models with Multec single-point fuel injection) – renewal

12   The valve is located under the water deflector on the engine compartment bulkhead (photo).
13   To remove the valve, lift the water deflector to expose the valve, then disconnect the three hoses, noting their locations to ensure correct refitting, and withdraw the valve from the bulkhead (release the securing clip, where applicable).
14   Refitting is a reversal of removal, ensuring that the hoses are reconnected correctly, as noted before removal.

Fuel tank vent valve (models with Multec multi-point fuel injection) – renewal

15   The procedure is as described in paragraphs 12 to 14 inclusive for models with single-point fuel injection.

Fuel tank vent valve (models with Motronic M 1.5.2 fuel injection) – renewal

16   The valve is located in a bracket attached to the rear of the cylinder head.
17   Disconnect the battery negative lead.
18   Disconnect the wiring plug from the fuel tank vent valve.
19   Disconnect the two hoses from the valve, noting their locations to ensure correct refitting.
20   Unclip the valve from its bracket, and withdraw it.
21   Refitting is a reversal of removal, ensuring that the hoses are reconnected as noted before removal.

Fuel tank vent valve (models with Motronic M 2.5 fuel injection) – renewal

22   The fuel tank vent valve is located at the rear left-hand side of the engine (photo).

47.22 Fuel tank vent valve – Motronic M 2.5 fuel injection system

23   Disconnect the battery negative lead.
24   Disconnect the wiring plug from the valve.
25   Disconnect the two hoses from the valve, noting their locations to aid refitting.
26   Remove the securing screw, and withdraw the valve from its bracket.
27   Refitting is a reversal of removal, ensuring that the hoses are reconnected as noted before removal.

Exhaust gas recirculation system

Testing

28   Start the engine, and run it until it reaches normal operating temperature.
29   Stop the engine, and remove the airbox from the top of the fuel injection unit, as described in Section 37 in Part B of this Chapter.
30   Connect an accurate tachometer to the engine in accordance with the equipment manufacturer's instructions.
31   Disconnect the vacuum hose from the valve, then start the engine and record the idle speed.
32   Disconnect the vacuum hose from the valve, then apply vacuum to the valve using a suitable vacuum hand pump. When the vacuum is applied, the idle speed should drop by at least 100 rpm.

33   If the idle speed does not drop as described previously, firstly, check the valve vacuum hose for obstructions and leaks. Clean the hose or renew it if necessary.
34   If the hose is in good condition, and a fault is still suspected, it is likely that the valve is faulty. In this case, clean and if necessary renew the valve as described in the following paragraphs.
35   Disconnect the tachometer, reconnect the vacuum hose and refit the airbox on completion.

Exhaust gas recirculation valve – cleaning and renewal

36   It is recommended that the valve is cleaned as follows annually.
37   Remove the airbox from the top of the fuel injection unit, as described in Section 37 in Part A of this Chapter.
38   Disconnect the vacuum hose from the valve.
39   Unscrew the two securing bolts, and withdraw the valve from the inlet manifold. Recover the gasket.
40   Carefully clean the mating faces of the inlet manifold and the valve using a stiff brush.
41   If the original valve is to be refitted, clean all deposits from the valve seat using a brush or a pointed tool. Take great care not to damage the valve seat.
42   Refit the valve using a new gasket, then refit the vacuum hose and the airbox.

Chapter 5 Ignition system

Contents

Specifications

General

System type:*
Carburettor engine (14 NV)	Bosch High Energy Ignition (HEI) inductive discharge system
1.4 and 1.6 litre single-point fuel injection engines (C 14 NZ and C 16 NZ) ...	Multec Multi-Spark Timing System (MSTS) with 'Hall-effect' distributor
1.4 litre multi-point fuel injection engine (C 14 SE)	Multec Multi-Spark Timing System (MSTS) with crankshaft speed/position sensor
1.6 litre multi-point fuel injection engine (C 16 SE)	Multec Multi-Spark Timing System (MSTS) with Direct Ignition System (DIS) and crankshaft speed/position sensor
1.8 litre engine (C 18 NZ)	Multec Multi-Spark Timing System (MSTS) with crankshaft speed/position sensor
2.0 litre SOHC engine (C 20 NE)	Motronic M 1.5.2 with crankshaft speed/position sensor
DOHC engine (C 20 XE)	Motronic M 2.5 with 'Hall-effect' distributor and crankshaft speed/position sensor

*For details of engine code location, see 'Buying spare parts and vehicle identification numbers'.
Firing order 1–3–4–2
Location of No 1 cylinder .... Timing belt end of engine

Distributor

Direction of rotor arm rotation .... Clockwise (viewed from cap)

Ignition timing (stroboscopic, at idle speed, vacuum hose disconnected):

Carburettor engine (14 NV)*	5° BTDC
Fuel injection engines:**	
All except 2.0 litre engines	10° BTDC
C 20 NE (SOHC) engine*	13 to 17° BTDC
C 20 XE (DOHC) engine*	14 to 18° BTDC

*For details of engine code location, see 'Buying spare parts and vehicle identification numbers'.
**Controlled by electronic control unit – no adjustment possible

Torque wrench setting

	Nm	lbf ft
Spark plugs	25	18

1 General information and precautions

General information

The ignition system is responsible for igniting the air/fuel mixture in each cylinder at the correct moment, in relation to engine speed and load. A number of different types of ignition systems are fitted to models within the Astra range, ranging from a basic breakerless electronic system, to a fully-integrated engine management system controlling both ignition and fuel injection systems. Each system is described in further detail later in this Section.

The ignition system is based on feeding low-tension voltage from the battery to the coil, where it is converted into high-tension voltage. The high-tension voltage is powerful enough to jump the spark plug gap in the cylinders many times a second under high compression pressures, providing that the system is in good condition. The low-tension (or primary) circuit consists of the battery, the lead to the ignition switch, the lead from the ignition switch to the low-tension coil windings, and also to the supply terminal on the electronic module, and the lead from the low-tension coil windings to the control terminal on the electronic module. The high-tension (or secondary) circuit consists of the high-tension coil windings, the HT (high-tension) lead from the coil to the distributor cap (where applicable), the rotor arm (where applicable), the HT leads to the spark plugs, and the spark plugs.

The system functions in the following manner. Current flowing through the low-tension coil windings produces a magnetic field around the high-tension windings. As the engine rotates, a sensor produces an electrical impulse which is amplified in the electronic module and used to switch off the low-tension circuit.

The subsequent collapse of the magnetic field over the high-tension windings produces a high-tension voltage, which is then fed to the relevant spark plug(s), either directly from the coil, or via the distributor cap and rotor arm, as applicable. The low-tension circuit is automatically switched on again by the electronic module, to allow the magnetic field to build up again before the firing of the next spark plug(s). The ignition is advanced and retarded automatically, to ensure that the spark occurs at the correct instant in relation to the engine speed and load.

HEI (High-Energy Ignition) system – 1.4 litre carburettor engine

This system is the least-sophisticated system fitted to the model range, and comprises a breakerless distributor and an electronic switching/amplifier module in addition to the coil and spark plugs.

The electrical impulse which is required to switch off the low-tension circuit is generated by a magnetic trigger coil in the distributor.

The ignition advance is a function of the distributor, and is controlled both mechanically and by a vacuum-operated system.

Multec MSTS (Microprocessor-controlled Spark Timing System) – single-point fuel injection engines

This system controls both the ignition and fuel injection systems, and comprises a 'Hall-effect' distributor (1.4 and 1.6 litre engines) or a crankshaft speed/position sensor (1.8 litre engine), a manifold pressure sensor, a coolant temperature sensor, a throttle position sensor, an exhaust gas oxygen sensor, and the Multec electronic control unit, in addition to the coil, electronic module, and spark plugs.

On 1.4 and 1.6 litre engines, the electrical impulse which is required to switch off the low-tension circuit is generated by a sensor in the distributor.

On 1.8 litre engines, the electrical impulse which is required to switch off the low-tension circuit is generated by a crankshaft speed/position sensor, which is activated by a toothed wheel on the crankshaft. The distributor consists simply of a rotor arm and distributor cap, and is used solely to distribute the HT current to the spark plugs.

Engine load information is supplied to the Multec control unit by a pressure sensor, which is connected to the fuel injection unit by a vacuum pipe. Additional information is supplied by a coolant temperature sensor, a throttle position sensor, and an exhaust gas oxygen sensor.

The control unit selects the optimum ignition advance setting based on the information received from the sensors. The degree of advance can thus be constantly varied to suit the prevailing engine conditions. The control unit also provides outputs to control the fuel injection system, which is described in Chapter 4.

Multec MSTS (Microprocessor-controlled Spark Timing System) – Multec multi-point fuel injection engines

The system is similar to that described previously for single-point fuel injection engines, but note the following differences.

The system comprises a crankshaft speed/position sensor, a manifold pressure sensor, a coolant temperature sensor, an intake air temperature sensor, an exhaust gas oxygen sensor, and the Multec electronic control unit, in addition to the coil(s) and spark plugs.

The electrical impulse which is required to switch off the low-tension circuit is generated by a crankshaft speed/position sensor, similar to that described previously for 1.8 litre single-point fuel injection engines.

On 1.4 litre engines, the distributor consists simply of a rotor arm and distributor cap, and is used solely to distribute the HT current to the spark plugs.

On 1.6 litre engines, a DIS (Direct Ignition System) module is used in place of the distributor and the coil. The DIS module is attached to the camshaft housing in the position normally occupied by the distributor, and consists of two ignition coils and an electronic control module, housed in a cast casing. Each ignition coil supplies two spark plugs with HT voltage – one spark is provided in a cylinder with its piston on the compression stroke, and one spark is provided to a cylinder with its piston on the exhaust stroke. This means that a 'wasted spark' is supplied to one cylinder during each ignition cycle, but this has no detrimental effect. This system has the advantage that there are no moving parts – therefore there is no wear, and the system is largely maintenance-free.

Additional information is supplied to the Multec electronic control unit by an intake air temperature sensor, mounted in the inlet manifold.

Bosch Motronic M 1.5.2 system – 2.0 litre SOHC engines

This system controls both the ignition and fuel injection systems.

The Motronic electronic control unit receives information from a crankshaft speed/position sensor (similar to that described previously for 1.8 litre single-point fuel injection engines), an air mass meter, an engine coolant temperature sensor, a throttle position sensor, an intake air temperature sensor, and an exhaust gas oxygen sensor.

The electrical impulse which is required to switch off the low-tension circuit is generated by a crankshaft speed/position sensor, similar to that described previously for 1.8 litre single-point fuel injection engines.

The distributor consists simply of a rotor arm and distributor cap, and is used solely to distribute the HT current to the spark plugs.

The control unit selects the optimum ignition advance setting, based on the information received from the sensors. The degree of advance can thus be constantly varied to suit the prevailing engine conditions. The control unit also provides outputs to control the fuel injection system, which is described in Chapter 4.

Bosch Motronic M 2.5 system – DOHC engines

The system is similar to the Motronic M 1.5.2 system described previously, with the following differences.

In addition to the crankshaft speed/position sensor, a 'Hall-effect' distributor is used. The electrical impulse which is required to switch off the ignition low-tension circuit is generated by the crankshaft speed/position sensor, and the sensor in the distributor provides a cylinder recognition signal.

Additionally, the electronic control module receives information from a cylinder block-mounted knock sensor (see Chapter 4), which senses 'knocking' (or pre-ignition) just as it begins to occur, enabling the module to retard the ignition timing, thus preventing engine damage.

Precautions

Refer to the precautions to be observed when working on models fitted with an electronic control unit, given in Chapter 4, Section 24.

Warning: *The HT voltage generated by an electronic ignition system is extremely high and, in certain circumstances, could prove fatal. Take care to avoid receiving electric shocks from the HT side of the ignition system. Do not handle HT leads, or touch the distributor or coil, when the engine is running. If tracing faults in the HT circuit, use well-insulated tools to manipulate live leads. Persons with surgically-implanted cardiac pacemaker devices should keep well clear of the ignition circuits, components and test equipment.*

2   Ignition system – testing

Note: *Refer to the warning given in Section 1 of this Chapter before proceeding.*

Carburettor engines

General

1   The components of the electronic ignition system are normally very reliable; most faults are far more likely to be due to loose or dirty connections or to 'tracking' of HT voltage due to dirt, dampness or damaged insulation than to the failure of any of the system components. **Always** check all wiring thoroughly before condemning an electrical component, and work methodically to eliminate all other possibilities before deciding that a particular component is faulty.
2   The practice of checking for a spark by holding the live end of an HT lead a short distance away from the engine is not recommended – not only is there a high risk of a powerful electric shock, but the coil or electronic module may be damaged.

Engine fails to start

3   If the engine either will not turn over at all, or only turns over very slowly, check the battery and starter motor. Connect a voltmeter across the battery terminals (meter positive probe to battery positive terminal), disconnect the ignition coil HT lead from the distributor cap and earth it, then note the voltage reading obtained while turning over the engine on the starter for around ten seconds (no more). If the reading obtained is less than approximately 8 volts, check the battery, starter motor and charging system (see Chapter 12).
4   If the engine turns over at normal speed, but will not start, check the HT circuit by connecting a timing light (following the equipment manufacturer's instructions) and turning the engine over on the starter motor; if the light flashes, voltage is reaching the spark plugs, so these should be checked first. If the light does not flash, check the HT leads themselves, followed by the distributor cap, carbon brush and rotor arm (see Section 3). Additionally, use an ohmmeter or continuity tester to check that there is no continuity between any of the distributor cap contacts. Similarly, check that there is no continuity between the rotor arm body and its metal contact – note that the arm has a built-in resistance.
5   If there is a spark, check the fuel system for faults (see Chapter 4).
6   If there is still no spark, check the voltage at the ignition coil ' + ' terminal (black wires), which should be the same as the battery voltage (ie, at least 11.5 volts). If the voltage at the coil is significantly (more than 1.0 volt) less than that at the battery, check the feed back through the fusebox and ignition switch to the battery and its earth until the fault is found.
7   If the feed to the coil is sound, check the coil windings, as described in Section 4. Renew the coil if faulty, but be careful to check carefully the condition of the LT connections themselves before doing so, to ensure that the fault is not due to dirty or loose connections.
8   If the coil is in good condition, the fault is probably within the electronic module or the distributor. To check the module and distributor, connect a suitable test meter across the coil LT terminals, in accordance with the equipment manufacturer's instructions. If the ignition is switched on, and the engine is turned over on the starter motor, the meter voltage readings should fluctuate each time the module triggers an HT pulse in the coil. If the meter reading fluctuates as the engine is turned over, the electronic module and the distributor are sound.
9   If the electronic module and distributor are sound, and the entire LT circuit is in good condition, the fault, if it lies in the ignition system, must be in the HT circuit components. These should be checked carefully, as outlined previously.

Engine misfires

10   An irregular misfire suggests either a loose connection or intermittent fault in the primary circuit, or an HT fault on the coil side of the rotor arm.
11   With the ignition switched off, check carefully through the system, ensuring that all connections are clean and securely fastened. If the equipment is available, check the LT circuit, as described previously in paragraphs 6 to 8 inclusive.
12   Check that the coil, the distributor cap and the HT leads are clean and dry. Check the leads themselves and the spark plugs (by

substitution if necessary), then check the distributor cap, carbon brush and rotor arm (see Chapter 1).
13   Regular misfiring is almost certainly due to a fault in the distributor cap, HT leads or spark plugs. Use a timing light (see paragraph 4) to check whether HT voltage is present at all leads.
14   If HT voltage is not present on any particular lead, the fault will be in that lead or in the distributor cap. If HT voltage is present on all leads, the fault will be in the spark plugs; check and renew them if there is any doubt about their condition.
15   If no HT voltage is present, check the coil, as the secondary windings may be breaking down under load.

Fuel injection engines

Note: *The test information given in this Section applies only to engines fitted with a conventional ignition system – ie, all except the 1.6 litre multi-point fuel injection (C 16 SE) engine. Due to the construction of the coil/electronic module unit used on this engine, testing should only be carried out using the appropriate test equipment available to a Vauxhall/Opel dealer.*

General

16   The general comments made above apply equally to the fuel injection engines, but note that extreme care should be taken when testing the system, as the electronic control unit is very sensitive, and if damaged, it may prove very costly to renew.
17   If in any doubt as to test procedures, or if the correct equipment is not available, entrust testing and fault diagnosis to a Vauxhall/Opel dealer. It is far better to pay the labour charges involved in having the car checked by someone suitably qualified, than to risk damage to the system or yourself.

Engine fails to start

18   Check whether the fault lies in the ignition system, by following the procedure described in paragraphs 3 and 4, and check the HT circuit as described.
19   If the HT circuit appears to be sound, the feed to the coil can be checked as described in paragraph 6. Note that the electronic control unit controls the coil feed. **Do not** attempt to 'test' the electronic control unit with anything other than the appropriate test equipment, which will be available only at a suitably-equipped Vauxhall/Opel dealer. If any of the wires are to be checked which run to the electronic control unit (although this is not recommended without the correct test equipment), always first unplug the relevant connector from the control unit (with the ignition switched off) so that there is no risk of the unit being damaged by the application of incorrect voltages from the test equipment.
20   If all components have been checked for signs of obvious faults, such as dirty or loose connections, damp, or 'tracking', and have been tested as far as possible, but the system is still thought to be faulty, the vehicle must be taken to a Vauxhall/Opel dealer for testing using the appropriate equipment.

Engine misfires

21   Refer to paragraphs 10 to 15, but note that the possible causes of partial failures which may result in a misfire are far too numerous to be eliminated without using suitable test equipment. Once the ignition system components have been checked for signs of obvious faults, such as dirty or loose connections, damp, or 'tracking', and have been tested as far as possible, but the system is still thought to be faulty, take the vehicle to a Vauxhall/Opel dealer for the full engine management system to be tested using the appropriate equipment.

3   Distributor – removal, overhaul and refitting

Carburettor engine

Removal

1   Disconnect the battery negative lead.
2   If necessary, identify each HT lead for position to aid correct refitting, then disconnect the leads from the spark plugs by pulling on the connectors, not on the leads. Similarly, disconnect the HT lead from the coil. Pull the leads from the clips on the camshaft cover.

3.4 Disconnecting the distributor wiring plug – carburettor engine

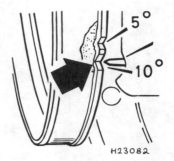

Fig. 5.1 Timing pointer on rear timing belt cover aligned with 10° BTDC notch in crankshaft pulley – carburettor engine (Sec 3)

3   Release the two securing clips using a screwdriver, and lift the distributor cap, complete with HT leads, from the distributor.
4   Disconnect the distributor wiring plug (photo).
5   Disconnect the vacuum pipe from the diaphragm unit on the side of the distributor.
6   If the original distributor is to be refitted, make alignment marks between the distributor body and the camshaft housing, so that the distributor can be refitted in its original position.
7   Using a suitable socket or spanner on the crankshaft pulley bolt, or by engaging top gear (manual gearbox) and pushing the vehicle backwards or forwards as necessary (with the handbrake released!), turn the crankshaft to bring No 1 piston to the firing point. No 1 piston is at the firing point when:

(a)   The timing pointer on the rear timing belt cover is aligned with the 10° BTDC notch in the crankshaft pulley – see Fig. 5.1.
(b)   The tip of the rotor arm is pointing to the position occupied by the No 1 cylinder HT lead terminal in the distributor cap.
(c)   The rotor arm is aligned with the notch in the distributor body (remove the rotor arm and plastic shield, then refit the rotor arm to check the alignment with the notch).

8   Unscrew the clamp nut and remove the clamp plate, then withdraw the distributor from the camshaft housing (photos).

Overhaul

9   With the distributor removed, pull off the rotor arm, and remove the plastic shield.
10   Although the top bearing plate can be removed after unscrewing the two securing screws – this is of academic interest, as other than the vacuum diaphragm unit, no spares are available for the distributor, and no adjustments are required.

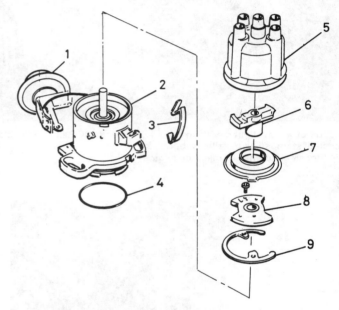

Fig. 5.2 Exploded view of distributor fitted to carburettor models (Sec 3)

1   Vacuum diaphragm unit
2   Body
3   Cap retaining clip
4   Seal ring
5   Distributor cap
6   Rotor arm
7   Plastic shield
8   Top bearing plate
9   Abutment ring

3.8A Unscrew the clamp nut ...

3.8B ... remove the clamp plate ...

3.8C ... and withdraw the distributor – carburettor engine

3.28 Removing the distributor cap – 1.4 litre single-point fuel injection engine

3.29 Disconnecting the distributor wiring plug – 1.4 litre single-point fuel injection engine

3.30A Alignment marks (circled) between distributor body and camshaft housing 1.4 litre single-point fuel injection engine

3.30B Rotor arm aligned with arrow (circled) stamped on distributor body – 1.4 litre single-point fuel injection engine

3.30C Remove the plastic shield ...

3.30D ... and check that the rotor arm is aligned with the notch (circled) in the distributor body rim – 1.4 litre multi-point fuel injection engine

3.30E Removing the clamp plate ...

3.30F ... and withdrawing the distributor – 1.4 litre multi-point fuel injection engine

11   If desired, the vacuum diaphragm unit can be removed by extracting the two securing screws and unhooking the operating arm from the distributor baseplate. Note that the screws are of differing lengths; the longer screw also secures one of the distributor cap clips.

12   The vacuum unit can be tested by applying suction to the vacuum port, and checking that the operating rod moves into the unit as suction is applied. Remove the suction, and check that the operating rod returns to its original position. If the operating rod does not move as described, renew the vacuum unit.

13   Check the distributor cap for corrosion of the segments, and for signs of tracking, indicated by a thin black line between the segments. Make sure that the carbon brush in the centre of the cap moves freely, and stands proud of the surface of the cap. Renew the cap if necessary.

14   If the metal portion of the rotor arm is badly burnt or loose, renew it. If slightly burnt or corroded, it may be cleaned with a fine file.

15   Examine the seal ring at the rear of the distributor body, and renew if necessary.

16   Reassembly is a reversal of dismantling, ensuring that the vacuum unit operating arm is correctly engaged with the peg on the baseplate several attempts may be required to reconnect it.

Refitting

17   Commence refitting by checking that No 1 cylinder is still at the firing point (see paragraph 7). The relevant timing marks should be aligned. If the engine has been turned whilst the distributor has been removed, check that No 1 cylinder is on its firing stroke by removing No 1 cylinder spark plug and placing a finger over the plug hole. Turn the crankshaft until compression can be felt which indicates that No 1 piston is rising on its compression stroke. Continue turning the crankshaft until the relevant timing marks are in alignment.

18   Turn the rotor arm to the position noted in paragraph 7 (c), and hold the rotor arm in this position as the distributor is fitted, noting that the distributor driveshaft will only engage with the camshaft in one

position. If the original distributor is being refitted, align the marks made on the distributor body and camshaft housing before removal.
19 Refit the clamp plate and nut, but do not fully tighten the nut at this stage.
20 Remove the rotor arm, then refit the plastic shield and the rotor arm.
21 Reconnect the vacuum pipe to the diaphragm unit.
22 Reconnect the distributor wiring plug.
23 Refit the distributor cap, ensuring that the HT leads are correctly reconnected.
24 Reconnect the battery negative lead.
25 Check and if necessary adjust the ignition timing, as described in Chapter 1.

1.4 and 1.6 litre fuel injection engines
Removal
26 Proceed as described in paragraphs 1 and 2.
27 Note that various types of distributor may be fitted, depending on model.
28 Loosen the two securing screws, or release the two securing clips using a screwdriver, as applicable, and remove the distributor cap, complete with HT leads, from the distributor (photo).
29 Where applicable, disconnect the distributor wiring plug (photo).
30 Proceed as described in paragraphs 6 to 8 inclusive, noting the following points (photos):

(a) Some distributors may already have alignment marks on the distributor body and camshaft housing.
(b) On certain distributors, No 1 piston is at the firing point when the rotor arm is aligned with the TDC arrow stamped on the distributor body (in place of a notch in the distributor body).

Overhaul
31 On some Bosch distributors, the plastic drive collar can be renewed if necessary after driving out the securing roll pin (photo), but otherwise no spare parts are available for the distributors, and if faulty, the complete unit must be renewed. The distributor cap and rotor arm can be examined as described in paragraphs 13 and 14.

Refitting
32 Where applicable, examine the condition of the O-ring seal at the base of the distributor, and renew if necessary.
33 Proceed as described in paragraphs 17 to 24 inclusive, noting the points made in paragraph 30.

1.8 and 2.0 litre SOHC engines
34 The distributor consists simply of a cap, rotor arm and plastic shield, mounted on the end of the camshaft housing, which can be removed as follows.

Removal
35 Proceed as described in paragraphs 1 and 2.
36 Using a suitable Torx socket, unscrew the three captive securing screws (photo), and withdraw the distributor cap (complete with HT leads) from the distributor.
37 Withdraw the plastic shield from the rotor arm housing. The shield is an interference fit in the housing, via an O-ring seal located in a groove in its periphery. Ease out the shield, taking care not to damage the rotor arm (photo).
38 Using a suitable Allen key or hexagon bit, extract the two securing screws and withdraw the rotor arm, leaving the metal rotor hub in the housing (photos).

Overhaul
39 Examine the distributor cap and rotor arm as described in paragraphs 13 and 14.

Refitting
40 Examine the O-ring on the plastic shield, and renew if necessary.
41 Refitting is a reversal of removal, noting that the rotor arm can only be fitted in one position. If necessary, turn the metal rotor hub so that the screw holes align with those in the rotor arm and the end of the camshaft. Ensure that the HT leads are correctly reconnected.

DOHC engine
Removal
42 Disconnect the battery negative lead.

3.31 Driving out the distributor drive collar roll pin – 1.4 litre multi-point fuel injection engine

3.36 Unscrewing a distributor cap securing screw – 2.0 litre SOHC engine

3.37 Removing the plastic shield from the rotor arm housing – 2.0 litre SOHC engine

3.38A Extract the securing screws ...

3.38B ... and withdraw the rotor arm – 2.0 litre SOHC engine

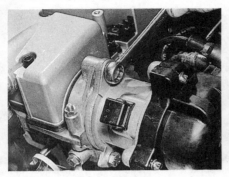

3.46A Unscrewing a distributor securing bolt – DOHC engine

3.46B Offset peg (A) engages with hole (B) in camshaft

4.3 Disconnecting the HT lead from the coil – 1.4 litre multi-point fuel injection engine

43   Remove the securing screws and lift the spark plug cover from the camshaft cover, then disconnect the HT leads from the spark plugs, and unclip the leads from the bracket on the end of the camshaft cover. Also disconnect the HT lead from the coil. Identify the leads for position if necessary, to aid refitting.

44   Using a suitable Torx socket, unscrew the three captive securing screws, and withdraw the distributor cap (complete with HT leads) from the distributor.

45   Disconnect the distributor wiring plug.

46   Unscrew the two bolts securing the distributor to the cylinder head, and withdraw the distributor. Note that the offset peg on the distributor drive engages with the corresponding hole in the end of the camshaft (photos).

Overhaul

47   No spare parts are available for the distributor, and if faulty, the complete unit must be renewed. The distributor cap and rotor arm can be examined as described in paragraphs 13 and 14.

Refitting

48   Examine the condition of the O-ring seal at the base of the distributor, and renew if necessary.

49   Refitting is a reversal of removal, noting that the distributor can only be fitted in one position.

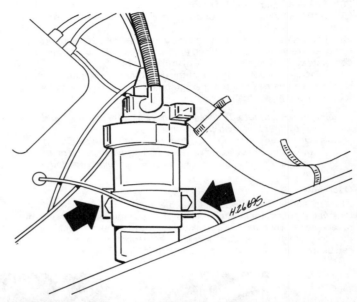

Fig. 5.3 Cylindrical type ignition coil mounting bolts (arrowed) (Sec 4)

4   Ignition coil – removal, testing and refitting

All except 1.6 litre multi-point fuel injection engine
Removal

1   The coil is mounted on the left-hand side of the engine compartment, in front of the suspension turret.

2   Disconnect the battery negative lead.

3   Disconnect the HT lead from the coil (photo).

4   Disconnect the LT wires from the coil, and/or disconnect the coil wiring plug, as applicable (photo). Note that the LT wires may be secured with spade connectors or by nuts depending on model. Where applicable, make a note of the LT wire connections to aid refitting.

5   Where applicable, disconnect the wiring plug from the ignition amplifier module mounted under the coil (photo).

6   Unscrew the two coil securing bolts, and withdraw the coil, complete with the amplifier module and mounting plate, where applicable (photo). Note that on certain models fitted with power steering, one of the coil securing bolts also secures the power steering fluid reservoir bracket. Also note the location of the coil suppressor which may be secured by one of the coil securing screws on certain models.

4.4 Disconnecting the coil wiring plug ...

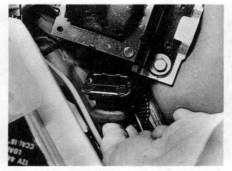

4.5 ... and the amplifier module wiring plug – 1.4 litre multi-point fuel injection engine

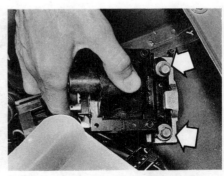

4.6 Ignition coil securing bolts (arrowed) – 1.4 litre multi-point fuel injection engine

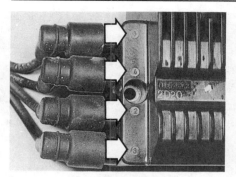

4.14 HT lead cylinder numbers (arrowed) marked on coil (coil removed) – 1.6 litre multi-point fuel injection engine

4.15 Disconnecting the coil wiring plug – 1.6 litre multi-point fuel injection engine

4.16 Unscrewing a coil securing screw – 1.6 litre multi-point fuel injection engine

7   Where applicable, disengage the coil from the amplifier module mounting plate.
8   On models with a cylindrical type coil, the mounting clamp can be removed from the coil by loosening the clamp nut.

Testing

9   Connect an ohmmeter between both LT terminals, and check the primary windings for continuity. Connect the ohmmeter between the HT terminal and either LT terminal, and check the secondary windings for continuity. If there is no continuity, the coil should be renewed.
10   Using an ohmmeter or a continuity tester, check that there is no continuity between the HT terminal and the coil body. If there is continuity, the coil should be renewed.

Refitting

11   Refitting is a reversal of removal, ensuring that (where applicable) the coil suppressor is in position before fitting the coil securing bolts. Ensure that all wiring is correctly reconnected as noted before removal, and that all connections are secure.

1.6 litre multi-point fuel injection engine

Removal

12   The coil is mounted on the left-hand end of the camshaft housing, in the position normally occupied by the distributor.
13   Disconnect the battery negative lead.
14   Disconnect the HT leads from the coil, noting their locations to ensure correct refitting. Note that the HT lead cylinder numbers are stamped into the coil casing (photo).
15   Disconnect the coil wiring plug (photo).
16   Unscrew the three Torx type securing screws, and remove the coil from its mounting plate (photo).

Testing

17   Due to the construction of the coil, testing should be carried out using the appropriate test equipment available to a Vauxhall/Opel dealer.

Refitting

18   Refitting is a reversal of removal.

5   Ignition amplifier module – removal and refitting

Removal

1   Where applicable, the amplifier module is located on a bracket under the ignition coil.

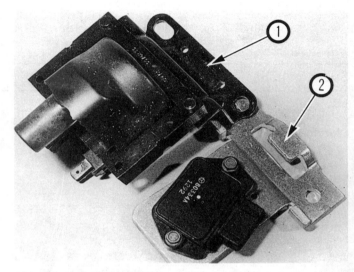

5.3 Ignition coil (1) and amplifier module mounting bracket (2) removed from vehicle

2   Remove the ignition coil and amplifier module mounting bracket, as described in Section 4.
3   The module can be removed from the mounting plate by unscrewing the two securing screws (photo).

Refitting

4   Before refitting the module, special heat-sink compound should be applied to the mounting plate to improve heat dissipation. If a new module is being fitted, it should be supplied with suitable heat sink compound. Similar compounds can be purchased from DIY electrical shops.
5   Refit the coil mounting plate and coil assembly, as described in Section 4.

6   Electronic control unit – removal and refitting

Refer to the relevant Section of Chapter 4.

Chapter 6 Clutch

Contents

Specifications

Type.. Single dry plate, operated by cable

Clutch disc
Diameter:
    1.4 litre engines .... 190.0 mm
    1.6 litre engines .... 200.0 mm
    1.8 litre and 2.0 litre SOHC engines.. 216.0 mm
    DOHC engines .... 228.0 mm
Lining thickness (new – all models) .... 3.5 mm

Torque wrench settings

	Nm	lbf ft
Differential housing cover plate bolts:		
Steel plate	30	22
Alloy plate	18	13
Clutch bellhousing cover plate bolts	7	5
Clutch cover-to-flywheel bolts	15	11
Clutch release fork-to-pivot shaft clamp bolt	35	26
Gearbox endplate bolts:		
M7 bolts	15	11
M8 bolts	20	15
Input shaft socket-headed screw	15	11

1 General information

All manual gearbox models are fitted with a single dry plate clutch, which consists of five main components; friction disc, pressure plate, diaphragm spring, cover and release bearing.

The friction disc is free to slide along the splines of the gearbox input shaft, and is held in position between the flywheel and the pressure plate by the pressure exerted on the pressure plate by the diaphragm spring. Friction lining material is riveted to both sides of the friction disc, and spring cushioning between the friction linings and the hub absorbs transmission shocks, and helps to ensure a smooth take-up of power as the clutch is engaged.

The diaphragm spring is mounted on pins, and is held in place in the cover by annular fulcrum rings.

The release bearing is located on a guide sleeve at the front of the gearbox, and the bearing is free to slide on the sleeve, under the action of the release arm which pivots inside the clutch bellhousing.

The release arm is operated by the clutch pedal, via a cable. As wear takes place on the friction disc over a period of time, the clutch pedal will rise progressively, relative to its original position. No periodic adjustment of the clutch cable is specified by the manufacturers.

When the clutch pedal is depressed, the release arm is actuated by means of the cable. The release arm pushes the release bearing forwards, to bear against the centre of the diaphragm spring, thus pushing the centre of the diaphragm spring inwards. The diaphragm spring acts against the fulcrum rings in the cover, and so as the centre of the spring is pushed in, the outside of the spring is pushed out, so allowing the pressure plate to move backwards away from the friction disc.

When the clutch pedal is released, the diaphragm spring forces the pressure plate into contact with the friction linings on the friction disc, and simultaneously pushes the friction disc forwards on its splines, forcing it against the flywheel. The friction disc is now firmly sandwiched between the pressure plate and the flywheel, and drive is taken up.

On certain models, the clutch assembly, release bearing and guide sleeve oil seal can be renewed without removing the engine or gearbox from the vehicle.

2 Clutch cable – removal and refitting

Removal

1 Working in the engine compartment, measure the length of the threaded rod protruding through the plastic block at the release arm end

2.1 Measuring the length of protruding threaded rod at the end of the clutch cable

2.2 Removing the clip from the threaded rod at the release arm

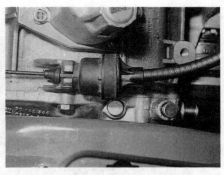

2.3 Clutch cable attachment to lug on bellhousing

3.3 Clutch pedal pivot locking clip (arrowed)

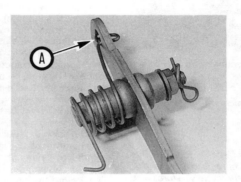

3.5A Clutch pedal components assembled as when in place in vehicle. Clutch cable is retained by return spring at 'A'

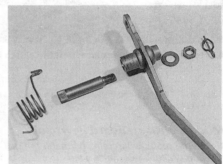

3.5B Clutch pedal pivot components

of the cable (photo). This will enable approximate presetting of the cable when refitting.

2   Remove the clip from the threaded rod at the release arm, then slide the rod from the release arm (photo). Push the release arm towards the engine, and if necessary slacken the cable adjuster, to aid removal.

3   Pull the cable assembly from the lug on the clutch bellhousing (photo).

4   Working inside the vehicle, release the securing clips, and remove the lower trim panel from the driver's footwell.

5   Unhook the return spring from the clutch pedal, and disconnect the cable end from the pedal. Note that the end of the return spring retains the cable end in the pedal. Access is limited, and it may prove easier to remove the clutch pedal, as described in Section 3, before disconnecting the cable.

6   The cable assembly can now be withdrawn into the engine compartment, by pulling it through the bulkhead. Take care not to damage the bulkhead grommet as the cable is withdrawn.

Refitting

7   Refitting is a reversal of removal, bearing in mind the following points.

8   Position the threaded rod so that the length of thread protruding through the plastic block is as noted before removal, then adjust the cable as described in Chapter 1.

9   Ensure that the bulkhead grommet is correctly seated.

3   Clutch pedal – removal and refitting

Removal

1   Proceed as described in Section 2, paragraphs 1 and 2.

2   Working inside the vehicle, release the securing clips, and remove the lower trim panel from the driver's footwell.

3   Remove the locking clip from the right-hand end of the pedal pivot shaft (photo), then unscrew the pedal retaining nut and recover the washer(s).

4   Push the pivot shaft out of the pedal bracket (to the left), then lower the pedal and return spring. Note the position of any washers and/or spacers on the pivot shaft, so that they can be refitted in their original positions.

5   Disconnect the cable end from the pedal by releasing the return spring, and withdraw the pedal and return spring from the vehicle (photos).

Refitting

6   Refitting is a reversal of removal, but before inserting the pedal pivot shaft, smear the surface with a little molybdenum disulphide grease.

7   On completion, adjust the clutch cable if necessary, as described in Chapter 1.

4   Clutch assembly – removal, inspection and refitting

Warning: *Dust created by clutch wear and deposited on the clutch components may contain asbestos, which is a health hazard. DO NOT blow it out with compressed air, or inhale any of it. DO NOT use petrol (or petroleum-based solvents) to clean off the dust. Brake system cleaner or methylated spirit should be used to flush the dust into a suitable receptacle. After the clutch components are wiped clean with rags, dispose of the contaminated rags and cleaner in a sealed, marked container.*

Note: *Certain 1.6 litre and DOHC engines have been progressively fitted with a 'pot' flywheel during production, and this practice may be adopted on other models in the future. The 'pot' flywheel is significantly thicker than the standard item, and consequently there is insufficient clearance between the flywheel and the clutch bellhousing to enable the clutch to be removed with the engine and gearbox in the vehicle. Before attempting to remove the clutch, remove the clutch bellhousing cover*

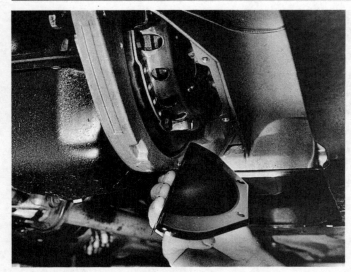

4.2 Removing the cover plate from the clutch bellhousing

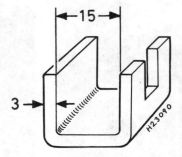

Fig. 6.1 Clutch pressure plate retaining clamp dimensions – in mm (Sec 4)

plate and examine the flywheel to ascertain which type is fitted, then proceed as follows, according to flywheel type.

Models with standard flywheel

Note: *The manufacturers recommend the use of special tools for this procedure, although suitable alternatives can be improvised as described in the text. It is suggested that this Section is read thoroughly before work commences, in order that suitable tools can be made available as required.*

Removal

1   Where applicable, remove the left-hand front wheel trim, then loosen the roadwheel bolts. Apply the handbrake, jack up the front of the vehicle, and support securely on axle stands (see *'Jacking, towing and wheel changing'*). Remove the roadwheel for improved access. On DOHC engine models, remove the engine undershield with reference to Chapter 11, Section 25.

2   Unscrew the securing bolts, and remove the cover plate from the base of the clutch bellhousing (photo).

3   For improved access, remove the wheel arch liner, as described in Chapter 11, Section 25.

4   Unscrew the retaining nut, and disconnect the earth strap from the gearbox endplate, where applicable (photo).

5   Place a suitable container beneath the gearbox endplate, to catch the oil which will be released, then unscrew the securing bolts and remove the endplate (photo). Note the location of the bolts (including the stud for the earth strap, where applicable), as two different lengths are used.

6   Recover the gasket.

7   Extract the circlip from inside the end of the gearbox input shaft, using a pair of circlip pliers (photo).

8   Using a twelve-point splined key, unscrew the bolt from the end of the input shaft (photo).

9   The input shaft can now be pulled out of engagement with the splined hub of the clutch friction disc. The manufacturers specify the use of special tools for this operation (tool Nos KM-556-1-A and KM-556-4), but an alternative can be improvised as shown (photos). The tool bolts into place on the end of the gearbox, using the endplate securing bolts. Tool dimensions will vary according to gearbox type.

10   Alternatively, screw an M7 bolt into the end of the input shaft, and use the bolt to pull the shaft out to its stop. It is likely that the input shaft will be a very tight fit, in which case it may prove difficult to withdraw, without using the special tool previously described. In extreme cases, a slide hammer can be attached to the end of the shaft to enable it to be withdrawn – although this is not to be recommended, as damage to the gearbox components may result.

11   Before the clutch assembly can be removed, the pressure plate must be compressed against the tension of the diaphragm spring, otherwise the assembly will be too thick to be withdrawn through the space between the flywheel and the edge of the bellhousing.

12   Three special clamps are available from the manufacturers for this purpose (tool No KM-526-A), but suitable alternatives can be made up from strips of metal. The clamps should be U-shaped, and conform to the dimensions given below, and in Fig. 6.1. Bevel the edges of the clamps to ease fitting, and cut a slot in one of the U-legs to clear the pressure plate rivets.

    Thickness of metal strip – 3.0 mm
    Distance between U-legs – 15.0 mm

13   Have an assistant depress the clutch pedal fully, then fit each clamp securely over the edge of the cover/pressure plate, engaging the clamps in the apertures around the rim of the cover (photos). Turn the crankshaft using a suitable socket or spanner on the pulley/sprocket bolt, to bring each clamp location into view.

14   Once the clamps have been fitted, have the assistant release the clutch pedal.

15   Progressively loosen and remove the six bolts and spring washers which secure the clutch cover to the flywheel. As previously, turn the crankshaft to bring each bolt into view. Where applicable (and if the original clutch is to be refitted), note the position of the mark on the flywheel which aligns with the notch in the rim of the clutch cover (photos).

4.4 Earth strap on gearbox endplate

4.5 Removing the gearbox endplate

4.7 Extract the circlip (arrowed) from the end of the gearbox input shaft

4.8 Unscrew the bolt from the end of the input shaft

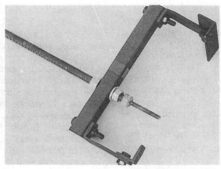

4.9A Improvised tool for disengaging gearbox input shaft from clutch

4.9B Disengaging the input shaft from the clutch using the improvised tool

4.13A Fitting a suitable clamp ...

4.13B ... to compress the clutch pressure plate prior to removal

4.15A Loosening a clutch cover-to-flywheel bolt

4.15B Stamped mark on flywheel (arrowed) aligned with notch in clutch cover

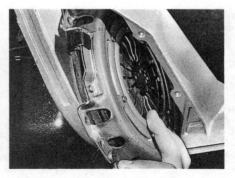

4.16 Withdrawing the clutch assembly from the bellhousing

16   The clutch assembly can now be withdrawn downwards from the bellhousing (photo). Be prepared to catch the clutch friction disc, which may drop out of the cover as it is withdrawn, and note which way round the friction disc is fitted. The greater projecting side of the hub faces away from the flywheel.
17   The pressure plate can be compressed against the tension of the diaphragm spring, in a vice fitted with soft jaw protectors, in order to remove the clamps.

Inspection

18   With the clutch assembly removed, clean off all traces of dust using a dry cloth. Although most friction discs now have asbestos-free linings, some do not, and it is wise to take suitable precautions; asbestos dust is harmful, and must not be inhaled.
19   Examine the linings of the clutch disc for wear and loose rivets, and the disc for distortion, cracks, broken torsion springs and worn splines. The surface of the friction linings may be highly glazed, but, as long as the friction material pattern can be clearly seen, this is satisfactory. If there is any sign of oil contamination, indicated by a continuous, or

patchy, shiny black discolouration, the disc must be renewed. The source of the contamination must be traced and rectified before fitting new clutch components; typically, a leaking crankshaft oil seal or gearbox input shaft oil seal – or both – will be to blame (renewal procedures are given in Chapters 2 and 7 respectively). The disc must also be renewed if the lining thickness has worn down to, or just above, the level of the rivet heads.
20   Check the machined faces of the flywheel and pressure plate. If either is grooved, or heavily scored, renewal is necessary. The pressure plate must also be renewed if any cracks are apparent, or if the diaphragm spring is damaged or its pressure suspect.
21   With the clutch removed, it is advisable to check the condition of the release bearing, as described in Section 5.

Refitting

Note: *The circlip in the end of the input shaft, and the gearbox endplate gasket should be renewed on reassembly.*

22   Some replacement clutch assemblies are supplied with the pressure plate already compressed using the three clamps described in

paragraph 12. If this is not the case, the pressure plate should be compressed against the tension of the diaphragm spring, using a vice fitted with soft jaw protectors, and the clamps used during removal should be fitted.

23   It is important to ensure that no oil or grease gets onto the friction disc linings, or the pressure plate and flywheel faces. It is advisable to refit the clutch assembly with clean hands, and to wipe down the pressure plate and flywheel faces with a clean rag before assembly begins.

24   Apply a smear of molybdenum disulphide grease to the splines of the friction disc hub, then offer the disc to the flywheel, with the greater projecting side of the hub facing away from the flywheel. Hold the friction disc against the flywheel while the cover/pressure plate assembly is offered into position.

25   The input shaft must now be pushed through the hub of the friction disc, until its end engages in the spigot bearing in the end of the crankshaft. **Under no circumstances** must the shaft be hammered home, as gearbox damage may result. If the input shaft cannot be pushed home by hand, steady pressure should be exerted on the end of the shaft. The manufacturers specify the use of a special tool for this operation (tool No KM-564), but the improvised tool used to withdraw the shaft during the removal procedure can be used by repositioning the nut as shown.

26   With the input shaft pushed fully home, position the cover/pressure plate assembly so that the mark on the flywheel is in alignment with the notch on the rim of the clutch cover, then refit and progressively tighten the six clutch cover-to-flywheel bolts (ensuring that the spring washers are fitted) in a diagonal sequence. Turn the crankshaft, using a suitable socket or spanner on the pulley/sprocket bolt, to gain access to each bolt in turn, and finally tighten all the bolts to the specified torque.

27   Have an assistant depress the clutch pedal, then remove the three clamps from the edge of the cover/pressure plate, again turning the crankshaft for access to each clamp.

28   Once the clamps have been removed, have the assistant release the clutch pedal.

29   Refit the screw to the end of the gearbox input shaft, then fit a new circlip.

30   Using a new gasket, refit the gearbox endplate, and tighten the securing bolts to the specified torque. Where applicable, ensure that the studded bolt which retains the earth strap is fitted to its correct location, as noted during removal.

31   Where applicable, reconnect the gearbox earth strap, and fit the retaining nut.

32   Refit the cover plate to the base of the clutch bellhousing, and tighten the securing bolts. Where applicable, refit the wheel arch liner.

33   Refit the roadwheel, then lower the vehicle to the ground and finally tighten the roadwheel bolts. Refit the wheel trim, where applicable, and on DOHC engine models, refit the engine undershield.

34   Check the clutch cable adjustment, as described in Chapter 1.

35   Check and if necessary top-up the gearbox oil level, as described in Chapter 1.

Models with 'pot' flywheel

Removal

36   Due to the size of the 'pot' flywheel, there is insufficient space for the clutch to be withdrawn through the aperture in the clutch bellhousing, as described previously for models with a standard flywheel.

37   Unless the complete engine/gearbox assembly is to be removed from the vehicle and separated for major overhaul (see Chapter 2), access to the clutch can be obtained by removing the engine (Chapter 2) or the gearbox (Chapter 7).

38   With the engine or gearbox removed, proceed as follows.

39   Where applicable (and if the original clutch is to be refitted), note the position of the mark on the flywheel which aligns with the notch in the rim of the clutch cover, then progressively unscrew the six bolts and spring washers which secure the clutch cover to the flywheel.

40   With all the bolts removed, lift off the clutch assembly. Be prepared to catch the friction disc as the cover assembly is lifted from the flywheel, and note which way round the friction disc is fitted. The greater projecting side of the hub should face away from the flywheel.

Inspection

41   Proceed as described in paragraphs 18 to 21 inclusive for models with a standard flywheel.

Refitting

42   Proceed as described in paragraphs 23 and 24.

43   Fit the clutch cover assembly, where applicable aligning the mark on the flywheel with the notch in the rim of the clutch cover. Insert the six bolts and spring washers, and tighten them finger-tight, so that the friction disc is gripped, but can still be moved.

44   The friction disc must now be centralised, so that when the engine and gearbox are mated, the gearbox input shaft splines will pass through the splines in the friction disc hub.

45   Centralisation can be carried out by inserting a round bar or a long screwdriver through the hole in the centre of the friction disc, so that the end of the bar rests in the spigot bearing in the centre of the crankshaft. Where possible, use a blunt instrument, but if a screwdriver is used, wrap tape around the blade to prevent damage to the bearing surface. Moving the bar sideways or up and down as necessary, move the friction disc in whichever direction is necessary to achieve centralisation. With the bar removed, view the friction disc hub in relation to the hole in the centre of the crankshaft and the circle created by the ends of the diaphragm spring fingers. When the hub appears exactly in the centre, all is correct. Alternatively, if a clutch alignment tool can be obtained, this will eliminate all the guesswork, and obviate the need for visual alignment.

46   Tighten the cover retaining bolts gradually in a diagonal sequence, to the specified torque. Remove the alignment tool.

47   Refit the engine or the gearbox, as described in the relevant Chapter.

48   On completion, check the clutch cable adjustment, as described in Chapter 1.

5 Clutch release bearing – removal, inspection and refitting

Note: *Refer to the note at the beginning of Section 4 before proceeding.*

Removal

1   On models with a standard flywheel, access to the release bearing can be obtained with the engine and gearbox in the vehicle, after removing the clutch assembly as described in Section 4, although access is improved if the gearbox is removed.

2   On models with a 'pot' flywheel, the gearbox must be removed for access to the release bearing. Unless the complete engine/gearbox assembly is to be removed from the vehicle and separated for major overhaul (see Chapter 2), access to the clutch is most easily obtained by removing the gearbox, as described in Chapter 7.

3   Unscrew the clamp bolt securing the release fork to the release arm pivot shaft (photo).

5.3 Unscrewing the clamp bolt securing the release fork to the release arm pivot shaft (model with standard flywheel)

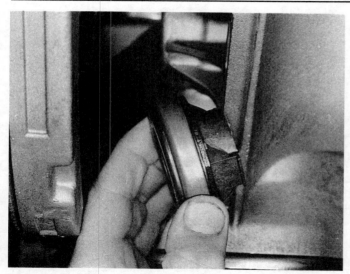

5.5 Withdrawing the clutch release bearing (model with standard flywheel)

4   If not already done, disconnect the clutch cable from the release arm, by removing the clip from the threaded rod, and then sliding the threaded rod from the release arm.

5   Pull the release arm pivot shaft up and out of the bellhousing, then withdraw the release fork and the bearing (photo). Where necessary, slide the bearing from the release fork, and where applicable, pull the bearing from the plastic collar.

6   If desired, the gearbox input shaft oil seal can be renewed after removing the release bearing guide sleeve, as described in Chapter 7.

Inspection

7   Spin the release bearing, and check it for excessive roughness. Hold the outer race, and attempt to move it laterally against the inner race. If any excessive movement or roughness is evident, renew the bearing. If a new clutch has been fitted, it is wise to renew the release bearing as a matter of course.

8   The nylon bushes supporting the release arm pivot shaft can be renewed if necessary (this is likely to be difficult if the gearbox is still in the vehicle), by tapping them from their lugs in the bellhousing using a suitable drift. Drive the new bushes into position, ensuring that their locating tabs engage with the slots in the bellhousing lugs.

Refitting

9   Refitting of the release bearing and arm is a reversal of the removal procedure, bearing in mind the following points.

10   Lightly smear the inner surfaces of the release arm pivot bushes, and the outer surfaces of the release bearing guide sleeve, with molybdenum disulphide grease.

11   Where applicable, fit the release bearing to the plastic collar, then fit the release bearing and fork together, and tighten the release fork clamp bolt to the specified torque.

12   Refit the clutch as described in Section 4, or refit the gearbox as described in Chapter 7, as applicable.

13   On completion, check the clutch cable adjustment as described in Chapter 1.

Chapter 7 Transmission

Contents

Specifications

Part A: Manual gearbox

Type .... Five forward speeds and one reverse, synchromesh on all forward gears. Integral differential

Manufacturer's designation
1.4 litre carburettor and single-point fuel injection engine models .... F 10/5
1.4 litre multi-point fuel injection and 1.6 litre engine models:
    All except 'Si' and 'GT' models.. F 13/5
    'Si' and 'GT' models .... F 13/5 CR
1.8 litre engine models:
    All except 'GT' models.. F 16/5
    'GT' models .... F 16/5 CR
2.0 litre SOHC engine models:
    All except 'GT', 'SRi' and 'GSi' models .... F 16/5
    'GT', 'SRi' and 'GSi' models .... F 16/5 CR
2.0 litre DOHC engine models.. F 20/5 CR

Ratios
F 10/5 and F 13/5 gearboxes:
    Final drive .... 4.18 : 1
    1st.. 3.55 : 1
    2nd... 1.96 : 1
    3rd.. 1.30 : 1
    4th.. 0.89 : 1
    5th.. 0.71 : 1
    Reverse .... 3.31 : 1
F 13/5 CR gearbox:
    Final drive .... 3.94 : 1
    1st.. 3.55 : 1
    2nd... 2.14 : 1
    3rd.. 1.43 : 1
    4th.. 1.12 : 1
    5th.. 0.89 : 1
    Reverse .... 3.31 : 1

Ratios (continued)
F 16/5 gearbox:
- Final drive:
  - 1.8 litre engine models .... 3.72 : 1
  - 2.0 litre engine models .... 3.55 : 1
- 1st .... 3.55 : 1
- 2nd .... 1.95 : 1
- 3rd .... 1.28 : 1
- 4th .... 0.89 : 1
- 5th .... 0.71 : 1
- Reverse .... 3.33 : 1

F 16/5 CR and F 20/5 CR gearboxes:
- Final drive:
  - 1.8 litre engine models .... 3.72 : 1
  - 2.0 litre SOHC engine models .... 3.55 : 1
  - 2.0 litre DOHC engine models .... 3.42 : 1
- 1st .... 3.55 : 1
- 2nd .... 2.16 : 1
- 3rd .... 1.48 : 1
- 4th .... 1.13 : 1
- 5th .... 0.89 : 1
- Reverse .... 3.33 : 1

Torque wrench settings

	Nm	lbf ft
Gear selector rod clamp bolt	15	11
Gearchange lever housing-to-floor pan bolts	6	4
Speedometer drivegear retaining plate bolt	4	3
Clutch release bearing guide sleeve bolts	5	4
Reversing light switch	20	15
Left-hand engine/transmission mounting-to-transmission bracket bolts	60	44
Left-hand engine/transmission mounting-to-body bolts*	65	48
Engine/transmission mounting bracket-to-transmission bolts	60	44
Rear engine/transmission mounting-to-crossmember bolts	40	30
Rear engine/transmission mounting-to-transmission bracket bolts	45	33
Engine-to-transmission bolts	75	55
Differential housing cover plate bolts:		
Steel plate	30	22
Alloy plate	18	13
Gearbox endplate bolts:		
M7 bolts	15	11
M8 bolts	20	15
Input shaft socket-headed screw	15	11

Part B: Automatic transmission
Type .... Hydrodynamic torque converter with electronically-controlled mechanical lock-up system, two epicyclic gearsets giving four forward speeds and reverse, integral final drive. Gearchanging under full electronic control, with three 'driving modes' selectable

Manufacturer's designation .... AF 20

Torque wrench settings

	Nm	lbf ft
Fluid drain plug	45	33
Fluid cooler pipe union bolts	22	16
Dipstick tube nut	20	15
Starter inhibitor/reversing light switch securing nut	25	18
Starter inhibitor swtich/reversing light switch-to-selector lever shaft nut	8	6
Actuating lever-to-selector lever shaft nut	16	12
Selector cable clamp bolt	6	4
Input/ouput speed sensor securing screws	6	4
Fluid temperature sensor	25	18
Fluid temperature sensor shield nuts	25	18
Torque converter-to-driveplate bolts*	50	37
Transmission bellhousing cover plate bolts	7	5
Engine-to-transmission bolts	75	55
Left-hand engine/transmission mounting-to-transmission bolts	60	44
Left-hand engine/transmission mounting-to-body bolts*	65	48

*Use new bolts

Part A: Manual gearbox

1   General information

A five-speed gearbox is fitted to all models. Six different types of gearbox are used, depending on the model and the power output of the engine fitted (see Specifications), but there are only minor internal differences between the gearbox types.

Drive from the clutch is picked up by the input shaft, which runs in parallel with the mainshaft. The input shaft and mainshaft gears are in constant mesh, and selection of gears is by sliding synchromesh hubs, which lock the appropriate mainshaft gear to the mainshaft.

The 5th speed components are located in an extension housing at the end of the gearbox.

Reverse gear is obtained by sliding an idler gear into mesh with two straight-cut gears on the input shaft and mainshaft.

All the forward gear teeth are helically-cut, to reduce noise and to improve wear characteristics.

The differential is mounted in the main gearbox casing, and drive is transmitted to the differential by a pinion gear on the end of the mainshaft. The inboard ends of the driveshafts locate directly into the differential. The gearbox and differential unit share the same lubricating oil.

Gear selection is by a floor-mounted gearchange lever, via a remote control linkage.

2   Gearbox oil – draining and refilling

Draining

1   On DOHC engine models, remove the engine undershield as described in Chapter 11, Section 25.
2   Place a suitable container under the differential cover plate, then unscrew the securing bolts, and withdraw the cover plate, allowing the gearbox oil to drain into the container.
3   Refit the differential cover plate, and tighten the securing bolts when the oil has drained.
4   On DOHC engine models, do not refit the engine undershield until the gearbox has been refilled with oil.

Refilling

5   Proceed as described for the gearbox oil level check in Chapter 1.

3   Gearchange linkage/mechanism – adjustment

Note: *A new plug should be fitted to the gear linkage adjuster hole in the gear selector cover on completion of adjustment.*

1   Working in the engine compartment, loosen the clamp bolt securing the gear selector rod to the clamp sleeve (photo).
2   Extract the plug from the adjuster hole in the gear selector cover (photo).
3   Looking towards the engine compartment bulkhead, grip the gear selector rod, and twist it clockwise until a 4.5 mm diameter twist drill can be inserted through the adjuster hole in the gear selector cover, to engage with the hole in the selector lever (photo).
4   Working inside the vehicle, pull back on the front edge of the gearchange lever gaiter, and free its lower end from the centre console, to allow access to the base of the gearchange lever.
5   The help of an assistant will now be required, to hold the gearchange lever in neutral in the 1st/2nd gear plane. The lever should be resting against the reverse stop, and the arrow and notch should be aligned as shown (photo).
6   Without moving the gearchange lever, tighten the clamp bolt securing the gear selector rod to the clamp sleeve in the engine compartment.

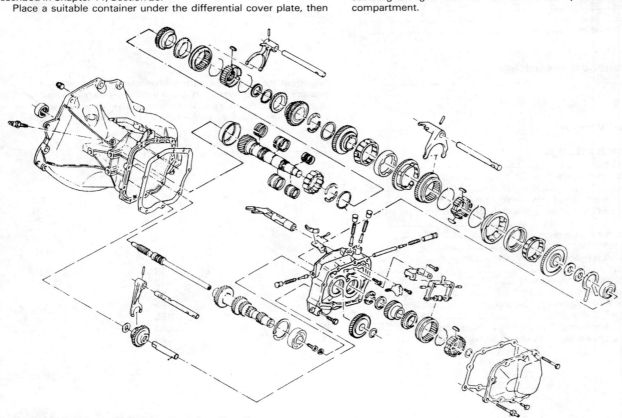

Fig. 7.1 Exploded view of F 16/5 type gearbox (Sec 1)

H23098

3.1 Gear selector rod-to-clamp sleeve clamp bolt (arrowed)

3.2 Extract the plug from the adjuster hole ...

3.3 ... and insert a twist drill to engage with the selector lever

7   Referring to Fig. 7.2, check that the free play between the hook (A) and the stop (B) at the base of the gearchange lever is as specified.
8   Refit the gearchange lever gaiter to the centre console.
9   Remove the twist drill from the adjuster hole in the gear selector cover, and seal the hole with a **new** plug.
10   Finally check that all gears can be engaged easily with the vehicle at rest, engine running, and clutch pedal depressed.

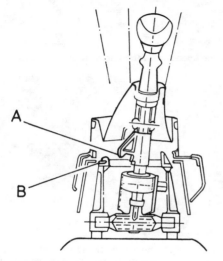

3.5 Arrow on gearchange lever aligned with notch in reverse stop

4   Gearchange linkage/mechanism – removal, overhaul and refitting

Gearchange lever

Removal

1   Ensure that the lever is in the neutral position.
2   Pull back on the front edge of the gearchange lever gaiter, and free its lower end from the centre console to allow access to the base of the lever.
3   Release the clip from the base of the lever shaft, then withdraw the pivot pin, and lift out the lever (photos).

Overhaul

4   To renew the gearchange lever gaiter and/or the knob, proceed as follows.
5   On models with a plastic lever knob, immerse the knob in hot water (approximately 80°C) for a few minutes, then twist the knob and tap it from the lever. On models with a leather-covered lever knob, clamp the lever in a vice fitted with soft jaw protectors, and place an open-ended spanner under the metal insert at the bottom of the knob, then tap the knob from the lever, using the spanner as an insulator to protect the knob. There is a strong possibility that the knob will be destroyed during the removal process.
6   If renewing the gaiter, slide the old gaiter from the lever, and fit the new one. Use a little liquid detergent to aid fitting if necessary.
7   Refit the knob (or fit the new knob, as applicable). When fitting a plastic knob, preheat it in hot water, as during removal. When fitting a leather-covered knob, preheat the metal insert at the base of the knob using a hair drier or hot-air gun. Ensure that the knob is fitted the correct way round.

Refitting

8   Refitting is a reversal of removal.

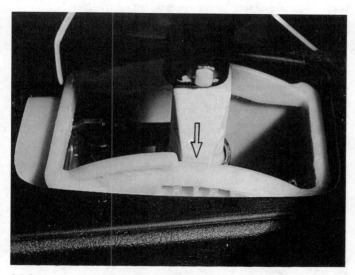

Fig. 7.2 Gearchange lever free play between hook (A) and stop (B) should be a maximum of 3.0 mm (Sec 3)

H23091

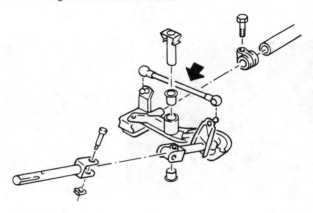

H23092

Fig. 7.3 Gear selector linkage components – link rod arrowed (Sec 4)

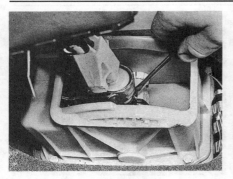

4.3A Release the clip from the base of the gearchange lever shaft, ...

4.3B ... then withdraw the pivot pin

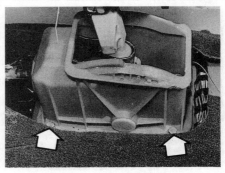

4.12 Gear lever housing securing bolts (arrowed)

Gearchange lever housing assembly

Removal

9   Working in the engine compartment, loosen the clamp bolt securing the gear selector rod to the clamp sleeve.

10   Remove the gearchange lever, as described previously in this Section.

11   Remove the centre console, as described in Chapter 11.

12   Unscrew the four bolts securing the gearchange lever housing to the floorpan (photo).

13   The housing and clamp sleeve can now be withdrawn. Pull the assembly towards the rear of the vehicle, to feed the clamp sleeve through the bulkhead. As the clamp sleeve is fed through the bulkhead, have an assistant remove the clamp from the end of the clamp sleeve in the engine compartment, to avoid damage to the rubber boot on the bulkhead.

Overhaul

14   If desired, the rubber boot can be renewed by pulling the old boot from the bulkhead, and pushing the new boot into position, ensuring that it is correctly seated.

15   The clamp sleeve bush in the gearchange lever housing can be renewed after sliding the clamp sleeve from the housing. Prise the bush insert from the front of the housing, then prise the bush from the insert. Fit the new bush using a reversal of the removal procedure, but lubricate the inside of the bush with a little silicone grease.

Refitting

16   Refitting of the assembly is a reversal of removal, but before tightening the clamp bolt, adjust the gear selector linkage as described in Section 3.

Gear selector linkage

Removal

17   Loosen the clamp bolt securing the clamp sleeve to the linkage.

18   Prise off the securing clip, then withdraw the pivot pin from the linkage universal joint.

19   Release the spring clip, the pull the bellcrank pivot pin from the bracket on the rear engine/gearbox mounting.

20   Withdraw the linkage from the vehicle.

Overhaul

21   Check the linkage components for wear, and renew as necessary. The pivot bushes can be renewed by prising out the old bushes and pressing in the new, and the link can be renewed by pulling it from the balljoints. Further dismantling is not recommended.

Refitting

22   Refitting is a reversal of removal, but before tightening the clamp bolt, adjust the gear selector linkage as described in Section 3.

5.2 Disconnecting the speedometer cable from the gearbox

5.3A Unbolt the retaining plate ...

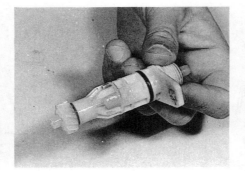

5.3B ... and withdraw the speedometer drive assembly

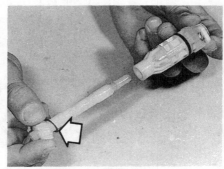

5.4 Withdrawing the speedometer driven gear from its sleeve. Note thrustwasher (arrowed)

5 Speedometer drive – removal and refitting

Removal

1 Where applicable, disconnect the battery negative lead, and disconnect the wiring plug from the vehicle speed sensor.
2 Unscrew the securing sleeve, and disconnect the speedometer cable from the top of the gearbox (photo).
3 Unbolt the retaining plate, and withdraw the speedometer drive assembly (photos).
4 If desired, the speedometer driven gear can be withdrawn from its sleeve, in which case note the thrustwasher under the gear (photo).

Refitting

5 If the driven gear has been removed from the sleeve, lubricate the gear shaft with a little silicon grease, then slide the gear into the sleeve, ensuring that the thrustwasher is in place on the gear shaft.
6 Inspect the O-ring seal on the sleeve, and renew if worn or damaged.
7 Further refitting is a reversal of removal.

6 Oil seals – renewal

Differential side (driveshaft) oil seals

Note: *A balljoint separator tool will be required for this operation. The driveshaft snap-ring(s) and lower arm-to-suspension strut balljoint locking pin(s) must be renewed on reassembly.*

1 Jack up the front of the vehicle, and support securely on axle stands, then remove the roadwheel (see 'Jacking, towing and wheel changing').
2 Drain the gearbox oil, as described in Section 2.
3 Extract the locking pin, then unscrew the castellated nut from the lower arm-to-suspension strut balljoint.
4 Using a balljoint separator tool, disconnect the lower arm-to-suspension strut balljoint.
5 A suitable tool will now be required to release the inner end of the

driveshaft from the differential. To release the right-hand driveshaft, a flat steel bar with a good chamfer on one end can be used. On certain models, the left-hand driveshaft may be more difficult to release, and a suitable square- or rectangular-section bar will be required.
6 Lever between the driveshaft and the differential housing to release the driveshaft snap-ring from the differential. Oil will probably be released as the driveshaft is withdrawn from the differential, even though the gearbox has been drained. Support the driveshaft by suspending it with wire or string, and do not allow it to hang under its own weight.
7 Prise the now-exposed oil seal from the differential, using a screwdriver or similar instrument (photo).
8 Smear the sealing lip of the new oil seal with a little gearbox oil, then using a metal tube or socket of suitable diameter, drive the new seal into the differential until the outer surface of the seal is flush with the outer surface of the differential casing (photo).
9 Fit a new snap-ring to the inboard end of the driveshaft, then push the driveshaft into the differential as far as possible.
10 Place a screwdriver or similar tool on the weld bead of the inner driveshaft joint, **not** the metal cover, and drive the shaft into the differential until the retaining snap-ring engages positively. Pull on the **outer** circumference of the joint to check the engagement.
11 Reconnect the lower arm-to-suspension strut balljoint, then fit the castellated nut and tighten to the specified torque. Secure the nut with a new locking pin.
12 Refit the roadwheel, then lower the vehicle to the ground, and finally tighten the roadwheel bolts. Refit the wheel trim, where applicable.
13 Refill the gearbox with oil, as described in Section 2.

Input shaft (clutch) oil seal

Note: *A new clutch release bearing guide sleeve O-ring must be used on refitting.*

14 Remove the clutch release bearing and fork, as described in Chapter 6.
15 Unscrew the securing bolts, and withdraw the clutch release bearing guide sleeve from the bellhousing. Recover the O-ring which fits between the guide sleeve and the bellhousing (photos).
16 Drive the old oil seal from the guide sleeve (photo), and fit a new

6.7 Prising out a differential side oil seal

6.8 Driving a new differential side oil seal into position

6.15A Withdraw the clutch release bearing guide sleeve ...

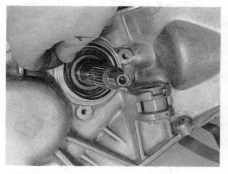
6.15B ... and recover the O-ring

6.16 Driving the oil seal from the clutch release bearing guide sleeve

7.4 Reversing light switch wiring connector (arrowed)

seal using a suitable tube or socket. Press the new seal into position – do not drive it in, as the seal is easily damaged.

17   Fill the space between the lips of the new seal with lithium-based grease, then refit the guide sleeve, using a new O-ring. The O-ring should be fitted dry.

18   Refit the guide sleeve to the bellhousing, and tighten the securing bolts.

19   Refit the clutch release bearing and fork, as described in Chapter 6.

7   Reversing light switch – removal, refitting and testing

Testing

1   The reversing light circuit is operated by a plunger-type switch, mounted in the front of the gearbox casing.

2   To test the switch, disconnect the wiring, and use a suitable meter or a battery-and-bulb test circuit to check for continuity between the switch terminals. Continuity should only exist when reverse gear is selected. If this is not the case, and there are no obvious breaks or other damage to the wires, the switch is faulty and must be renewed.

Removal

3   The reversing light switch is located in the front of the gearbox casing, and is accessible from the engine compartment.

4   Disconnect the battery negative lead, then disconnect the wiring from the switch (photo).

5   Unscrew the switch from the gearbox.

Refitting

6   Refitting is a reversal of removal.

8   Manual gearbox – removal and refitting

Note: *This is an involved procedure, and it is easier in many cases to remove the gearbox with the engine as an assembly, as described in Chapter 2. If removing the gearbox on its own, it is suggested that this Section is read through thoroughly before commencing work. Various components must be renewed on reassembly, suitable equipment will be required to support the engine, and a special tool will be required to engage the gearbox input shaft with the clutch on refitting.*

Removal

1   Disconnect the battery negative lead.

2   Working in the engine compartment, loosen the clamp bolt securing the gear selector rod to the linkage, then pull the selector tube towards the engine compartment bulkhead to separate it from the linkage.

3   Remove the retaining clip, then slide the clutch cable from the release lever, pushing the release lever back towards the bulkhead if necessary, to allow the cable to be disconnected. Pull the cable support from the bracket on the gearbox casing, then move the cable to one side out of the way, taking note of its routing.

4   Disconnect the wiring from the reversing light switch, which is located at the front of the gearbox casing, above the left-hand mounting bracket.

5   Where applicable, disconnect the wiring from the vehicle speed sensor.

6   Unscrew the securing sleeve, and disconnect the speedometer cable from the top of the gearbox.

7   Unscrew and remove the three upper engine-to-gearbox bolts, noting the locations of any brackets or clips attached to the bolts.

8   The engine must now be supported from its left-hand lifting bracket. Ideally, the engine should be supported using a strong wooden or metal beam, resting on blocks positioned securely in the channels at the sides of the engine compartment. The Vauxhall/Opel special tool designed specifically for this purpose is shown in Fig. 7.4. Alternatively, the engine can be supported using a suitable hoist and lifting tackle, but in this case, the hoist must be of such a design to enable the engine to be supported with the vehicle raised off the ground, leaving sufficient clearance to withdraw the gearbox from under the front of the vehicle.

9   Jack up the front of the vehicle, and support securely on axle stands (see '*Jacking, towing and wheel changing*'. Note that the vehicle must be raised sufficiently high to enable the gearbox to be withdrawn from under the front of the vehicle.

10   On DOHC engine models, remove the engine undershield, with reference to Chapter 11, Section 25.

11   Ensure that the engine is adequately supported, as described in paragraph 8, then remove the front suspension subframe, as described in Chapter 10.

12   Drain the gearbox oil, as described in Section 2.

13   A suitable tool will now be required to release the inner ends of the driveshafts from the differential. To release the right-hand driveshaft, a flat steel bar with a good chamfer on one end can be used. On certain models, the left-hand driveshaft may be more difficult to release, and a suitable square- or rectangular-section bar may be required.

14   Lever between the driveshaft and the differential housing to release the driveshaft snap-ring from the differential. Oil will probably be released as the driveshaft is withdrawn from the differential, even though the gearbox has been drained. Support the driveshafts by

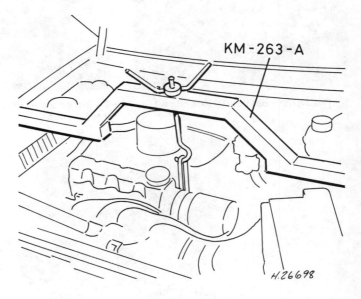

Fig. 7.4 Vauxhall/Opel special tool No KM-263 used to support engine (Sec 8)

suspending them with wire or string, and do not allow them hang under their own weight.

15   Where applicable, unscrew the retaining nut, and disconnect the earth strap from the gearbox endplate.

16   Place a suitable container beneath the gearbox endplate, to catch the oil which will be released, then unscrew the securing bolts and remove the endplate. Note the location of the bolts (including the stud for the earth strap, where applicable), as two different lengths are used.

17   Recover the gasket.

18   Extract the circlip from the end of the gearbox input shaft, using a pair of circlip pliers.

19   Using a twelve-point splined key, unscrew the bolt from the end of the input shaft.

20   The input shaft can now be pulled out of engagement with the splined hub of the clutch friction disc. The manufacturers specify the use of special tools for this operation (tool Nos KM-556-1-A and KM-556-4, but an alternative can be improvised – see Chapter 6, Section 4 for details). The tool bolts into place on the end of the gearbox, using the endplate securing bolts. Tool dimensions will vary according to gearbox type.

21   Alternatively, screw an M7 bolt into the end of the input shaft, and use the bolt to pull the shaft out to its stop. It is likely that the input shaft will be a very tight fit, in which case it may prove difficult to withdraw, without using the special tool previously described. In extreme cases, a slide hammer can be attached to the end of the shaft to enable it to be withdrawn, although this is not to be recommended, as damage to the gearbox components may result.

22   Support the gearbox with a trolley jack, with an interposed block of wood to spread the load.

23   Remove the left-hand engine/gearbox mounting completely, by unscrewing the two bolts securing the rubber mounting to the vehicle body, and the three bolts securing the mounting bracket to the gearbox.

24   Unscrew the securing bolts, and remove the cover plate from the base of the clutch bellhousing.

25   Ensure that the gearbox is adequately supported, then unscrew and remove the remaining engine-to-gearbox bolts.

26   The gearbox can now be lowered and withdrawn from under the front of the vehicle. The help of an assistant will greatly ease this operation.

Refitting

Note: *New left-hand engine/gearbox mounting-to-body bolts, new driveshaft snap-rings, and a new gearbox endplate gasket must be used on refitting.*

27   Before commencing the refitting operations, check that the two original bolts which secured the left-hand engine/gearbox mounting to the vehicle body rotate freely in their threaded bores in the body. If necessary, re-cut the threaded bores, using an M10 x 1.25 mm tap.

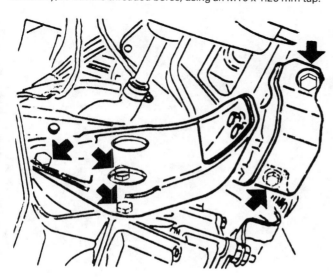

Fig. 7.5 Remove the left-hand engine/gearbox mounting by unscrewing the five bolts (arrowed) (Sec 8)

28   Commence refitting by positioning the gearbox under the front of the vehicle, and support with a trolley jack and interposed block of wood, as during removal.

29   Raise the gearbox sufficiently to enable the lower engine-to-gearbox bolts to be fitted, then refit the bolts, but do not fully tighten them at this stage.

30   Refit the left-hand engine/gearbox mounting, using two new bolts to secure the rubber mounting to the vehicle body. Tighten all bolts to the specified torque.

31   Tighten the previously-fitted lower engine-to-gearbox bolts to the specified torque, then withdraw the trolley jack from under the gearbox.

32   The gearbox input shaft must now be pushed through the hub of the clutch friction disc, until its end engages in the spigot bearing in the end of the crankshaft. **Under no circumstances** must the shaft be hammered home, as gearbox damage may result. If the input shaft cannot be pushed home by hand, steady pressure should be exerted on the end of the shaft. The manufacturers specify the use of a special tool for this operation (tool No KM-564), but the improvised tool used to withdraw the shaft during the removal procedure can be used by repositioning the nut (see Chapter 6).

33   Refit the bolt to the end of the input shaft, then fit a new circlip.

34   Using a new gasket, refit the gearbox endplate, and tighten the securing bolts to the specified torque. Where applicable, ensure that the studded bolt which retains the earth strap is fitted to its correct location, as noted during removal.

35   Where applicable, reconnect the gearbox earth strap, and fit the retaining nut.

36   Refit the cover plate to the base of the clutch bellhousing, and tighten the securing bolts.

37   Fit new snap-rings to the inboards end of the driveshafts, then push the driveshafts into the differential as far as possible.

38   Place a screwdriver or similar tool on the weld bead of each inner driveshaft joint, **not** the metal cover, and drive the shaft into the differential until the retaining snap-ring engages positively. Pull on the **outer** circumference of the joint to check the engagement.

39   Refit the front suspension subframe, as described in Chapter 10.

40   Refit the front wheels.

41   If a hoist and lifting tackle has been used to support the engine, either disconnect the lifting tackle, or lower the hoist sufficiently to enable the vehicle to be lowered to the ground.

42   Lower the vehicle to the ground, and remove or disconnect the equipment used to support the engine, if not already done.

43   Refit the three upper engine-to-gearbox bolts, and tighten them to the specified torque.

44   Reconnect the speedometer cable, and tighten the securing sleeve.

45   Where applicable, reconnect the wiring to the vehicle speed sensor.

46   Reconnect the reversing light switch wiring.

47   Refit the clutch cable support to the bracket on the gearbox casing, then reconnect the cable to the release lever, and adjust the cable as described in Chapter 1. Ensure that the cable is routed as noted during removal.

48   Reconnect the gear selector rod to the linkage, then adjust the linkage as described in Section 3, before tightening the clamp bolt.

49   Refill the gearbox with oil, as described in Chapter 1.

50   Reconnect the battery negative lead.

9   Manual gearbox overhaul – general information

The complete overhaul of a manual gearbox is a complicated task, requiring a number of special tools, and previous experience is a great help. It is therefore recommended that owners remove the gearbox themselves, if wished, but then either fit a new or reconditioned unit, or have the existing unit overhauled by a Vauxhall/Opel dealer or gearbox specialist.

The dismantling of the gearbox into its major assemblies is a reasonably straightforward operation, and can be carried out to enable an assessment of wear or damage to be made (suitable exploded views of the gearboxes are provided to assist owners who wish to undertake this). From this assessment, a decision can be taken as to whether or not to proceed with a full overhaul. Note however that any overhaul work will require the dismantling and reassembly of many small and intricate assemblies, as well as the taking of certain measurements to assess wear. This will require a number of special tools, and previous experience will prove invaluable. As a minimum, the following tools will be required:

Internal and external circlip pliers
A selection of pin punches
A selection of Torx and splined bits
A bearing puller
A hydraulic press
A slide hammer
A selection of heat-sensitive marker pencils

While the *'Fault diagnosis'* Section at the beginning of this manual should help to isolate most gearbox faults to enable a decision to be taken on what course of action to follow, remember that economic considerations may rule out an apparently-simple repair. For example, a common reason for gearbox dismantling is to renew the synchromesh units, wear or faults in these assemblies being indicated by noise when changing gear. Jumping out of gear or similar gear selection faults may be due to worn selector forks, or synchro-sleeves. General noise during operation may be due to worn bearings, shafts or gears. The cumulative cost of renewing all worn components may make it more economical to renew the gearbox complete.

To establish whether gearbox overhaul is economically viable, first establish the cost of a complete replacement gearbox, comparing the cost of a new unit with that of an exchange reconditioned unit (if available), or even a good secondhand unit (with a guarantee) from a vehicle breaker. Compare these costs with the likely cost of the replacement parts which will be required if the existing gearbox is overhauled; do not forget to include all items which must be renewed when they are disturbed, such as oil seals, O-rings, roll pins, circlips, snap-rings, etc.

Part B: Automatic transmission

10 General information

A 4-speed fully-automatic transmission is available as an option on certain Astra models. The transmission consists of a torque converter, an epicyclic geartrain and hydraulically-operated clutches and brakes. The differential is integral with the transmission, and is similar to that used in manual gearbox models.

The torque converter provides a fluid coupling between the engine and transmission which acts as an automatic 'clutch', and also provides a degree of torque multiplication when accelerating.

The epicyclic geartrain provides either one of the four forward gear ratios, or reverse gear, according to which of its component parts are held stationary or allowed to turn. The components of the geartrain are held or released by brakes and clutches, which are activated by a hydraulic control unit. A fluid pump within the transmission provides the necessary hydraulic pressure to operate the brakes and clutches.

The transmission is electronically-controlled, and three driving modes; 'Economy', 'Sport' and 'Winter' are provided. The transmission electronic control unit operates in conjunction with the engine electronic control unit to control the gearchanges. The electronic control unit receives information on transmission fluid temperature, throttle position, engine coolant temperature, and input-versus-output speed. The control unit controls the hydraulically-operated clutches and brakes via four solenoids. The control system can also retard the engine ignition timing, via the engine electronic control unit, to allow smoother gearchanges.

Fig. 7.6 Cutaway view of AF 20 automatic transmission (Sec 10)

1 Torque converter
2 Converter clutch
3 Fluid pump
4 Multi-plate brake
5 Multi-plate brake
6 Valve body assembly
7 Multi-plate brake
8 Multi-plate clutch
9 Multi-plate clutch
10 Free-wheel mechanism
11 Free-wheel mechanism
12 Free-wheel mechanism
13 Multi-plate clutch
14 Brake band
15 Differential

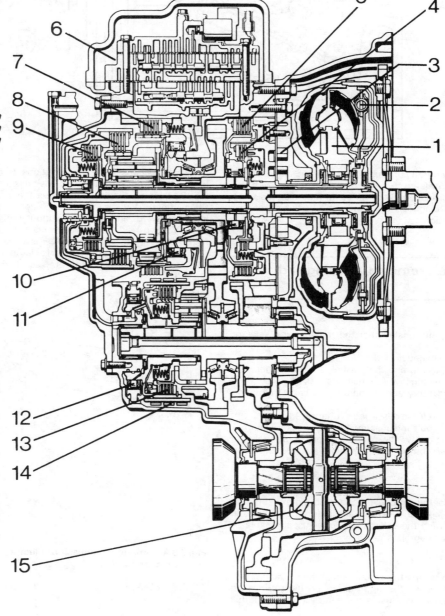

Fig. 7.7 Automatic transmission electronic control system (Sec 10)

1   Distributor
2   Transmission fluid temperature
    sensor
3   Starter inhibitor/reversing light
    switch
4   Connection for
    pressure-regulating solenoids
5   Transmission input speed sensor
6   Transmission output sensor
7   Speedometer cable connection
8   Throttle position sensor
9   Engine electronic control unit
10 Automatic transmission
    electronic control unit
11 'Winter' mode switch
12 'Economy/Sport' mode switch
13 Kickdown switch
14 Brake light switch

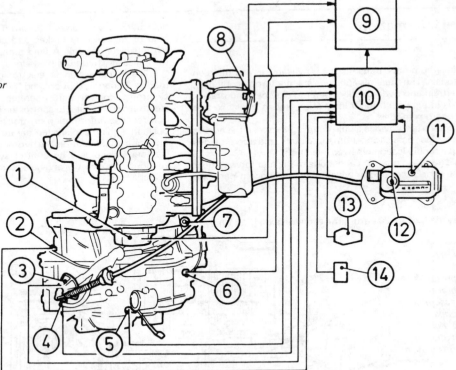

Due to the complexity of the automatic transmission, any repair or overhaul work must be entrusted to a Vauxhall/Opel dealer, with the necessary specialist equipment and knowledge for fault diagnosis and repair. Refer to the Fault diagnosis Section at the beginning of this manual for further information.

11   Selector cable – removal, refitting and adjustment

Removal

1   Apply the handbrake, and ensure that the transmission selector lever is in position 'P'.
2   Disconnect the battery negative lead.
3   Remove the retaining clamp and the washer, and disconnect the selector cable from the actuating lever on the transmission.
4   Unscrew the securing nuts, and withdraw the cable mounting bracket from the transmission.
5   Remove the centre console, as described in Chapter 11.
6   Slacken the cable clamp bolt and unscrew the cable locknut (items 1 and 2 in Fig. 7.8), then withdraw the cable, and pull it through the bulkhead into the engine compartment, prising out the bulkhead grommet where necessary.

Refitting

7   Refitting is a reversal of the removal procedure, but make sure that the bulkhead grommet is correctly located, and before tightening the cable clamp bolt and refitting the selector cover, adjust the cable as described in the following paragraphs.

Adjustment

8   Working in the engine compartment, check that the actuating lever on the transmission moves to the appropriate position, while an assistant moves the selector lever inside the vehicle through the full

range of positions. Note that positions 'P' and 'N' are marked on the transmission, but the remaining positions are unmarked.
9   If adjustment is required, move the selector lever to position 'P'. Check that the lever is locked in position 'P' by attempting to move the lever backwards and forwards without lifting the lever knob.
10 Working inside the vehicle, release the transmission selector cover from the centre console (the cover is secured by clips on either side), then rotate the cover until the cable clamp bolt aperture is visible.
11 Using a long-reach socket, slacken the cable clamp bolt   see Fig. 7.9.

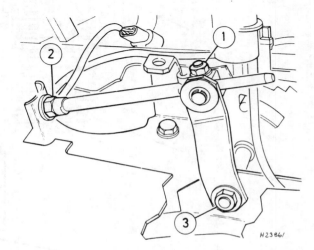

Fig. 7.8 Automatic transmission selector cable connection at selector lever (Sec 11)

1   Cable clamp bolt   3   Lever pivot nut
2   Cable locknut

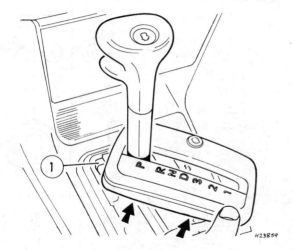

Fig. 7.9 Automatic transmission selector cable adjustment – selector cover clips arrowed (Sec 11)

1 *Long-reach socket can be inserted through aperture to slacken cable clamp bolt*

12   Again working in the engine compartment, turn the actuating lever on the transmission to the right (ie, towards the battery holder), until it reaches its stop.
13   Attempt to turn the front roadwheels, and check that the parking pawl engages, locking the wheels in position.
14   Have the assistant hold the actuating lever against the stop, while the cable clamp bolt inside the vehicle is tightened to the specified torque.
15   Recheck the selector operation, as described in paragraph 1.
16   Refit the selector cover on completion.

12   Selector lever assembly – removal and refitting

Removal

1   Apply the handbrake, and ensure that the transmission selector lever is in position 'P'.
2   Disconnect the battery negative lead.
3   Release the transmission selector cover from the centre console (the cover is secured by clips at either side). Pull the illumination light bulb holder from the selector cover, and disconnect the transmission 'Winter' mode switch wiring connector.
4   Slacken the selector cable clamp bolt and unscrew the cable locknut (items 1 and 2 in Fig. 7.8), then disconnect the cable from the selector lever assembly.
5   Disconnect the transmission 'Economy/Sport' mode switch wiring connector.
6   Unscrew the securing nut, and slide the selector lever from the end of the pivot shaft, then withdraw the assembly.
7   No attempt should be made to dismantle the assembly.

Refitting

8   Refitting is a reversal of removal, but on completion, adjust the cable as described in Section 11.

13   Speedometer drive – removal and refitting

The procedure is as described for the manual gearbox in Part A, Section 5 of this Chapter.

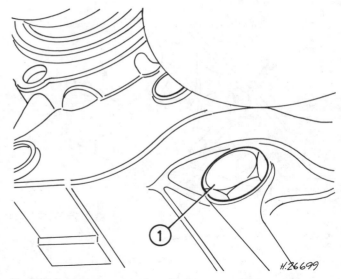

Fig. 7.10 Automatic transmission fluid drain plug (1) (Sec 14)

14   Differential side (driveshaft) oil seals – renewal

The procedure is as described for the manual gearbox in Part A, Section 6 of this Chapter, bearing in mind the following points.

(a) *Drain the transmission fluid into a suitable container by removing the drain plug located at the lower right-hand side of the transmission housing – see Fig. 7.10.*
(b) *Smear the sealing ring of the new oil seal with transmission fluid.*
(c) *On completion, refill the transmission through the dipstick tube with the correct quantity and type of fluid, and check the level as described in Chapter 1.*

15   Fluid cooler – general information

The transmission fluid cooler is an integral part of the radiator assembly, and removal and refitting is described in Chapter 3.
The hoses running from the transmission to the cooler should be checked at regular intervals, and renewed if there is any doubt about their condition.
Always take note of the pipe and hose connections before disturbing them, and take note of the hose routing.
To minimise the loss of fluid, and to prevent the entry of dirt into the system, clamp the hoses before disconnecting them, and plug the unions once the hoses have been disconnected.
When reconnecting the hoses, ensure that they are connected to their original locations, and route them so that they are not kinked or twisted. Also allow for the movement of the engine on its mountings, ensuring that the hoses will not be stretched or fouled by surrounding components.
Always renew the sealing washers if the banjo union bolts are disturbed, and tighten the bolts to their specified torque wrench setting. Be particularly careful when tightening the cooler unions.

16   Kickdown switch – removal, refitting and adjustment

Removal

1   Disconnect the battery negative lead.
2   Release the carpet from the retainer under the throttle pedal, and lift the carpet to expose the switch mounting.

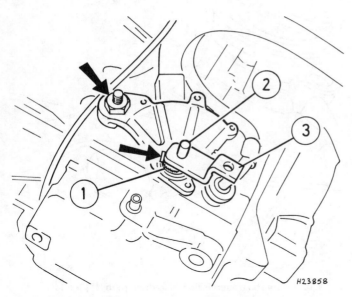

Fig. 7.11 Starter inhibitor/reversing light switch (Sec 17)

1   Large nut   3   Actuating lever
2   Selector lever shaft
Arrows indicate switch mountings

3   Disconnect the switch wiring, then unclip the switch from its retainer.

Refitting

4   Refitting is a reversal of removal, but push the switch into the retainer as far as the stop, and check the switch adjustment as described in the following paragraphs.

Adjustment

5   Working in the engine compartment, where applicable, remove the airbox from the top of the fuel injection unit, to enable the throttle valve to be observed.
6   Have an assistant depress the throttle pedal until it contacts the switch on the vehicle floor, then check that the throttle valve is fully open, and that the pedal acts squarely on the centre of the switch button.
7   If the pedal/switch button contact point requires adjustment, this must be carried out by resetting the throttle stop screw and then adjusting the cable free play – see Chapter 4.

17   Starter inhibitor/reversing light switch – removal, refitting and adjustment

Removal

Note: *The dipstick tube O-ring must be renewed on refitting.*

1   Apply the handbrake and select position 'N' with the gear selector lever.
2   Disconnect the battery negative lead.
3   Working in the engine compartment, unscrew the securing nut from the starter inhibitor/reversing light switch mounting stud, and withdraw the dipstick tube upwards from the transmission.
4   Remove the retaining clamp and the washer, and disconnect the selector cable from the actuating lever on the transmission.
5   Disconnect the wiring from the switch.
6   Using pliers to counterhold the shaft, unscrew the nut securing the actuating lever to the selector lever shaft, then remove the locking plate and unscrew the large nut and washer securing the switch to the shaft.
7   Unscrew the nut securing the switch to the transmission, and withdraw the switch.

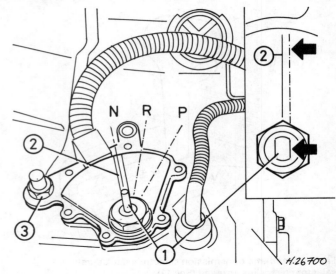

Fig. 7.12 Starter inhibitor/reversing light switch adjustment (Sec 17)

1   Selector lever shaft   3   Switch securing nut
2   Groove in switch housing
Arrows show shaft in alignment with groove in switch housing

Refitting

8   Ensure that the selector lever shaft is in position 'N' (the third detent from the front). Lower the switch onto the shaft and rotate it until the shaft's flattened surface is aligned with the groove in the switch housing, then refit the nut which secures the switch to the transmission, and tighten it to the specified torque.
9   Refit the washer, then refit and tighten the large nut securing the switch to the selector lever shaft. Tighten the nut to the specified torque wrench setting, then refit the locking plate.
10   Refit the nut securing the actuating lever to the selector lever shaft. Use pliers to counterhold the shaft as the nut is tightened, as during removal.
11   Refit the dipstick tube, using a new O-ring, then refit and tighten the securing nut.
12   Reconnect the switch wiring, and the battery negative lead.
13   Reconnect the selector cable to the actuating lever on the transmission, and adjust the cable as described in Section 11.

Adjustment

14   Remove the retaining clamp and the washer, and disconnect the selector cable from the actuating lever on the transmission.
15   Move the actuating lever fully to the right against the stop, then turn the lever back two notches to position 'N' – see Fig. 7.12.
16   Observe the end of the selector lever shaft. The shaft's flattened surface should be aligned with the groove in the switch housing. If necessary, loosen the nut securing the switch to the transmission ('3' in Fig. 7.12), and turn the switch until the alignment is correct.
17   On completion of adjustment, tighten the switch securing nut to the specified torque.
18   Reconnect the selector cable to the actuating lever on the transmission, and adjust the cable as described in Section 11.

18   Transmission 'mode' switches – removal and refitting

'Economy'/'Sport' mode switch
Removal

1   Remove the selector lever assembly as described in Section 12.
2   Using a length of welding rod or a similar tool inserted through the lower end of the selector lever, push out the switch.
3   Note the wiring connections, then carefully unsolder the wires from the switch.

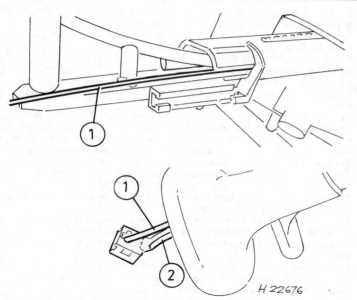

Fig. 7.13 Using welding rod (1) to push switch from top of selector lever – unsolder wire connections (2) (Sec 18)

Refitting

4   Refitting is a reversal of removal, but ensure that the wiring connections are correct, as noted before removal, and refit the selector lever assembly as described in Section 12.

'Winter' mode switch

Removal

5   Disconnect the battery negative lead.
6   Release the transmission selector cover from the centre console (the cover is secured by clips on either side), then carefully push the switch from the selector cover, and disconnect the wiring plug.

Refitting

7   Refitting is a reversal of removal.

19   Fluid temperature sensor – removal and refitting

Removal

Note: *A new sensor sealing ring must be used on refitting.*

1   Disconnect the battery negative lead.
2   Unscrew the two securing nuts, and remove the sensor shield from the front of the transmission.
3   Disconnect the sensor wiring connector.
4   Unscrew the sensor, and withdraw it from the transmission. Be prepared for fluid spillage, and plug the aperture in the transmission to prevent dirt ingress and minimise fluid loss. Recover the sealing ring.

Refitting

5   Refitting is a reversal of removal, using a new sealing ring. On completion, check the fluid level and top-up if necessary as described in Chapter 1.

20   Input/output speed sensors – removal and refitting

Removal

Note: *A new sensor sealing ring must be used on refitting.*

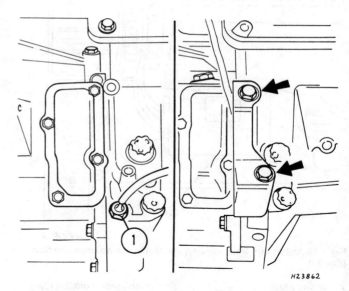

Fig. 7.14 Remove the sensor shield (securing nuts arrowed) for access to the fluid temperature sensor (1) (Sec 19)

1   The speed sensors are located in the upper face of the transmission casing. The input speed sensor is nearest to the left-hand end of the transmission.
2   Disconnect the battery negative lead.
3   Disconnect the relevant wiring connector.
4   Unscrew the sensor securing screw, and withdraw the sensor from the transmission. Be prepared for fluid spillage, and plug the aperture in the transmission to prevent dirt ingress and minimise fluid loss. Recover the sealing ring.

Refitting

5   Refitting is a reversal of removal, using a new sealing ring. On completion, check the fluid level and top-up if necessary, as described in Chapter 1.

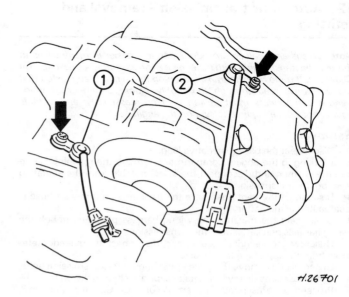

Fig. 7.15 Transmission input speed (1) and output speed (2) sensor locations (Sec 20)

Securing screws arrowed

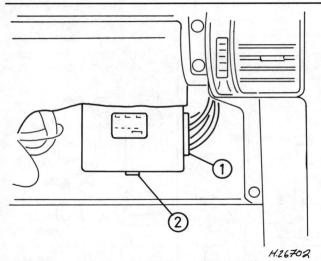

Fig. 7.16 Automatic transmission electronic control unit location (Sec 21)

1   Wiring plug   *2   Control unit-to-bracket clip*

21   Electronic control unit – removal and refitting

Removal

1   The electronic control unit is located behind the glovebox on the passenger's side of the facia.
2   Disconnect the battery negative lead.
3   Remove the glovebox as described in Chapter 11.
4   Disconnect the wiring plug from the control unit.
5   Release the control unit from its securing bracket, and withdraw it from the facia.

Refitting

6   Refitting is a reversal of removal.

22   Automatic transmission – removal and refitting

Note: *This is an involved procedure, and it is easier in many cases to remove the transmission with the engine as an assembly, as described in Chapter 2. If removing the transmission on its own, it is suggested that this Section is read through thoroughly before commencing work. Various components must be renewed on reassembly, and suitable equipment will be required to support the engine.*

Removal

1   Disconnect the battery negative lead.
2   Working in the engine compartment, remove the retaining clamp and the washer, and disconnect the selector cable from the actuating lever on the transmission.
3   Disconnect the vent hose from the transmission (the vent hose is located below the battery tray).
4   Disconnect the transmission wiring harness plug, and unbolt the wiring harness bracket(s) from the transmission.
5   Unscrew the securing sleeve, and disconnect the speedometer cable from the top of the transmission.
6   Unscrew and remove the three upper engine-to-transmission bolts, noting the locations of any brackets or clips attached to the bolts.
7   Proceed as described in Part A of this Chapter, Section 8, paragraphs 8 to 14, noting the following points.

   (a)   Substitute 'transmission' for 'gearbox'.
   (b)   Drain the transmission fluid by removing the drain plug located at the lower right-hand side of the transmission housing – see Fig. 7.10.

8   Clamp the transmission fluid cooler hoses, then disconnect them from the transmission, noting their locations. Be prepared for fluid spillage, and plug the open ends of the hoses and transmission to minimise fluid loss and prevent dirt ingress.
9   Unbolt and remove the transmission bellhousing cover plate.
10   If the original torque converter and driveplate are to be refitted, make alignment marks between the torque converter and the driveplate, to ensure that the components are reassembled in their original positions.
11   Working through the bottom of the bellhousing, unscrew the three torque converter-to-driveplate bolts. It will be necessary to turn the crankshaft using a suitable spanner or socket on the crankshaft pulley or sprocket bolt (as applicable), to gain access to each bolt in turn through the aperture. Use a screwdriver or a similar tool to jam the driveplate ring gear, preventing the driveplate from rotating as the bolts are loosened. Discard the bolts.
12   Support the transmission with a trolley jack, with an interposed block of wood to spread the load.
13   Remove the left-hand engine/transmission mounting completely, by unscrewing the two bolts securing the rubber mounting to the vehicle body, and the three bolts securing the mounting bracket to the transmission.
14   Ensure that the transmission is adequately supported, then unscrew and remove the remaining engine-to-transmission bolts. Ensure that the torque converter is held firmly in place in the transmission casing as the engine and transmission are separated, otherwise it could fall out, resulting in fluid spillage and possible damage. Retain the torque converter while the transmission is removed by bolting a strip of metal across the transmission bellhousing end face.
15   The transmission can now be lowered and withdrawn from under the front of the vehicle. The help of an assistant will greatly ease this operation.

Refitting

Note: *New torque converter-to-driveplate bolts must be used on refitting, and if the original torque converter is being used, an M10 x 1.25 mm tap will be required. New left-hand engine/transmission mounting-to-body bolts, and new driveshaft snap-rings, must be used on refitting.*

16   If the original torque converter is being refitted, commence refitting by recutting the torque converter-to-driveplate bolt threads in the torque converter using an M10 x 1.25 mm tap.
17   If a new transmission is being fitted, the manufacturers recommend that the radiator fluid cooler passages are flushed clean before the new transmission is installed. Ideally, compressed air should be used (in which case, ensure that adequate safety precautions are taken), but alternatively, the cooler can be flushed with clean automatic

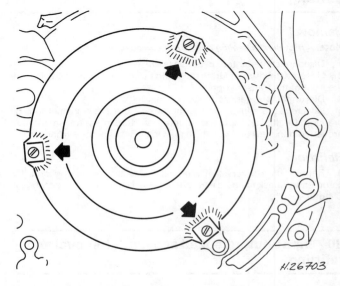

Fig. 7.17 Torque converter-to-driveplate bolt threads (arrowed) must be recut on refitting (Sec 22)

transmission fluid until all the old fluid has been expelled, and fresh fluid runs clear from the cooler outlet.

18 Commence refitting by positioning the transmission under the front of the vehicle, and support with a trolley jack and interposed block of wood, as during removal.

19 Where applicable, remove the strip of metal retaining the torque converter in the transmission, and hold the torque converter in position as the transmission is mated to the engine.

20 Raise the transmission sufficiently to enable the upper and lower engine-to-transmission bolts to be fitted, but do not tighten them fully at this stage. Ensure that any brackets or clips noted during removal are in place on the bolts.

21 Refit the left-hand engine/transmission mounting, using two new bolts to secure the rubber mounting to the vehicle body. Tighten all bolts to the specified torque.

22 Tighten the previously-fitted engine-to-transmission bolts to the specified torque, then withdraw the trolley jack from under the transmission.

23 If the original torque converter and driveplate have been refitted, carefully turn the crankshaft to align the marks made before removal, before fitting the torque converter-to-driveplate bolts.

24 Fit **new** torque converter-to-driveplate bolts, and tighten them to the specified torque. Turn the crankshaft for access to each bolt in turn, and prevent the driveplate from turning as during removal.

25 Refit the transmission bellhousing cover plate.

26 Proceed as described in Part A of this Chapter, Section 8, paragraphs 37 to 42 inclusive.

27 Reconnect the transmission fluid cooler hoses to the transmission, using new sealing washers.

28 Reconnect the speedometer drive cable to the transmission.

29 Refit the transmission wiring harness brackets, and reconnect the wiring harness plug.

30 Reconnect the transmission vent hose.

31 Reconnect the selector cable to the actuating lever on the transmission, and adjust the cable as described in Section 11.

32 Refill the transmission with the specified type and quantity of fluid through the dipstick tube.

33 Reconnect the battery negative lead.

34 On completion, check the transmission fluid level and top-up if necessary, as described in Chapter 1.

23 Automatic transmission overhaul – general information

In the event of a fault occurring on the transmission, it is first necessary to determine whether it is of an electrical, mechanical or hydraulic nature, and to achieve this, special test equipment is required. It is therefore essential to have the work carried out by a Vauxhall/Opel dealer if a transmission fault is suspected.

Do not remove the transmission from the car for possible repair before professional fault diagnosis has been carried out, since most tests require the transmission to be in the vehicle.

Chapter 8 Driveshafts

Contents

Specifications

Type...
Unequal-length open shafts, with constant velocity joint at each end. Certain models have vibration damper fitted to right-hand shaft

Driveshaft joint grease specification ....
Vauxhall/Opel grease No 19 41 521 (Duckhams LBM 10)

Torque wrench settings

	Nm	lbf ft
Front hub nut:*		
Stage 1	130	96
Stage 2	Loosen nut fully	Loosen nut fully
Stage 3	20	15
Stage 4	Angle-tighten a further 90°	Angle-tighten a further 90°
Lower arm-to-suspension strut balljoint nut	70	52

Refer to Section 2

1 General information

Drive from the differential is taken to the roadwheels by two open driveshafts with a constant velocity joint at each end.

The driveshafts are splined at both ends. The inner ends fit into the differential, and are retained by snap-rings, while the outer ends fit into the front hubs, and are retained by the front hub nuts.

The right-hand driveshaft is longer than the left-hand one, due to the position of the differential. Certain models have a two-piece vibration damper fitted to the right-hand driveshaft.

2 Driveshafts – removal and refitting

Removal

Note: *A balljoint separator tool will be required for this operation. The following components must be renewed when refitting the driveshaft: hub nut, washer and split pin, driveshaft retaining snap-ring, and lower arm- to-suspension strut balljoint nut locking pin.*

1 Jack up the front of the vehicle and support securely on axle stands (see *'Jacking, towing and wheel changing'*). Remove the relevant roadwheel.
2 Extract the split pin from the castellated hub nut on the end of the driveshaft.
3 The hub nut must now be loosened. The nut is extremely tight, and a suitable extension bar will be required to loosen it. To prevent the driveshaft from turning, insert two roadwheel bolts, and insert a metal bar between them to counterhold the hub (see photos 2.19A and B).

4 Remove the hub nut and washer from the driveshaft (photo).
5 Extract the locking pin, then unscrew the castellated nut from the lower arm-to-suspension strut balljoint (photos).
6 Using a balljoint separator tool, disconnect the lower arm-to-suspension strut balljoint (photo).
7 On DOHC engine models, remove the engine undershield, as described in Chapter 11, Section 25.

2.4 Removing the hub nut and washer from the driveshaft

2.5A Extract the locking pin (arrowed) ...

2.5B ... then remove the balljoint castellated nut

2.6 Using a balljoint separator tool to disconnect the balljoint

2.9 Using a steel bar to release the end of the driveshaft from the differential

2.11 Withdrawing the outer end of the driveshaft from the hub

2.13 Driveshaft vibration damper (arrowed) – DOHC engine model viewed through right-hand wheel arch

8   A suitable tool will now be required to release the inner end of the driveshaft from the differential. To release the right-hand driveshaft, a flat steel bar with a good chamfer on one end can be used. The left-hand driveshaft may prove more difficult to release, and a suitable square- or rectangular-section bar may be required.

9   Lever between the driveshaft and the differential housing to release the driveshaft snap-ring from the differential (photo). Have a suitable container available, to catch the oil which will be released as the

driveshaft is withdrawn from the differential. Support the driveshaft by suspending it with wire or string, and do not allow it to hang under its own weight.

10   Plug the opening in the differential, to prevent further oil loss and dirt ingress.

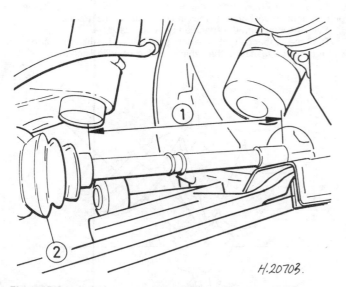

Fig. 8.1 Driveshaft damper weight distance from outer joint gaiter (2) (Sec 2)

1 = 268.0 to 270.0 mm

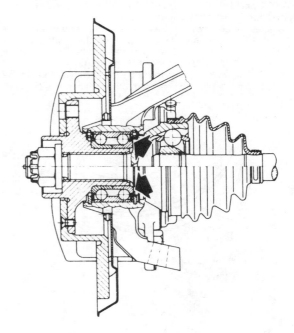

Fig. 8.2 Sectional view of front hub assembly (Sec 2)

Clean the contact faces (arrowed) of the driveshaft and wheel bearing

2.16 Always renew driveshaft retaining snap-ring on refitting

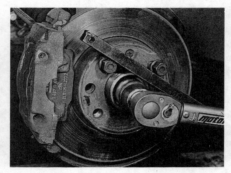

2.19A Tighten the hub nut to the specified torque ...

2.19B ... then through the specified angle (see Specifications)

11   Withdraw the outer end of the driveshaft from the hub, and remove the driveshaft from the vehicle (photo). It should be possible to pull the driveshaft from the hub by hand, but if necessary tap the end of the shaft with a soft-faced mallet to release it. **Do not** *use heavy blows, as damage to the driveshaft joints may result.*
12   **Do not** *allow the vehicle to rest on its wheels with one or both driveshaft(s) removed, as damage to the wheel bearing(s) may result.* If moving the vehicle is unavoidable, temporarily insert the outer end of the driveshaft(s) in the hub(s) and tighten the hub nut(s): in this case, the inner end(s) of the driveshaft(s) must be supported, for example by suspending with string from the vehicle underbody. **Do not** *allow the driveshaft to hang down under its own weight.*
13   Certain models have a two-piece vibration damper fitted to the right-hand driveshaft (photo). If the damper is removed for any reason, it is important to refit it so that the distance between the inner end of the outer joint gaiter and the outer face of the damper is as shown in Fig. 8.1.

Refitting

14   Before refitting a driveshaft, make sure that the contact faces of the shaft and the wheel bearing are absolutely clean – see Fig. 8.2.
15   Commence refitting by applying a little molybdenum disulphide grease to the driveshaft splines, then insert the outer end of the shaft into the hub. Fit a new washer, and screw on a new hub nut finger-tight.
16   Fit a new snap-ring to the inboard end of the driveshaft (photo), then remove the plug from the opening in the differential, and push the driveshaft into the differential as far as possible.
17   Place a screwdriver or similar tool on the weld bead of the inner driveshaft joint, **not** the metal cover, and drive the shaft into the differential until the retaining snap-ring engages positively. Pull on the **outer** circumference of the joint to check the engagement.
18   Reconnect the lower arm-to-suspension strut balljoint, then fit the castellated nut, and tighten to the specified torque. Secure the nut with a new locking pin.

19   Tighten the new hub nut to the specified torque, in the stages given in the Specifications. Prevent the driveshaft from turning as during removal (photos). If the holes in the driveshaft for the split pin do not line up with any of the slots in the nut, loosen (**do not** tighten) the nut, until the holes line up with the nearest slots to enable the split pin to be fitted. Use a new split pin, bending over the ends of the pin to secure it.
20   Refit the roadwheel, then lower the vehicle to the ground.
21   Check and if necessary top-up the gearbox oil/transmission fluid level, as described in Chapter 1.
22   On DOHC engine models, refit the engine undershield.

3   Driveshaft joint – renewal

Note: *Check to ensure that a new securing circlip is supplied when ordering a new driveshaft joint.*

1   A worn driveshaft joint must be renewed, as it cannot be overhauled. If driveshaft joint wear is apparent on a vehicle in which the driveshaft has covered in excess of 48 000 miles (80 000 km), the manufacturers recommend that the complete driveshaft is renewed.
2   With the driveshaft removed as described in Section 2, release the metal securing band, and slide the rubber gaiter from the worn joint.
3   Using circlip pliers, expand the circlip which secures the joint to the driveshaft – see Fig. 8.3.
4   Using a soft-faced mallet, tap the joint from the driveshaft – Fig. 8.4.
5   Ensure that a new circlip is fitted to the new joint, then tap the new joint onto the driveshaft until the circlip engages in its groove.
6   Pack the joint with the specified type of grease.
7   Refit the rubber gaiter to the new joint, with reference to Section 4.
8   Refit the driveshaft to the vehicle, as described in Section 2.

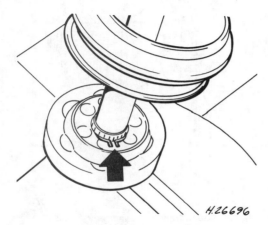

H.26696

Fig. 8.3 Driveshaft joint retaining circlip (arrowed) (Sec 3)

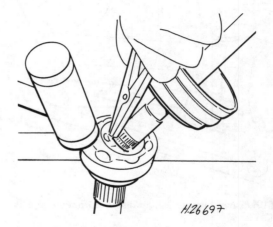

H.26697

Fig. 8.4 Tapping joint from driveshaft (Sec 3)

4 Driveshaft joint gaiter – renewal

1   With the driveshaft removed as described in Section 2, remove the relevant joint as described in Section 3. Note that if both gaiters on a driveshaft are to be renewed, it is only necessary to remove one joint.
2   Release the remaining securing band, and slide the gaiter from the driveshaft.
3   Clean the old grease from the joint, then repack the joint with the specified type of fresh grease. If excessively-worn or damaged, the driveshaft joint should be renewed, with reference to Section 3 if necessary.
4   Slide the new gaiter onto the driveshaft so that the smaller diameter opening is located in the groove in the driveshaft.
5   Refit the joint, using a new securing circlip. Tap the joint onto the driveshaft until the circlip engages in its groove.
6   Slide the gaiter over the joint, then squeeze the gaiter to expel as much air as possible.
7   Secure the gaiter using new securing bands. To fit a securing band, wrap it around the gaiter, and while pulling on the band as tight as possible, engage the lug on the end of the band with one of the slots. Use a screwdriver if necessary to push the band as tight as possible before engaging the lug and slot. Finally tighten the band by compressing the raised square portion of the band with pliers.

5 Driveshaft overhaul – general information

If any of the checks in Chapter 1 reveal wear in any driveshaft joint, first remove the roadwheel trim or wheel centre cap, as applicable. If the driveshaft nut staking is still effective, the nut should be correctly tightened. If in doubt, use a torque wrench to check that the nut is securely fastened and re-stake it (see Section 2), then refit the wheel trim or centre cap, as applicable. Repeat this check on the remaining driveshaft nut.

Road test the vehicle, and listen for a metallic clicking from the front as the vehicle is driven slowly in a circle on full steering lock. If a clicking noise is heard, this indicates wear in the outer constant velocity joint. This means that the joint must be renewed, as overhaul is not possible (see Section 3).

If vibration, consistent with road speed, is felt through the vehicle when accelerating, there is a possibility of wear in the inner constant velocity joints.

Chapter 9 Braking system

Contents

Specifications

System type

Conventional braking system ....   Front discs and rear drums, with vacuum servo assistance, dual hydraulic circuit split diagonally, pressure-regulating valves in rear hydraulic circuits. Cable-operated handbrake on rear wheels

ABS ....   Front and rear discs, with vacuum servo assistance, operated via hydraulic modulator, dual hydraulic circuit split front/rear, pressure-regulating valves in rear hydraulic circuit. Cable-operated handbrake on rear wheels

Front brakes

Type:
    All except 2.0 litre engine models..   Solid discs with floating calipers
    2.0 litre engine models ....   Ventilated discs with floating calipers
Disc diameter:
    1.4 and 1.6 litre engine models..   236.0 mm
    1.8 and 2.0 litre engine models..   256.0 mm
Disc thickness:
    New:
        1.4 and 1.6 litre engine models ....   12.7 mm
        1.8 litre engine models ....   20.0 mm
        2.0 litre engine models ....   24.0 mm
    Minimum permissible thickness after machining:*
        1.4 and 1.6 litre engine models ....   10.7 mm
        1.8 litre engine models ....   18.0 mm
        2.0 litre engine models ....   22.0 mm
    Minimum permissible thickness (at which point discs must be renewed):
        1.4 and 1.6 litre engine models ....   9.7 mm
        1.8 litre engine models ....   17.0 mm
        2.0 litre engine models ....   21.0 mm
Maximum disc run-out..   0.1 mm
*When this dimension is reached, only one further new set of pads is permissible, then renew the discs.

Rear brakes

Type:
    Models with conventional braking system .... Drums
    Models with ABS .... Solid discs
Drum brakes:
    Drum internal diameter:
        New .... 200.0 mm
        Maximum permissible diameter after machining .... 201.0 mm
Disc brakes:
    Disc diameter .... 270.0 mm
    Disc thickness:
        New .... 10.0 mm
        Minimum permissible thickness after machining* .... 8.0 mm
        Minimum permissible thickness (at which point discs must be
        renewed) .... 7.0 mm
        Maximum disc run-out .... 0.1 mm

When this dimension is reached, only one further new set of pads is permissible, then renew the discs.

Torque wrench settings

	Nm	lbf ft
Caliper and wheel cylinder bleed nipples..	6	4
Brake fluid pipe union nuts...	16	12
Front brake fluid hose-to-caliper union bolt......................................	40	30
Front caliper guide bolts	30	22
Front caliper bracket-to-hub carrier bolts...	95	70
Brake master cylinder-to-servo nuts	22	16
Vacuum servo securing bolts	22	16
Vacuum servo-to-mounting bracket nuts	20	15
ATE type master cylinder stop-screw	6	4
Front brake disc securing screw	4	3
Rear brake disc securing screw	8	6
Front brake disc shield screws..	4	3
Brake drum securing screw	4	3
Rear wheel cylinder bolts	9	7
Rear caliper mounting bolts...	80	59
Rear brake backplate/hub unit securing nuts (use new nuts):		
Stage 1	50	37
Stage 2	Angle-tighten a further 30°	Angle-tighten a further 30°
Stage 3	Angle-tighten a further 15°	Angle-tighten a further 15°
Handbrake lever securing bolts	20	15
Pressure-regulating valve securing screws (Estate and Van models)	20	15
ABS hydraulic modulator securing nuts...	8	6
ABS wheel sensor securing bolt..	8	6

---

1 General information and precautions

General information

The footbrake operates on all four wheels. Solid or ventilated disc brakes are fitted at the front, and self-adjusting drum or solid disc brakes are fitted at the rear, depending on model. Actuation is hydraulic, with vacuum servo assistance. The handbrake is cable-operated, and acts on the rear wheels only.

The hydraulic system is split into two circuits. On non-ABS (Anti-lock Braking System) models, the system is split diagonally, and on ABS models, the system is split front and rear. In the event of a hydraulic fluid leak in one circuit, the remaining circuit will still function, so that some braking capability remains.

The hydraulic fluid supply to the rear brakes is regulated so that the front brakes always lock first under heavy braking (this reduces the danger of the car spinning). On Saloon and Hatchback models, the fluid pressure to the rear brakes is controlled by two valves, one for each brake, which are mounted on the rear underbody of the vehicle. On Estate and Van models, the fluid pressure to the rear brakes is controlled by a single load-dependent valve, which acts depending on the loading of the rear suspension.

The brake servo is of the direct-acting type, fitted between the pedal and the master cylinder. The servo is powered by vacuum developed in the inlet manifold. Should the servo fail, the brakes will still operate, but increased pedal pressure will be required.

ABS (Anti-lock Braking System) is fitted as standard on certain models, and is available as an option for all others. The system comprises an electronic control unit, roadwheel sensors, hydraulic modulator, and the necessary valves and relays. Disc brakes are fitted to all four wheels. The purpose of the system is to prevent wheel(s) locking during heavy brake applications. This is achieved by automatic release of the brake on the locked wheel, followed by reapplication of the brake. This procedure is carried out several times a second by the hydraulic modulator. The modulator is controlled by the electronic control unit, which itself receives signals from the wheel sensors, which monitor the locked or unlocked state of the wheels. The two front brakes are modulated separately, but the two rear brakes are modulated together. The ABS unit is fitted between the brake master cylinder and the brakes, the vacuum servo and master cylinder being of similar type for both non-ABS and ABS models.

The front wheel sensors are mounted on the hub carriers, and monitor the rotation of the wheels via toothed discs on the driveshafts. The rear wheel sensors are integral with the rear hub units.

Should the ABS develop a fault, it is recommended that a complete test is carried out by a Vauxhall/Opel dealer, who will have the necessary specialist diagnostic equipment.

On DOHC engine models, the ABS wheel sensors also send signals to the traction control system, which is described in Chapter 4.

Precautions

General

When working on any part of the system, work carefully and methodically; also observe scrupulous cleanliness when overhauling any part of the hydraulic system. Always renew components (in axle sets, not just on one wheel, where applicable) if in doubt about their condition, and use only Vauxhall/Opel replacement parts, or at least those of known good quality. Note the warnings given in *'Safety first'* and at the relevant points in this Chapter concerning the dangers of asbestos dust and hydraulic fluid.

ABS

If the ABS develops a fault, the complete system should be tested by a Vauxhall/Opel dealer, who will have the necessary specialist equipment to make a quick and accurate diagnosis of the problem. Due to the special equipment required, it is not practical for the DIY mechanic to carry out the test procedure.

To prevent possible damage to the electronic control unit, always disconnect the control unit wiring plug before carrying out electrical welding work.

It is recommended that the control unit is removed if the vehicle is to be subjected to high temperatures, as may be encountered (for instance) during certain paint-drying processes.

If using steam-cleaning equipment, do not aim the water/steam jet directly at the control unit.

Do not disconnect the control unit wiring plug with the ignition switched on.

Do not use a battery booster to start the engine.

After working on the ABS system components, ensure that all wiring plugs are correctly reconnected, and have the complete system tested by a Vauxhall/Opel dealer using the dedicated ABS test equipment, at the earliest opportunity.

2   Hydraulic system – bleeding

Note: *Hydraulic fluid is poisonous; wash off immediately and thoroughly in the case of skin contact, and seek immediate medical advice if any fluid is swallowed or gets into the eyes. Certain types of hydraulic fluid are inflammable, and may ignite when allowed into contact with hot components; when servicing any hydraulic system, it is safest to assume that the fluid IS inflammable, and to take precautions against the risk of fire as when handling petrol. Hydraulic fluid is also an effective paint stripper, and will attack certain plastics; if any is spilt, it should be washed off immediately using copious quantities of fresh water. Finally, it is hygroscopic (it absorbs moisture from the air) – old fluid may be contaminated and unfit for further use. When topping-up or renewing the fluid, always use the recommended type, and ensure that it comes from a freshly-opened, sealed container.*

General

1   The efficient operation of any hydraulic system is only possible after removing all air from the components and circuit. If any of the hydraulic components in the braking system have been removed or disconnected, or if the fluid level has been allowed to fall appreciably, it is inevitable that air will have been introduced into the system. The removal of all this air from the hydraulic system is essential if the brakes are to function correctly, and the process of removing it is known as 'bleeding'.

2   During the bleeding procedure, add only clean, unused hydraulic fluid of the recommended type; never re-use fluid that has already been bled from the system. Ensure that sufficient fluid is available before starting work.

3   If there is any possibility of incorrect fluid already being present in the system, the complete hydraulic circuit must be flushed with fresh fluid of the correct type, and new fluid seals should be fitted to all the components.

4   If hydraulic fluid has been lost from the system, or air has entered due to a leak, ensure that the fault is rectified before proceeding further.

5   Park the vehicle on level ground, stop the engine, and select first or reverse gear on manual gearbox models (or 'P' on models with automatic transmission) then chock the wheels and release the handbrake.

6   Check that all pipes and hoses are secure, unions tight and bleed nipples closed. Clean any dirt from around the bleed nipples.

7   Top-up the hydraulic fluid reservoir to the 'MAX' level line, refit the cap loosely, and maintain the fluid level above the 'MIN' level line throughout the procedure, or there is a risk of further air entering the system through the reservoir.

8   There are a number of one-man, do-it-yourself brake bleeding kits currently available from motor accessory shops. It is recommended that one of these kits is used whenever possible, as they greatly simplify the bleeding operation, and also reduce the risk of expelled air and fluid being drawn back into the system. If such a kit is not available, the basic (two-man) method must be used, which is described in detail later in this Section. Note that Vauxhall/Opel recommend the use of a pressure-bleeding kit when bleeding the braking system.

9   If a kit is to be used, prepare the car as described previously, and follow the kit manufacturer's instructions, as the procedure may vary slightly according to the type being used. Generally, instructions for using a kit will be as outlined below in the relevant sub-Section.

10   Whichever method is used, if the complete system is to be bled, the same sequence must be followed (paragraphs 11 and 12) to ensure the removal of all air from the system.

Bleeding sequence

11   Where an operation has only affected one circuit of the hydraulic system (the system is split diagonally on non-ABS models, and front and rear on models with ABS), then it will only be necessary to bleed the relevant circuit. If the master cylinder has been disconnected and reconnected, or the fluid level has been allowed to fall appreciably, then the complete system must be bled.

12   If the complete system is to be bled, then it should be done working in the following sequence.

Non-ABS models

   (a)   *Right-hand front brake.*
   (b)   *Right-hand rear brake.*
   (c)   *Left-hand front brake.*
   (d)   *Left-hand rear brake.*

Models with ABS

   (a)   *Right-hand front brake.*
   (b)   *Left-hand front brake.*
   (c)   *Right-hand rear brake.*
   (d)   *Left-hand rear brake.*

Bleeding – basic (two-man) method

13   Gather together a clean glass jar, a suitable length of plastic or rubber tubing which will fit the bleed nipples tightly, and a ring spanner to fit the nipples. The help of an assistant will also be required.

14   Remove the dust cap from the first nipple in the sequence (photos). Fit the spanner and tube to the nipple, place the other end of the tube in the jar, and pour in sufficient fluid to cover the end of the tube.

15   Ensure that the hydraulic fluid reservoir level is maintained at least above the 'MIN' level mark throughout this procedure.

16   Have the assistant fully depress the brake pedal several times to build up pressure, then maintain it on the final stroke.

17   While pedal pressure is maintained, unscrew the bleed nipple (approximately one turn) and allow the fluid to flow into the jar. The assistant should maintain pedal pressure, pushing the pedal down to the floor if necessary, and should not release the pedal until instructed to do so. When the flow stops, tighten the bleed nipple again, instruct the assistant to release the pedal slowly, and recheck the reservoir fluid level.

18   Repeat the steps given in paragraphs 16 and 17 until the fluid emerging from the bleed nipple is free from air bubbles.

19   When no more air bubbles appear, tighten the bleed nipple securely, remove the tube and spanner, and refit the dust cap. Do not overtighten the bleed nipple.

20   Repeat the procedure on the remaining nipples in the sequence, until all air is removed from the system and the brake pedal feels firm again.

Bleeding – using a one-way valve kit

21   As the name implies, these kits consist of a length of tubing with a one-way valve fitted to prevent expelled air and fluid being drawn back into the system; some kits include a translucent container which can be positioned so that the air bubbles can be more easily seen flowing from the end of the tube (photo).

22   The kit is connected to the bleed nipple, which is then opened. The user returns to the driver's seat and depresses the brake pedal with a smooth, steady stroke and slowly releases it. This is repeated until the expelled fluid is free from air bubbles.

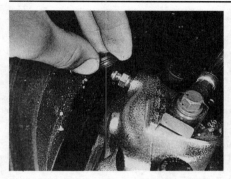

2.14A Removing the dust cap from a front brake caliper bleed nipple

2.14B Removing the dust cap from a rear wheel cylinder bleed nipple – model with rear drum brakes

2.21 Bleeding the brake hydraulic system using a typical one-way valve kit

23 Note that although these kits simplify the work, it is easy to forget the hydraulic fluid reservoir fluid level; ensure that the level is maintained above the 'MIN' level mark at all times, or more air will be drawn into the system.

Bleeding – using a pressure-bleeding kit

24 These kits are usually operated by the pressurised air contained in the spare tyre, although note that it will probably be necessary to reduce the pressure to a lower limit than normal; refer to the instructions supplied with the kit.
25 By connecting a pressurised, fluid-filled container to the hydraulic fluid reservoir, bleeding can be carried out simply by opening each nipple in turn (in the specified sequence) and allowing the fluid to flow out until no more air bubbles can be seen in the expelled fluid.
26 This method has the advantage that the large reservoir of fluid provides an additional safeguard against air being drawn into the system during bleeding.
27 Pressure-bleeding is particularly effective when bleeding 'difficult' systems, or when bleeding the complete system at the time of routine fluid renewal.

All methods

28 When bleeding is complete, and firm pedal feel is restored, wash off any spilt fluid, tighten the bleed nipples securely and refit their dust caps. Do not overtighten the bleed nipples.
29 Check the hydraulic fluid level, and top-up if necessary (Chapter 1).
30 Discard any hydraulic fluid which has been bled from the system; it will not be fit for re-use.
31 Depress the brake pedal in the normal way to check its 'feel'. If it feels at all spongy, air must still be present in the system, and further bleeding is required. Failure to bleed satisfactorily after a reasonable repetition of the bleeding procedure may be due to worn master cylinder seals.

3 Hydraulic pipes and hoses – inspection, removal and refitting

Note: Refer to the note at the beginning of Section 2 before proceeding.

Inspection

1 The hydraulic fluid pipes, hoses, hose connections and pipe unions should be regularly examined.
2 First check for signs of leakage at the pipe unions, then examine the flexible hoses for signs of cracking, chafing and fraying.
3 The rigid brake pipes should be examined carefully for signs of dents, corrosion or other damage. Corrosion should be scraped off, and if the depth of pitting is significant, the pipes should be renewed. This is particularly likely in those areas underneath the vehicle body where the pipes are exposed and unprotected.

Removal

4 If any section of pipe or hose is to be removed, the loss of fluid may be reduced by removing the hydraulic fluid reservoir filler cap, placing a piece of polythene over the filler neck and securing it tightly with an elastic band. If a section of pipe is to be disconnected from the master cylinder, the reservoir should be emptied by syphoning out the fluid or drawing out the fluid with a pipette. Alternatively, flexible hoses can be sealed, if required, using a proprietary brake hose clamp (photo), while metal pipe unions can be plugged (if care is taken not to allow dirt into the system), or capped immediately they are disconnected.
5 To remove a section of pipe, unscrew the union nuts at each end of the pipe, and release the pipe from the clips attaching it to the body. Some union nuts can be very tight, particularly if they are exposed to road dirt, etc, under the vehicle. If an open-ended spanner is used, burring of the flats on the nuts is not uncommon, and for this reason it is preferable to use a split ring spanner which will engage all the flats. If such a spanner is not available, self-locking grips may be used, although this is NOT recommended.
6 To remove a flexible hose, first clean the ends of the hose and the surrounding area, then unscrew the union nut(s)/bolt(s), as applicable, from the hose end(s). Where applicable, unclip the hose from its mounting bracket, and withdraw the hose (photo).
7 Brake pipes with flared ends and union nuts in place can be obtained individually or in sets, from Vauxhall/Opel dealers or accessory shops. The pipe is then bent to shape, using the old pipe as a guide, and is ready for fitting to the car.

Refitting

8 Refitting the pipes and hoses is a reversal of removal. Make sure that brake pipes are securely supported in their clips, and ensure that the hoses are not kinked. Check also that the hoses are clear of all suspension components and underbody fittings, and will remain clear during movement of the suspension and steering. After refitting, remove the polythene from the reservoir, and bleed the brake hydraulic system as described in Section 2.

3.4 Using a brake hose clamp will minimise fluid loss when brake flexible hoses are disconnected

3.6 Typical brake pipe-to-flexible hose union

4   Front brake pads – renewal

Warning: *Renew both sets of front brake pads at the same time – never renew the pads on only one wheel, as uneven braking may result. Note that the dust created by wear of the pads may contain asbestos, which is a health hazard. Never blow it out with compressed air, and do not inhale it. A suitable filtering mask should be worn when working on the brakes. DO NOT use petroleum-based solvents to clean brake parts – use brake cleaner or methylated spirit only.*

1   Apply the handbrake, then jack up the front of the vehicle, and support securely on axle stands (see *'Jacking, towing and wheel changing'*).

2   Where applicable, pull the pad wear sensor from the inboard pad, and disconnect the wiring at the connector under the wheel arch, next to the suspension strut (photo). Note the wire routing.

3   Using a screwdriver, prise the pad retaining clip from the outboard edge of the caliper, noting how it is located (photo).

4   Prise out the two guide bolt dust caps from the inboard edge of the caliper, then using a suitable Allen key or hexagon bit, unscrew the guide bolts, and lift the caliper and inboard pad from the bracket (photos). Recover the outboard brake pad. Suspend the caliper body with wire or string, to avoid straining the brake fluid hose.

5   Pull the inboard pad from the caliper piston, noting that it is retained by a clip attached to the pad backing plate (photo).

6   Brush the dirt and dust from the caliper, but take care not to inhale it. Carefully remove any rust from the edge of the brake disc.

7   In order to accommodate the new thicker pads, the caliper piston must be depressed fully into its cylinder bore, using a flat metal bar such as a tyre lever. Do not lever between the piston and disc to depress the piston. The action of depressing the piston will cause the fluid level in the reservoir to rise, so to avoid spillage, syphon out some fluid using a (clean) old battery hydrometer or a pipette.

8   Check that the cutaway recesses in the piston are positioned vertically. If necessary, carefully turn the piston to its correct position.

9   Apply a little brake grease to the contact surfaces of the new brake pads.

10   Fit the new inboard pad to the caliper piston, ensuring that the clip is correctly located.

11   Locate the outboard pad on the caliper bracket, with the friction material facing the disc.

12   Refit the caliper to the bracket, and tighten the guide bolts to the specified torque (photo).

13   Refit the guide bolt dust caps.

14   Refit the pad retaining clip, locating it as noted before removal (photo).

15   Where applicable, fit a new pad wear sensor to the inboard pad, and connect the wiring at the connector under the wheel arch. Route the wiring as noted during removal.

4.2 Pad wear sensor (and ABS wheel sensor) wiring connectors (arrowed) under front wheel arch

4.3 Removing the pad retaining clip from the edge of the caliper

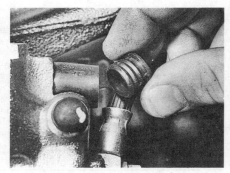

4.4A Prise out the dust caps ...

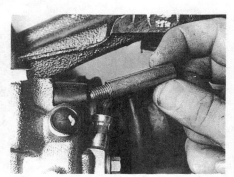

4.4B ... then remove the caliper guide bolts ...

4.4C ... and withdraw the caliper and inboard pad

4.5 Pulling the inboard pad from the caliper piston

4.12 Tightening a caliper guide bolt

4.14 Pad retaining clip correctly positioned on caliper

16   Repeat the operations on the remaining side of the vehicle.
17   Refit the roadwheels and lower the vehicle to the ground.
18   Apply the footbrake several times to position the pads against the discs.
19   Check and if necessary top-up the brake fluid level.
20   New pads should be carefully bedded-in and, where possible, heavy braking should be avoided during the first 100 miles (160 km) or so after fitting new pads.

5 Front brake caliper – removal, overhaul and refitting

Note: *Refer to the note at the beginning of Section 2, and the warning concerning brake dust at the beginning of Section 4 before proceeding. Before dismantling a caliper, check that suitable replacement parts can be obtained, and retain the old components to compare them with the new ones.*

Removal

1   Apply the handbrake, then jack up the front of the vehicle, and support securely on axle stands (see *'Jacking, towing and wheel changing'*).
2   Remove the brake pads, as described in Section 4.
3   Working under the bonnet, remove the brake fluid reservoir cap, and secure a piece of polythene over the filler neck with a rubber band, or by refitting the cap. This will reduce the loss of fluid during the following procedure.
4   Unscrew the brake fluid hose union bolt from the rear of the caliper, and disconnect the hose. Recover the two sealing rings from the union bolt (one either side of the hose end fitting). Be prepared for fluid

spillage, and plug the open ends to prevent dirt ingress and further fluid loss.
5   Withdraw the caliper body from the vehicle.
6   If desired, the caliper bracket can be removed from the hub carrier by unscrewing the two securing bolts (photo).

Overhaul

7   Brush the dirt from the caliper, but take care not to inhale it.
8   Using a screwdriver, carefully prise the dust seal from the end of the piston and the caliper body, and remove it.
9   Place a thin piece of wood in front of the piston to prevent it from falling out of its bore and sustaining damage, then apply low air pressure – eg from a foot pump – to the hydraulic fluid union hole in the rear of the caliper body, to eject the piston from its bore.
10   Remove the wood, and carefully withdraw the piston.
11   Carefully prise the seal from the groove in the caliper piston bore, using a plastic or wooden instrument – see Fig. 9.1.
12   Inspect the surfaces of the piston and its bore in the caliper for scoring, or evidence of metal-to-metal contact. If evident, renew the complete caliper assembly.
13   If the piston and bore are in good condition, discard the seals and obtain a repair kit, which will contain all the necessary renewable items.
14   Clean the piston and cylinder bore with brake fluid or methylated spirit – nothing else.
15   Commence reassembly by fitting the dust seal into the caliper bore.
16   Locate the dust seal in its groove in the piston. Dip the piston in clean brake fluid, and insert it squarely into the cylinder. Check that the cutaway recesses in the piston are positioned vertically. If necessary, carefully turn the piston to its correct position.
17   When the piston has been partially depressed, engage the dust seal with the rim of the caliper bore.

5.6 Caliper bracket securing bolts (arrowed)

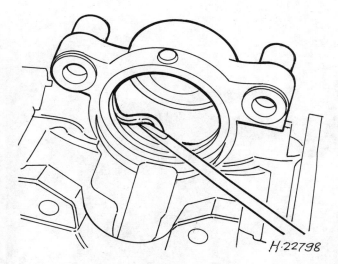

Fig. 9.1 Prising the seal from the groove in the front caliper piston bore (Sec 5)

18   Push the piston further into its bore, but not as far as the stop, ensuring that it does not jam.
19   If desired, the guide bolt sleeves can be renewed. Extract the nylon compression sleeve from within each rubber, then carefully compress the rubber shoulder, and push the rubber through the hole in the caliper body to remove it from the inboard end.
20   Fit the new sleeves using a reversal of the removal procedure.

Refitting

Note: *New sealing rings must be used on the fluid hose union bolt on refitting.*

21   Where applicable, refit the caliper bracket to the hub carrier, and tighten the securing bolts to the specified torque.
22   Reconnect the brake fluid hose union, using new sealing rings on the union bolt.
23   Refit the brake pads, as described in Section 4.
24   Remove the polythene from the brake fluid reservoir filler neck, and bleed the relevant brake hydraulic circuit, as described in Section 2.
25   Refit the roadwheel and lower the vehicle to the ground.

6   Brake disc – inspection, removal and refitting

Note: *Refer to the warning concerning brake dust at the beginning of Section 4 before proceeding.*

Inspection

1   If checking a front disc, apply the handbrake, and if checking a rear disc, chock the front wheels, then jack up the relevant end of the vehicle, and support securely on axle stands (see *'Jacking, towing and wheel changing'*).
2   Check that the brake disc securing screw is tight, then fit a spacer approximately 10.0 mm thick to one of the roadwheel bolts, and refit and tighten the bolt in the hole opposite the disc securing screw – see Fig. 9.2.
3   Rotate the brake disc, and examine it for deep scoring or grooving. Light scoring is normal, but if excessive, the disc should be removed and either renewed or machined (within the specified limits) by a suitable engineering works.
4   Using a dial gauge, or a flat metal block and feeler gauges, check that the disc run-out does not exceed the figure given in the Specifications.
5   If the disc run-out is excessive, remove the disc as described later in this Section, and check that the disc-to-hub surfaces are perfectly clean.
6   With the disc removed, check the hub run-out. If the run-out exceeds the maximum specified for disc run-out, it is likely that the hub bearings are severely worn or damaged. Refer to Chapter 10 for details of renewal.

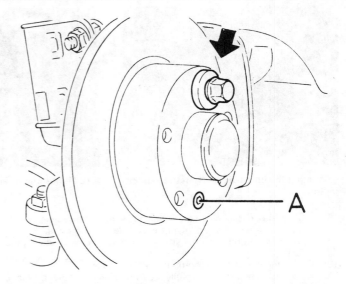

Fig. 9.2 Refit a wheel bolt and spacer (arrowed) opposite the disc securing screw (A) before checking brake disc run-out (Sec 6)

7   Refit the disc, and check the disc run-out again. If the hub bearings are in good condition, the fault must lie with the disc, which should be renewed.

Removal
Front disc

8   Where applicable, remove the roadwheel bolt and spacer used when checking the disc.
9   Remove the brake pads, as described in Section 4.
10   Unscrew the two securing bolts, and remove the caliper bracket.
11   Remove the securing screw (photo), and withdraw the disc from the hub.

Rear disc

12   Where applicable, remove the roadwheel bolt and spacer used when checking the disc.
13   Remove the brake pads, as described in Section 11.
14   Remove the brake caliper with reference to Section 12, but leave the hydraulic pipe connected. Move the caliper to one side, and suspend it using wire or string to avoid straining the pipe.
15   Remove the securing screw, and withdraw the disc from the hub (photo). If the disc is tight, collapse the handbrake shoes by inserting a screwdriver through the adjuster hole in the disc and turning the adjuster wheel.

6.11 Unscrewing a front brake disc securing screw

6.15 Removing a rear brake disc

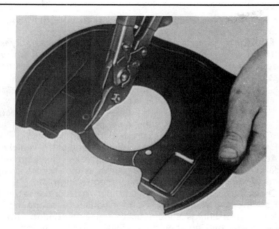

Fig. 9.3 Cutting a section of metal from a new front brake disc shield prior to fitting (Sec 7)

Refitting

16   Refitting is a reversal of removal, but make sure that the mating faces of the disc and hub are perfectly clean. Refit the brake pads as described in Section 4 or 11, as applicable.

7 Front brake disc shield – removal and refitting

Note: *Refer to the warning concerning brake dust at the beginning of Section 4 before proceeding.*

Removal

1   Apply the handbrake, then jack up the front of the vehicle, and support securely on axle stands. Remove the relevant roadwheel.

2   Remove the brake disc, as described in Section 6.

3   Using a screwdriver inserted through the holes in the hub flange, extract the three screws securing the disc shield to the hub carrier.

4   Using plate shears or an alternative suitable tool, cut a section of metal from the rear edge of the shield to enable the shield to be withdrawn over the hub, then remove the shield.

Refitting

5   If a new shield is to be fitted, cut out a section of metal, as during removal of the old shield, to enable the shield to be fitted. De-burr the cut edges, and coat them with anti-corrosion paint.

6   Further refitting is a reversal of removal; refit the brake disc as described in Section 6.

8 Rear brake shoes – renewal

Note: *Renew both sets of rear brake shoes at the same time – never renew the shoes on one wheel, as uneven braking may result. Refer to the warning concerning brake dust at the beginning of Section 4 before proceeding.*

1   Chock the front wheels, then jack up the rear of the vehicle and support securely on axle stands (see *'Jacking, towing and wheel changing'*). Remove the rear roadwheels.

2   Working on one side of the vehicle, remove the brake drum, as described in Section 9.

3   Note the location and orientation of all components before dismantling, as an aid to reassembly.

4   Clean the dust and dirt from the drum and shoes, but take care not to inhale it.

5   Remove the shoe hold-down pins, springs and cups by depressing the cups and turning them through 90° using a pair of pliers (photos). Note that the hold-down pins are removed through the rear of the backplate.

6   Disconnect the handbrake cable from the operating lever (photo).

8.5A Release the shoe hold-down cup ...

8.5B ... and withdraw the cup and spring

8.6 Disconnecting the handbrake cable from the operating lever (hub removed for clarity)

8.8 Rubber band fitted to wheel cylinder to retain pistons

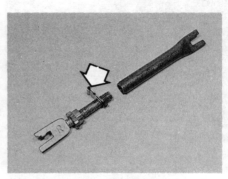

8.15 Right-hand brake shoe adjuster components – thermoclip arrowed

7   The upper and lower return springs may now be unhooked and the shoes removed separately, or the assembly of shoes, adjuster strut and springs may be removed together. The second course of action is particularly easy if the hub is removed – see Chapter 10. Take care not to damage the wheel cylinder rubber boots. Before removing the return springs, note the position and orientation of the springs and adjuster strut.

8   If the shoes are to be removed for some time, fit a stout rubber band or a spring clip to the wheel cylinder, to prevent the pistons from being pushed out of their bores (photo). In any event, **do not** press the brake pedal while the drum is removed.

9   Clean the dust and dirt from the brake backplate, but take care not to inhale it.

10   Apply a small amount of brake grease to the shoe rubbing areas on the backplate.

11   If the linings removed were contaminated with brake fluid or grease, investigate and rectify any source of contamination before fitting new linings (wheel cylinder or hub bearing oil seal leaking).

12   Although linings are available separately (without shoes), renewal of the shoes complete with linings is to be preferred, unless the necessary skills and equipment are available to fit new linings to the old shoes.

13   If not already done, dismantle the shoes, strut and springs. Note the position and orientation of the components.

14   If both brake assemblies are dismantled at the same time, take care not to mix up the components. Note that the left-hand and right-hand adjuster components are marked; the threaded rod is marked 'L' or 'R', and the other 'handed' components are colour-coded black for the left-hand side, and silver for the right-hand side.

15   Dismantle and clean the adjuster strut. Apply a smear of silicone-based grease to the adjuster threads. If new brake linings or shoes are to be fitted, the thermoclip on the adjuster strut must also be renewed (photo).

16   Examine the return springs. If they are distorted, or if they have seen extensive service, renewal is advisable. Weak springs may cause the brakes to bind.

17   If a new handbrake operating lever was not supplied with the new shoes (where applicable), transfer the lever from the old shoes. The lever may be secured with a pin and circlip, or by a rivet, which will have to be drilled out.

18   If the components are to be refitted as an assembly, assemble the new shoes, springs and adjuster components. Expand the adjuster strut to ease fitting.

19   Offer the shoes to the brake backplate. Be careful not to damage the wheel cylinder boots, or to displace the pistons. Remember to remove the rubber band or spring clip from the wheel cylinder, where applicable.

20   When the shoes are in position, insert the hold-down pins and secure them with the springs and cups.

21   Reconnect the handbrake cable, then refit the hub, where applicable.

22   If fitting the shoes and springs together as an assembly is found too difficult, it is possible to fit the shoes and secure them with the hold-down pins, then to introduce the adjuster strut and fit the return springs and adjuster.

23   Back off the adjuster wheel to reduce the length of the strut, until the brake drum will pass over the shoes.

24   Make sure that the handbrake operating lever is correctly positioned, with the pin on the edge of the shoe web, not riding on top of it, then refit and secure the brake drum (photo).

25   Repeat the operations on the remaining side of the vehicle.

26   Adjust the brakes by operating the footbrake at least fifteen times. A clicking noise will be heard at the drums, as the automatic adjusters operate. When the clicking stops, adjustment is complete.

27   Check the handbrake cable adjustment, as described in Section 19.

28   Refit the roadwheels, and lower the vehicle to the ground.

29   New brake linings should be carefully bedded-in and, where possible, heavy braking should be avoided during the first 100 miles (160 km) or so after fitting new linings.

9   Rear brake drum – removal, inspection and refitting

Note: *Refer to the warning concerning brake dust at the beginning of Section 4 before proceeding.*

Removal

1   Chock the front wheels, then jack up the rear of the vehicle and support securely on axle stands (see *'Jacking, towing and wheel changing'*).

2   Fully release the handbrake.

3   Extract the drum securing screw (photo), and remove the drum. If the drum is tight, remove the plug from the inspection hole in the brake backplate, and push the handbrake operating lever towards the brake shoe to move the shoes away from the drums. If necessary, slacken the handbrake cable adjuster (see Section 19).

Inspection

4   Brush the dirt and dust from the drum, taking care not to inhale it.

5   Examine the internal friction surfaces of the drum. If they are deeply-scored, or so worn that the drum has become ridged to the width of the shoes, then both drums must be renewed.

8.24 Rear drum brake components correctly assembled. Hub removed for clarity

9.3 Removing a brake drum securing screw

6   Regrinding of the friction surface is not recommended, since the internal diameter of the drum will no longer be compatible with the shoe friction material contact diameter.

Refitting

7   Refit the brake drum and tighten the securing screw. If necessary back off the adjuster wheel until the drum will pass over the shoes.
8   Adjust the brakes by operating the footbrake a number of times. A clicking noise will be heard at the drum as the automatic adjuster operates. When the clicking stops, adjustment is complete.
9   Refit the roadwheel and lower the vehicle to the ground.

10   Rear wheel cylinder – removal, overhaul and refitting

Note: *Refer to the note at the beginning of Section 2, and the warning concerning brake dust at the beginning of Section 4 before proceeding. Before dismantling a wheel cylinder, check that suitable replacement parts can be obtained, and retain the old components to compare them with the new ones.*

Removal

1   Chock the front wheels, then jack up the front of the vehicle and support securely on axle stands (see *'Jacking, towing and wheel changing'*). Remove the relevant roadwheel.
2   Remove the brake drum, as described in Section 9.
3   Using a pair of pliers, unhook the upper return spring from the brake shoes, noting its orientation, then push the upper ends of the shoes apart until they are clear of the wheel cylinder.
4   Working under the bonnet, remove the brake fluid reservoir cap, and secure a piece of polythene over the filler neck with a rubber band, or by refitting the cap. This will reduce the loss of fluid during the following procedure.
5   Unscrew the brake fluid pipe union nut from the rear of the wheel cylinder, and disconnect the pipe (photo). Take care not to strain the pipe. Be prepared for fluid spillage, and plug the open ends to prevent dirt ingress and further fluid loss.
6   Unscrew the two securing bolts from the rear of the brake backplate, and withdraw the wheel cylinder.

Overhaul

7   Brush the dirt and dust from the wheel cylinder, but take care not to inhale it.
8   Pull the rubber dust seals from the ends of the cylinder body.

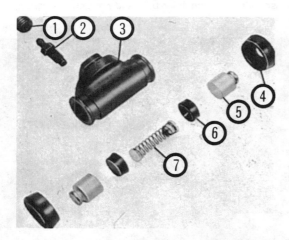

Fig. 9.4 Exploded view of a rear brake wheel cylinder (Sec 10)

1 Dust cap	5 Piston
2 Bleed nipple	6 Piston seal
3 Cylinder body	7 Spring
4 Dust seal	

10.5 Unscrewing the fluid pipe union nut from the rear wheel cylinder

9   The pistons will normally be ejected by the pressure of the coil spring, but if they are not, tap the end of the cylinder body on a piece of wood, or apply low air pressure – eg, from a foot pump – to the hydraulic fluid union hole in the rear of the cylinder body, to eject the pistons from their bores.
10   Inspect the surfaces of the pistons and their bores in the cylinder body for scoring, or evidence of metal-to-metal contact. If evident, renew the complete wheel cylinder assembly.
11   If the pistons and bores are in good condition, discard the seals and obtain a repair kit, which will contain all the necessary renewable items.
12   Lubricate the piston seals with clean brake fluid, and insert them into the cylinder bores, with the spring between them, using finger pressure only.
13   Dip the pistons in clean brake fluid, and insert them into the cylinder bores.
14   Fit the dust seals, and check that the pistons can move freely in their bores.

Refitting

15   Refit the wheel cylinder to the backplate, and tighten the securing bolts.
16   Reconnect the brake fluid pipe to the cylinder, and tighten the union nut.
17   Push the brake shoes against the pistons, then refit the upper return spring as noted before removal.
18   Refit the brake drum, and tighten the securing screw. If necessary, back off the adjuster wheel until the drum will pass over the shoes.
19   Remove the polythene from the brake fluid reservoir filler neck, and bleed the relevant brake hydraulic circuit, as described in Section 2.
20   Adjust the brakes by operating the footbrake a number of times. A clicking noise will be heard at the drum as the automatic adjuster operates. When the clicking stops, adjustment is complete.
21   Refit the roadwheel and lower the vehicle to the ground.

11   Rear brake pads (models with rear disc brakes) – renewal

Note: *Refer to the warning concerning brake dust at the beginning of Section 4 before proceeding.*

1   Chock the front wheels, then jack up the rear of the vehicle and support securely on axle stands (see *'Jacking, towing and wheel changing'*). Remove the rear roadwheels.
2   Note how the anti-rattle spring is located, then drive out the upper and lower pad retaining pins from the outside of the caliper using a suitable pin punch (photos).

11.2A Rear brake pad anti-rattle spring correctly located. Note lower pad retaining pin has been partially removed

11.2B Driving out the upper pad retaining pin

11.5 Removing the rear inboard brake pad

11.8 Checking a rear caliper piston cutaway recess angle with a card template

3   Remove the anti-rattle spring.
4   Push the pads away from the disc slightly then, using a pair of pliers, withdraw the outboard pad and, where applicable, the anti-squeal shim which fits between the pad and the caliper body.
5   Withdraw the inboard pad (photo) and, where applicable, the anti-squeal shim.
6   Brush the dust and dirt from the caliper, but take care not to inhale it. Carefully remove any rust from the edge of the brake disc.
7   In order to accommodate the new thicker pads, the caliper piston must be depressed fully into its cylinder bore, using a flat metal bar such as a tyre lever. Do not lever between the piston and the disc to depress the piston. The action of depressing the piston will cause the fluid level in the reservoir to rise, so to avoid spillage, syphon out some fluid using a (clean) old battery hydrometer or a teat pipette.
8   Check that the cutaway recesses in the pistons are positioned downwards, at approximately 23° to the horizontal. A template made of card may be used to check the setting (photo). If necessary, carefully turn the pistons to their correct positions.
9   Apply a little brake grease to the top and bottom edges of the backplates on the new brake pads.
10   Locate the new pads and the anti-squeal shims in the caliper. Ensure that the friction material faces the disc, and check that the pads are free to move slightly.
11   Locate the anti-rattle spring on the pads, then insert the pad retaining pins from the inside edge of the caliper, while depressing the spring. Tap the pins firmly into the caliper.
12   Repeat the operations on the remaining side of the vehicle.
13   Refit the roadwheels, and lower the vehicle to the ground.
14   Apply the footbrake hard several times to position the pads against the discs.
15   Check and if necessary top-up the brake fluid level.

16   New brake pads should be carefully bedded-in and, where possible, heavy braking should be avoided during the first 100 miles (160 km) or so after fitting new pads.

12   Rear brake caliper (models with rear disc brakes) – removal, overhaul and refitting

Note: *Refer to the note at the beginning of Section 2, and the warning concerning brake dust at the beginning of Section 4 before proceeding. Before dismantling a caliper, check that suitable replacement parts can be obtained, and retain the old components to compare them with the new ones.*

Removal

1   Chock the front wheels, then jack up the rear of the vehicle and support securely on axle stands (see *'Jacking, towing and wheel changing'*). Remove the relevant roadwheel.
2   Remove the brake pads, as described in Section 11.
3   Working under the bonnet, remove the brake fluid reservoir cap, and secure a piece of polythene over the filler neck with a rubber band, or by refitting the cap. This will reduce the loss of fluid during the following procedure.
4   Unscrew the brake fluid pipe union nut from the rear of the caliper, and disconnect the pipe. Take care not to strain the pipe. Be prepared for fluid spillage, and plug the open ends to prevent dirt ingress and further fluid loss.
5   Unscrew the two mounting bolts and withdraw the caliper from the vehicle (photo).

12.5 Rear brake caliper mounting bolts (arrowed)

Overhaul

6 Brush the dirt and dust from the caliper, but take care not to inhale it.
7 Note that no attempt must be made to separate the two halves of the caliper.
8 Using a screwdriver, prise the dust seal retaining clips from the piston dust seals, then carefully prise off the dust seals.
9 Using a suitable clamp, clamp one of the pistons in its fully-retracted position, then apply low air pressure – eg from a foot pump – to the hydraulic fluid union hole in the rear of the caliper body, to eject the remaining piston from its bore. Take care not to drop the piston, as it may result in damage.
10 Temporarily close off the bore of the removed piston, using a suitable flat piece of wood or similar improvised tool, then remove the clamp from the remaining piston, and again apply air pressure to the caliper union to eject the piston.
11 Carefully prise the seals from the grooves in the caliper piston bores, using a plastic or wooden instrument.
12 Inspect the surfaces of the pistons and their bores in the caliper for scoring, or evidence of metal-to-metal contact. If evident, renew the complete caliper assembly.
13 If the pistons and bores are in good condition, discard the seals, and obtain a repair kit, which will contain all the necessary renewable items. Also obtain a tube of brake cylinder paste.
14 Clean the piston and cylinder bore with brake fluid or methylated spirit – nothing else.
15 Apply a little brake cylinder paste to the pistons, cylinder bores, and piston seals.
16 Commence reassembly by fitting the seals to the grooves in the caliper bores.
17 Locate the dust seals in their grooves in the pistons, then insert the pistons carefully into their bores until they enter the seals. It may be necessary to rotate the pistons to prevent them from jamming in the seals.
18 When the pistons have been partially depressed, engage the dust seals with the rims of the caliper bores, and refit the retaining clips.

Refitting

19 Refit the caliper, and tighten the securing bolts to the specified torque.
20 Reconnect the brake fluid pipe to the caliper, and tighten the union nut.
21 Refit the brake pads, as described in Section 11.
22 Refit the roadwheel, and lower the vehicle to the ground.
23 Remove the polythene from the brake fluid reservoir filler neck, and bleed the relevant brake hydraulic circuit, as described in Section 2.

13 Handbrake shoes (models with rear disc brakes) – renewal

Note: *Refer to the warning concerning brake dust at the beginning of Section 4 before proceeding.*

1 Jack up the vehicle, and support on axle stands positioned under the body side members (see *'Jacking, towing and wheel changing'*).
2 Remove the brake disc, as described in Section 6.
3 Clean the dust and dirt from the various components, but take care not to inhale it.
4 Disconnect the handbrake cable and the return spring from the handbrake operating lever at the brake backplate (photo). If necessary, slacken the handbrake cable adjustment, with reference to Section 19.
5 Remove the shoe hold-down pins, springs and cups by depressing the cups and turning them through 90° using a pair of pliers. Note that the hold-down pins are removed through the rear of the brake backplate.
6 The shoes, adjuster, handbrake operating lever and return springs can now be removed together as an assembly.
7 Note the position and orientation of all components, then unhook the upper and lower return springs from the shoes, and recover the handbrake operating lever and the adjuster.
8 Apply a little brake grease to the threads of the adjuster, then screw

13.4 Handbrake cable and return spring connection to handbrake operating lever – model with rear disc brakes

it together to its minimum length. Also apply a little brake grease to the shoe rubbing areas on the backplate.
9 Fit one of the new brake shoes, and secure it to the backplate with the hold-down pin, spring and cup.
10 Locate the handbrake operating lever in position.
11 Fit the remaining brake shoe, and secure with the hold-down pin, spring and cup.
12 Hook the upper return spring onto the shoes.
13 Fit the adjuster between the lower ends of the shoes, as noted before dismantling, then fit the lower return spring.
14 Reconnect the handbrake cable and the return spring to the handbrake operating lever.
15 Refit the brake disc, as described in Section 6, but do not refit the roadwheel at this stage.
16 Repeat the operations on the remaining side of the vehicle.
17 Check the handbrake cable adjustment, as described in Section 19.
18 Refit the roadwheels, and lower the vehicle to the ground.

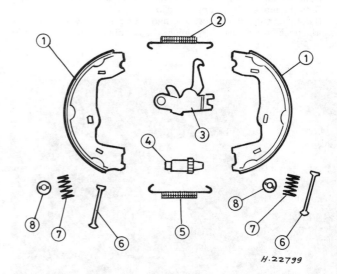

Fig. 9.5 Rear handbrake shoe components – models with rear disc brakes (Sec 13)

1 Brake shoes
2 Upper return spring
3 Handbrake operating lever
4 Adjuster
5 Lower return spring
6 Hold-down pin
7 Hold-down spring
8 Hold-down cup

14 Rear brake backplate – removal and refitting

Models with rear drum brakes
Removal
1 Chock the front wheels, then jack up the rear of the vehicle, and support securely on axle stands (see 'Jacking, towing and wheel changing'). Remove the relevant roadwheel.
2 Remove the brake shoes, as described in Section 8.
3 Remove the rear wheel cylinder, as described in Section 10.
4 Using a suitable pair of pliers, prise out the clip securing the handbrake cable to the backplate.
5 Remove the rear hub unit, as described in Chapter 10, and withdraw the backplate.

Refitting
6 Fit the backplate and the rear hub unit, with reference to Chapter 10, using new nuts tightened in the three stages given in the Specifications.
7 Locate the handbrake cable in the backplate, and refit the securing clip.
8 Refit the rear wheel cylinder, as described in Section 10.
9 Refit the brake shoes, as described in Section 8.
10 Before refitting the roadwheel and lowering the vehicle to the ground, check and if necessary adjust the handbrake, as described in Section 19.
11 Bleed the relevant brake hydraulic circuit, as described in Section 2.

Models with rear disc brakes
Removal
12 Proceed as described in paragraph 1.
13 Remove the brake disc, as described in Section 6.
14 Remove the handbrake shoes, as described in Section 13.
15 Remove the rear hub unit, as described in Chapter 10, and withdraw the brake backplate.

Refitting
16 Fit the backplate and the rear hub unit, with reference to Chapter 10, using new nuts tightened in the three stages given in the Specifications.
17 Refit the handbrake shoes, as described in Section 13.
18 Refit the brake disc, as described in Section 6.
19 Before refitting the roadwheel and lowering the vehicle to the ground, check and if necessary adjust the handbrake, as described in Section 19.

15 Brake pedal – removal and refitting

Removal
1 Disconnect the battery negative lead.
2 Remove the lower trim panel from the driver's footwell.
3 Disconnect the wiring plug from the brake light switch, then twist the switch anti-clockwise and remove it from its bracket.
4 Pull the spring clip from the right-hand end of the servo fork-to-pedal pivot pin (photo).
5 Using a suitable pair of pliers, pull back the end of the pedal return spring from the pedal, to enable the servo fork-to-pedal pivot pin to be removed. Withdraw the pivot pin (photo).
6 Pull the locking clip from the left-hand end of the pedal pivot pin.
7 Unscrew the nut from the left-hand end of the pivot pin, then slide the pivot pin from the right-hand end of the pedal mounting bracket. If necessary, tap the end of the pivot pin with a soft-faced hammer to free the splines from the mounting bracket. Recover any washers which may be positioned on the pivot pin, noting their locations.
8 Withdraw the pedal and return spring.

Refitting
9 Refitting is a reversal of removal, bearing in mind the following points.
10 Ensure that the pedal return spring is correctly located on the pedal before refitting.
11 Coat the pedal pivot pin with a little molybdenum disulphide grease.
12 Ensure that any washers on the pedal pivot pin are positioned as noted before removal.

16 Vacuum servo unit – testing, removal and refitting

Right-hand-drive models
Testing
1 To test the operation of the servo unit, depress the footbrake four or five times to exhaust the vacuum, then start the engine while keeping the footbrake depressed. As the engine starts, there should be a noticeable 'give' in the brake pedal as vacuum builds up. Allow the engine to run for at least two minutes, and then switch it off. If the brake

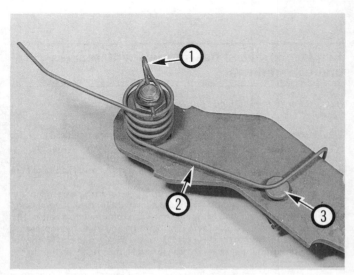

15.5 Brake pedal assembly removed from vehicle

1 *Locking clip*
2 *Pedal return spring*
3 *Pedal pivot pin*

15.4 Brake servo fork-to-pedal pivot pin spring clip (arrowed)

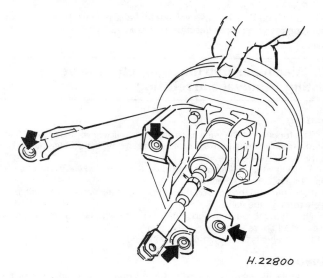

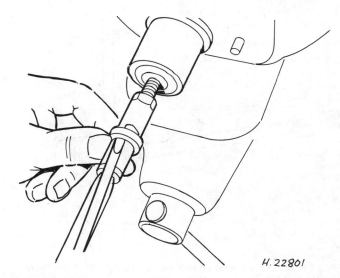

Fig. 9.6 Brake servo and mounting bracket removed showing securing nut locations (arrowed) – left-hand-drive models (Sec 16)

Fig. 9.7 Prising out the securing clip to remove the operating fork from the servo operating rod sleeve – left-hand-drive models (Sec 16)

pedal is now depressed again, it should be possible to detect a hiss from the servo when the pedal is depressed. After about four or five applications, no further hissing will be heard, and the pedal will feel considerably firmer.

Removal

Note: *When refitting, some suitable sealing compound (Vauxhall/Opel No 15 03 294, or equivalent) will be required to coat the mating faces of the servo mounting bracket, and suitable thread-locking compound will be required to coat the servo securing bolts.*

2   Disconnect the battery negative lead.
3   Working inside the vehicle, release the securing clips, and remove the lower trim panel from the driver's footwell.
4   Disconnect the wiring plug from the brake light switch, then twist the switch anti-clockwise and remove it from its bracket.
5   Pull the spring clip from right-hand end of the servo fork-to-pedal pivot pin.
6   Using a suitable pair of pliers, pull back the end of the pedal return spring from the pedal, to enable the servo fork-to-pedal pin to be removed. Withdraw the pivot pin.
7   Remove the windscreen cowl trim panel, as described in Chapter 11, then remove the windscreen wiper motor and linkage, as described in Chapter 12.
8   Remove the washer fluid reservoir, as described in Chapter 12.
9   Disconnect the vacuum pipe from the brake servo.
10   Unscrew the two securing nuts, and carefully withdraw the brake master cylinder from the studs on the servo. Move the master cylinder forwards slightly, taking care not to strain the brake pipes.

11   Remove the two plugs covering the servo securing bolts from the cowl panel (photo).
12   Using a suitable Allen key or hexagon bit, unscrew the servo securing bolts and remove them completely (photo), then lift the servo complete with mounting bracket from the bulkhead. Note that the bracket may stick to the bulkhead, as it is fitted with sealing compound.
13   If desired, the mounting bracket can be removed from the servo by unscrewing the four securing nuts. Note that the bracket will stick to the servo, as it is fitted with sealing compound.
14   The servo cannot be overhauled, and if faulty, the complete unit must be renewed.

Refitting

15   Before refitting the servo, check that the operating fork dimension is correct, as follows.
16   Measure the distance from the end face of the servo casing to the centre of the pivot pin hole in the end of the operating fork. The distance should be 147.70 mm. To make accurate measurement easier, insert a bolt or bar of suitable diameter through the pivot pin hole, and measure to the centre of the bolt or bar (photo).
17   If adjustment is necessary, slacken the locknut, turn the fork to give the specified dimension, then tighten the locknut.
18   Coat the mating surfaces of the mounting bracket with sealing compound (Vauxhall/Opel No 15 03 294, or equivalent), then refit the bracket to the servo.
19   Coat the threads of the servo securing bolts with thread-locking fluid, then fit the servo to the bulkhead and tighten the securing bolts.
20   Refit the securing bolt cover plugs to the cowl panel.

16.11 Plug removed from cowl panel to expose brake servo securing bolt

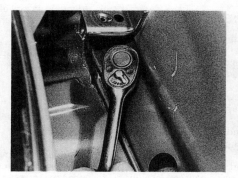

16.12 Unscrewing a brake servo securing bolt

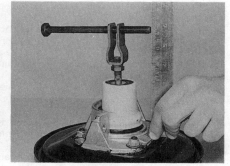

16.16 Measuring the servo operating fork dimension using a bolt inserted through the pivot pin hole

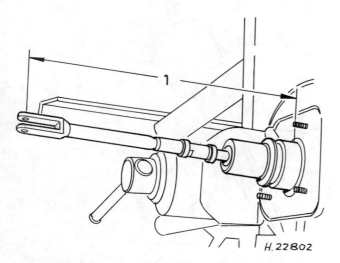

Fig. 9.8 Brake servo operating fork dimension (1) – left-hand-drive models (Sec 16)

21   Refit the master cylinder to the servo, and tighten the securing nuts to the specified torque.
22   Reconnect the vacuum pipe to the servo.
23   Refit the washer fluid reservoir.
24   Refit the windscreen wiper motor and linkage, as described in Chapter 12, then refit the windscreen cowl trim panel.
25   Further refitting is a reversal of removal. On completion, check the operation of the servo, as described in paragraph 16.

Left-hand-drive models

Testing
26   Refer to paragraph 1.

Removal
Note: *New self-locking nuts will be required when refitting the servo mounting bracket to the bulkhead.*
27   Proceed as described in paragraphs 2 to 6 inclusive.
28   Disconnect the vacuum pipe from the brake servo.
29   Unscrew the two securing nuts, and carefully withdraw the brake master cylinder from the studs on the servo. Move the master cylinder forwards slightly, taking care not to strain the brake pipes.
30   Unscrew the four servo bracket securing nuts from the bulkhead (a flexible socket coupling will be required to reach the lower bolt), then tilt the servo/bracket assembly, and withdraw it upwards from the engine compartment.
31   If desired, the mounting bracket can be removed from the servo by unscrewing the four securing nuts. The rubber sleeve can now be removed from the brake servo if desired.
32   To remove the operating fork from the servo operating rod sleeve, prise out the securing clip.

Refitting
33   Before refitting the servo, check that the operating fork dimension is correct, as follows.
34   Measure the distance from the end face of the servo casing to the centre of the pivot pin hole in the end of the operating fork. The distance should be 255.5 mm – see Fig. 9.8. To make accurate measurement easier, insert a bolt or bar of suitable diameter through the pivot pin hole, and measure to the centre of the bolt or bar.
35   If adjustment is necessary, slacken the locknut on the operating rod sleeve, turn the fork to give the specified dimension, then tighten the locknut.
36   Where applicable, refit the rubber sleeve, and refit the servo to the mounting bracket. Tighten the servo-to-mounting bracket nuts to the specified torque.
37   Lower the servo and mounting bracket and servo assembly into position, then refit the assembly to the bulkhead, using new self-locking nuts, and tighten the nuts to the specified torque.
38   Refit the master cylinder to the servo, and tighten the securing nuts to the specified torque.

39   Reconnect the vacuum pipe to the servo.
40   Further refitting is a reversal of removal. On completion, check the operation of the servo, as described in paragraph 1.

17   Vacuum servo unit non-return valve – testing, removal and refitting

Testing
1   The function of the valve is to allow air to flow in one direction only, out of the servo unit. If the valve allows air to flow in both directions, it is faulty, and must be renewed.
2   To test the valve, first remove the hose/valve assembly, as described later in this Section.
3   Blow through the hose on the servo side of the valve; air should pass freely through the valve.
4   Now blow through the hose on the inlet manifold side of the valve; no air should pass through.
5   If the valve is faulty, it must be renewed.

Removal
6   The plastic valve is located in the vacuum hose running from the inlet manifold to the brake servo.
7   Although the valve is available separately from the hoses, in order to remove the valve, the hoses must be cut, and therefore renewed on reassembly. If the valve is to be renewed, it is therefore easier to remove the complete hose/valve assembly, and renew it complete.
8   To remove the assembly, carefully unplug the hose adaptor from the vacuum servo unit, then unscrew the hose union from the inlet manifold, and withdraw the assembly.

Refitting
9   Refitting is a reversal of removal, but when reconnecting the hose adaptor to the servo, take care not to damage or distort the sealing grommet, and on completion, start the engine and check for air leaks.

18   Master cylinder – removal, overhaul and refitting

Note: *Refer to the note at the beginning of Section 2 before proceeding.*

Removal
1   Disconnect the battery negative lead.
2   Depress the footbrake pedal several times to dissipate the vacuum in the servo unit.
3   Disconnect the wiring plug from the brake fluid level sensor in the reservoir filler cap.
4   If possible, use a pipette or a (clean) old battery hydrometer to remove the brake fluid from the reservoir. This will reduce the loss of fluid later in the procedure.
5   Position a suitable container beneath the master cylinder, to catch the brake fluid which will be released.
6   Identify the brake fluid pipes for position, then unscrew the union nuts and disconnect the pipes from the master cylinder.
7   Unscrew the two securing nuts, and withdraw the master cylinder from the studs on the vacuum servo unit.
8   Clean the external surfaces of the cylinder, then using a screwdriver, carefully prise the fluid reservoir and its seals from the top of the cylinder.

Overhaul
Note: *Before contemplating overhaul of the master cylinder, check that suitable replacement parts can be obtained, and retain the old components to compare them with the new ones.*

9   If desired, on models with a conventional (non-ABS) braking system, the master cylinder can be overhauled, as described in the following paragraphs. No overhaul of the master cylinder is possible on models with ABS.
10   With the master cylinder removed, proceed as follows, according to type.

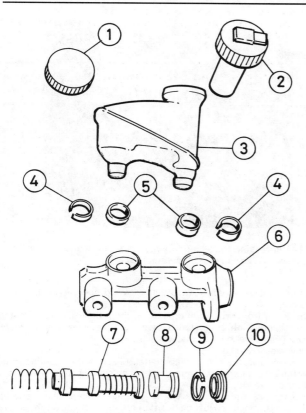

Fig. 9.9 Exploded view of GMF type master cylinder (Sec 18)

1	*Filler cap (standard)*
2	*Filler cap (with fluid level sensor)*
3	*Fluid reservoir*
4	*Fluid reservoir retaining clips*
5	*Fluid reservoir seals*
6	*Cylinder body*
7	*Secondary piston and springs*
8	*Primary piston*
9	*Circlip*
10	*Sealing ring*

GMF type master cylinder

11   Clamp the master cylinder in a soft-jawed vice.
12   Carefully prise out the sealing ring from the end of the cylinder bore.
13   Depress the primary piston slightly using a suitable piece of wood or plastic, then hold the piston in the depressed position by inserting a smooth pin or rod of 3.0 mm diameter through the primary fluid reservoir port in the cylinder.
14   Extract the circlip from the end of the cylinder bore using a screwdriver. Take care not to damage the piston or cylinder bore.
15   Withdraw the pin or rod retaining the piston.
16   Withdraw the primary piston assembly from the cylinder, if necessary tapping the cylinder on a wooden block to free the piston from the bore.
17   Apply low air pressure – eg from a foot pump – to the front fluid reservoir port in the cylinder, to eject the secondary piston assembly.
18   Clean all the components, in clean brake fluid or methylated spirit only, and examine them for wear and damage. In particular, check the surfaces of the pistons and cylinder bore for scoring and corrosion. If the bore shows signs of wear, renew the complete master cylinder assembly.
19   If the cylinder bore is in good condition, obtain a repair kit, which will contain all the necessary renewable items. A Vauxhall/Opel dealer will be able to supply a pre-assembled kit of parts, which should be fitted as follows.
20   Lubricate the cylinder bore with clean brake fluid or brake grease, then clamp the cylinder in a soft-jawed vice, with the bore horizontal.
21   Remove the plug from the end of the assembly tube, and insert the short part of the tube into the cylinder bore as far as the shoulder on the tube.
22   Use a suitable piece of wood or plastic to push the components out

Fig. 9.10 Holding the primary piston depressed while extracting the circlip from the cylinder body – GMF type master cylinder (Sec 18)

of the tube and into the cylinder bore, then hold the primary piston in the depressed position by inserting the pin or rod used during dismantling through the cylinder primary fluid reservoir port.
23   Fit a new circlip to the end of the cylinder bore, ensuring that it seats correctly, and that the piston is free to move.
24   Depress the primary piston, and withdraw the pin or rod from the fluid reservoir port.
25   Fit a new sealing ring to the end of the cylinder bore.

ATE type master cylinder

26   Clamp the master cylinder in a soft-jawed vice.
27   Carefully prise out the sealing ring from the end of the cylinder bore.
28   Depress the primary piston slightly using a suitable piece of wood or plastic, then extract the circlip from the end of the cylinder bore.
29   Withdraw the primary piston assembly, noting the location of the stop-washers.
30   Depress the secondary piston, again using a piece of wood or plastic, and withdraw the stop-screw from the end of the cylinder body – see Fig. 9.12.
31   Withdraw the secondary piston assembly from the cylinder, if necessary tapping the cylinder on a wooden block to free the piston from the bore.
32   Clean all the components, using clean brake fluid or methylated spirit only, and examine them for wear and damage. In particular, check the surfaces of the pistons and cylinder bores for scoring and corrosion. If the bore shows signs of wear, renew the complete master cylinder assembly.
33   If the cylinder bore is in good condition, obtain a repair kit, which will contain all the necessary renewable items. A Vauxhall/Opel dealer will supply a pre-assembled kit of parts, which should be fitted as follows.
34   Lubricate the cylinder bore with clean brake fluid or brake grease, then clamp the cylinder in a soft-jawed vice, with the bore horizontal.
35   Fit a new sealing ring to the stop-screw, then screw it into the cylinder body a little way, but not so far that it protrudes into the bore.
36   Remove the plugs from the ends of the assembly tube, then remove all the components from the short part of the tube, and push the short part into the long part until they are flush.
37   Insert the assembly tube into the cylinder bore as far as the collar on the short sleeve, then use a piece of wood or plastic to push the secondary piston assembly into the bore until it contacts the end of the cylinder.
38   Lightly tighten the stop-screw, then withdraw the piece of wood or plastic and the assembly tube, and fully tighten the stop-screw.
39   Reposition the master cylinder in the vice, with the bore facing upwards.
40   Smear the primary piston skirt and the seal grooves with the special grease provided in the repair kit. Fit the stop-washer to the piston.
41   Adjust the assembly tube so that the end of the long part is flush with the inner shoulder of the short part.

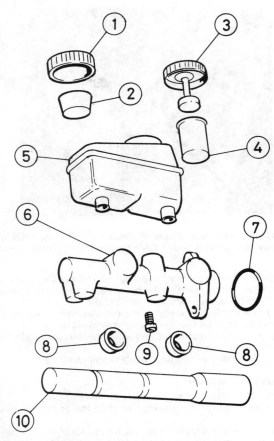

Fig. 9.11 Exploded view of ATE type master cylinder (Sec 18)

1   *Filler cap (standard)*
2   *Strainer*
3   *Filler cap (with fluid level sensor)*
4   *Guide sleeve for float*
5   *Fluid reservoir*
6   *Cylinder body*
7   *Sealing ring*
8   *Fluid reservoir seals*
9   *Stop-screw*
10 *Repair kit assembly tube*

42   Fit the front seal to the primary piston, with the open end of the seal facing the front of the master cylinder.
43   Place the assembly tube over the cylinder to compress the seal, insert the piston and tube part way into the bore, and withdraw the tube.
44   Place the intermediate ring on the primary piston, then fit the remaining seal using the assembly tube as described previously.
45   Place the stop-washer on the primary piston, then depress the piston slightly using a piece of wood or plastic, and fit a new circlip to the end of the cylinder bore. Ensure that the circlip is correctly seated, and that the piston is free to move.
46   Fit a new sealing ring to the end of the cylinder bore.

Refitting

47   Refitting is a reversal of removal, but on completion, bleed the complete brake hydraulic system, as described in Section 2.

19   Handbrake – adjustment

Models with rear drum brakes

1   The handbrake will normally be kept in correct adjustment by the self-adjusting action of the rear brake shoes. However, due to cable stretch over a period of time, the travel of the handbrake lever may

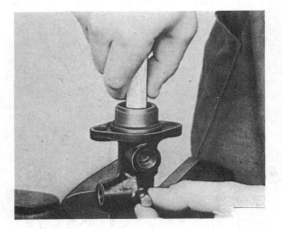

Fig. 9.12 Depressing the secondary piston while extracting the stop-screw – ATE type master cylinder (Sec 18)

become excessive, in which case the following operations should be carried out.
2   Chock the front wheels, then jack up the rear of the vehicle, and support securely on axle stands (see *'Jacking, towing and wheel changing'*). Remove the rear roadwheels.
3   Fully release the handbrake.
4   On models with a catalytic converter, unscrew the securing nuts, and withdraw the exhaust centre box heat shield by carefully sliding it round the centre box.
5   Turn the adjuster nut on the now-exposed cable adjuster (photo), until the brake shoes can just be heard to rub when the rear wheels are turned by hand in the normal direction of rotation.
6   Loosen the adjuster nut until the wheels are just free to turn.
7   The handbrake must start to operate with the lever on the second notch of the ratchet.
8   On completion of adjustment, check the handbrake cables for free movement, and apply a little grease to the adjuster threads to prevent corrosion.
9   Where applicable, refit the exhaust heat shield.
10   Refit the roadwheels, and lower the vehicle to the ground.

Models with rear disc brakes

11   Chock the front wheels, then jack up the rear of the vehicle, and support securely on axle stands (see *'Jacking, towing and wheel changing'*). Remove the rear roadwheels.
12   Pull the handbrake lever as far as the second notch on the ratchet.

19.5 Handbrake cable adjuster nut (arrowed)

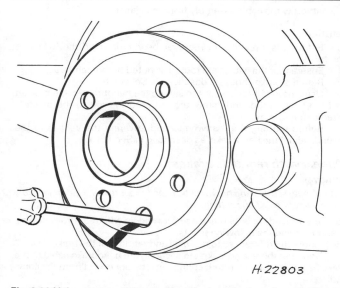

Fig. 9.13 Using a screwdriver to turn the handbrake adjuster wheel – models with rear disc brakes (Sec 19)

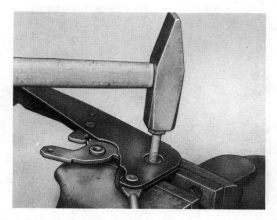

Fig. 9.14 Driving out the handbrake lever ratchet segment securing sleeve (Sec 20)

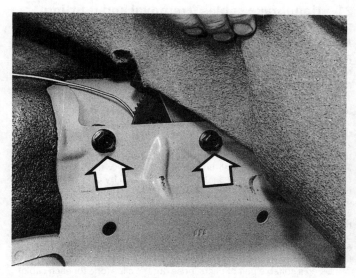

20.8 Carpet pulled back to expose handbrake lever securing bolts (arrowed)

13   On models with a catalytic converter, unscrew the securing nuts, and withdraw the exhaust centre box heat shield by carefully sliding it round the centre box.

14   Loosen the nut on the now-exposed cable adjuster.

15   Using a screwdriver inserted through the adjuster hole in one of the discs, turn the adjuster wheel until the brake shoes can just be heard to rub when the disc is turned by hand in the normal direction of rotation – see Fig. 9.13.

16   Turn the adjuster wheel back until the disc is just free to turn.

17   Repeat paragraphs 15 and 16 on the remaining side of the vehicle.

18   Tighten the nut on the cable adjuster until the brake shoes just begin to operate. Check that the shoes operate equally on both wheels.

19   Fully release the handbrake, then apply it again.

20   The discs must lock when the handbrake lever reaches the sixth notch on the ratchet. If necessary, turn the nut on the adjuster to achieve this.

21   Where applicable, refit the exhaust heat shield.

22   Refit the roadwheels, and lower the vehicle to the ground.

20   Handbrake lever – removal, overhaul and refitting

Removal

Note: *A new self-locking nut must be used to secure the handbrake cable to the operating rod on refitting.*

1   Disconnect the battery negative lead.

2   Jack up the vehicle, and support on axle stands positioned under the body side members (see *'Jacking, towing and wheel changing'*).

3   On models with a catalytic converter, unscrew the securing nuts, and withdraw the exhaust centre box heat shield by carefully sliding it round the centre box.

4   Note the length of exposed thread on the now-exposed handbrake cable adjuster, then remove the adjuster nut to enable the cable bracket to be disconnected from the handbrake lever operating rod.

5   Disconnect the cable bracket from the operating rod, and slide the rubber sealing grommet from the underbody and the operating rod.

6   Remove the passenger's seat on right-hand-drive models, or the driver's seat on left-hand-drive models (as applicable), as described in Chapter 11, Section 26. Pay particular attention to the warning given regarding the seat belt tensioner mechanism.

7   Remove the centre console, as described in Chapter 11.

8   Carefully lift up the carpet around the handbrake lever housing, to expose the two handbrake lever securing bolts (photo). Alternatively, slits can be cut in the carpet for access to the bolts, if desired.

9   Unscrew the securing bolts, and withdraw the handbrake lever sufficiently to disconnect the handbrake 'on' warning light switch wiring.

10   Disconnect the wiring, and withdraw the handbrake lever and operating rod from the vehicle.

Overhaul

11   A worn ratchet segment can be renewed by driving the securing sleeve from the handbrake lever, using a metal rod or a bolt of suitable diameter.

12   Drive the new sleeve supplied with the new segment into the lever to permit a little play between the segment and lever.

13   If desired, a new pawl can be fitted if the original pivot rivet is drilled out.

14   Rivet the new pawl so that it is still free to move.

15   The handbrake 'on' warning light switch can be removed from the lever assembly after unscrewing the securing bolt.

Refitting

16   Refitting is a reversal of removal, bearing in mind the following points.

17   Refit the seat as described in Chapter 11, Section 26.

18   Use a new self-locking nut to secure the handbrake cable bracket to the operating rod, and screw the nut onto the rod to the position noted before removal.

19   Before lowering the vehicle to the ground, adjust the handbrake, as described in Section 19.

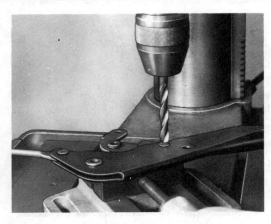

Fig. 9.15 Drilling out the handbrake lever pawl pivot pin (Sec 20)

21   Handbrake cables – removal and refitting

Models with rear drum brakes

Removal

Note: *A new self-locking nut must be used to secure the handbrake cable to the operating rod on refitting.*

1   The handbrake cable assembly consists of two cables (one running to each rear brake assembly), attached to a bracket on the handbrake lever operating rod. The two cables cannot be removed separately, and the complete cable assembly must therefore be removed as a unit.

2   Jack up the vehicle, and support on axle stands positioned under the body side members (see *'Jacking, towing and wheel changing'*).

3   On models with a catalytic converter, unscrew the securing nuts, and withdraw the exhaust centre box heat shield by carefully sliding it round the centre box.

4   Note the length of exposed thread on the now-exposed handbrake cable adjuster, then remove the adjuster nut to enable the cable bracket to be disconnected from the handbrake lever operating rod.

5   Disconnect the cable bracket from the operating rod.

6   Remove the brake shoes, and disconnect the handbrake cables from the shoes, as described in Section 8.

7   Using a suitable pair of pliers, prise out the clips (one for each cable) which secure the handbrake cables to the brake backplates (photo).

8   Detach the cables from the guides on the underbody and rear suspension. Note that the cables can be fed through certain guides, but in some cases, the guide brackets must be bent away from the underbody to allow the cable to be withdrawn.

9   Withdraw the cable assembly from the vehicle.

Refitting

10   Refitting is a reversal of removal, bearing in mind the following points.

11   Ensure that the cables are routed as noted before removal.

12   Refit the brake shoes, as described in Section 8.

13   Use a new self-locking nut to secure the handbrake cable bracket to the operating rod, and screw the nut onto the rod to the position noted before removal.

14   Before refitting the roadwheels and lowering the vehicle to the ground, adjust the handbrake, as described in Section 19.

Models with rear disc brakes

Removal

Note: *A new self-locking nut must be used to secure the handbrake cable to the operating rod on refitting.*

15   The procedure is as described for models with rear drum brakes, bearing in mind the following points.

16   Ignore the references to removal and refitting of the brake drum.

17   Note that there is no lockplate securing the handbrake cable to the brake backplate, but the return spring must be unhooked from the cable end.

Refitting

18   Refitting is a reversal of removal, bearing in mind the following points.

19   Ensure that the cables are routed as noted before removal.

20   Use a new self-locking nut to secure the handbrake cable bracket to the operating rod, and screw the nut onto the rod to the position noted before removal.

21   Before refitting the roadwheels and lowering the vehicle to the ground, adjust the handbrake, as described in Section 19.

22   Rear brake pressure-regulating valve – removal, refitting and adjustment

Saloon and Hatchback models

Note: *Refer to the note at the beginning of Section 2 before proceeding. Note also that the valves must only be renewed in pairs, and both valves must be of the same calibration.*

Removal

1   Two valves are fitted, one for each hydraulic circuit, located under the rear of the vehicle (photo).

21.7 Removing a handbrake cable securing clip (arrowed) from the brake backplate – model with rear drum brakes

22.1 Rear brake pressure-regulating valve (arrowed) – Hatchback model

2 Chock the front wheels, then jack up the rear of the car and support securely on axle stands (see *'Jacking, towing and wheel changing'*).
3 Working under the bonnet, remove the brake fluid reservoir cap, and secure a piece of polythene over the filler neck with a rubber band, or by refitting the cap. This will reduce the loss of fluid during the following procedure.
4 Working under the rear of the vehicle, unscrew the union nut, and disconnect the brake pipe from one of the valves. Be prepared for fluid spillage, and plug the open end of the pipe to prevent dirt ingress and further fluid spillage.
5 Similarly, disconnect the flexible hose from the valve.
6 Pull the valve retaining clip from the bracket on the underbody, noting that on certain models, the retaining clip also secures the ABS sensor wiring, and withdraw the valve.
7 Repeat the procedure for the remaining valve.

Refitting

8 Refitting is a reversal of removal, but on completion, remove the polythene from the brake fluid reservoir filler neck, and bleed the complete hydraulic system, as described in Section 2.

Adjustment

9 The valves are calibrated at the factory, and no adjustment is possible.

Estate and Van models

Removal

10 A single tandem valve is used, which is located under the rear of the vehicle, above the rear suspension torsion beam.
11 Proceed as described in paragraphs 2 and 3.
12 Unhook the spring from the valve operating lever.
13 Unscrew the union nuts, and disconnect the brake pipes from the valve. Be prepared for fluid spillage, and plug the open ends of the pipes to prevent dirt ingress and further fluid spillage. Note that the union nuts differ in size, to ensure correct reconnection.
14 Remove the two securing screws, and withdraw the valve from its bracket on the underbody.
15 If the valve is to be renewed, the protective shield should be removed from the old valve and transferred to the new valve. The shield is secured by a single nut.

Refitting

16 Fit the valve to the bracket on the underbody, and tighten the two securing bolts.
17 Reconnect the two brake pipes to the valve, and tighten the union nuts. Note that the two union nuts differ in size; also take care not to overtighten the nuts.
18 Reconnect the spring to the valve operating lever.
19 Refit the roadwheels, and lower the vehicle to the ground.
20 Bleed the complete hydraulic system, as described in Section 2, then refer to Chapter 1 and adjust the valve.

Adjustment

21 Refer to Chapter 1.

23 Brake light switch – removal and refitting

Removal

1 Disconnect the battery negative lead.
2 Release the securing clips, and remove the lower trim panel from under the driver's side facia.
3 Disconnect the wiring plug from the brake light switch, then twist the switch anti-clockwise and remove it from its bracket.
4 No adjustment of the switch is possible, except by bending the bracket, which is not recommended.

Refitting

5 Refitting is a reversal of removal.

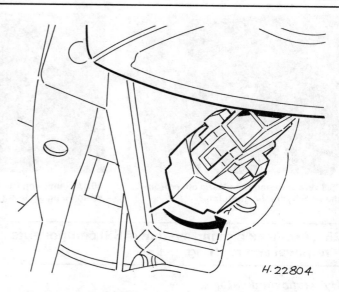

H.22804

Fig. 9.16 Twist the brake light switch anti-clockwise to remove it from its bracket (Sec 23)

24 Braking system warning lights – general information

Brake lights

1 The brake light circuit is controlled by a plunger-type switch mounted on the brake pedal bracket.
2 If the switch is thought to be faulty, it can be tested by disconnecting the its wires and connecting either a multi-meter (set to the resistance function) or a battery-and-bulb test circuit, across the switch terminals. The switch should allow current to flow only when its plunger is extended. If the switch is faulty, it must be renewed.
3 Details for removal and refitting of the switch are given in Section 23.

Low fluid level warning light

4 The warning light circuit is activated by a float-type sensor attached to the hydraulic fluid reservoir filler cap.
5 If the sensor is thought to be faulty, unscrew the filler cap, and connect the test equipment described in paragraph 2 across the sensor terminals on the cap. The sensor should allow current to flow only when the float is hanging at the bottom of its travel. If the sensor is faulty, the complete filler cap/sensor assembly must be renewed.

Handbrake 'on' warning light

6 The warning light is activated by a plunger-type switch mounted at the base of the handbrake lever.
7 The switch should illuminate whenever the handbrake is applied, and should extinguish when the handbrake is released.
8 If the switch is thought to be faulty, remove it as described in Section 20, and connect the test equipment described previously in paragraph 2. The switch should only allow current to flow only when the plunger is fully extended. If the switch is faulty, it must be renewed.

ABS warning light

9 The ABS warning light will illuminate when the ignition is first switched on, and should extinguish after a few seconds. If the warning light stays on, or comes on whilst driving, this indicates a fault in the system. The vehicle is still safe to drive (the conventional braking system will still be effective); however, at the earliest opportunity, take the vehicle to a Vauxhall/Opel dealer, and have the complete system tested using the dedicated test equipment.

Check control unit warnings

10 On models fitted with a check control system, warnings are provided to indicate front disc pad wear, and brake light bulb failure. Further details of this system can be found in Chapter 12.

25.3 Withdrawing the plastic cover from the ABS hydraulic modulator

25.4A Removing the ABS control unit wiring plug securing screw

25.4B Disconnecting the ABS solenoid valve wiring plug

25 Anti-lock braking system (ABS) components – removal and refitting

Hydraulic modulator

Note: *Refer to the note at the beginning of Section 2 before proceeding.*

Removal

1   Disconnect the battery negative lead.
2   Remove the brake fluid reservoir cap, and secure a piece of polythene over the filler neck with a rubber band, or by refitting the cap. This will reduce the loss of fluid during the following procedure.
3   Remove the securing screw, and withdraw the plastic cover from the hydraulic modulator (photo).
4   Disconnect the control unit wiring plug, and the solenoid valve wiring plug. Note that the control unit wiring plug is secured by a screw (photos).
5   Unscrew the brake fluid pipe union nuts, and disconnect the pipes from the modulator. Be prepared for fluid spillage, and plug the open ends to prevent dirt ingress and further fluid loss. Move the pipes just clear of the modulator, taking care not to strain them.
6   Unscrew the three securing nuts (see Fig. 9.17), then tilt the modulator slightly, and withdraw it upwards from its bracket, sufficiently to gain access to the earth lead securing nut at the lower front edge of the modulator (photo).
7   Unscrew the securing nut and disconnect the earth lead, then withdraw the modulator from the vehicle, taking care not to spill brake fluid on the vehicle paintwork.
8   If a new modulator is to be fitted, pull the two relays from the top of the old modulator, and transfer them to the new unit. No attempt must be made to dismantle the modulator.

Refitting

9   Before refitting the modulator, check that the bolts securing the mounting bracket to the body panel are tight, and that the modulator rubber mountings are in good condition. Renew the rubber mountings if necessary.
10   Refitting is a reversal of removal, bearing in mind the following points.
11   Make sure that the earth lead is reconnected before fitting the modulator to its mounting bracket.
12   On completion, remove the polythene sheet from the brake fluid reservoir filler neck, and bleed the complete hydraulic system, as described in Section 2.
13   Check that the ABS warning light extinguishes when first starting the engine after the modulator has been removed. At the earliest opportunity, take the vehicle to a Vauxhall/Opel dealer, and have the complete system tested using the dedicated test equipment.

Front wheel sensor

Removal

14   Disconnect the battery negative lead.
15   Apply the handbrake, then jack up the front of the vehicle, and support securely on axle stands (see *'Jacking, towing and wheel changing'*).
16   Unclip the sensor wiring connector from the retaining clip under the wheel arch, then separate the two halves of the wiring connector, prising them apart with a screwdriver if necessary.
17   Using a suitable Allen key or hexagon bit, unscrew the bolt securing the wheel sensor to the mounting bracket (photo), then carefully lever the sensor from the bracket using a screwdriver. Recover the sealing ring.

25.6 ABS hydraulic modulator earth lead and securing nut

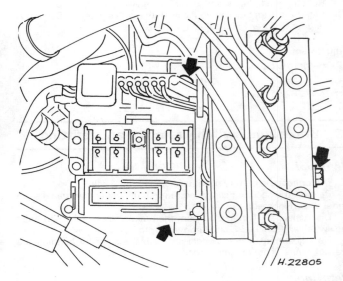

Fig. 9.17 ABS hydraulic modulator securing nuts (arrowed) (Sec 25)

H.22805

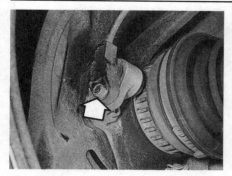

25.17 ABS front wheel sensor securing bolt (arrowed)

25.22 ABS rear wheel sensor (arrowed)

25.31 ABS relays (arrowed)

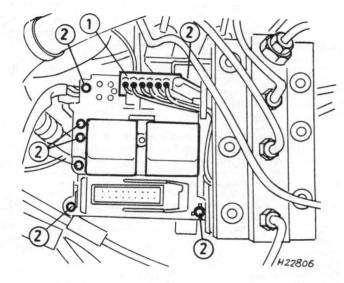

Fig. 9.18 ABS electronic control unit wiring plug (1) and securing screws (2) (Sec 25)

Refitting

18 Examine the condition of the sealing ring, and renew if necessary.
19 Refitting is a reversal of removal, bearing in mind the following points.
20 Smear a little grease on the sensor casing before fitting it to the bracket.
21 Check that the ABS warning light extinguishes when first starting the engine. At the earliest opportunity, take the vehicle to a Vauxhall/Opel dealer, and have the complete system tested using the dedicated test equipment.

Rear wheel sensor

22 The rear wheel sensors are integral with the rear hub assemblies, and cannot be separated from the hub assemblies (photo). For details of rear hub removal and refitting, refer to Chapter 10.

Electronic control unit

Removal

Note: Refer to the precautions concerning the ABS system given in Section 1 before proceeding.

23 Ensure that the ignition is switched off, then disconnect the battery negative lead.
24 The module is attached to the hydraulic modulator assembly in the engine compartment.
25 Remove the securing screw, and withdraw the plastic cover from the hydraulic modulator.
26 Disconnect the control unit wiring plug, and the solenoid valve wiring plug.
27 Remove the two relays from the top of the assembly.
28 Disconnect the remaining wiring plug from the control unit.
29 Unscrew the seven securing screws, and withdraw the control unit from the modulator assembly.

Refitting

30 Refitting is a reversal of removal, but take care not to overtighten the control unit securing screws.

Relays

Removal

31 Two relays are used, one for the solenoid valve, and one for the pump motor; both relays are mounted on the control unit (photo).
32 Disconnect the battery negative lead.
33 Remove the securing screw, and withdraw the plastic cover from the hydraulic modulator.
34 Pull out the appropriate relay.

Refitting

35 Refitting is a reversal of removal.
36 Check that the ABS warning light extinguishes when first starting the engine. At the earliest opportunity, take the vehicle to a Vauxhall/Opel dealer, and have the complete system tested using the dedicated test equipment.

Chapter 10 Suspension and steering

Contents

Specifications

Front suspension

Type	Independent, with MacPherson struts and anti-roll bar

Rear suspension

Type	Semi-independent torsion beam, with trailing arms, coil springs and telescopic shock absorbers. Anti-roll bar on certain models. Twin anti-roll bars on DOHC engine models. Manual level control system standard on certain models, optional on others
Rear wheel toe setting (not adjustable)	10' toe-out to 40' toe-in
Rear wheel camber angle (not adjustable)	2°10' negative to 1°10' negative

Steering

Type	Rack-and-pinion. Power assistance standard on certain models, optional on others
Turns lock-to-lock:	
Manual steering	4.11
Power steering	3.43
Camber angle (laden* – not adjustable)	1°50' negative to 0°20' negative
Maximum camber variation between sides	1°00'
Castor angle (laden* – not adjustable):	
Saloon and Hatchback models	1°15' positive to 3°15' positive
Estate and Van models	0°30' positive to 2°30' positive
Maximum castor variation between sides	1°
Toe setting	0°25' toe-out to 0°5' toe-out

*For the purposes of these figures, a vehicle is considered to be 'laden' when it has a load equivalent to 70.0 kg in each front seat.

Roadwheels

Type .... Steel or alloy (standard on certain models, optional on others)
Size .... 5 1/2J x 13, 5 1/2J x 14 or 6J x 15

Tyres

Size:
  5 1/2J x 13 wheels .... 155 R13 78S/T or 175/70 R13 82T/H
  5 1/2J x 14 wheels .... 175/65 R14 82T/H, 185/60 R14 82H, 185/60 R14 82T or
                                        195/60 R14 85H*
  6J x 15 wheels 205/50 R15 85V

*Only permissible for use with Vauxhall/Opel snow chains

	Front	Rear
Pressures (cold):		

Note: *The following pressures are intended as a guide only – refer to your vehicle handbook, or a Vauxhall/Opel dealer for the latest recommendations.*

Saloon and Hatchback models:	Front	Rear
Normal load (up to 3 passengers):		
1.4 and 1.6 litre engine models	1.9 bars (27 lbf/in^2)	1.6 bars (23 lbf/in^2)
1.8 litre engine models	2.1 bars (30 lbf/in^2)	1.8 bars (26 lbf/in^2)
2.0 litre SOHC engine models	2.3 bars (33 lbf/in^2)	2.0 bars (29 lbf/in^2)
2.0 litre DOHC engine models	2.3 bars (33 lbf/in^2)	2.2 bars (32 lbf/in^2)
Full-load:		
1.4 and 1.6 litre engine models	2.1 bars (30 lbf/in^2)	2.3 bars (33 lbf/in^2)
1.8 litre engine models	2.3 bars (33 lbf/in^2)	2.5 bars (36 lbf/in^2)
2.0 litre engine models	2.5 bars (36 lbf/in^2)	2.7 bars (39 lbf/in^2)
Estate and Van models:		
Normal load (up to 3 passengers):		
1.4 and 1.6 litre engine models	1.9 bars (27 lbf/in^2)	1.7 bars (24 lbf/in^2)
1.8 and 2.0 litre engine models	2.1 bars (30 lbf/in^2)	1.9 bars (27 lbf/in^2)
Full-load:		
1.4 and 1.6 litre engine models	2.1 bars (30 lbf/in^2)	3.0 bars (43 lbf/in^2)
1.8 and 2.0 litre engine models	2.3 bars (33 lbf/in^2)	3.2 bars (46 lbf/in^2)

Torque wrench settings

Front suspension	Nm	lbf ft
Lower arm-to-suspension strut balljoint nut	70	52
Suspension strut upper mounting nuts	30	22
Front hub nut:*		
Stage 1	130	96
Stage 2	Loosen nut fully	Loosen nut fully
Stage 3	20	15
Stage 4	Angle-tighten a further 90°	Angle-tighten a further 90°
Suspension strut piston rod nut	70	52
Suspension strut ring nut	200	148
Lower arm-to-front subframe (horizontal) pivot bolt	110	81
Lower arm damper weight bolts (where applicable)	20	15
Balljoint-to-lower arm nuts	60	44
Anti-roll bar-to-subframe bolts	20	15
Anti-roll bar-to-lower arm locknuts**	20	15
Subframe-to-underbody bolts:**		
Front bolts (not applicable to certain early left-hand-drive models – see Section 10)	115	85
Centre bolts (front bolts on early left-hand-drive models – see Section 10)	170	125
Rear bolts:		
Stage 1	100	74
Stage 2	Angle-tighten a further 75°	Angle- tighten a further 75°
Stage 3	Angle-tighten a further 15°	Angle- tighten a further 15°

Rear suspension	Nm	lbf ft
Rear hub unit securing nuts:**		
Stage 1	50	37
Stage 2	Angle-tighten a further 30°	Angle-tighten a further 30°
Stage 3	Angle-tighten a further 15°	Angle-tighten a further 15°
Shock absorber top mounting nut (Saloon and Hatchback models)	20	15
Shock absorber lower mounting bolt (Saloon and Hatchback models)	70	52
Shock absorber lower mounting nut (Estate and Van models)	12	9
Shock absorber upper mounting bolt	70	52
Main anti-roll bar securing bolts:**		
Stage 1	30	22
Stage 2	Angle-tighten a further 30°	Angle-tighten a further 30°
Stage 3	Angle-tighten a further 15°	Angle-tighten a further 15°
Additional anti-roll bar securing bolts (DOHC engine models):**		
Stage 1	60	44
Stage 2	Angle-tighten a further 60°	Angle-tighten a further 60°
Stage 3	Angle-tighten a further 15°	Angle-tighten a further 15°
Trailing arm-to-underbody fixings	105	77

Torque wrench settings (continued)

	Nm	lbf ft
Steering		
Steering wheel retaining nut	25	18
Steering shaft-to-rubber coupling pinch-bolt	22	16
Steering column fixings	22	16
Steering gear pinion-to-rubber coupling pinch-bolt..................	22	16
Steering gear-to-bulkhead fixings..	22	16
Tie-rod-to-steering gear bolts	95	70
Tie-rod end clamp bolts..	20	15
Tie-rod end-to-suspension strut balljoint nut	60	44
Steering gear pinion nut	40	30
Steering gear damper adjuster locknut	60	44
Power steering pump mounting bolts:		
1.4 and 1.6 litre engine models..	30	22
1.8 and 2.0 litre engine models:		
Bolts 'A' and 'C' in Fig. 10.22...	25	18
Bolt 'B' in Fig. 10.22...	40	30
Power steering pump pulley bolts (1.4 and 1.6 litre engine models)	25	18
Power steering fluid pipe unions...	28	21
Roadwheels		
Roadwheel bolts...	90	66

*Refer to Section 2.
**Use new bolts/nuts, as applicable.

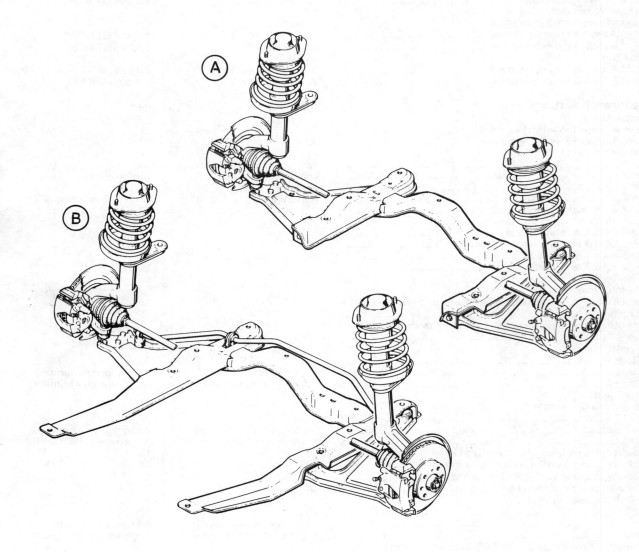

Fig. 10.1 Front suspension layout (Sec 1)

A   Early left-hand-drive models (see Section 10)   B   Later left-hand-drive and all right-hand-drive models

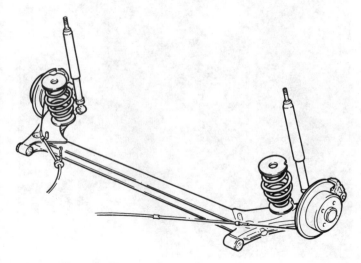

Fig. 10.2 Rear suspension layout – Saloon and Hatchback models with rear disc brakes (Sec 1)

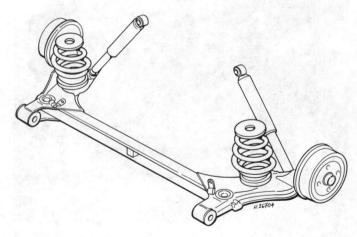

Fig. 10.3 Rear suspension layout – Estate and Van models with rear drum brakes (Sec 1)

1   General information

The front suspension consists of MacPherson struts, lower arms, and an anti-roll bar. The lower arms and the anti-roll bar are mounted on a detachable U-shaped front subframe, which also carries the rear engine/transmission mounting.

Each lower arm is attached to the subframe by a horizontal front bush and a vertical rear bush.

The hub carriers are mounted between the lower ends of the MacPherson struts and the lower arms, and carry the double-row ball type wheel bearings and the brake assemblies.

The rear suspension is of semi-independent type, consisting of a torsion beam and trailing arms, with double-conical coil springs and telescopic shock absorbers, and (on certain models) an anti-roll bar. The front ends of the trailing arms are attached to the vehicle underbody by horizontal bushes, and the rear ends are located by the shock absorbers, which are bolted to the underbody at their upper ends. The coil springs are mounted independently of the shock absorbers, and act directly between the trailing arms and the underbody. Certain models are fitted with an anti-roll bar, which is mounted between the torsion beam and the trailing arms. DOHC engine models are fitted with twin rear anti-roll bars. On all models, each rear wheel bearing, hub and stub axle assembly is manufactured as a sealed unit, which cannot be dismantled.

A manual rear suspension level control system is available on Estate and Van models. The system operates using compressed air-filled shock absorbers. The rear suspension level is adjusted by altering the air pressure in the shock absorbers, via a valve located in the luggage compartment.

The steering gear is of rack-and-pinion type. Movement is transmitted to the front wheels via tie-rods, which are connected to the rack through a sliding sleeve at their inner ends, and to the suspension struts via balljoints at their outer ends.

The steering column consists of an outer column which incorporates a deformable section, and a shaft connected to a flexible coupling at its lower end.

Power steering is fitted as standard to certain models, and is available as an option on others. The power steering is hydraulically-operated, and pressure is supplied by a fluid pump driven via a drivebelt from the engine crankshaft. On 1.8 and 2.0 litre models, fluid cooler pipes are mounted beneath the radiator to keep the temperature of the hydraulic fluid within operating limits.

2   Front suspension strut – removal and refitting

Removal

Note: *A balljoint separator tool will be required during this procedure. The*

tie-rod end balljoint nut, lower arm-to-suspension strut balljoint nut locking pin, and the hub nut, washer and split pin, must be renewed on refitting.

1   Apply the handbrake, then jack up the front of the vehicle and support securely on axle stands (see 'Jacking, towing and wheel changing'). Remove the relevant roadwheel.
2   Where applicable, remove the ABS wheel sensor from the hub carrier, with reference to Chapter 9 if necessary, and disconnect the wiring from the strut.
3   Remove the brake caliper from the hub carrier, as described in Chapter 9. The caliper can be suspended out of the way, using wire or string, to avoid the need to disconnect the hydraulic fluid hose.
4   Unscrew and remove the self-locking nut from the tie-rod end-to-suspension strut balljoint.
5   Using a balljoint separator tool, disconnect the tie-rod end-to-suspension strut balljoint.
6   Extract the split pin from the castellated hub nut on the end of the driveshaft.
7   The hub nut must now be loosened. The nut is extremely tight, and a suitable extension bar will be required to loosen it. To prevent the driveshaft from turning, insert two roadwheel bolts, and insert a metal bar between them to counterhold the hub.
8   Remove the hub nut and washer from the driveshaft.
9   Extract the locking pin, then unscrew the castellated nut from the lower arm-to-suspension strut balljoint.
10   Using a balljoint separator tool, disconnect the lower arm-to-suspension strut balljoint.
11   Withdraw the outer end of the driveshaft from the hub. It should be possible to pull the driveshaft from the hub by hand, but if necessary tap the end of the shaft with a soft-faced mallet to release it. **Do not** *use heavy blows, as damage to the driveshaft joints may result.* Support the driveshaft by suspending it with wire or string – **do not** allow the driveshaft to hang down under its own weight.
12   Working in the engine compartment, unscrew the two nuts securing the suspension strut to the suspension turret (photo). Support the suspension strut as the nuts are unscrewed, as once the nuts have been removed, the strut is free to drop from the vehicle.
13   Withdraw the suspension strut/hub carrier assembly from the vehicle (photo).

Refitting

14   Locate the top end of the strut in the suspension turret, then refit the securing nuts and tighten them to the specified torque.
15   Apply a little molybdenum disulphide grease to the driveshaft splines, then insert the outer end of the shaft into the hub. Fit a new washer, and screw on a new hub nut finger-tight.
16   Reconnect the lower arm-to-suspension strut balljoint, then fit the castellated nut, and tighten to the specified torque. Secure the nut with a new locking pin.

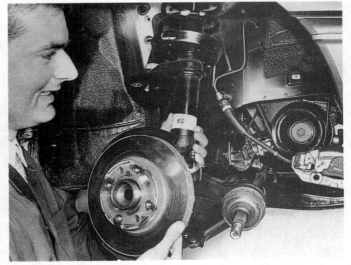

2.12 Suspension strut securing nuts (arrowed)

2.13 Withdrawing the suspension strut/hub carrier assembly

17   Tighten the new hub nut to the specified torque, in the stages given in the Specifications. Prevent the driveshaft from turning as during removal. If the holes in the driveshaft for the split pin do not line up with any of the slots in the nut, loosen (**do not** tighten) the nut, until the holes line up with the nearest slots to enable the split pin to be fitted. Use a new split pin, bending over the ends of the pin to secure it.
18   Reconnect the tie-rod balljoint to the suspension strut, and tighten a new self-locking nut to the specified torque.
19   Refit the brake caliper to the hub carrier, as described in Chapter 9.
20   Where applicable, refit the ABS wheel sensor to the hub carrier, with reference to Chapter 9 if necessary, and reconnect the wiring to the strut.
21   Refit the roadwheel, and lower the vehicle to the ground.
22   On completion, check and if necessary adjust the front wheel alignment, as described in Section 36.

6   Lift off the strut upper mounting rubber and the bearing.
7   Lift off the upper spring seat and damper ring, then carefully release the spring compressor and remove the spring. Note which way round the spring is fitted.
8   Slide the bellows, and the rubber buffer which fits inside the bellows, from the strut.

3   Front suspension strut – overhaul

Note: *A spring compressor tool will be required for this operation.*
1   With the strut removed as described in Section 2, proceed as follows.
2   The hub, wheel bearing and brake disc shield can be removed, as described in Section 4.
3   With the suspension strut resting on a bench or clamped in a vice, fit a spring compressor tool, and compress the coil spring to relieve the pressure on the upper spring seat. Ensure that the compressor tool is securely located on the spring in accordance with the tool manufacturer's instructions.
4   Prise out the plastic cover from the top of the strut.
5   Hold the strut piston rod with a suitable socket, and unscrew the piston rod nut.

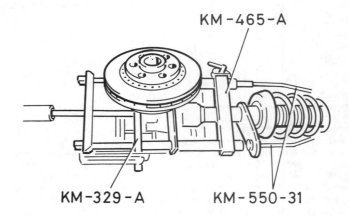

KM–465–A

KM–329–A   KM–550–31

H.26705

Fig. 10.4 Vauxhall/Opel spring compressor tool components in position on front suspension strut (Sec 3)

3.9A One method of unscrewing the suspension strut ring nut

3.9B Removing the ring nut ...

3.10 ... and withdrawing the shock absorber cartridge

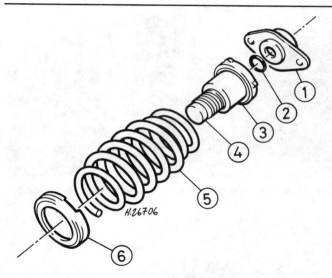

Fig. 10.5 Front suspension strut components (Sec 3)

1   Upper mounting rubber
    assembly
2   Bearing
3   Upper spring seat and
    damper ring
4   Bellows and rubber buffer
5   Spring
6   Lower spring seat

9   To remove the shock absorber cartridge, the ring nut must be unscrewed from the top of the strut tube. This nut is extremely tight. One method which can be used to unscrew the nut is to invert the strut and clamp the nut in a vice, then lever the strut round using a long bar and a bolt passed through the tie-rod bracket (photos).
10   With the ring nut removed, the shock absorber cartridge can be withdrawn (photo).
11   The shock absorber can be tested by clamping the lower end in a vice, then fully extending and contracting the shock absorber several times. Any evidence of jerky movement or lack of resistance indicates the need for renewal.
12   Examine all components for wear or damage, and renew as necessary. Pay particular attention to the mounting rubber and the bearing.
13   Commence reassembly by sliding the shock absorber cartridge into the strut and refitting the ring nut. Do not remove the wax coating from the nut.

14   Clamp the strut in a vice, and tighten the ring nut to the specified torque, using a suitably-large long-reach socket.
15   Refit and compress the coil spring, ensuring that the lower end of the spring rests against the lug on the lower spring seat.
16   Refit the rubber buffer and the bellows.
17   Refit the upper spring seat and the damper ring.
18   Lubricate the bearing with a little grease, then refit it with the visible part of the bearing race uppermost.
19   Refit the strut upper mounting rubber.
20   Counterhold the strut piston rod, and tighten the piston rod nut to the specified torque. This can be achieved by holding the piston rod using a splined key fitted to a torque wrench, and tightening the nut using a spanner until the specified torque is reached.
21   Carefully release and remove the spring compressor tool, ensuring that the spring seats correctly at top and bottom. Ensure that the lower end of the spring still rests against the lug on the lower spring seat.
22   Refit the strut, as described in Section 2.

4   Front hub bearing – renewal

Note; *The bearing will probably be destroyed during the removal operation. The use of a suitable puller will greatly ease the procedure.*
1   Remove the relevant suspension strut/hub carrier assembly, as described in Section 2.
2   Unscrew the securing screw, and remove the brake disc from the hub.
3   Support the hub carrier on two metal bars positioned as shown in Fig. 10.6 then, using a metal bar of suitable diameter, press or drive the hub from the wheel bearing. Alternatively, screw two roadwheel bolts into the hub and, using progressively thicker packing pieces, tighten the bolts to force the hub from the bearing. Note that one half of the inner bearing race will remain on the hub .
4   Using a suitable puller, pull the half inner bearing race from the hub (photo). Alternatively, support the bearing race on suitably-thin metal bars, and press or drive the hub from the bearing race.
5   Remove the three securing screws (photo), and lift the brake disc shield from the hub carrier.
6   Extract the inner and outer bearing retaining circlips (photo).
7   Using a suitable puller, pull the bearing from the hub carrier, applying pressure to the outer race. Alternatively, support the hub carrier, and press or drive out the bearing.
8   Before installing the new bearing, thoroughly clean the bearing location in the hub carrier, and fit the outer bearing retaining circlip ('A' in Fig. 10.7). Note that the circlip tabs should be positioned towards the bottom of the hub carrier.

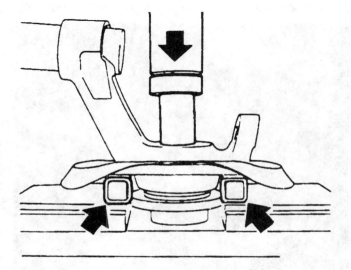

Fig. 10.6 Pressing the front hub from the wheel bearing (Sec 4)

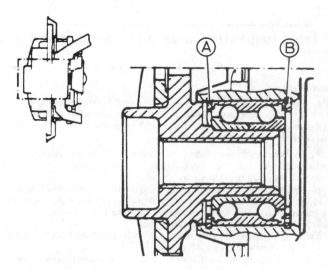

Fig. 10.7 Cross-sectional view of front wheel bearing/hub assembly (Sec 4)

A   Outer bearing retaining circlip   B   Inner bearing retaining circlip

4.4 Removing the half inner bearing race from the hub

4.5 Removing a brake disc shield securing screw

4.6 Extracting the outer bearing retaining circlip

4.9 Fitting a new front wheel bearing using a socket, nut, bolt, washers, and a length of bar

4.12 Drawing the hub into the bearing using improvised tools

9   Press or drive the new bearing into position until it contacts the outer circlip, applying pressure to the outer race (photo).
10   Fit the inner bearing retaining circlip, with the tabs positioned towards the bottom of the hub carrier.
11   Fit the brake disc shield.
12   Press or draw the hub into the bearing. The bearing inner track **must** be supported during this operation. This can be achieved using a suitable socket, long bolt, washer, and a length of bar as shown (photo).
13   Refit the brake disc.
14   Refit the suspension strut/hub carrier assembly, as described in Section 2.

5   Front suspension lower arm – removal and refitting

Removal

Note: *A balljoint separator tool will be required for this operation. The lower arm rear pivot bolt, lower arm-to-suspension strut balljoint nut locking pin, and anti-roll bar-to-lower arm securing nuts and locknuts must be renewed on refitting.*

1   Apply the handbrake, then jack up the front of the vehicle, and support securely on axle stands (see *'Jacking, towing and wheel changing'*). Remove the relevant roadwheel.
2   Unscrew and discard the nuts securing the end of the anti-roll bar to the lower arm. Note that the nut which rests against the dished washer is a conventional nut, and the second nut is a locknut. Recover the dished washers and the mounting rubbers.
3   Extract the locking pin, then unscrew the castellated nut from the lower arm-to-suspension strut balljoint.
4   Using a balljoint separator tool, disconnect the lower arm-to-suspension strut balljoint.
5   Unscrew and remove the two pivot bolts securing the lower arm to the subframe (photo). Note that the rear pivot bolt also secures the subframe to the underbody. Both bolts are very tight, and a suitable extension bar will probably be required to loosen them.

6   Pull the lower arm from the subframe, and withdraw it from the vehicle.

Refitting

7   Note that on certain models, a damper weight may be bolted to the right-hand lower arm. If the right-hand lower arm is to be renewed on such a vehicle, it is important to ensure that the damper weight is transferred to the new arm.
8   Note that the metal sleeves in the rear mounting bush can be discarded when refitting the lower arm.
9   Commence refitting by pushing the lower arm into position in the subframe.
10   Fit the two pivot bolts, then hold the lower arm in a horizontal position, and tighten the bolts to the specified torque. Note that a new

5.5 Lower arm front pivot bolt (arrowed)

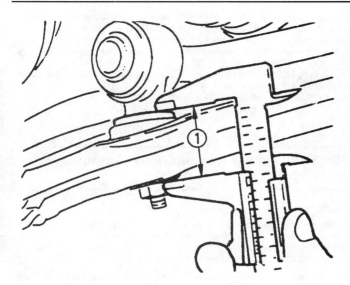

Fig. 10.8 Front anti-roll bar rubber bush compression (1) should be 38.0 to 39.0 mm (Sec 5)

rear pivot bolt must be used, and the new bolt must be tightened to the specified torque in the three stages given in the Specifications.

11   Reconnect the lower arm-to-suspension strut balljoint, and tighten the castellated nut to the specified torque. Secure the nut with a new locking pin.

12   Reconnect the end of the anti-roll bar to the lower arm, noting that the dished washers which retain the mounting rubbers should be fitted with their concave sides facing towards the lower arm.

13   Fit a new anti-roll bar-to-lower arm securing nut, and tighten it to give the specified rubber bush compression shown in Fig. 10.8. If necessary, renew the rubber bushes.

14   Fit a new anti-roll bar-to-lower arm locknut, and tighten it to the specified torque.

15   Refit the roadwheel and lower the vehicle to the ground.

16   On completion, check and if necessary adjust the front wheel alignment, as described in Section 36.

6   Front suspension lower arm bushes – renewal

1   Remove the lower arm, as described in Section 5.
2   The bushes are a tight fit in the lower arm, and must be pressed out.
3   If a press is not available, the bushes can be drawn out using a long bolt, nut, washers and a suitable diameter socket or length of metal tubing.
4   The vertical bush should be pressed out through the top of the lower arm, from below, and the horizontal bush should pressed out towards the front of the lower arm, from the rear.
5   Lubricate the new bushes using soapy water, then fit them to the lower arm, using the method described in paragraph 3.
6   The new vertical bush should be pressed into the lower arm from below, and the new horizontal bush should be pressed into the lower arm from front to rear. The horizontal bush should project from the lower arm equally at both ends.
7   Refit the lower arm, as described in Section 5.

7   Front suspension lower arm balljoint – renewal

Note: *Three special bolts, spring washers and nuts (available from Vauxhall/Opel dealers) will be required when fitting the new balljoint.*

1   Remove the lower arm, as described in Section 5.
2   Mount the lower arm in a vice, then drill the heads from the three rivets which secure the balljoint to the lower arm, using a 12.0 mm diameter drill.

3   If necessary, tap the rivets from the lower arm, then remove the balljoint.
4   The new balljoint should be fitted using three special bolts, spring washers and nuts, available from a Vauxhall/Opel parts centre.
5   Ensure that the balljoint is fitted the correct way up, noting that the securing nuts should be positioned on the underside of the lower arm.
6   Tighten the balljoint-to-lower arm nuts to the specified torque.
7   Refit the lower arm, as described in Section 5.

8   Front anti-roll bar – removal and refitting

Removal

Note: *Suitable equipment will be required to support the engine during this procedure. The rear subframe securing bolts, and the anti-roll bar-to-lower arm securing nuts and locknuts, must be renewed on refitting.*

1   Before removing the anti-roll bar, the engine must be supported from its left-hand lifting bracket. Ideally, the engine should be supported using a strong wooden or metal beam resting on blocks positioned securely in the channels at the sides of the engine compartment. The Vauxhall/Opel special tool designed specifically for this purpose is shown in Fig. 7.4 in Chapter 7. Alternatively, the engine can be supported using a suitable hoist and lifting tackle, but in this case, the hoist must be of such a design as to enable the engine to be supported with the vehicle raised off the ground, leaving sufficient clearance to lower the front subframe.

2   Apply the handbrake, then jack up the front of the vehicle, and support securely on axle stands (see *'Jacking, towing and wheel changing'*). Remove the front roadwheels.

3   On DOHC engine models, remove the engine undershield, as described in Chapter 11, Section 25.

4   If desired, for improved access, remove the front section of the exhaust system, as described in Chapter 4.

5   Working under the vehicle, unscrew and remove the nuts securing the ends of the anti-roll bar to the lower arms. Recover the dished washers and mounting rubbers (photo).

6   Ensure that the engine is adequately supported, then unscrew and remove the two nuts and washers securing the engine/transmission rear mounting to the subframe.

7   Support the subframe on a trolley jack, with an interposed wooden beam to spread the load.

8   Unscrew and remove the two rear and two centre bolts securing the subframe to the vehicle underbody. Note that the rear bolts also secure the lower arms to the subframe. The bolts are very tight, and a suitable extension bar will probably be required to loosen them. **Note:** *On certain early left-hand-drive models, a short front subframe was used, which was secured by four bolts instead of six. On these models, remove all four*

8.5 Front anti-roll bar-to-lower arm securing nuts (arrowed)

subframe securing bolts, and lower the complete subframe from the vehicle.

9   Loosen, but do not remove, the two front subframe-to-underbody securing bolts (not applicable to certain early left-hand-drive models – see note in paragraph 8).

10   Carefully lower the subframe until the anti-roll bar-to-subframe bolts are accessible, then unscrew and remove the bolts.

11   Lift the anti-roll bar from the subframe and the lower arms, and withdraw it from the vehicle.

Refitting

12   If desired, the anti-roll bar mounting bushes can be renewed, as described in Section 9.

13   Refitting is a reversal of removal, bearing in mind the following points.

14   When refitting the subframe to the underbody, use new rear securing bolts, and tighten them to the specified torque in the three stages given in the Specifications.

15   Reconnect the ends of the anti-roll bar to the lower arms, noting that the dished washers which retain the mounting rubbers should be fitted with their concave sides facing towards the lower arm.

16   Fit new anti-roll bar-to-lower arm securing nuts, and tighten them to give the specified rubber bush compression shown in Fig. 10.8. If necessary, renew the rubber bushes.

17   Fit new anti-roll bar-to-lower arm locknuts, and tighten them to the specified torque.

18   Tighten all nuts and bolts to the specified torques.

19   Where applicable, refit the front section of the exhaust system, with reference to Chapter 4.

9   Front anti-roll bar bushes – renewal

Note: *The use of a balljoint separator tool will greatly ease this procedure.*

1   Remove the anti-roll bar, as described in Section 8.

2   If an anti-roll bar end link bush (between the end link and the anti-roll bar) requires renewal, the complete end link must be renewed.

3   To remove an end link, mount the anti-roll bar in a vice, then, using a balljoint separator tool and progressively thicker packing pieces, remove the end link from the end of the anti-roll bar. Alternatively, the end link can be removed by driving it from the anti-roll bar using light hammer blows on a suitable drift, although this is likely to cause damage to the end link unless carried out with extreme care.

4   If necessary, repeat the procedure on the remaining end link.

5   With either end link removed, the anti-roll bar-to-subframe mounting bushes can be renewed if desired, by sliding the bushes along

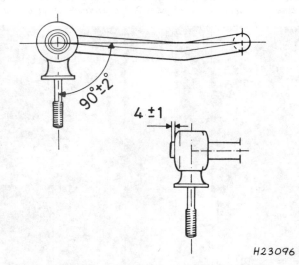

Fig. 10.9 Correct position of end link on front anti-roll bar (Sec 9)

Dimensions in mm

the bar and manipulating them until they can be withdrawn from the end of the bar. Fit the new bushes in a similar way.

6   Press or drive the end link(s) onto the anti-roll bar, to the position shown in Fig. 10.9. Use a suitable metal tube or socket to avoid damage to the end link(s).

7   Before refitting the anti-roll bar, examine the anti-roll bar-to-lower arm bushes, and renew if necessary.

8   Refit the anti-roll bar, as described in Section 8.

10   Front suspension subframe – removal and refitting

Removal

Note: *Suitable equipment will be required to support the engine during this procedure; a balljoint separator tool will also be required. The subframe securing bolts, and the lower arm-to-suspension strut balljoint nut locking pins, must be renewed on refitting.*

1   The subframe is removed complete with the lower arms and the anti-roll bar, as an assembly.

2   Before removing the subframe, the engine must be supported from its left-hand lifting bracket. Ideally, the engine should be supported using a strong wooden or metal beam resting on blocks positioned securely in the channels at the sides of the engine compartment. The Vauxhall/Opel special tool designed specifically for this purpose is shown in Fig. 7.4 in Chapter 7. Alternatively, the engine can be supported using a suitable hoist and lifting tackle, but in this case, the hoist must be of such a design as to enable the engine to be supported with the vehicle raised off the ground, leaving sufficient clearance to withdraw the subframe from under the front of the vehicle.

3   Apply the handbrake, then jack up the front of the vehicle and support securely on axle stands (see *'Jacking, towing and wheel changing'*). Remove the front roadwheels.

4   On DOHC engine models, remove the engine undershield, as described in Chapter 11, Section 25.

5   Remove the front section of the exhaust system, with reference to Chapter 4. On DOHC engine models, where applicable, unbolt the oil cooler hose bracket from the right-hand side of the subframe.

6   Working on one side of the vehicle, extract the locking pin, then unscrew the castellated nut from the lower arm-to-suspension strut balljoint.

7   Using a balljoint separator tool, disconnect the lower arm-to-suspension strut balljoint.

8   Repeat paragraphs 6 and 7 for the remaining lower arm.

9   Ensure that the engine is adequately supported, then unscrew and remove the two nuts and washers securing the rear engine/transmission mounting to the subframe.

10   Support the subframe on a trolley jack, with an interposed wooden beam to prevent the subframe from tipping as it is withdrawn.

11   Unscrew and remove the six bolts securing the subframe to the vehicle underbody. *Note that on certain early left-hand-drive models, a short front subframe was used, which was secured by four bolts instead of six. On these models, remove all four subframe securing bolts.* Note that the rear bolts also secure the lower arms to the subframe (photos). The bolts are very tight, and a suitable extension bar will probably be required to loosen them.

12   Lower the jack supporting the subframe, and withdraw the assembly from under the front of the vehicle.

13   If desired, the anti-roll bar and/or the lower arms can be removed from the subframe, with reference to Section 8 and/or Section 5, as applicable.

Refitting

14   Refitting is a reversal of removal, bearing in mind the following points.

15   If the anti-roll bar and/or the lower arms have been removed from the subframe, refit them with reference to Sections 8 and/or Section 5, as applicable.

16   Fit new subframe securing bolts, and tighten them to the specified torque given in the Specifications. Note that the rear subframe/lower arm securing bolts must be tightened in three stages.

10.11A Front subframe front securing bolt (arrowed)

10.11B Front subframe centre and rear securing bolts (arrowed)

17 Secure the lower arm-to-suspension strut balljoint nuts with new locking pins.

18 Refit the front section of the exhaust system, with reference to Chapter 4 and, where applicable, on DOHC engine models, refit the oil cooler bracket to the subframe, followed by the engine undershield.

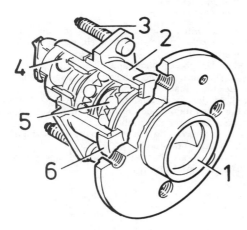

Fig. 10.10 Sectional view of rear hub assembly (Sec 11)

1 Hub
2 Stub axle
3 Threaded bolt
4 Dust cap with integral ABS wheel sensor
5 Bearings
6 Oil seal

11 Rear hub – removal and refitting

Removal

Note: *The hub unit securing nuts must be renewed on refitting.*

1 Chock the front wheels, then jack up the rear of the vehicle and support securely on axle stands (see *'Jacking, towing and wheel changing'*). Remove the relevant roadwheel.

2 On models with rear drum brakes, remove the brake drum, as described in Chapter 9.

3 On models with rear disc brakes, remove the brake caliper and the brake disc, as described in Chapter 9. The caliper can be suspended out of the way, using wire or string, to avoid the need to disconnect the hydraulic fluid pipe.

4 On models with rear disc brakes, disconnect the return spring from the handbrake shoe lever and the brake backplate.

5 On models with ABS, disconnect the ABS sensor wiring plug at the rear of the hub assembly.

6 Unscrew the four securing nuts, and withdraw the hub assembly (photos). On models with rear disc brakes, the hub assembly can be withdrawn complete with the brake backplate, in which case, detach the handbrake cable from the handbrake shoe lever as the hub assembly is withdrawn. On models with rear drum brakes, the brake backplate can be left attached to the rear suspension torsion beam.

Refitting

7 Refitting is a reversal of removal, bearing in mind the following points.

8 New hub unit securing nuts must be used, and they must be tightened in the three stages given in the Specifications. Note that a socket extension and a universal joint may be required, to enable the use of an angle gauge (photo).

11.6A Rear hub securing nuts (arrowed) – model with rear drum brakes

11.6B Removing a rear hub – model with rear drum brakes

11.8 Tightening a rear hub nut using an angle gauge

12.2 Unscrewing a rear shock absorber top mounting nut while counterholding the piston rod – Hatchback model

12.4 Rear shock absorber lower securing bolt – Hatchback model

9   On models with rear disc brakes, where applicable, make sure that the handbrake cable and the return spring are correctly reconnected.
10   On models with rear disc brakes, refit the brake disc and the brake caliper as described in Chapter 9.
11   On models with rear drum brakes, refit the brake drum as described in Chapter 9.
12   Before refitting the roadwheel and lowering the vehicle to the ground, check the handbrake cable adjustment, as described in Chapter 9.

12   Rear shock absorber – removal, inspection and refitting

Note: *Only one shock absorber should be removed at a time. Shock absorbers should be renewed in pairs.*

Saloon and Hatchback models
Removal
1   Working in the luggage compartment, pull the plastic cover from the shock absorber top mounting.
2   Counterhold the shock absorber piston rod, and unscrew the shock absorber top mounting nut (photo). Remove the washer and the upper mounting rubber.
3   For improved access, drive the rear of the vehicle up onto ramps, and chock the front wheels. Alternatively, chock the front wheels, then jack up the rear of the vehicle, and support securely on axle stands (see *'Jacking, towing and wheel changing'*). If the vehicle is jacked up, the relevant trailing arm **must be** supported with a jack as the vehicle is raised, to prevent the trailing arm being forced down by the coil spring.
4   Unscrew and remove the bolt securing the lower end of the shock absorber to the trailing arm (photo).
5   Compress the shock absorber by hand, if necessary prising the lower end to free it from the trailing arm.
6   Withdraw the shock absorber from under the vehicle, and recover the remaining mounting rubber and the spacer sleeve from the top of the shock absorber.

Inspection
7   Examine the shock absorber mounting rubbers for wear or damage, and renew if necessary.
8   The shock absorber can be tested by clamping the lower mounting eye in a vice, then fully extending and compressing the shock absorber several times. Any evidence of jerky movement or lack of resistance indicates the need for renewal.

Refitting
9   Refitting is a reversal of removal, but tighten the shock absorber lower mounting bolt to the specified torque.

Estate and Van models
Removal
10   On models with manual rear suspension level control, depressurise the system by releasing the air through the valve in the luggage compartment.
11   Proceed as described in paragraph 3.
12   Where applicable, disconnect the manual suspension level control air line from the shock absorber.
13   Counterhold the shock absorber piston rod, and unscrew the shock absorber lower mounting nut from the trailing arm. Remove the washer and the upper mounting rubber.
14   Unscrew and remove the bolt securing the upper end of the shock absorber to the vehicle underbody.
15   Compress the shock absorber by hand, if necessary prising the upper end to free it from the body.

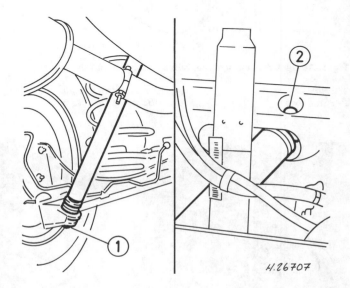

Fig. 10.11 Rear shock absorber mountings – Estate and Van models (Sec 12)

1   Lower mounting   *2   Upper mounting*

16   Withdraw the shock absorber from under the vehicle, and recover the remaining mounting rubber and the spacer sleeve from the lower end of the shock absorber.

Inspection

17   Proceed as described in paragraphs 7 and 8, but clamp the upper mounting eye in the vice when testing the shock absorber.

Refitting

18   Refitting is a reversal of removal, bearing in mind the following points.
19   Where applicable, ensure that the shock absorber is fitted with the air line union facing the correct way round.
20   Tighten the shock absorber upper mounting bolt to the specified torque.
21   On models with manual rear suspension level control, pressurise the system to 0.8 bars, and check for air leaks.

13   Rear shock absorber mounting rubbers – renewal

Note: *Only one shock absorber should be disconnected at a time.*

Saloon and Hatchback models

1   The mounting bush in the shock absorber lower eye is not available separately, and if worn or damaged, the complete shock absorber must be renewed.
2   The shock absorber upper mounting rubbers can be renewed without removing the shock absorber as follows.
3   Proceed as described in Section 12, paragraphs 1 and 2.
4   With the roadwheels resting on the ground, jack up the rear of the vehicle slightly, to enable the shock absorber to be compressed sufficiently by hand to release the top mounting from the body.
5   Remove the remaining mounting rubber from the top of the shock absorber.
6   Fit the new mounting rubbers using a reversal of the removal procedure.

Estate and Van models

7   The mounting bush in the shock absorber upper eye is not available separately, and if worn or damaged, the complete shock absorber must be renewed.
8   The shock absorber lower mounting rubbers can be renewed without removing the shock absorber as follows.
9   On models with manual rear suspension level control, depressurise the system by releasing the air through the valve in the luggage compartment.
10   Counterhold the shock absorber piston rod, and unscrew the shock absorber lower mounting nut from the trailing arm. Remove the washer and mounting rubber.
11   Compress the shock absorber by hand sufficiently to release the lower end from the trailing arm.
12   Remove the remaining mounting rubber and the spacer sleeve from the lower end of the shock absorber.
13   Fit the new mounting rubbers using a reversal of the removal procedure.
14   On models with manual rear suspension level control, pressurise the system to 0.8 bars on completion.

14   Rear suspension coil spring – removal and refitting

Note: *Due to the design of the rear suspension, it is important to note that only one coil spring should be removed at a time. Note that the rear springs should be renewed in pairs, and if the springs are to be renewed, it is advisable to renew the spring damping rubbers at the same time.*

Removal

1   On models with manual rear suspension level control, depressurise the system by releasing the air through the valve in the luggage compartment.
2   Chock the front wheels, then jack up the rear of the vehicle, and support securely on axle stands (see *'Jacking, towing and wheel changing'*).
3   Raise the relevant trailing arm slightly using a jack.
4   Unscrew and remove the bolt and washer securing the lower end of the shock absorber to the trailing arm, and free the lower end of the shock absorber.
5   Carefully lower the jack supporting the trailing arm, and remove the coil spring and its damping rubbers. Lever the trailing arm downwards slightly if necessary to remove the spring.

Refitting

6   Refitting is a reversal of removal, bearing in mind the following points.
7   Ensure that the spring locates correctly on the trailing arm and the underbody.
8   Tighten the shock absorber lower mounting bolt to the specified torque.
9   If the springs are to be renewed, repeat the procedure on the remaining side of the vehicle.
10   On models with manual rear suspension level control, pressurise the system to 0.8 bars on completion.

15   Rear anti-roll bar(s) – removal and refitting

Main anti-roll bar
Removal

Note: *New anti-roll bar securing nuts and bolts must be used on refitting.*

1   On all models fitted with a rear anti-roll bar, the anti-roll bar is located inside the rear suspension torsion beam. On DOHC engine models, an additional rear anti-roll bar is fitted, which is bolted to the exterior of the torsion beam – removal and refitting is described in the following sub-Section.
2   Chock the front wheels, then jack up the rear of the vehicle, and support securely on axle stands (see *'Jacking, towing and wheel changing'*). Remove one of the rear roadwheels.
3   Working at one end of the anti-roll bar, counterhold the securing bolt, while unscrewing the securing nut (photo).
4   Repeat the procedure for the remaining securing nut at the other end of the anti-roll bar.
5   Prise the anti-roll bar insulation rubber from the centre of the torsion beam (photo).
6   Working at the side of the vehicle from which the wheel has been removed, draw the anti-roll bar out through the end of the torsion beam.

Refitting

7   Refitting is a reversal of removal, bearing in mind the following points.
8   To ease refitting, lightly coat the anti-roll bar with a lubricant, such as light oil.
9   Ensure that the insulation rubber is correctly refitted to the centre of the torsion beam.
10   Use new anti-roll bar securing nuts and bolts. Counterhold the securing nuts, while tightening the bolts in the three stages given in the Specifications.

Additional anti-roll bar (DOHC engine models)
Removal

Note: *New anti-roll bar securing nuts and bolts must be used on refitting.*

11   To improve access, chock the front wheels, then jack up the rear of the vehicle, and support securely on axle stands (see *'Jacking, towing and wheel changing'*).
12   Unscrew the four securing bolts – two at each end of the anti-roll bar (photo) – while counterholding the nuts, and lower the anti-roll bar from the torsion beam.

15.3 Rear anti-roll bar securing nut and bolt

15.5 Rear anti-roll bar insulation rubber (arrowed)

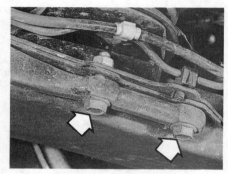

15.12 Additional rear anti-roll bar securing bolts (arrowed) – DOHC engine model

Refitting

13   Refitting is a reversal of removal, but use new securing nuts and bolts. Counterhold the securing nuts, while tightening the bolts in the three stages given in the Specifications.

16   Rear suspension torsion beam/trailing arms assembly – removal and refitting

Removal

1   Chock the front wheels, then jack up the rear of the vehicle, and support securely on axle stands (see 'Jacking, towing and wheel changing'). Remove the rear roadwheels.
2   On models with manual rear suspension level control, depressurise the system by releasing the air through the valve in the luggage compartment.
3   On models with a catalytic converter, unbolt and remove the exhaust centre box heat shield.
4   Note the length of exposed thread on the now-exposed handbrake cable adjuster, then remove the adjuster nut to enable the cable bracket to be disconnected from the handbrake lever operating rod.
5   Release the handbrake cables from the brackets on the underbody.
6   Working in the engine compartment, remove the filler cap from the brake hydraulic fluid reservoir, then place a piece of polythene across the top of the reservoir filler hole, and refit the filler cap. This will minimise fluid loss when the brake lines are disconnected.
7   Disconnect the flexible hoses from the rigid brake pipes at the front edge of each trailing arm. Be prepared for fluid loss, and plug the open ends of the pipes and hoses, to prevent dirt ingress and further fluid loss.
8   Where applicable, disconnect the wiring plugs from the ABS wheel sensors, and release the wiring from the brackets on the trailing arms.
9   On Estate and Van models, disconnect the brake pressure-regulating valve spring from the bracket on the torsion beam.
10   Loosen, but **do not** remove, the nuts and bolts securing the front ends of the trailing arms to the vehicle underbody (photo).
11   Support the torsion beam with a trolley jack and interposed block of wood. Position the jack securely under the centre of the torsion beam.
12   On Saloon and Hatchback models, unscrew and remove the bolts securing the lower ends of the shock absorbers to the trailing arms.
13   On Estate and Van models, counterhold the shock absorber piston rods, and unscrew the nuts securing the lower ends of the shock absorbers to the trailing arms.
14   Gently lower the jack supporting the torsion beam, until the coil springs can be removed. Remove the coil springs, with reference to Section 14 if necessary.
15   Ensure that the torsion beam is adequately supported, then remove the nuts and bolts securing the front ends of the trailing arms to the vehicle underbody. The help of an assistant will greatly ease this task – ensure that the torsion beam does not slip off the jack.
16   Withdraw the torsion beam/trailing arms assembly from under the rear of the vehicle.
17   If desired, the brake components can be removed from the trailing arms, with reference to the relevant Sections of Chapter 9. The hub units can be removed with reference to Section 11, and where

16.10 Trailing arm-to-underbody securing nut (arrowed) viewed through rear wheel arch

applicable, the anti-roll bar(s) can be removed with reference to Section 15.
18   If necessary, the trailing arm bushes can be renewed, with reference to Section 17.

Refitting

19   Commence reassembly by refitting any components which were removed from the torsion beam/trailing arms assembly, with reference to the relevant Sections of this Chapter and/or Chapter 9, as applicable.
20   Support the torsion beam/trailing arms assembly on the trolley jack, and position the assembly under the rear of the vehicle.
21   Raise the jack, and fit the bolts and nuts which secure the front ends of the trailing arms to the underbody. Do not fully tighten the fixings at this stage.
22   Refit the coil springs, with reference to Section 14 if necessary.
23   Raise the rear ends of the trailing arms, and refit the bolts or nuts, as applicable, securing the lower ends of the shock absorbers to the trailing arms. Tighten the fixings to the specified torque, counterholding the shock absorber piston rod on Estate and Van models. Withdraw the jack from under the rear of the vehicle.
24   Where applicable, reconnect the ABS wheel sensor wiring, and refit the wiring to the brackets on the trailing arms.
25   Remove the plugs from the brake pipes and hoses, and reconnect the unions.
26   Refit the handbrake cables to the brackets on the underbody, then reconnect the handbrake cable bracket to the handbrake lever operating rod.
27   Fit a new handbrake cable adjuster nut, and screw the nut onto the rod to the position noted before removal. Check the handbrake adjustment, as described in Chapter 9.

28 On models with a catalytic converter, refit the exhaust centre box heat shield.
29 On Estate and Van models, reconnect the brake pressure-regulating valve spring to the bracket on the torsion beam.
30 Refit the roadwheels, and lower the vehicle to the ground.
31 On models with manual rear suspension level control, pressurise the system to 0.8 bars.
32 Remove the chocks from the front wheels.
33 Ensure that the vehicle is parked on level ground, then with the equivalent of a load of 70.0 kg in each front seat, 'bounce' the vehicle to settle the suspension.
34 Without disturbing the position of the vehicle, place chocks at the front and rear edges of the front wheels, to prevent the vehicle from moving.
35 Working under the rear of the vehicle, tighten the fixings securing the front ends of the trailing arms to the underbody to the specified torque.
36 Finally, recheck the handbrake cable adjustment, then remove the polythene from beneath the brake hydraulic fluid reservoir cap, and bleed the complete brake hydraulic system, as described in Chapter 9.
37 On Estate and Van models, check the adjustment of the brake pressure-regulating valve, as described in Chapter 1.

17 Rear suspension trailing arm bushes – renewal

Note: *Trailing arm bushes should always be renewed in pairs – ie, on both sides of the vehicle.*

1 The trailing arm bushes can be renewed without removing the torsion beam/trailing arms assembly from the vehicle, as follows.
2 Chock the front wheels, then jack up the rear of the vehicle, and support securely on axle stands (see *'Jacking, towing and wheel changing'*). Remove the rear roadwheels.
3 On models with manual rear suspension level control, depressurise the system by releasing the air through the valve in the luggage compartment.
4 On Estate and Van models, disconnect the brake pressure-regulating valve spring from the bracket on the torsion beam.
5 Unclip the flexible hoses and the rear ends of the rigid brake pipes from the vehicle underbody. Also unclip the handbrake cables and ABS sensor wiring, where applicable.
6 Support the torsion beam with a trolley jack and interposed block of wood. Position the jack under the centre of the torsion beam.
7 Unscrew and remove the nuts and bolts securing the trailing arms to the underbody.
8 Gently lower the jack until the trailing arm bushes are accessible, then support the torsion beam on axle stands. Take care not to strain the brake pipes.
9 A special Vauxhall/Opel tool is available for removal and refitting of the bushes, but a suitable alternative can be improvised using a long

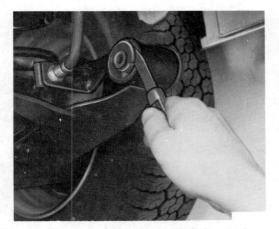

Fig. 10.12 Cutting the inner flange from a trailing arm bush (Sec 17)

bolt, nut, washers, and a length of suitable-diameter metal tubing or a socket.
10 Where applicable, prior to removing a bush, cut the flange from the inner end of the bush using a sharp knife – see Fig. 10.12.
11 Removal of the bush will be made easier if the bush housing in the trailing arm is heated to approximately 70°C using a heat gun or a hairdryer. **Do not** use a naked flame, due to the close proximity of the fuel tank.
12 Draw the bush from the trailing arm using the tool described in paragraph 8.
13 Lubricate the new bush with a little soapy water, then draw it into position, ensuring that the narrow part of the bush points upwards.
14 Repeat the procedure on the remaining trailing arm.
15 Raise the torsion beam using the jack, and fit the bolts and nuts which secure the front ends of the trailing arms to the underbody. Do not fully tighten the fixings at this stage. Withdraw the axle stands.
16 Clip the rigid brake pipes and the flexible hoses to the vehicle underbody.
17 On Estate and Van models, reconnect the brake pressure-regulating valve spring to the bracket on the torsion beam.
18 Proceed as described in Section 16, paragraphs 30 to 35 inclusive.
19 On Estate and Van models, check the adjustment of the brake pressure-regulating valve, as described in Chapter 1.

18 Rear suspension level control system – general information

The suspension level control system is manually-operated, and the level is adjusted by altering the air pressure in the rear shock absorbers, via a valve located in the luggage compartment.
For safety reasons, if the vehicle is to be driven fully-loaded, the level control system must not be fully-pressurised with the vehicle in the unladen condition.
To adjust the system, proceed as follows.
With the vehicle unladen, use a tyre pressure gauge on the air valve to check that the system pressure is 0.8 bars. Adjust if necessary.
With the vehicle standing on a level surface, measure the distance from the centre of the rear bumper to the ground. Subtract 50.0 mm from the distance measured, and note the new value.
Load the vehicle, and if necessary increase the pressure in the system until the noted value for the bumper height is reached. **Do not** exceed a pressure of 5.0 bars.
After unloading the vehicle, depressurise the system to the minimum pressure of 0.8 bars.
Do not drive an unladen vehicle with the system fully-pressurised.

19 Rear suspension level control system components – removal and refitting

Air valve
Removal
1 Working in the luggage compartment, pull back the floor covering for access to the air valve.
2 Fully depressurise the system.
3 Remove the cap and retaining sleeve from the valve, then compress the retaining lugs and push the valve downwards, taking care not to damage the air lines.
4 Unscrew the air line unions from the valve, and then withdraw the valve from the vehicle.

Refitting
5 Refitting is a reversal of removal, but on completion, pressurise the system and check for air leaks.

Air lines
Removal
6 To remove an air line, first fully depressurise the system.

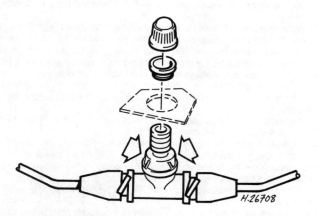

Fig. 10.13 Rear suspension level control system air valve. Compress retaining lugs (arrowed) to remove valve (Sec 19)

7   Unscrew the unions at the shock absorber and air valve, then release the air line from the clips on the vehicle underbody.

Refitting

8   Refitting is a reversal of removal, but on completion, pressurise the system and check for air leaks.

Shock absorbers

9   Removal and refitting of the shock absorbers is covered in Section 12.

20   Steering wheel – removal and refitting

Removal

Note: *A suitable two-legged puller will be required for this operation.*

1   Disconnect the battery negative lead.
2   Set the front wheels in the straight-ahead position, and unless it is unavoidable, do not move them until the steering wheel has been refitted.
3   Prise the horn push pad from the centre of the steering wheel, and disconnect the wiring.
4   Using a screwdriver, prise back the tabs on the lockwasher securing the steering wheel retaining nut.
5   Unscrew and remove the steering wheel retaining nut and the lockwasher.
6   Make alignment marks between the steering wheel and the end of the column shaft.

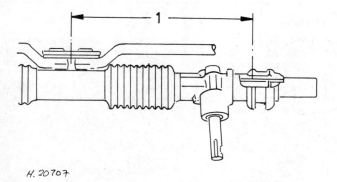

Fig. 10.14 Steering gear centralised for setting of steering wheel straight-ahead position – right-hand-drive shown (Sec 21)

1 = 325.0 mm

7   A suitably-small two-legged puller must now be fitted to the steering wheel in order to pull it from the column shaft. Note that the steering wheel is a very tight fit on the shaft.

Refitting

8   Commence refitting by gently tapping the steering wheel into position on the column shaft, using a suitable metal tube or socket, and ensuring that the marks made before removal are aligned. Before tapping the wheel fully home, check the centralisation, as described in Section 21.
9   Refit the lockwasher and the steering wheel retaining nut, and tighten the nut to the specified torque. Bend up the lockwasher tabs to secure the nut.
10   Refit the horn push pad, ensuring that the wiring is securely connected, and reconnect the battery negative lead.

21   Steering wheel – centralising

1   The steering straight-ahead position is achieved when the reference dimension between the centre of the tie-rod-to-steering gear bolt locking plate(s), and the centre of the rib on the right-hand steering gear mounting clamp (right-hand-drive models), or the left-hand steering gear mounting clamp (left-hand-drive models), as applicable, is as shown in Fig. 10.14. In this position, the flexible rubber coupling upper pinch-bolt should lie horizontally on top of the steering shaft – see Fig. 10.15.
2   Check that the steering wheel is centralised.
3   If the steering wheel is off-centre by more than 5°, it should be removed, then moved the required number of splines on the column shaft to achieve centralisation, and refitted as described in Section 20.

22   Steering column lock – removal and refitting

Removal

1   Disconnect the battery negative lead.
2   Remove the steering column shrouds, as described in Chapter 11, Section 32.
3   Insert the ignition key into the ignition switch, and turn it to position 'II'.
4   Insert a thin rod into the hole in the lock housing, then press the rod to release the detent spring, and pull out the lock cylinder using the key (photo).

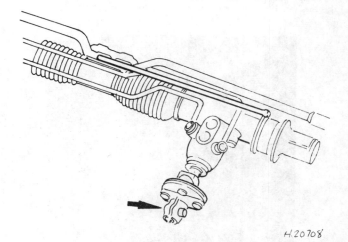

Fig. 10.15 Flexible coupling upper pinch-bolt alignment (arrowed) with steering gear centralised – right-hand-drive shown (Sec 21)

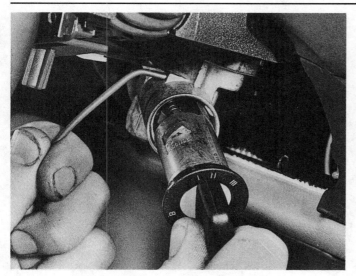

22.4 Removing the steering column lock cylinder

5   Removal and refitting of the lock housing is described in Section 24, as part of the steering column dismantling and reassembly procedure.

Refitting

6   Where applicable, refit the lock housing as described in Section 24.
7   Refit the lock cylinder, with the key in position 'II', by simply pushing it into position in the housing. Turn the key back to position '0', and remove it.
8   Further refitting is a reversal of removal.

23   Steering column – removal and refitting

Removal

Note: *A bolt/stud extractor will be required for this operation. A new shear-head bolt must be used on refitting.*

1   Disconnect the battery negative lead.
2   Set the front wheels in the straight-ahead position.
3   Working in the driver's footwell, release the securing clips, and remove the lower trim panel.
4   Remove the steering wheel as described in Section 20, for improved access.
5   Remove the steering column lock, as described in Section 22.
6   Depress the retaining clips, release the two stalk switches from the steering column, then disconnect the wiring plugs, and withdraw the switches.
7   Unclip the fusebox cover, and unclip the blanking cover from the aperture in the facia panel below the steering column.
8   Working at the lower end of the steering shaft, unscrew and remove

the upper pinch-bolt securing the steering shaft to the flexible rubber coupling.
9   Locate the plastic disc, which should be fitted loosely to the lower end of the steering shaft, and push it up the shaft until it engages with the steering column tube (photo).
10   Using a suitable socket and extension bar, unscrew the bolt securing the steering column to the facia bracket (photo).
11   Two fixings must now be extracted from the column upper mounting bracket. A conventional nut is used on one side of the column (the left-hand side on right-hand-drive models, or the right-hand side on left-hand-drive models), and a shear-head type bolt is used on the remaining side.
12   The shear-head type bolt must be removed by centre-punching, drilling off the head, and then using a suitable bolt/stud extractor (sometimes called 'easy-outs'). When drilling the bolt, take care not to damage the facia panel (photo).
13   Withdraw the column assembly into the vehicle interior, and then remove it from the vehicle. Handle the column carefully, avoiding knocks or impact of any kind, which may damage the collapsible section of the column.
14   If desired, the column can be dismantled as described in Section 24.

Refitting

15   Commence refitting by ensuring that the roadwheels are still in the straight-ahead position, and that the plastic disc on the steering shaft is engaged with the column tube.
16   The flexible coupling should be positioned so that the upper pinch-bolt will be horizontal on top of the steering shaft.
17   Offer the column into position, and reconnect the flexible coupling. Refit the pinch-bolt, but do not fully tighten it at this stage.
18   Loosely fit the upper mounting fixings, using a new shear-head bolt.
19   Refit the bolt securing the steering column to the facia bracket, and tighten to the specified torque.
20   Tighten the upper mounting fixings. The shear-head bolt should be tightened until the head breaks off, and the conventional nut should be tightened to the specified torque.
21   Pull upwards on the steering shaft until the shaft contacts the bearing stop, then tighten the flexible coupling upper pinch-bolt.
22   Prise the plastic centring disc from the base of the column tube, and leave it loose on the steering shaft.
23   Further refitting is a reversal of the removal procedure. Refit the steering wheel, as described in Section 20.
24   On completion, first manoeuvre the vehicle at low speed, then carry out a test drive along a route with several corners, and check that the steering mechanism operates smoothly.

24   Steering column – dismantling and reassembly

Dismantling

1   If the steering column is in position in the vehicle, proceed as described in Section 22, paragraphs 1 to 4 inclusive.

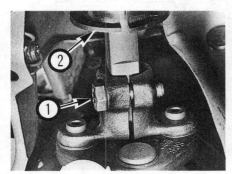

23.9 Steering shaft flexible rubber coupling pinch-bolt (1) and plastic disc (2)

23.10 Steering column-to-facia bracket securing bolt (arrowed) viewed through instrument panel aperture

23.12 Drilling out the steering column shear-head bolt – right-hand-drive model

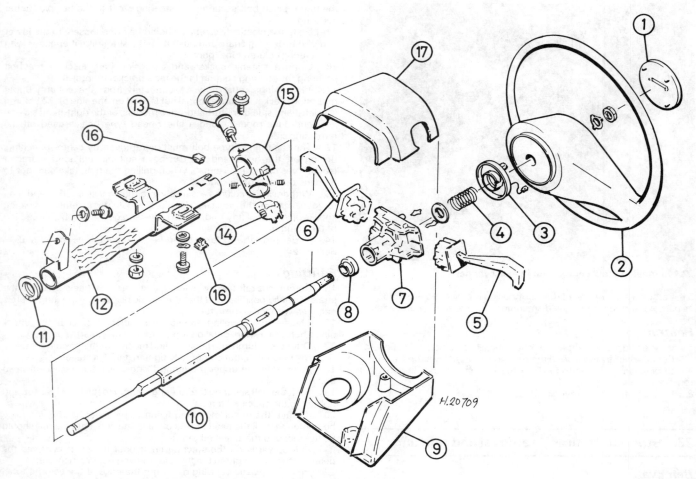

Fig. 10.16 Exploded view of steering column and associated components (Sec 24)

1 Horn push pad	6 Wash/wipe switch	10 Steering shaft	14 Lock barrel
2 Steering wheel	7 Switch housing	11 Centralising plastic disc	15 Lock housing
3 Cam assembly	8 Bearing	12 Column tube	16 Switch housing safety plugs
4 Spring	9 Lower column shroud	13 Lock barrel	17 Upper column shroud
5 Lighting switch			

2   Prise out the ignition switch housing safety plugs, then turn the housing anti-clockwise, and pull it from the steering column.

3   The bearing can be removed from the ignition switch housing by prising apart the two bearing fixing catches, and pressing or driving out the bearing with a piece of suitable diameter tubing on the bearing outer race. When pressing in the new bearing, make sure that the thrustwasher and contact springs are correctly located – see Fig. 10.17.

4   The ignition switch is secured to the lock housing by two grub screws. Remove the screws to extract the switch. It is recommended that the switch and the lock cylinder are not both removed at the same time, otherwise their mutual alignment will be lost.

5   If the steering column is in position in the vehicle, unscrew and remove the upper pinch-bolt from the steering shaft flexible coupling in the driver's footwell.

6   Withdraw the steering shaft from the steering column tube.

Reassembly

7   Commence reassembly by fitting the plastic centring disc, which will be supplied with a new column or steering shaft, into the base of the column tube.

8   Insert the shaft into the column tube, and if the column is in position in the vehicle, engage the bottom end of the shaft with the flexible coupling and refit the upper pinch-bolt, but do not tighten it at this stage.

9   Where applicable, refit the ignition switch, and tighten the grub screws.

10   Refit the ignition switch housing, using new safety plugs.

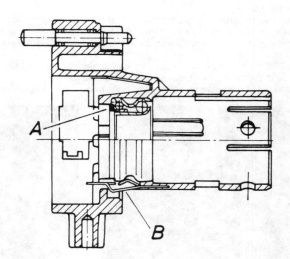

Fig. 10.17 Sectional view of ignition switch housing (Sec 24)

A Thrustwasher   B Contact springs

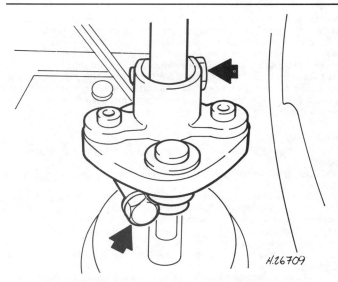

Fig. 10.18 Steering shaft flexible rubber coupling pinch-bolts (arrowed) (Sec 25)

11   If the column is in position in the vehicle, pull upwards on the steering shaft until the shaft contacts the bearing stop, then tighten the flexible coupling upper pinch-bolt. Ensure that the roadwheels are in the straight-ahead position, and that the flexible coupling is positioned so that the upper pinch-bolt is horizontal on top of the steering shaft.
12   Where applicable, further reassembly is a reversal of dismantling. Refit the steering wheel, as described in Section 20.
13   On completion, first manoeuvre the vehicle at low speed, then carry out a test drive along a route with several corners, and check that the steering mechanism operates smoothly.

25   Steering shaft flexible rubber coupling – renewal

1   Set the front wheels in the straight-ahead position.
2   Working in the driver's footwell, release the securing clips, and remove the lower trim panel.
3   Unscrew and remove the two pinch-bolts securing the rubber coupling to the steering shaft and the steering gear pinion shaft.
4   Unscrew the bolts securing the steering gear to the bulkhead in the engine compartment, then move the steering gear away from the bulkhead sufficiently to disconnect the coupling from the steering gear pinion.
5   Pull the coupling from the steering shaft, noting which way round it is fitted.
6   Check that the steering wheel and the front wheels are still in the straight-ahead position.
7   Fit the coupling to the steering gear pinion, and tighten the clamp bolt.
8   Push the steering gear back into position on the bulkhead, ensure that the steering shaft engages with the coupling, then tighten the steering gear securing bolts to the specified torque.
9   Pull upwards on the steering shaft until the shaft contacts the bearing stop, then tighten the flexible coupling upper pinch-bolt.
10   Check that the steering wheel is centralised, as described in Section 21.

26   Steering gear rubber bellows – renewal

Note: *New bellows securing clips will be required when refitting.*
1   Remove the steering gear, as described in Section 27.
2   Remove the mounting clamp and rubber from the left-hand end of the steering gear on right-hand-drive models, or from the right-hand end of the steering gear on left-hand-drive models, as applicable.
3   On power steering gear, disconnect the fluid pipe unions from the

left-hand end of the steering gear (right-hand-drive models), or the right-hand end of the steering gear (left-hand-drive models).
4   Remove the outer bellows securing clips from each end of the steering gear, then slide off the bellows/tube assembly.
5   Remove the inner bellows securing clips, and separate the bellows from the tube.
6   Fit the new bellows to the tube, using new clips. The clips should be positioned so that when the steering gear is fitted to the vehicle, the ends of the clips point upwards.
7   Fit the bellows/tube assembly to the steering gear, and secure with new clips, again positioned with the ends of the clips pointing upwards. Ensure that the bellows are not twisted.
8   On power steering gear, reconnect the fluid pipe unions, using new O-rings.
9   Refit the mounting clamp and rubber, then refit the steering gear, as described in Section 27.

27   Steering gear – removal and refitting

Removal

Note: *New steering gear-to-bulkhead bolts, and a new tie-rod-to-steering gear locking .plate must be used on refitting. On models with power steering, the fluid hose-to-pipe O-ring(s) must be renewed on refitting.*

1   Disconnect the battery negative lead.
2   Set the front wheels in the straight-ahead position.
3   Where applicable, remove the airbox from the top of the carburettor or throttle body (see Chapter 4).
4   Remove the coolant expansion tank, as described in Chapter 3. On certain models, it may be possible to move the expansion tank sufficiently to allow access for removal of the steering gear without disconnecting the hoses.
5   Where applicable, disconnect the wiring harness from the anti-theft alarm switch on the left-hand suspension turret, and move the harness clear of the steering gear. Alternatively, the switch can be removed.
6   Prise the locking plate from the tie-rod-to-steering gear bolts, then unscrew and remove the bolts, and recover the washers and spacer plate (photo).
7   On models with power steering, disconnect the fluid hoses from the pipes at the left-hand side of the engine compartment (next to the coolant expansion tank location). Recover the O-ring(s) where applicable. Be prepared for fluid spillage, and plug the open ends of the pipes and hoses to prevent dirt ingress and further fluid loss.
8   Working in the driver's footwell, release the securing clips, and remove the lower trim panel.
9   Unscrew and remove the upper pinch-bolt securing the steering shaft to the flexible rubber coupling.
10   Working in the engine compartment, unbolt the two clamps

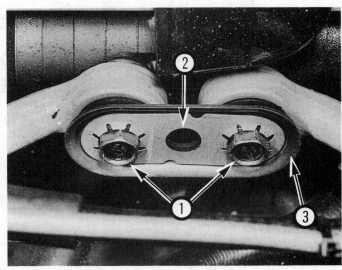

27.6 Tie-rod-to-steering gear bolts (1), locking plate (2) and spacer plate (3)

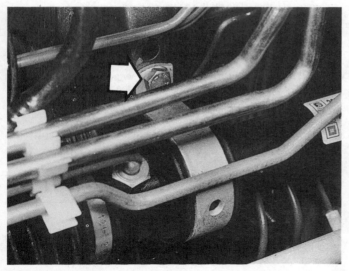

27.10 Steering gear clamp bolt (arrowed) – model with power steering

securing the steering gear to the bulkhead (photo), then push the right-hand end of the steering gear through the large rubber grommet in the right-hand wheel arch, and manipulate the steering gear upwards out of the engine compartment. The help of an assistant may be required to release the flexible rubber coupling from the steering shaft as the steering gear is withdrawn. Note that on some models, various wires and hoses may be secured to the steering gear with cable ties – ensure that, where applicable, all wires and hoses are freed before the steering gear is removed.

Refitting

11   Refitting is a reversal of removal, bearing in mind the following points.

12   Use new mounting bolts to secure the steering gear clamps to the bulkhead.

13   Reconnect the flexible rubber coupling to the steering shaft (with the rack and steering wheel centralised) so that the upper pinch-bolt lies horizontally on top of the steering shaft – see Fig. 10.15.

14   On models with power steering, renew the O-ring(s) when reconnecting the fluid hoses to the pipes.

15   The tie-rod-to-steering gear locking plate must be renewed on refitting.

16   Where applicable, after refitting the expansion tank, top-up the coolant level as described in Chapter 1.

17   On models with power steering, on completion, bleed the hydraulic system, as described in Section 29.

18   On completion, check the steering wheel centralisation, as described in Section 21.

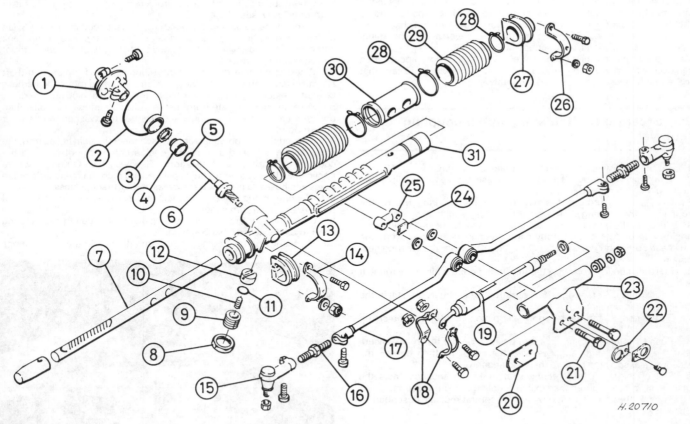

H.20710

Fig. 10.19 Exploded view of manual steering gear (Sec 28)

1 Flexible coupling	9 Adjuster screw	17 Tie-rod	24 Guide plate
2 Rubber cover	10 Spring	18 Steering damper clamp	25 Sliding bar
3 Locking ring	11 O-ring	19 Steering damper	26 Mounting clamp
4 Pinion nut	12 Damper slipper	20 Spacer plate	27 Mounting rubber
5 O-ring	13 Mounting rubber	21 Tie-rod-to-steering gear bolt	28 Bellows securing clip
6 Pinion	14 Mounting clamp	22 Locking plate (alternative type)	29 Bellows
7 Rack	15 Tie-rod end		30 Tube
8 Locknut	16 Tie-rod adjuster pin	23 Steering damper tube	31 Rack housing

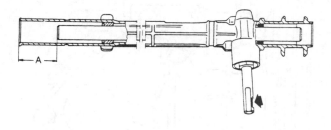

Fig. 10.20 Correct position of pinion cut-out (arrowed) (Sec 28)

A = 61.0 mm

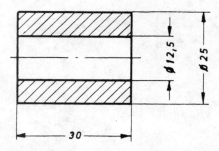

Fig. 10.21 Distance piece for damper slipper adjustment (Sec 28)

All dimensions in mm

28   Steering gear – overhaul

Manual steering gear

Note: *The pinion nut locking ring, damper slipper seal, and rack housing sealing cap must be renewed on reassembly.*

1   Remove the steering gear, as described in Section 27, and remove the mounting rubbers and clamps.
2   Clean away all external dirt.
3   Release the outer bellows securing clips from each end of the steering gear, then slide off the bellows/tube assembly.
4   Extract the sliding bar and the guide plate from the rack.
5   Release the locknut from the rack adjuster screw.
6   Unscrew and remove the adjuster screw, and extract the coil spring, seal and damper slipper.
7   Unscrew and remove the lower pinch-bolt from the flexible rubber coupling, then remove the coupling and the rubber boot from the pinion.
8   Extract the pinion nut locking ring, then unscrew the pinion nut and extract the seal.
9   Withdraw the rack and the pinion.
10   Drive the metal sealing cap from the end of the rack housing, using a long rod.
11   Further dismantling is not possible. If the rack bushes or pinion needle bearing are worn, the complete rack housing must be renewed. The pinion can only be renewed complete with the ball bearing.
12   Clean away old lubricant, then apply grease (Vauxhall/Opel grease No 19 48 588, or equivalent) to all moving components. Insert a further 50.0 g of the grease between the rack bushes inside the housing.
13   Insert the rack into the housing, and locate it so that the end furthest from the pinion is positioned as shown in Fig. 10.20.
14   Fit the pinion so that, when meshed with the rack, its cut-out is positioned at right-angles to the rack housing, facing towards the right-hand end of the housing on right-hand-drive models, or the left-hand end of the housing on left-hand-drive models, as applicable – see Fig. 10.20.
15   Apply grease to the pinion ball bearing, then screw in the pinion nut and tighten it to the specified torque.
16   Fit a new pinion nut locking ring, driving it into place using a piece of metal tubing or a suitable socket.
17   The damper slipper adjustment must now be set. Make up two tubular distance pieces to the dimensions shown in Fig. 10.21.
18   Using the tie-rod-to-steering gear bolts, secure the sliding bar, guide plate and distance pieces to the rack.
19   Fit a new damper slipper seal, then fit the damper slipper and the coil spring into their hole. Screw in the adjuster screw until some resistance is felt – a target turning torque of 5 Nm (3.7 lbf ft) is specified.
20   From this position, back off the adjuster screw by between 20° and 40°. Check that the rack moves freely throughout its entire travel.
21   Without disturbing the adjuster screw, fit the locknut and tighten it to the specified torque. This can be achieved by counterholding the adjuster screw using a suitable socket fitted to a torque wrench, and turning the locknut with a spanner until the specified torque is reached. Take care not to move the adjuster screw.

22   Tap a new sealing cap into the end of the rack housing.
23   Remove the tie-rod-to-steering gear bolts, and the distance pieces.
24   Refit the bellows/tube assembly, and secure the bellows with new clips. Position the clips so that when the steering gear is installed in the vehicle, the ends of the clips point upwards, and ensure that the bellows are not twisted.
25   Refit the steering gear mounting rubbers and clamps, noting that the right-hand mounting clamp (right-hand-drive models), or the left-hand mounting clamp (left-hand-drive models), as applicable, fits with the concave end of the clamp pointing downwards with the steering gear installed in the vehicle.
26   Refit the rubber boot and the flexible rubber coupling to the pinion, and tighten the pinch-bolt.
27   Refit the steering gear, as described in Section 27, but before finally tightening the mounting bolts and reconnecting the tie-rods, check the steering wheel centralisation, as described in Section 21. If the pinion position is incorrect (ie the upper flexible rubber coupling pinch-bolt position is not as specified), then the pinion will have to be withdrawn from the steering gear and moved as necessary to correct the setting.
28   After refitting the steering gear, first manoeuvre the vehicle at low speed, then carry out a test drive along a route with several corners. The steering should show a well-defined self-centring action. If not, the rack damper slipper has been over-adjusted, and must be reset. The steering gear must be removed again to enable adjustment to be carried out.

Power steering gear

29   Overhaul of the power steering gear is not recommended by the manufacturers.
30   Fluid leaks from the hydraulic fluid pipe unions can normally be corrected by renewing the union seals with the rack installed.
31   Bellows renewal is covered in Section 26.
32   Adjustment of the power steering gear should not be attempted.
33   Any faults with the steering gear should be referred to a Vauxhall/Opel dealer, although renewal of the complete assembly will probably be the only course of action available.

29   Power steering hydraulic system – bleeding

1   With the engine stopped, initially fill the reservoir to the level of the 'MAX' mark on the dipstick attached to the reservoir filler cap.
2   Start the engine, and immediately top-up the fluid level to the 'MIN' mark on the dipstick. **Do not** allow the reservoir to run dry at any time. The help of an assistant will ease this operation.
3   With the engine running at idle speed, turn the steering wheel slowly two or three times approximately 45° to the left and right of the centre, then turn the wheel twice from lock to lock. Do not hold the wheel on either lock, as this imposes strain on the hydraulic system.
4   Stop the engine, and check the fluid level. With the fluid at operating temperature (80°C), the level should be on the 'MAX' mark, and with the fluid cold (20°C), the level should be on the 'MIN' mark. Top-up if necessary.

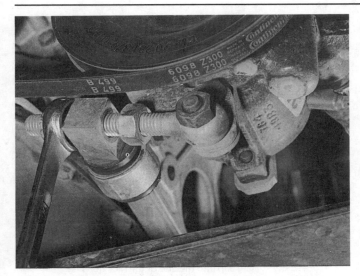

30.4 Adjusting the length of the power steering pump threaded rod – 2.0 litre engine

30   Power steering pump drivebelt – removal, refitting and adjustment

1.4 and 1.6 litre models
1   The power steering pump is driven by the alternator drivebelt.
2   Drivebelt removal, refitting and adjustment procedures are given in Chapter 12.

1.8 and 2.0 litre models
3   Slacken the adjuster and mounting bolts shown in Fig. 10.22.
4   Slacken the adjuster nuts, and adjust the length of the threaded rod in order to remove or tension the belt as desired (photo).
5   To tension the belt, Vauxhall/Opel specify the use of a special gauge, but the correct belt tension can be approximated by adjusting the length of the threaded rod to give a belt deflection of approximately 10.0 mm under moderate thumb pressure, at the midpoint of the belt run between the pulleys. If in doubt, err on the slack side, as an excessively-tight belt may cause pump damage.
6   Tighten the adjuster nuts, and tighten the adjuster and mounting bolts to the specified torque on completion.
7   If a new drivebelt has been fitted, recheck the tension after a few hundred miles.

31   Power steering pump – removal and refitting

1.4 and 1.6 litre engine models
Removal
Note: *A new fluid pipe union O-ring must be used on refitting.*
1   For improved access, remove the air cleaner casing from the right-hand front wing, as described in Chapter 4.
2   Remove the alternator/power steering pump drivebelt, as described in Chapter 12.
3   Counterhold the power steering pump pulley, using an old drivebelt, then unscrew the three pulley securing bolts, and remove the pulley (photo).
4   To improve access, remove the upper outer timing belt cover, as described in Chapter 2.
5   Disconnect the fluid pipe union and the flexible fluid hose from the pump. Be prepared for fluid spillage, and plug or cover the open ends of the pump, pipe and hose, to prevent dirt ingress and further fluid loss (photos).
6   Carefully manipulate the pump from its location, and withdraw it from the engine compartment, taking care not to damage the paintwork, as there is very little clearance for the pump to pass through the space between the engine and the bodywork (photo).

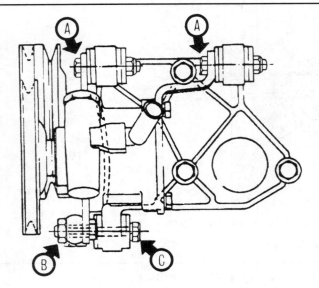

Fig. 10.22 Power steering pump mounting and adjuster bolts (arrowed) must be loosened to adjust drivebelt tension – 1.8 and 2.0 litre engine models (Sec 30)

For A, B and C see 'Torque wrench settings' in Specifications

7   No overhaul of the pump is possible, and if faulty, a new unit must be fitted.

Refitting
8   Refitting is a reversal of removal, but renew the O-ring when reconnecting the fluid pipe union (photo), and tension the alternator/power steering pump drivebelt, as described in Chapter 12.
9   On completion, top-up the fluid level, and bleed the fluid circuit as described in Section 29.

1.8 and 2.0 litre models
Removal
Note: *A new fluid pipe union O-ring must be used on refitting.*

10   Remove the power steering pump drivebelt, as described in Section 30.
11   Disconnect the fluid pipe union and the flexible fluid hose from the

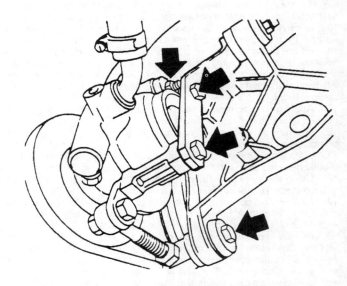

Fig. 10.23 Power steering pump mounting bolts (arrowed) – 1.8 and 2.0 litre engine models (Sec 31)

31.3 Removing the power steering pump pulley – 1.6 litre engine

31.5A Unscrewing the power steering pump fluid pipe union (arrowed) – 1.6 litre engine

31.5B Power steering pump fluid pipe and hose ends covered to prevent dirt ingress and fluid loss

31.6 Removing the power steering pump – 1.6 litre engine

31.8 Renew the power steering pump fluid pipe O-ring (arrowed) on refitting

pump. Be prepared for fluid spillage, and plug the open ends of the pump, pipe and hose, to prevent dirt ingress and further fluid loss.

12   Unscrew and remove the four mounting bolts shown in Fig. 10.23. Recover the nuts, and take care not to lose the rubber insulators which fit into the mounting bracket.

13   Withdraw the pump from the vehicle.

14   No overhaul of the pump is possible, and if faulty, a new unit must be fitted.

Refitting

15   Refitting is a reversal of removal, but renew the O-ring when reconnecting the fluid pipe union, and before finally tightening the pump mounting bolts, tension the drivebelt, as described in Section 30.

16   On completion, top-up the fluid level, and bleed the fluid circuit as described in Section 29.

32   Power steering fluid reservoir – removal and refitting

Removal

1   The reservoir can be removed from the mounting bracket by unscrewing the clamp screw and removing the clamp.

2   Have a suitable container ready to catch the fluid, then disconnect the fluid hoses from the reservoir, and drain the fluid. Plug the open ends of the hoses, to prevent dirt ingress and further fluid loss.

3   If desired, the mounting bracket can be unbolted from the body panel, but note that on certain models, the bolts securing the bracket also secure the ignition coil and suppressor – refer to Chapter 3 if necessary. Where applicable, unclip the brake fluid pipes and any wiring from the bracket before removal.

Refitting

4   Refitting is a reversal of removal, but on completion, bleed the fluid circuit, as described in Section 29.

33   Power steering fluid cooler pipes – removal and refitting

Removal

Note: *New fluid pipe union O-rings must be used on refitting.*

1   For improved access, apply the handbrake, then jack up the front of the vehicle, and support securely on axle stands (see *'Jacking, towing and wheel changing'*).

2   On DOHC engine models, remove the engine undershield, as described in Chapter 11, Section 25.

3   Disconnect the fluid cooler pipe unions (photo). Be prepared for fluid

33.3 Power steering fluid cooler pipes (arrowed) viewed from underneath vehicle – 1.6 litre engine model

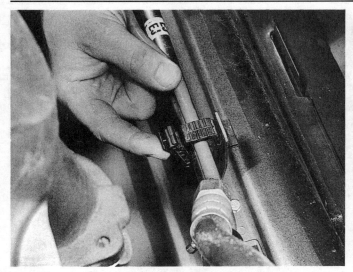

33.4 Releasing a power steering fluid cooler pipe securing clip (viewed from above with radiator removed) – 1.6 litre engine model

spillage, and plug the open ends of the pipes, to prevent dirt ingress and further fluid loss. Recover the O-rings.

4   Release the three plastic clips securing the pipes to the lower body panel (photo), then manipulate the pipes from the engine compartment.

Refitting

5   Refitting is a reversal of removal, but renew the O-rings when reconnecting the fluid pipe unions.

6   On completion, top-up the fluid level, and bleed the fluid circuit as described in Section 29.

34   Tie-rod end/balljoint – removal and refitting

Removal

Note: *A balljoint separator tool will be required for this operation. A new tie-rod end balljoint nut must be used on refitting.*

1   Apply the handbrake, then jack up the front of the vehicle and support securely on axle stands (see *'Jacking, towing and wheel changing'*). Remove the relevant front roadwheel.

2   Loosen the tie-rod end clamp bolt, which secures the tie-rod end to the threaded adjuster pin on the tie-rod (photo).

34.4 Using a balljoint separator tool to disconnect the tie-rod end-to-suspension strut balljoint

34.2 Tie-rod end viewed from underneath

1   *Tie-rod end clamp bolt*   3   *Tie-rod clamp bolt*
2   *Threaded adjuster pin*

3   Unscrew the self-locking nut from the tie-rod end-to-suspension strut balljoint.

4   Using a balljoint separator tool, disconnect the tie-rod end-to-suspension strut balljoint (photo).

5   Note the position of the tie-rod end on the adjuster pin, either by marking the pin with paint or tape, or by counting the number of threads exposed, then unscrew the tie-rod end from the tie-rod.

6   Note that the tie-rod ends are 'handed'. The right-hand tie-rod end is marked 'R', but the left-hand tie-rod end has no marking.

Refitting

7   Commence refitting by screwing the tie-rod end onto the adjuster pin to approximately the same position as was noted during removal.

8   Reconnect the tie-rod end balljoint to the suspension strut, and tighten a new self-locking nut to the specified torque.

9   Tighten the tie-rod end clamp bolt.

10   Refit the roadwheel and lower the vehicle to the ground.

11   Check the front wheel alignment, as described in Section 36, and adjust if necessary. No harm will result from driving the vehicle a short distance to have the alignment checked.

35   Tie-rod – removal and refitting

Removal

Note: *A new tie-rod end-to-steering gear locking plate, and where applicable, a new tie-rod end balljoint nut, must be used on refitting.*

1   The tie-rod can either be removed leaving the tie-rod end in place, or as an assembly with the tie-rod end.

2   Apply the handbrake, then jack up the front of the vehicle and support securely on axle stands (see *'Jacking, towing and wheel changing'*). Remove the relevant front roadwheel.

3   If the tie-rod is to be removed complete with the tie-rod end, proceed as described in Section 34, paragraphs 3 and 4.

4   If the tie-rod is to be removed independently of the tie-rod end, loosen the tie-rod clamp bolt, which secures the tie-rod to the threaded adjuster pin on the tie-rod end.

5   Prise the locking plate from the tie-rod end-to-steering gear bolts, then unscrew and remove the bolts, and recover the washers and spacer plate.

6   If the tie-rod is being removed complete with the tie-rod end, the assembly can now be withdrawn from the vehicle.

7   If the tie-rod is to be removed independently of the tie-rod end, note the position of the tie-rod end on the adjuster pin, either by marking the pin with paint or tape, or by counting the number of threads exposed,

then unscrew the tie-rod from the tie-rod end, and withdraw it from the vehicle.

Refitting

8   Refitting is a reversal of removal, bearing in mind the following points.
9   The tie-rod-to-steering gear bolt locking plate must be renewed on refitting.
10   If the tie-rod is being refitted complete with the tie-rod end, reconnect the tie-rod end balljoint to the suspension strut, and tighten a new self-locking nut to the specified torque.
11   If the tie-rod is being refitted with the tie-rod end already in place on the vehicle, screw the tie-rod onto the adjuster pin to approximately the same position as noted during removal, and tighten the clamp bolt.
12   On completion, check the front wheel alignment, as described in Section 36, and adjust if necessary. No harm will result from driving the vehicle a short distance to have the alignment checked.

36   Wheel alignment and steering angles – general information

1   Accurate front wheel alignment is essential for precise steering and handling, and for even tyre wear. Before carrying out any checking or adjusting operations, make sure that the tyres are correctly inflated, that all steering and suspension joints and linkages are in sound condition, and that the wheels are not buckled or distorted, particularly around the rims. It will also be necessary to have the vehicle positioned on flat, level ground, with enough space to push the car backwards and forwards through about half its length.
2   Front wheel alignment consists of four factors:
Camber is the angle at which the roadwheels are set from the vertical, when viewed from the front or rear of the vehicle. Positive camber is the angle (in degrees) that the wheels are tilted outwards at the top from the vertical.
Castor is the angle between the steering axis and a vertical line when viewed from each side of the vehicle. Positive castor is indicated when the steering axis is inclined towards the rear of the vehicle at its upper end.
Steering axis inclination is the angle, when viewed from the front or rear of the vehicle, between the vertical and an imaginary line drawn between the upper and lower front suspension strut mountings.
Toe setting is the amount by which the distance between the front inside edges of the roadwheels differs from that between the rear inside edges, when measured at hub height. If the distance between the front edges is less than at the rear, the wheels are said to 'toe-in'. If it is greater than at the rear, the wheels are said to 'toe-out'.
3   Camber, castor and steering axis inclination are set during manufacture, and are not adjustable. Unless the vehicle has suffered accident damage, or there is gross wear in the suspension mountings or joints, it can be assumed that these settings are correct. If for any reason it is believed that they are not correct, the task of checking them should be left to a Vauxhall/Opel dealer, who will have the necessary special equipment needed to measure the small angles involved.
4   It is, however, within the scope of the home mechanic to check and adjust the front wheel toe setting. To do this, a tracking gauge must first be obtained. Two types of gauge are available, and can be obtained from motor accessory shops. The first type measures the distance between the front and rear inside edges of the roadwheels, as previously described, with the vehicle stationary. The second type, known as a 'scuff plate', measures the actual position of the contact surface of the tyre, in relation to the road surface, with the vehicle in motion. This is achieved by pushing or driving the front tyre over a plate, which then moves slightly according to the scuff of the tyre, and shows this movement on a scale. Both types have their advantages and disadvantages, but either can give satisfactory results if used correctly and carefully. Alternatively, a tracking gauge can be fabricated from a length of steel tubing, suitably cranked to clear the sump and clutch bellhousing, with a setscrew and locknut at one end.
5   Many tyre specialists will also check toe settings free, or for a nominal charge.
6   Make sure that the steering is in the straight-ahead position when making measurements.
7   If adjustment is found to be necessary, clean the ends of the tie-rods in the area around the adjustment pin and clamp bolts.

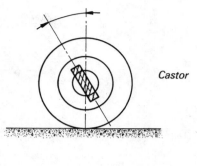

Castor

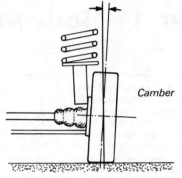

Camber

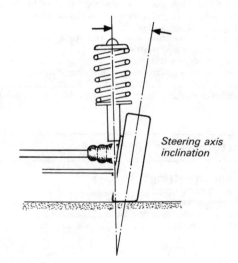

Steering axis inclination

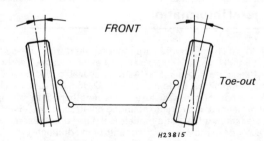

FRONT

Toe-out

H23815

Fig. 10.24 Wheel alignment and steering angles (Sec 36)

8   Slacken the clamp bolts (one on each tie-rod balljoint, and one on each tie-rod), and turn the adjustment pin on each tie-rod by the same amount in the same direction. Only turn each pin by a quarter of a turn at a time before rechecking.
9   When adjustment is correct, tighten the clamp bolts to the specified torque. Check that the tie-rod lengths are equal to within 5.0 mm, and that the steering wheel spokes are in the correct straight-ahead position.

Chapter 11 Bodywork and fittings

Contents

Specifications

Torque wrench settings

	Nm	lbf ft
Tailgate hinge-to-body bolts	20	15
Seat belt mounting bolts	35	26
Seat belt height adjuster securing bolts	20	15
Front seat securing bolts	20	15

1 General information

The bodyshell and floorpan are manufactured from pressed-steel, and together make up the vehicle's structure (monocoque), without the need for a separate chassis. The Astra is available in 4-door Saloon, 3- and 5door Hatchback, 5- door Estate and 2-door Van body styles.

Various areas of the structure are strengthened to provide for suspension, steering and engine mounting points, and load distribution. One notable feature of all Astra models is the use of tubular reinforcing bars in the doors, to provide the occupants with additional protection in the event of a side impact.

Extensive corrosion protection is applied to all new vehicles. Various anti-corrosion preparations are used, including galvanising, zinc phosphatisation, and PVC underseal. Protective wax is injected into the box sections and other hollow cavities.

Extensive use is made of plastic for peripheral components, such as the radiator grille, bumpers and wheel trims, and for much of the interior trim.

Interior fittings are to a high standard on all models, and a wide range of optional equipment is available throughout the range.

2 Maintenance – bodywork and underframe

Cleaning the vehicle's exterior

The general condition of a vehicle's bodywork is the one thing that significantly affects its value. Maintenance is easy but needs to be regular. Neglect, particularly after minor damage, can lead quickly to further deterioration and costly repair bills. It is important also to keep watch on those parts of the vehicle not immediately visible, for instance the underbody, inside all the wheel arches and the lower part of the engine compartment.

The basic maintenance routine for the bodywork is washing – preferably with a lot of water, from a hose. This will remove all the loose solids which may have stuck to the vehicle. It is important to flush these off in such a way as to prevent grit from scratching the finish. The wheel arches and underbody need washing in the same way to remove any accumulated mud, which will retain moisture and tend to encourage rust, particularly in Winter, when it is essential that any salt (from that put down on the roads) is washed off. Paradoxically enough, the best time to clean the underbody and wheel arches is in wet weather, when the mud is thoroughly wet and soft. In very wet weather, the underbody is usually cleaned automatically of large accumulations; this is therefore a good time for inspection.

If the vehicle is very dirty, especially underneath or in the engine compartment, it is tempting to use one of the pressure-washers or steam-cleaners available on garage forecourts; while these are quick and effective, especially for the removal of the accumulation of oily grime which sometimes is allowed to become thick in certain areas, their usage does have some disadvantages. If caked-on dirt is simply blasted off the paintwork, its finish soon becomes scratched and dull, and the pressure can allow water to penetrate door and window seals and the lock mechanisms; if the full force of such a jet is directed at the vehicle's underbody, the wax-based protective coating can easily be damaged, and water (with whatever cleaning solvent is used) could be forced into crevices or components that it would not normally reach. Similarly, if such equipment is used to clean the engine compartment, water can be forced into the components of the fuel and electrical systems, and the protective coating can be removed that is applied to many small components during manufacture; this may therefore actually *promote* corrosion (especially inside electrical connectors) and initiate engine problems or other electrical faults. Also, if the jet is pointed directly at any of the oil seals, water can be forced past the seal lips and into the engine or transmission. Great care is required, therefore, if such equipment is used and, in general, regular cleaning by such methods should be avoided.

A much better solution in the long term is just to flush away as much loose dirt as possible using a hose alone, even if this leaves the engine compartment looking 'dirty'. If an oil leak has developed, or if any other accumulation of oil or grease is to be removed, there are one or two excellent grease solvents available, such as Holts Engine Cleaner or Holts Foambrite, which can be brush-applied. The dirt can then be simply hosed off. Take care to replace the wax-based protective coat, if this was affected by the solvent.

Normal washing of the vehicle's bodywork is best carried out using cold or warm water, with a proprietary vehicle shampoo such as Holts Turtle Wax Zipwax or Turtle Extra Car Wash and Wax. Remove dead insects with products such as Holts Fly Squash Remover; tar spots can be removed either by using white spirit, followed by soapy water to remove all traces of spirit, or by using Holts Body + Plus Tar Remover. Try to keep water out of the bonnet air intakes, and check afterwards that the heater air inlet box drain tube is clear, so that any water has drained out of the box.

After washing the paintwork, wipe off with a chamois leather to give an unspotted clear finish. A coat of clear protective wax polish, such as one of the many excellent Turtle Wax polishes, will give added protection against chemical pollutants in the air. If the paintwork sheen has dulled or oxidised, use a cleaner/polisher combination such as Turtle Extra to restore the brilliance of the shine. This requires a little effort, but such dulling is usually caused because regular washing has been neglected. Care needs to be taken with metallic paintwork, as special non-abrasive cleaner/polisher is required to avoid damage to the finish. Brightwork should be treated in the same way as paintwork.

Windscreens and windows can be kept clear of the smeary film which often appears, by the use of proprietary glass cleaner like Holts Mixra. Never use any form of wax or other body or chromium polish on glass.

Exterior paintwork and body panels check

Once the vehicle has been washed, and all tar spots and other surface blemishes have been cleaned off, check carefully all paintwork, looking closely for chips or scratches; check with particular care vulnerable areas such as the front (bonnet and spoiler) and around the wheel arches. Any damage to the paintwork must be rectified as soon as possible, to comply with the terms of the manufacturer's cosmetic and anti-corrosion warranties; check with a Vauxhall/Opel dealer for details.

If a chip or (light) scratch is found that is recent and still free from rust, it can be touched-up using the appropriate touch-up pencil; these can be obtained from Vauxhall/Opel dealers or from the Holts Dupli-Color Color Touch range. Any more serious damage, or rusted stone chips, can be repaired as described in Section 4, but if damage or corrosion is so severe that a panel must be renewed, seek professional advice as soon as possible.

Always check that the door and ventilator opening drain holes and pipes are completely clear, so that water can drain out.

Underbody sealer check

The wax-based underbody protective coating should be inspected annually, preferably just prior to Winter, when the underbody should be washed down as thoroughly but gently as possible (see the above concerning steam cleaners, etc.) and any damage to the coating repaired using Holts Undershield; if any of the body panels are disturbed for repair or renewed, do not forget to replace the coating and to inject wax into door panels, sills, box sections, etc., to maintain the level of protection provided by the vehicle manufacturer.

3 Maintenance – upholstery and carpets

Mats and carpets should be brushed or vacuum-cleaned regularly, to keep them free of grit. If they are badly stained, remove them from the vehicle for scrubbing or sponging, and make quite sure they are dry before refitting.

Fabric-trimmed seats and interior trim panels can be kept clean by wiping with a damp cloth and Turtle Wax Carisma. If they do become stained (which can be more apparent on light-coloured upholstery) use a little liquid detergent and a soft nail brush to scour the grime out of the grain of the material. Do not forget to keep the headlining clean in the same way as the (fabric) upholstery.

When using liquid cleaners of any sort inside the vehicle, do not over-wet the surfaces being cleaned. Excessive damp could get into the seams and padded interior, causing stains, offensive odours or even rot. If the inside of the vehicle gets wet accidentally, it is worthwhile taking some trouble to dry it out properly, particularly where carpets are involved. *Do not leave oil/paraffin-burning or electric heaters inside the vehicle for this purpose.*

4 Minor body damage – repair

Note: *The photographic sequence between pages 32 and 33 illustrates the operations detailed in the following sub-Sections. For more detailed information about bodywork repair, the Haynes Publishing Group publish a book by Lindsay Porter called 'The Car Bodywork Repair Manual'. This incorporates information on such aspects as rust treatment, painting and glass-fibre repairs, as well as details on more ambitious repairs involving welding and panel-beating.*

Repair of minor scratches in bodywork

If the scratch is very superficial and does not penetrate to the metal of the bodywork, repair is very simple. Lightly rub the area of the scratch with a paintwork renovator, such as Turtle Wax New Color Back, or a very fine cutting paste, like Holts Body + Plus Rubbing Compound, to remove loose paint from the scratch and to clear the surrounding bodywork of wax polish. Rinse the area with clean water.

Apply touch-up paint, such as Holts Dupli-Color Color Touch, or a paint film, such as Holts Autofilm, to the scratch using a fine paint brush; continue to apply fine layers of paint until the surface of the paint in the scratch is level with the surrounding paintwork. Allow the new paint at least two weeks to harden, then blend it into the surrounding paintwork by rubbing the scratch area with a paintwork renovator, such as Turtle Wax New Color Back, or a very fine cutting paste, like Holts Body + Plus Rubbing Compound. Finally, apply wax polish from one of the Turtle Wax range of wax polishes.

Where the scratch has penetrated right through to the metal of the bodywork, causing the metal to rust, a different repair technique is required. Remove any loose rust from the bottom of the scratch with a penknife, then apply rust-inhibiting paint, such as Turtle Wax Rust Master, to prevent the formation of rust in the future. Using a rubber or nylon applicator, fill the scratch with bodystopper paste, such as Holts Body + Plus Knifing Putty. If required, this paste can be mixed with cellulose thinners, such as Holts Body + Plus Cellulose Thinners, to provide a very thin paste which is ideal for filling narrow scratches. Before the stopper-paste in the scratch hardens, wrap a piece of smooth cotton rag around the top of a finger. Dip the finger in cellulose thinners, such as Holts Body + Plus Cellulose Thinners, and quickly sweep it across the surface of the stopper-paste in the scratch; this will ensure that the surface of the stopper-paste is slightly hollowed. The scratch can now be painted over as described earlier in this Section.

Repair of dents in bodywork

When deep denting of the vehicle's bodywork has taken place, the first task is to pull the dent out, until the affected bodywork almost attains its original shape. There is little point in trying to restore the original shape completely, as the metal in the damaged area will have stretched on impact, and cannot be reshaped fully to its original contour. It is better to bring the level of the dent up to a point which is about 3 mm below the level of the surrounding bodywork. In cases where the dent is very shallow anyway, it is not worth trying to pull it out at all. If the underside of the dent is accessible, it can be hammered out gently from behind, using a mallet with a wooden or plastic head. Whilst doing this, hold a suitable block of wood firmly against the outside of the panel, to absorb the impact from the hammer blows and thus prevent a large area of the bodywork from being 'belled-out'.

Should the dent be in a section of the bodywork which has a double skin or some other factor making it inaccessible from behind, a different technique is called for. Drill several small holes through the metal inside the area – particularly in the deeper sections. Then screw long self-tapping screws into the holes just sufficiently for them to gain a good purchase in the metal. Now the dent can be pulled out by pulling on the protruding heads of the screws with a pair of pliers.

The next stage of the repair is the removal of the paint from the damaged area, and from an inch or so of the surrounding 'sound' bodywork. This is accomplished most easily by using a wire brush or abrasive pad on a power drill, although it can be done just as effectively by hand using sheets of abrasive paper. To complete the preparation for filling, score the surface of the bare metal with a screwdriver or the tang of a file, or alternatively, drill small holes in the affected area. This will provide a really good 'key' for the filler paste.

To complete the repair, see the Section on filling and respraying.

Repair of rust holes or gashes in bodywork

Remove all paint from the affected area, and from an inch or so of the surrounding 'sound' bodywork, using an abrasive pad or a wire brush on a power drill. If these are not available, a few sheets of abrasive paper will do the job most effectively. With the paint removed, you will be able to judge the severity of the corrosion, and therefore decide whether to renew the whole panel (if this is possible) or to repair the affected area. New body panels are not as expensive as most people think, and it is often quicker and more satisfactory to fit a new panel than to attempt to repair large areas of corrosion.

Remove all fittings from the affected area except those which will act as a guide to the original shape of the damaged bodywork (eg headlight shells, etc.). Then, using tin snips or a hacksaw blade, remove all loose metal and any other metal badly affected by corrosion. Hammer the edges of the hole inwards, in order to create a slight depression for the filler paste.

Wire brush the affected area to remove the powdery rust from the surface of the remaining metal. Paint the affected area with rust-inhibiting paint, such as Turtle Wax Rust Master; if the back of the rusted area is accessible, treat this also.

Before filling can take place, it will be necessary to block the hole in some way. This can be achieved by the use of aluminium or plastic mesh, or aluminium tape.

Aluminium or plastic mesh or glass-fibre matting, such as Holts Body + Plus Glass-Fibre Matting, is probably the best material to use for a large hole. Cut a piece to the approximate size and shape of the hole to be filled, then position it in the hole so that its edges are below the level of the surrounding bodywork. It can be retained in position by several blobs of filler paste around its periphery.

Aluminium tape should be used for small or very narrow holes. Pull a piece off the roll, and trim it to the approximate size and shape required; pull off the backing paper (if used) and stick the tape over the hole – it can be overlapped if the thickness of one piece is insufficient. Burnish down the edges of the tape with the handle of a screwdriver or similar, to ensure that the tape is securely attached to the metal underneath.

Bodywork repairs – filling and respraying

Before using this Section, see the Sections on dent, deep scratch, rust hole and gash repairs.

Many types of bodyfiller are available, but generally speaking those proprietary kits which contain a tin of filler paste and a tube of resin hardener (such as Holts Body + Plus, or Holts No-Mix which can be used directly from the tube) are best for this type of repair. A wide, flexible plastic or nylon applicator will be found invaluable for imparting a smooth and well-contoured finish to the surface of the filler.

Mix up a little filler on a clean piece of card or board – measure the hardener carefully (follow the maker's instructions on the pack) otherwise the filler will set too rapidly or too slowly. Alternatively, Holts No-Mix can be used straight from the tube without mixing, but daylight is required to cure it. Using the applicator, apply the filler paste to the prepared area; draw the applicator across the surface of the filler to achieve the correct contour and to level the surface. As soon as a contour that approximates to the correct one is achieved, stop working the paste – if you carry on too long, the paste will become sticky, and begin to 'pick-up' on the applicator. Continue to add thin layers of filler paste at twenty-minute intervals, until the level of the filler is just proud of the surrounding bodywork.

Once the filler has hardened, the excess can be removed using a metal plane or file. From then on, progressively-finer grades of abrasive paper should be used, starting with a 40-grade production paper and finishing with a 400-grade wet-and-dry paper. Always wrap the abrasive paper around a flat rubber, cork, or wooden block – otherwise the surface of the filler will not be completely flat. During the smoothing of the filler surface, the wet-and-dry paper should be periodically rinsed in water. This will ensure that a very smooth finish is imparted to the filler at the final stage.

At this stage, the 'dent' should be surrounded by a ring of bare metal, which in turn should be encircled by the finely 'feathered' edge of the good paintwork. Rinse the repair area with clean water, until all of the dust produced by the rubbing-down operation has gone.

Spray the whole area with a light coat of primer, either Holts Body + Plus Grey or Red Oxide Primer – this will show up any imperfections in the surface of the filler. Repair these imperfections with fresh filler paste or bodystopper, and once more smooth the surface with abrasive paper. If bodystopper is used, it can be mixed with cellulose thinners to form a really thin paste which is ideal for filling small holes. Repeat this spray-and-repair procedure until you are satisfied that the surface of the filler and the feathered edge of the paintwork are perfect. Clean the repair area with clean water, and allow to dry fully.

The repair area is now ready for final spraying. Paint spraying must be carried out in a warm, dry, windless and dust-free atmosphere. This condition can be created artificially if you have access to a large indoor working area, but if you are forced to work in the open, you will have to pick your day very carefully. If you are working indoors, dousing the floor in the work area with water will help to settle the dust which would otherwise be in the atmosphere. If the repair area is confined to one body panel, mask off the surrounding panels; this will help to minimise the effects of a slight mis-match in paint colours. Bodywork fittings (eg chrome strips, door handles, etc.) will also need to be masked off. Use genuine masking tape and several thicknesses of newspaper for the masking operations.

Before starting to spray, agitate the aerosol can thoroughly, then spray a test area (an old tin, or similar) until the technique is mastered. Cover the repair area with a thick coat of primer; the thickness should be built up using several thin layers of paint rather than one thick one. Using 400-grade wet-and-dry paper, rub down the surface of the primer until it is really smooth. While doing this, the work area should be thoroughly doused with water, and the wet-and-dry paper periodically rinsed in water. Allow to dry before spraying on more paint.

Spray on the top coat using Holts Dupli-Color Autospray, again building up the thickness by using several thin layers of paint. Start spraying in the centre of the repair area and then, with a side-to-side motion, work outwards until the whole repair area and about 50 mm of the surrounding original paintwork is covered. Remove all masking material ten to fifteen minutes after spraying on the final coat of paint.

Allow the new paint at least two weeks to harden. After this time, using a paintwork renovator such as Turtle Wax New Color Back (or a very fine cutting paste, like Holts Body + Plus Rubbing Compound) blend the edges of the paint into the existing paintwork. Finally, apply wax polish from one of the Turtle Wax range of wax polishes.

Plastic components

With the use of more and more plastic body components by the vehicle manufacturers (eg bumpers, spoilers and in some cases major body panels), rectification of more serious damage to such items has

6.5 Front bumper side securing screws (arrowed)

6.6 Front bumper-to-body front panel securing nut

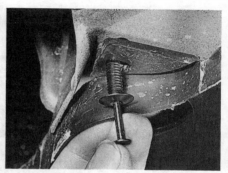

6.7 Removing a front bumper securing clip

become a matter of either entrusting repair work to a specialist in this field, or renewing complete components. Repair of such damage by the DIY owner is not really feasible, owing to the cost of the equipment and materials required for effecting such repairs. The basic technique involves making a groove along the line of the crack in the plastic using a rotary burr in a power drill. The damaged part is then welded back together by using a hot air gun to heat up and fuse a plastic filler rod into the groove. Any excess plastic is then removed, and the area rubbed down to a smooth finish. It is important that a filler rod of the correct plastic is used, as body components can be made of a variety of different types (eg polycarbonate, ABS, polypropylene).

Damage of a less-serious nature (abrasions, minor cracks, etc.) can be repaired by the DIY owner using a two-part epoxy filler repair material such as Holts Body + Plus, or Holts No-Mix which can be used directly from the tube. Once mixed in equal proportions (or applied direct from the tube in the case of Holts No-Mix), this is used in similar fashion to the bodywork filler used on metal panels. The filler is usually cured in twenty to thirty minutes, ready for sanding and painting.

If the owner is renewing a complete component himself, or if he has repaired it with epoxy filler, he will be left with the problem of finding a suitable paint for finishing which is compatible with the type of plastic used. At one time, the use of a universal paint was not possible, owing to the complex range of plastics encountered in body component applications. Standard paints, generally speaking, will not bond satisfactorily to plastic or rubber, but Holts Professional Spraymatch paints to match any plastic or rubber finish can be obtained from dealers. However, it is now possible to obtain a plastic body parts finishing kit which consists of a pre-primer treatment, a primer, and coloured top coat. Full instructions are normally supplied with a kit, but basically the method of use is to first apply the pre-primer to the component concerned, and allow it to dry for up to thirty minutes. Then the primer is applied, and left to dry for about an hour before finally applying the special coloured top coat. The result is a correctly-coloured component where the paint will flex with the plastic or rubber, a property that standard paint does not normally possess.

5 Major body damage – repair

Where serious damage has occurred, or large areas need renewal due to neglect, it means that complete new panels will need welding-in; this is best left to professionals. If the damage is due to impact, it will also be necessary to check completely the alignment of the bodyshell; this can only be carried out accurately by a Vauxhall/Opel dealer using special jigs. If the body is left misaligned, it is primarily dangerous (as the car will not handle properly) and secondly, uneven stresses will be imposed on the steering, suspension and possibly transmission, causing abnormal wear or complete failure, particularly to items such as the tyres.

6 Front and rear bumpers – removal and refitting

Front bumper

Removal

1   The bumper is removed as a complete assembly with the front trim panel; on models with front foglights, disconnect the battery negative lead and disconnect the foglight wiring plugs.
2   If desired, for improved access, apply the handbrake, then jack up the front of the vehicle, and support securely on axle stands (see *Jacking, towing and wheel changing*).
3   Remove the radiator grille, as described in Section 7.
4   Working under the wheel arches, remove the screws and/or clips, as applicable, securing the rear edges of the bumper to the wheel arch liners.
5   Unscrew the two screws securing each side of the bumper to the brackets on the body (photo).
6   Unscrew the two nuts (one at each side of the bumper) securing the bumper to the body front panel (photo). Recover the washers.
7   Remove the four plastic clips securing the lower edge of the bumper to the lower body panel. To remove the clips, prise out the central pins, using a screwdriver if necessary, then pull the clips from the bumper (photo).
8   Carefully withdraw the bumper from the vehicle.

Refitting

9   Refitting is a reversal of removal.

Rear bumper

Removal

10   The bumper is removed as a complete assembly with the rear trim panel.
11   On Saloon and Hatchback models, remove the rear number plate light(s), as described in Chapter 12.

H.22806

Fig. 11.1 Rear bumper securing screw and nut locations (Sec 6)

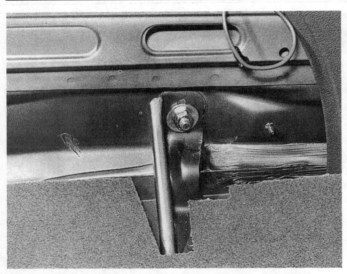

6.14 Rear bumper-to-rear body panel securing nut – Hatchback model

12   Working under the wheel arches, unscrew the two screws securing each side of the bumper to the brackets on the body.
13   Where applicable, remove the rear luggage compartment trim panel for access to the bumper-to-rear body panel nuts. On Estate and Van models, note that it will be necessary to lift the spare wheel cover for access to one of the bumper securing nuts.
14   Unscrew the two bumper-to-rear body panel nuts (one at each side of the bumper) (photo). Recover the washers.
15   Carefully withdraw the bumper from the vehicle.

Refitting
16   Refitting is a reversal of removal.

7   Radiator grille – removal and refitting

Removal
1   Open the bonnet.
2   Carefully lever the top of the grille forwards to release the upper securing clips (photo).
3   Using a suitable screwdriver, carefully release the clips from each end of the grille, below the headlights (photo).
4   Slide the grille towards the right-hand side of the vehicle, to release the lower securing clips, then lift the grille from the vehicle (photo).
5   Where applicable, disconnect the fluid hoses from the headlight washer nozzles, which are integral with the grille panel.
6   Carefully manipulate the grille from the front panel, and withdraw it from the vehicle.

Refitting
7   Refitting is a reversal of removal, ensuring that all the clips are positively engaged.

7.2 Releasing a radiator grille upper securing clip

7.3 Radiator grille end securing clip released from below headlight

7.4 Radiator grille lower securing clip released from body front panel

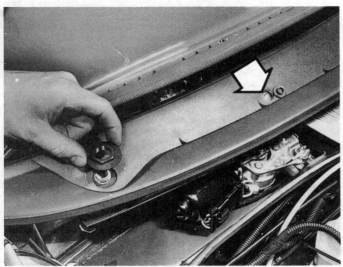

8.4 Removing a windscreen cowl panel securing screw nut from the wiper arm spindle. Cowl panel securing screw arrowed

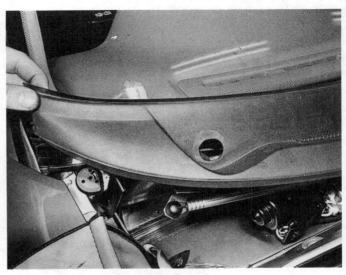

8.5 Removing the windscreen cowl panel

8 Windscreen cowl panel – removal and refitting

Removal

1 Open the bonnet.
2 Remove the windscreen wiper arms, as described in Chapter 12.
3 Unscrew the two large nuts from the windscreen wiper arm spindles.
4 Prise the two screw covers from the cowl panel, and remove the securing screws (photo).
5 Note how the cowl panel engages with the weatherseal at the base of the windscreen, then carefully release the ends of the cowl panel from the scuttle (the ends of the panel are secured with Velcro strips), and withdraw the panel from the vehicle (photo).

Refitting

6 Refitting is a reversal of removal, bearing in mind the following points.
7 Ensure that the panel is correctly engaged with the weatherseal.
8 Make sure that the ends of the panel are securely held by the Velcro strips.
9 Refit the windscreen wiper arms as described in Chapter 12.

9 Bonnet and hinges – removal and refitting

Bonnet

Removal

1 Open the bonnet and support it in the fully-open position.
2 Disconnect the windscreen washer fluid hose from the connector in the bonnet. It is advisable to tie a length of string to the connector, to prevent it from slipping into an inaccessible position in the bonnet.
3 If the original bonnet is to be refitted, mark the position of the hinges on the bonnet, to alignment on refitting.
4 Carefully pull back the insulation blocks from the bonnet hinges.
5 With the help of an assistant, support the weight of the bonnet, then unscrew the securing bolts from the hinges, and lift the bonnet from the vehicle. If the bonnet is to be refitted, rest it carefully on rags or cardboard, to avoid damaging the paint.

Refitting

6 Refitting is a reversal of removal, bearing in mind the following points.

7 If a new bonnet is to be fitted, transfer all the serviceable fixings (rubber buffers, lock strikers, etc.) to it.
8 Where applicable, align the hinges with the previously-made marks on the bonnet.
9 If the lock striker has been disturbed, adjust it to the dimension shown in Fig. 11.3, then tighten the locknut.
10 If necessary, adjust the hinge bolts and the front rubber buffers until a good fit is obtained with the bonnet shut.

Hinge

Removal

Note: *To secure the hinge on refitting, a bolt and washer assembly will be required, which can be obtained from a Vauxhall/Opel dealer.*
11 Remove the bonnet, as described previously in this Section.
12 Remove the windscreen cowl panel, as described in Section 8.
13 The bonnet hinges are riveted to the body panels, and to remove a hinge, it will be necessary to drill or grind off the rivet head.
14 With the rivet head removed, tap the rivet from the hinge assembly, and withdraw the hinge.

Refitting

15 When refitting the hinge, a bolt and washer assembly must be used to replace the rivet used originally.
16 Secure the hinge using the bolt and washer assembly (available from a Vauxhall/Opel dealer), ensuring that the components are located as shown in Fig. 11.2.
17 Refit the windscreen cowl panel, with reference to Section 8.
18 Refit the bonnet as described previously in this Section.

10 Bonnet lock components – removal and refitting

Bonnet lock hook

Removal

1 The bonnet lock hook is riveted to the bonnet, and removal involves drilling out the rivet.

Refitting

2 Refitting is a reversal of removal, using a new rivet.

Lock striker

Removal

3 To remove the lock striker from the bonnet, loosen the locknut, then unscrew the striker, and recover the washer and spring.

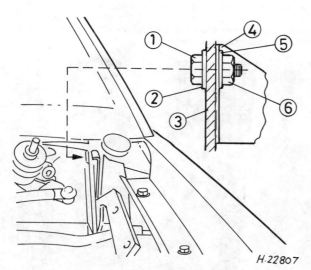

Fig. 11.2 Bonnet hinge-to-body fixing components (Sec 9)

1 Bolt
2 Spring washer
3 Hinge
4 Body bracket
5 Washer
6 Nut

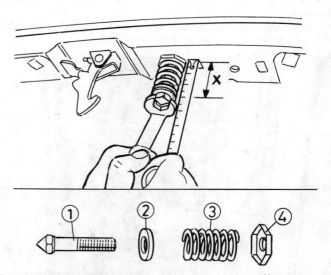

Fig. 11.3 Bonnet lock striker adjustment (Sec 10)   H.22808

1 Striker
2 Washer
3 Coil spring
4 Locknut
X = 40 to 45 mm

Refitting

4   Refitting is a reversal of removal, but adjust the striker dimension as shown in Fig. 11.3 before tightening the locknut.

Locking spring

Removal

5   Disconnect the end of the bonnet release cable from the spring, then unhook the end of the spring from the slot in the front body panel, taking care not to damage the paint.

Refitting

6   Refitting is a reversal of removal.

11   Bonnet release cable – removal and refitting

Removal

1   Open the bonnet, and support it in the fully-open position.
2   Unscrew the release cable clip from the front body panel.
3   Disconnect the end of the release cable from the locking spring under the front body panel.
4   Disconnect the release cable from the release lever in the driver's footwell. If necessary, remove the release lever from its retainer for access to the cable end.
5   Pull the cable assembly through the grommet in the engine compartment bulkhead and into the engine compartment.
6   Note the routing of the cable, then release the cable from any remaining clips and cable ties, and withdraw it from the engine compartment.

Refitting

7   Refitting is a reversal of removal, but ensure that the cable is correctly routed, and on completion, check the release mechanism for satisfactory operation.

12   Doors – removal, refitting and adjustment

Front door

Removal

1   To remove a door, open it fully and support it under its lower edge on blocks or axle stands covered with pads of rag.

12.2 Front door wiring connector

2   Disconnect the wiring connector from the front edge of the door. To release the connector, twist the locking collar, then pull the connector from the socket in the door (photo).
3   Using a suitable punch, drive the large roll-pin from the door check arm pivot (photo).
4   Where applicable, remove the plastic covers from the hinge pins, then drive out the pins using a suitable punch. Have an assistant support the door as the pins are driven out, then withdraw the door from the vehicle.

Refitting

5   Refitting is a reversal of removal, using a new check-link roll-pin.

Adjustment

6   The door hinges are welded onto the door frame and the body pillar, so that there is no provision for adjustment or alignment.
7   If the door can be moved up and down on its hinges due to wear in the hinge pins or their holes, it may be possible to drill out the holes and fit slightly oversize pins. Consult a Vauxhall/Opel dealer for further advice.
8   Door closure may be adjusted by altering the position of the lock striker on the body pillar, using an Allen key or a suitable hexagon bit.

Rear door

Removal

9   On models with central locking, Remove the door inner trim panel, as described in Section 30, and disconnect the wiring connector inside the door. Note the routing of the wiring, and the location of the wiring connector, then carefully feed the wiring through the grommet in the front edge of the door.
10   Proceed as described in paragraphs 3 and 4.

Refitting

11   Refitting is a reversal of removal, using a new check-link roll-pin.
12   Where applicable, ensure that the wiring and the connector are routed and located as noted during removal.

13   Door handle and lock components – removal and refitting

Door interior handle

Removal

1   Remove the door inner trim panel, as described in Section 30.
2   Using a screwdriver, carefully release the retaining clips and pull the handle assembly from the door, then unhook the operating rod, and withdraw the assembly (photos).

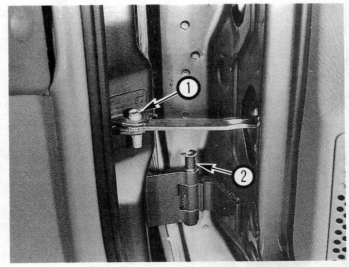

12.3 Front door check-link roll-pin (1) and hinge pin (2)

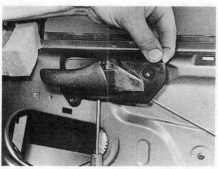

13.2A Releasing a front door interior handle retaining clip

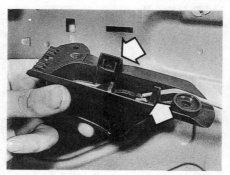

13.2B Front door interior handle retaining clips (arrowed)

13.5 Front door exterior handle securing nuts (1) and central locking microswitch (2)

Refitting

3   Refitting is a reversal of removal, but check the mechanism for satisfactory operation before refitting the door inner trim panel, then refit the trim panel with reference to Section 30.

Front door exterior handle

Removal

4   Remove the door inner trim panel, and peel back the plastic insulating sheet for access to the handle, as described in Section 30.
5   Unscrew the two nuts securing the exterior handle to the door (photo).
6   Where applicable, unclip the central locking microswitch from the rear edge of the exterior handle assembly.
7   Release the two lower retaining clips, then manipulate the outer plastic section of the exterior handle assembly through the outside of the door, and disconnect the operating rod (photo).
8   Withdraw the inner section of the exterior handle assembly from the inside of the door, and disconnect the lock cylinder operating rod.

Refitting

9   Refitting is a reversal of removal, but check the operation of the mechanism before refitting the door inner trim panel, and refit the trim panel with reference to Section 30.

Rear door exterior handle – Saloon and Hatchback models

Removal

10   Remove the door inner trim panel, and peel back the plastic insulating sheet for access to the handle, as described in Section 30.

13.7 Withdrawing the outer section of a front door exterior handle

11   Pull the weatherstrips from the inside and outside lower edges of the window aperture.
12   Unscrew the upper window rear guide rail securing bolt, which is accessible at the rear edge of the window aperture.
13   Unscrew the lower window rear guide rail securing bolt (Torx type), which is accessible through the inner door skin, then withdraw the guide rail from the door. Where applicable, the weatherstrip can be left attached to the guide rail, in which case, position the guide rail to one side out of the way, taking care not to damage the vehicle paintwork.
14   Unscrew the two nuts securing the exterior handle to the door.
15   Release the two lower retaining clips, then manipulate the exterior handle assembly through the outside of the door, and disconnect the operating rods.

Refitting

16   Proceed as described in paragraph 9.

Rear door exterior handle – Estate models

Removal

17   Remove the door inner trim panel, and peel back the plastic insulating sheet for access to the handle, as described in Section 30.
18   Unscrew the two nuts securing the exterior handle to the door.
19   Release the two lower retaining clips, then manipulate the exterior handle assembly through the outside of the door, and disconnect the operating rods.

Refitting

20   Proceed as described in paragraph 9.

Front door lock

Removal

21   Remove the door inner trim panel, and peel back the plastic insulating sheet from the rear edge of the door, as described in Section 30.
22   Unscrew the window rear guide rail securing bolt from the rear edge of the door, then manipulate the guide rail out through the lower aperture in the door.
23   Where applicable, reach in through the door aperture and unclip the plastic cover from the lock.
24   Working through the apertures in the door, disconnect the three operating rods from the lock assembly.
25   On models with central locking, disconnect the battery negative lead (if not already done), then reach in through the door aperture, and disconnect the wiring plug from the central locking motor (photo).
26   Unscrew the three Torx screws securing the lock assembly to the rear edge of the door, then manipulate the lock assembly (complete with the lock button operating rod, and the central locking motor, where applicable) around the window regulator mechanism, and out through the lower door aperture (photos).

Refitting

27   Refitting is a reversal of removal, but check the operation of the door lock, handle and window regulator mechanisms before refitting the door trim panel, and refit the trim panel with reference to Section 30. If the lock operation is not satisfactory, note that the exterior handle operating rod can be adjusted by turning the knurled plastic adjuster wheel at the end of the rod.

13.25 Disconnecting the central locking motor wiring plug from a front door lock

13.26A Unscrewing a front door lock securing screw

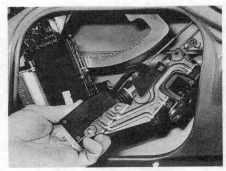

13.26B Withdrawing a front door lock assembly through the lower door aperture

Rear door lock – Saloon and Hatchback models

Removal

28   Fully lower the window, then remove the door inner trim panel and the plastic insulating sheet, as described in Section 30.

29   Pull the weatherstrips from the inside and outside lower edges of the window aperture.

30   Unscrew the upper window rear guide rail securing bolt, which is accessible at the rear edge of the window aperture.

31   Unscrew the lower window rear guide rail securing bolt (Torx type), which is accessible through the inner door skin, then withdraw the guide rail from the door. Where applicable, the weatherstrip can be left attached to the guide rail, in which case, position the guide rail to one side out of the way, taking care not to damage the vehicle paintwork.

32   Where applicable, reach in through the door aperture, and unclip the plastic cover from the lock.

33   Working through the apertures in the door, disconnect the operating rods from the lock assembly.

34   On models with central locking, disconnect the battery negative lead (if not already done), and disconnect the wiring plug from the central locking motor.

35   Unscrew the three Torx screws securing the lock assembly to the rear edge of the door, then manipulate the lock assembly (complete with the lock button operating rod, and the central locking motor, where applicable) around the window regulator mechanism, and out through the lower door aperture.

Refitting

36   Proceed as described in paragraph 27.

Rear door lock – Estate models

Removal

37   Fully lower the window, then remove the door inner trim panel and the plastic insulating sheet, as described in Section 30.

38   Working at the top of the window aperture, remove the two upper rear window rear guide rail securing screws.

39   Working at the bottom of the window aperture, remove the lower rear window guide securing screw, then remove the rear window guide securing bolt and nut, and withdraw the window guide upwards through the window aperture.

40   Proceed as described in paragraphs 32 to 35 inclusive.

Refitting

41   Proceed as described in paragraph 27.

Front door lock cylinder

Removal

42   Remove the door exterior handle, as described in earlier in this Section.

43   Insert the key into the lock, then extract the circlip from the end of the lock cylinder (photo).

44   Withdraw the lock cylinder using the key, and recover the lever assembly.

Refitting

45   Refitting is a reversal of removal, but check the operation of the

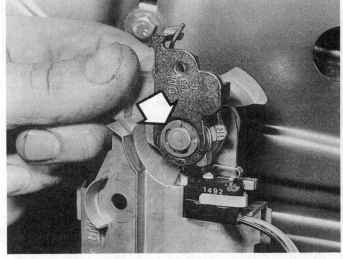

13.43 Front door lock cylinder securing circlip (arrowed)

door lock, handle and window regulator mechanism before refitting the door trim panel, and refit the trim panel with reference to Section 30.

Lock striker

Removal

46   The lock striker is screwed into the door pillar on the body.

47   Before removing the striker, mark its position, so that it can be refitted in exactly the same position.

48   To remove the striker, simply unscrew the securing screw using a suitable Allen key or hexagon bit.

Refitting

49   Refitting is a reversal of removal, but if necessary, adjust the position of the striker to achieve satisfactory closing of the door.

Central locking components

50   Refer to Section 19.

14   Door window glass and regulators – removal and refitting

Front door window glass

Removal

1   Remove the door inner trim panel and the plastic insulating sheet, as described in Section 30.

14.2A Removing the weatherstrip from the inside of the front door window aperture

14.2B Removing the weatherstrip from the outside of the front door window aperture (door mirror removed)

14.3A Unscrewing the window rear guide rail securing bolt from the front door ...

14.3B ... and withdrawing the rear guide rail

14.5 Prising the end stop from the front door window glass guide channel

14.6A Unscrewing a front door window lower guide rail securing bolt ...

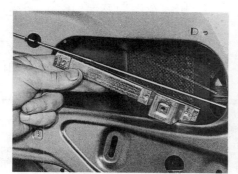

14.6B ... and withdrawing the lower guide rail

14.7 Withdrawing the front door window glass

2   Pull the weatherstrips from the inside and outside lower edges of the window aperture. Note that on certain models, it may be necessary to remove the door mirror (see Section 21) to enable removal of the outside weatherstrip (photos).
3   Unscrew the window rear guide rail securing bolt from the rear edge of the door, then manipulate the guide rail out through the lower aperture in the door (photos).
4   Where applicable, reconnect the battery negative lead and the electric window switch wiring, and lower the window until the metal guide channel at the bottom edge of the window glass is accessible through the door aperture.
5   Prise the plastic end stop from the window glass guide channel (photo).
6   Unscrew the two securing bolts, and remove the window lower guide rail from the door (photos).
7   Manipulate the window regulator mechanism as necessary, and tilt the window glass forwards until it can be withdrawn from outside the door through the window aperture (photo).

Refitting

8   Refitting is a reversal of removal, but adjust the angle of the lower guide rail by means of the two securing screws until smooth operation of the window is achieved, and refit the door inner trim panel with reference to Section 30.

Rear door window glass – Saloon and Hatchback models

Removal

9   Fully lower the window, then remove the door inner trim panel and the plastic insulating sheet, as described in Section 30.
10   Pull the weatherstrips from the inside and outside lower edges of the window aperture.
11   Unscrew the upper window rear guide rail securing bolt, which is accessible at the rear edge of the window aperture.
12   Unscrew the lower window rear guide rail securing bolt (Torx type), which is accessible through the inner door skin, then withdraw

14.12 Upper (1) and lower (2) rear door window rear guide rail securing bolts – Hatchback model

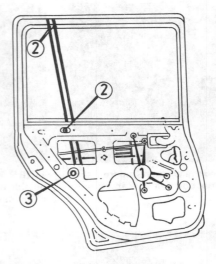

Fig. 11.4 Rear door rear window guide fixings – Estate models (Sec 14)

2   Screws   3   Nut and bolt
Also shown are the window regulator securing rivets (1)

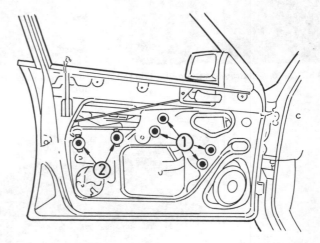

Fig. 11.5 Front door window regulator securing rivets (1), and window lower guide rail securing bolts (2) (Sec 14)

the guide rail from the door (photo). Where applicable, the weatherstrip can be left attached to the guide rail, in which case, position the guide rail to one side out of the way, taking care not to damage the vehicle paintwork.
13   Manipulate the window regulator mechanism as necessary, and tilt the window glass forwards until it can be withdrawn from outside the door through the window aperture.

Refitting
14   Refitting is a reversal of removal, but refit the door inner trim panel with reference to Section 30.

Rear door window sliding glass – Estate models
Removal
15   Proceed as described in paragraphs 9 and 10.
16   Remove the window regulator mechanism, as described later in this Section.
17   Working at the top of the window aperture, remove the two upper rear window rear guide rail securing screws.
18   Working at the bottom of the window aperture, remove the lower rear window guide securing screw, then remove the rear window guide securing bolt and nut, and withdraw the window guide upwards through the window aperture.
19   Withdraw the window glass upwards through the window aperture.

Refitting
20   Refitting is a reversal of removal, but refit the window regulator mechanism as described later in this Section, and refit the door inner trim panel with reference to Section 30.

Rear door window fixed glass – Estate models
Removal
21   Remove the sliding glass, as described previously in this Section.
22   Pull the fixed glass forwards from its surround, and withdraw it from the door.

Refitting
23   Refitting is a reversal of removal.

Front door window regulator
Removal
24   Lower the window approximately halfway, then remove the door inner trim panel and the plastic insulating sheet, as described in Section 30.

25   Support the window in the half-open position by placing a wooden prop under it, ensuring that the prop is clear of the regulator mechanism.
26   Drill out the four rivets securing the regulator mechanism to the door, using an 8.5 mm diameter drill (photo). Take care not to damage the door panel.
27   Prise the plastic end stop from the window glass guide channel.
28   Unscrew the two securing bolts, and remove the window lower guide rail from the door.
29   On models with electric windows, disconnect the battery negative lead (if not already done), then disconnect the wiring plug from the window motor (photo).
30   Carefully manipulate the window regulator assembly out through the aperture in the door (photo).

Refitting
31   Refitting is a reversal of removal, bearing in mind the following points.
32   Ensure that the regulator arms are correctly positioned in the guide rails before securing the regulator assembly to the door.
33   Secure the regulator assembly to the door, using new rivets (photo).

14.26 Drilling out a front door window regulator securing rivet

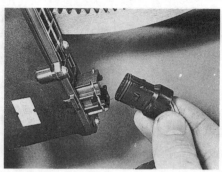

14.29 Disconnecting a front door electric window motor wiring plug

14.30 Withdrawing a front door window regulator assembly

14.33 Fit new rivets to secure the front door window regulator assembly

14.36A Front door window regulator assembly upper ...

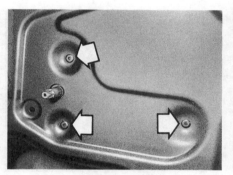

14.36B ... and lower securing rivets (arrowed)

34   Adjust the angle of the lower guide rail by means of the two securing screws, until smooth operation of the window is achieved.
35   Refit the door inner trim panel with reference to Section 30.

Rear door window regulator

Removal

36   Proceed as described in paragraphs 24 to 26 inclusive, and paragraphs 29 and 30, noting that the assembly is secured by five rivets (two upper and three lower rivets) (photos).

Refitting

37   Refitting is a reversal of removal, bearing in mind the following points.
38   Ensure that the regulator arm is correctly positioned in the guide rail before securing the regulator assembly to the door.
39   Secure the regulator assembly to the door using new rivets.
40   Check the regulator mechanism for satisfactory operation before refitting the door trim panel, then refit the panel with reference to Section 30.

Electric window components

41   Refer to Section 20.

15   Boot lid and hinges (Saloon models) – removal and refitting

Boot lid

Removal

1   Open the boot lid fully.
2   On models with central locking, disconnect the battery negative lead, then disconnect the wiring from the lock motor. If the original boot lid is to be refitted, first tie a length of string to the end of the wiring. Feed

the wiring through the boot lid, then untie the string, leaving it in position in the boot lid to assist refitting.
3   Mark the position of the hinges on the boot lid.
4   With the help of an assistant, support the weight of the boot lid, then unscrew the securing bolts from the hinges (photo), and lift the boot lid from the vehicle.

Refitting

5   If a new boot lid is to be fitted, transfer all the serviceable fittings (rubber buffers, lock mechanism, etc.) to it.
6   Refitting is a reversal of removal, bearing in mind the following points.
7   Align the hinges with the previously-made marks on the boot lid.
8   Where applicable, draw the central locking motor wiring through the boot lid, using the string.
9   If necessary, adjust the hinge bolts and the rubber buffers until a good fit is obtained with the boot lid shut.
10   If necessary, adjust the position of the lock striker on the body, to achieve satisfactory lock operation.

Hinge

Removal

11   Remove the boot lid, as described previously in this Section.
12   Remove the rear quarter trim panel, as described in Section 30.
13   Note the position of the hinge counterbalance spring in the bracket on the body, so that it can be refitted in its original position, then unhook the spring from the body (photo). Use a suitable lever to release the spring if necessary.
14   Unscrew the securing bolt (photo), and remove the hinge from the body.

Refitting

15   Refitting is a reversal of removal, bearing in mind the following points.
16   Ensure that the counterbalance spring is positioned as noted before removal.
17   Refit the boot lid as described previously in this Section.

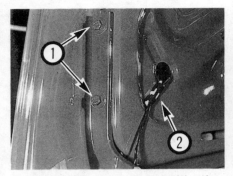

15.4 Boot lid hinge securing bolts (1) and central locking motor wiring (2) – Saloon model

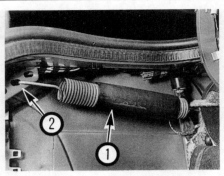

15.13 Boot lid hinge spring (1) – note position of spring in bracket (2) – Saloon model

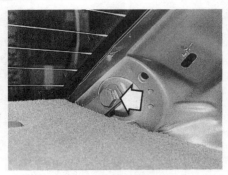

15.14 Boot lid hinge-to-body securing bolt (arrowed) – Saloon model

16.5 Boot lid lock – Saloon model

16.9 Lock cylinder securing nut (arrowed) – Saloon model

16.13 Boot lid lock striker securing bolt

16   Boot lid handle and lock components (Saloon models) – removal and refitting

Handle

Removal

1   Open the boot lid, then remove the four securing screws, and withdraw the lock cylinder assembly cover panel.
2   Unscrew the two securing nuts, then withdraw the handle from outside the boot lid. Note that the securing nuts also secure the lock cylinder assembly to the boot lid.

Refitting

3   Refitting is a reversal of removal.

Lock

Removal

4   Proceed as described in paragraph 1.
5   Unscrew the two securing bolts, and withdraw the lock from the boot lid (photo).

Refitting

6   Refitting is a reversal of removal, but if necessary, adjust the position of the lock striker on the body, to achieve satisfactory lock operation.

Lock cylinder

Removal

7   Open the boot lid fully.
8   Remove the four securing screws, and withdraw the lock cylinder assembly cover panel.
9   Unscrew the two securing nuts (photo), and withdraw the lock cylinder assembly, unhooking the lock operating rod(s) as the assembly

is withdrawn. Note that the securing nuts also secure the boot lid handle.
10   No spare parts are available for the lock cylinder assembly, and if faulty, the complete assembly must be renewed.

Refitting

11   Refitting is a reversal of removal.

Lock striker

Removal

12   The lock striker is screwed into the lower body panel.
13   Remove the securing screws, then unclip the rear boot trim panel to expose the lock striker securing bolt (photo).
14   Before removing the striker, mark its position, so that it can be refitted in exactly the same position.
15   To remove the striker, simply unscrew the securing screw.

Refitting

16   Refitting is a reversal of removal, but if necessary, adjust the position of the striker to achieve satisfactory closing of the boot lid.

Central locking motor

17   Refer to Section 19.

17   Tailgate, hinges and support struts – removal and refitting

Tailgate

Removal

1   Open the tailgate fully.
2   Disconnect the battery negative lead.
3   Remove the securing screws, and withdraw the tailgate rear trim panels.

17.7 Tailgate hinge pin securing clip (arrowed) – Hatchback model

17.22 Prising out a tailgate support strut balljoint clip – Hatchback model

4   Disconnect all the relevant wiring now exposed, and disconnect the washer fluid hose from the washer nozzle.
5   If the original tailgate is to be refitted, tie string to the ends of all the relevant wires, and if necessary the washer fluid hose, then feed the wiring and the hose through the top of the tailgate. Untie the string, leaving it in position in the tailgate to assist refitting.
6   Have an assistant support the weight of the tailgate, then disconnect the tailgate support struts from their mounting balljoints, with reference to paragraph 22.
7   Prise the securing clips from the ends of the tailgate hinge pins (photo).
8   With the tailgate adequately supported, tap the hinge pins from the hinges, using a suitable punch, and carefully lift the tailgate from the vehicle.

Refitting
9   If a new tailgate is to be fitted, transfer all serviceable components (rubber buffers, lock mechanism, etc.) to it.
10   Refitting is a reversal of removal, bearing in mind the following points.
11   If the original tailgate is being refitted, draw the wiring and washer fluid hose (where applicable) through the tailgate, using the string.
12   If necessary, adjust the rubber buffers to obtain a good fit when the tailgate is shut.
13   If necessary, adjust the position of the lock striker on the body, to achieve satisfactory lock operation.

Hinge

Removal
14   Remove the tailgate as described previously in this Section.
15   Prise off the rear roof trim panel, taking care not to break the securing clips (see Section 29), and lower the rear headlining slightly for access to the tailgate hinge securing screws.
16   Mark the hinge position on the body.
17   Unscrew the securing screws, and withdraw the hinge.

Refitting
18   Refitting is a reversal of removal, bearing in mind the following points.
19   Align the hinges with the previously-made marks on the body.
20   Refit the tailgate as described previously in this Section.

Support strut

Removal
21   Open the tailgate fully, and have an assistant support it.
22   Release the strut from its mounting balljoints by prising the spring clips a little way out (photo), and pulling the strut off the balljoints.

Refitting
23   Refitting is a reversal of removal.

18   Tailgate handle and lock components – removal and refitting

Handle – Hatchback models

Removal
1   Open the tailgate, then remove the securing screws and withdraw the tailgate rear trim panel.
2   Working through the aperture in the tailgate, unscrew the two securing nuts, then withdraw the handle from outside the tailgate. Note that the securing nuts also secure the lock cylinder assembly.

Refitting
3   Refitting is a reversal of removal.

Handle – Estate and Van models

Removal
4   Proceed as described in paragraph 1.
5   Remove the tailgate lock cylinder assembly, as described later in this Section.
6   Remove the tailgate wiper motor, as described in Chapter 12.
7   Remove the rear number plate lights, as described in Chapter 12.
8   Working through the apertures in the tailgate, unscrew the four securing nuts, and withdraw the handle from outside the tailgate.

Refitting
9   Refitting is a reversal of removal, but refit the tailgate wiper motor as described in Chapter 12.

Lock

Removal
10   Proceed as described in paragraph 1.
11   Working through the aperture in the tailgate, disconnect the operating rod(s) from the lock (photo).
12   Unscrew the securing screws (three on Hatchback models, four on Estate models), and withdraw the lock (photo).

Refitting
13   Refitting is a reversal of removal, but if necessary, adjust the position of the lock striker on the body, to achieve satisfactory lock operation.

Lock cylinder

Removal
14   Remove the securing screws, and withdraw the tailgate rear trim panel.
15   Disconnect the operating rod(s) from the lock cylinder assembly (photo).

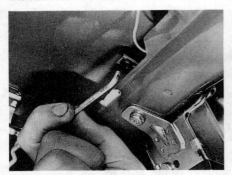

18.11 Disconnecting a tailgate lock operating rod – Hatchback model

18.12 Removing the tailgate lock – Hatchback model

18.15 Disconnecting an operating rod from the lock cylinder assembly – Hatchback model

18.16 Lock cylinder assembly securing nuts (arrowed) – Hatchback model

18.22 Tailgate lock striker – Hatchback model

16   Unscrew the two securing nuts (photo), and withdraw the lock cylinder assembly. Note that on Hatchback models, the securing nuts also secure the tailgate handle.
17   No spare parts are available for the lock cylinder assembly, and if faulty, the complete assembly must be renewed.

Refitting
18   Refitting is a reversal of removal.

Lock striker
Removal
19   The lock striker is screwed into the lower body panel.
20   Where applicable, extract the securing screws, and remove the luggage compartment rear trim panel for access to the lock striker securing bolts.
21   Before removing the striker, mark its position, so that it can be refitted in exactly the same position.
22   To remove the striker, simply unscrew the securing screws (photo).

Refitting
23   Refitting is a reversal of removal, but if necessary, adjust the position of the striker to achieve satisfactory closing of the tailgate.

Central locking motor
24   Refer to Section 19.

19   Central locking components – removal and refitting

Electronic control unit
Removal
1   The control unit is located behind the right-hand footwell side/sill trim panel.

2   Disconnect the battery negative lead.
3   Remove the footwell side/sill trim panel, as described in Section 30.
4   Where applicable, unscrew the two securing nuts, and pull the wiring plug bracket from the footwell.
5   Pull the two securing clips from the studs in the footwell, and pull the carpet back from the studs to expose the control unit (photos).
6   Unscrew the two securing screws, and lift the unit from its location in the footwell, then disconnect the wiring plug and withdraw the unit.

Refitting
7   Refitting is a reversal of removal.

Operating microswitches
Removal
8   The microswitches are mounted inside the front doors, at the rear of the exterior handle assemblies.
9   Remove the door inner trim panel, and peel back the plastic insulating sheet sufficiently to gain access to the exterior handle, as described in Section 30.
10   Unclip the microswitch from the rear edge of the exterior handle assembly, disconnect the switch wiring connector from the door wiring harness, then withdraw the switch (photo).

Refitting
11   Refitting is a reversal of removal, but refit the door inner trim panel as described in Section 30.

Door lock operating motor
Removal
12   Remove the door lock, as described in Section 13.
13   Disconnect the lock operating rod from the motor.
14   Remove the two securing screws, and withdraw the motor from the lock assembly (photo).

Refitting
15   Refitting is a reversal of removal.

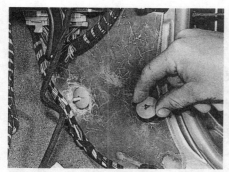

19.5A Pull the securing clips from the studs in the footwell ...

19.5B ... and pull the carpet back to expose the central locking electronic control unit (arrowed)

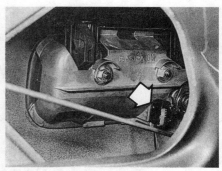

19.10 Central locking operating microswitch (arrowed)

19.14 Central locking motor securing screws (arrowed)

19.19 Disconnecting the wiring plug from the boot lid lock operating motor – Saloon model

19.20A Boot lid lock operating motor – Saloon model

19.20B Removing a tailgate lock operating motor – Hatchback model

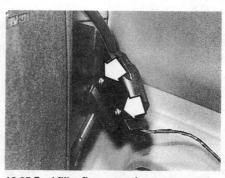

19.25 Fuel filler flap operating motor securing screws (arrowed) – Saloon model

Boot lid/tailgate lock operating motor

Removal

16   Disconnect the battery negative lead.

17   Open the boot or tailgate, as applicable.

18   Remove the securing screws, and withdraw the lock cylinder assembly cover panel (Saloon models), or the tailgate rear trim panel (Hatchback and Estate models).

19   Disconnect the wiring plug from the motor (photo).

20   Unscrew the two securing screws, and withdraw the motor from the boot lid or tailgate, as applicable, unhooking the lock operating rod as the motor is withdrawn (photos).

Refitting

21   Refitting is a reversal of removal.

Fuel filler flap operating motor – Saloon and Estate models

Removal

22   Disconnect the battery negative lead.

23   Release the right-hand luggage compartment side trim panel from the body, with reference to Section 30.

24   Disconnect the motor wiring plug.

25   Remove the two securing screws, then carefully manipulate the motor from its location, disengaging the operating rod as the unit is withdrawn (photo).

Refitting

26   Refitting is a reversal of removal.

Fuel filler flap lock operating motor – Hatchback models

Removal

27   Disconnect the battery negative lead.

28   Remove the luggage compartment right-hand side trim panel, with reference to Section 30.

29   Remove the right-hand rear light cluster, as described in Chapter 12.

19.30 Pulling back the carpet to expose the fuel filler flap lock operating motor bracket securing screws – Hatchback model

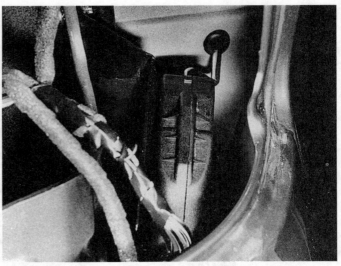

19.31 Fuel filler flap operating motor viewed through rear light cluster aperture

30   Pull back the carpet from the wheel arch to expose the two lock motor bracket securing screws (photo).
31   Remove the securing screws, then carefully manipulate the motor and bracket assembly from its location, disengaging the operating rod as the unit is withdrawn. Manipulate the unit out through the rear light cluster aperture, and disconnect the wiring plug (photo).
32   If desired, the motor can be separated from the bracket by removing the securing screws.

Refitting
33   Refitting is a reversal of removal.

20   Electric window components – removal and refitting

Operating switches
Removal
1   The switches are located in the driver's and passenger's doors.

2   Remove the door inner trim panel, as described in Section 30.
3   With the wiring connector disconnected, carefully prise the switch assembly from the trim panel (photo).

Refitting
4   Refitting is a reversal of removal, but refit the door inner trim panel as described in Section 30.

Operating motors
Removal
5   Remove the door window regulator, as described in Section 14.
6   To remove the motor assembly from the regulator, unscrew the three securing screws (photo).
7   No spare parts are available for the motor assembly, and if faulty, the complete unit must be renewed.

Refitting
8   Refitting is a reversal of removal, but refit the regulator as described in Section 14.

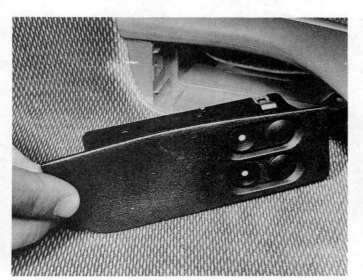

20.3 Removing the electric window operating switch from the driver's door

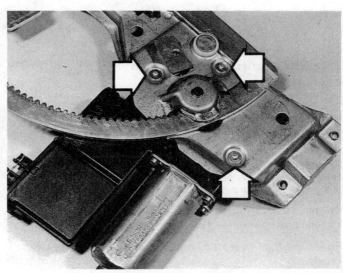

20.6 Electric window operating motor securing screws (arrowed)

21.3 Door mirror trim panel freed from front edge of door – electric mirror

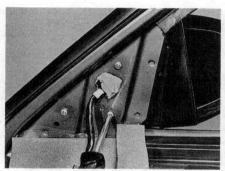

21.4 Unscrewing a door mirror securing screw – electric mirror

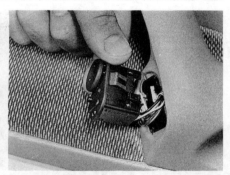

21.9 Removing the electric mirror operating switch from the door inner trim panel

21 Mirrors – overhaul, removal and refitting

Door mirror
Removal

1   On models with electric mirrors, disconnect the battery negative lead.
2   Where applicable, on models with manually-adjustable mirrors, pull off the adjuster lever.
3   Prise the mirror trim panel from the inside front edge of the door, and disconnect the wiring from the loudspeaker mounted in the trim panel (photo).
4   Extract the three now-exposed securing screws, and withdraw the mirror assembly from the door. On models with electric mirrors, disconnect the wiring plug (photo).

Refitting

5   Refitting is a reversal of removal, but ensure that the rubber weatherseal is correctly located on the mirror housing.

Glass renewal

6   If desired, the mirror glass can be removed for renewal without removing the mirror. On models with electric mirrors, disconnect the battery negative lead before proceeding.
7   Carefully prise the glass from its balljoints using a screwdriver, and where applicable, disconnect the heater wires from the glass. Take care, as the glass is easily broken if forced.
8   To refit, simply push the glass onto the balljoints (ensuring that the heater wires are connected, where applicable).

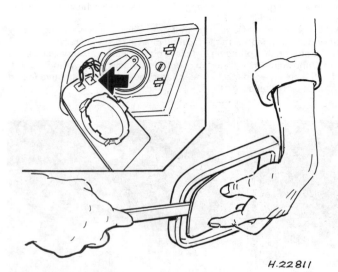

H.22811

Fig. 11.6 Prising the mirror glass from an electric mirror – heater wires arrowed (Sec 21)

Electric mirror operating switch removal and refitting

9   The switch can be prised from the door inner trim panel, after removing the door inner trim panel (as described in Section 30) and disconnecting the wiring plug (photo).
10   After refitting the switch, refit the door inner trim panel as described in Section 30.

Electric motor removal and refitting

11   Remove the mirror glass, as described previously in this Section.
12   Extract the three motor securing screws, disconnect the wiring plug, then withdraw the motor.
13   Refitting is a reversal of removal, but ensure that the wiring is routed behind the motor, to avoid interfering with the adjustment mechanism.

Interior rear-view mirror
Removal

14   The mirror can be removed from its mounting plate on the windscreen, after unscrewing the mounting screw using a 2 mm Allen key.
15   The mounting plate is fixed to the windscreen using a special adhesive, and should not be disturbed unless absolutely necessary. Note that there is a risk of cracking the windscreen glass if an attempt is made to remove a securely-bonded mounting plate.

Refitting

16   If necessary, the special adhesive required to fix the mounting plate to the windscreen can be obtained from a Vauxhall/Opel dealer.

22 Windscreen and rear window glass – general information

With the exception of the rear quarter windows, all fixed glass is bonded in position, using a special adhesive.
Special tools, adhesives and expertise are required for successful removal and refitting of glass fixed by this method. Such work must therefore be entrusted to a Vauxhall/Opel dealer, a windscreen specialist, or other competent professional.

23 Rear quarter windows – removal and refitting

Removal

Note: *The manufacturers recommend the use of new plastic nuts to secure the glass on refitting.*

1   Remove the rear quarter trim panel, as described in Section 30.
2   Have an assistant support the quarter window from outside the vehicle, then unscrew the plastic securing nuts (photo), and the bolts, and push the window from the body.

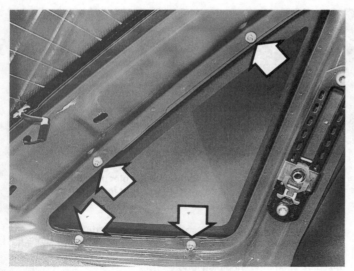

23.2 Rear quarter window securing nuts (arrowed)

Refitting

3   Refitting is a reversal of removal, but ensure that the seal on the rear of the glass is seated correctly against the body as the window is fitted, and use new plastic nuts to secure the glass.

24   Sunroof components – removal and refitting

Note: *The sunroof is a complex piece of equipment, consisting of a large number of components. It is strongly recommended that the sunroof mechanism is not disturbed unless absolutely necessary. If the sunroof mechanism is faulty, or requires overhaul, consult a Vauxhall/Opel dealer for advice.*

Glass panel

Removal

1   Push the sunshade fully rearwards, and open the glass panel halfway.
2   Extract the four securing screws from the front edge of the guide rail plastic surround, and withdraw the surround down through the sunroof aperture (photos).
3   Move the glass panel forwards, and open it to its tilt position.
4   Prise the plastic trim strips from the guide rails, to expose the glass panel securing screws (photo).
5   Extract the three securing screws from each guide rail (photo) and where applicable, recover the lockwashers.
6   Carefully lift the glass panel from the roof aperture, taking care not to damage the vehicle paintwork.

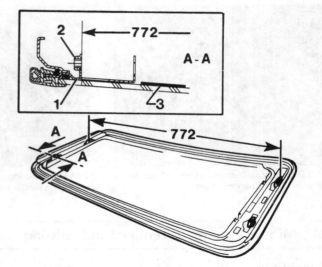

Fig. 11.7 Sunroof glass panel mounting flange dimension (Sec 24)

1   Mounting flange
2   Nut
3   Protective foil

A – A   Cross-section cutting
point
Dimensions in mm

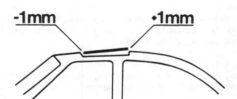

Fig. 11.8 Sunroof glass panel fitting position (Sec 24)

Refitting

7   Refitting is a reversal of removal, bearing in mind the following points.
8   Before refitting the glass panel, measure the distance between the mounting flanges. Bend the flanges if necessary to achieve the desired dimension – see Fig. 11.7.
9   Where applicable, ensure that the glass panel securing screw lockwashers engage with the locating pins on the guide rails.
10   Before fully tightening the glass panel securing screws, close the panel, and adjust its position to give the dimensions shown in Fig. 11.8.
11   If a new glass panel has been fitted, peel off the protective foil on completion of adjustment.

24.2A Extract the four securing screws ...

24.2B ... and withdraw the sunroof guide rail plastic surround

24.4 Prising a plastic trim strip from the guide rail

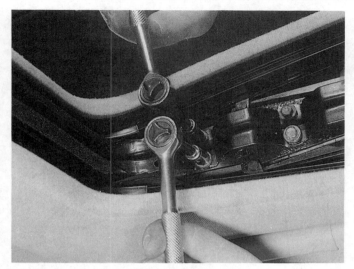

24.5 Loosening a glass panel securing screw

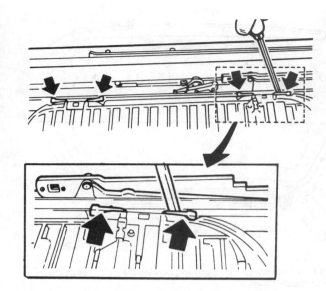

Fig. 11.9 Sunshade spring clip locations (arrowed) (Sec 24)

Gutter

Removal

12 Remove the glass panel, as described previously in this Section.
13 Extract the two securing screws, then lift the gutter from the roof aperture.

Refitting

14 Refit the gutter to the roof aperture at an angle, pushing it up to the stop on both sides until the retaining lugs engage with the gutter guides.
15 Refit and tighten the securing screws.
16 Refit and adjust the glass panel, as described previously in this Section.

Sunshade

Removal

17 Remove the glass panel and the gutter, as described previously in this Section.
18 Carefully prise the four sunshade spring clips out of the roof guides (using a plastic or wooden implement to avoid damage), then withdraw the sunshade from the guides – see Fig. 11.9.

Refitting

19 Refitting is a reversal of removal, but ensure that the spring clips engage correctly with the roof guides.

Crank drive

Removal

20 Prise out the trim, and unscrew the crank handle securing screw. Prise the crank from the drive spindle.
21 Disconnect the battery negative lead, then prise the courtesy light from the roof trim panel, and disconnect the wiring.
22 Remove the two trim panel securing screws, and withdraw the trim panel from the roof.
23 Extract the two securing screws, and remove the crank drive assembly.

Refitting

24 Refitting is a reversal of removal, bearing in mind the following points.
25 Before finally tightening the crank handle, the crank drive must be adjusted as follows.
26 Temporarily refit the crank handle, and position it so that it faces forwards, then depress the locking button.
27 Remove the crank handle and turn the crank drive pinion anti-clockwise by hand as far as the stop.
28 Refit the crank handle so that it faces directly forwards, then tighten the securing screw and refit the trim.

25 Body exterior fixings – removal and refitting

Wheel arch liners

1 The plastic wheel arch liners are secured by a combination of self-tapping screws and plastic nuts and clips. Removal and refitting is self-evident, bearing in mind the following points.
2 Some of the securing clips may be held in place using a central pin, which must be tapped out to release the clip.
3 The clips are easily broken during removal, and it is advisable to obtain a few spare clips for possible use when refitting.
4 Certain models may have additional underbody shields and splashguards fitted, which may be attached to the wheel arch liners.

Engine undershield (DOHC engine models)

5 Apply the handbrake, then jack up the front of the vehicle, and support securely on axle stands (see 'Jacking, towing and wheel changing').
6 Extract the two securing screws, and remove the oil filter access panel.
7 Working around the edges of the undershield, remove the

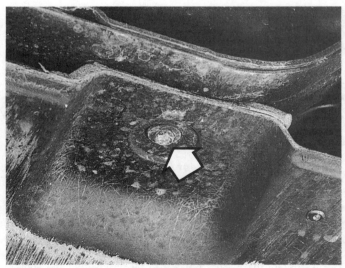

25.7 Engine undershield securing screw (arrowed)

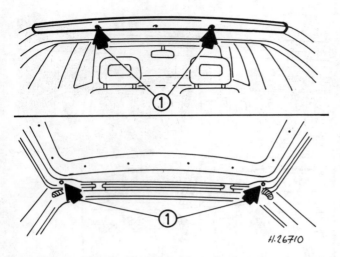

H.26710

Fig. 11.10 Tailgate spoiler securing screws (1) – all except DOHC engine models (Sec 25)

self-tapping screws which secure the shield to the underbody, noting that some of the screws may also secure the wheel arch liners (photo).
8   With the help of an assistant, pull the shield from the vehicle, and place it to one side to avoid damage.
9   Refitting is a reversal of removal.

Fuel filler flap

10   Open the flap for access to the two securing screws.
11   Remove the securing screws and withdraw the flap.
12   Refitting is a reversal of removal.

Boot lid spoiler – Saloon models
Removal
13   Open the boot lid, then remove the securing screws, and withdraw the lock assembly cover panel.
14   Unscrew the three bolts and eight nuts securing the spoiler to the boot lid.
15   On certain models, the spoiler may be retained with adhesive tape, in which case great care must be taken to avoid damage to the paintwork as the spoiler is removed. One solution is to heat the tape using a hot air gun or a hairdryer, until the heat softens the adhesive sufficiently to enable the spoiler to be easily removed. Take care that the heat does not damage the surrounding paintwork.
16   Withdraw the spoiler from the boot lid.

Refitting
17   Where applicable, clean off all traces of adhesive using white spirit, then wash the area with warm soapy water to remove all traces of spirit. If adhesive tape is used to secure the spoiler, ensure that the relevant surfaces are completely clean, and free from dirt and grease.
18   If adhesive tape is used to refit the spoiler, follow the instructions supplied for refitting (consult a Vauxhall/Opel dealer if necessary). It may be necessary to use a heat source, as during removal, to soften the adhesive before the tape is applied.
19   Refit the spoiler, ensuring that it is correctly aligned before pressing firmly into position, and tighten the securing nuts and bolts.
20   Refit the lock assembly cover panel on completion.

Tailgate spoiler – all except DOHC engine models
Removal
21   Working outside the tailgate, remove the two spoiler securing screws.
22   Open the tailgate, and unscrew the two remaining screws from the corners of the tailgate.
23   Refer to paragraph 15.
24   Withdraw the spoiler.
25   If desired, the washer nozzle can be prised from the spoiler mounting bracket once the spoiler has been withdrawn.

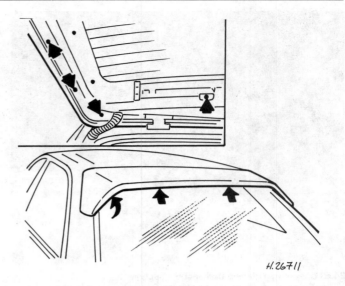

H.26711

Fig. 11.11 Tailgate spoiler fixings (arrowed) – DOHC engine models (Sec 25)

26   If desired, the spoiler mounting bracket can be removed from the tailgate after unscrewing the securing nuts and screws.

Refitting
27   Where applicable, refit the spoiler mounting bracket and the washer nozzle, using a reversal of the removal procedure.
28   Refer to paragraphs 17 and 18.
29   Refit the spoiler, ensuring that it is correctly aligned before pressing firmly into position, and tighten the securing bolts.

Tailgate spoiler – DOHC engine models
Removal
30   Open the tailgate, then remove the securing screws, and withdraw the tailgate upper inner trim panel.
31   Working inside the tailgate, and at the outer lower edge of the spoiler, remove the six bolts and four nuts securing the spoiler to the tailgate.
32   Proceed as described in paragraphs 23 to 26 inclusive.

Refitting
33   Proceed as described in paragraphs 27 to 29 inclusive.

Side rubbing strips
Removal
34   Apply masking tape along the edge of the strip to be removed, as an aid to correct alignment on refitting.
35   Using a hot air gun or a hairdryer, heat the trim strip until the heat softens the adhesive sufficiently to enable the trim strip to be easily removed. Take care that the heat does not damage the surrounding paintwork.

Refitting
36   Clean off all traces of adhesive using white spirit, then wash the area with warm soapy water to remove all traces of spirit. Ensure that the surface to which the new strip is to be fitted is completely clean, and free from dirt and grease.
37   Use the heat gun or hairdryer to heat the new trim strip to approximately 80°C, then peel off the protective foil, and press the trim strip firmly into position, using the masking tape as a guide. Remove the masking tape when the strip is secured.

Badges
Removal
38   The various badges are secured with adhesives. To remove them, either soften the adhesive using a hot air gun or hairdryer (taking care to avoid damage to the paintwork), or separate the badge from the body by 'sawing' through the adhesive using a length of nylon cord.

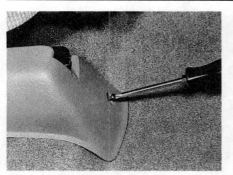

26.1 Removing the securing screw from the outer seat rail trim

26.2 Releasing the clips from the inner seat rail trim piece

26.3 Inserting the safety fork into its slot in the seat belt tensioner cylinder

Refitting

39   Clean off all traces of adhesive using white spirit, then wash the area with warm soapy water to remove all traces of spirit. Ensure that the surface to which the new badge is to be fastened is completely clean, and free from grease and dirt.

40   Use the hot air gun to soften the adhesive on the new badge, then press it firmly into position.

Side skirts and additional spoilers

41   On certain models, bodykits may be fitted, comprising side skirts and an additional tailgate spoiler.

42   These components are secured by a combination of screws, adhesive and rivets. Although the basic principles described in this Section for other similar components apply, it is advisable to entrust removal and refitting to a Vauxhall/Opel dealer or a bodywork specialist, as great care is required to avoid damage to the surrounding paintwork and the components themselves.

---

26   Seats – removal and refitting

Front seat

Warning: *The seat belt tensioners fitted to the front seat assemblies may cause injury if triggered inadvertently. Before carrying out any work on the front seats, the safety fork must be inserted into the seat belt tensioner cylinder, to prevent the possibility of the tensioner being triggered (see paragraphs 3 and 4 below). Seats should always be transported and installed with the safety fork in place. If a seat is to be disposed of, the tensioner must be triggered before the seat is removed from the vehicle, by inserting the safety fork, and striking the tensioner tube sharply with a hammer. If the tensioner has been triggered due to a sudden impact or accident, the unit must be renewed, as it cannot be reset. Due to safety considerations, tensioner renewal should be entrusted to a Vauxhall/Opel dealer.*

Removal

Note: *The manufacturers recommend the use of new bolts when refitting the seats.*

1   Remove the single securing screw from the front edge of the outer seat rail trim (photo), then withdraw the trim.

2   Release the securing clips, and unclip the trim from the rear edge of the inner seat rail (photo).

3   Locate the plastic safety fork for the seat belt tensioner, which is usually taped to the outside of the tensioner cylinder (photo).

4   Insert the safety fork into the slot provided in the tensioner cylinder, ensuring that the fork engages securely.

5   Remove the four bolts which secure the seat rails to the floor, then withdraw the seat, complete with rails (photos). Recover the washers and plates.

6   Withdraw the seat, complete with the rails, from the vehicle.

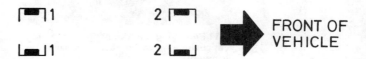

Fig. 11.12 Tightening sequence for front seat bolts (Sec 26)

7   If desired, the seat can be separated from the rails for attention to the adjustment mechanism.

Refitting

8   Refitting is a reversal of removal, bearing in mind the following points.

9   Use new seat securing bolts, and tighten them in the sequence shown in Fig. 11.12.

10   Before refitting the trim panels to the seat rails, remove the safety fork from the seat belt tensioner cylinder, and tape it to the outside of the cylinder.

Rear seat cushion

Removal

11   With the seats in their raised position, where applicable, unclip the trim panel from the front of the hinge (photo).

12   Prise the securing clips from the ends of the hinge pins (photo), then withdraw the pins from the hinges.

13   With the hinge pins removed, the seat cushion can be withdrawn from the vehicle.

Refitting

14   Refitting is a reversal of removal.

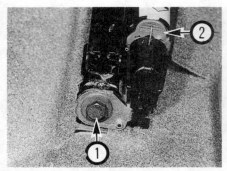

26.5A Front outer seat rail securing bolt (1) – note seat belt tensioner safety fork (2) engaged in slot

26.5B Rear outer seat rail securing bolt – note washer and plate

26.5C Rear inner seat rail securing bolt

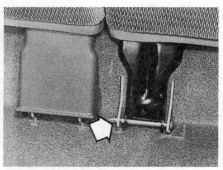

26.11 Removing the trim panel from a rear seat cushion hinge – note securing clip (arrowed)

26.12 Rear seat cushion hinge pin securing clip (arrowed)

Rear seat back

Removal

15   Fold down the seat back.
16   Carefully release the securing clips, using a suitable forked tool or a screwdriver, and pull back the trim covering the hinges on the seat back.
17   Unscrew the two bolts at each side, securing the seat back to the hinges, then withdraw the seat back from the vehicle.

Refitting

18   Refitting is a reversal of removal.

27   Front seat belt tensioner system – general information

    All Astra models are fitted with a front seat belt tensioner system, which is designed to instantaneously take up any slack in the seat belt in the case of a sudden frontal impact, therefore reducing the possibility of injury to the front seat occupants. Each front seat is fitted with its own system, the components of which are mounted in the seat frame.
    The seat belt tensioner is triggered by a frontal impact causing a deceleration of six times the force of gravity or greater. Lesser impacts, including impacts from behind, will not trigger the system.
    When the system is triggered, a pre-tensioned spring draws back the seat belt via a cable attached to a fulcrum, which acts on the seat belt stalk mounted on the seat frame. The cable and fulcrum can move by up to 80.0 mm, which therefore reduces the slack in the seat belt around the shoulders and waist of the occupant by a similar amount.
    There is a risk of injury if the system is triggered inadvertently when working on the vehicle, and it is therefore strongly recommended that any work involving the seat belt tensioner system is entrusted to a Vauxhall/Opel dealer. Refer to the warning given at the beginning of Section 26 before contemplating any work on the front seats.

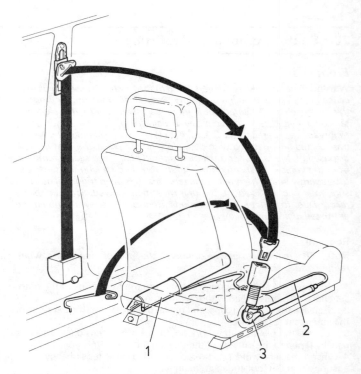

Fig. 11.13 Front seat belt tensioner system (Sec 27)

1 Spring   *3   Fulcrum*
2 Cable

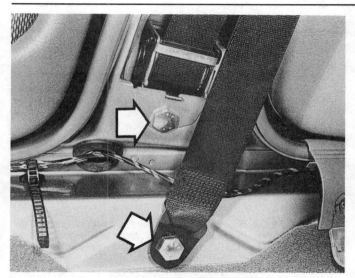

28.4 B-pillar lower trim panel removed to expose inertia reel unit and seat belt lower mounting securing bolts (arrowed)

28 Seat belt components – removal and refitting

Front seat belt – all models except 3-door Hatchback

Removal

1   Remove the B-pillar lower trim panel, as described in Section 30.
2   Prise off the trim, and unbolt the seat belt upper mounting from the B-pillar. Recover the spacer.
3   Unbolt the lower seat belt mounting from the body, and recover the spacer and washers, noting their locations.
4   Unscrew the securing bolt (photo), withdraw the inertia reel unit from the B-pillar, then withdraw the seat belt assembly from the vehicle.

Refitting

5   Refitting is a reversal of removal, but make sure that the belt is fitted untwisted, and ensure that the washers and spacers on the upper and lower mountings are fitted as noted before removal. Tighten all fixings to the specified torque.

Front seat belt – 3-door Hatchback models

Removal

6   Prise off the trim, and unbolt the seat belt upper mounting from the B-pillar. Recover the spacer.
7   Remove the rear side trim panel, as described in Section 30.
8   Unscrew the securing bolt, withdraw the inertia reel unit from the B-pillar, then withdraw the seat belt assembly from the vehicle.

Refitting

9   Refitting is a reversal of removal, but tighten all fixings to the specified torque.

Front seat belt height adjuster

Removal

10   Remove the B-pillar upper trim panel, as described in Section 30.
11   Remove the two Torx type securing bolts, and withdraw the height adjuster assembly from the B-pillar.

Refitting

12   Refitting is a reversal of removal, but ensure that the height adjuster is fitted the correct way up. The top of the adjuster is marked with two arrows, which should point towards the vehicle roof.

Front seat belt tensioner

13   The front seat belt tensioner mechanism is mounted on the front seat frame. Due to safety considerations (refer to the warning at the beginning of Section 26), no attempt should be made to carry out work on the tensioner mechanism. Any problems should be referred to a Vauxhall/Opel dealer.

Rear seat belt

Removal

14   Fold the rear seat cushion forwards for access to the seat belt lower mountings.
15   Prise up the carpet to expose the seat belt lower mounting bolt(s), then unscrew the relevant bolt(s) from the floor. Note the location of any spacers and washers on the mounting bolt(s).
16   If removing one of the side inertia reel seat belts, proceed as follows.
17   Prise off the trim, and unbolt the seat belt upper mounting from the body pillar (photo). Recover the spacer.
18   **On Saloon and 5-door Hatchback models,** remove the rear quarter trim panel, as described in Section 30.
19   **On 3-door Hatchback models,** remove the rear parcel shelf support panel, as described in Section 30.
20   **On Estate and Van models,** remove the luggage compartment side trim panel, with reference to Section 30.
21   **On Saloon models,** remove the luggage compartment side trim panel, with reference to Section 30.
22   Unscrew the inertia reel unit securing bolt – accessible from the luggage compartment on Saloon models (photos) – remove the inertia reel unit from the body, then withdraw the seat belt assembly from the vehicle.

Refitting

23   Refitting is a reversal of removal, but make sure that the belt is fitted untwisted, and ensure that the washers and spacers on the upper (where applicable) and lower mountings are fitted as noted before removal (photo). Tighten all fixings to the specified torque.

Rear seat belt height adjuster

24   The procedure is as described in paragraphs 10 to 12 for the front seat belt height adjuster, but for access to the height adjuster, remove the rear quarter trim panel (see Section 30) instead of the B-pillar trim panel (photo).

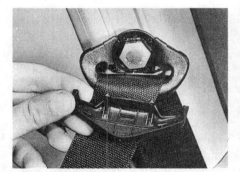

28.17 Prising the trim from a rear seat belt upper mounting

28.22A Rear seat belt inertia reel securing bolt (arrowed) – 5-door Hatchback model

28.22B Rear seat belt inertia reel securing bolt (arrowed) – Saloon model

28.23 Fitting a rear seat belt upper mounting spacer and washer

28.24 Rear seat belt height adjuster assembly

29   Interior trim – general information

Interior trim panels

1   The interior trim panels are all secured using either screws or various types of plastic fasteners.
2   To remove a panel, study it carefully, noting how it is secured. Often, other panels or ancillary components must be removed before a particular panel can be withdrawn, such as seat belt mountings, grab handles, etc.
3   Once any such components have been removed, check that there are no other panels overlapping the one to be removed; usually there is a sequence that has to be followed, which will become obvious on close inspection.
4   Remove all obvious fasteners, such as screws, many of which may have plastic covers fitted. If the panel cannot be freed, it is probably secured by hidden clips or fasteners on the rear of the panel. Such fasteners are usually situated around the edge of the panel, and can be prised up to release them. Note that plastic clips can break quite easily, so it is advisable to have a few replacement clips of the correct type available for refitting. Generally, the best way of releasing such clips is to use a suitable forked tool (photo). If this is not available, an old, broad-bladed screwdriver with the edges rounded-off and wrapped in insulating tape will serve as a good substitute.
5   The following Section and the accompanying illustrations and photographs describe removal and refitting of all the major trim panels. Note that the type and number of fasteners used often varies during the production run of a particular model, and differences may be noted to the procedures provided for certain vehicles.
6   When removing a panel, **never** use excessive force, or the panel may be damaged. Always check carefully that all fasteners have been removed or released before attempting to withdraw a panel.

29.4 Using a forked tool to remove a trim panel securing clip

7   Refitting is the reverse of the removal procedure; secure the fasteners by pressing them firmly into place, and ensure that all disturbed components are correctly secured to prevent rattles. If adhesives were found at any point during removal, use white spirit to remove all traces of old adhesive, then wash off all traces of spirit using soapy water. Use a suitable trim adhesive (a Vauxhall/Opel dealer should be able to recommend a proprietary product) on reassembly.

Carpets

8   The passenger compartment floor carpet is in divided into two pieces, front and rear, and each section is secured by plastic clips.
9   Carpet removal and refitting is reasonably straightforward, but very time- consuming due to the fact that many of the adjoining trim panels must be removed first, as must components such as the seats and their mountings, the centre console, etc.

Headlining

10   The headlining is clipped to the roof, and can be withdrawn only once all fittings such as the grab handles, sunvisors, sunroof trim (where applicable), door pillar trim panels, rear quarter trim panels, weatherseals, etc, have been removed or prised clear.
11   Note that headlining removal requires considerable skill and patience if it is to be carried out without damage, and is therefore best entrusted to an expert.

30   Interior trim panels – removal and refitting

Front door inner trim panel

Removal

1   Disconnect the battery negative lead.
2   Prise the trim plate from the door lock button in the top rear edge of the door, then pull the lock button from the operating rod (photos).
3   On models with manually-operated windows, release the securing clip, and remove the window regulator handle. To release the securing clip, insert a length of wire with a hooked end between the handle and the trim bezel on the door trim panel, and manipulate it to free the securing clip from the handle. Take care not to damage the door trim panel. Recover the trim bezel.
4   Where applicable (manually-adjustable mirrors), pull off the door mirror adjuster lever, then prise the door mirror trim panel from the door, and disconnect the wiring from the loudspeaker mounted in the trim panel.
5   Prise the door mirror switch (driver's door), electric window switch (passenger door), or the blanking plate, as applicable, from the door handle surround to expose the upper door trim panel securing screw. Remove the screw (photo).
6   Remove the five remaining trim panel securing screws, which are located along the bottom edge of the door (three screws), and around the bottom edge of the armrest/handgrip (two screws) (photos).
7   The plastic clips securing the trim panel to the door must now be released. This can be done using a screwdriver, but it is preferable to use a forked tool, to minimise the possibility of damage to the trim panel and the clips. The clips are located around the outer edge of the trim panel.
8   Once the clips have been released, pull the trim panel away from the door.

30.2A Prise the trim plate from the door lock button ...

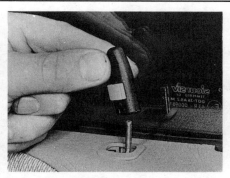

30.2B ... and pull the lock button from the operating rod

30.5 Unscrewing the front door inner trim panel upper securing screw

30.6A Removing a front door inner trim panel lower securing screw

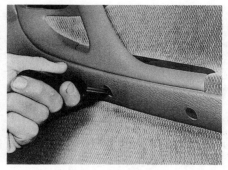

30.6B Removing a front door inner trim panel securing screw from armrest/handgrip

9   When working on models with electric door mirrors and/or electric windows, it will be necessary to disconnect the wiring plugs as the trim panel is withdrawn. Note the position of the wiring connector(s) in the bracket(s) on the door (photos).

10   Withdraw the trim panel from the door.

11   If desired, the plastic insulating sheet can be peeled from the door (photo). Peel the sheet back slowly to prevent damage to the sealant, and take care not to damage the sheet.

Refitting

12   Refitting is a reversal of removal, bearing in mind the following points.

13   If the plastic insulating sheet has been removed from the door, make sure that it is refitted intact, and securely fixed to the door. If the sheet was removed carefully, there should be no need to use new sealant when refitting the sheet. If the sheet is damaged or detached, rainwater may leak into the vehicle or damage the door trim.

14   Where applicable, ensure that the wiring connector(s) is/are positioned correctly in the bracket(s) on the door before refitting the trim panel.

15   Ensure that all the trim panel securing clips engage as the panel is refitted, and if any of the clips were broken during removal, renew them on refitting.

Rear door inner trim panel

Removal

16   Proceed as described in paragraphs 2 and 3 (photo).

17   Prise the plastic surround from the door interior handle (photo).

18   Prise the trim panel from the lower rear edge of the window aperture (photo).

19   Remove the four trim panel securing screws. Two are located at the bottom edge of the door, and two are located under the armrest (photo).

20   Proceed as described in paragraphs 7 and 8.

30.9A Front door inner trim panel removed to expose wiring connectors

30.9B Electric door mirror wiring connector locates under foam padding

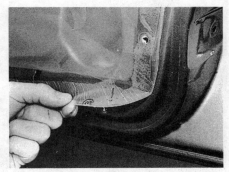

30.11 Peeling the plastic insulating sheet from the door

30.16 Removing the rear window regulator handle – securing clip arrowed

30.17 Removing the plastic surround from the rear door interior handle

30.18 Removing the trim panel from the edge of the rear door window aperture

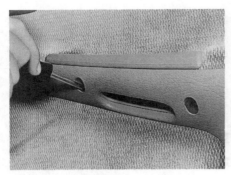

30.19 Removing a rear door inner trim panel securing screw

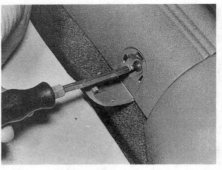

30.23 Unscrewing a front footwell side/sill trim panel securing screw

21   Withdraw the trim panel from the door.

Refitting
22   Proceed as described in paragraphs 12 to 15 inclusive.

Front footwell side/sill trim panel
Removal
23   Working along the sill, prise down the three cover panels, and remove the three securing screws (photo).
24   Working at the upper front edge of the panel, prise out the cover

and extract the remaining securing screw, then withdraw the panel (photos).

Refitting
25   Refitting is a reversal of removal.

Rear sill trim panel – all models except 3-door Hatchback
Removal
26   Fold the rear seat cushion forwards.

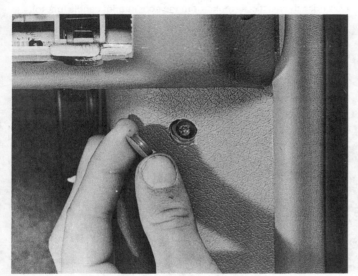

30.24A Removing the cover from the front side/sill trim panel securing screw

30.24B Removing a front side/sill trim panel (front seat removed)

30.30 Removing the seat belt mounting rail securing bolt and spacer plate – 3-door Hatchback model

30.31 Removing the seat belt mounting rail – 3-door Hatchback model

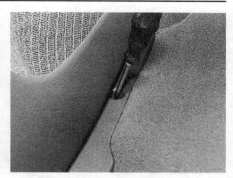

30.33A Remove the rear sill trim panel rear ...

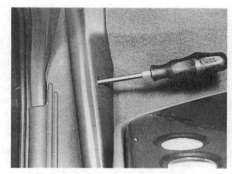

30.33B ... and front securing screws ...

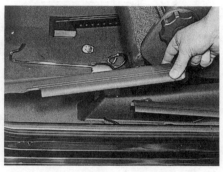

30.33C ... and withdraw the panel – 3-door Hatchback model

27 Working along the sill, prise down the two cover panels and remove the two securing screws, then withdraw the panel.

Refitting
28 Refitting is a reversal of removal.

Rear sill trim panel – 3-door Hatchback models
Removal
29 Prise down the covers, and remove the two rear securing screws from the front footwell side/sill trim panel.
30 Prise down the cover, and unscrew the bolt securing the seat belt lower mounting rail to the sill. Recover the spacer plate (photo).
31 Pull the rear of the seat belt mounting rail from the hole in the sill trim panel, and if desired, slip the lower end of the seat belt webbing from the rail (photo).
32 Fold the rear seat cushion forwards.
33 Prise out the covers, and extract the two trim panel securing screws, then carefully withdraw the panel, sliding the front edge of the panel from under the front footwell side/sill trim panel (photos).

Refitting
34 Refitting is a reversal of removal, tightening the seat belt mounting rail bolt to the specified torque.

A-pillar trim panel
Removal
35 Prise out the cover, and remove the securing screw from the top of the trim panel.
36 Carefully prise the panel from the pillar to release the two securing clips.

Refitting
37 Refitting is a reversal of removal.

B-pillar lower trim panel – all models except 3-door Hatchback
Removal
38 Prise down the cover, and remove the front securing screw from the rear sill trim panel.
39 Open the front and rear doors, and prise the weatherseals from the edges of the B-pillar.

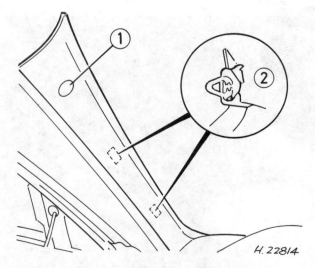

Fig. 11.14 A-pillar trim panel fixings (Sec 30)

1 Screw and cover   2 Clips

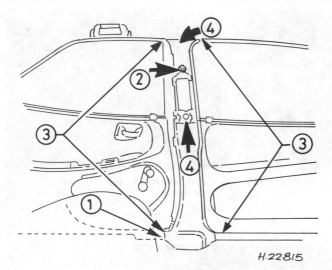

Fig. 11.15 B-pillar trim panel fixings – all models except 3-door Hatchback (Sec 30)

1 *Rear sill panel securing screw*   3 *Weatherseals*
2 *Seat belt upper mounting bolt*   4 *Trim panel securing screws*

40   Carefully prise the panel from the pillar, recovering the securing clips, where applicable.

Refitting
41   Refitting is a reversal of removal.

B-pillar upper trim panel – all models except 3-door Hatchback

Removal
42   Remove the B-pillar lower trim panel, as described previously in this Section.
43   Prise off the trim, and unbolt the seat belt upper mounting from the B- pillar. Recover the spacer.
44   Prise out the covers, and remove the two securing screws from the upper trim panel (one at the top and one at the bottom).
45   Carefully prise the panel from the pillar.

Refitting
46   Refitting is a reversal of removal, tightening the seat belt mounting to the specified torque.

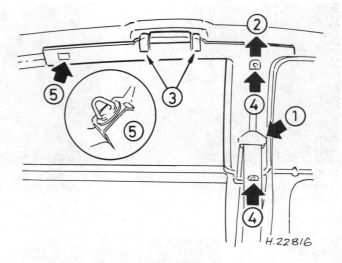

Fig. 11.16 B-pillar upper trim panel fixings – 3-door Hatchback models (Sec 30)

1 *Seat belt upper mounting*   3 *Grab handle*
    bolt   4 *Trim panel securing screws*
2 *Coat hook*   5 *Trim panel securing clip*

B-pillar upper trim panel – 3-door Hatchback models
Removal
47   Remove the rear side trim panel, as described later in this Section.
48   Prise off the trim, and unbolt the seat belt upper mounting from the B- pillar. Recover the spacer.
49   Extract the two securing screws, and remove the grab handle from the top of the B-pillar upper trim panel.
50   Extract the securing screw, and remove the coat hook from the B-pillar.
51   Prise out the cover, and remove the lower securing screw from the trim panel.
52   Carefully prise the panel from the body, releasing the clip from the rear end of the panel as it is withdrawn.

Refitting
53   Refitting is a reversal of removal, tightening the seat belt mounting to the specified torque.

30.56 Unscrewing a rear side trim panel securing screw – 3-door Hatchback model

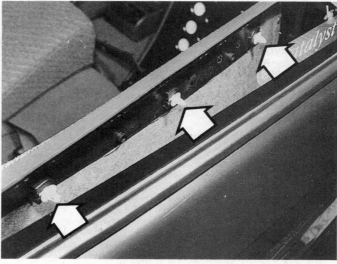

30.57 Rear side trim panel removed to expose securing clips (arrowed – viewed through rear window) – 3-door Hatchback model

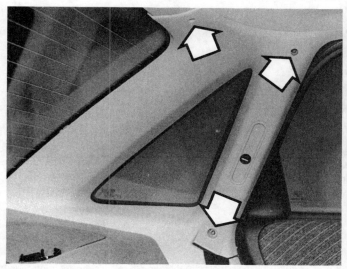

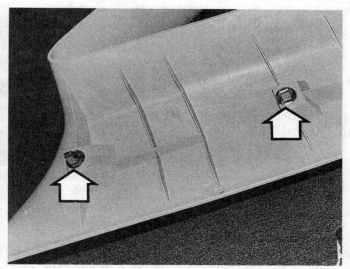

30.69 Rear quarter trim panel securing screw locations (arrowed) – Saloon model

30.70 Rear quarter trim panel removed to show two of the securing clips (arrowed) – Saloon model

Rear side trim panel – 3-door Hatchback models

Removal

54 Remove the rear sill trim panel, as described previously in this Section.

55 Open the door, and carefully pull the weatherseal from the front of the rear trim panel.

56 Prise out the cover, and remove the securing screw from the rear of the side trim panel (photo).

57 Carefully pull the panel from the body to release the securing clips (photo).

Refitting

58 Refitting is a reversal of removal.

Rear parcel shelf support panel – 3-door Hatchback models

Removal

59 Open the tailgate, then remove the parcel shelf, and fold the rear seat back forwards.

60 Working in the luggage compartment, disconnect the wiring from the loudspeaker.

61 Working inside the rear of the vehicle, where applicable prise out the cover, and remove the trim panel securing screw.

62 Working in the luggage compartment, remove the five remaining panel securing screws.

63 Carefully pull the panel from the body, releasing the retaining clip at the front of the panel as it is pulled free.

64 Pass the seat belt webbing and the wiring through the holes in the panel, and withdraw the panel from the vehicle.

Refitting

65 Refitting is a reversal of removal.

Rear quarter trim panel – Saloon models

Removal

66 Fold the rear seat back forwards.

67 Prise off the trim, and unbolt the seat belt upper mounting from the C- pillar. Recover the spacer.

68 Open the rear door, and carefully prise the weatherseal from the front edge of the trim panel.

69 Where applicable, prise out the covers, and remove the three trim panel securing screws (two upper screws, and one lower screw) (photo).

70 Carefully pull the panel from the body to release the securing clips, passing the seat belt webbing through the slot in the panel as it is withdrawn (photo).

Refitting

71 Refitting is a reversal of removal, tightening the seat belt mounting to the specified torque.

Rear quarter (C-pillar) trim panel – 3-door Hatchback models

Removal

72 Prise off the trim, and unbolt the seat belt upper mounting from the C-pillar. Recover the spacer.

73 Open the tailgate, and carefully prise the weatherseal from the rear edge of the trim panel.

74 Prise out the covers, remove the three securing screws, then withdraw the panel.

Refitting

75 Refitting is a reversal of removal, tightening the seat belt mounting to the specified torque.

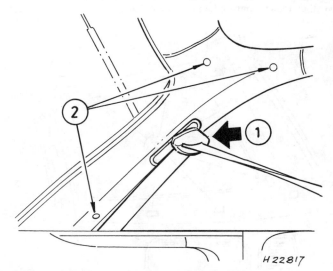

Fig. 11.17 Rear quarter (C-pillar) trim panel fixings – 3-door Hatchback models (Sec 30)

1   Seat belt upper mounting

2   Trim panel securing screws and covers

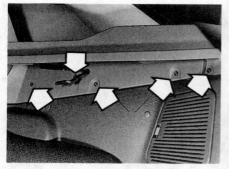

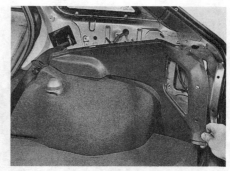

30.81 Rear quarter trim panel securing screws (arrowed) – 5-door Hatchback model

30.82 Removing the rear quarter trim panel – 5-door Hatchback model

30.93 Removing the luggage compartment side trim panel – 5-door Hatchback model

Rear quarter trim panel – 5-door Hatchback models

Removal

76   Remove the rear parcel shelf, and fold the rear seat back forwards.
77   Prise off the trim, and unbolt the seat belt upper mounting from the C-pillar. Recover the spacer.
78   Open the rear door and the tailgate, and carefully prise the weatherseals from the edges of the trim panel.
79   Working in the luggage compartment, disconnect the wiring from the loudspeaker.
80   Working inside the rear of the vehicle, where applicable prise out the covers, and remove the four trim panel securing screws.
81   Working in the luggage compartment, remove the five remaining panel securing screws (photo).
82   Carefully pull the panel from the body, releasing the retaining clip at the front of the panel as it is pulled free (photo).
83   Pass the seat belt webbing and the wiring through the holes in the panel, and withdraw the panel from the vehicle.

Refitting

84   Refitting is a reversal of removal, tightening the seat belt mounting to the specified torque.

Rear quarter trim panel – Estate models

Removal

85   Fold the rear seat back forwards.
86   Prise off the trim, and unbolt the seat belt upper mounting from the C-pillar. Recover the spacer.
87   Open the rear door and the tailgate, and carefully prise the weatherstrips from the edges of the trim panel.

88   Where applicable, remove the luggage retaining net and the luggage compartment cover.
89   Prise off the covers, and remove the three trim panel securing screws.
90   Carefully pull the panel from the body to release the securing clips, and withdraw the panel from the vehicle.

Refitting

91   Refitting is reversal of removal, tightening the seat belt mounting to the specified torque.

Luggage compartment, tailgate and boot lid trim panels

92   The luggage compartment trim panels on all models are secured by a combination of plastic clips and/or screws. Removal and refitting of the panels is self-explanatory, bearing in mind the points made in Section 29, and the following additional points.
93   To remove the luggage compartment side trim panel on Hatchback and Estate models, it will first be necessary to remove the rear quarter trim panel, as described previously in this Section (photo).
94   Various fittings, such as the luggage compartment light, and the first aid kit retaining strap bolt, may have to be removed before certain panels can be freed.

---

31   Centre console – removal and refitting

Removal

1   Disconnect the battery negative lead.
2   Carefully prise the rear ashtray from the centre console.

Fig. 11.18 Rear quarter trim panel fixings – Estate models (Sec 30)

H.26712

1   Securing screws and covers   2   Clips

31.3 Removing the central storage tray from the centre console

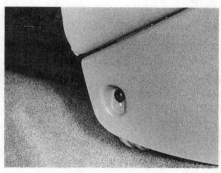

31.6 Rear ashtray removed to expose rear centre console securing screws

31.7 Central storage tray removed to expose centre console securing screws (arrowed)

31.8 Centre console front securing screw

3   Similarly, remove the central storage tray from the centre console (photo). Note that on models fitted with heated front seats and/or electronic traction control, it will be necessary to disconnect the battery negative lead and then disconnect the wiring from the relevant switches located in the storage tray, before the tray can be removed.

4   Release the handbrake lever gaiter from the centre console, and on manual gearbox models, release the gear lever gaiter from the centre console.

5   On models with automatic transmission, release the transmission selector cover from the centre console (the cover is secured by clips at either side). Pull the illumination light bulbholder from the selector cover, and disconnect the transmission 'Winter' mode switch wiring connector.

6   Remove the two securing screws from the rear ashtray housing (photo).

7   Remove the two securing screws from the central storage tray housing (photo).

8   Remove the two screws from the front of the centre console assembly – one screw on each side (photo), then slide the assembly rearwards, and pull the cigarette lighter plug and the illumination bulb from the rear of the assembly.

9   Withdraw the assembly, manipulating the gear lever gaiter/selector lever and cover (as applicable) through the aperture in the centre console, and sliding the handbrake lever gaiter from the assembly as it is withdrawn.

Refitting

10   Refitting is a reversal of removal.

32   Facia panels – removal and refitting

Note: *When removing facia panels, note the locations of the securing screws, as several different types of screw are used.*

Facia centre panel assembly

Removal

1   Disconnect the battery negative lead.

2   Remove the steering column shrouds and the instrument panel surround, as described later in this Section.

3   Remove the lighting control stalk (right-hand-drive models), or the wash/wipe control stalk (left-hand-drive models), as applicable, as described in Chapter 12.

4   Remove the hazard warning light switch, as described in Chapter 12.

5   Remove the radio/cassette player, and the multi-function display, as described in Chapter 12.

6   Remove the centre facia ventilation nozzles, as described in Chapter 3, Section 11.

7   Working through the centre facia ventilation nozzle apertures, carefully release the securing clip, using a screwdriver or a similar tool, and disconnect the vent flap actuating rod (photo).

8   Remove the two lower facia panel securing screws, visible at the bottom of the panel (photo).

9   Carefully pull off the heater air distribution and temperature control switch knobs, to expose two of the facia panel securing screws, then extract the screws (photos).

10   Turn the heater blower switch knob to position '3', then insert a small screwdriver or a suitable rod through the hole in the bottom of the

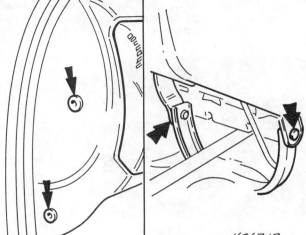

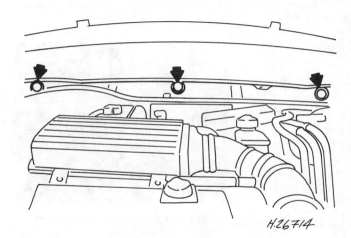

Fig. 11.19 Facia internal fixing screws (arrowed) (Sec 32)

Fig. 11.20 Facia panel bulkhead fixing bolts (arrowed) (Sec 32)

32.7 Releasing the centre facia ventilation vent flap actuating rod

32.8 Unscrewing a facia centre panel lower securing screw

32.9A Pull off the heater switch knobs ...

32.9B ... and extract the facia centre panel securing screws

32.11 Unscrewing a facia centre panel upper securing screw

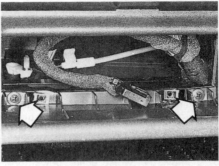

32.12 Multi-function display removed to expose facia centre panel securing screws (arrowed)

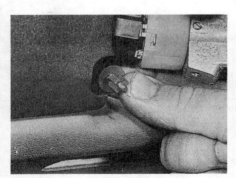

32.13 Removing the facia centre panel securing clip

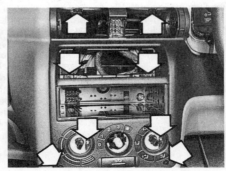

32.14A Facia centre panel securing screws (arrowed)

32.14B Withdrawing the facia centre panel assembly

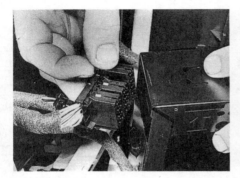

32.14C Disconnecting the radio/cassette unit wiring plug ...

32.14D ... and the hazard warning light switch wiring plug from the rear of the facia centre panel assembly

32.20A Prise out the covers ...

32.20B ... to expose the front steering column shroud securing screws

32.21 Unscrewing a steering column shroud lower securing screw

switch knob to depress the knob retaining clip. Pull the knob from the switch.
11   Remove the two upper facia panel securing screws, accessible through the centre facia ventilation nozzle apertures (photo).
12   Remove the two centre facia panel securing screws, accessible through the multi-function display aperture (photo).
13   Carefully pull out the facia panel securing clip, accessible from behind the right-hand side (right-hand-drive models), or the left-hand side (left-hand-drive models) of the panel, as applicable (photo).
14   The facia centre panel assembly can now be carefully withdrawn from the facia. As the assembly is withdrawn, disconnect the radio aerial lead, the radio/cassette unit wiring plug, and the hazard warning light switch wiring plug from the rear of the assembly (photos).

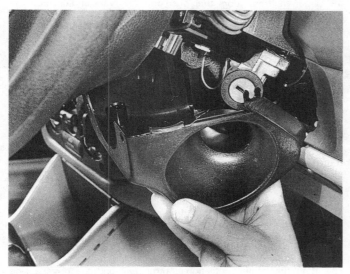

32.23 Withdrawing the lower steering column shroud

Refitting
15   Refitting is a reversal of removal, bearing in mind the following points.
16   Make sure that all electrical plugs are securely reconnected to the rear of the assembly, and as the assembly is refitted, feed the multi-function display wiring through the multi-function display aperture, to aid subsequent reconnection.
17   Ensure that the centre vent flap actuating rod is securely reconnected, before refitting the ventilation nozzles.

Steering column shrouds
Removal
18   Disconnect the battery negative lead.
19   Turn the steering wheel to expose the two front steering column shroud securing screw covers.
20   Prise out the covers, then remove the securing screws (photos).
21   Working under the lower steering column shroud, remove the three lower securing screws, noting their locations, as the screws are of different lengths (photo).
22   Pull the rubber grommet from the ignition switch.
23   Unclip the lower shroud from the upper shroud (two clips at the back, and one each side), and withdraw the lower shroud (photo).
24   Unhook the stalk switch gaiters from the upper shroud, and withdraw the upper shroud (photo).

Refitting
25   Refitting is a reversal of removal, but ensure that the stalk switch gaiters and ignition switch grommet are correctly located, and make sure that the lower shroud securing screws are refitted to their original locations.

Instrument panel surround
Removal
26   Remove the steering column shrouds, as described earlier in this Section.
27   Where applicable, prise out the screw covers, then remove the four (two upper and two lower) securing screws, and withdraw the instrument panel surround (photos).

32.24 Withdrawing the upper steering column shroud

32.27A Unscrewing an instrument panel surround lower securing screw

32.27B Withdrawing the instrument panel surround

Refitting
28   Refitting is a reversal of removal.

Ventilation nozzles
29   Refer to Chapter 3, Section 11.

Driver's side ventilation nozzle housing
30   This housing also houses the lighting switch, headlight aim adjustment switch, and foglight switch(es). Removal and refitting of the panel is described in Chapter 3, Section 11.

Passenger's side ventilation nozzle housing
31   Refer to Chapter 3, Section 11.

Glovebox
Removal
32   With the glovebox lid closed, unscrew the two lower securing screws, which are accessible below the glovebox.
33   Open the glovebox lid, and prise the glovebox light from its location in the side of the glovebox. If desired, disconnect the wiring, and remove the light assembly.
34   Unscrew the two upper securing screws, which are now accessible at the top of the glovebox.
35   Withdraw the glovebox from the facia, feeding the light through the aperture in the side of the glovebox as it is withdrawn (photo).

Refitting
36   Refitting is a reversal of removal.

Glovebox lock cylinder
Removal
37   Squeeze the two securing lugs together, and remove the cover from the glovebox catch.
38   Insert the key into the lock cylinder, then turn the key and cylinder to the locked position, and pull the lock cylinder from its housing using the key.

Refitting
39   Refitting is a reversal of removal.

Footwell lower trim panels
Removal
40   The footwell lower trim panels are attached to the bottom of the facia by plastic securing clips.
41   To remove a panel, release the clips by turning them with a suitable screwdriver, then withdraw the panel from underneath the facia.

Refitting
42   Refitting is a reversal of removal.

Complete facia assembly
Removal
43   Disconnect the battery negative lead.
44   Remove the centre console, as described in Section 31.
45   Remove the facia centre panel assembly, the steering column

32.35 Withdrawing the glovebox assembly

shrouds, the footwell lower trim panels, the glovebox, and the instrument panel surround, as described earlier in this Section.
46   Remove the heater/ventilation control unit, and the driver's side ventilation nozzle housing, as described in Chapter 3.
47   Remove the steering wheel, as described in Chapter 10.
48   Remove the steering column stalk switches, the instrument panel, and the fusebox, as described in Chapter 12.
49   Open the front doors, then prise out the covers, and unscrew the two securing screws from each side of the facia.
50   Working under the centre of the facia, unscrew the two lower facia securing screws from the mounting bracket.
51   Remove the windscreen wiper motor and linkage, as described in Chapter 12.
52   Unscrew the three facia panel securing bolts from the engine compartment bulkhead.
53   With the aid of an assistant, withdraw the facia assembly into the interior of the vehicle, and carefully disconnect all wiring and hoses from the rear of the facia.
54   Check that all relevant wiring and hoses have been disconnected, then manipulate the facia out through one of the front door apertures.

Refitting
55   Refitting is a reversal of removal, bearing in mind the following points.
56   Make sure that all relevant wiring and hoses are securely reconnected, and routed so that they are not under strain.
57   Refit the windscreen wiper motor and linkage as described in Chapter 12.
58   Refit the instrument panel as described in Chapter 12.
59   Refit the steering wheel as described in Chapter 10.
60   Refit the heater/ventilation control unit, and the driver's side ventilation nozzle housing, as described in Chapter 3.
61   Refit the facia centre panel assembly, as described earlier in this Section.

Chapter 12 Electrical system

Contents

Specifications

System type .... 12-volt, negative earth

Battery
Type... Maintenance-free (sealed-for-life) lead-acid
Battery capacity .... 36, 44, 66, or 70 Ah

Alternator
Type.. Bosch or Delco-Remy
Output .... 55 or 70 amps, depending on model
Minimum brush length:
    Bosch type alternator (all except code number 0 120 488 193 .... 5.0 mm protrusion
    Bosch type alternator (code number 0 120 488 193)......................... 11.0 to 12.0 mm protrusion
    Delco-Remy type alternator... 12.0 mm overall length

Starter motor

Type	Pre-engaged Bosch, Delco-Remy or Valeo
Brush minimum length:	
Bosch DM type starter motor	3.0 mm
Bosch DW type starter motor	8.0 mm
Delco-Remy type starter motor (all except code number 09 000 756)	4.0 mm
Delco-Remy type starter motor (code number 09 000 756)	8.5 mm
Valeo type starter motor	No data available at time of writing

Fuses – fusebox with 30 fuse locations

Fuse No	Rating (amps)	Circuit(s) protected
1	20	Central door locking
2	20	Fuel pump
3	30	Horn, windscreen and tailgate wash/wipe systems
4	10	Left-hand headlight dipped beam, left-hand headlight aim adjustment motor, bulb failure sensor
5	10	Right-hand headlight dipped beam, right-hand headlight aim adjustment motor, bulb failure sensor
6	10	Automatic transmission ECU, anti-lock braking system ECU
7	10	Warning lights, 'headlights on' warning buzzer, electric mirrors, glovebox light, radio/cassette player, facia switch illumination bulbs, heated rear window
8	20	Tow bar coupling
9		Unused
10		Unused
11		Unused
12	10	Left-hand headlight main beam
13	10	Right-hand headlight main beam, headlight main beam warning light
14	15	Electronic traction control ECU
15	30	Electric window motors
16		Unused
17	20	Front foglights
18	10	Left-hand sidelight, left-hand tail light, bulb failure sensor
19	10	Right-hand sidelight, right-hand tail light, number plate light(s), bulb failure sensor, facia switch illumination bulbs, centre console switch illumination bulbs, radio/cassette player, headlight washer pump, 'headlights on' warning buzzer
20	20	Central door locking, carburettor automatic choke, automatic transmission switch, reversing lights, cigarette lighter, seat heating
21		Unused
22	10	Anti-theft alarm horn
23		Unused
24	20	Electric aerial, direction indicators, radio/cassette player, interior lights
25	10	Automatic transmission ECU
26		Unused
27	10	Daytime running lights (Norway and Sweden only)
28	10	Rear foglights
30	20	Heated rear window

Fuses – fusebox with 28 fuse locations

All fuse ratings and circuits protected as for fusebox with 30 fuse locations, except for the following.

Fuse No	Rating (amps)	Circuit(s) protected
9	15	Electronic traction control ECU
10	30	Electric window motors
11	10	Rear foglights
14	30	Heater blower motor
15	30	Cooling fan
16	30	Heated rear window
22		Unused
23	30	Headlight washer system

Torque wrench settings

	Nm	lbf ft
Alternator mounting bolts:		
M8 bolts	30	22
M10 bolts	40	30
Starter motor mounting bolts:		
1.4 and 1.6 litre engines	25	18
1.8 and 2.0 litre engines:		
Engine side	45	33
Transmission side	75	55

1 General information and precautions

Warning: *Before carrying out any work on the electrical system, read through the precautions given in 'Safety first!' at the beginning of this manual.*

The electrical system is of the 12-volt negative earth type, and consists of a 12-volt battery, an alternator with integral voltage regulator, a starter motor and related electrical accessories, components and wiring.

The battery is of the 'maintenance-free' (sealed-for-life) type, and is charged by the alternator, which is belt-driven from a crankshaft-mounted pulley.

The starter motor is of the pre-engaged type, incorporating an integral solenoid. On starting, the solenoid moves the drive pinion into engagement with the flywheel ring gear before the starter motor is energised. Once the engine has started, a one-way clutch prevents the motor armature being driven by the engine until the pinion disengages from the flywheel.

Further details of the various systems are given in the relevant Sections of this Chapter. While some repair procedures are given, the usual course of action is to renew the component concerned. The owner whose interest extends beyond mere component renewal should obtain a copy of the *'Automobile Electrical & Electronic Systems Manual'*, available from the publishers of this manual.

It is necessary to take extra care when working on the electrical system to avoid damage to semi-conductor devices (diodes and transistors), and to avoid the risk of personal injury. In addition to the precautions given in *'Safety first!'* at the beginning of this manual, observe the following when working on the system.

Always remove rings, watches, etc., before working on the electrical system. Even with the battery disconnected, capacitive discharge could occur if a component's live terminal is earthed through a metal object. This could cause a shock or nasty burn.

Do not reverse the battery connections. Components such as the alternator, fuel injection/ignition system electronic control unit (where applicable), or any other components having semi-conductor circuitry could be irreparably damaged.

If the engine is being started using jump leads and a slave battery, connect the batteries *positive-to-positive* and *negative-to-negative* (see *'Booster battery (jump) starting'*). This also applies when connecting a battery charger.

Never disconnect the battery terminals, the alternator, any electrical wiring or any test instruments when the engine is running.

Do not allow the engine to turn the alternator when the alternator is not connected.

Never 'test' for alternator output by 'flashing' the output lead to earth.

Never use an ohmmeter of the type incorporating a hand-cranked generator for circuit or continuity testing.

Always ensure that the battery negative lead is disconnected when working on the electrical system.

Before using electric-arc welding equipment on the car, disconnect the battery, alternator and components such as the fuel injection/ignition system electronic control unit (where applicable), to protect them from the risk of damage.

2 Electrical fault-finding – general information

Note: *Refer to the precautions given in 'Safety first!' and in Section 1 of this Chapter before starting work. The following tests relate to testing of the main electrical circuits, and should not be used to test delicate electronic circuits (such as engine management systems, anti-lock braking systems, etc), particularly where an electronic control module is used. Refer to Chapter 4, Section 24 for precautions to be observed when working on models fitted with electronic control units.*

General

1   A typical electrical circuit consists of an electrical component, any switches, relays, motors, fuses, fusible links or circuit breakers related to that component, and the wiring and connectors which link the component to both the battery and the chassis. To help to pinpoint a problem in an electrical circuit, wiring diagrams are included at the end of this manual.

2   Before attempting to diagnose an electrical fault, first study the appropriate wiring diagram to obtain a complete understanding of the components included in the particular circuit concerned. The possible sources of a fault can be narrowed down by noting if other components related to the circuit are operating properly. If several components or circuits fail at one time, the problem is likely to be related to a shared fuse or earth connection.

3   Electrical problems usually stem from simple causes, such as loose or corroded connections, a faulty earth connection, a blown fuse, a melted fusible link, or a faulty relay (refer to Section 13 for details of testing relays). Visually inspect the condition of all fuses, wires and connections in a problem circuit before testing the components. Use the wiring diagrams to determine which terminal connections will need to be checked, in order to pinpoint the trouble-spot.

4   The basic tools required for electrical fault-finding include a circuit tester or voltmeter (a 12-volt bulb with a set of test leads can also be used for certain tests); a self-powered test light (sometimes known as a continuity tester); an ohmmeter (to measure resistance); a battery and set of test leads; and a jumper wire, preferably with a circuit breaker or fuse incorporated, which can be used to bypass suspect wires or electrical components. Before attempting to locate a problem with test instruments, use the wiring diagram to determine where to make the connections.

5   To find the source of an intermittent wiring fault (usually due to a poor or dirty connection, or damaged wiring insulation), a 'wiggle' test can be performed on the wiring. This involves wiggling the wiring by hand to see if the fault occurs as the wiring is moved. It should be possible to narrow down the source of the fault to a particular section of wiring. This method of testing can be used in conjunction with any of the tests described in the following sub-Sections.

6   Apart from problems due to poor connections, two basic types of fault can occur in an electrical circuit – open-circuit, or short-circuit.

7   Open-circuit faults are caused by a break somewhere in the circuit, which prevents current from flowing. An open-circuit fault will prevent a component from working, but will not cause the relevant circuit fuse to blow.

8   Short-circuit faults are caused by a 'short' somewhere in the circuit, which allows the current flowing in the circuit to 'escape' along an alternative route, usually to earth. Short-circuit faults are normally caused by a breakdown in wiring insulation, which allows a feed wire to touch either another wire, or an earthed component such as the bodyshell. A short-circuit fault will normally cause the relevant circuit fuse to blow.

Finding an open-circuit

9   To check for an open-circuit, connect one lead of a circuit tester or voltmeter to either the negative battery terminal or a known good earth.

10   Connect the other lead to a connector in the circuit being tested, preferably nearest to the battery or fuse.

11   Switch on the circuit, bearing in mind that some circuits are live only when the ignition switch is moved to a particular position.

12   If voltage is present (indicated either by the tester bulb lighting or a voltmeter reading, as applicable), this means that the section of the circuit between the relevant connector and the battery is problem-free.

13   Continue to check the remainder of the circuit in the same fashion.

14   When a point is reached at which no voltage is present, the problem must lie between that point and the previous test point with voltage. Most problems can be traced to a broken, corroded or loose connection.

Finding a short-circuit

15   To check for a short-circuit, first disconnect the load(s) from the circuit (loads are the components which draw current from a circuit, such as bulbs, motors, heating elements, etc).

16   Remove the relevant fuse from the circuit, and connect a circuit tester or voltmeter to the fuse connections.

17   Switch on the circuit, bearing in mind that some circuits are live only when the ignition switch is moved to a particular position.

18   If voltage is present (indicated either by the tester bulb lighting or a voltmeter reading, as applicable), this means that there is a short-circuit.

19   If no voltage is present, but the fuse still blows with the load(s) connected, this indicates an internal fault in the load(s).

Finding an earth fault

20　The battery negative terminal is connected to 'earth' – the metal of the engine/transmission unit and the car body – and most systems are wired so that they only receive a positive feed, the current returning via the metal of the car body. This means that the component mounting and the body form part of that circuit. Loose or corroded mountings can therefore cause a range of electrical faults, ranging from total failure of a circuit, to a puzzling partial fault. In particular, lights may shine dimly (especially when another circuit sharing the same earth point is in operation), motors (eg wiper motors or the radiator cooling fan motor) may run slowly, and the operation of one circuit may have an apparently-unrelated effect on another. Note that on many vehicles, earth straps are used between certain components, such as the engine/transmission and the body, usually where there is no metal-to-metal contact between components due to flexible rubber mountings, etc.

21　To check whether a component is properly earthed, disconnect the battery, and connect one lead of an ohmmeter to a known good earth point. Connect the other lead to the wire or earth connection being tested. The resistance reading should be zero; if not, check the connection as follows.

22　If an earth connection is thought to be faulty, dismantle the connection, and clean back to bare metal both the bodyshell and the wire terminal or the component earth connection mating surface. Be careful to remove all traces of dirt and corrosion, then use a knife to trim away any paint, so that a clean metal-to-metal joint is made. On reassembly, tighten the joint fasteners securely; if a wire terminal is being refitted, use serrated washers between the terminal and the bodyshell, to ensure a clean and secure connection. When the connection is re-made, prevent the onset of corrosion in the future by applying a coat of petroleum jelly or silicone-based grease. Alternatively, (at regular intervals) spray on a proprietary ignition sealer such as Holts Damp Start, or a water-dispersant lubricant such as Holts Wet Start.

3　Battery – testing and charging

Note: *The following information refers only to the maintenance-free type battery fitted as original equipment by the manufacturers.*

1　Topping-up and testing of the electrolyte in each battery cell is not possible. The condition of the battery can therefore only be tested by observing the battery condition indicator.

2　The battery condition indicator is located in the top of the battery casing, and indicates the condition of the battery by its colour. If the indicator shows green, then the battery is in a good state of charge. If the indicator turns darker, eventually to black, then the battery requires charging, as described later in this Section. If the indicator shows clear/yellow, then the electrolyte level in the battery is too low to allow further use, and the battery should be renewed. **Do not** attempt to charge, load or jump-start a battery when the indicator shows clear/yellow.

3　If the battery is to be charged, remove it from the vehicle and charge it as follows.

4　The maintenance-free type battery takes considerably longer to fully recharge than the standard type, the time taken being dependent on the extent of discharge.

5　A constant-voltage type charger is required; connect it up and set it to 13.9 to 14.9 volts, with a charge current below 25 amps.

6　If the battery is to be charged from a fully-discharged state (less than 12.2 volts output), have it recharged by a Vauxhall/Opel dealer or a competent automotive electrician, as the charge rate is high, and constant supervision during charging is necessary.

4　Battery – removal and refitting

Removal

1　The battery is located at the front left-hand corner of the engine compartment.

2　Disconnect the lead(s) at the negative (earth) terminal by unscrewing the retaining nut and removing the terminal clamp.

3　Disconnect the positive terminal lead(s) in the same way.

4　Unscrew the clamp bolt sufficiently to enable the battery to be lifted from its location. Keep the battery upright, to avoid spilling electrolyte on the bodywork.

Refitting

5　Refitting is a reversal of removal, but smear petroleum jelly on the terminals when reconnecting the leads, and always reconnect the positive lead first, and the negative lead last.

5　Charging system – testing

Note: *Refer to the warnings given in 'Safety first!' and in Section 1 of this Chapter before starting work.*

1　If the ignition warning light fails to illuminate when the ignition is switched on, first check the alternator wiring connections for security. If satisfactory, check that the warning light bulb has not blown, and that the bulbholder is secure in its location in the instrument panel. If the light still fails to illuminate, check the continuity of the warning light feed wire from the alternator to the bulbholder. If all is satisfactory, the alternator is at fault, and should be renewed or taken to an auto-electrician for testing and repair.

2　If the ignition warning light illuminates when the engine is running, stop the engine and check that the drivebelt is correctly tensioned (Section 6) and that the alternator connections are secure. If all is so far satisfactory, check the alternator brushes and slip rings (see Section 8). If the fault persists, the alternator should be renewed, or taken to an auto-electrician for testing and repair.

3　If the alternator output is suspect even though the warning light functions correctly, the regulated voltage may be checked as follows.

4　Connect a voltmeter across the battery terminals and start the engine.

5　Increase the engine speed until the voltmeter reading remains steady; the reading should be approximately 12 to 13 volts, and no more than 14 volts.

6　Switch on as many electrical accessories (eg, the headlights, heated rear window and heater blower) as possible, and check that the alternator maintains the regulated voltage at around 13 to 14 volts.

7　If the regulated voltage is not as stated, the fault may be due to worn brushes, weak brush springs, a faulty voltage regulator, a faulty diode, a severed phase winding, or worn or damaged slip rings. The brushes and slip rings may be checked (see Section 8), but if the fault persists, the alternator should be renewed or taken to an auto-electrician for testing and repair.

6　Alternator drivebelt – removal, refitting and tensioning

Removal

1　Disconnect the air intake trunking from the air cleaner, and from the airbox or the throttle body, as applicable, and remove it for improved access.

2　On 1.4 and 1.6 litre engine models with power steering, the alternator drivebelt also drives the power steering pump.

3　To remove the belt on 1.8 and 2.0 litre engine models, first remove the power steering pump drivebelt, as described in Chapter 10.

4　Loosen the alternator mounting nuts and bolts sufficiently to allow the alternator to be pivoted in towards the engine (photo).

5　Slide the belt from the pulleys.

Refitting

6　Fit the belt around the pulleys, ensuring that the belt is of the correct type if it is being renewed, and take up the slack in the belt by swinging the alternator away from the engine and lightly tightening the mounting nuts and bolts.

7　On 1.8 and 2.0 litre engine models, refit and tension the power steering pump drivebelt, as described in Chapter 10.

8　Tension the alternator drivebelt as described in the following paragraphs.

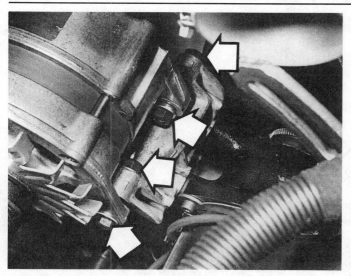

6.4 Lower alternator mounting nuts and bolts (arrowed). Viewed with top alternator mounting disconnected – Bosch alternator

Tensioning

9   Correct tensioning of the drivebelt will ensure that it has a long life. Beware, however, of overtightening, as this can cause excessive wear in the alternator.

10   Refer to paragraphs 1 and 2.

11   Although special tools are available for checking the belt tension, a good approximation can be achieved if the belt is tensioned so that there is approximately 13.0 mm of free movement under firm thumb pressure at the mid-point of the longest run between pulleys.

12   With the mounting bolts just holding the unit firm, lever the alternator away from the engine using a wooden lever at the mounting bracket end until the correct tension is achieved, then tighten the mounting nuts and bolts. **On no account** lever at the free end of the alternator, as serious internal damage could be caused.

13   Refit the air trunking.

14   When a new belt has been fitted, it will probably stretch slightly when it is first run, and the tension should be rechecked and if necessary adjusted after approximately 250 miles (400 km) of running.

7   Alternator – removal and refitting

Removal

1   Disconnect the battery leads.

2   For improved access, disconnect the air trunking from the air cleaner, and from the airbox or throttle body, as applicable, and remove it.

3   Disconnect the wires from their terminals on the rear of the alternator, noting their locations, or disconnect the wiring plug, as applicable (photo).

4   Remove the drivebelt, as described in Section 6.

5   Unscrew the two mounting bolts and nuts, and recover any washers and insulating bushes, noting their locations. Note the earth strap attached to the top mounting bolts on certain models (photo).

6   Withdraw the alternator (photo), taking care not to knock or drop it, as this can cause irreparable damage.

Refitting

7   Refitting is a reversal of removal, bearing in mind the following points.

8   Where applicable, ensure that the earth lead is in place on the top mounting bolt.

9   Refit and tension the drivebelt, as described in Section 6.

8   Alternator brushes and regulator – inspection and renewal

Delco-Remy type alternator

1   The brush holder and voltage regulator are combined in a single assembly. For access to the assembly, the alternator must be partially dismantled as follows. If the voltage regulator is faulty, the complete assembly must be renewed.

2   Remove the alternator as described in Section 7.

3   Scribe a line across the drive end housing and the slip ring end housing, to ensure correct alignment when reassembling.

4   Unscrew the three through-bolts, and prise the drive end housing and rotor away from the slip ring end housing and stator (photo).

5   Check the condition of the slip rings, and if necessary clean with a rag or very fine glass paper (photo).

6   Remove the three nuts and washers securing the stator leads to the rectifier, and lift away the stator assembly (photo).

7   Remove the terminal screw, and lift out the diode assembly.

8   Extract the two screws securing the brush holder and voltage regulator to the slip ring end housing, and remove the brush holder assembly. Note the insulation washers under the screw heads.

9   Check that the brushes move freely in their guides, and that the brush lengths are within the limits given in the Specifications. If any doubt exists regarding the condition of the brushes, the best policy is to renew them.

10   To fit new brushes, unsolder the old brush leads from the brush holder, and solder on the new leads in exactly the same place.

11   Check that the new brushes move freely in the guides.

12   Before refitting the brush holder assembly, retain the brushes in the retracted position using a stiff piece of wire or a twist drill.

13   Refit the brush holder assembly so that the wire or drill protrudes through the slot in the slip ring end housing, and tighten the securing screws.

14   Refit the diode assembly and the stator assembly to the housing, ensuring that the stator leads are in their correct positions, and refit the terminal screw and nuts.

15   Assemble the drive end housing and rotor to the slip ring end housing, ensuring that the previously-made marks are still aligned. Insert and tighten the three through-bolts.

16   Pull the wire or drill, as applicable, from the slot in the slip ring end housing, so that the brushes rest on the rotor slip rings (photo).

7.3 Wiring connections (arrowed) at rear of alternator – Bosch alternator

7.5 Earth strap (arrowed) attached to top alternator mounting bolts

7.6 Withdrawing the alternator

Fig. 12.1 Exploded view of Delco-Remy type alternator (Sec 8)

1　Pulley nut (not fitted to all
　　models)
2　Pulley
3　Fan
4　Drive end housing
5　Bearing
6　Bearing retainer
7　Rotor
8　Through-bolt
9　Slip ring end housing
10　Brush holder/voltage
　　regulator assembly
11　Diode assembly
12　Stator

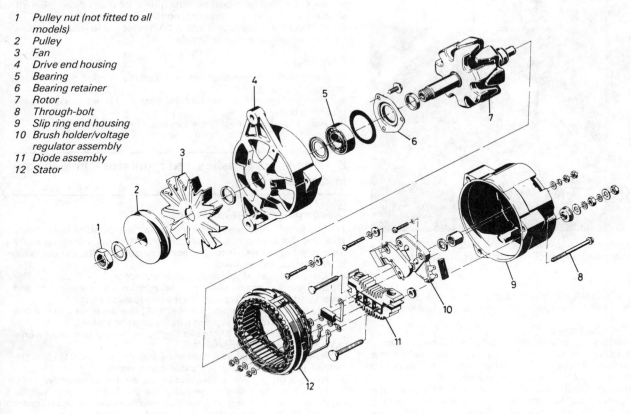

Fig. 12.2 Exploded view of Bosch type alternator (Sec 8)

1　Pulley nut
2　Pulley
3　Fan
4　Drive end housing
5　Bearing
6　Bearing retainer
7　Through-bolts
8　Brush holder/voltage
　　regulator assembly
9　Slip ring end housing
10　Stator endplate
11　Stator
12　Bearing
13　Rotor

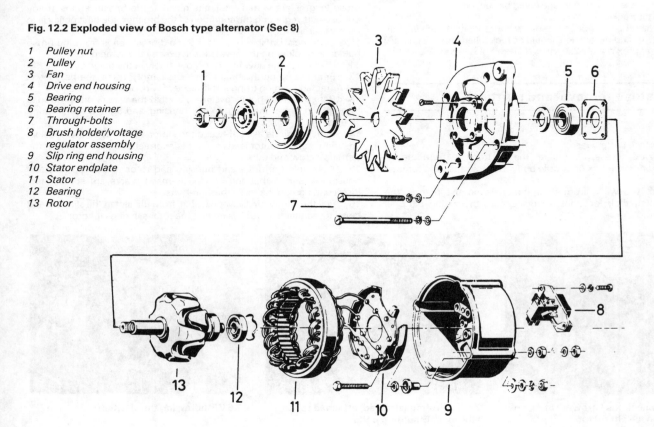

8.4 Separating the drive end housing from the slip ring end housing – Delco-Remy alternator

8.5 Alternator slip rings (arrowed) – Delco-Remy alternator

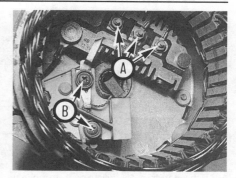

8.6 Stator lead securing nuts (A) and brush holder/voltage regulator securing screws (B) – Delco-Remy alternator

8.16 Removing drill bit used to hold brushes in retracted position

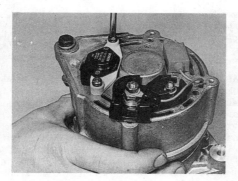

8.22A Remove the securing screws ...

8.22B ... and withdraw the brush holder/voltage regulator – Bosch alternator

17 Refit the alternator, as described in Section 7.

Bosch type alternator

18 The brush holder and voltage regulator are combined in a single assembly, which is bolted to the rear of the alternator. If the voltage regulator is faulty, the complete assembly must be renewed.

19 Disconnect the air trunking from the air cleaner, and from the airbox or throttle body, as applicable, and remove it for improved access.

20 Disconnect the battery negative lead.

21 If desired, to improve access further, the alternator can be removed, as described in Section 7.

22 Remove the two securing screws, and withdraw the brush holder/voltage regulator assembly (photos).

23 Check that the brushes move freely in their guides, and that the brush lengths are within the limits given in the Specifications (photo). If any doubt exists regarding the condition of the brushes, the best policy is to renew them as follows.

24 Hold the brush wire with a suitable pair of pliers, and unsolder it from the brush holder. Lift away the brush. Repeat for the remaining brush.

25 Note that whenever new brushes are fitted, new brush springs should also be fitted.

26 With the new springs fitted to the brush holder, insert the new brushes, and check that they move freely in their guides. If they bind, lightly polish with a very fine file or glass paper.

27 Solder the brush wire ends to the brush holder, taking care not to allow solder to pass to the stranded wire.

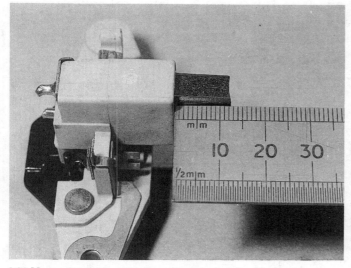

8.23 Measuring the length of an alternator brush – Bosch alternator

8.28 Alternator slip rings (arrowed) – Bosch alternator

28   Check the condition of the slip rings, and if necessary clean them with a rag or very fine glass paper (photo).
29   Refit the brush holder/voltage regulator assembly, and tighten the securing screws.
30   Where applicable, refit the alternator, as described in Section 7.
31   Reconnect the battery leads.
32   Refit the air trunking.

9   Starting system – testing

Note: *Refer to the precautions given in 'Safety first!' and in Section 1 of this Chapter before starting work.*

1   If the starter motor fails to operate when the ignition key is turned to the appropriate position, the following possible causes may be to blame.

   (a)   The battery is faulty.
   (b)   The electrical connections between the switch, solenoid, battery and starter motor are somewhere failing to pass the necessary current from the battery through the starter to earth.
   (c)   The solenoid is faulty.
   (d)   The starter motor is mechanically or electrically defective.

2   To check the battery, switch on the headlights. If they dim after a few seconds, this indicates that the battery is discharged – recharge (see Section 3) or renew the battery. If the headlights glow brightly, operate the ignition switch and observe the lights. If they dim, then this indicates that current is reaching the starter motor, therefore the fault must lie in the starter motor. If the lights continue to glow brightly (and no clicking sound can be heard from the starter motor solenoid), this indicates that there is a fault in the circuit or solenoid – see following paragraphs. If the starter motor turns slowly when operated, but the battery is in good condition, then this indicates that either the starter motor is faulty, or there is considerable resistance somewhere in the circuit.
3   If a fault in the circuit is suspected, disconnect the battery leads (including the earth connection to the body), the starter/solenoid wiring and the engine/transmission earth strap. Thoroughly clean the connections, reconnect the leads and wiring, then use a voltmeter or test light to check that full battery voltage is available at the battery positive lead connection to the solenoid, and that the earth is sound. Smear petroleum jelly around the battery terminals to prevent corrosion – corroded connections are amongst the most frequent causes of electrical system faults.
4   If the battery and all connections are in good condition, check the circuit by disconnecting the wire from the solenoid blade terminal. Connect a voltmeter or test light between the wire end and a good earth (such as the battery negative terminal), and check that the wire is live when the ignition switch is turned to the 'start' position. If it is, then the circuit is sound – if not, proceed to paragraph 5.

5   The solenoid contacts can be checked by connecting a voltmeter or test light between the battery positive feed connection on the starter side of the solenoid, and earth. When the ignition switch is turned to the 'start' position, there should be a reading or lighted bulb, as applicable. If there is no reading or lighted bulb, the solenoid is faulty and should be renewed.
6   If the circuit and solenoid are proved sound, the fault must lie in the starter motor. Begin checking the starter motor by removing it (see Section 10), and checking the brushes (see Section 11). If the fault does not lie in the brushes, the motor windings must be faulty. In this event, the starter motor can be overhauled as described in Section 11, but check on the availability and cost of spares before proceeding, as it may prove more economical to obtain a new or exchange motor.

10   Starter motor – removal and refitting

Removal

1   Disconnect the battery negative lead.
2   Apply the handbrake, then jack up the front of the vehicle, and support securely on axle stands (see *'Jacking, towing and wheel changing'*).
3   On DOHC engine models, remove the engine undershield, as described in Chapter 11, Section 25.
4   Note the wiring connections on the solenoid, then disconnect them (photo).
5   Where applicable, unscrew the bolt securing the starter motor mounting bracket to the cylinder block.
6   Unscrew the two starter motor mounting bolts, noting that the top bolt on 1.8 and 2.0 litre models is fitted from the gearbox side, and also secures the wiring harness bracket (photo). Where applicable, also note the location of the engine earth strap, which may be secured by one of the starter motor mounting bolts on certain models.
7   Withdraw the starter motor.

Refitting

8   Refitting is a reversal of removal, but where applicable, ensure that the wiring harness bracket is in place on the top mounting bolt, and tighten all bolts to the specified torque.

11   Starter motor – overhaul

Bosch DM type starter motor

1   With the starter motor removed from the vehicle and cleaned, grip the unit in a vice fitted with soft jaw protectors.

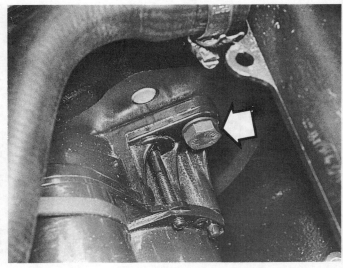

10.4 Starter motor solenoid wiring connections   **10.6 Starter motor mounting bolt (arrowed) – viewed from above**

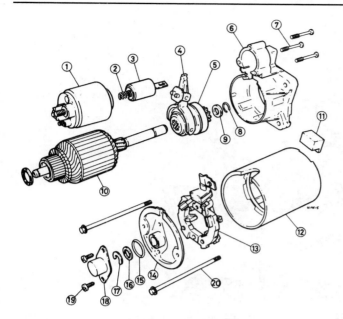

Fig. 12.3 Exploded view of Bosch DM type starter motor (Sec 11)

1	Solenoid yoke	11	Rubber insert
2	Solenoid return spring	12	Yoke
3	Solenoid armature	13	Brush plate
4	Actuating arm	14	Commutator end plate
5	Drive pinion and clutch	15	Seal
	assembly	16	Shim
6	Drive end housing	17	C-clip
7	Solenoid securing screws	18	Commutator end housing
8	C-clip		cap
9	Thrust collar	19	Securing screw
10	Armature	20	Through-bolt

2   Unscrew the nuts from the ends of the through-bolts, and remove the mounting bracket, where applicable.

3   Remove the nut and washer securing the field winding lead to the solenoid stud, and unhook the lead from the stud.

4   Remove the two screws securing the commutator end plate cap, then remove the cap and rubber seal.

5   Wipe any grease from the armature shaft, then remove the C-clip and shims from the end of the shaft.

6   Unscrew the two through-bolts, and lift off the commutator end plate.

7   Release the brush holders, complete with brushes, by pushing the brush holders towards the commutator and unclipping them from the brush plate. Withdraw the brush plate.

8   Separate the drive end housing and armature from the yoke by tapping them apart with a soft-faced hammer.

9   Remove the three securing screws, and withdraw the solenoid yoke, then unhook the solenoid armature from the actuating arm and remove the armature.

10   Remove the rubber insert from the drive end housing, then unscrew the actuating arm pivot retaining nut and slide the pivot pin (bolt) from the housing.

11   Withdraw the armature assembly, complete with actuating arm, from the drive end housing. Unhook the actuating arm from the drive pinion flange.

12   To remove the drive pinion from the armature shaft, drive the thrust collar down the shaft, using a suitable tube drift, to expose the C-clip. Remove the clip from its groove, and slide the thrust collar and drive pinion from the shaft. Do not grip the clutch assembly in a vice during this procedure, as damage will result.

13   Examine the components, and renew as necessary.

14   If the brushes have worn to less than the specified minimum length, renew them as a set. To renew the brushes, the leads must be unsoldered from the terminals on the brush plate, and the leads of the new brushes must be soldered to the terminals.

15   The commutator face should be clean, with no burnt spots. Where

necessary, burnish with fine glass paper (**not** emery), and wipe with a fuel-moistened cloth. If the commutator is in very bad condition, it can be skimmed on a lathe, provided its diameter is not reduced excessively. If recutting the insulation slots, take care not to cut into the commutator metal.

16   Renew the commutator end plate and drive end housing bushes, which are of the self-lubricating type, and should be soaked in clean engine oil for at least twenty minutes before installation. Drive out the old bushes, whilst supporting the end plate/housing using a suitable drift.

17   Accurate checking of the armature, commutator and field coil windings and insulation requires the use of special test equipment. If the starter motor was inoperative when removed from the vehicle, and the previous checks have not highlighted the problem, then it can be assumed that there is a continuity or insulation fault, and the unit should be renewed.

18   Commence reassembly by sliding the drive pinion and thrust collar onto the armature shaft. Fit the C-clip into its groove, and then use a two-legged puller to draw the thrust collar over the clip.

19   Refit the actuating arm to the drive pinion flange, then refit the armature assembly and actuating arm to the drive end housing.

20   Refit the actuating arm pivot pin (bolt), and secure with the retaining nut. Fit the rubber insert into the drive end housing.

21   Apply a little lithium-based grease to the solenoid armature hook, then locate the hook over the actuating arm in the drive end housing. Ensure that the solenoid armature return spring is correctly positioned, then guide the solenoid yoke over the armature. Align the yoke with the drive end housing, and fit the three securing screws.

22   Guide the yoke over the armature, and tap onto the drive end housing.

23   Position the brush plate over the end of the armature shaft, then assemble the brush holders, brushes and springs, ensuring that the brush holder clips are securely located. The brush plate will be positively located when the through-bolts are fitted.

24   Guide the commutator end plate into position, and fit the through-bolts.

25   Slide the armature into its bearings so that the shaft protrudes as far as possible at the commutator bearing end.

26   Fit sufficient shims to the end of the armature shaft to eliminate endfloat when the C-clip is fitted, then fit the clip.

27   Fit the rubber seal to the commutator end plate, then apply a little lithium-based grease to the end of the armature shaft and refit the end plate cap, securing with the two screws.

28   Reconnect the field winding lead to the solenoid stud, and secure with the nut and washer.

29   Refit the mounting bracket to the through-bolts, and secure with the two nuts, where applicable.

Bosch DW type starter motor

30   With the starter motor removed from the vehicle and cleaned, grip the unit in a vice fitted with soft jaw protectors.

31   Unscrew the nuts from the ends of the through-bolts, and remove the mounting bracket, where applicable.

32   Remove the two securing screws (photo), and withdraw the armature shaft cover.

33   Remove the C-clip and spacer from the end of the armature shaft (photos).

34   Unscrew the two through-bolts, and lift off the commutator end plate (photos).

35   Remove the securing nut, and disconnect the wiring from the solenoid terminal (photo).

36   Withdraw the complete yoke and armature assembly from the drive end housing (photo).

37   Retain the brushes in the brush holders using a large socket or metal tube, then remove the brush plate from the armature shaft (photos).

38   Withdraw the armature from the yoke (photo).

39   Extract the three securing screws, and remove the solenoid yoke from the drive end housing (photos).

40   Recover the spring, then unhook the solenoid armature from the actuating arm (photos).

41   Withdraw the complete pinion and clutch assembly from the drive end housing (photo).

42   To remove the drive pinion from the shaft, proceed as described in paragraph 12.

Fig. 12.4 Exploded view of Bosch DW type starter motor (Sec 11)

1 Solenoid yoke
2 Solenoid return spring
3 Solenoid armature
4 Actuating arm
5 Drive end housing
6 Drive pinion and clutch
   assembly
7 Spacer
8 Ring gear and carrier
9 Output shaft and planet
   gear assembly
10 Circlip
11 Through-bolt
12 Commutator end plate
13 C-clip
14 Shim
15 Commutator end plate
16 Brush plate
17 Yoke
18 Rubber block
19 Armature

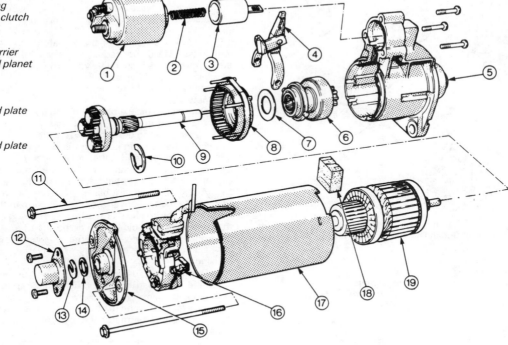

11.32 Removing an armature shaft cover screw – Bosch DW type starter motor

11.33A Remove the C-clip (arrowed) ...

11.33B ... and the spacer – Bosch DW type starter motor

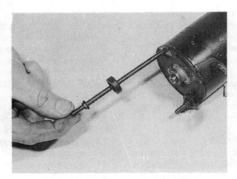

11.34A Unscrew the two through-bolts ...

11.34B ... remove them ...

11.34C ... and lift off the commutator end plate – Bosch DW type starter motor

11.35 Disconnecting the wiring from the solenoid terminal – Bosch DW type starter motor

11.36 Withdraw the yoke and armature assembly – Bosch DW type starter motor

11.37A Place a large socket over the end of the armature ...

11.37B ... then slide the brushes onto it – Bosch DW type starter motor

11.37C Brushes retained in brush holders by socket – Bosch DW type starter motor

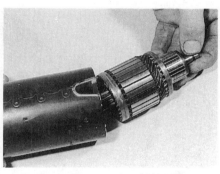

11.38 Withdraw the armature from the yoke – Bosch DW type starter motor

11.39A Extract the securing screws ...

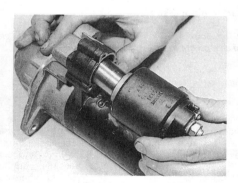

11.39B ... and remove the solenoid yoke from the drive end housing ...

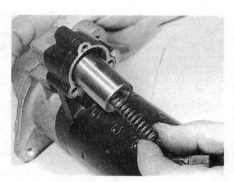

11.40A ... recover the spring ...

11.40B ... and unhook the solenoid armature – Bosch DW type starter motor

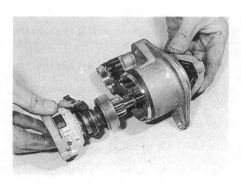

11.41 Withdrawing the pinion and clutch assembly – Bosch DW type starter motor

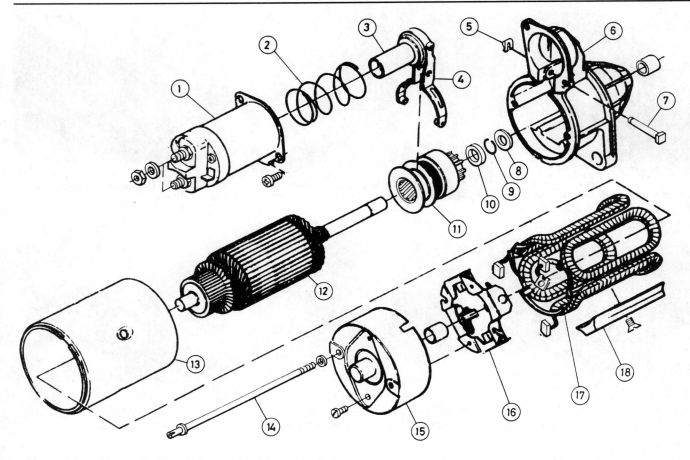

Fig. 12.5 Exploded view of Delco-Remy type starter motor (Sec 11)

1	Solenoid yoke	6	Drive end housing
2	Solenoid return spring	7	Actuating arm pivot pin
3	Solenoid armature	8	Shim
4	Actuating arm	9	C-clip
5	Pivot pin clip	10	Thrust collar

11	Drive pinion and clutch assembly	15	Commutator end housing
12	Armature	16	Brush plate
13	Yoke	17	Field coils
14	Through-bolt	18	Permanent magnet

43   Examine the components and renew as necessary.

44   To renew the brushes, the leads must be unsoldered from the terminals on the brush plate, and the leads of the new brushes must be soldered to the terminals.

45   Proceed as described in paragraphs 15 to 17 inclusive.

46   Commence reassembly by refitting the drive pinion to the shaft, as described in paragraph 18.

47   Refit the pinion and clutch assembly into the drive end housing, ensuring that the ring gear carrier and rubber block are correctly located.

48   Apply a little lithium-based grease to the end of the solenoid armature, and reconnect it to the actuating arm.

49   Ensure that the solenoid armature return spring is correctly positioned, then guide the solenoid yoke over the armature, and refit the three securing screws.

50   With the brush components assembled to the brush plate, and the brushes retained in their holders using a socket or tube as during removal, position the brush plate over the end of the armature shaft, and withdraw the socket or tube.

51   Insert the armature into the yoke, making sure that the brush plate stays in place, and engage the rubber insulator with the cut-out in the yoke.

52   Refit the yoke and the armature assembly to the drive end housing, aligning the sun gear with the planet gears.

53   Reconnect the wiring to the solenoid terminal, and fit the securing nut.

54   Refit the commutator end plate, and secure with the two through-bolts.

55   Refit the spacer and C-clip to the end of the armature shaft, then smear the end of the shaft with a little lithium-based grease.

56   Fit the armature shaft cover, and secure with the two screws.

57   Refit the mounting bracket to the through-bolts, and secure with the two nuts, where applicable.

Delco-Remy type starter motor

58   With the starter motor removed from the vehicle and cleaned, grip the unit in a vice fitted with soft jaw protectors.

59   Unscrew the nuts from the ends of the through-bolts, and remove the mounting bracket, where applicable.

60   Unscrew and remove the two through-bolts which hold the components of the starter motor assembly together (photo).

61   Extract the two small screws which secure the commutator end housing to the brush plate (photo), then lift off the commutator end housing.

62   Lift the brush retaining springs to remove the positive brushes from the brush holders, then lift the brush plate from the commutator (photo).

63   Remove the two securing screws, and withdraw the solenoid yoke and spring from the drive end housing (photo).

64   Extract the clip from the actuating arm pivot pin, then tap the pivot pin from the drive end housing (photos).

65   Remove the solenoid armature and the actuating arm, then unhook the actuating arm from the armature.

66   Separate the drive end housing and armature from the yoke by tapping them apart with a soft-faced hammer.

11.60 Unscrew the through-bolts ...

11.61 ... and extract the two small screws – Delco-Remy type starter motor

11.62 Lift the brush plate from the commutator – Delco-Remy type starter motor

11.63 Withdrawing the solenoid yoke and spring – Delco-Remy type starter motor

11.64A Extract the clip from the actuating arm pivot pin ...

11.64B ... then withdraw the pivot pin – Delco-Remy type starter motor

67   Proceed as described in paragraphs 12 to 18 inclusive.
68   Hook the actuating arm onto the solenoid armature, then refit the armature and actuating arm to the drive end housing.
69   Tap the actuating arm pivot pin into the drive end housing, and refit the retaining clip.
70   Refit the solenoid yoke and spring, and secure with the two screws.
71   Guide the yoke over the armature, and tap onto the drive end housing.
72   Refit the brushes to the brush holders, then position the brush plate on the commutator.
73   Fit the commutator end housing, and fit the two screws securing the end housing to the brush plate.

74   Refit the two through-bolts.
75   Where applicable, refit the mounting bracket, and secure with the two nuts.

Valeo type starter motor

76   At the time of writing, no information was available regarding overhaul of the Valeo type starter motor.

12   Fusebox – removal and refitting

Removal

1   Disconnect the battery negative lead.
2   Pull off the fusebox cover.
3   Unscrew the two securing screws (photo), then release the assembly from the retaining brackets, and lower the assembly sufficiently to enable the wiring plugs to be disconnected.
4   Disconnect the wiring plugs, carefully noting their locations if there is likely to be any confusion on refitting, then withdraw the assembly from the facia.

Refitting

5   Refitting is a reversal of removal.

13   Fuses and relays – testing and renewal

Fuses

1   Fuses are designed to break a circuit when a predetermined current is reached, in order to protect components which may be damaged by excessive current flow. Any excessive current flow will be due to a fault in the circuit – usually a short-circuit (see Section 2).

12.3 Fusebox cover removed to expose securing screws (arrowed)

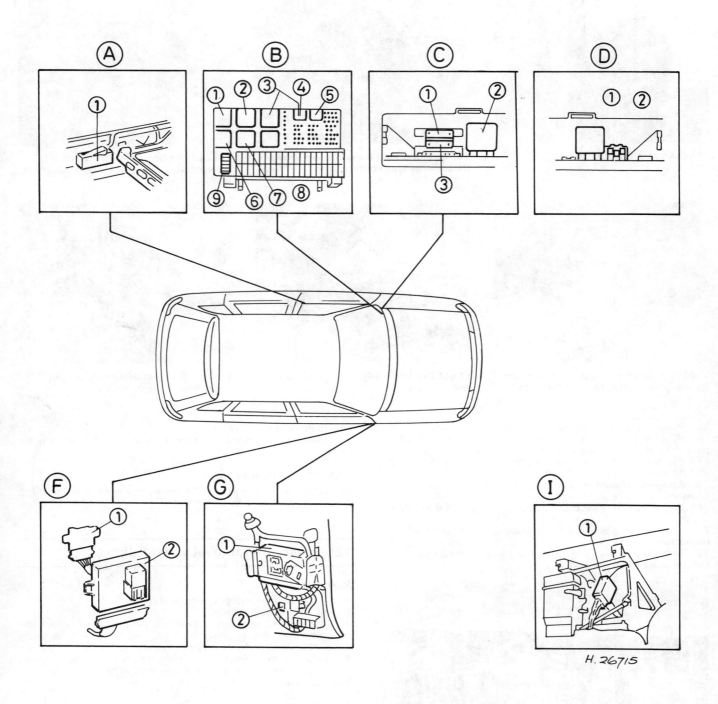

Fig. 12.6 Schematic view of fuse and relay locations (Sec 13)

A   Right-hand sill panel
   1 *Electronic traction control*
     ECU
B   Fusebox – front view
   1 *Door mirror heater relay*
   2 *Direction indicator relay*
   3 *Tailgate wash/wipe relay*
   4 *Front foglight relay*
   5 *Rear foglight relay*

   6 *Windscreen wash/wipe*
     relay
   7 *Heated rear window relay*
   8 *Warning buzzer*
   9 *Diagnostic plug*
C   Fusebox – rear view
   1 *Cooling fan fuse*
   2 *Starter motor relay*
   3 *Heater blower motor fuse*

D   Fusebox – rear view
   1 *Starter motor relay*
   2 *Anti-theft alarm fuse*
F   Right-hand footwell
   1 *Central door locking*
  ECU
   2 *Anti-theft alarm ECU*

G   Right-hand footwell
   1 *Engine management ECU*
   2 *Fuel pump relay*
I   Steering column bracket
   1 *Driving light relay (Sweden*
     and Norway only)

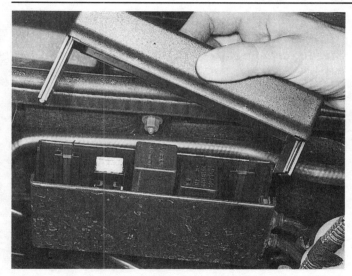

13.3 Removing the cover from the secondary fusebox on the engine compartment bulkhead – DOHC engine model

2   The main fuses are located in the fusebox, at the lower driver's side of the facia, under a removable cover.
3   On certain models, additional fuses are located in a secondary fusebox mounted on the engine compartment bulkhead (photo).
4   The circuits protected by the various fuses are marked on the inside of the panel cover.
5   A blown fuse can be recognised from its melted or broken wiring.
6   To remove a fuse, first ensure that the relevant circuit is switched off.
7   Pull off the fusebox cover, and pull the relevant fuse from its location in the fusebox.
8   Before renewing a blown fuse, try to trace and rectify the cause, and

always use a fuse of the correct rating. Fuses rarely blow without good reason – don't renew the same fuse more than once without finding the source of the problem. If the same fuse is blowing regularly, it could be that the associated wiring is getting too hot, with attendant fire risks (see 'The vehicle electrical system' in 'Safety first!'). Never substitute a fuse of a higher rating, or make temporary repairs using wire or metal foil, as more serious damage or even fire could result.
9   Note that the fuses are colour-coded as follows. Refer to the Specifications for details of the fuse ratings and the circuits protected.

Red	10A
Blue	15A
Yellow	20A
Green	30A

Relays

10   A relay is an electrically-operated switch, which is used for the following reasons.

(a)   A relay can switch a heavy current remotely from the circuit in which the current is flowing, therefore allowing the use of lighter gauge wiring and switch contacts.
(b)   A relay can receive more than one control input, unlike a mechanical switch.
(c)   A relay can have a 'timer' function – eg, intermittent wiper relay.

11   The main relays are located in the fusebox, above the fuses (photo). Additional relays are located in various positions, as shown in the accompanying illustrations.
12   If a circuit controlled by a relay develops a fault, and the relay is suspect, operate the circuit. If the relay is functioning, it should be possible to hear the relay click as it is energised. If this is the case, the fault lies with the components or wiring in the system. If the relay is not being energised, then either the relay is not receiving a main supply or switching voltage, or the relay itself is faulty. (Do not overlook the relay socket terminals when tracing faults.) Testing is by the substitution of a known good unit, but be careful; while some relays are identical in appearance and in operation, others look similar, but perform different functions.

Fig. 12.7 Schematic view of fuse and relay locations (Sec 13)

A   **Left-hand rear wing**
 1   Electric aerial relay
B   **Engine compartment bulkhead**
 1   Headlight wash system fuse
 2   Headlight wash system relay
 3   Horn relay
 4   Horn fuse
C   **Engine compartment**
 1   Anti-lock braking system ECU

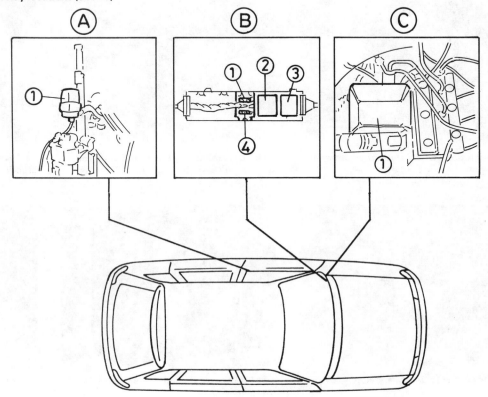

H.22819

13.11 Relays located above fuses in fusebox

14   Switches – removal and refitting

Ignition switch

Removal

1   Disconnect the battery negative lead.
2   Remove the steering column shrouds, as described in Chapter 11.
3   The ignition switch is secured to the steering lock housing by two grub screws.
4   Disconnect the wiring, and remove the screws to extract the switch (photos). It is recommended that the switch and the lock cylinder are not both removed at the same time, or their mutual alignment will be lost.

Refitting

5   Refitting is a reversal of removal.

Steering column stalk switches

Removal

6   Proceed as described in paragraphs 1 and 2.
7   Depress the retaining clips, and release the relevant switch from the steering column (photo).
8   Disconnect the wiring plug(s) and withdraw the switch (photo).

Refitting

9   Refitting is a reversal of removal.

Lighting switch

Removal

10   Disconnect the battery negative lead.
11   Insert a small screwdriver or suitable rod through the hole in the bottom of the switch knob to depress the knob retaining clip (photo). Pull the knob from the switch.
12   Press the two now-exposed switch securing clips towards the switch spindle (photo), then pull the switch from the facia and disconnect the wiring plug.
13   Note that the switch assembly cannot be dismantled, and if any part of the switch is faulty, the complete assembly must be renewed.

Refitting

14   Refitting is a reversal of removal.

Facia pushbutton switches

Removal

15   Disconnect the battery negative lead.
16   Using a screwdriver, carefully prise the switch from the facia, taking care not to damage the facia trim, and where applicable disconnect the wiring plug (photos).

Refitting

17   Refitting is a reversal of removal.

14.4A Ignition switch grub screw location (arrowed)

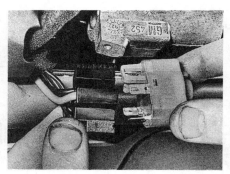

14.4B Disconnecting the wiring plug from the ignition switch

14.7 Withdrawing a stalk switch from the steering column

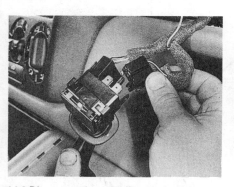

14.8 Disconnecting a stalk switch wiring plug

14.11 Releasing the lighting switch knob retaining clip

14.12 Removing the lighting switch

14.16A Carefully prise the switch free ...

14.16B ... and withdraw it from the facia

Headlight aim adjustment switch

18   The procedure is as described previously in this Section for the facia pushbutton switches.

Hazard warning flasher switch

Removal

19   Disconnect the battery negative lead.
20   Move the switch to the 'on' position.
21   Using a screwdriver, carefully prise off the switch button to expose the switch.
22   Again using a screwdriver, carefully prise the switch from its housing.

Refitting

23   Refitting is a reversal of removal.

Horn switch

24   Carefully prise the centre pad from the steering wheel, and disconnect the wire.

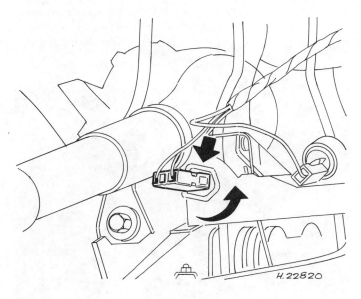

Fig. 12.8 Brake light switch location (arrowed) – twist switch anti-clockwise to remove (Sec 14)

25   If desired, the horn switch contact assembly can be removed from the centre of the steering wheel, after removing the steering wheel as described in Chapter 10.

Brake light switch

Removal

26   Disconnect the battery negative lead.
27   Working in the driver's footwell, release the securing clips, and remove the lower trim panel.
28   The switch is mounted in a bracket next to the steering column, at the top of the brake pedal.
29   Disconnect the wiring plug from the switch.
30   Twist the switch anti-clockwise, and withdraw it from the bracket.

Refitting

31   Refitting is a reversal of removal, but note that the brake lights should come on when the brake pedal is pressed down by about 15.0 to 20.0 mm. The switch can only be adjusted by carefully bending the mounting bracket, but this is not recommended.

Handbrake 'on' warning light switch

32   The procedure is described in Chapter 9, as part of the handbrake lever removal, overhaul and refitting procedure.

Reversing light switch

33   The procedure is described in Chapter 7.

Low oil pressure warning light switch

Removal

34   The switch is screwed into the end of the oil pump, on the inlet manifold side of the engine.
35   Disconnect the battery negative lead.
36   On most models, access to the switch can be obtained from above, but on some models improved access can be obtained by jacking up the front of the vehicle, and supporting securely on axle stands (see *'Jacking, towing and wheel changing'*), then removing the right-hand roadwheel. On DOHC engine models, remove the access hatch from the engine undershield (photo).
37   Disconnect the wiring from the switch.
38   Place a suitable container under the switch to catch the oil which will be released as the switch is removed.
39   Using a suitable spanner, unscrew the switch. Be prepared for oil spillage, and plug the hole in the oil pump to minimise oil loss and prevent dirt ingress.

Refitting

40   Refitting is a reversal of removal, but on completion check and if necessary top-up the engine oil level as described in Chapter 1.

14.36 Low oil pressure warning light switch viewed from underneath vehicle – DOHC engine model

Heater blower motor switch

41   The procedure is described in Chapter 3.

Central locking operating switches

42   The procedure is described in Chapter 11.

Electric window operating switches

43   The procedure is described in Chapter 11.

Electric door mirror switch

44   The procedure is described in Chapter 11.

Seat heating switches

45   The procedure is as described previously in this Section for the facia pushbutton switches.

Courtesy light switches

Removal

46   The courtesy light switches are located in the door pillars, at the front of the doors.

47   Disconnect the battery negative lead.
48   Open the relevant door.
49   Remove the securing screw, then pull the switch from the door pillar, and disconnect the wiring. If there is a danger of the wiring falling back inside the door pillar, tie a piece of string to it.

Refitting

50   Refitting is a reversal of removal.

Luggage compartment light switch

51   The switch is located at the bottom of the tailgate on Hatchback, Estate and Van models, and at the front left-hand corner of the luggage compartment on Saloon models (photos).
52   Removal and refitting is as described previously in this Section for the courtesy light switches.

Glovebox light switch

53   The switch is integral with the light assembly, and is operated by the left-hand glovebox hinge.
54   Removal and refitting of the assembly is described in Section 16.

Electronic traction control manual override switch

55   The procedure is described in Chapter 4.

Automatic transmission switches

56   Refer to Chapter 7.

15   Bulbs (exterior lights) – renewal

General

1   Whenever a bulb is renewed, note the following points.

(a)   Disconnect the battery negative lead before starting work.
(b)   Remember that if the light has recently been in use, the bulb may be extremely hot.
(c)   Always check the bulb contacts and/or holder (as applicable). Ensure that there is clean metal-to-metal contact between the bulb contacts and the contacts in the holder, and/or the holder and the wiring plug. Clean off any corrosion or dirt before fitting a new bulb.
(d)   Always ensure that the new bulb is of the correct rating, and that it is completely clean before fitting; this applies particularly to headlight bulbs.

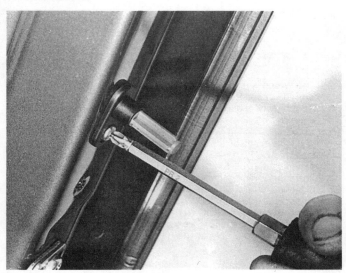

14.51A Removing the luggage compartment light switch securing screw – Hatchback model

14.51B Luggage compartment light switch location – Saloon model

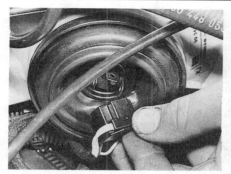

15.2 Disconnecting the wiring plug from a headlight bulb

15.4 Removing a headlight bulb

15.8 Removing a sidelight bulbholder

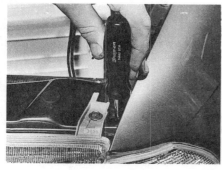

15.11 Loosening a front direction indicator unit securing screw

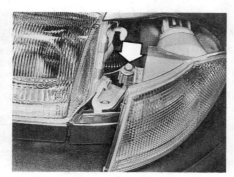

15.12 Front direction indicator unit withdrawn, exposing securing screw (arrowed)

15.13 Removing a front direction indicator light bulbholder

Headlight

2   Working in the engine compartment, pull the wiring plug from the rear of the headlight bulb (photo).
3   Pull the rubber cover from the rear of the headlight.
4   Release the bulb retaining spring clip, then grasp the bulb by its contacts and carefully withdraw it from the headlight unit (photo).
5   When handling the new bulb, use a tissue or clean cloth to avoid touching the glass with the fingers; moisture and grease from the skin can cause blackening and rapid failure of this type of bulb. If the glass is accidentally touched, wipe it clean using methylated spirit.
6   Refitting is a reversal of removal, but make sure that the locating lugs on the bulb engage with the cut-outs in the headlight reflector, and ensure that the rubber cover is securely located over the rear of the headlight unit.

Front sidelight

7   Working in the engine compartment, locate the sidelight bulbholder, which is positioned in the lower rear of the headlight unit, on the side nearest the radiator grille.
8   Push the bulbholder into the headlight unit, and twist it anti-clockwise to remove it (photo).
9   The bulb is a push-fit in the holder.
10   Refitting is a reversal of removal.

Front direction indicator light

11   Working in the engine compartment, loosen, but do not remove the screw securing the top of the direction indicator unit to the headlight (photo).
12   Withdraw the direction indicator unit forwards from the front wing, taking care not to strain the wiring (photo).
13   Push the bulbholder into the light unit, and twist it anti-clockwise to remove it (photo).
14   The bulb is a bayonet fit in the bulbholder.
15   Refitting is a reversal of removal.

15.16 Removing the front direction indicator side repeater light lens

Front direction indicator side repeater light

16   Twist the light lens anti-clockwise, and pull it from the light (photo).
17   The bulb is a push-fit in the light.
18   Refitting is a reversal of removal, but ensure that the rubber sealing ring is correctly seated between the lens and the body panel.

Front foglight

19   To improve access, apply the handbrake, then jack up the front of the vehicle, and support securely on axle stands (see *'Jacking, towing and wheel changing'*).

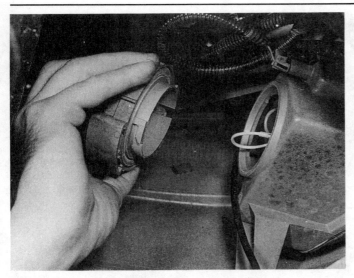

15.20 Removing the rear cover from a front foglight

20   Remove the plastic cover from the rear of the light unit by twisting it anti-clockwise, and pulling it free (photo).
21   Release the retaining clip, then withdraw the bulb and disconnect the wiring.
22   Refitting is a reversal of removal.

Rear light cluster

23   Working in the luggage compartment, unclip the cover from the rear of the light unit.
24   On Saloon and Hatchback models, release the securing lug, and on Estate and Van models, squeeze the two securing clips towards the centre of the bulbholder, then withdraw the bulbholder from the light unit, taking care not to strain the wiring (photos).

25   The bulbs are a bayonet fit in the bulbholder (photo). Note that the brake/tail light bulb has offset bayonet pins, so that it can only be fitted in one position; ensure that the correct type of replacement is obtained.
26   Refitting is a reversal of removal.

Rear number plate light

Saloon and Hatchback models (except DOHC engine models)
27   Using a thin-bladed screwdriver, carefully prise the light surround from the bumper (photo).
28   Pull the light assembly from the bumper, taking care not to strain the wiring.
29   Unclip the cover from the light unit, to expose the bulb (photo).
30   The bulb is a bayonet fit in the light unit.
31   Refitting is a reversal of removal.

DOHC engine models
32   Proceed as described in paragraph 27.
33   Remove the bulb by carefully prising it from its location with a screwdriver.
34   Refitting is a reversal of removal.

Estate and Van models
35   Remove the two screws securing the relevant light to the tailgate handle assembly, and lower the light from the tailgate.
36   Carefully prise the bulb from the light.
37   Refitting is a reversal of removal.

16   Bulbs (interior lights) – renewal

General
1   Refer to Section 15, paragraph 1.

Courtesy lights and rear reading lights
2   Using a thin-bladed screwdriver, carefully prise the light from its

15.24A Rear light bulbholder securing lug (arrowed) – Hatchback model

15.24B Removing a rear light bulbholder – Saloon model

15.25 Removing a rear light bulb – Hatchback model

15.27 Prising the rear number plate light surround from the bumper – Hatchback model

15.29 Removing the cover from the rear number plate light unit

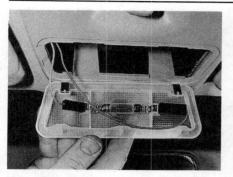

16.2A Withdrawing the front courtesy light to expose the bulb

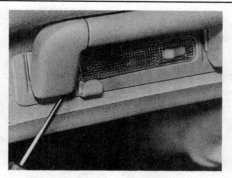

16.2B Prising a rear reading light from its location

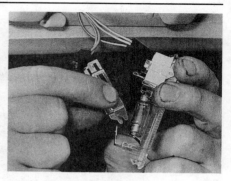

16.3 Unclipping the shield from a rear reading light bulb

16.5 Glovebox light assembly withdrawn from its location

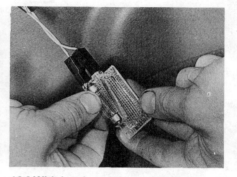

16.6 Withdrawing a luggage compartment light bulb

location (photos).
3   Where applicable, unclip the shield from the bulb, then remove the bulb by carefully prising it from the contacts in the light unit (photo).
4   Refitting is a reversal of removal.

Glovebox light
5   Proceed as described previously in this Section for the courtesy light (photo).

Luggage compartment light
6   Proceed as described previously in this Section for the courtesy light (photo).

Instrument illumination and warning light bulbs
7   The procedure is described in Section 21.

Heater/ventilation control illumination light bulb
8   The procedure is described as part of the heater/ventilation control unit removal and refitting procedure in Chapter 3.

Cigarette lighter illumination light bulb
9   The procedure is described as part of the cigarette lighter removal and refitting procedure in Section 26.

Facia panel/centre console switch illumination bulbs
10   If a bulb fails in one of these switches, the complete switch assembly must be renewed as described in Section 14, as no individual spare parts are available.

17   Exterior light units – removal and refitting

Headlight unit
Removal
1   Disconnect the battery negative lead.
2   Remove the radiator grille panel, as described in Chapter 11.

3   Working in the engine compartment, loosen, but do not remove the screw securing the top of the direction indicator unit to the headlight.
4   Withdraw the direction indicator unit forwards from the front wing, and disconnect the wiring plug.
5   Disconnect the wiring plugs from the headlight bulb, sidelight bulb, and headlight aim adjustment motor.
6   Remove the three securing screws (two upper screws, and a single lower screw), and withdraw the headlight unit (photos).
7   With the exception of bulbs and the aim adjustment motor, no headlight components are available separately, and if faulty or damaged, the complete unit must be renewed.

Refitting
8   Refitting is a reversal of removal, but on completion have the headlight beam alignment checked, with reference to Section 18.

Front direction indicator unit
Removal
9   Disconnect the battery negative lead.
10   Proceed as described in paragraphs 3 and 4.

Refitting
11   Refitting is a reversal of removal.

Front direction indicator side repeater light
Removal
12   Disconnect the battery negative lead.
13   Remove the wheel arch liner, as described in Chapter 11, Section 25.
14   Working in the engine compartment, locate the repeater light wiring connector, and separate the two halves of the connector.
15   Working under the wheel arch, depress the retaining tabs and manipulate the light unit through the outside of the wing, pulling the wiring and the grommet from the inner wing panel (photo).
16   The lens can be removed from the light by twisting it to release the retaining clips.
17   Check the condition of the rubber sealing ring, and renew if necessary.

Refitting
18   Refitting is a reversal of removal.

17.6A Headlight securing screws (arrowed)

17.6B Withdrawing a headlight

21 Working behind the front spoiler, disconnect the foglight wiring plug.
22 Unscrew the three securing screws (two at the bottom of the light, and one well-hidden above the light), and withdraw the light from the front bumper/spoiler assembly (photo).

Refitting
23 Refitting is a reversal of removal.

Rear light cluster
Removal
24 Disconnect the battery negative lead.
25 Working in the luggage compartment, unclip the cover from the rear of the light unit.
26 On Saloon and Hatchback models, release the securing lug, and on Estate and Van models, squeeze the two securing clips towards the centre of the bulbholder, then withdraw the bulbholder from the light unit, taking care not to strain the wiring.
27 On Saloon and Hatchback models, remove the four light cluster securing screws, and on Estate and Van models, remove the three securing screws (one upper screw, and two lower screws), and withdraw the light cluster from outside the rear wing panel (photos).
28 Note that the lens cannot be renewed separately, and if damaged, the complete light cluster must be renewed.

Refitting
29 Refitting is a reversal of removal.

Rear number plate light – Saloon and Hatchback models
Removal
30 Using a thin-bladed screwdriver, carefully prise the light surround from the bumper.

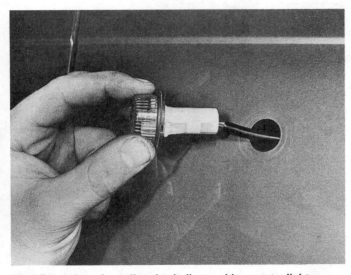

17.15 Removing a front direction indicator side repeater light

Front foglight
Removal
19 Disconnect the battery negative lead.
20 For improved access, apply the handbrake, then jack up the front of the vehicle, and support securely on axle stands (see *'Jacking, towing and wheel changing'*).

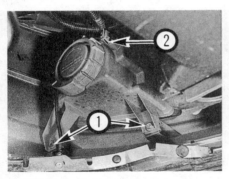

17.22 Front foglight lower securing screws (1) and wiring plug (2)

17.27A Rear light cluster securing screws (arrowed) – Saloon model

17.27B Removing a rear light cluster – Hatchback model

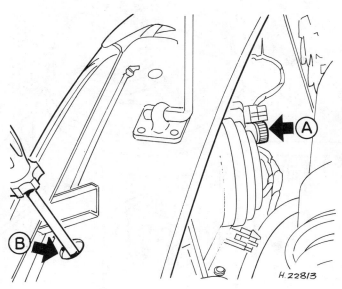

Fig. 12.9 Headlight beam adjustment screws (Sec 18)

A *Vertical adjustment* B *Horizontal adjustment*

31   Pull the light assembly from the bumper, and disconnect the wiring.

Refitting
32   Refitting is a reversal of removal.

Rear number plate light – Estate and Van models
Removal
33   Remove the two screws securing the relevant light assembly to the tailgate handle.
34   Pull the light assembly from the handle, and disconnect the wiring.

Refitting
35   Refitting is a reversal of removal.

18   Headlight beam alignment – general information

1   It is advisable to have the headlight beam alignment checked and if necessary adjusted by a Vauxhall/Opel dealer using optical beam-setting equipment. Correct alignment of the headlight beams is most important, not only to ensure good vision for the driver, but also to protect other drivers from being dazzled.
2   The headlight beam height may be adjusted to compensate for the load being carried by using the headlight aim adjustment control on the facia. The settings provided by this control are as follows.

0   *Driver's seat occupied.*
1   *All seats occupied.*
2   *All seats occupied and load in luggage compartment.*
3   *Driver's seat occupied and load in luggage compartment.*

3   In an emergency, adjustment of the headlights may be made by turning the adjuster screws on the top and rear of each headlight unit. The top screw controls horizontal adjustment, and the rear screw controls vertical adjustment.
4   If an adjustment is made, the alignment should be checked using suitable beam-setting equipment at the earliest opportunity. Note that when using beam-setting equipment, the headlight aim adjustment control should be set to position '0'.

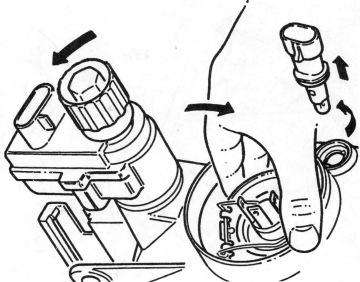

Fig. 12.10 Remove the sidelight bulbholder, turn the headlight aim adjustment motor, and push the reflector assembly to one side (Sec 19)

19   Headlight aim adjustment motor – removal and refitting

Removal
1   Remove the headlight unit, as described in Section 17.
2   Remove the sidelight bulbholder assembly, with reference to Section 15 if necessary.
3   Turn the motor through approximately 60° towards the top of the headlight, then carefully push the headlight reflector assembly away from the motor, and hold it in position, so that the motor and the balljoint are pushed partially out of the headlight assembly – see Fig. 12.10.

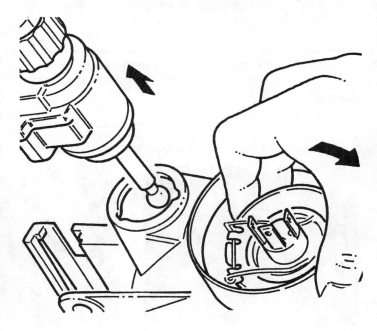

Fig. 12.11 Pull the headlight aim adjustment motor from the headlight – 'Carello' type headlight (Sec 19)

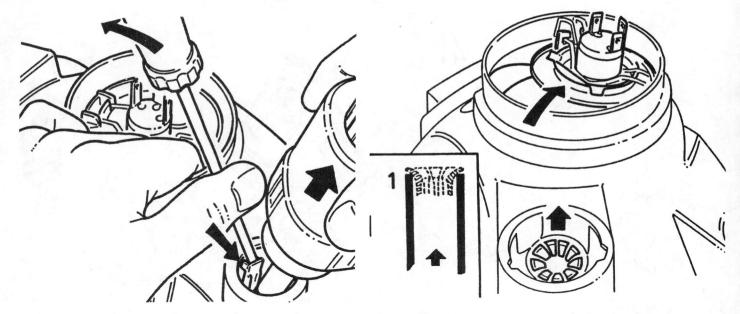

Fig. 12.12 Release the headlight aim adjustment motor balljoint using a screwdriver – 'Bosch' type headlight (Sec 19)

Fig. 12.13 The ball socket (1) must be open before pushing the headlight aim adjustment motor balljoint into place – 'Carello' type headlight (Sec 19)

4   On models with 'Carello' type headlights, carefully pull the motor and balljoint assembly from the headlight.
5   On models with 'Bosch' type headlights, release the balljoint using a small screwdriver, then carefully pull the motor and balljoint assembly from the headlight.

Refitting

6   Carefully push the headlight reflector assembly away from the motor location, ensuring that on models with 'Carello' type headlights, the ball socket is open, as shown in Fig. 12.13 (otherwise irreparable damage could be caused to the headlight), and hold the reflector in position while pushing the motor balljoint into place.
7   With the balljoint reconnected, lock the motor in position by twisting it towards the bottom of the headlight.
8   Refit the sidelight bulbholder, then refit the headlight as described in Section 17.

20   Instrument panel – removal and refitting

Removal

1   Disconnect the battery negative lead.
2   Working in the engine compartment, unscrew the securing sleeve, and disconnect the speedometer cable from the gearbox/transmission.
3   Remove the steering column shrouds, as described in Chapter 11.

4   Where applicable, prise out the screw covers, then remove the four (two upper and two lower) securing screws, and withdraw the instrument panel surround.
5   Remove the three (one upper and two lower) instrument panel securing screws (photo), and carefully pull the instrument panel forwards from the facia.
6   Push down (towards the back of the speedometer) on the catch securing the speedometer cable to the rear of the speedometer, and release the speedometer cable (photo).
7   Release the retaining clips, and disconnect the wiring plugs from the rear of the instrument panel (photo).
8   Withdraw the instrument panel.

Refitting

9   Refitting is a reversal of removal, but ensure that the speedometer cable is not twisted or kinked between the instrument panel and the bulkhead as the panel is refitted.

21   Instrument panel components – removal and refitting

General

1   With the instrument panel removed as described in Section 20, proceed as follows.

20.5 Unscrewing a lower instrument panel securing screw

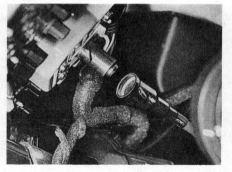

20.6 Speedometer cable disconnected from speedometer

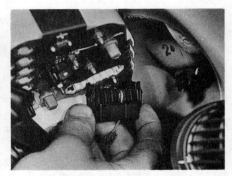

20.7 Disconnecting a wiring plug from the rear of the instrument panel

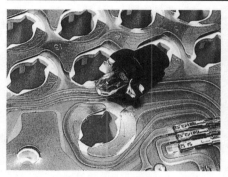

21.2 Warning light bulb withdrawn from its location in the instrument panel

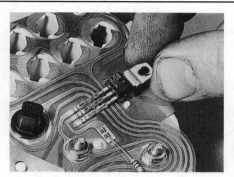

21.5 Pulling the instrument panel voltage stabiliser from the printed circuit board

21.8 Releasing an instrument panel shroud retaining clip

Panel illumination and warning light bulbs

Removal

2   Twist the relevant bulbholder anti-clockwise, and withdraw it from the printed circuit board on the rear of the instrument panel (photo).
3   The bulbs are integral with the bulbholders, and must be renewed as a unit.

Refitting

4   Refitting is a reversal of removal.

Voltage stabiliser

Removal

5   Remove the single securing screw from the rear of the instrument panel, then pull the voltage stabiliser from the contacts on the printed circuit board (photo).

Refitting

6   Refitting is a reversal of removal, but take care not to damage the contacts on the voltage stabiliser and printed circuit board.

Fuel and temperature gauges – models without tachometer

Removal

7   Pull the tripmeter reset pin from the front of the panel.

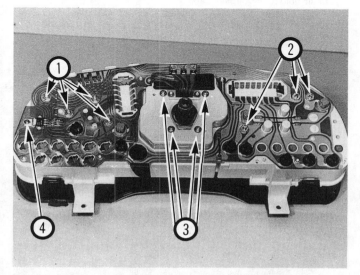

21.11 Rear view of instrument panel – model with tachometer

1   Fuel and temperature gauge securing nuts
2   Tachometer securing nuts
3   Speedometer securing screws
4   Voltage stabiliser securing screw

8   Release the two retaining clips at the top of the panel, and remove the panel shroud (photo).
9   Unscrew the two securing nuts, and withdraw the relevant gauge through the front of the instrument panel.

Refitting

10   Refitting is a reversal of removal.

Fuel and temperature gauge assembly – models with tachometer

11   The procedure is as described in paragraphs 7 to 10 inclusive, except that the gauge assembly is secured by four nuts (photo).

Tachometer

12   The procedure is as described in paragraphs 7 to 10 inclusive, except that the tachometer is secured by three nuts.

Speedometer

Removal

13   Proceed as described in paragraphs 7 and 8.
14   Extract the four securing screws from the rear of the panel, and withdraw the speedometer from the front of the panel.

Refitting

15   Refitting is a reversal of removal.

Printed circuit board

Removal

16   Remove all bulbs and instruments, and the voltage stabiliser, as described previously in this Section.
17   Carefully peel the printed circuit board from the instrument panel.

Refitting

18   Refitting is a reversal of removal, but ensure that the printed circuit board is seated correctly on the rear of the instrument panel.

22   Clock/multi-function display – removal and refitting

Removal

1   Disconnect the battery negative lead.
2   Remove the radio/cassette player, as described in Section 34.
3   Remove the rubber mat from the tray in front of the clock/multi-function display (photo).
4   Remove the two central now-exposed screws (photo).
5   Reach up through the radio/cassette player aperture, and push the clock/multi-function display from the facia (photo).
6   Disconnect the wiring plug, and withdraw the unit.

22.3 Removing the rubber mat from the tray in front of the clock/multi-function display

22.4 Unscrewing a clock/multi-function display securing screw

22.5 Pushing the clock/multi-function display from the facia

Refitting

7   Refitting is a reversal of removal, but refit the radio/cassette player as described in Section 34.

23   Auxiliary warning system – general information

The auxiliary warning system displays information on the multi-function display, to warn the driver of low engine oil level, low engine coolant level, low washer fluid level, brake pad wear, brake light bulb failure, and dipped headlight beam/tail light bulb failure.

Warnings are displayed automatically on the multi-function display, and the warnings will override any other information displayed.

Removal and refitting procedures for the auxiliary warning system components are given in Section 24.

24   Auxiliary warning system components – removal and refitting

Control module

1   The control module is integral with the multi-function display. Refer to Section 22 for details of removal and refitting.

Multi-function display

2   Refer to Section 22.

Coolant level sensor

Removal

Warning: *Do not attempt to remove the expansion tank filler cap/coolant level sensor assembly while the engine is hot, as there is a high risk of scalding. If the filler cap/coolant level sensor assembly must be removed before the engine and radiator have fully cooled (even though this is NOT recommended), the pressure in the cooling system must first be relieved. Cover the cap with a thick layer of cloth, to avoid scalding, and slowly unscrew the filler cap until a hissing sound can be heard. When the hissing has stopped, indicating that the pressure has reduced, slowly unscrew the filler cap until it can be removed; if more hissing sounds are heard, wait until they have stopped before unscrewing the cap completely. At all times, keep well away from the filler cap opening.*

3   The coolant level sensor is integral with the expansion tank filler cap.
4   Before removing the filler cap/coolant level sensor assembly, disconnect the battery negative lead, and disconnect the wiring plug from the top of the sensor.

Refitting

5   Refitting is a reversal of removal.

Washer fluid level sensor

Removal

6   If possible, drain the fluid reservoir by operating the washers, to minimise fluid loss when the level sensor is removed.
7   Disconnect the battery negative lead.
8   Disconnect the wiring plug from the sensor, which is mounted in the side of the washer fluid reservoir.
9   Unscrew the sensor from the reservoir.

Refitting

10   Refitting is a reversal of removal.

Brake fluid level sensor

Note: *Hydraulic fluid is poisonous; wash off immediately and thoroughly in the case of skin contact, and seek immediate medical advice if any fluid is swallowed or gets into the eyes. Certain types of hydraulic fluid are inflammable, and may ignite when allowed into contact with hot components; it is safest to assume that the fluid IS inflammable, and to take precautions against the risk of fire as when handling petrol. Hydraulic fluid is also an effective paint stripper, and will attack certain plastics; if any is spilt, it should be washed off immediately using copious quantities of fresh water.*

Removal

11   The brake fluid level warning sensor is integral with the brake hydraulic fluid reservoir filler cap.
12   Before removing the filler cap/level sensor assembly, disconnect the battery negative lead, and disconnect the wiring plug from the top of the sensor.

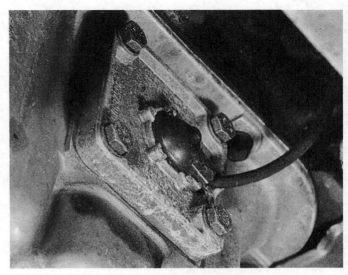

24.14 Engine oil level sensor location – DOHC engine

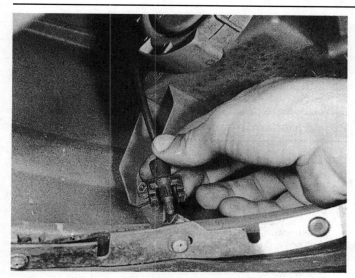

24.26 Unclipping the outside air temperature sensor from the spoiler

Refitting

13   Refitting is a reversal of removal.

Engine oil level sensor
Removal

14   The engine oil level sensor is located in the front face of the sump (photo).
15   On DOHC engine models, remove the access hatch from the engine undershield.
16   Disconnect the battery negative lead, then disconnect the wiring plug from the sensor.
17   Place a suitable container under the sump, to catch any oil which may be released as the sensor is unscrewed.
18   Unscrew the securing screws, and withdraw the sensor from the sump.
19   Recover the sealing ring.

Refitting

20   Refitting is a reversal of removal, but before refitting the sensor, examine the condition of the sealing ring, and renew if necessary.

Brake pad wear sensors

21   The sensors take the form of wires located in the front brake pads.
22   Removal and refitting are described in Chapter 9 as part of the front brake pad renewal procedure.

Outside air temperature sensor
Removal

23   The sensor is clipped into the lower edge of the front spoiler.
24   Disconnect the battery negative lead.
25   For improved access, apply the handbrake, then jack up the front of the vehicle, and support securely on axle stands (see 'Jacking, towing and wheel changing').
26   Unclip the sensor from the spoiler, then disconnect the wiring connector, noting its location (photo).

Refitting

27   Refitting is a reversal of removal, ensuring that the wiring connector is located as noted before removal.

25   Trip computer – general information

The trip computer displays information on the multi-function display, to indicate fuel consumption, average speed, range, outside air temperature, and elapsed time (stopwatch). The information to be displayed is selected using two pushbuttons on the end of the right-hand steering column stalk switch.

The trip computer operates in conjunction with the auxiliary warning system, and any warning display will take priority over the trip computer display.

Details for removal and refitting of the auxiliary warning system components are given in Section 24.

26   Cigarette lighter – removal and refitting

Removal

1   Disconnect the battery negative lead.
2   Remove the centre console, as described in Chapter 11.
3   To remove the cigarette lighter assembly, simply pull it from the illumination ring assembly. If desired, the illumination ring assembly can be removed, by pulling it from the housing after depressing the retaining clips.

Refitting

4   Refitting is a reversal of removal.

27   Horn – removal and refitting

Models with single-tone horn
Removal

1   Disconnect the battery negative lead.
2   Remove the radiator grille, as described in Chapter 11.
3   Disconnect the wiring from the rear of the horn.
4   Unscrew the securing nut, and withdraw the horn from its bracket (photo).

Refitting

5   Refitting is a reversal of removal.

Models with multi-tone horns
Removal

6   Disconnect the battery negative lead.
7   Apply the handbrake, then jack up the front of the vehicle, and support securely on axle stands (see 'Jacking, towing and wheel changing').
8   Working at the front of the left-hand wheel arch, disconnect the wiring from the relevant horn.

27.4 Horn location viewed with radiator grille panel removed (securing nut arrowed) – model with single-tone horn

27.9 Horn location (arrowed) – model with multi-tone horns

9   Unscrew the relevant securing nut, and withdraw the horn from its bracket (photo).
10   On certain models, access to the horn mounting nuts may be easier if the complete horn assembly is first removed by unscrewing the bracket securing nut.

Refitting
11   Refitting is a reversal of removal.

28   Speedometer drive cable – removal and refitting

Removal
1   Remove the instrument panel, as described in Section 20.
2   Carefully pull the speedometer cable through the bulkhead into the engine compartment, noting its routing. It will probably be necessary to prise the cable grommet from the bulkhead.
3   The cable can now be withdrawn from the vehicle, noting its routing so that it can be refitted in the same position.

29.2A Unscrewing a windscreen wiper arm securing nut

Refitting
4   Refitting is a reversal of removal, ensuring that the cable is correctly routed. Make sure that the cable is not kinked or twisted between the instrument panel and the bulkhead as the instrument panel is refitted, and ensure that the cable grommet is securely located in the bulkhead.

29   Wiper arms – removal and refitting

Removal
1   The wiper motor should be in the parked position before removing the wiper arm. Mark the position of the blade on the glass with adhesive tape, as a guide to refitting.
2   Lift the hinged cover, and remove the nut and washer securing the arm to the spindle (photos).
3   Prise the arm from the spindle, using a screwdriver if necessary – take care not to damage the trim or paintwork.

Refitting
4   Refitting is a reversal of removal, positioning the arms so that the blades align with the tape applied to the glass before removal. Note that the driver's side windscreen wiper blade is fitted with a wind deflector.

30   Windscreen wiper motor and linkage – removal and refitting

Removal
1   Disconnect the battery negative lead.
2   Remove the windscreen wiper arms with reference to Section 29.
3   Remove the scuttle water deflector panels, noting how they are located over the flanges on the scuttle (photos).
4   Remove the windscreen cowl panel, as described in Chapter 11.
5   Disconnect the wiring plug from the motor (photo).
6   Unscrew the three securing bolts, and withdraw the complete motor and linkage assembly from the scuttle (photo).

Refitting
7   Refitting is a reversal of removal, bearing in mind the following points.
8   Refit the windscreen cowl panel, as described in Chapter 11.
9   Refit the windscreen wiper arms with reference to Section 29.

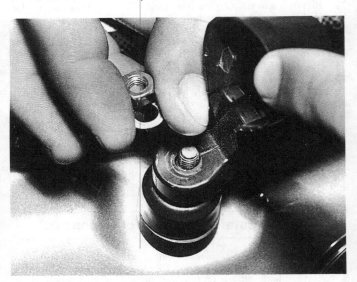

29.2B Removing the tailgate wiper arm securing nut and washer – Hatchback model

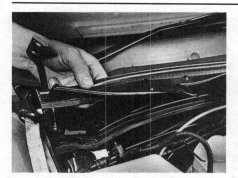
30.3A Removing the front ...

30.3B ... and rear water deflector panels from the scuttle

30.5 Disconnecting the wiring plug from the windscreen wiper motor

30.6 Withdrawing the windscreen wiper motor and linkage assembly

5   Locate the motor wiring connector, and separate the two halves of the connector (photo).
6   Unscrew the two securing bolts, noting the locations of any earth wires secured by the bolts (photo), and withdraw the motor assembly from the tailgate. Note that the spindle mounting rubbers may be released from the tailgate as the assembly is withdrawn.

Refitting

7   Refitting is a reversal of removal, ensuring that the spindle mounting rubbers are correctly located in the tailgate aperture, and that any earth wires are located as noted before removal.

32   Windscreen/tailgate washer system components – removal and refitting

Fluid reservoir
Removal
1   Disconnect the battery negative lead.
2   Working in the engine compartment, disconnect the wiring plug(s) from the fluid pump(s) in the reservoir.
3   Disconnect the fluid hose(s) from the pump(s). Be prepared for fluid spillage.
4   Remove the securing screw from the front right-hand edge of the reservoir, and withdraw the reservoir from the engine compartment.

Refitting
5   Refitting is a reversal of removal.

Fluid pump
Removal
6   Disconnect the battery negative lead.
7   Working in the engine compartment, disconnect the wiring plug from the pump.
8   Disconnect the fluid hose(s) from the pump. Be prepared for fluid spillage.

31   Tailgate wiper motor and linkage – removal and refitting

Removal
1   Disconnect the battery negative lead.
2   Remove the tailgate wiper arm, as described in Section 29.
3   Remove the plastic cover from the end of the wiper spindle, then unscrew the spindle nut and recover the washer (photo).
4   Remove the tailgate trim panel, as described in Chapter 11, Section 30.

31.3 Removing the plastic cover from the tailgate wiper spindle – Hatchback model

31.5 Tailgate wiper motor wiring connector – Hatchback model

31.6 Tailgate wiper motor securing bolts (arrowed)

9   Pull the pump from the reservoir, being prepared for fluid spillage if the reservoir still contains fluid.

Refitting

10   Examine the condition of gauze filter at the end of the pump pick-up tube, and clean or renew if necessary.
11   Refitting is a reversal of removal, ensuring that the pump is securely seated in the reservoir.

Windscreen washer nozzle
Removal

12   Carefully prise the nozzle from the bonnet, taking care not to damage the paintwork.
13   Disconnect the fluid hose, and withdraw the nozzle.

Refitting

14   To refit, reconnect the washer hose to the nozzle, and push the nozzle into its locating hole.
15   The nozzle can be adjusted by inserting a pin into the jet, and swivelling it to the required position.

Tailgate washer nozzle – Hatchback models
Removal

16   The washer nozzle can be removed after removing the tailgate spoiler as described in Chapter 11. Take care to prevent the end of the fluid hose from dropping into the tailgate.

Refitting

17   Refitting is a reversal of removal, but refit the spoiler as described in Chapter 11, and note that the nozzle can be adjusted by inserting a pin into the jet and swivelling it to the desired position.

Tailgate washer nozzle – Estate models
Removal

18   Open the tailgate, and remove the upper tailgate interior trim panel, with reference to Chapter 11, Section 30.
19   Disconnect the fluid hose from the rear of the nozzle, then push the nozzle out through the tailgate.

Refitting

20   Refitting is a reversal of removal.

33   Headlight washer system components – removal and refitting

Washer nozzles
Removal

1   Remove the radiator grille, as described in Chapter 11.

2   Remove the two securing screws, and withdraw the nozzles from the radiator grille.

Refitting

3   Refitting is a reversal of removal.
4   The nozzles can be adjusted by inserting a pin into the jet, and swivelling it to the desired position.

Fluid reservoir
Removal

5   The headlight washer fluid reservoir is located at the rear left-hand corner of the engine compartment.
6   Disconnect the battery negative lead.
7   Working in the engine compartment, unscrew the filler neck from the top of the reservoir.
8   Remove the wheel arch liner, as described in Chapter 11, Section 25.
9   Remove the three reservoir securing screws, and manipulate the reservoir as necessary to disconnect the pump wiring plug and the fluid hose. Be prepared for fluid spillage as the hose is disconnected.
10   Withdraw the reservoir from under the wheel arch.

Refitting

11   Refitting is a reversal of removal.

Fluid pump
Removal

12   Remove the fluid reservoir, as described previously in this Section.
13   Pull the pump from the reservoir, being prepared for fluid spillage if the reservoir still contains fluid.

Refitting

14   Examine the condition of the pump-to-reservoir sealing grommet, and renew if necessary.
15   Refitting is a reversal of removal.

34   Radio/cassette player – removal and refitting

Removal

1   All the radio/cassette players fitted to the Astra range have DIN standard fixings. Two special tools, obtainable from in-car entertainment specialists, are required for removal.
2   Disconnect the battery negative lead.
3   Unscrew the four grub screws from the corners of the radio/cassette player, using a suitable Allen key or hexagon bit (photo).

34.3 Unscrewing a grub screw from the radio/cassette player

34.5 Withdrawing the radio/cassette player from the facia

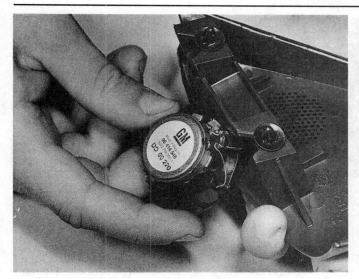

35.4 Removing a front treble loudspeaker from the mirror trim panel

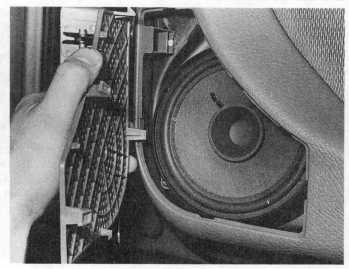

35.7 Removing the front bass loudspeaker trim panel from the door

4   Insert the tools into the holes exposed by removal of the grub screws, and push them until they snap into place. Pull the tools rearwards (away from the facia) to release the unit.
5   Pull the unit forwards, and withdraw it from the facia (photo).

Refitting

6   To refit the radio/cassette player, simply push the unit into the facia until the retaining lugs snap into place, then refit the grub screws.

35 Loudspeakers – removal and refitting

Front treble loudspeaker ('tweeter')
Removal

1   Disconnect the battery negative lead.
2   Carefully prise the door mirror trim panel from the door.
3   Disconnect the wiring plug from the loudspeaker.
4   Carefully push the loudspeaker from its location in the trim panel (photo).

Refitting

5   Refitting is a reversal of removal.

Front bass loudspeaker ('woofer')
Removal

6   Disconnect the battery negative lead.

7   Carefully unclip the loudspeaker trim panel from the door to expose the loudspeaker (photo).
8   Remove the three securing screws, then withdraw the loudspeaker from the door and disconnect the wiring.

Refitting

9   Refitting is a reversal of removal.

Rear loudspeaker – Saloon models
Removal

10   Disconnect the battery negative lead.
11   Working in the luggage compartment, disconnect the wiring plug from the loudspeaker.
12   Working inside the vehicle, carefully prise the loudspeaker cover from the rear parcel shelf (slide the cover towards the centre of the vehicle to remove it) (photo).
13   Unscrew the four now-exposed loudspeaker securing screws, and carefully withdraw the loudspeaker into the luggage compartment (photo).

Refitting

14   Refitting is a reversal of removal.

Rear loudspeaker – Hatchback models
Removal

15   Disconnect the battery negative lead.
16   Working in the luggage compartment, disconnect the wiring plug from the loudspeaker.
17   Remove the four securing screws, and withdraw the loudspeaker from under the rear parcel shelf (photo).

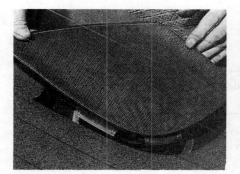

35.12 Removing the rear loudspeaker cover from the parcel shelf (viewed through rear window) – Saloon model

35.13 Removing a rear loudspeaker securing screw (viewed through rear window) – Saloon model

35.17 Removing a rear loudspeaker – Hatchback model

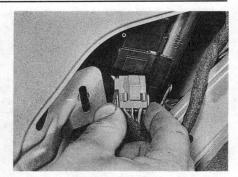

**36.9A Electric aerial earth lead (arrowed) –
Hatchback model**

**36.9B Lower the aerial to disconnect the
aerial lead (arrowed) ...**

**36.9C ... and the motor wiring plug –
Hatchback model**

Refitting
18   Refitting is a reversal of removal.

Rear loudspeaker – Estate and Van models
Removal
19   Disconnect the battery negative lead.
20   Remove the tailgate lower trim panel, as described in Chapter 11, Section 30.
21   Remove the three securing screws, then withdraw the loudspeaker from the tailgate, and disconnect the wiring.

Refitting
22   Refitting is a reversal of removal.

36   Radio aerial – removal and refitting

Saloon models
Removal
1   On models fitted with an electrically-operated aerial, make sure that the aerial is fully retracted, then disconnect the battery negative lead.
2   Remove the luggage compartment rear trim panel, and the left-hand side trim panel, as described in Chapter 11, Section 30.

**36.10 Withdrawing the aerial assembly through the rear light
cluster aperture – Hatchback model**

3   Where applicable, remove the screw securing the aerial earth lead to the body panel.
4   Remove the screw securing the lower end of the aerial to the body panel, then pull the aerial through the grommet in the rear wing panel, and lower it sufficiently to disconnect the aerial lead and, where applicable, the motor wiring plug.
5   Withdraw the aerial into the luggage compartment.

Refitting
6   Refitting is a reversal of removal, but ensure that the aerial grommet is correctly seated in the rear wing panel.

Hatchback models (except DOHC engine models)
Removal
7   Proceed as described in paragraphs 1 and 2.
8   Remove the left-hand rear light cluster, as described in Section 17.
9   Proceed as described in paragraphs 3 and 4 (photos).
10   Carefully manipulate the aerial assembly to enable it to be withdrawn from the vehicle through the rear light cluster aperture (photo).

Refitting
11   Refer to paragraph 6.

Estate and DOHC engine models
Removal
12   Remove the headlining, with reference to Chapter 11.
13   Working through the access hole in the roof, disconnect the aerial lead from the base of the aerial.
14   Unscrew the aerial securing nut, and withdraw the aerial from the roof.

Refitting
15   Refitting is a reversal of removal.

37   Anti-theft alarm system – general information

Certain models are fitted with an anti-theft alarm system as standard equipment.

The alarm system operates in conjunction with the central locking system switches, and is triggered by opening of the doors, bonnet, and boot lid/tailgate, or by interference with the radio/cassette player.

The alarm features a self-diagnostic function, and any faults should be referred to a Vauxhall/Opel dealer, who will have access to the necessary specialist diagnostic equipment.

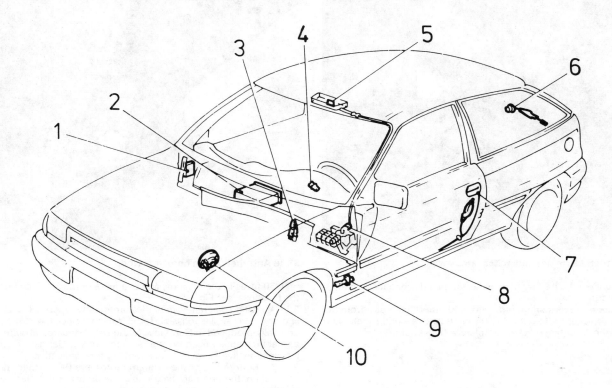

Fig. 12.14 Anti-theft alarm system (Sec 37)

1	Electronic control unit	4	Ignition switch	7	Door lock switch	9	Courtesy light switch
2	Radio/cassette sensor	5	LED integral with courtesy light	8	Relay (isolates starter	10	Horn
3	Bonnet switch	6	Tailgate/boot lid switch		motor)		

38 Anti-theft alarm system components – removal and refitting

Electronic control unit
Removal
1   The control unit is located behind the right-hand footwell side/sill trim panel.
2   Disconnect the battery negative lead.
3   Remove the footwell side/sill trim panel, as described in Chapter 11, Section 30.
4   Unscrew the two plastic securing nuts, then lift the control unit from the footwell, disconnect the wiring plug, and withdraw the unit.

Refitting
5   Refitting is a reversal of removal.

Bonnet switch
Removal
6   Disconnect the battery negative lead.
7   Using a screwdriver, carefully release the securing clip, and withdraw the switch from its bracket on the suspension turret (photo).
8   Disconnect the wiring plug, and withdraw the switch.

Refitting
9   Refitting is a reversal of removal.

Horn
Removal
10   The horn is located on the left-hand inner front wing panel, next to the battery (photo).

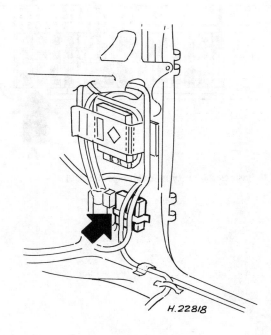

Fig. 12.15 Anti-theft alarm electronic control unit location (arrowed) in right-hand footwell (Sec 38)

38.7 Anti-theft alarm bonnet switch (arrowed)

11   Disconnect the battery negative lead, then disconnect the wiring from the horn.
12   Unscrew the securing nut, and withdraw the horn from its mounting bracket. Alternatively, unscrew the securing bolt, and withdraw the mounting bracket complete with the horn.

Refitting

13   Refitting is a reversal of removal.

39 Wiring diagrams – explanatory notes

1   Two wiring diagrams are provided, one diagram for early models

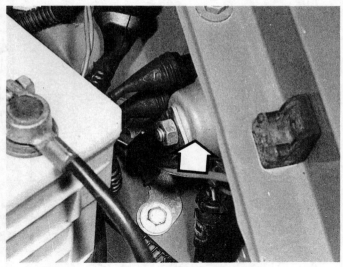

38.10 Anti-theft alarm horn (arrowed)

with 30 fuses in the fusebox, and one for later models with 28 fuses in the fusebox – see Fig. 12.16.
2   The wiring diagrams are of the current flow type, each circuit being shown in the simplest possible form. Note that since the diagrams were originally produced in Germany (to the DIN standard), all wire colours and abbreviations used on the diagrams are in German; refer to the information given above the diagram key for clarification.
3   The bottom line of the diagram represents the earth (or negative) connection; the numbers below this line are track numbers, enabling circuits and components to be located using the key.
4   The lines at the top of the diagram represent live feed (or positive) connection points. The line marked '30' is live at all times, that marked '15' is live only when the ignition is switched on.
5   Numbers on the diagram which are framed in square boxes at the end of a wire indicate the track reference number at which that particular wire is continued. At the point indicated, another framed number will appear, referring back to the previous circuit.

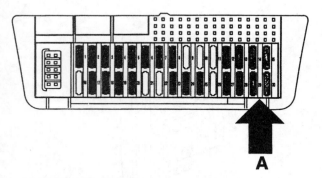

A

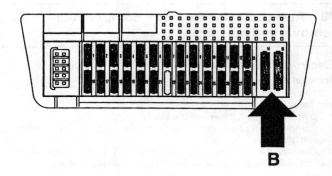

B

Fig. 12.16 Early and later type fuseboxes (Sec 39)

A   Early models with 30 fuses

B   Later models with 28 fuses

Explanation of abbreviations used

Note: *Note: The following list is included for guidance only – a comprehensive list was not available at time of writing.*

ABS	Anti-lock braking system	LWR	Headlamp range control
AC	Air conditioning	M1.5	Fuel injection (Bosch Motronic M1.5)
AT	Automatic transmission	M2.5	Fuel injection (Bosch Motronic M2.5)
ATC	Automatic temperature control	MID	Multi-information display
AZV	Trailer hitch	MOT	Motronic system (general)
BR	On-board computer	MT	Manual transmission
CC	Check control	MUL	Fuel injection (Multec)
CRC	Cruise control	N	Norway
D	Diesel	NSL	Rear foglight
DID	Dual information display	NSW	Foglight
DIS	Direct ignition system	OEL	Oil level check (oil pressure)
DS	Theft protection	OPT	Optional equipment
DWA	Anti-theft warning system	PBSL	Parking/brake lockout
DZM	Tachometer	P/N	Park/Neutral (starter inhibitor – automatic transmission)
EFC	Electric folding roof (Convertible)	POT	Potentiometer
EKS	Pinch guard (electric windows)	RC	Ride control
EMP	Radio/cassette	RFS	Reversing lights
ETC	Electronic traction control	RHD	Right-hand drive
EUR	Euronorm engine	S	Sweden
EZ+	El Plus with self-diagnosis	SD	Sliding sunroof
EZV	Ecotronic	SH	Seat heating
FH	Electric windows	SRA	Headlight washer
GB	Great Britain	TANK	Fuel gauge
HRL	Luggage compartment lamp	TD	Turbodiesel
HS	Heated rear window	TEMP	Temperature gauge
HW	Rear screen wiper	TFL	Day running lights
HZG	Heating	TKS	Door courtesy light switch
INS	Instrument	TSZI	High-energy ignition (HEI)
IRL	Interior light	VGS	Carburettor
KAT	Catalytic converter	WEG	Mileometer frequency sensor
KBS	Wiring harness	WHR	Vehicle level control
KV	Contact, distributor	WS	Warning buzzer
L3.1	Fuel injection (Bosch L3.1-Jetronic)	ZV	Central locking
LCD	LCD instrument	ZYL	Cylinder
LHD	Left-hand drive	4WD	Four-wheel-drive

Wiring identification

Example: GE WS 1.5
GE – Basic colour
WS – Identification colour
1.5 – Wire cross-section (mm^2)

Colour code

BL	Blue
BR	Brown
GE	Yellow
GN	Green
GR	Grey
HBL	Light blue
LI	Lilac
RT	Red
SW	Black
VI	Violet
WS	White

Circuit interconnections

A framed number – eg 180 – refers to a grid reference (track) at which the circuit is continued

Key to wiring diagrams

Not all items fitted to all models
*Models with earlier 30-fuse type fusebox
**Models with later 28-fuse type fusebox

No	Description	Track
E01	Sidelight, left	604
E02	Tail light, left	501, 602
E03	Number plate light	613 to 616
E04	Sidelight, right	609
E05	Tail light, right	503, 611
E07	Headlight main beam, left	629
E08	Headlight main beam, right	631
E09	Headlight dipped beam, left	505, 630
E10	Headlight dipped beam, right	507, 632
E11	Instrument lighting	546
E12	Automatic transmission selector illumination	296, 297
E13	Luggage compartment light	687
E14	Interior light	689, 750, 752
E15	Glovebox light	857
E16	Cigarette lighter illumination	855
E17	Reversing light, left	698
E18	Reversing light, right	699
E19	Heated rear window	756
E20	Foglight, front left	650
E21	Foglight, front right	651
E24	Foglight, rear left	645
E25	Seat heating, left	860
E27	Rear reading light, left	692
E28	Rear reading light, right	694
E30	Seat heating, right	864
E34	Heater control illumination	756
E39	Foglight, rear right	646
F01 to F28	Fuses in (28-fuse type) fusebox	Various
F01 to F30	Fuses in (30-fuse type) fusebox	Various
F14**	Heater blower fuse ('maxi' type)	762
F35	Voltage stabiliser	548
F36	Fuel filter heating fuse (diesel, engine compartment)	450, 495
F38**	Anti-theft alarm horn fuse	743
F41	Glow plug fuse ('maxi' type, engine compartment)	440, 487
F42	Fuse, radiator cooling fan	120
F45	Horn fuse	830
F46*	Heater blower fuse ('maxi' type)	762
F48*	Anti-theft alarm horn fuse	743
G01	Battery	100
G02	Alternator	115
G06	Alternator (diesel)	469 to 472
H01	Radio/cassette	571 to 587
H02	Horn (single-tone)	826
H03	Direction indicator warning light	554
H04	Oil pressure warning light	561
H05	Brake fluid warning light	563
H06	Hazard flashers warning light	674
H07	Alternator/no-charge warning light	565
H08	Headlight main beam warning light	558
H09	Stop-light, left	509, 659
H10	Stop-light, right	511, 660
H11	Direction indicator light, front left	675
H12	Direction indicator light, rear left	676
H13	Direction indicator light, front right	683
H14	Direction indicator light, rear right	684
H15	Low fuel/fuel reserve warning light	551
H16	Glow plug warning light	539
H17	Trailer direction indicator warning light	542
H18	Horn (twin-tone)	830
H19	Headlights 'on' warning buzzer	695, 696
H21	Handbrake 'on' warning light	566
H25	Heated mirror warning light	842
H26	ABS warning light	537
H30	Engine warning light	559

No	Description	Track
H33	Direction indicator side repeater light, left	679
H34	Direction indicator side repeater light, right	681
H37	Loudspeaker, front left	576, 577
H38	Loudspeaker, front right	581, 582
H39	Loudspeaker, rear left	576, 577
H40	Loudspeaker, rear right	581, 582
H42	Automatic transmission warning light	540
H47	Anti-theft alarm horn	743
H48	Horn (twin-tone)	832
H51	Electronic traction control (ETC) warning light	538
H52	Tweeter, front left	576
H53	Tweeter, front right	581
K01	Heated rear window relay	756, 757
K03	Relay, starter (anti-theft warning unit, 70A)	111, 112
K05	Front foglight relay	651, 652
K08	Intermittent wiper relay (windscreen)	803 to 806
K10	Direction indicator flasher unit	670 to 672
K20	Ignition module/ignition coil	137 to 141, 170 to 172, 239, 240, 302, 303, 362 to 365
K25	Glow time relay (70A)	437 to 440
K30	Intermittent wiper relay (tailgate)	813 to 815
K35	Heated mirror relay	847 to 849
K37	Central door locking control unit	705 to 711
K57	Multec single-point control unit	175 to 194, 211 to 230, 242 to 261
K58	Fuel pump relay (Multec single-point)	196, 197, 231, 232, 261, 262, 332, 333
K59	Day running light relay	619 to 625
K61	Motronic control unit	367 to 397, 402 to 426
K63	Twin-tone horn relay	829, 830
K68	Fuel injection unit relay	395 to 399, 428 to 432
K76	Glow time control unit	479 to 484
K77	Glow plug relay	486, 487
K78	Pre-resistor relay	489, 490
K79	Charging indicator relay	472 to 474
K80	Fuel filter heating relay (diesel)	449, 450, 494, 495
K82	Engine speed relay	444, 445
K85	Automatic transmission control unit	271 to 294
K89	Rear foglight relay	639 to 641
K91	Multec multi-point control unit	305 to 332, 345
K94	Anti-theft alarm control unit	737 to 750
K95	ETC system control unit	926 to 941
K97	Headlight washer delay relay	820 to 822
L01	Ignition coil	138, 172, 205, 239, 303, 362, 406
L02	Ignition coil (DIS)	338 to 343
M01	Starter motor	105, 106
M02	Windscreen wiper motor	801 to 804
M03	Heater blower motor	761 to 763
M04*	Radiator cooling fan motor	120, 123
M04**	Radiator cooling fan motor	120, 123, 127
M08	Tailgate wiper motor	811 to 813
M15	Electric window motor, front passenger door	783, 785
M18	Central locking motor, driver's door	706 to 709
M19	Central locking motor, left rear door	717 to 719
M20	Central locking motor, right rear door	721 to 723
M21	Fuel pump	197, 232, 262, 333, 399, 429
M24	Headlight washer pump	822
M26	Electric aerial motor	587, 588
M26.1	Electric aerial motor relay	590
M30	Electric mirror (driver's side)	838 to 841
M31	Electric mirror (passenger side)	844 to 847
M32	Central locking motor, front passenger door	717 to 720
M33	Idle speed actuator/power unit	377, 378, 414, 415
M39	Headlight levelling motor, left	592 to 594
M40	Headlight levelling motor, right	596 to 598
M41	Central locking motor, fuel filler flap	725, 726
M47	Electric window motor, driver's door	773 to 776
M55	Windscreen/tailgate washer pump	817

No	Description	Track
M60	Central locking motor, boot lid/tailgate	726, 728
M65	Throttle valve actuator (ETC system)	930 to 934
M66	Idle air stepper motor	178 to 181, 215 to 218, 249 to 252, 314 to 317
P01	Fuel gauge	550
P02	Coolant temperature gauge	553
P04	Fuel level sensor	550
P05	Coolant temperature sensor	553
P07	Tachometer	543
P12	Coolant temperature sensor	371 to 373, 413
P13	Ambient air temperature sensor	524
P14	Distance sensor	478, 479
P17	Wheel sensor, front left	910, 953
P18	Wheel sensor, front right	913, 956
P19	Wheel sensor, rear left	916, 959
P20	Wheel sensor, rear right	919, 962
P21	Distance sensor	556
P23	MAP sensor	188 to 190, 217 to 219, 249 to 251, 319 to 321
P25	Bulb test sensor	500 to 513
P27	Brake pad wear sensor, front left	516
P28	Brake pad wear sensor, front right	516
P29	Inlet manifold temperature sensor	315, 410
P30	Coolant temperature sensor	186, 215, 247, 317
P32	Exhaust gas oxygen sensor (heated)	392, 393, 426, 427
P33	Exhaust gas oxygen sensor	190, 229, 256, 330
P34	Throttle valve potentiometer	191 to 193, 221 to 223, 252 to 254, 323 to 325, 411, 412
P35	Crankshaft impulse sensor	244 to 246, 311 to 313, 381, 383, 421 to 423
P38	Automatic transmission fluid temperature sensor	290
P44	Air mass meter	394 to 398, 417 to 419
P45	Automatic transmission engine speed sensor	287, 288
P46	Knock sensor	385, 386
P47	Hall sensor (cylinder identification)	388, 389
P48	Automatic transmission distance sensor	285, 286
P55	Coolant temperature sensor	482
P57	Aerial	587
P58	Anti-theft alarm glass breakage sensor, rear left	754
P59	Anti-theft alarm glass breakage sensor, rear right	754
R02	Carburettor pre-heating	135
R03	Cigarette lighter	854
R05	Glow plugs	438 to 440, 485 to 487
R19*	Pre-resistor, radiator cooling fan motor	123
R19**	Pre-resistor, radiator cooling fan motor	123, 127
R22	Glow plug pre-resistor	490
S01	Ignition/starter switch	105, 106
S02	Light switch assembly	
S02.1	Light switch	604 to 607
S02.2	Interior light switch	689
S02.3	Instrument lighting dimmer	533
S03	Heater blower/heated rear window switch	760 to 764
S05	Direction indicator switch assembly	
S05.2	Headlight dipped beam switch	630 to 631
S05.3	Direction indicator switch	682 to 684
S07	Reversing light switch	698
S08	Stop-light switch	660
S09	Wiper switch assembly	
S09.2	Intermittent wiper switch (windscreen)	801 to 804
S09.5	Tailgate wash/wipe switch	814 to 816
S010	Automatic transmission selector switch	271 to 277
S011	Brake fluid level switch	563
S013	Handbrake 'on' switch	566
S014	Oil pressure sender/switch	561
S015	Luggage compartment light switch	687

No	Description	Track
S017	Courtesy light switch, front passenger door	694
S021	Front foglight switch	652 to 654
S022	Rear foglight switch	645 to 647
S029**	Coolant temperature switch	120
S030	Seat heating switch, front left	860 to 862
S031	Courtesy light switch, left rear door	691
S032	Courtesy light switch, right rear door	692
S033	ETC system switch	929, 930
S034	Multi-information display switch	526, 527
S037	Electric window switch assembly (in driver's door)	
S037.1	Electric window switch, driver's window	774, 775
S037.2	Electric window switch, passenger window	772 to 777
S041	Anti-theft locking switch, driver's door	702 to 704
S042	Front passenger door locking switch	714
S047	Courtesy light switch, driver's door	695, 696
S052	Hazard warning light (hazard flashers) switch	672 to 676
S055	Seat heating switch, front right	864 to 866
S064	Horn switch	826
S068	Electric mirror switch assembly	
S068.1	Electric mirror adjustment switch	836 to 840
S068.2	Electric mirror heating switch	842
S068.3	Electric mirror left/right selector switch	836 to 841
S078	Electric window switch assembly (in passenger door)	782 to 785
S082	Washer fluid level switch	518
S088*	Coolant temperature switch	119 to 124
S088**	Coolant temperature switch	123 to 128
S093	Coolant level switch	520
S095	Engine oil level switch	522
S098	Headlight levelling switch	591 to 593
S104	Automatic transmission kickdown switch	289
S105	Automatic transmission 'Winter' switch	293 to 295
S106	Automatic transmission 'Economy'/'Sport' switch	288
S107	Throttle valve switch	374 to 379
S120	Anti-theft alarm bonnet switch	739
S127	Boot lid/tailgate central locking switch	735
U04	ABS hydraulic unit	
U04.1	Pump motor relay	902, 903, 945, 946
U04.2	Solenoid valve relay	904, 905, 947, 948
U04.3	Pump motor	902, 945
U04.4	Diode	905, 948
U04.5	Solenoid valve, front left	909, 952
U04.6	Solenoid valve, front right	911, 954
U04.7	Solenoid valve, rear axle	913, 956
U04.8	ABS control unit	906 to 912, 949 to 963
U12	Heated fuel filter assembly	449, 450, 494, 495
U13	Automatic transmission solenoid valve block	280 to 283
U14	Clock display unit	515 to 533
U15	Clock/radio display unit	515 to 533
U16	Clock/radio/computer display unit	515 to 533
U17	Aerial amplifier	584, 585
V01	Brake fluid level test bulb diode	564
V03	Anti-theft alarm light/diode	749
X01	Trailer socket	606, 607, 657, 658
X02 to X90	Wiring connectors	Various
Y05	Fuel solenoid valve	442, 476
Y07	Fuel injectors	323 to 330, 380 to 387, 416 to 423
Y10	Distributor (HEI system)	174 to 179
Y23	Distributor (HEI system)	140 to 144, 201 to 208
Y30	Cold start acceleration valve	445
Y32	Single-point fuel injector	181, 212, 244
Y33	Distributor (MHDI system)	237, 303 to 305, 361 to 363, 401
Y34	Fuel tank ventilation valve	391, 422

Key to wiring diagrams (continued)

Not all items fitted to all models
*Models with earlier 30-fuse type fusebox
**Models with later 28-fuse type fusebox

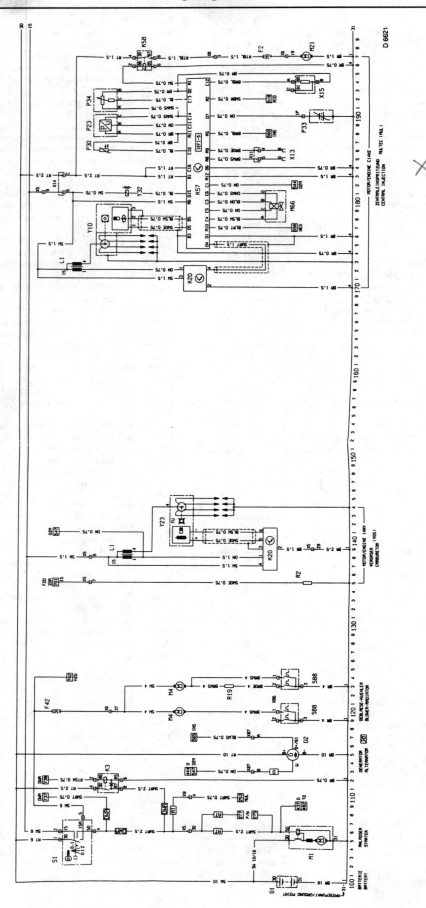

Wiring diagram for models with 30 fuses in fusebox (up to approximately February 1992)

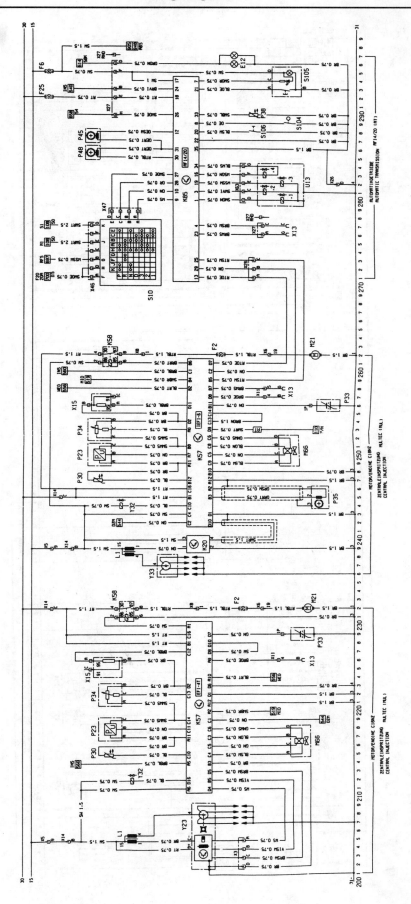

Wiring diagram for models with 30 fuses in fusebox (up to approximately February 1992) – continued

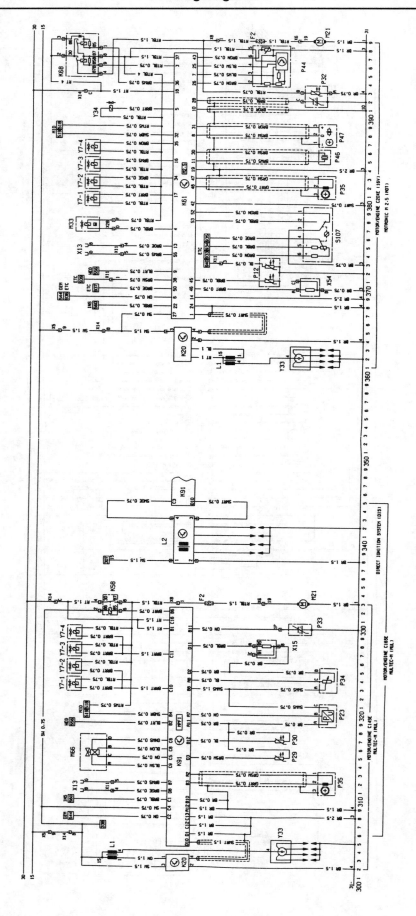

Wiring diagram for models with 30 fuses in fusebox (up to approximately February 1992) – continued

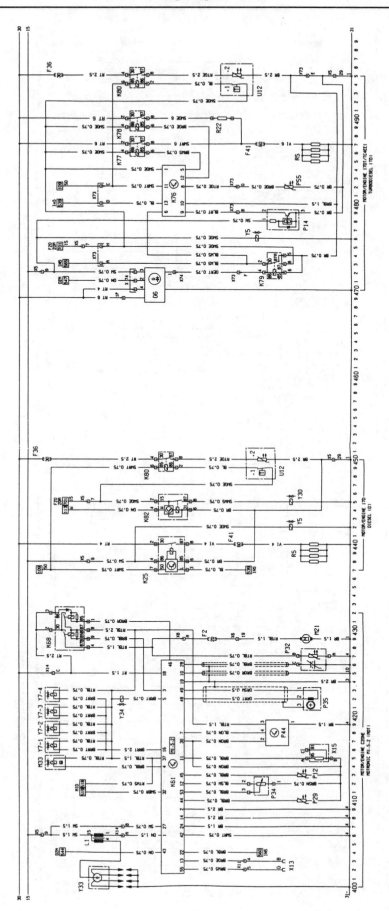

Wiring diagram for models with 30 fuses in fusebox (up to approximately February 1992) – continued

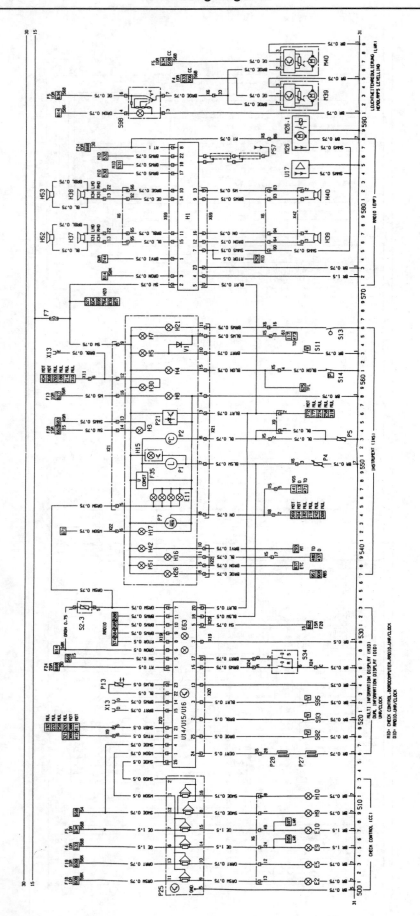

Wiring diagram for models with 30 fuses in fusebox (up to approximately February 1992) – continued

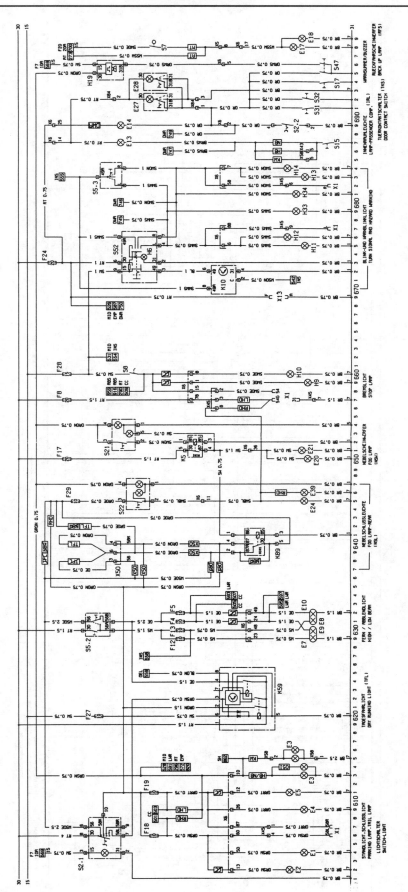

Wiring diagram for models with 30 fuses in fusebox (up to approximately February 1992) – continued

Wiring diagram for models with 30 fuses in fusebox (up to approximately February 1992) – continued

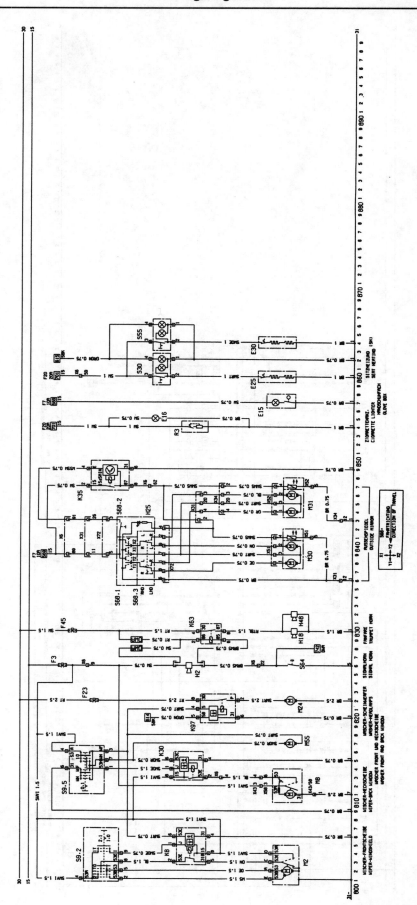

Wiring diagram for models with 30 fuses in fusebox (up to approximately February 1992) – continued

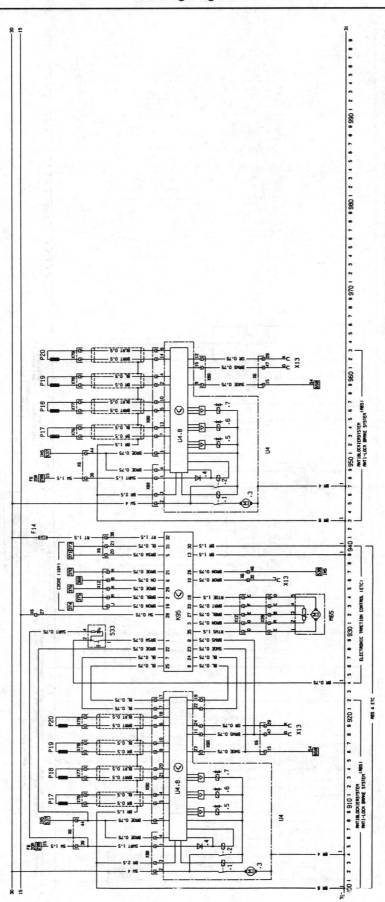

Wiring diagram for models with 30 fuses in fusebox (up to approximately February 1992) – continued

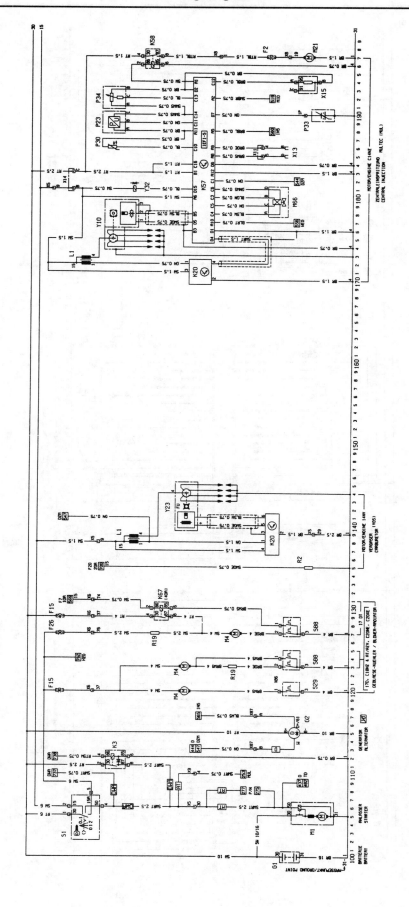

Wiring diagram for models with 28 fuses in fusebox (from approximately March 1992)

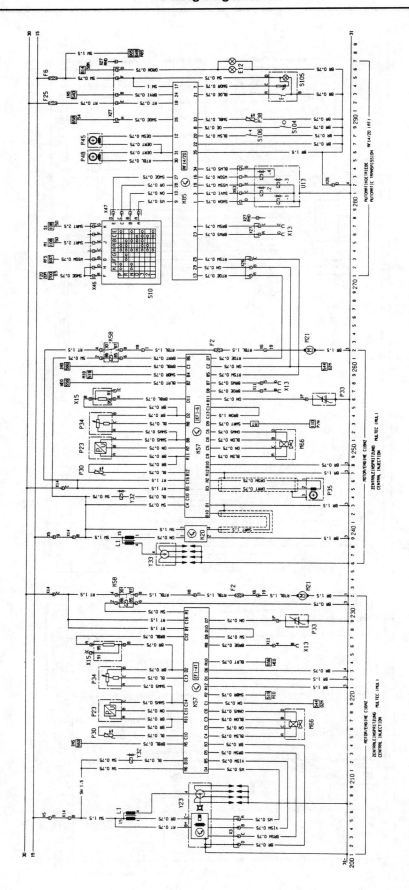

Wiring diagram for models with 28 fuses in fusebox (from approximately March 1992) – continued

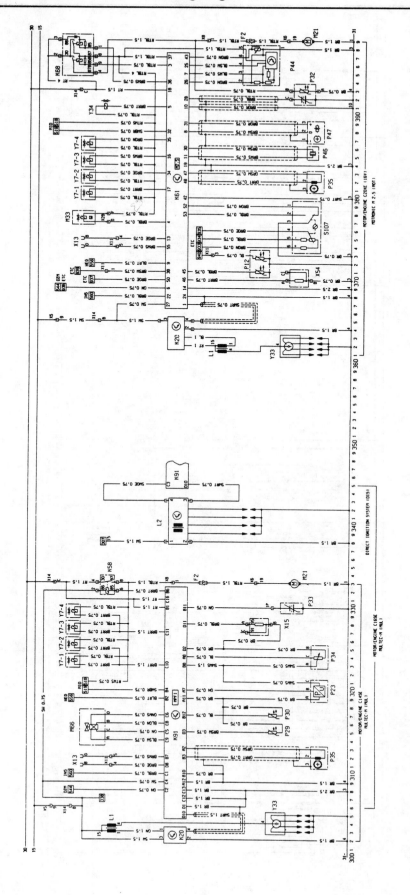

Wiring diagram for models with 28 fuses in fusebox (from approximately March 1992) – continued

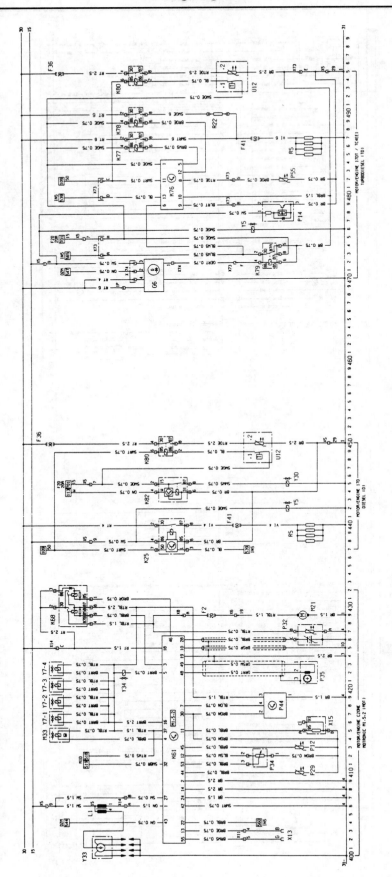

Wiring diagram for models with 28 fuses in fusebox (from approximately March 1992) – continued

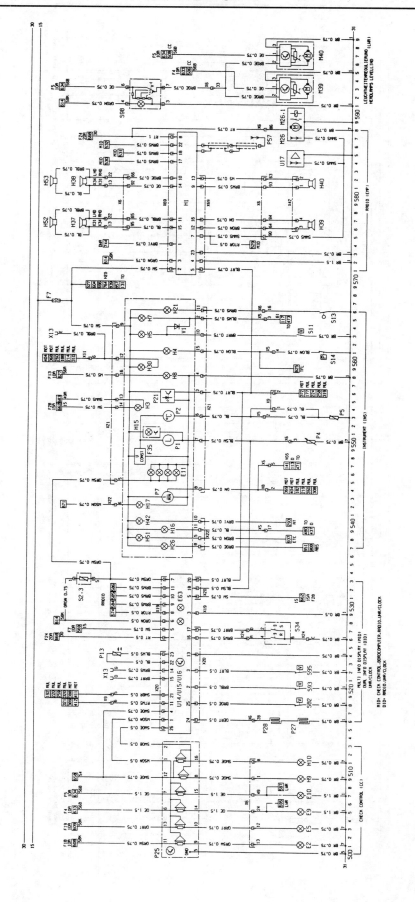

Wiring diagram for models with 28 fuses in fusebox (from approximately March 1992) – continued

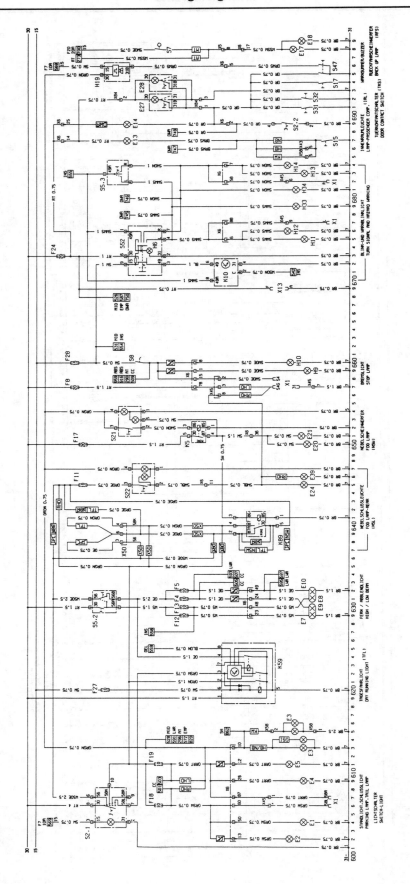

Wiring diagram for models with 28 fuses in fusebox (from approximately March 1992) – continued

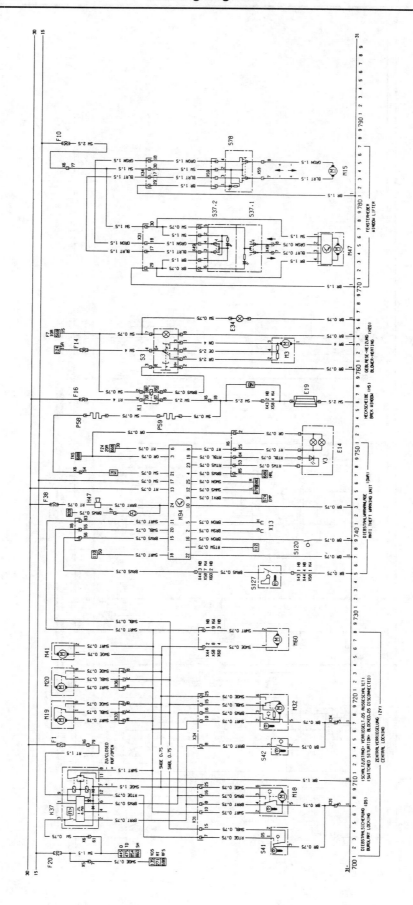

Wiring diagram for models with 28 fuses in fusebox (from approximately March 1992) – continued

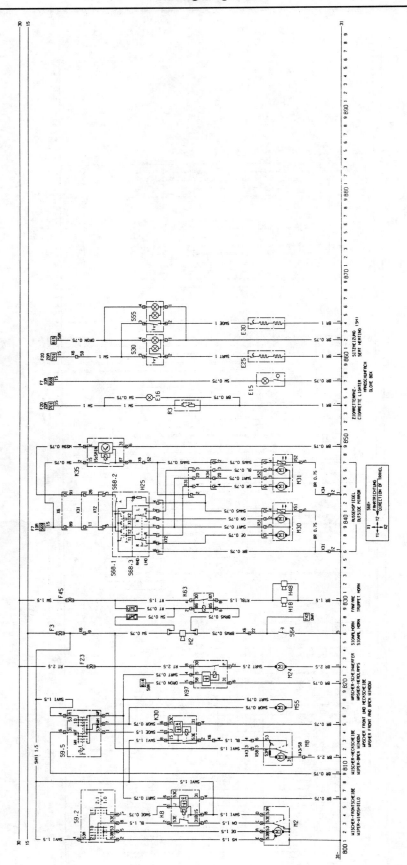

Wiring diagram for models with 28 fuses in fusebox (from approximately March 1992) – continued

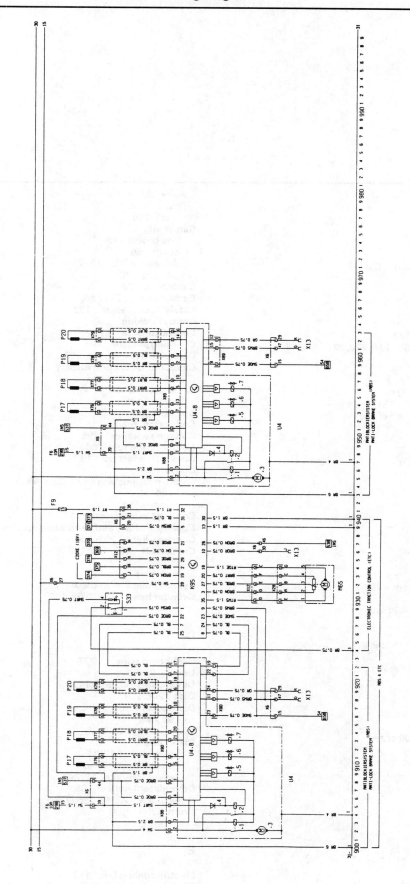

Wiring diagram for models with 28 fuses in fusebox (from approximately March 1992) – continued

Index

FUEL INJECTION UNITS.
ROCHESTER MULTEC.

1) FUEL INJECTION UNIT RES = 1.8Ω (INC 0.2 LEAD RES OF METER)

2) MAP SENSOR   C   B   A

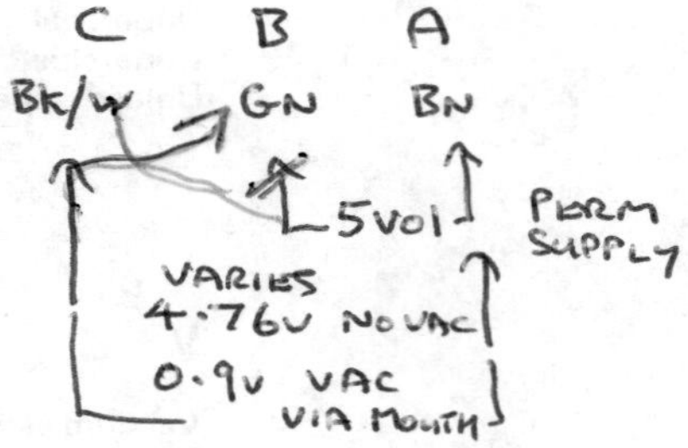

Bk/w   GN   BN

5 VOLT   PERM SUPPLY

VARIES
4.76v NO VAC
0.9v VAC VIA MOUTH

3) THROTTLE POSITION SENSOR.

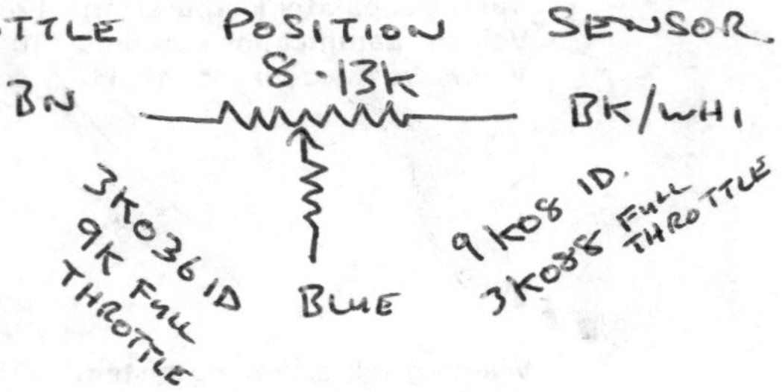

BN   8.13k   Bk/WHI

3K036 ID
9K FULL THROTTLE

BLUE

9K08 ID.
3K088 FULL THROTTLE

4) IDLE STEPPER MOTOR.

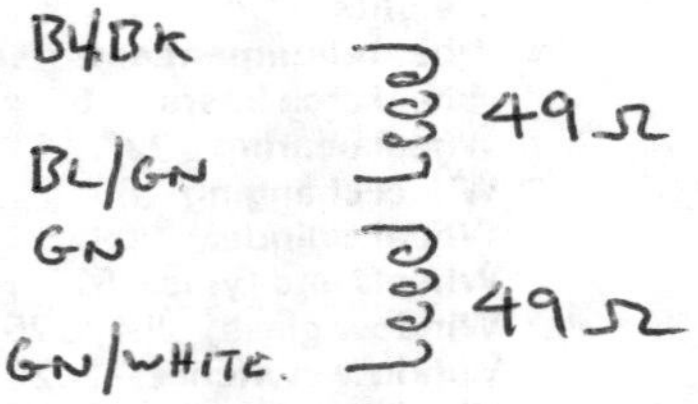

B4/BK

BL/GN   49Ω

GN

GN/WHITE.   49Ω

5) TEMP SENDER (ECU). ——— FROM RTD BOOK PAGE 329

0°C	4k4	—	6k6
20°C	2k2	—	2k8
40°C	1k	—	1k4
80°C	270R	—	380R

COLD   3k7
L WARM   1k1

☐ ↙ ☐   OK610
☐↓ ☐   OK416
☐ ↓ ☐   OK282
☐ ↓ ☐   OK228
☐ ↓ ☐   OK218
☐ ↓ ☐   OK193